September 8–12, 2016
Melbourne, VIC, Australia

**Association for
Computing Machinery**

Advancing Computing as a Science & Profession

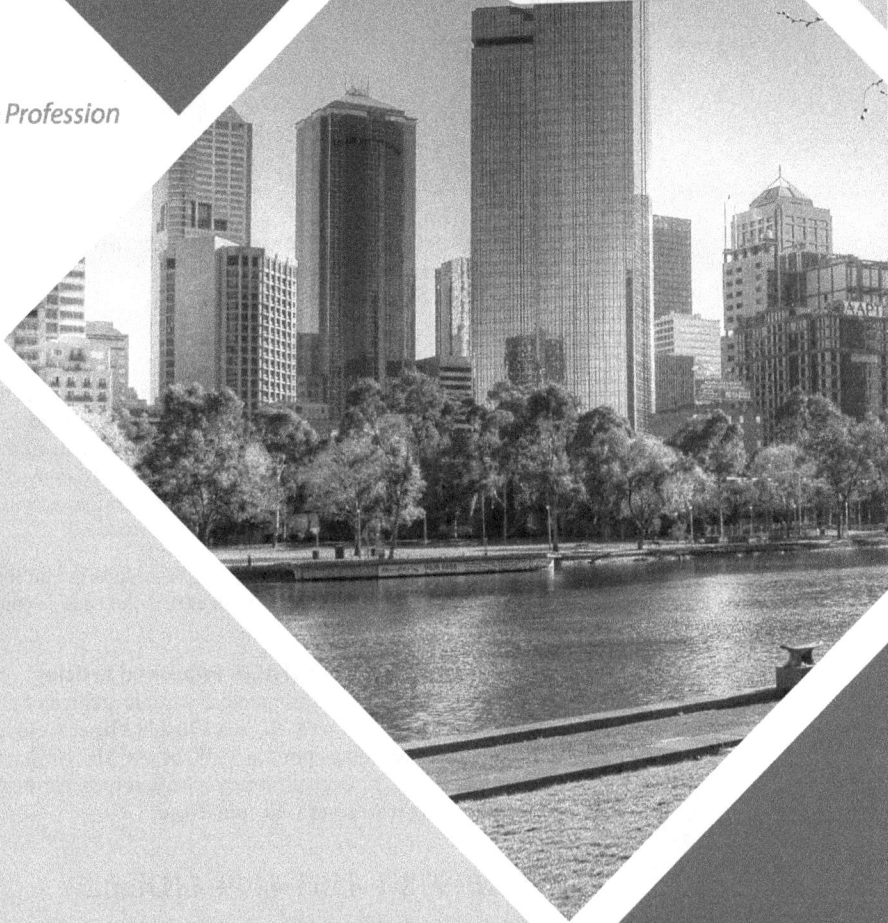

ICER'16

Proceedings of the 2016 ACM Conference on
International Computing Education Research

Sponsored by:
ACM SIGCSE

Supported by:
Monash University

Association for Computing Machinery

Advancing Computing as a Science & Profession

The Association for Computing Machinery
2 Penn Plaza, Suite 701
New York, New York 10121-0701

Notice to Past Authors of ACM-Published Articles

ISBN: 978-1-4503-4449-4 (Digital)

ISBN: 978-1-4503-4625-2 (Print)

Additional copies may be ordered prepaid from:

ACM Order Department
PO Box 30777
New York, NY 10087-0777, USA

Phone: 1-800-342-6626 (USA and Canada)
+1-212-626-0500 (Global)
Fax: +1-212-944-1318
E-mail: acmhelp@acm.org
Hours of Operation: 8:30 am – 4:30 pm ET

Printed in the USA

ICER 2016 Chairs' Welcome

We warmly welcome you to the twelfth annual International Computing Education Research conference (ICER 2016), sponsored by the ACM Special Interest Group on Computer Science Education. This year ICER will be held in Melbourne, Australia, and will be located in the Monash University Law Chambers in the city centre of Melbourne.

The ICER conference has been steadily growing. This year there were a record number of research paper submissions with a total of 102 papers submitted and 26 papers accepted for an acceptance rate of 25%. The papers were double-blind reviewed by an international program committee. The review process was overseen by a meta-review team consisting of three conference co-chairs (Sheard, Dorn and Tenenberg) and the two associate chairs. Our paper authors represent eight different countries: Australia, Canada, Finland, Germany, India, Netherlands, United Kingdom and USA.

Associated with ICER 2016 is a Doctoral Consortium with 18 doctoral students who are working on computing education research projects and a Work in Progress workshop where 9 participants will receive in-depth feedback on their proposals for computing education research projects.

The ICER program is organized around nine paper presentation sessions with a variety of computing education topics such as understanding how students code, identifying students at risk, assessment benchmarking, and programming tools and IDEs. We have continued ICER's well established single-track format with time allocated for audience discussion to each paper presentation. In addition, there will be 4 lightning talks with posters, 4 lightning talks, and 6 posters, with additional poster presentations from the Doctoral Consortium participants.

A highlight of the conference is our keynote speaker Associate Professor Richard Buckland from the University of New South Wales. Richard is an award winning computing educator with many innovations in online and face-to-face teaching. His keynote address *Affective and Cognitive – Designing Educational Experiences that Transform,* will explore teaching and learning in the affective domain.

The ICER conference chairs would like to thank the team of volunteers who have contributed to the organization and running of this event. We would particularly like to thank the submission chair, Simon, for keeping the submissions and reviewing running so smoothly, and the associate chairs, Peter Hubwieser and Chris Hundhausen, for their work on the meta-reviewing.

We hope you have a wonderful time at ICER 2016.

Judy Sheard
ICER 2016 Chair
Monash University
Caulfield East, VIC, Australia

Josh Tenenberg
ICER 2016 Co-Chair
University of Washington at Tacoma
Tacoma, WA, USA

Donald Chinn
ICER 2016 Co-Chair
University of Washington at Tacoma
Tacoma, WA, USA

Brian Dorn
ICER 2016 Co-Chair
University of Nebraska at Omaha
Omaha, NE, USA

Table of Contents

Keynote Address
Session Chair: Judy Sheard *(Monash University)*

Papers: Perceptions of CS Study and Careers
Session Chair: Brian Dorn *(University of Nebraska at Omaha)*

Papers: Programming Tools and IDEs
Session Chair: Sally Fincher *(University of Kent at Canterbury)*

Papers: Understanding How Students Code
Session Chair: Simon *(University of Newcastle)*

Papers: Assessment
Session Chair: Mark Guzdial *(Georgia Institute of Technology)*

Papers: Errors and At Risk Students
Session Chair: Colleen Lewis *(Harvey Mudd College)*

Papers: Situating Computing Education Research
Session Chair: William Doane *(IDA Science & Technology Policy Institute)*

Papers: Learning Experiences, Curriculum and Resources
Session Chair: Donald Chinn *(University of Washington at Tacoma)*

Papers: Influences on Student Performance
Session Chair: Katrina Falkner *(University of Adelaide)*

Papers: Tools, Techniques and Learning

Session Chair: Chris Hundhausen *(Washington State University)*

Doctoral Consortium

Session Chair: Anthony Robins *(University of Otago)*

ICER 2016 Conference Organization

General and Program Chairs: Judy Sheard *(Monash University, Australia)*
Josh Tenenberg *(University of Washington Tacoma, USA)*
Donald Chinn *(University of Washington Tacoma, USA)*
Brian Dorn *(University of Nebraska at Omaha, USA)*

Associate Program Chairs: Peter Hubwieser *(Technische Universität München, Germany)*
Chris Hundhausen *(Washington State University, USA)*

Lightning Talk and Poster Chairs: Leo Porter *(University of California San Diego, USA)*
Katrina Falkner *(University of Adelaide, Australia)*

Work in Progress Workshop Chairs: Colleen Lewis *(Harvey Mudd College, USA)*
Sally Fincher *(University of Kent, UK)*

Doctoral Consortium Chairs: Anthony Robins *(University of Otago, New Zealand)*
Ben Shapiro *(University of Colorado, USA)*

Local Arrangements Committee: Michael Morgan *(Monash University, Australia)*
Matthew Butler *(Monash University, Australia)*

Submissions Chair: Simon *(University of Newcastle, Australia)*

Website and Social Media Chairs: Jan Erik Moström *(Umeå University, Sweden)*
Nickolas Falkner *(University of Adelaide, Australia)*

Program Committee: Christine Alvarado *(University of California San Diego, USA)*
Michal Armoni *(Weizmann Institute of Science, Rehovot, Israel)*
Cynthia Bailey Lee *(Stanford University, USA)*
Tiffany Barnes *(North Carolina State University, USA)*
Andrew Begel *(Microsoft Research, USA)*
Yifat Ben-David Kolikant *(The Hebrew University of Jerusalem, Israel)*
Jonas Boustedt *(Hogskolan i Gavle, Sweden)*
Neil Brown *(University of Kent, UK)*
Kevin Buffardi *(California State University Chico, USA)*
Matthew Butler *(Monash University, Australia)*
Tzu-Yi Chen *(Pomona College, USA)*
Donald Chinn *(University of Washington Tacoma, USA)*
Michael Clancy *(University of California Berkeley, USA)*
Tony Clear *(Auckland University of Technology, New Zealand)*
Steve Cooper *(Stanford University, USA)*
Quintin Cutts *(University of Glasgow, UK)*

Program Committee (continued):

Adrienne Decker *(Rochester Institute of Technology, USA)*
Stephen Edwards *(Virginia Tech, USA)*
Allison Elliott Tew *(AET Consulting, USA)*
Katrina Falkner *(University of Adelaide, Australia)*
Nickolas Falkner *(University of Adelaide, Australia)*
Sally Fincher *(University of Kent, UK)*
Kathi Fisler *(Worcester Polytechnic Institute, USA)*
Sue Fitzgerald *(Metropolitan State University, USA)*
David Ginat *(Tel Aviv University, Israel)*
Sara (Esper) Guthals *(ThoughtSTEM, USA)*
Mark Guzdial *(Georgia Institute of Technology, USA)*
Brian Hanks *(BFH Educational Consulting, USA)*
Michael Hewner *(Rose-Hulman Institute of Technology, USA)*
Petri Ihantola *(University of Tampere, Finland)*
Yasmin Kafai *(University of Pennsylvania, USA)*
Päivi Kinnunen *(Aalto University, Finland)*
Maria Knobelsdorf *Universität Hamburg, Germany)*
Gary Lewandowski *(Xavier University, USA)*
Michael Lee *(New Jersey Institute of Technology, USA)*
Colleen Lewis *(Harvey Mudd College, USA)*
Raymond Lister *(University of Technology, Sydney)*
Andrew Luxton-Reilly *(University of Auckland, New Zealand)*
Lauri Malmi *(Aalto University, Helsinki, Finland)*
Robert McCartney *(University of Connecticut, USA)*
Michael Morgan *(Monash University, Australia)*
Thomas Park *(Drexel University, USA)*
Leo Porter *(University of California San Diego, USA)*
Brad Richards *(University of Puget Sound, USA)*
Kate Sanders *(Rhode Island College, USA)*
Carsten Schulte *(Freie Universität Berlin, Germany)*
Ben Shapiro *(Tufts University, USA)*
Beth Simon *(Coursera, USA)*
Juha Sorva *(Aalto University, Finland)*
Jamie Spacco *(Knox College, USA)*
Andreas Stefik *(University of Nevada Las Vegas, USA)*
Leigh Ann Sudol-Delyser *(NYC Foundation for CS Education, USA)*
Ian Utting *(University of Kent, UK)*
Tammy Vandegrift *(University of Portland, USA)*
Ángel Velázquez-Iturbide *(Universidad Rey Juan Carlos, Spain)*
Tammy Vandegrift *(University of Portland, USA)*
Aman Yadav *(Michigan State University, USA)*
Daniel Zingaro *(University of Toronto, Canada)*

ICER 2016 Sponsor & Supporter

Sponsor:

Supporter: MONASH University

Affective and Cognitive – Designing Educational Experiences that Transform

Richard Buckland
University of New South Wales, Australia
richardb@unsw.edu.au

"In the educational literature, nearly every author introduces their paper by stating that the affective domain is essential for learning, but it is the least studied, most often overlooked, the most nebulous and the hardest to evaluate of Bloom's three domains" - Kirk (2007)

Working in the cognitive domain is familiar and easy to measure. Affective learning outcomes are harder to achieve and much harder to measure and assure. Yet to transform our students into effective holistic learners with the potential to change the world around them it is the affective domain (belief, personal change, motivation, …) that is essential. Unfortunately these are also the aspects of learning that are most at risk in the online revolution currently disrupting education.

For example, to teach entrepreneurship we could design lessons so that students learn facts about famous entrepreneurs, so that they learn and know how to apply the formal academic models that have been developed to describe effective entrepreneurial behaviour. Further the students could learn to make and justify sensible decisions given real world case studies, and to be able to assess the business actions of others. Yet would any of these things give us confidence they will be effective entrepreneurs? Probably not.

Likely to become an effective entrepreneur students will need to know more than the theory of how to be an entrepreneur - they will also need to act as an entrepreneur, to take key risks, to avoid other key risks, to be persistent, to persevere, to make connections and build relationships and networks, to see opportunities and then to seize them with both hands. They will need to be transformed not only in what they know, but also in who they are.

In this talk we will look at what it is to learn and to teach in the Affective domain. We will look at Affective course learning outcomes, Affective alignment in assessment, and consider how to design and deliver effective Affective education both face to face and online.

BIO

Richard Buckland is Associate Professor in Computer Security, Cybercrime, and Cyberterror at the University of New South Wales, Australia. He has a love for teaching and a deep faith in the potential of all students. He has taught over ten thousand students face to face including K-12, undergraduate, postgraduate and professional students, and hundreds of thousands of students electronically. He has a passionate belief in the importance of education, of learning, of thinking.

Richard has been awarded ten peer reviewd teaching awards. He was named the Australian ICT educator of the year in 2013 (iAwards) and in 2008 was the Engineering Educator of the Year for Australia and New Zealand (AAEE).

Richard's online computing lectures have had over two million views and in 2012 he ran the first Australian MOOC "The Art of Computing". He is currently teaching a Cyber Security MOOC of 17,000 students. He is co-founder of OpenLearning.com the constructivist open MOOC and flipped classroom platform designed to delight students as well as teachers.

ICER '16, September 08-12, 2016, Melbourne, VIC, Australia
ACM 978-1-4503-4449-4/16/09.
http://dx.doi.org/10.1145/2960310.2960311

When Everyone Knows CS is the Best Major

Decisions about CS in an Indian context

Michael Hewner
Rose–Hulman Institute of Technology
5500 Wabash Avenue
Terre Haute IN, USA
hewner@rose-hulman.edu

Shitanshu Mishra
Indian Institute of Technology Bombay
Powai, Mumbai - 400076
Maharashtra, India
shitanshu@iitb.ac.in

ABSTRACT

Much of the existing work on student experiences in the CS major focuses on CS in American and European contexts. This paper explores the experience of CS students who – due to India's unusual educational system, joined CS with very little knowledge about CS outside of its reputation. The study was a grounded–theory based interview study based on 20 students at 2 tiers of schools in India. Results suggest that although students generally enjoyed the CS content of their courses, they had a great deal of concern about the lack of freedom in professional programming. This is surprising considering the highly positive view of CS jobs is what initially seems to attract students to the major. We contrast this with educational findings in other contexts and discuss the educational implications of the result.

Categories and Subject Descriptors

K.3.2 [**Computers and Education**]: Computer and Information Science Education — Curriculum

Keywords

Curriculum, India, International

1. INTRODUCTION

> "Parents force their children to take [Computer Science]. In India, every parent wants to made their children either doctor or engineer — not any other thing. Every parent tries this. So I chose engineering and my [admission exam rank] was good enough so I can pick CS in IIT . . . if you are doing good, you have to choose CS."
>
> —Indian student explaining how they choose CS

CS enrollments have massively increased at many schools in the US [26] and elsewhere. Although some research suggests that students currently entering into the major are not

ICER '16, September 08 - 12, 2016, Melbourne, VIC, Australia

© 2016 Copyright held by the owner/author(s). Publication rights licensed to ACM.
ISBN 978-1-4503-4449-4/16/09. . . $15.00

DOI: http://dx.doi.org/10.1145/2960310.2960318

academically weaker than in years with poorer enrollment [19] there is no doubt that CS is pulling from a wider pool of applicants. Although many students select CS based on some experience in the discipline or some intrinsic interest, others choose CS for other more mysterious reasons.

One place that is familiar with high CS enrollments is India. In India, CS at the top engineering schools is so popular that in 2014, 85 of the top 100 ranked engineering students in India chose CS as their major [18]. As each major has a cap for student admission, for most having the opportunity to enroll in CS is an unlikely dream. Previous research on affect in CS has focused mostly on places like the US: areas where students can easily choose their major and select it based on personal interest. In India, intrinsic interest is not a major aspect of student major selection. As this paper will explore, social and curricular factors conspire to have give CS a (probably undeserved) reputation as the "best major". This paper presents the results of a qualitative grounded theory based study of CS students at two colleges in India, exploring the affective results of CS's overwhelming popularity with students.

What initially attracts students to the major is a mix of reputation and the promise of certain (and lucrative) employment. This attracts students even if they have no experience with CS and are uncertain they will like it. In India, it is not usually possible to change majors so the choice of major is a four year commitment. Luckily, based on our interviews, students do come to enjoy Computer Science. Unfortunately, they also retain serious misgivings about a lack of freedom in industry jobs and relatively little clarity about what alternatives exist.

This paper proposes to analyze how students with low exposure to CS and pre–college interest experience the major. We focus on two questions:

1. What makes Indian students with little CS experience select CS?

2. After exposure to CS, what do Indian students think about pursuing CS after graduation?

Although the results presented here are specifically about students in an Indian context, the issues raised should be of interest anywhere with a similar educational context: high stakes exams, little pre–college CS exposure, and a strong social focus on finding high paying stable employment. This paper first presents method and results, then discusses similarities and differences with related work, and concludes with a discussion and educational implications.

2. METHOD

The study was an open–ended qualitative study designed to understand what students views on CS, how they selected the major, and their plans for the future. This work was a replication of Hewner's study [9, 10] of CS students in the US context. The primary data for this study came from interviews with undergraduate CS majors at 2 tiers of schools: (i) Indian Institute of Technology Bombay (IIT) is a prestigious engineering institute, (ii) Mumbai University (MU) are two mid–tier general colleges. We interviewed 14 IIT students and 6 MU students. The interviews were between 35 and 60 minutes.

Recruitment was done through presentations in CS classes. Students were asked to volunteer and not offered compensation. Participation was generally greater than 33% so self–section bias should be limited. When selecting students to interview, we used the grounded theory practice of theoretical sampling [4]. In theoretical sampling, a researcher begins with an initial population to interview and then selects future candidates based on what would further help elaborate the developing theory. This allows the researcher to discover factors that seem to have an effect on interview responses and pursue them. However, this method does not have validity as a statistically representative sample to ascribe characteristics to particular sub–populations.

We selected students to interview in order to get a range of academic success, gender, and (as the study developed) career plans. Students were interviewed at all stages of their undergraduate careers (and one graduate student), with particular focus on 2nd and 3rd year students.

The initial interviews focused on questions about students' experiences in the classroom, their views about computer science and reasons for selecting it as major, and their plans for the future. The initial question–set was similar to those used by Hewner [9] but as the theory developed focus changed over time. The interviews also added greater focus on students' pre–college decision making; especially near 10th year (when they choose a specialization) and after college placement exams (when they choose a specific school and major). The interviews attempted to be as non–leading as possible: with questions like "tell me about how you decided to go into engineering". However, encouraging the students to be as detailed as possible ("Would you say you had decided on engineering before 10th year, or did you decide at that time?") tended to open up more information about conflicts or concerns in those times.

2.1 Checks to Ensure Validity

When attempting to understand student conceptions, there is a risk of misinterpretation and bias. This is a common problem in qualitative research; even when participants and researchers act in good faith, it is difficult to understand when backgrounds and assumptions are different. There are a variety of techniques to mitigate this risk [16]. The main technique used was reviewing coding and analysis between researchers to consider other possible interpretations. We generally would both review the transcripts of interviews, one researcher would code it and present summaries/notes of their view the most relevant sections to the other. Oftentimes this discussion would go back to the source and cause re–coding. This is not the same as formal inter-rater reliability, but that level of exactness is not possible given that the codes themselves are in flux in the qualitative process.

2.2 Grounded Theory Analysis

The theory of student conceptions presented here was developed based on line–by–line analysis of interview transcripts. Our process was based on the approach outlined by Charmaz [4]:

1. First, the researcher develops initial codes that describe what is being expressed in each line of the data.

2. Second, the researcher goes back through the body of research accumulated and selects 'focused' codes that explain larger segments of the data.

3. Third, the focused codes are abstracted into categories in a tentative theory that is then checked against other parts of the data to test its explanatory power. There are several techniques to help the researcher attempt to develop the categories in this larger theory: axial coding [6], theoretical coding [4], and situational maps [5].

4. Steps 1–3 continue until saturation: where new interviews do not significantly elaborate the existing theory.

A subset of codes are shown as an example in fig. 1. These codes give insight of the theory about "reasons for choosing CS". The upper table in the figure shows the 'focused' codes. The lower table shows the 'initial' codes which were grouped as "CS is the best major".

Choosing Engineering			CS is the Best Major	Parents and Relatives
Interest in Maths	Limited choice	Not serious about non-CS		
5	3	3	11	5

Good jobs	The brand	Flexible major	If you do well in exams
7	5	3	4

Figure 1: Example of a codes. Numbers are the frequencies of interviews in which any code appeared

Below is a demonstration of the analysis process explained using an excerpt from one of the interview.

> "[Tech companies] are looking for a person who can work in their scenario ... they have the assignments with some organizations. They need people who are [intelligent] and people who can work for them without any — I won't say ideas — endeavor of their own ... They won't explore they won't create something of their own and they won't try to think in a different way ... Yeah, I definitely wouldn't like to work [in a place like that]."

So in the initial pass this was coded as "wanting input into the creative/design process". This code was shared with a few other quotes that had a similar concern about just being given specifications and not having input. As analysis continued this was incorporated into a larger focused code of "autonomy", which was part of a larger section on student future goals.

However, about half way through the process, a second pass was done and codes were reorganized. We recognized commonalities between this quote and other concerns that jobs would be algorithmically uninteresting, or that managers would make excessive demands. These issues were motivating most students to seriously consider alternatives to work in industry. All these ideas became part of the larger "Wanting Freedom" category that forms a key part of our theory of student future desires.

3. REASONS FOR CHOOSING CS

3.1 Choosing Engineering

"Well it's basically after 10th you need to decide [which general area to go into] ... practice for the competitive exams. After [my 10th year] I wanted to go engineering. Basically that was building up in my mind a long time since [year] 9 maybe. Cause I was interested in mathematics my parents and my sister and my entire family they're all doctors but I preferred mathematics no matter what. The most – what can you say – prominent branch in mathematics is engineering."

To understand major selection at Indian colleges, it's first necessary to understand India's exam system. College (and major) admission are entirely based on performance on one of several exams students take in their 12th year of schooling. Students prepare for these exams by enrolling in exam–prep schools in their 11th and 12th year: the entirely of those two years is devoted to exam preparation.

There are four different categories of exams: engineering, science, commerce, and arts. As a result, the first decision students need to make is which exam track they wish to prepare for in 10th year.

All the students we interviewed selected an engineering exam track (otherwise they would not have entered the CS major). Generally, the decision seemed very straightforward from them. Commonly they framed the decision as a choice between engineering and medicine (science) – the two most prestigious choices – occasionally they also entertained pure mathematics (science exam) as an option.

Parents and relatives were frequently involved in the decision. This ranged from students who felt they could choose freely but parents made some suggestion to students who felt that they were forced to choose between engineering and medicine and had no other option. Regardless of the level of involvement, students generally did not consider this a tough decision and made it pretty casually. As noted by Hewner in his CS study [10] and replicated with Indian students, just because an educational decision is important does not mean students will spend a lot of time (or research) making it. Students did not have a specific branch of engineering selected at this time. Skill with math was often cited as a factor in their decision, but rarely experience with or interest in technology.

3.2 Choosing a College and Major

When 12th year exam results are in, students apply to a particular major within a particular college. Priority is determined by exam grade. The type of college largely determines its reputation, so for example students would definitely prefer IIT to MU simply based on the kind of college it is. Once a school's pre–determined number of major slots

are filled, no more students can enter that major in that school. Students know it is almost impossible to change majors after entering a school, so this major choice is binding.

The result of this system is that students generally have very little knowledge about what colleges or majors will be available to them until exam results are in. Students may well have to choose either a more prestigious college or a preferred major. As a result, most students did not consider what area of engineering they were most interested in until they received their exam results. The engineering exam itself consists of mathematics, physics, and chemistry questions; exam-prep schools therefore did not attempt to educate students about the various branches of engineering.

3.3 No Strong Vision

"Actually I was really interested for computers. When I was in 11th 10th grade I knew the basics of computers but I did not have the knowledge that what happens in if I take engineering in Computer Science. I did not have that knowledge. But I was interested towards it somehow — intuition you can say. So I took that computer science engineering in my bachelors ... I used to play a lot of games."

Similar to previous studies of US students [10], students did not have a concrete career goal when they selected their major (or even when I interviewed them). Given that it is almost impossible to transfer between majors after admission, one might expect that students would devote energy to researching the possible majors in detail, but this does not seem to be the case.

Some of the students we interviewed has some previous interest in technology. The majority of the involvement was very limited though – playing games, using webpages etc. None had done any serious programming (i.e. a full year long course) or significant hobbyist projects. This contrasts with Hewner's work [10] in which many students had at least some exposure pre–college. Furthermore, because they did not know what degrees would be available to them until they saw the exam results, none had planned on CS in particular until that time.

A few students did research into the topics and course content of the various degree programs before selecting the major. For them, the discrete math and algorithm side of CS was most attractive. But this was definitely the exception: most students did not do research before choosing their major. Even the students who did research still did not generally have a specific post graduation goal at the time of entering their degree.

3.4 CS is the Best Major

"It's more like a tradition. If you are among the top rankers in IIT it's like you generally prefer Computer Science. So you can say that unless you're very much interested in some other field which I wasn't — and Computer Science it looks like you can get a deal out of it. ...I think it's the placements mostly like we do have rankings in every department from IIT so CS is mostly tops in it in terms of placement ...So it's a kind of tradition building up and that's because of the placements we get. CS people get maximum placements, the highest packages. Plus I think CS is also the most intriguing branch as per me at least. It is a branch that really fancies me. Like algorithms, programming ..."

The idea that "everyone knew" CS was the best major was by far the most commonly cited reason for students deciding to enter the CS major. Although initially it seemed like students might be simply interested in getting high salary jobs (i.e. "placements" or "packages") post graduation, this idea turned out to be more complicated. We think there are several aspects that combine to make CS so strongly appealing.

When students were asked to reflect on why CS was considered "the best major", high salaries was always the first explanation. This was a bit strange because students in general did seem to consider money a major consideration elsewhere in their decision making process. When considering jobs near graduation, for example, salary generally seemed to be important but secondary to ensuring that the job itself was enjoyable.

Part of the appeal of good packages seems to be job security; high packages signal high demand and therefore the certainty of finding a reasonable job. Several students mentioned that, if they chose some other field they might have difficulty getting a job. This was mentioned even at the prestigious IIT , which likely has good placement in all fields. There is a sense in which, if they chose another degree path for capricious reasons, they might someday regret having given up the opportunity for a "sure thing" in a CS degree.

Another aspect of it is the competitiveness of the degree programs themselves act as a signifier of intelligence/prestige. No student we interviewed directly attributed their choice of CS to interest in prestige, but a few confided that they suspected their classmates of having such motives. Some mentioned that they appreciated the flexibility of an engineering degree: it allows graduate study abroad or can allow entrance into competitive MBA programs. Some students definitely choose CS because of this flexibility and even admitted they planned on future careers in business that did not use their CS knowledge directly, but this was uncommon in the students we interviewed.

Of course, students don't evaluate each of these aspects of "CS is the best major" intellectually. For most students, no particular relative or friend told them about CS: this idea has been casually absorbed from newspapers, conversations, etc. All this amounts to is a feeling that they have an unusual opportunity to be able to choose CS (because most students can't) and that they would need a particularly good reason not to take advantage of it. Because students don't often have particular experience with any engineering discipline when they apply, this feeling becomes a major factor in their decision.

3.5 Parents and Relatives

"Actually my Dad had a dream, to see somebody who can actually go to IIT ...I planned to clear [the entrance exam], and then I thought I'll do some Math [and not go to IIT] ...After [the exam], when I got rank, my cousin, he told me that there is a lot of scope of math in Computer

Science, and in Electrical Engineering as well. [He] told me that [CS and EE would be more useful in life]."

In talking with Indian instructors and school administrators, it seems to be a common refrain that Indian students enter CS because their conservative parents think it is a good idea. Based on our interviews, that does not seem to be borne out. In fact, parents and relatives' involvement in the major decision making process was extremely diverse: everything from no input whatsoever to heavy involvement even with post–graduation plans. Moreover, students don't need their parents involvement to act conservatively: the factors outlined in "CS is the best major" affect the students strongly even without the parents.

Most of the students we interviewed said that their families made suggestions but that in the end they were free to choose for themselves. Some students, when probed further, admitted that certain options (e.g. commerce or arts) would cause arguments or were implicitly disallowed. Other students insisted that they had almost complete control over their educational decisions, however, and that their parents would be supportive regardless.

Even when parents were heavily involved, students also were willing to stand up to their parents if necessary. One student's parents favored a civil engineering degree as opposed to CS, and actually used the student's credentials to log on to the college website and pick the degree they favored. Later, the student secretly changed the degree section back. This kind of fighting was definitely the exception, however: most times students and parents were on the same page in terms of goals.

3.6 Summary

There is no single factor motivating students to study CS. Students did not have a particular long–term careers in view. Students did not usually have experience with CS. Students did also not choose CS for cynical reasons: although good career prospects were a positive aspect of CS (and students were aware of it), no students seemed to be strictly looking for the best paying job. Family input was involved, but no students felt strictly forced by their families into CS. Instead, the choice of CS was motivated by the fact that the students did not have a particular concrete goal, and CS has a good reputation. Despite the fact that choice of a particular major was a 4 year commitment, students made the decision fairly casually.

4. ENJOYING CS

"Mainly in the 3rd semester... like when I was working on a project in the lab, data structure lab, so we have to complete a project basically. There we created new games.. also created [a] search engine... for Ubuntu... We got the feel that, what is in CS, and how can we use the CS. Like in the 1st semester I [didn't] know what CS was.."

Most of the students did not have exposure to Computer Science before starting college. Further, students did not seem to primarily use the potential for enjoyment as their reason for choosing the major. Despite this, almost all of the students said they had come to enjoy the field of Computer Science and the content of their classes. Of course, many students had a few CS courses they did not enjoy, but their overall view of the field was interested and positive.

The process of enjoying CS took time for many (but not all students) students: many students cited 2-3 semesters. Students felt that in their intro classes they did not fully understand what they were learning. But even though students did not generally have much freedom to choose courses, later courses in the curriculum generally persuaded them of CS's potential.

We observed a marked difference between IIT and MU students in reasons for liking CS. For IIT students, CS's mathematical nature was a great draw. Students often talked about discovering importance of algorithms and the enjoyment of coming up with a novel approach. They mentioned they liked the activity of coding as well but it was usually secondary. This may be partly a result of the exam system: students entrance exams focused on mathematics, physics, and chemistry. All three have a strong mathematical component so it's not too surprising that top scorers would enjoy mathematics.

For MU students, the activity of programming was definitely more primary. MU would usually say that they like solving a problem by writing good programs: not distinguishing between the design of the algorithm and coding itself. Even non-programming courses had a strong focus on eventually writing code: "Even in Operating Systems, you need to program and then only you can use any OS concept ...".

Both groups perceived CS as broader than they originally expected and involved with many challenging problems. They cited application domains like artificial intelligence, multi-processing, and data analysis. Of course students were aware abstractly that Computer Science was involved in these activities before starting the major, but many commented that understanding the complexity behind these various systems was beyond what they had anticipated when they chose CS.

5. CONCERNS ABOUT CAREERS IN CS

The story thus far seems relatively positive. Students decide to major in Computer Science with relatively little exposure, relying in part on CS's good reputation as "the best major". In their CS classes, students learn the discipline and generally find it enjoyable (which is good, because they can't switch majors). Surely then they are looking forward to a career in industry?

Many students had significant concerns about jobs in industry. They were considering them, but many had negative perceptions about working in CS. Both IIT and MU students viewed many industry jobs as uncreative and demanding, and most hoped to (in various ways) find an alternative that allowed them greater "freedom". Following findings are the parts of larger "Wanting Freedom" focused code.

5.1 Negative View of CS Jobs

> Student: "I want not to do coding in a Google can: 4x4 can only coding. It should have some adventure, something — not just coding. Not only C++. It's related to coding but not only coding. . . . You know?"

> Interviewer: "Do you have an idea of what other thing than coding you'd like to be working on?"
>
> Student: "I like to do many stuffs — I don't know. I have no absolute explanation for it."

What are the problems with CS jobs, given CS's reputation for the best packages — many jobs and high salaries? Students still perceived that the jobs paid reasonably and were available (although some MU students did worry at least in part about finding any job at all). Students' reasons were different but they share some common themes:

1. Students were concerned that most CS jobs were just to implement features decided by someone else — that they would have no say in the design or feature set.

2. Students were concerned that they would be solving technically or algorithmically trivial problems.

3. Students were concerned they would be required to work long hours.

4. Students were concerned their environment would be conservative: that they would be forced to work regular business hours or have a dress code.

5. In general, that a industry CS job would be boring or that unreasonable demands would be forced on them by management.

On the whole, students view CS jobs as stifling and monotonous. This perception was not confined to a few "bad jobs/ managers/ companies" out there: instead it was the view that the majority of jobs available had these negative characteristics. This was true for both IIT and MU students: some IIT students felt that industry jobs would be good for lower tier school graduates, but in fact both groups shared similar concerns.

These views were not, in general, based on direct experience with industry jobs: MU students did not usually get internships and most IIT students we interviewed had more research–oriented summer work (if any). Similar to the perception of CS as the "best major", these views were described as things that "everybody knows" or as coming from senior students — but not usually a specific senior with a specific bad experience. Students with actual work experience tended to be more positive about industry jobs.

5.2 Alternatives to Bad CS Jobs

Students concerned about potential bad jobs suggested several alternatives. In each case, the alternative seemed chosen to focus on the perceived main failing of industry jobs (i.e. a student concerned with having a unreasonable boss might want to start a startup or maybe get and MBA and become a boss themselves). Mostly, these alternatives were pretty speculative: e.g. students who wished to start startups did not have an idea yet, students who wished to go to graduate school did not have an area of specialization, etc.

5.2.1 Facebook, Microsoft and Google

> "But then there are these jobs which are not just about coding in which you also have to put your minds — there are various algorithms. . . you

have this graph search on Facebook that is one of the coolest things I have seen till now on Facebook. There are people designing these algorithms...So all that requires some mind...there are all kinds of jobs in a company so I would personally prefer using my brain to some extent for these things and not just do some naive coding."

One group was strangely absent from student complaints about bad work environments: large American companies. Especially for students concerned about technologically interesting work, these companies were perceived to be able to guarantee algorithmically interesting technical focus. No Indian company had a similarly high reputation and indeed being Indian seemed to be a detriment to students' perception.

Perhaps unsurprisingly given students' view of the company's technical focus, students perceived the main way to get these desirable jobs was through excelling in algorithm-focused interview questions. This was seen as very difficult: several students acknowledged they would like to work at these companies but probably would not be able to. The process itself seemed surprisingly similar to the college entrance exams: students perceived the jobs as desirable but did not know the details. They felt the main way to get them was by competing in a another high–stakes examination.

5.2.2 Your Own Startup

For students primarily interested in being their own boss, creating a startup was a common plan. Interestingly, no students interviewed expressed interest in joining an existing Indian startup, even though apparently such startups frequently recruited on campuses.

Students who were interested in starting their own business often planned to do so after working in industry for several years (2 years was the generally quoted number). They felt that this would allow them to understand how business worked and save some money beforehand. A few mentioned that this might also please families concerned about their long–term careers.

5.2.3 Social Services and MBAs

One of the unusual characteristics of Indian engineering degrees is that they were perceived as a good way to prepare for entering Social Services: government jobs that were considered highly prestigious and depended on doing well on another national examination. Though a few students mentioned this as a possible alternative, this option generally seemed more popular with students' parents than students themselves, although it was viewed as helping society in a way an ordinary industry job did not.

Another possibility seemed to be continuing in school to get an MBA: this option was particularly popular among MU students. Managers were perceived as not being subject to the same limiting constraints as ordinary employees. Students planning to go for an MBA felt learning a technical field like CS would be beneficial in understanding technology from a business sense, but generally saw themselves as moving into a pure-management role after the MBA.

5.2.4 Graduate School

For both MU and IIT students continuing on to graduate school, especially graduate school abroad, was considered a strong alternative. Students generally had little experience with academic careers, so their expectations of graduate school varied quite a bit between students:

1. Some viewed academic careers as method of focusing on some technically challenging sub–discipline.

2. Some viewed foreign schools as better than Indian schools and hoped to learn more, eventually perhaps securing a desirable foreign job.

3. Some viewed it as an opportunity to work without deliverables and invent something new.

5.3 Summary

Indian students have negative perceptions of industry CS work. In many ways, these perceptions mirror the feelings of non–CS–majors elsewhere [24, 2]: that CS work is uncreative, stuck behind a computer etc. What is surprising is that these negative opinions of CS jobs can coexist with excitement and interest about the academic content of CS. Students like the academic topics of CS, but much of the negative association of CS work remain – even in India, where the promise of excellent (i.e. highly stable and high paying) jobs is one of the main factors attracting students to CS in particular.

As alternatives to the negative aspects of CS jobs, students considered a wide variety of alternatives that gave them more freedom. However, similar to before entering the major, students views of the future were very speculative. Although many students felt strongly they did not want a CS industry job, almost none had a well researched alternative in mind.

As far as the career advising offered by the schools is concerned, these schools have training and placement cells, but no students mentioned ever about using them for advisory purposes.

6. RELATION TO EXISTING WORK

A lot research exists on how students select majors. [23, 15, 13] In a study performed by Serapilgia and Lenox [21], several categories of factors that affect the decision of women to enter into a course of study in Information Science programs were found, viz., influence by male role models; introduction to computers in the home and school; interest in problem solving; early exposure to computers/technology; greater opportunity for higher salaries. Stinebrickner and Stinebrickner [22] found that "over-optimism about completing a degree" affected student choice of the major. Pedro et al. [20] found the indicators such as student knowledge, performance and gaming behaviours which vary among students who choose different college majors. Zimmerman et al.[25] found that the factors influenced the students choice of CS major were "money", "knowing someone in the CS field", and "experience with computers". To the best of our knowledge there is a dearth of such research for India like educational context. Moreover the Indian context differs in two very significant ways from these places: (i) students have much less freedom in choosing a major; and (ii) Indian students have this feeling about CS being particularly great.

In some ways, the Indian students seem similar to what we've seen in the past – in other ways they are different:
Vague vision of the future. Similar to the students in Hewner's study of CS students [10], Indian students did not

choose their major with a vision of a career post graduation. In Hewner's studies, students chose their courses based on personal interest, which did not seem as strong in the Indian students. However, what is consistent is that forcing students to make high–stakes decisions earlier (specialization choice in Hewner's work, 4–year degree in an Indian context) encouraged students to chose in a casual and somewhat arbitrary fashion.

Pre–college perceptions of CS. Pre–college work suggests that before college many US students are interested in computing careers [7] but generally speaking do not have a strong idea of what Computer Science is [3]. This seems very similar to what we observed with Indian students pre–college recollections (although clearly CS is vastly more popular major in India). Despite the importance of decisions about majors in the Indian context, approaches to learning about potential majors seems relatively similar.

Most commonly cited reason for opting for CS major was the idea that "everyone knew" CS was the best major. This reconfirms and further elaborates on the findings by Holmegaard et al., [12] that the choice of major is not an isolated individual event but its a social process.

One key area that Indian students obviously do differ from counterparts studied in previous work is in their potential to be exposed to CS prior to selecting the CS major. At this point, many countries are either requiring CS to all post-secondary students (e.g. Israel, Russia) or at least increasing its availability as an elective (e.g. New Zealand, Sweden). [1] In a study based on United States students, CS education in school is itself a strong predictor for student STEM major choices. [14] In India, the fact that the last few years of high school occur at exam prep schools make it very unlikely a student would have had formal pre–college CS experience. Even if the student had the opportunity, they would not have been able to be sure they would get into a CS program so they would not be likely to pursue it seriously.

In–college perceptions of CS. One result that definitely exists across cultural contexts is that CS majors are excited about the academic content Computer Science. Even though Indian students did not know much about CS before they selected the field, they enjoyed it. Similarly, previous work asking students to write about CS has prompted them to talk about how broad and enjoyable it is. [11] Biggers et al. study also found that compared to CS majors who left the discipline, majors who stayed were talked significantly more about how broad and exciting it was. [2] Yardi and Bruckman also found CS professionals to be upbeat in their estimation of the CS field. [24]

In contrast Indian students' perceptions of CS industry jobs seemed more similar to impressions attributable to either those who left the CS major in Bigger's survey [2] or pre–college students not planning to major in Yardi and Bruckman's work. [24] But student concern about post graduation careers did not seem motivated by bad experiences in the classroom, which Hewner identified as a primary motivator of long–career decision making. [10]

6.1 Academia and Industry in India

There is some research that suggests that the negative perception of CS industry jobs in Indian students may be related to pedagogy. Introducing industry–oriented topics like software engineering may be more difficult because recruiting professors with industry experience is particularly difficult in the developing world [17]. As a result, the disconnect that always exists between academia and industry is exacerbated and professors avoid talking about software engineering and industrial topics. When the topics are presented, they focus on theory and don't take into account actual local practices. This leads students to view them as inauthentic and boring [17]. Garg and Varma did an analysis of CS curricula and found that software engineering topics were de-emphasized and also tended to be taught in lecture style separated from projects (which were graded on CS content – not technique) [8]. So part of negative views of industrial software development may have been absorbed implicitly from professors.

7. DISCUSSION

7.1 Impact of Educational System

Many structures of the Indian educational system contributes to some of the unusual results seen here:

1. The national exam system forces students to specialize in engineering/science/others well before they have a concrete career plan

2. Being accepted into particular college majors at application time causes students to wait on deciding on a major until exam results are returned, making it impossible for students to explore their major before college begins

3. Policies which limit major change to only a few students restrict students who discover their major is not a good fit

4. The application process to both colleges and jobs encourage students to view career paths as competing for a small number of "guaranteed good" spots, rather than differentiating themselves

As with similar policies in the US [10], it seems clear that requiring students to make high–stakes decisions before they have a clear plan does not encourage them to make the decision more carefully. The Indian system forces decisions on things like engineering vs. science etc. as early at year 10. Similarly, in year 12 they must commit to a major from a limited list of choices after getting their exam results. Both decisions are high–stakes, but because students don't really know enough to make a well–reasoned decision they make them quite casually.

In Indian school administrators and educators often voice dissatisfaction with the way students make major decisions, and they usually blame parents demanding students make conservative choices. Based on these interviews, however, it seems more likely that the college application/exam process forcing students to decide very early is causing students to pick in very similar and conservative ways.

As educators, we often don't have a mechanism to change national education policies. But there are a lot of individual school policies that exacerbate the problem of high–stakes choices early. At the school level, policies which restrict students changing their mind seem to cause unnecessary problems. At IIT for example, despite the fact that all majors have a common introductory sequence, the number of students allowed to enter or leave a major are strictly limited.

Even if a student wishes to leave a popular major like CS, they could be limited even if individuals in the destination major are willing to switch to CS. Little support for double–majors, minors, and other outside–of–discipline classwork further limit student options.

On the individual level, high stakes exams seem to have encouraged a very similar strategic approach among students. Even taking for granted that CS has the best packages on average, surely there is some advantage to being a top–tier chemist as opposed to a below average computer scientist? Although most students we interviewed find the perception of CS to be overblown, they nonetheless tend to follow the conventional wisdom (although, admittedly, this is skewed by our sample).

7.2 Envisioning a Future in CS

One of the most interesting results of the study was the discovery that students could be excited about CS concepts while at the same time have a great deal of concern about careers in CS. It almost seemed like the negative stereotypes associated with the CS major itself observed in other countries [24] had been transposed to programming jobs in the Indian context. Strangely, no student mentioned concerns about these negative jobs until after entering the major, despite the fact that the availability and compensation of these jobs are part of what make the major so popular.

Given our data, it's impossible to know if student perceptions of industry jobs are inaccurate or if Indian programming jobs are as uncreative and demanding as students imagine. Either way, it seems that the widespread negative perception of industry jobs is causing a recruitment problem for Indian technology companies.

Based on Garg and Varma's work in Indian Software Engineering education [8], it may be that students are inheriting part of their distaste for Indian industry work from their professors/curricula. This is one area where pedagogical changes in the curricula or teaching style might benefit students. Both IIT and MU students had described class experiences designed to give a feel for industry–style development. More emphasis in the curriculum might help reduce the concerns of students about the boring nature of industry jobs.

Furthermore, beyond industry jobs in particular, Indian students seemed to have a strong desire for career opportunities that provide a greater amount of freedom. Freedom and an enjoyable job does not seem to be a concern for students in the initial choice of college and degree, yet it seems a dominant factor as they examine career options near graduation. As students look into alternatives, they don't have much information.

For example, students who are considering applying for graduate school abroad have little idea what they ought to be doing (outside presumably of performing well on standardized tests like the GRE). As a result, student perceptions of graduate work seems to be a mix of the accurate (e.g. you can specialize in a particular subdomain and choose your own projects) and the fantastical (e.g. you have no accountability and are just supposed to produce innovative ideas). In some cases students have desires that can probably be accommodated within the space of possible CS jobs (e.g. the desire to do something good for the community as a whole) but make plans that seem outlandish (e.g. somehow funding and managing a hospital).

The Indian educational system seems to be effectively solving the problem of taking students who don't know much about CS and presenting it a way they enjoy in their classes at both IIT and MU . But students seem to have difficulty taking those enjoyable classroom experiences and finding realistic career opportunities they feel they will also enjoy. If students could find a realistic career goal and understand what sorts of things they ought to be doing in and outside the classroom to pursue it, then it seems like students might be able to pursue CS with even more confidence and success.

8. CONCLUSION

In this paper we have focused on two questions:

1. What makes Indian students with little CS experience select CS?

2. After exposure to CS, what do Indian students think about pursuing CS after graduation?

In answer to the first question, CS college education in India is in an interesting position. The major is extremely popular, but most students are not being forced in the major by their parents or cynically picking to maximize financial returns. Certainly, CS's reputation as the "best major" and a unusual opportunity influences many students. The constraints imposed by the engineering testing system make it difficult for students to foster independent interests in engineering before starting college. Despite this, students mostly seem to have approached CS with great curiosity and in general seemed to enjoy the discipline and their classes.

In answer to the second question, despite CS's reputation for the best salaries and jobs, most students seemed concerned about the transition to industry. Indian CS industry jobs were perceived as uncreative and demanding. Students were considering perceived alternatives like graduate work, American technical firms, startups, and even non–CS career paths. Although freedom did not seem to be a major goal of students as they chose their college/major, it seems significant as they consider post–college careers.

More broadly, this work suggests that policies that force students to make high–stakes decisions early cause strange education effects. In the Indian case, it contributes to students perception of CS as the "best" major and its very high popularity. In general, ensuring that school policies to allow later term decisions about goals may allow for less random student decision making.

This work also suggests that students can be enjoying the academic content of their CS courses while at the same time having great trepidation with regard to CS jobs. In this Indian case, this suggests a greater a better connection between industry and academia and more explicit school support for other options could help. Beyond India specifically, it suggests a greater attention to student post-graduation careers might be worthwhile.

Although this study has focused on the specific details of the Indian context, there are many countries with similar educational structures (e.g. high stakes exams that entirely control college admissions) that may find similar reactions in their own students. Even for educators with a different context, India provides an interesting example of the ways in which a superficially good thing (overwhelming popularity of the CS major) can have unusual effects.

9. REFERENCES

[1] Special issue on computing education in (k-12) schools. *Trans. Comput. Educ.*, 14(2), 2014.

[2] M. Biggers, A. Brauer, and T. Yilmaz. Student perceptions of computer science. In *Proceedings of SIGCSE 2008*, pages 402–406, Portland, 2008. ACM.

[3] L. Carter. Why students with an apparent aptitude for computer science don't choose to major in computer science. In *Proceedings of SIGCSE 2006*, pages 27–31, Houston, Texas, USA, 2006. ACM.

[4] K. Charmaz. *Constructing Grounded Theory.* Sage Publications Ltd, 1 edition, Jan. 2006.

[5] A. Clarke. *Situational Analysis: Grounded Theory After the Postmodern Turn.* Sage Publications, 2005.

[6] J. Corbin and A. C. Strauss. *Basics of Qualitative Research.* Sage Publications, Inc, 3rd edition, 2008.

[7] W. E. Foundation and ACM. New image for computing: Report on market research. http://www.acm.org/membership/NIC.pdf, 2009.

[8] K. Garg and V. Varma. Software engineering education in india: Issues and challenges. In *Software Engineering Education and Training, 2008. CSEET '08. IEEE 21st Conference on*, pages 110–117, April 2008.

[9] M. Hewner. Undergraduate conceptions of the field of computer science. ICER '13, pages 107–114, New York, 2013. ACM.

[10] M. Hewner. How cs undergraduates make course choices. ICER '14, pages 115–122, New York, NY, USA, 2014. ACM.

[11] M. Hewner and M. Guzdial. Attitudes about computing in postsecondary graduates. In *Proceeding of ICER 2008*, pages 71–78, Sydney, Australia, 2008. ACM.

[12] H. T. Holmegaard, L. M. Ulriksen, and L. M. Madsen. The process of choosing what to study: A longitudinal study of upper secondary students' identity work when choosing higher education. *Scandinavian Journal of Educational Research*, 58(1):21–40, 2014.

[13] S. W. Kim, K.-E. Brown, and V. L. Fong. Credentialism and career aspirations: How urban chinese youth chose high school and college majors. *Comparative Education Review*, 60(2):000–000, 2016.

[14] A. Lee. Determining the effects of computer science education at the secondary level on stem major choices in postsecondary institutions in the united states. *Computers & Education*, 88:241–255, 2015.

[15] T. Lenox, G. Jesse, and C. R. Woratschek. Factors influencing students decisions to major in a computer-related discipline. *Information Systems Education Journal*, 10(6):63, 2012.

[16] Y. S. Lincoln and E. G. Guba. *Naturalistic inquiry.* Sage, 1985.

[17] R. Osman. Teaching software engineering in developing countries: A position paper. In *Computer Software and Applications Conference (COMPSAC), 2012 IEEE 36th Annual*, pages 648–653, July 2012.

[18] Y. Rao and H. Chhapia. IIT–bombay first choice for 44 out of top 50 rankers. *Times of India*, July 2, 2014.

[19] M. Sahami and C. Piech. As cs enrollments grow, are we attracting weaker students? In *SIGCSE 2016*, SIGCSE '16, pages 54–59, New York, NY, USA, 2016. ACM.

[20] M. O. San Pedro, R. S. Baker, N. T. Heffernan, and J. L. Ocumpaugh. Exploring college major choice and middle school student behavior, affect and learning: what happens to students who game the system? In *Proceedings of the Fifth International Conference on Learning Analytics And Knowledge*, pages 36–40. ACM, 2015.

[21] C. P. Serapiglia and T. L. Lenox. Factors affecting women's decisions to pursue an is degree: A case study. *Information Systems Education Journal, galley*, 9:1420, 2010.

[22] R. Stinebrickner and T. Stinebrickner. A major in science? initial beliefs and final outcomes for college major and dropout. *The Review of Economic Studies*, page rdt025, 2013.

[23] X. Wang. Why students choose stem majors motivation, high school learning, and postsecondary context of support. *American Educational Research Journal*, page 0002831213488622, 2013.

[24] S. Yardi and A. Bruckman. What is computing?: bridging the gap between teenagers' perceptions and graduate students' experiences. In *Proceedings of the third international workshop on Computing education research*, pages 39–50, Atlanta, Georgia, USA, 2007. ACM.

[25] T. G. Zimmerman, D. Johnson, C. Wambsgans, and A. Fuentes. Why latino high school students select computer science as a major: Analysis of a success story. *ACM Transactions on Computing Education (TOCE)*, 11(2):10, 2011.

[26] S. Zweben and B. Bizot. 2014 taulbee survey. In *Computing Research News*, volume 27, 2015.

Perceived Instrumentality and Career Aspirations in CS1 Courses: Change and Relationships with Achievement

Markeya S. Peteranetz
Abraham E. Flanigan
Duane F. Shell
University of Nebraska-Lincoln
114 Teachers College Hall
Lincoln, Nebraska 68588
1-402-472-8331
markeya.dubbs@huskers.unl.edu,
abrahamflanigan@gmail.com,
dshell2@unl.edu

Leen-Kiat Soh
University of Nebraska-Lincoln
122E Avery Hall
Lincoln, Nebraska 68588
1-402-472-6738
lksoh@cse.unl.edu

ABSTRACT

We explored CS1 students' perceived instrumentality (PI) for the course and aspirations for a career related to CS. Perceived instrumentality refers to the connection one sees between a current activity and a future goal. There are two types of PI: endogenous and exogenous. Endogenous instrumentality refers to the perception that mastering new information or skills is important for achieving distal goals. Exogenous instrumentality refers to the perception that obtaining an external reward (such as a grade) is essential for obtaining future goals. We investigated (1) how students' PI and career aspirations changed over the course of a semester, (2) how these changes differed as a function of course enrollment and major (CS or not), (3) the relationship between PI and career aspirations, and (4) whether PI and career aspirations predicted academic achievement. Overall and for most subgroups, exogenous instrumentality increased significantly and endogenous instrumentality decreased significantly across the semester, though the degree of change varied among some subgroups. Career aspirations decreased overall and for most subgroups, but CS majors showed a much smaller decrease than non-majors, and students in a CS/business honors course showed an overall increase in career aspirations. Finally, students' achievement outcomes were predicted by their PI and career aspirations. These findings contribute to the literature on motivation in CS1 courses and points to PI as a promising avenue for influencing student motivation. Implications for student motivation and retention in CS and other STEM courses are also discussed.

Categories and Subject Descriptors

K.3.2. [Computers and Education]: Computer and Information Science Education

ICER'16, September 8–12, 2016, Melbourne, VIC, Australia.
© 2016 ACM. ISBN 978-1-4503-4449-4/16/09…$15.00.
DOI: http://dx.doi.org/10.1145/2960310.2960320

General Terms

Performance, Human factors, Theory

Keywords

Perceived instrumentality; Career aspirations; CS1

1. INTRODUCTION

In today's rapidly advancing technological environment, the need to attract and retain students in STEM majors is possibly greater than ever before [22, 31]. It has been proposed that career opportunities in STEM-related fields will grow at nearly twice the rate as opportunities in non-STEM fields between 2008 and 2018 [22]. The need for more post-secondary students to major and graduate in STEM fields, especially computer science (CS), is widely recognized, [3, 22] and there is increasing recognition of the need for computational thinking both for CS and across the broader spectrum of STEM and non-STEM disciplines [29].

To address these needs, considerable effort has been focused on attracting and retaining students in CS. These include efforts to engage and motivate non-CS majors [5]; instructional strategies such as pair programming, peer-based instruction, and media computation [21]; using personal robots [16]; project-based instruction with different tracks [10]; and framing an appropriate classroom climate to reduce student anxiety about their status among peers and encourage them to co-learn and speak up in class [2]. But, despite these efforts, enrollment and persistence in CS continues to be problematic, with enrollments actually declining over the past decade [18].

This lack of progress indicates a need to better understand the motivations of students who are taking CS courses and how their motivation is contributing to their success and retention. Many aspects of student motivation in CS courses have been examined including goal orientation [7], mindsets [4], and self-efficacy [25], and these motivators influence both student engagement and achievement. The purpose of this study was to investigate two relatively understudied motivators in CS courses: perceived instrumentality (PI) and career aspirations. PI and career aspirations differ from previously studied motivators because they reflect motivation related to distal outcomes such as career success rather than proximal outcomes such as course achievement. As a result, PI and career aspirations provide a different perspective on student motivation.

We examined PI [6, 11, 12, 17], and specifically considered (a) how PI changes over the semester in introductory CS1 courses and (b) how that change potentially affects students learning and achievement. Although prior studies have found that PI is associated with student achievement in undergraduate CS1 courses, results have differed depending on whether PI was assessed at the beginning [27] or the end [24] of the course, with findings not always corresponding to expectations based on PI theory [6, 12]. These different findings from the beginning and end of the semester assessments suggest that important changes in students' PI occur during the semester. Our study is designed to examine these possible changes and the impact of those changes on student achievement to help resolve these conflicting prior findings.

The second motivator we investigated is future career aspiration. Prior studies in engineering have found that the extent to which students aspire to a career in engineering influences their achievement, engagement, and persistence [1, 8]. Specifically, future career aspirations have been found to be associated with how much students perceive a specific course as instrumental to their future [8]. No studies of career aspirations have been done in CS, however. Our study is designed to fill this gap by examining change in students' future aspirations for using CS and computational thinking in their career across the semester in CS1 classes and examining how changes in career aspirations are associated with PI.

2. THEORETICAL FRAMEWORK

2.1 Perceived Instrumentality

Perceived instrumentality refers to a task-specific evaluation of how a current learning activity connects to future goals [11, 12, 14, 28]. Prior research has found that motivation and achievement are enhanced when students see a connection between present tasks and their future goals [6, 13, 14, 28].

Researchers have proposed two types of instrumentality: endogenous and exogenous instrumentality. Endogenous instrumentality is the perception that mastering new information or skills is important for achieving personally meaningful distal goals [12]. An example of endogenous instrumentality is an aspiring software engineering trying to master the concepts taught in her introductory programming course because she sees them as essential for success in her future career in software engineering. Exogenous instrumentality refers to the perception that there is only a utilitarian connection between the attained outcome of a course or activity (such as the grade) and achievement of future goals [12]. A CS major may be motivated to earn an A in their biology course because they see a need for a high GPA for future graduate school or employment; but, have no personal interest in learning biology for personal growth. Theoretical formulations of PI [12, 14, 28] generally hold that endogenous PI is the more powerful positive motivator because instrumentality for learning course material for personal growth is a source of intrinsic motivation. While the utility-based motivation from exogenous PI can be positively motivating, this motivation is based on an extrinsic/external reward, and an extrinsic reward alone can be a poor motivator.

In one study examining students in CS1 courses, students' PI for the course at the end of the semester was found to be associated with higher student grades and learning [24]. Endogenous PI was associated with higher grades and learning; exogenous PI was associated with lower grades and learning. A similar pattern was found for engagement and self-directed learning. These findings were consistent with theoretical formulations of PI [12, 14, 28]

that propose that endogenous PI is a more powerful positive motivator and provide evidence that exogenous PI may be problematic. Similar findings were obtained from studies examining student profiles of motivated, self-regulation and engagement in CS1 courses [19, 26]. Students in adaptive profiles (strategic, knowledge building) associated with high achievement were much higher in endogenous PI than students in more dysfunctional profiles (apathetic, surface learning, learned helpless) associated with lower achievement. Students in dysfunctional profiles also typically had higher exogenous than endogenous PI.

Contrary findings, however, emerged in a study of students' entering course motivation in CS1 courses and their grades and retention [27]. Consistent with prior findings and theory, higher exogenous PI at the start of the semester was negatively associated with final course grades; however, contrary to expectations from prior studies, higher endogenous PI at the start of the semester was also negatively associated with final course grades. The only exception was for an honors course where entering endogenous PI was positively associated with final grades.

In this paper, we addressed these contradictory findings concerning students' entering and end-of-course PI by examining how their endogenous and exogenous PI changed across the semester and whether this change differed for students in CS1 courses tailored for different student populations.

2.2 Career Aspirations

Research has found that students who make a connection between academic courses and activities and their potential future selves experience increased motivation towards current tasks and higher levels of academic achievement [6, 14, 15]. Students are more motivated for a CS course if they can envision themselves in a CS-related job and aspire to pursue that job. Research in engineering has found that students who maintained high future career aspirations tended to view their engineering coursework more favorably than their peers but that students had changes in these aspirations over time [1]. Also, aspirations related to a future career in engineering have been related to higher perceptions of endogenous instrumentality for engineering coursework [8].

These studies suggest important links between career aspirations and PI for courses, especially endogenous PI. These links have not been extensively examined, and importantly, have not been examined at all in CS. Our current study sought to address this lack of research by examining changes in career aspirations across the semester in introductory CS1 courses along with how changes in aspirations might be related to changes in endogenous and exogenous PI.

3. THE PRESENT STUDY

The purpose of this study was to investigate how PI and career aspirations of undergraduates in a suite of CS1 courses changed across the semester. Moreover, we explored how these changes were associated with students' learning outcomes. The central research question guiding this study was: *How dynamic are undergraduate computer science students' PI and career aspirations in CS1 courses?* The following specific research questions were examined:

1. How do students' endogenous and exogenous PI in CS1 courses and their career aspirations change from the beginning to the end of the semester?

2. Do changes in students' PI and career aspirations across the semester differ as a function of course enrollment or major?

3. What is the relationship between undergraduate students' career aspirations and their endogenous and exogenous PI for a CS1 course?

4. How do changes in PI and career aspirations across the semester relate to students' CS1 learning outcomes?

4. METHODS

4.1 Participants

Participants in this study were 621 undergraduates (538 males; 83 females) from a suite of CS1 courses at a large Midwestern university. Participants included 297 freshmen, 184 sophomores, 72 juniors, 51 seniors, and 17 who identified as "other." Of these participants, 447 (383 males; 64 females) provided complete data and were included in the analysis. Participants were recruited from a suite of CS1 courses that catered to different undergraduate student populations. Specifically, the suite consisted of separate courses tailored for: CS majors ($n = 72$), engineering majors ($n = 205$), a combination of computer, engineering, and physical science majors ($n = 108$), humanities majors ($n = 6$), and interdisciplinary business/CS honors students ($n = 56$). Core content was the same for all courses, but courses were tailored for the different majors with different programming languages, lab exercises, and programming assignments. The study was approved by the University Institutional Review Board (IRB#: 20120111818EP).

4.2 Instruments

4.2.1 Perceived Instrumentality (PI)

PI was measured using the Perceptions of Instrumentality Scale [11, 19, 26]. *Endogenous PI* (4 items) assesses the perceived instrumentality of learning the course content for obtaining distal goals (e.g., "What I gain from this class will shape my future."). *Exogenous PI* (4 items) assesses the utility of attaining course grades for achieving distal goals (e.g., "The only thing useful to me in this class is the grade I get."). Students indicated their agreement with each question using a 5-point Likert scale ranging from 1 (*strongly disagree*) to 5 (*strongly agree*). Endogenous and exogenous PI scale scores were computed as the mean of the items in each scale. Cronbach's alpha reliability estimates for the endogenous and exogenous PI scales were .92 and .93 respectively.

4.2.2 Career Aspirations

Career aspirations were assessed with an instrument based on the Project for the Analysis of Learning and Achievement in Mathematics (PALMA) [20]. The original scales were for high school math students and were rephrased for post-secondary CS by the researchers. Participants responded to three items assessing aspirations to use CS concepts and skills in their future career (e.g., "In whatever career I choose, I would like to work in a job that uses computer science applications, programming, or computational thinking."; "In my career, I would like to work with projects that involve a lot of computer science applications, programming, or computational thinking.") at both the beginning and end of the semester. Participants indicated their agreement to each item using a 5-point Likert scale ranging from 1 (*strongly disagree)* to 5 (*strongly agree)*. The career aspirations score was computed as the mean of the three scale items. Cronbach's alpha reliability estimate for the scale was .95.

4.2.3 Course Achievement Measures

To investigate how changes in PI and career aspirations predict students' academic outcomes, final course grades and performance on a computational thinking knowledge test were used as the barometers of achievement.

4.2.3.1 Course Grades

While completing the informed consent sheet, participants granted the researchers permission to obtain access to their final course grades. Course grades were obtained from the instructor's final grade roster for each course. The grading is on a 13-point scale from F (0.0) to A/A+ (both 4.0). Because raw grades are not directly comparable across courses, grades were z-score standardized within each course prior to analysis.

4.2.3.2 Computational Thinking Knowledge Test

All courses in the suite of introductory CS courses from which participants were recruited include the same basic core of computer science topics. To create a common measure of retention of these core topics that could be used across all of the courses, a Web-based, 13-item test of computational thinking and CS knowledge containing a blend of conceptual and problem-solving questions was developed by computer science and engineering faculty. The test addresses common core content including selection, looping, arrays, functions, algorithms, search, and sorting. Information on the test development can be found in [19, 26]. The Cronbach's alpha estimate for the knowledge test was .73.

4.3 Procedures

This study took place as part of a larger NSF-funded study focused on improving students' abilities to learn computational thinking by incorporating computational and creative thinking exercises into undergraduate CS courses, including CS1 courses. Participants in the study CS1 classes completed the Perceptions of Instrumentality Scale and career aspirations items during lab or lecture sessions during the first week of the semester. During the last two weeks of the semester, participants repeated the beginning-of-semester instruments and completed the Computational Thinking Knowledge Test in lab or lecture sessions. All of the surveys were completed using the Survey Monkey® online survey tool. After the semester ended, students' final course grades were obtained from the instructors' final grade rosters for each course.

4.4 Analysis Procedures

All data analysis was performed using SPSS v. 21 and 22. Multivariate analysis of variance (MANOVA) and univariate analysis of variance (ANOVA) were done using the General Linear Model repeated measures procedure and the One-way ANOVA procedure. Linear regression analyses were conducted using the Linear Regression procedure.

5. RESULTS

The present study explored (a) whether CS1 students' endogenous and exogenous PI and career aspirations changed across the course of the semester, (b) the possibility of course enrollment and major as moderators of change in PI and career aspirations, (c) the relationship between PI and career aspirations, and (d) how changes in PI and career aspirations could be used to predict course achievement, as measured by standardized course grades and computational thinking knowledge test scores. Changes in sample sizes reflect changes in the number of participants who provided relevant data at each time point. Note that in this section we present the analyses and results. In Section 6, we summarize the findings with implications for CS education.

5.1 How do students' endogenous and exogenous PI of CS1 courses and their career aspirations change from the beginning to the end of the semester?

To determine whether participants' endogenous and exogenous PI changed from the beginning to the end of the semester, a repeated-measures MANOVA was conducted. Overall for all participants, PI changed significantly from the beginning of the semester until the end (Wilks' $\lambda = .751$, $F(2, 441) = 73.163$, $p < .001$, partial $Eta^2 = .249$). Univariate follow-up tests revealed that there was a significant change for both endogenous ($F(1, 442) = 139.059$, $p < .001$, partial $Eta^2 = .239$) and exogenous ($F(1, 442) = 71.578$, $p < .001$, partial $Eta^2 = .139$) instrumentality. Endogenous instrumentality scores decreased across the semester from a mean of 3.91 at the beginning of the semester to 3.47 at the end. Exogenous instrumentality scores increased across the semester from a mean of 2.19 at the beginning of the semester to 2.57 at the end. These findings indicate that *students' perceived instrumentality for learning the course material in their CS1 course was decreasing while their instrumentality for the utility of grades was increasing.*

To determine whether participants' career aspirations changed from the beginning to the end of the semester, a repeated-measures ANOVA was conducted. Overall for all participants, career aspirations changed significantly from the beginning of the semester until the end (Wilks' $\lambda = .961$, $F(1, 440) = 18.073$, $p < .001$, partial $Eta^2 = .039$): career aspirations decreased from a mean of 3.43 at the beginning of the semester to 3.25 at the end. This finding suggests that *introductory CS1 students' aspirations to pursue a career that utilized a substantial amount of computer science applications and computational thinking declined during the semester of taking their CS1 course.*

5.2 Do changes in students' PI and career aspirations across the semester differ as a function of course enrollment or major?

Course enrollment and major were examined as possible moderators of the changes in PI and career aspirations. Other important possible moderators (viz., gender) are not reported because the limited number of individuals in some subgroups reduced statistical power and led to difficulty in interpreting results.

5.2.1 Course Enrollment

The CS1 humanities course was not included in any between-class analyses because of the low number of participants in that course ($n = 6$). Mixed MANOVA was used to test whether changes in students' PI differed as a function of course enrollment. Group means for endogenous and exogenous instrumentality at the beginning and end of the semester are shown in Table 1. The main effect of time was significant (Wilks' $\lambda = .842$, $F(2, 432) = 40.608$, $p < .001$, partial $Eta^2 = .158$) as was the main effect of course enrollment (Wilks' $\lambda = .746$, $F(6, 864) = 22.733$, $p < .001$, partial $Eta^2 = .136$). The interaction between course enrollment and change in PI was also significant (Wilks' $\lambda = .945$, $F(6, 864) = 22.733$, $p < .001$, partial $Eta^2 = .028$), indicating that change in PI across the semester was different in different courses. Univariate follow-up analyses revealed that both main effects and the interaction effect were significant for both endogenous and exogenous instrumentality (results summarized in Table 2). As shown in Table 1, *all courses except for the Business/CS Honors course showed substantial shifts in both endogenous and exogenous instrumentality* (Cohen's Ds from ± 0.24 to 0.68). Significant pairwise comparisons between courses are also shown in Table 1.

Mixed ANOVA was used to test whether changes in students' career aspirations differed as a function of course enrollment. Group means for career aspirations at the beginning and end of the semester are shown in Table 1. The main effect of time was significant (Wilks' $\lambda = .987$, $F(1, 437) = 5.840$, $p < .05$, partial $Eta^2 = .013$), as was the main effect of course ($F(3, 437) = 53.808$, $p < .001$, partial $Eta^2 = .270$), indicating career aspirations for the entire sample changed across the semester, and career aspirations varied among courses. The interaction between course enrollment and time was also significant (Wilks' $\lambda = .977$, $F(3, 437) = 3.371$, $p < .05$, partial $Eta^2 = .023$), indicating that change in career aspirations across the semester was different across courses. *Post-hoc analyses revealed that students in the course for interdisciplinary honors students experienced an increase in career aspirations, but students in all other courses experienced a decrease in career aspirations. Furthermore, students in the course for engineering majors experienced the greatest decrease in aspirations for having jobs or projects in their career that involve using CS and computational thinking.* Significant pairwise comparisons between courses are also shown in Table 1.

Table 1. Changes Across the Semester in Perceived Instrumentality and Career Aspirations by Course

	CS Majors	CS/PS Majors	Engineering Majors	Business/CS Honors	All Courses
	($n = 69$)	($n = 107$)	($n = 205$)	($n = 56$)	($n = 437$)
Endogenous					
Initial	4.29 (0.70)	4.00 (0.70)	3.58 (0.81)	4.46 (0.50)	3.91 (0.80)
End	3.86 (0.92)	3.64 (1.03)	2.98 (0.96)	4.36 (0.63)	3.46 (1.05)
Overall	4.08 (0.81)[a]	3.82 (0.87)[bd]	3.28 (0.89)[abc]	4.41 (0.57)[cd]	3.69 (0.93)
Cohen's D	-0.53	-0.41	-0.68	-0.18	-0.48
Exogenous					
Initial	2.08 (0.89)	2.18 (0.77)	2.41 (0.87)	1.64 (0.61)	2.20 (0.86)
End	2.32 (1.08)	2.49 (1.13)	2.97 (1.01)	1.71 (0.69)	2.59 (1.10)
Overall	2.20 (0.99)[eh]	2.34 (0.95)[fi]	2.69 (0.94)[ghi]	1.68 (0.65)[efg]	2.40 (0.98)
Cohen's D	0.24	0.32	0.60	0.11	0.40
Career Aspirations	($n = 72$)	($n = 108$)	($n = 205$)	($n = 56$)	($n = 441$)
Initial	3.92 (0.90)	3.55 (0.86)	3.02 (0.76)	4.10 (0.93)	3.43 (0.93)
End	3.80 (1.09)	3.42 (1.09)	2.71 (0.95)	4.19 (0.93)	3.25 (1.15)
Overall	3.86 (1.00)[jm]	3.49 (0.98)[kmn]	2.87 (0.86)[jkl]	4.15 (0.93)[ln]	3.34 (1.04)
Cohen's D	-0.12	-0.13	-0.36	0.10	-0.17

Note. M(SD). Course means with different subscripts are different at $p < .05$ in pairwise comparisons.

Table 2. Summary of Univariate Follow-Up Test Results

	F	p	Partial Eta^2
Course Enrollment			
Endogenous			
Time	78.819	<.001	.154
Course	45.779	<.001	.241
Time*Course	6.571	<.001	.044
Exogenous			
Time	33.865	<.001	.073
Course	26.442	<.001	.155
Time*Course	5.270	.001	.035
Major in CS			
Endogenous			
Time	111.952	<.001	.202
Major	272.484	<.001	.382
Time*Major	6.571	<.001	.044
Exogenous			
Time	54.072	<.001	.109
Major	130.666	<.001	.229
Time*Major	27.275	<.001	.058

Table 3. Changes Across the Semester in Perceived Instrumentality and Career Aspirations by Major

	CS Majors/ Intending	Non-Majors	All Students
	($n = 173$)	($n = 270$)	($n = 443$)
Endogenous			
Beginning	4.40 (0.54)	3.59 (0.78)	3.91 (0.80)
End	4.27 (0.63)	2.95 (0.93)	3.47 (1.05)
Cohen's D	-0.22	-0.75	-0.47
Exogenous			
Beginning	1.82 (0.74)	2.43 (0.84)	2.19 (0.86)
End	1.92 (0.93)	3.00 (0.99)	2.57 (1.10)
Cohen's D	0.12	0.62	0.39
Career Aspirations	($n = 177$)	($n = 270$)	($n = 447$)
Beginning	4.07 (0.83)	3.02 (0.73)	3.44 (0.93)
End	4.13 (0.89)	2.68 (0.91)	3.25 (1.15)
Cohen's D	0.07	-0.41	-0.18

5.2.2 Major in CS

Mixed MANOVA was used to test whether changes in students' PI differed as a function of majoring or intending to major in CS (referred to as "major"). Group means for endogenous and exogenous instrumentality at the beginning and end of the semester are shown in Table 3. The main effect of time was significant (Wilks' $\lambda = .788$, $F(2, 440) = 59.230$, $p < .001$, partial Eta$^2 = .212$) as was the main effect of major (Wilks' $\lambda = .618$, $F(2, 440) = 136.065$, $p < .001$, partial Eta$^2 = .382$). The interaction between major and time was also significant (Wilks' $\lambda = .891$, $F(2, 440) = 26.833$, $p < .001$, partial Eta$^2 = .109$), indicating that change in PI across the semester differed between those majoring or intending to measure in CS and those not intending to major in CS. Univariate follow-up analyses revealed that both main effects and the interaction effect were significant for both endogenous and exogenous instrumentality (results summarized in Table 2). As shown in Table 3, *students **not** intending to major in CS experienced a larger increase in exogenous instrumentality and a larger decrease in endogenous instrumentality than students majoring or intending to major in CS.*

Mixed ANOVA was used to test whether changes in students' career aspirations differed as a function of major. Group means for career aspirations at the beginning and end of the semester are shown in Table 1. The analysis revealed a significant interaction between changes in career aspirations across the semester and plans to major in CS (Wilks' $\lambda = .949$, $F(1, 439) = 23.468$, $p < .001$, partial Eta$^2 = .051$). *Participants who planned on majoring in CS experienced a slight increase in career aspirations, whereas participants who did not plan on majoring in CS experienced a more substantial decrease.*

5.3 What is the relationship between undergraduate students' career aspirations and their endogenous and exogenous PI for a CS1 course?

We used two-step regressions to examine the relationship between PI and career aspirations. The two types of instrumentality were tested in separate regression analyses. In the first step of each analysis, we regressed PI at the end of the semester on PI at the beginning of the semester. In the second step, we added career aspirations at the beginning of the semester and change in career aspirations as predictors. Change in career aspirations was calculated by subtracting participants' beginning of semester scores from their end of semester scores, so that positive values indicate an increase in career aspirations across the semester. This allowed us to determine whether initial career aspirations or a change in career aspirations were related to final instrumentality, after controlling for initial instrumentality.

5.3.1 Endogenous Instrumentality

In the first step, endogenous instrumentality at the beginning of the semester significantly predicted endogenous instrumentality at the end of the semester ($R^2 = .439$, $F(1, 441) = 344.904$, $p < .001$). Adding initial career aspirations and change in career aspirations significantly improved the model, ($R^2_{change} = .180$, $F_{change}(2, 439) = 103.558$, $p < .001$). Initial endogenous instrumentality ($\beta = 0.430$, $t = 11.204$, $p < .001$), initial career aspirations ($\beta = 0.356$, $t = 9.031$, $p < .001$), and change in career aspirations ($\beta = 0.422$, $t = 13.531$, $p < .001$) were all significant predictors. That is, after accounting for initial endogenous instrumentality, *initial career aspirations and change in career aspirations contributed significantly to the prediction of end-of-semester endogenous instrumentality.* As expected from theory, *higher aspirations of a career that involved CS at the start of the course and an increase in such aspirations was associated with higher endogenous instrumentality at the end of the course.*

5.3.2 Exogenous Instrumentality

In the first step, exogenous instrumentality at the beginning of the semester significantly predicted exogenous instrumentality at the end of the semester ($R^2 = .304$, $F(1, 441) = 192.572$, $p < .001$). Adding initial career aspirations and change in career aspirations significantly improved the model, ($R^2_{change} = .169$, $F_{change}(2, 439) = 70.551$, $p < .001$). Initial exogenous instrumentality ($\beta = 0.375$, $t = 9.680$, $p < .001$), initial career aspirations ($\beta = -0.366$, $t = -9.223$, $p < .001$), and change in career aspirations ($\beta = -0.358$, $t = -9.860$, $p < .001$) were all significant predictors. That is, after accounting for initial exogenous instrumentality, *initial career aspirations and change in career aspirations contributed significantly to the prediction of end-of-semester exogenous instrumentality.* As expected from theory, *higher aspirations of a career that involved CS at the start of the course and an increase in such aspirations was associated with lower exogenous instrumentality at the end of the course.*

5.4 How do changes in PI and career aspirations across the semester relate to students' CS1 learning outcomes?

Regression analysis was used to examine the relationships between participants' initial PI, changes in PI across the semester, and standardized final course grades. Changes in instrumentality were calculated by subtracting initial scores from final scores, so that positive values indicate stronger PI at the end of the semester. The overall model was significant ($R^2 = .041$, $F(4, 432) = 4.662$, $p = .001$). Only change in endogenous instrumentality was a significant predictor of standardized course grades (see Table 4). An increase in endogenous PI across the semester was associated with higher course grades ($\beta = 0.146$, $t = 2.444$, $p = .015$).

A parallel analysis was conducted using computational thinking knowledge test scores as the criterion variable. The overall model was significant ($R^2 = .156$, $F(4, 411) = 18.974$, $p < .001$). Initial exogenous instrumentality ($\beta = -.374$, $t = -5.319$, $p < .001$) and change in exogenous instrumentality ($\beta = -0.255$, $t = -4.155$, $p < .001$) were significant predictors, and change in endogenous instrumentality ($\beta = 0.111$, $t = 1.923$, $p = .055$) trended toward significance (see Table 4). These results indicate that *lower exogenous instrumentality at the beginning of the semester and a decrease in exogenous instrumentality were associated with higher scores on the computational thinking knowledge test.*

Regression analysis was also used to examine the relationships between participants' initial career aspirations, changes in career aspirations across the semester, and standardized final course

Table 4. Relationships of Perceived Instrumentality and Career Aspirations with Achievement.

	β	t	p	R^2	Adj. R^2
Instrumentality					
Course grades				.041*	.033
Initial endogenous	-.048	-0.691	.490		
Initial exogenous	-.060	-0.824	.410		
Endogenous change	.146	2.444	.015		
Exogenous change	-.082	-1.291	.197		
Knowledge test				.156**	.148
Initial endogenous	-.106	-1.536	.125		
Initial exogenous	-.374	-5.319	<.001		
Endogenous change	.111	1.923	.055		
Exogenous change	-.255	-4.155	<.001		
Career Aspirations					
Course grades				.073**	.069
Initial aspirations	.050	1.060	.290		
Aspirations change	.278	5.860	<.001		
Knowledge test				.120**	.115
Initial aspirations	.273	5.766	<.001		
Aspirations change	.283	5.968	<.001		

Note. * $p < .01$, ** $p < .001$

grades. Changes in career aspirations were calculated by subtracting initial scores from final scores, so that positive values indicate stronger career aspirations at the end of the semester. The overall model was significant ($R^2 = .073$, $F(2, 438) = 17.249$, $p < .001$). Only change in career aspirations was a significant predictor of standardized course grades (see Table 4). *An increase in career aspirations across the semester was associated with higher course grades* ($\beta = 0.278$, $t = 5.860$, $p < .001$).

A parallel analysis was conducted using computational thinking knowledge test scores as the criterion variable. The overall model was significant ($R^2 = .120$, $F(2, 413) = 28.041$, $p < .001$). Initial aspirations ($\beta = .273$, $t = 5.766$, $p < .001$) and change in career aspirations ($\beta = .283$, $t = 5.968$, $p < .001$) were significant predictors (see Table 4). These results indicate that *higher career aspirations at the beginning of the semester and an increase in career aspirations were associated with higher scores on the computational thinking knowledge test.*

Taken together, these results indicate that *PI and career aspirations are more strongly related to the computational thinking knowledge test than standardized course grades.*

6. DISCUSSION

6.1 Grand Summary of Findings

The results of this study indicate that CS1 students' PI and career aspirations change from the beginning to the end of the semester. On average, perception of exogenous instrumentality increases, perception of endogenous instrumentality decreases, and aspirations to pursue a career in CS decreases. However, these trends differed as a function of course enrollment and major.

First, *overall levels of PI and patterns of change in PI were different in different courses.* Unsurprisingly, students in the course for CS majors and the course for students in the business/CS honors program reported the highest levels of endogenous instrumentality and the lowest levels of exogenous instrumentality at both the beginning and end of the semester. Because most students in these two classes have a major in CS or a minor in CS, it makes sense that they would see the content of their CS1 course as being meaningfully connected to their future goals (endogenous instrumentality) while placing less emphasis on only the utility of obtaining a grade for future goal attainment (exogenous instrumentality). Students in the business/CS honors program appeared to hold on to their initial higher endogenous PI and lower exogenous PI across the semester better than the CS majors as they exhibited less change in their PI during the semester. In contrast, students in the course for engineering majors reported the lowest levels of endogenous instrumentality and the highest levels of exogenous instrumentality at the beginning of the semester, and then proceeded to exhibit the greatest decrease in endogenous PI and increase in exogenous PI. In fact, at the end of the semester, they reported comparable levels of the two types of PI. This indicates that, compared to students in other courses, the students in the introductory CS course for engineering majors initially saw less of a connection between the learning the course content and their future goals, and over time their already weak perceived connection between the content and their goals weakened *further* still. At the same time, these students initially saw more of a utilitarian-only connection between getting a grade in the course and their future goals than did other students, and during the semester this utilitarian-only instrumentality increased *even more* than students in the other CS1 classes.

Second, *overall levels of career aspirations and change in career aspirations were different in different courses*. Aspirations to pursue a career that utilizes a substantial amount of CS applications and computational thinking decreased on average for the entire sample. Students in the business/CS honors program, however, demonstrated a small, but significant increase in their career aspirations, meaning they were more aspiring of a CS-related career at the end of class than when they started. Students in the course for engineering majors started with the lowest aspirations for having CS and computational thinking in their career and exhibited the greatest decrease in these career aspirations. And, students in the course for CS majors and the course for both CS and physical science majors exhibited similarly small declines in career aspirations, though students in the CS course reported higher career aspirations at both time points. In general, these results indicate that (1) students differ in the degree to which they aspire to pursue a career that utilizes a substantial amount of computer science applications and computational thinking when they enter their CS1 courses, and (2) while students in most of the CS1 courses decreased in career aspirations, students in at least one course increased in their CS career aspirations.

Third, *overall levels of PI, career aspirations, and patterns of change in PI and career aspirations differed according to whether or not students were majoring or intending to major in CS*. At both time points, students majoring or intending to major in CS reported lower exogenous instrumentality and higher endogenous instrumentality than those *not* intending to major in CS. The overall trend of increasing exogenous instrumentality and decreasing endogenous instrumentality was present in both groups, but the average changes were substantially larger for students who did not intend to major in CS. That is, *students majoring or intending to major in CS primarily felt that the CS1 course was connected to their future goals because of what they were learning in the course, rather than because of the impact their grade would have on their future. Students not intending to major in CS initially indicated similar perceptions, though the perceived connection between course content and future goals was weaker, and the perceived connection between grades and future goals was stronger*. By the end of the semester, the difference in magnitude for endogenous and exogenous instrumentality had vanished for students not intending to major in CS.

Additionally, students who did not intend to major in CS initially reported lower career aspirations than those majoring or intending to major in CS. By the end of the semester, *non-majors had even less of a desire to pursue a career that involved a substantial amount of CS applications and computational thinking; whereas, those majoring or intending to major in CS reported slightly higher aspirations for a career in CS*. These results suggest rather clearly that PI, career aspirations, and the way they change during a CS1 course differ substantially among those who are majoring or not majoring in CS.

Fourth, consistent with prior research and theory [1, 6, 8, 14, 15], *higher career aspirations significantly predicted higher endogenous PI and lower exogenous PI*. Importantly, our findings show that *students who increase in their aspirations for a CS-related career across the semester have higher instrumentality for learning the course content*.

Fifth, *PI and career aspirations were more strongly related to scores on the computational thinking knowledge test than standardized course grades*. Findings were consistent with prior studies showing PI and career aspirations to be associated with higher achievement and learning [6, 15, 24]. Interestingly, changes in endogenous instrumentality and changes in career aspirations were the only individually significant predictors of standardized course grades, and their predictive power was rather weak. However, exogenous instrumentality and career aspirations were both predictive of scores on the computational thinking knowledge test. That is, higher initial exogenous instrumentality and an increase in exogenous instrumentality were associated with lower scores, and higher career aspirations and an increase in career aspirations predicted higher scores. The computational thinking knowledge test is a cumulative test that targets deeper understanding and more long-term retention of the CS principles and skills taught in these CS1 courses, so it makes sense that weaker perceptions of the primary value of a course being in the grade one receives (rather than the content) and aspirations to pursue a career in CS would be associated with higher scores on this test.

The findings presented here must be interpreted in light of the limitations of this study. First, our sample was drawn from CS1 courses at a single institution. More research is needed to determine whether these findings can be generalized to more advanced CS courses or other institutions. Given that the sample in this study contained 447 students from a variety of programs enrolled in five different classes taught by five instructors, it is reasonable to believe the results could be replicated in other studies of undergraduate CS students. Furthermore, the CS1 courses from which our sample was drawn are tailored for different groups of students, which is fairly atypical of CS1 courses. It is unclear whether or how this tailoring and grouping of students might impact PI, career aspirations, and their change over time. Second, PI and career aspirations were only measured at the beginning or end of the semester, precluding the possibility of more complex analyses that can detect non-linear change over time. It is possible that the changes in PI and career aspirations do not follow a steady, monotonic trajectory, and future research examining PI and career aspirations at more than two time points should test for non-linear change.

6.2 Implications for CS Educators

There is concern about attracting and retaining students in STEM-related fields [22, 30], including CS [2, 10]. Given this concern, it is important for CS educators to be aware of how students might conceptualize the value of their CS1 courses. The findings from this study suggest students' conceptions of the connection between CS1 courses and their futures may change while students are taking the course. The decrease in endogenous PI and increase in exogenous PI suggests that students gradually see their grade in the course as more important and the content as less important. Previous research has connected PI to the use of adaptive learning strategies [13] and the amount of time spent studying [14], as well as academic achievement [24]. Therefore, intentionally fostering PI could be one way to increase meaningful long-term learning of CS content.

CS educators can positively influence undergraduate CS students' PI by helping them see the connections between course content and future goals. It is important to point out such connections because students who perceive the instrumentality of CS1 courses as primarily exogenous (i.e., the grade earned will impact their future) rather than endogenous (i.e., what is learned will impact their future) might be less likely to take additional CS courses and less likely to consider the possibility of majoring in CS. However, students who perceive the instrumentality of CS1 course content as primarily endogenous are probably more likely to take additional CS courses and more likely to consider majoring in CS.

Results of intervention studies [23] indicate that students' PI can be positively impacted through relatively short interventions that involve prompting students to think about direct connections between course material and their future goals. Though the connections between a course and students' futures may seem obvious to the instructor, students might not see those connections without external prompting. For example, an instructor could promote endogenous PI by having students respond to a brief writing prompt about how a concept or learning activity is connected to the types of problems they are likely to encounter in a future job. Having students share the connections they see can further expand students' understanding of how course content is connected to their futures. Activities such as this one can help students see the value in mastering the content of CS courses.

7. CONCLUSION

In this study, we found that CS1 students' PI and career aspirations changed over the course of a single semester. This is an important finding as it indicates that both PI and career aspirations are somewhat dynamic and influenced by students' experiences during the course. In general, students' experiences during the semester caused them to decrease in endogenous PI to learn the course material and increase in exogenous PI for the more utilitarian goal of getting a grade. Of course, within these general patterns, some students did increase in endogenous PI and decrease in exogenous PI and these patterns were associated with higher learning and achievement. Similarly, although on average career aspirations decreased across the semester, those students who increased in their career aspirations also increased in their endogenous PI and their learning of course material. Students who indicated majoring or intending to major/minor in CS were more resistant to declines in endogenous PI and actually increased in career aspirations; whereas non-CS majors had significant decreases in both. This suggests that the experiences in CS1 classes are generally positive for CS majors; but rather negative for non-CS majors, even when the primary course for non-majors (the engineering major course) was specifically tailored for these non-majors. Results help clarify the differences found for initial PI [27] and end-of-semester PI [24]. Because of the rather large changes in PI across the semester found in this study, it makes sense that students' initial PI might be relatively unassociated with course achievement.

Given the emphasis placed on retention in CS and other STEM-related courses [2, 10, 22, 30], particularly retention of underrepresented populations, we believe it is important for CS educators to understand the connections between PI and achievement in CS courses. By helping students see clear connections between what they are learning in a CS1 course and their future goals, CS educators may be able to positively impact student motivation, achievement, and retention in CS courses and computing-related majors.

There are at least two possibilities to generally explain the findings reported in this paper. The first is that students begin their CS1 course with somewhat inaccurate views about the field of CS, how computational thinking and CS may connect to their future career goals, what it means to be a computer scientist, and how they would use or apply CS knowledge in their careers. Then, as they complete their first CS course and learn more about CS, there is a shift in their understanding of how CS does or does not relate to these future goals. The second possibility is that students have an accurate understanding about the field of CS and how it connects to their future goals, but as they complete their first CS course, there is a shift in students' future goals. In the former case, constructing a more accurate representation of CS and its connection to future plans is what drives the shift in instrumentality and career aspirations. In the latter case, it is the shift in students' future plans that drives the change in instrumentality and career aspirations. Future research should explore these, and other, possible explanations for the shifts in PI and career aspirations during CS1 courses. Future research is also needed to identify (1) how changes in PI and career aspirations impact subsequent enrollment in CS courses, (2) the relationship between PI and career aspirations and retention in CS majors, and (3) whether similar shifts in PI and career aspirations occur in other STEM courses, including upper-level CS courses.

8. ACKNOWLEDGMENTS

This material is based upon work supported by the National Science Foundation under grant nos. 1431874 and 1122956.

9. REFERENCES

[1] Alpay, E., Ahearn, A. L., Graham, R. H., and Bull, A. M. J. 2008. Student enthusiasm for engineering: charting changes in student aspirations and motivation. *European J. of Engin. Ed.* 33(5-6), 573-585.

[2] Barker, L. J., M. O'Neill, and N. Kazim 2014. Framing Classroom Climate for Student Learning and Retention in Computer Science. In *Proc. of the 45th ACM Technical Symposium on Comp. Sci. Educ. (SIGCSE'2014)*, 319-324

[3] Committee on Prospering in the Global Economy of the 21st Century 2007. *Rising Above the Gathering Storm*. Washington, DC: National Academies Press

[4] Flanigan, A. E., Peteranetz, M. S., Shell, D. F., and Soh, L-K (2015). Exploring changes in computer science students' implicit theories of intelligence across the semester. In *Proc.of ICER'15 (Omaha, NE)*, 161-168.

[5] Forte, A., and M. Guzdial 2005. Motivation and Nonmajors in Computer Science: Identifying Discrete Audiences for Introductory Courses. *IEEE Trans. on Ed.*, 48(2), 248-253

[6] Greene, B. A., & DeBacker, T. K. 2004. Gender and orientations toward the future: Links to motivation. *Ed. Psych. Review* 16(2), 91-120.

[7] Hazley, M.P., Shell, D.F., Soh, L.K., Miller, L.D., Chiriacescu, V., and Ingraham, E. 2014. Changes in student goal orientations across the semester in undergraduate computer science courses in *Proceedings Frontiers in Education Conference*, (Madrid, Spain, 2014), IEEE, 1-7.

[8] Hilpert, J.C., Carrion, M.L, Husman, J., and Baughman, L. 2011. Engineering futures: Female students, careers, and work/life balance. Published in the conference proceedings of the *41st ASEE/IEEE Frontiers in Ed. Conference*.

[9] Hilpert, J.C., Husman, J., Stump, G.S., Kim, W., Chung, W.T., and Duggan, M.A. 2012. Examining students' future time perspective: Pathways to knowledge building. *Japanese Psych. Research* 54(3), 229-240

[10] Haungs, M., C. Clark, J. Clements, and D. Janzen 2012. Improving First-Year Success and Retention through Interest-Based CS0 Courses, in *Proc. 43rd ACM Technical Symposium on Comp. Sci. Educ.(SIGCSE'2012)*, 589-594.

[11] Husman, J., Derryberry, W.P, Crowson, H.M., and Lomax, R. 2004. Instrumentality, task value, and intrinsic motivation: Making sense of their independent interdependence. *Contemporary Educational Psychology* 29, 63-76.

[12] Husman, J. and Lens, W. 1999. The role of the future in student motivation. *Educational Psychologist* 34(2), 113-125.

[13] Husman, J. and Hilpert, J. 2007. The Intersection of Students' Perceptions of Instrumentality, Self-Efficacy, and Goal Orientations in an Online Mathematics Course. *Zeitschrift für Pädagogische Psychologie/ German Journal of Educational Psychology* 21, 229-239.

[14] Lens, W., Simons, J., and Dewitte, S. 2001. Student motivation and self-regulation as a function of future time perspective and perceived instrumentality. In S. Volet and S. Järvelä (Eds.) *Motivation and learning contexts: Theoretical advances and methodological implications.* (233-248). Pergamon Press.

[15] Leondari, A. 2007. Future time perspective, possible selves, and academic achievement. *New Directions for Adult and Continuing Ed.* 2007(114), 17-26.

[16] McGill, M. M. 2012. Learning to Program with Personal Robots: Influences on Student Motivation. *ACM Trans. on Comp. Educ.*,12(1), article 4.

[17] Miller, R.B., DeBacker, T.K., and Greene, B.A. 1999. Perceived instrumentality and academics: The link to task valuing. *J. of Instruc. Psych.* 26(4), 250-260.

[18] National Center for Education Statistics 2014. *Digest of Education Statistics.* Washington, DC: U.S. Dept. of Ed.

[19] Authors Suppressed for Anonymity.

[20] Pekrun, R., vom Hofe, R., Blum, W., Frenzel, A. C., Goetz, T., and Wartha, S. 2007. Development of mathematical competencies in adolescence: The PALMA longitudinal study. In M. Prenzel (Ed.), *Studies on the educational quality of schools* (pp. 17–37). Münster, Germany: Waxmann..

[21] Porter, L., M. Guzdial, C. McDowell, and B. Simon 2013. Success in Introductory Programming: What Works?, *Communications of the ACM*, 58(8), 34-36.

[22] President's Council of Advisors on Science and Technology 2012. *Engage to excel: Producing one million additional college graduates with degrees in science, technology, engineering, and mathematics.* Washington, DC: Executive Office of the President of the United States.

[23] Puruhito, K., Husman, J., Hilpert, J.C., Ganesh, T., and Stump, G. 2011. Increasing instrumentality without decreasing instructional time: An intervention for engineering students. Published in the *Conference Proceedings of the 41st ASEE/IEEE Frontiers in Education Conference.*

[24] Shell, D.F., Hazley, M.P., Soh, L.K., Ingraham, E., and Ramsay, S. 2013. Associations of students' creativity, motivation, and self-regulation with learning and achievement in college computer science courses in *Proceedings of the Frontiers in Education Conference*, (Oklahoma City, Oklahoma, 2013), IEEE, 1637-1643.

[25] Shell, D. F., Hazley, M. P., Soh, L.-K., Miller, L. D., Chiriacescu, V. and Ingraham, E. 2014. Improving learning of computational thinking using computational creativity exercises in a college CS1 computer science course for engineers. In *Proc. 44th Annual Frontiers in Ed. (FIE) Conference,* (Madrid, Spain), 3029-3035.

[26] Shell, D.F. and Soh, L.K. 2013. Profiles of motivated self-regulation in college computer science courses: Differences in major versus required non-major courses. *J. of Sci. Ed. and Tech.* 22 (Feb. 2013), 899-913. DOI= 10.1007/s10956-013-9437-9

[27] Shell, D. F., Soh, L.-K., Flanigan, A. E., and Peteranetz, M. S. 2016. Students' initial course motivation and their achievement and retention in college CS1 courses. *In Proc. 47th ACM Technical Symposium on Computer Science Education* (SIGCSE'2016) (Memphis, TN), 639-644).

[28] Simons, J., Dewitte, S., and Lens, W. 2004. The role of different types of instrumentality in motivation, study strategies, and performance: Know why you learn, so you'll know what you learn! *British Journal of Educational Psychology* 74, 343-360.

[29] Wing, J. 2006. Computational Thinking. *CACM,* 49, 33-35.

[30] Watkins, J., and Mazur, E. 2013. Retaining students in science, technology, engineering, and mathematics (STEM) majors. *J.l of Col. Sci. Teach.* 42(5), 36-41.

[31] Xie, Y. and Killewald, A. A. 2012. *Is American science in decline?* Cambridge, MA: Harvard University Press. doi:10.4159/harvard.9780674065048.

"I Don't Code All Day": Fitting in Computer Science When the Stereotypes Don't Fit

Colleen M. Lewis
Department of Computer Science
Harvey Mudd College
Claremont, CA, USA 91711
lewis@cs.hmc.edu

Ruth E. Anderson
Department of Computer Science & Engineering
University of Washington, Seattle
Seattle, WA, USA 98195-2350
rea@cs.washington.edu

Ken Yasuhara
Center for Engineering Learning & Teaching
University of Washington, Seattle
Seattle, WA, USA 98195-2183
yasuhara@uw.edu

ABSTRACT

Stereotypes of computer scientists are relevant to students' performance and feelings of belonging. While efforts exist to change these stereotypes, we argue that it may be possible to challenge a student's belief that stereotypes of computer scientists are relevant to whether they can become a computer scientist. In our previous work, we presented a model of five factors that influence students' decisions to major in computer science (CS). Data were collected from interviews with 31 students enrolled in introductory CS courses at two public universities in the United States. Here we elaborate on our grounded theory of one of these factors: how students assess their fit with CS. We describe how students measure their fit with CS in terms of the amount they see themselves as expressing the traits of singular focus, asocialness, competition, and maleness and how students make interpretations and decisions based upon these measurements. We found that students' interpretations were influenced by their attitudes toward the nature of stereotypes.

Keywords

Stereotypes; fit; major choice; grounded theory

1. INTRODUCTION

Enrollments in computer science (CS) are growing [29, 42], but as a field we have not made enough progress addressing the underrepresentation of women and minorities in CS [6, 24, 33]. Research to understand how students decide to major in CS [4, 5, 7, 21, 23, 26] can play an important role in identifying barriers students face and inform interventions.

This paper is an extension of our previous work [32] in which we interviewed 31 students who were enrolled in an introductory CS course at one of two large, public universities in the United States. In our previous work we developed a model of how students decided whether or not to pursue a major in CS based upon ability, fit, enjoyment, utility, and

opportunity cost. The previous work developed a grounded theory [47] to model the processes by which students assessed their ability and how they used that to inform their decision about majoring in CS [32]. In the current paper, we present a grounded theory of how students assess their fit with CS. Students' assessment of their fit was nuanced, but consistently intertwined with the following stereotypes of computer scientists:

- **singularly focused** - CS requires an obsession with CS, necessarily at the exclusion of having other interests or meeting personal needs.
- **asocial** - computer scientists do not have social skills and CS requires working in isolation.
- **competitive** - CS courses (and thus potentially the field as a whole) are competitive and CS work is done individually as opposed to in collaboration with others.
- **male** - success in CS requires one to identify as male, or men are innately more talented in CS than women.

Research shows that students' stereotypes about individuals within a field and sense of belonging within that field are relevant to their interest, persistence, and performance [8, 10, 22, 30, 45, 49, 54]. While some efforts seek to change these stereotypes of computer scientists [14, 39], we recommend an additional strategy of helping students understand the stereotypes as not based upon the nature of the work in CS. This recommendation is based upon participants who expressed awareness of stereotypes that did not fit them, but were not dissuaded by these stereotypes. This is consistent with the recommendations of Ashcraft and Ashcraft [2] who recommend educating students about the ways in which the current stereotypes of computer scientists were constructed [17, 18, 19, 38].

In addition to concrete recommendations for educators (Section 8) we present a model of how students assess their fit with CS. This helps connect quantitative studies about how students decide whether or not to major in CS with education research regarding how students construct their identity and see that identity in relation to others [44]. Our work challenges the fatalism in studies showing that students who identify themselves as dissimilar to stereotypes of a field are correspondingly less interested in the field [30]. Based upon our model, it appears feasible to help students understand stereotypes as stereotypes and not as prescriptions for computer scientists.

2. PREVIOUS RESEARCH

2.1 Research on CS Persistence and Attrition

While recent surges in enrollment [29, 42] may decrease the focus on students' decisions to major in CS, this research is still of crucial importance to making the field accessible to students who are underrepresented in CS. In the United States, it is well documented that people who identify as women, Black, Hispanic, American Indian, and/or Alaskan native are underrepresented in computing courses, degree programs, and careers [6, 24, 33]. This has motivated countless efforts to diversify computing (see [48, 56] for summaries) and research to understand barriers to students' access to computing [25, 33, 34].

Much of the research regarding students' interest in CS and how they select CS as a major has been quantitative [3, 4, 5, 7, 21, 23]. For example, a large-scale study of 1000 women found that these students' experience of social encouragement, self-perception, academic exposure, and career perception were the best predictors of their decision to pursue CS [23]. Kinnunen and Malmi identified lack of time and motivation, low comfort level in class, and prior commitment to a non-CS field as commonly cited reasons for students who dropped an introductory CS course [26]. Carter found that expectations of having to sit at a computer all day, prior interest in another major, and interest in a more "people-oriented" field were common reasons for disinterest in CS [7]. Barker and colleagues found that student-student interaction was the best predictor of students' plans to continue studying CS [3].

These findings motivate our current research to understand the mechanisms that shape these decisions. Qualitative research such as this can provide details to help educators apply the research within their own context. For example, Kinnunen and Simon [28] use grounded theory [27] to describe variation in the ways students interpret positive and negative programming experiences.

2.2 Research on Students' Belonging

Students' sense of belonging is widely recognized as relevant to persistence and engagement in academics [22, 46, 49]. The importance of belonging may be additionally influential for students who are underrepresented in the field and for students about whom negative stereotypes exist [45].

Research has consistently shown that stereotypes create barriers to access [12, 24, 45]. Stereotype threat [43, 45] describes the robust research finding that an individual's performance is depressed when poor performance on the task may be interpreted based upon a stereotype about some dimension of their identity. Cheryan and colleagues have done research on how students' interest in computing varies if they have interactions with people who fit stereotypes about computer scientists [10] or experiences within computer labs that look like stereotypical computer labs [8]. Master, Cheryan, and Meltzoff [35] argue that to increase girls' interest in CS, educational environments for CS should be redesigned to avoid current stereotypes of CS.

Ensmenger [17, 18, 19, 38] has documented the ways in which the stereotypical identity of a computer scientist has been constructed. While the work of computer scientists was originally feminized [38], it has been rebranded in ways that "reinforced the notion that there is a natural, historical, and inevitable connection between male forms of sociability and cognition and virtuoso computer programming ability." [19, p. 43]. In addition to this explicit masculine branding, Ensmenger identified that "the contemporary computer nerd is defined primarily by his consuming obsession with technology, his lack of conventional social skills, and inattention to his physical health and appearance." [19, p. 42].

Research suggests that even young children are aware of stereotypes [11], but researchers sometimes create a distinction between awareness of a stereotype and endorsement of that stereotype [12, 37, 45]. While research suggests that gaps between students' perception of themselves and scientists lead to decreased interest [30], we propose strategies that acknowledge those gaps, but encourage students to challenge the relevance of the stereotype.

2.3 Five Factors that Shape Decision to Major

In previous work [32], we identified five factors that appeared to shape students' decisions to major in CS or not:

- Their **ability** as related to CS: experience and expectations of success as CS majors
- Their **fit** between their identity and CS: the extent to which their own values and identity align with values and cultural expectations they associate with CS
- Their **enjoyment** of CS: how much they would enjoy majoring in CS
- The **utility** of CS: the extent to which CS would provide potential value to society or to them as individuals
- The **opportunity cost** associated with majoring in CS: practical constraints, as well as ways in which majoring in CS might restrict other plans

In this previous work [32], we selected a single factor, ability, and presented a grounded theory of how students assessed their ability within CS. In participants' discussion of their ability within CS, an important dimension of variability was whether or not students perceived ability within CS as innate or not. This dimension of variability aligned with Carol Dweck and colleagues' body of work that focuses extensively on students' beliefs about whether intelligence is innate [15, 55].

3. METHODS

3.1 Data Collection and Research Context

Interview data was collected in the U.S. at two large, public, research-focused universities. At University A, nine participants were recruited from UA-CS1 and eleven participants were recruited from UA-CS2. At University B, eleven participants were recruited from UB-CS1. All participants responded to a recruitment e-mail and were compensated $15. Of these 31 students, about one third intended to major in CS, and an additional third were unsure or intended to minor, with the rest not intending to major or minor. Just over half of the students in the sample were women. At UA, women were oversampled among volunteers and at UB no screening was done. Within the paper, participants are referred to using identifiers including university and course level and a pseudonym that we attempted to match to the gender they indicated on a demographic survey.

The interviews used a semi-structured interview protocol, which affords the interviewer the flexibility to pursue unanticipated topics but does not guarantee that all participants are asked the same questions [47]. Topics included students' experiences in the current CS course, academic interests, and interest in and preconceptions of CS. Interviews lasted 30-60 minutes and were audio recorded and transcribed.

3.2 Data Analysis: Grounded Theory

We selected grounded theory as an analytic approach to understand and document our participants' process of deciding to major in CS. Previous research has used quantitative methodologies to identify patterns in students' process of deciding to major in CS [3, 4, 5, 7, 21, 23], but the patterns that can be identified in these research studies must be specified a priori. The grounded theory methodology seeks to highlight and value participants' individual experiences rather than testing a hypothesis or identifying the prevalence of a particular experience in a population. In conducting a grounded theory analysis we sought to capture the variation and themes that are present in our data and develop explanatory theories of our participants' processes of deciding to major in CS. The grounded theories developed in this project can be seen as hypotheses that attempt to explain how students decide whether or not to major in CS.

The analysis presented in this paper builds upon our original analyses [32]. We began by reading all interview transcripts and coding the transcript using open coding, which is a process of identifying noteworthy patterns and documenting instances of these patterns. Throughout the analysis we refined the operational definitions that identified what would and would not be identified as an example of each code. We clustered our approximately 75 codes into 25 categories that were then clustered to identify five factors that shaped participants' decision to major in CS: ability, fit, enjoyment, utility, and opportunity cost.

In our previous work [32], we developed a grounded theory of students' assessment of their CS ability and the process by which this shaped their decision to major in CS. We now extend this previous work to develop a complementary grounded theory of how students assess the fit between their identity and CS.

Of the codes initially believed to be relevant to students' evaluation of their fit with CS, we conducted an additional set of axial coding, with specific attention on students' assessment of their fit. In this process we identified four characteristics within the factor of fit: singular focus, asocial, competition, and male.

We generated dozens of diagrams in an effort to articulate how stereotypes, hearsay, and experiences shaped participants' assessment of their fit with CS. We evaluated the extent to which each diagram (1) captured important themes within the interviews, (2) provided an explanatory model for the process of assessing fit with CS that was consistent with our interview data, and (3) distilled this complex process of assessing fit with CS to be comprehensible outside of our research team.

Competing diagrams were refined to attempt to best capture the process present in our interview data. Our resulting model (see Figure 1) is analogous to our previous model for students' assessment of CS ability, which was despite our generation of divergent models and our initial assumption that an analogous diagram would not capture the salient themes and variation in students' assessment of their fit with CS. Both models are a variant of a traditional diagram used in some grounded theory research [47], customized to our data.

3.3 Overlap of Ability and Fit

We expect that the five factors of ability, fit, enjoyment, utility, and opportunity cost are interdependent. In particular, students' assessment of their ability likely influences their assessment of their fit with CS. For example, Linda described her assessment of whether she fits with the major as directly tied to her experience of how difficult the course was: *"I was a little bit discouraged from how difficult [inaudible] for me. It felt kind of lonesome, a little bit. I think maybe that's what I was feeling - a little bit of separation from the others, the other people. Because at end of [CS1], I was really excited and I felt like, 'Oh yeah, I can fit here.' And [CS2] is like the test: Can you really fit here? It's like another CS weed-out, and I felt like I was being weeded out and kind of thrown by the wayside." (UA_CS2_103).* This quotation provides a concrete example of how assessment of fit and ability are interdependent. We have not included ability as a fifth characteristic of fit because students' assessment of their ability has been thoroughly discussed in our previous paper [32].

3.4 Selection of Category Names

The characteristics of singularly focused, asocial, competitive, and male were selected because they were discussed throughout our interviews. In selecting the characteristic names we made the decision to have them align with our understanding of the stereotypes about computer scientists [19]. However, some of our participants identified collaboration as a requirement for CS as opposed to competition. We have decided to consistently label the characteristics with the stereotyped label (e.g., competition) rather than the non-stereotyped label (e.g., collaboration). Research has identified the ways in which stereotypes of computer scientists also include race, sexuality, and social class [2, 19]. Despite the vital importance of understanding these dimensions of the stereotypes we do not discuss them in our paper because our participants were not asked about these and did not mention them explicitly. We recognize that individuals have multiple identities and that stereotypes about different dimensions of their identities intersect and interact [1, 20].

4. THEORETICAL FRAMEWORK

In our analysis of students' assessment of their fit with CS, we did not begin with a guiding theoretical framework. The interviews illustrate a complex process by which students considered characteristics of themselves and the characteristics they perceived as being important in CS. Based on what emerged from the interviews, we found that Sfard and Prusak's narrative theory of identity [44] provides a framework and vocabulary for understanding and describing this process of assessing fit and how it relates to major choice. Within this process that our participants described, we found that whether students described particular characteristics of computer scientists as required was important. We integrate this idea with the theory from Sfard and Prusak [44] by building upon research from Dweck and Colleagues [15, 31, 35, 36].

Sfard and Prusak define identities as narratives or stories about self that an individual tells to themselves or others. Rather than being innate, these identity narratives are constructed and modified (sometimes unconsciously) through social interaction. With this narrative definition, Sfard and

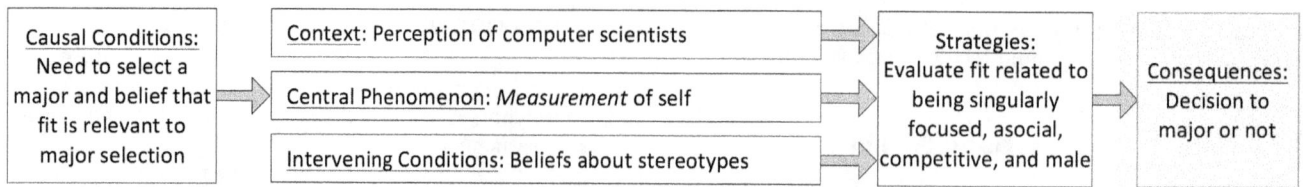

Figure 1: Diagram of grounded theory of students' assessment of fit with CS.

Prusak's theory describes how people form, modify, and express a variety of present and potential identities. Sfard and Prusak [44] also distinguish between two kinds of identities: actual and designated. An actual identity describes a person's present state, while a designated identity describes what could, at some point in the future, become part of their actual identity. Designated identities can be positive, in the sense that they reflect one's aspirations or sense of possible future selves, but they can also represent limitations on future selves or restrictions on what one can do or become. The language of "actual identity" may be misleading because it may be incorrectly interpreted as implying that there is a true identity. This would be a direct contradiction of the theory presented by Sfard and Prusak, which is that identities are socially constructed through narrative [44].

In terms of this framing, our interviews contain multiple narratives related to being or becoming a CS major or computer scientist. In the context of an interview about deciding to pursue CS, our participants' statements about the characteristics important to being a successful computer scientist can be seen as narratives about designated identities. In describing these CS designated identities, students often compared them explicitly or implicitly with their actual identities, providing some sense of the extent to which they see themselves fitting into CS.

The four characteristics of computer scientists that we highlight in this paper represent salient features of the CS designated identities described by our interviewees. Grounded in interview data, we not only detail student beliefs about these characteristics, but also propose a theory of how interest in the CS major is affected by actual and designated identities.

5. RESULTS

5.1 Overview of Model of Assessment of Fit

Figure 1 shows our grounded theory of how participants evaluated their fit with CS when deciding to major in CS or not. In the diagram we use the traditional grounded theory labels (underlined in Figure 1) [47]. Within the text below, we show these labels in parentheses. We identified the need to select a major and the belief that fit is relevant to major selection (Causal Conditions) as conditions that caused students to measure their self (Central Phenomenon, Section 5.2). The process of evaluating their fit (Strategies, Section 5.5) appeared to be shaped by three things:

- Students' assessment of self, i.e., what are the students' characteristics regarding being singularly focused, asocial, competitive, and male? (Central Phenomenon, Section 5.2)
- Students' beliefs about stereotypes, i.e., what is the relevance of stereotypes? (Intervening Conditions, Section 5.3)

- Students' perception of computer scientists, i.e., what are the characteristics of computer scientists regarding being singularly focused, asocial, competitive, and male? (Context, Section 5.4)

The outcome of students' evaluation of fit was their decision to major or not (Consequences, Section 5.6).

5.2 Central Phenomenon: Measuring Self

In this work, the central phenomenon is the student's narrative of themselves with respect to the four characteristics: singularly focused, asocial, competitive, and male. Students' narratives about themselves enable them to evaluate if they fit with their perception of the characteristics of computer scientists. We asked students to complete a demographic questionnaire, which asked them to identify their gender, but in designing the interviews did not seek to collect narratives about their actual identities related to being singularly focused, asocial, or competitive. The focus on these characteristics came out of the data analysis. Despite this, participants shared stories that included actual identities related to the four characteristics. For example, Ellie described herself as a *"people person"* (UB_CS1_11).

5.3 Intervening Conditions: Beliefs about Stereotypes

Through open coding we found that an important dimension of variation was whether or not students thought particular personal characteristics were required of computer scientists. This finding connected to the work of Dweck and colleagues (e.g., [15]), which describes students as either entity or incremental theorists. Entity theorists endorse the idea that intelligence is fixed, while incremental theorists endorse the idea that intelligence is malleable. Levy, Stroessner, and Dweck [31] generalize entity and incremental theorists as endorsing that a person's traits, and not just intelligence, are either fixed or malleable. Based upon this generalization, Levy, Stroessner, and Dweck evaluated the extent to which children with each theory engaged in social stereotyping. The researchers hypothesize that entity theorists may "believe that traits can be reliably inferred from small samples of behavior." [31, p. 1422]. This distinction between an individual's knowledge of stereotypes and their endorsement of those stereotypes is a common distinction [11, 13, 37]. The primary implication of this research is that educators should work to challenge the notion that characteristics of the CS stereotype are required by the field.

5.4 Context: Sources of Stereotypes

While students' perceptions of computer scientists are likely shaped by cultural stereotypes of computer scientists [19], we infer that participants made measurements of computer scientists through observations, information provided by others, and personal experience. The following details about the research contexts illuminates ways in which institutional structures can reinforce or dispel stereotypes.

5.4.1 Singularly Focused

Participants' appeared to measure the characteristic of computer scientists as singularly focused through observations, personal experience, and statements from friends and advisors.

- Melissa described observations of her close friends as *"doing the same thing every day, every night, and without sleep. And without eating anything."* (UA_CS2_104).
- Vanessa reported that *"And now I see why people are in lab all day"* (UB_CS1_02).
- Christine described that she heard *"Like 'oh we don't sleep' or they're like 'oh yeah we just sit in front of the computer all day.'"* (UB_CS1_09).
- In contrast, Isabella reported that the seminar leader: *"showed us that there are a lot of people who like CS, but they don't do it 24 hours, you know".* (UA_CS1_009).

Class time provided opportunities for students to interact with other students who might reinforce or challenge the stereotype of computer scientists being singularly focused. The workload expectations of the students' course or other courses within the major could also shape perception of whether being singularly focused is required.

5.4.2 Asocial

Participants measured the characteristic of asocial through observations of computer scientists and peers.

- Linda described her observation that her CS1 class is *"a very silent class"* and that there were *"not a lot of sociable people. There's definitely, there's definitely a few"* (UA_CS2_103).
- Jana characterized her family members working at a large software company by saying that *"all of them are introverts"* (UA_CS2_101).
- In contrast, Christine described the need for social and collaboration skills: *"you have to learn to work with other people because I mean the huge projects it's never like done by one person."* (UB_CS1_09).

Students' perceptions of whether CS requires being asocial may relate to the extent to which students interact within the course. At University A, students in CS1 and CS2 observe their peers during the three large lecture sessions, the one or two weekly quiz sections, and while working in the programming lab dedicated to the course. There is minimal interaction between students during the three weekly large lecture meetings. Assignments in the course are done individually and there is a strict anti-collaboration policy around submitted assignments. Students may ask questions of course staff in the programming lab and during quiz section. Students from UB had six hours of closed lab and a single hour of lecture a week. Graduate or undergraduate teaching assistants in the lab were told to encourage students to collaborate and students were allowed to pair program [51] on lab exercises, homework, and projects.

5.4.3 Competitive

Participants' measurements of the characteristic of competitive related to the structures of competition within classes and whether individuals were competitive.

- Linda expressed that the environment is *"definitely extremely competitive"* (UA_CS2_103).
- Dennis reported, *"I know that the admission rate is low for the CS dept."* (UA_CS1_004).
- Jana reported that students described her CS2 class as *"a weedout class"* (UA_CS2_101).
- In contrast, Gregory observed that his CS1 class *"always felt like the class was trying to kind of foster that interest in CS rather than - you know - weed people out of the class."* (UA_CS1_007).

Admission to the CS major is competitive at UA. Less than 25% of majors are accepted directly out of high school. Most prospective majors apply after two years of prerequisite coursework, and at the time of these interviews approximately 40% were accepted. At UB, there are two CS-related majors. One major is populated by students directly out of high school. The other major has had a competitive admissions process, but at the time of these interviews did not. When Linda discussed her difficulty finding students in her class to work with or talk to she said: *"it was either the students or it's just sort of the–the course, how it discourages collaboration on assignments . . . everyone's scared of that; they won't really say what they do for their assignments. They really won't talk about it"* (UA_CS2_103). When asked how big of an impact this had on the amount of collaboration in the course, Linda said: *"I felt that was one of the main problems, . . . I think it's good to make sure students aren't copying, but if those are the only assignments we get—one big one per week—and we can't work with each other really, because sharing ideas means kind of sharing code ideas, so code kind of comes up. It's just kind of scary. You don't really want to share ideas"* (UA_CS2_103). This suggests that perhaps course structure or policies could affect the perception that CS lacks collaboration.

5.4.4 Male

In our sample, only students who identified as female made comments about either the proportion of females in CS or whether one must be masculine to fit with CS.

- Xenia observed that *"there are a lot more guys"* (UB_CS1_04) in the CS major.
- Melissa observed that *"guys do perform better than girls in the CSE courses. At least [CS1] and [CS2]. And you can see that there are more guy TAs than the girl TAs. So - I think like in [CS2], I think, like more than 70%, at least that show up in the class, there are like 70% of guys."* (UA_CS2_104).

Melissa's observations were accurate that about 80% of the TAs and the students in her CS2 class were men. While participants may have been told about the gender make-up within the field or CS courses, they only reported observing the gender make-up and did not report personal experiences beyond observations of the gender make-up.

5.5 Strategies: Evaluating Fit

Students examined their fit with CS by interpreting their self-assessment of how much they reflected the characteristics of singular focus, asocial, competitive, and male relative to what they perceived as the requirements of the field of CS for these characteristics. These interpretations were shaped by students' internal beliefs about stereotypes as well as their context, such as observations in their CS courses and the experiences of their peers. To show the potential for these stereotypes to discourage participation we present examples where students assume these characteristics are required. To show narratives that may be helpful for supporting and encouraging students who perceive themselves as different from the stereotypes we present examples where students challenge or reject the requirement of these characteristics.

5.5.1 Singularly Focused

Explicit in a number of the participants' descriptions is that they believe that CS requires a singular focus. For example, Anthony, described computer scientists as needing to be *"disconnected"* from the world. Anthony expressed that there could be exceptions to this, but attributed these exceptions to differences in the difficulty of the work. He said: *"I can imagine people who are like successful in CS and they still can do good in this world. They can take care of their family and their health and lots of stuff. Just depends on how difficult the task is." (Anthony, UA_CS1_001)*. Although he identified exceptions, these exceptions do not challenge the underlying requirement of being *"disconnected"* from the world when facing difficult CS tasks. Another participant, Kendra, used language such as *"can't"* and *"have to"* to describe that computer scientists *"have to be able to make it their lifestyle; can't just do it as a side thing, have to be thinking about it all the time." (UA_CS1_102)*. For Anthony and Kendra, who describe the nature of the work as requiring a singular focus, the designated identity of a computer scientist was tied to being singularly focused.

In a few instances, individuals challenged the stereotypes or directly rejected them. Charles mentioned some of the stereotypes of computer scientists being singularly focused, but later he said: *"you also have to step back and just not be too stressed from it. I guess you have to be, to a degree, easy going ... You have to be able to detach yourself from your work." (UA_CS1_003)*. Isabella reported that her friends questioned her: *"'CS, really? I mean isn't that you just sit down and you code for hours'"(UA_CS1_009)*. She explicitly identifies this as a stereotype and says it does not describe her: *"That is kind of the stereotype of CS. They just code all day and work very hard. But you know I like working hard. But I am not, you know there are the stereotypical CS programmers. But I am not one of them. And you know I have fun, and go out and do other things. I don't code all day" (Isabella, UA_CS1_009)*. Orion described how he plans to be an exception to the stereotype of a singularly-focused computer scientist: *"I don't plan on becoming the recluse that stays in the basement with high-end technology. I'm going to be the guy with the high-end technology that still goes outdoors" (UA_CS2_106)*. The first set of cases (Anthony & Kendra) presented designated identities that included a singular focus as a necessary component. The second set of cases included a competing narrative to the singular focus (Charles) and two students who present a designated identity that does not conform to the stereotype (Isabella & Orion).

5.5.2 Asocial

Students connected the nature of the work of CS with being asocial or requiring a lack of a social life. Patrick said that one of the characteristics of a computer scientist is *"not having a social life so you can think about your programs all day" (UA_CS2_107)*. Jana expressed that not everyone can become a computer scientist because CS requires a particular *"mental outlook" (UA_CS2_101)*. She said: *"maybe that mental outlook includes them being introverts, because CS is very abstract, so maybe it's connected somehow." (Jana, UA_CS2_101)*. Similarly, Linda connected the nature of CS work to being asocial: *"[CS] takes a mind that likes being with themselves sort of, because it is pretty impersonal – or very you and the computer"(UA_CS2_103)*.

A few students' described concrete examples of exceptions to the stereotype of computer scientists as asocial. Brian described his CS lab as *"pretty loud" (UB_CS1_08)*. When asked if he liked this, he responded: *"I really like it cause it's just more fun that way. - cause then you're talking with everybody - you know - comparing programs and stuff" (UB_CS1_08)*. While Linda had expressed that the nature of CS work required being asocial, she sometimes defended the level of social interaction in CS. She reports that her roommates discouraged her from going into CS: *"they say I'm too sociable for this" (UA_CS2_103)*, but she contended that CS is *"what you make of it, based upon your personality and what you prefer" (Linda, UA_CS2_103)*.

5.5.3 Competitive

Several students felt that one would need to be competitive to thrive in CS. When asked if there was anything he found unappealing about the CS major, Gregory explains his belief that as you go into higher-level CS and mathematics classes there is more competition, *"I'm sure this is a misrepresentation, but my estimation is that people are less social and a little bit more competitive. They are - that there is less that spirit of collaboration than you might find in kind of a lower level of the class. And I guess that turns me off." (UA_CS1_007)*. Linda described that you can *"overcome the competition and challenge" (UA_CS2_103)*, which both endorses the expectation of competition and expresses a belief in her ability to operate within it.

Participants also described the requirement of collaboration in CS, which challenges the expectation that CS requires competition. For example, multiple students identified that a successful computer scientist must have *"communication skills" (Dennis, UA_CS1_004 and Emily, UA_CS1_005)*. Noah said that a successful computer scientist has to be *"able to work in a team and communicate with people" (UA_CS2_105)*. Christine expressed that a successful computer scientist needs to work with people: *"you have to learn to work with other people because I mean the huge projects it's never like done by one person." (UB_CS1_09)*. Heather described CS as *"individual" (UA_CS1_008)*, but her description of a successful computer scientist shows that she recognizes the value of collaborative work in CS: *"I could see someone who is successful being able to interact with a group of people, like lead a meeting, for example. Have good ideas. Be able to communicate, be open to other ideas. Teamwork." (Heather, UA_CS1_008)*.

5.5.4 Male

In our interviews, only female students mentioned how being male related to being successful in CS. Melissa was the most unambiguous in stating that it was an advantage for computer scientists to be male: *"I think just like the girls and guys have different kind of system of thinking, just like, I just think that guys are more used to thinking the way that the programming language is thinking. Like girls may like more of like English literature or like the other like music. And the guys more like those applications stuff like engineering, CS, or like stuff like EE. I think that is inherited. Like you are born with those characteristics." (UA_CS2_104).*

Three students at UA made statements that showed they clearly rejected the stereotype that you must be male to be successful in CS. For example: *"even though it is a male-dominated field, I feel like I have been getting along with people in that class. Most of my friends are guys in that class. (laughs) It is o.k."* (Heather, UA_CS1_008). Xenia noticed that there are more guys than girls in her class but she feels comfortable in the classroom and does not view that as a deterrent: *"my friend and I laugh about it, that's about it."* (UB_CS1_04)

5.6 Consequences: Decision to Major or Not

5.6.1 Singularly Focused

Participants connected the stereotypes of CS requiring a singular focus to their decisions to major in CS. For example, Andrew explained that CS was unappealing because *"I don't want to spend the whole day just sitting in the lab."* (UB_CS1_07). Similarly, Melissa explained: *"I am an outsider, so I think oh why are you just doing the same thing every day, every night, and without sleep. And without eating anything. It is kind of crazy."* (UA_CS2_104). Christine described how the stereotype of a singular focus and asocialness shaped her decision: *"I just think like maybe I don't get to see the sun too much and all I do is sit there and code. I'm just like doing it all on my own. That's kind of unappealing."* (UB_CS1_09).

5.6.2 Asocial

Participants linked the requirement of asocialness to their decisions to major in CS. For example, Jana had described being an introvert as part of the required *"mental outlook"* (UA_CS2_101) for a computer scientist. She explained that *"I'm not that much of an introvert"* and described that this made another major a *"much better fit"* (UA_CS2_101). Similarly, Tiffany expressed concern about the potential for social interaction: *"I don't know how much I would love working with computers exclusively or computers and a small group of people for a job. I would rather be working with more people rather than computers'* (UA_CS2_111). Ellie described CS as unappealing: *"it lacks more of that social aspect that I like a lot."* (UB_CS1_11). The stereotype was not universally discouraging, Heather described: *"Sometimes I just like working on my own, like without talking to other people, and I just get work done a lot faster."* (UA_CS1_008).

5.6.3 Competitive

Competition impacted students' interest in majoring in CS in multiple ways. When asked if there was anything he found unappealing about the CS major, Gregory explained that he expects more competition in higher level CS courses: *"And I guess that turns me off."* (UA_CS1_007). At UA the difficulty of getting into the CS major is something most students are aware of and dissuades some from applying to the major: *"After taking the course [UA CS2] and hearing about how competitive applications are and getting into the school is, I was like, 'oh okay, we know what I'm not majoring in' (laughs)"* (Rachel, UA_CS2_108).

5.6.4 Male

When asked if there were things about the CS major that did not appeal to her, Heather cited stereotypes as one negative: *"I'm not a fan of the stereotypes that people make about women in CS"* (UA_CS1_008). Heather felt that people often mentioned that she did not fit the stereotype: *"I mean every single person I have told that I am trying to major in CS has made some kind of comment about the way that they see me, and it kind of puts me off a little bit. (laughs)"* (UA_CS1_008). Despite this, Heather is planning on taking CS2 and applying to the CS major. Melissa went on at length about why *"guys do perform better than girls in the CSE courses"* and added that *"So, uh, I think if (CS2) was not in the requirements of my major, I think I won't consider to take these two courses."* (UA_CS2_104).

6. DISCUSSION

Our research reinforces previous research about the importance of students' feelings of belonging [8, 10, 22, 30, 45, 49, 50, 54]. This is particularly important for students about whom negative stereotypes exist [45] and any students who are underrepresented in CS based upon one or more dimensions of their identity. We reject assumptions that differences between a student's identities (i.e., actual identities [44]) and the stereotyped identities of computer scientists (i.e., designated identities [44]) must diminish students' interest.

Previous research [2] recommends teaching students about the development of the identity of a computer scientist, to show it is constructed rather than essential, "unmasking and raising awareness about the historical evolution of specific occupational identities." [2, p. 153].

At UA, a one-credit seminar exploring women in CS seeks to accomplish this. The course is offered to students taking CS1 or CS2 and provides an opportunity for students to visit local companies, attend research presentations, and meet current student CS majors and alumnae [16, 52]. One of the goals of the course was to: "Encourage a broad, accurate view of computer science and related fields." [53] The seminar made a point of dispelling common stereotypes about CS: "With every research visit we emphasized that computer science is more than just sitting in front of a computer all day. We felt that it was important to highlight the interactive, creative side of the computing field." [16, p. 10.905.5]

Four of our participants (Linda, Emily, Heather & Isabella) were enrolled in this seminar. Several of them mentioned it specifically when discussing stereotypes about CS.

Isabella attributed her rejection of the stereotype of singular focus as coming from information she gained in the seminar: *"This is where the seminar came in, at first I thought that wow. CS really isn't for me because all the kids that are in my [CS1] they have been programming since they were 7, they have programmed all of their lives. And like, they even do it as a hobby. And I mean I find CS fun, but I don't do it on the weekends you know. And that is o.k. And when I hit the seminar that was what I was afraid of going into CS, that I was competing against all of these people who programmed as a hobby you know. But the seminar, [the leader] showed us that there are a lot of people who like CS, but they don't do it 24 hours, you know. And they do other things and they are successful at it. It is o.k. to have other interests, and that is often a bonus to have other interests, because it opens your eyes to different things."* (UA_CS1_009). Isabella explicitly stated that the seminar has made her more interested in majoring in CS.

Heather was planning on majoring in CS and found the seminar helpful in terms of allowing her to meet more women interested in CS and to have some of her doubts about whether women can do CS addressed. People are surprised when she says she wants to major in CS and tell her that she does not fit the CS stereotype - telling her she should major in dance instead. Heather said she found the seminar useful *"because those were some of the doubts that I had myself. And it was nice to hear that other people had the same experiences, and have other people tell them that they could not be a CS major or that they would get in just because they were a woman. But when [the leaders] said 'that is not true, we do not consider that at all' that was good confirmation." (UA_CS1_008)*. When asked if the seminar had influenced her interest in majoring in CS, she replied: *"I think that has confirmed it a lot because I have seen people like myself in that class. Who are interested in, but not completely sure they want to do this. And again, they are women." (UA_CS1_008)*.

7. VALIDITY AND LIMITATIONS

Subjectivity is inherent in the process of interpretive qualitative research, but we attempted to address validity concerns in our study's analysis and presentation. All three researchers have experience teaching introductory CS courses and background in education research in CS. This meant that we were familiar with the language of CS, as well as the pedagogical context, which guided follow-up questions during interviews and aided data interpretation.

Interpretations presented here were the result of negotiations by at least two researchers who examined transcript data. In keeping with qualitative traditions, we offer the reader context and numerous quotes for our claims, allowing them to make judgments of validity. As is common with grounded theory work, our goal was not universal theory, so we make limited claims about the generalizability of our findings and the prevalence of observed phenomena. We do, however, expect that many of the complex relationships our theory describes apply to other settings.

One potential limitation was that participants were self-selected volunteers. However, the sample included roughly equal numbers of students intending to major, considering majoring or minoring, and not intending to major in CS, suggesting limited relevance of self-selection bias. A clearer limitation stems from our sole focus on the self-perceptions of students. Important as they are, we expect there are other influences on interest in majoring in CS that students are not conscious of or do not self-report for some other reason.

Finally, it should be noted that we only interviewed students who were currently taking a CS1 or CS2 course. Research has found that women who had not taken a CS course were more likely to mention a stereotype than women who had taken a CS course [9]. Thus we might expect the influence of stereotypes to be even more pronounced among that group, suggesting the importance of encouraging women to take CS courses.

8. CONCLUSION

Our previous work [32] identified five factors that students considered when deciding whether to major in CS: ability,
fit, enjoyment, utility, and opportunity cost. In this paper we elaborate on how students determine their fit with CS. We identified four characteristics some students felt were required for one to have in order to fit in CS: singularly focused on CS, asocial, competitive, and male. We found that some students were able to reject stereotypes about what was required to be a computer scientist, particularly when provided examples of computer scientists who themselves did not match these stereotypes. One intervention we observed having an impact on our interviewees was the women in CS seminar [16, 52] at UA. This course was successful in showing students that stereotypes they had about CS were not requirements of the field. While this seminar was offered as a separate course, elements of the course (e.g. explicit discussion of stereotypes, outside speakers) could be integrated into introductory CS courses. CS educators may also consider modifying aspects of their course to be sure they are sending accurate messages about what is required to be in CS. Having course staff describe outside interests can dispel the image that someone who does CS has no time for or interest in anything else. Providing opportunities during class or lab for students to interact with their peers and drawing a connection to interaction in the CS workplace can show that interaction and collaboration are a part of CS. Students' experience of competition at UA could be influenced by both the competitive admissions policies and restrictive collaboration policies. This pattern, while observed within a small sample, warrants departments using caution when implementing competitive admission requirements in response to over-enrollment [29, 41, 42]. Recruiting female TAs or female guest speakers could help challenge all students' association of computer scientists as men.

Although not discussed in this paper, in our previous work [32] we found enjoyment, utility, and opportunity cost also shaped students' decision to major in CS or not (see Section 2.3). The amount each of these factors affects each person's decision will vary and interact. For example, it seems likely that the amount someone expects they would enjoy majoring in CS is impacted by both their assessment of their ability and how well they fit with their notion of who a computer scientist is. For some students, the extent to which they see CS as providing potential value to society or to themselves (i.e., utility) will be an overwhelming factor in their decision to major in CS. Exposure to CS before college and multiple pathways into the CS major are critical to assuring that the opportunity cost associated with majoring in CS is not so high to dissuade students. At Stanford, research shows that women tended to take CS late in their college career [40], suggesting that it is important to get students who are underrepresented in CS to try it early.

One future direction would be to use our findings to inform a quantitative study to further validate causal relationships and document the prevalence of various beliefs and experiences. Our hope is that our work will directly inform the design and validation of interventions to help potential CS students make informed major choices.

9. ACKNOWLEDGMENTS

We would like to thank the participants from our study. The research reported here was supported in part by a grant from the National Science Foundation (Award 1339404).

10. REFERENCES

[1] J. Acker. Inequality regimes gender, class, and race in organizations. *Gender & society*, 20(4):441–464, 2006.

[2] K. L. Ashcraft and C. Ashcraft. Breaking the "glass slipper": What diversity interventions can learn from the historical evolution of occupational identity in ICT and commercial aviation. In *Connecting women*, pages 137–155. Springer, 2015.

[3] L. J. Barker, C. McDowell, and K. Kalahar. Exploring factors that influence computer science introductory course students to persist in the major. In *ACM SIGCSE Bulletin*, volume 41, pages 153–157. ACM, 2009.

[4] S. Beyer, K. Rynes, and S. Haller. Deterrents to women taking computer science courses. *Technology and Society Magazine, IEEE*, 23(1):21–28, 2004.

[5] R. Boyle, J. Carter, and M. Clark. What makes them succeed? Entry, progression and graduation in computer science. *Journal of Further and Higher Education*, 26(1):3–18, 2002.

[6] T. Camp. Computing, we have a problem.... *ACM Inroads*, 3(4):34–40, 2012.

[7] L. Carter. Why students with an apparent aptitude for computer science don't choose to major in computer science. *ACM SIGCSE Bulletin*, 38(1):27–31, 2006.

[8] S. Cheryan, V. C. Plaut, P. G. Davies, and C. M. Steele. Ambient belonging: how stereotypical cues impact gender participation in computer science. *Journal of personality and social psychology*, 97(6):1045, 2009.

[9] S. Cheryan, V. C. Plaut, C. Handron, and L. Hudson. The stereotypical computer scientist: Gendered media representations as a barrier to inclusion for women. *Sex roles*, 69(1-2):58–71, 2013.

[10] S. Cheryan, J. O. Siy, M. Vichayapai, B. J. Drury, and S. Kim. Do female and male role models who embody stem stereotypes hinder women's anticipated success in stem? *Social Psychological and Personality Science*, 2(6):656–664, 2011.

[11] D. Cvencek, A. N. Meltzoff, and A. G. Greenwald. Math–gender stereotypes in elementary school children. *Child development*, 82(3):766–779, 2011.

[12] D. Cvencek, N. S. Nasir, K. O'Connor, S. Wischnia, and A. N. Meltzoff. The development of math–race stereotypes:"they say chinese people are the best at math". *Journal of Research on Adolescence*, 25(4):630–637, 2015.

[13] P. G. Devine. Stereotypes and prejudice: their automatic and controlled components. *Journal of personality and social psychology*, 56(1):5, 1989.

[14] J. D'Onfro. *How this Googler is trying to shake up Hollywood's idea of who an 'engineer' is*, 2015. http://www.businessinsider.com/julie-ann-crommett-cs-in-the-media-2015-10.

[15] C. S. Dweck and E. L. Leggett. A social-cognitive approach to motivation and personality. *Psychological review*, 95(2):256, 1988.

[16] C. Eney and C. Hoyer. Making a difference on $10 a day: Creating a 'women in cse' seminar linked to cs1. In *Proceedings of the 2005 American Society for Engineering Education Annual Conference & Exposition*, pages 10.905.1–10.905.10. ASEE, 2005.

[17] N. L. Ensmenger. Letting the "computer boys" take over: Technology and the politics of organizational transformation. *International Review of Social History*, 48(S11):153–180, 2003.

[18] N. L. Ensmenger. *The computer boys take over: Computers, programmers, and the politics of technical expertise.* Mit Press, 2012.

[19] N. L. Ensmenger. Beards, sandals, and other signs of rugged individualism: Masculine culture within the computing professions. *Osiris*, 30(1):38–65, 2015.

[20] S. Fenstermaker and C. West. *Doing gender, doing difference: Inequality, power, and institutional change.* Psychology Press, 2002.

[21] J. Gal-Ezer, D. Shahak, and E. Zur. Computer science issues in high school: gender and more.... In *ACM SIGCSE Bulletin*, volume 41, pages 278–282. ACM, 2009.

[22] C. Goodenow. Classroom belonging among early adolescent students: relationships to motivation and achievement. *The Journal of Early Adolescence*, 13(1):21–43, 1993.

[23] Google for Education. *Women Who Choose Computer Science - What Really Matters*, 2014. https://docs.google.com/file/d/0B-E2rcvhnlQ-a1Q4VUxWQ2dtTHM/edit.

[24] Google for Education. *Images of Computer Science: Perceptions Among Students, Parents and Educators in the U.S.*, 2015. https://services.google.com/fh/files/misc/images-of-computer-science-report.pdf.

[25] Google for Education. *Searching for Computer Science: Access and Barriers in U.S. K-12 Education*, 2015. https://services.google.com/fh/files/misc/searching-for-computer-science_report.pdf.

[26] P. Kinnunen and L. Malmi. Why students drop out cs1 course? In *Proceedings of the second international workshop on Computing education research*, pages 97–108. ACM, 2006.

[27] P. Kinnunen and B. Simon. Building theory about computing education phenomena: a discussion of grounded theory. In *Proceedings of the 10th Koli Calling International Conference on Computing Education Research*, pages 37–42. ACM, 2010.

[28] P. Kinnunen and B. Simon. My program is ok–am i? computing freshmen's experiences of doing programming assignments. *Computer Science Education*, 22(1):1–28, 2012.

[29] J. Kurose. Booming undergraduate enrollments: a wave or a sea change? *ACM Inroads*, 6(4):105–106, 2015.

[30] J. D. Lee. Which kids can "become" scientists? Effects of gender, self-concepts, and perceptions of scientists. *Social Psychology Quarterly*, pages 199–219, 1998.

[31] S. R. Levy, S. J. Stroessner, and C. S. Dweck. Stereotype formation and endorsement: The role of implicit theories. *Journal of Personality and Social Psychology*, 74(6):1421, 1998.

[32] C. M. Lewis, K. Yasuhara, and R. E. Anderson. Deciding to major in computer science: A grounded theory of students' self-assessment of ability. In *Proceedings of the Seventh International Workshop on Computing Education Research*, ICER '11, pages 3–10, New York, NY, USA, 2011. ACM.

[33] J. Margolis, R. Estrella, J. Goode, J. J. Holme, and K. Nao. *Stuck in the shallow end: Education, race, and computing.* MIT Press, 2010.

[34] J. Margolis and A. Fisher. *Unlocking the clubhouse: Women in computing.* MIT press, 2003.

[35] A. Master, S. Cheryan, and A. N. Meltzoff. Computing whether she belongs: Stereotypes undermine girls' interest and sense of belonging in computer science. *Journal of Educational Psychology*, 108(3):424–437, 2016.

[36] A. Master, E. M. Markman, and C. S. Dweck. Thinking in categories or along a continuum: Consequences for children's social judgments. *Child development*, 83(4):1145–1163, 2012.

[37] C. McKown and M. J. Strambler. Developmental antecedents and social and academic consequences of stereotype-consciousness in middle childhood. *Child Development*, 80(6):1643–1659, 2009.

[38] T. J. Misa. *Gender codes: Why women are leaving computing.* John Wiley & Sons, 2011.

[39] National Center for Women and Information Technology and Televisa Foundation. *TECHNOLOchicas*, 2015. technolochicas.org.

[40] K. Redmond, S. Evans, and M. Sahami. A large-scale quantitative study of women in computer science at Stanford University. In *Proceeding of the 44th ACM Technical Symposium on Computer Science Education*, SIGCSE '13, pages 439–444, New York, NY, USA, 2013. ACM.

[41] E. Roberts. *A History of Capacity Challenges in Computer Science*, 2016. http://cs.stanford.edu/people/eroberts/CSCapacity.pdf.

[42] E. S. Roberts. Meeting the challenges of rising enrollments. *ACM Inroads*, 2(3):4–6, 2011.

[43] T. Schmader, M. Johns, and C. Forbes. An integrated process model of stereotype threat effects on performance. *Psychological review*, 115(2):336, 2008.

[44] A. Sfard and A. Prusak. Telling identities: In search of an analytic tool for investigating learning as a culturally shaped activity. *Educational researcher*, 34(4):14–22, 2005.

[45] C. M. Steele. A threat in the air: How stereotypes shape intellectual identity and performance. *American psychologist*, 52(6):613, 1997.

[46] J. Stout and B. Tamer. Collaborative learning eliminates the negative impact of gender stereotypes on women's self-concept. In *Proceedings for the Annual Meeting of the American Society for Engineering Education.*, 2016.

[47] A. Strauss, J. Corbin, et al. *Basics of qualitative research*, volume 15. Newbury Park, CA: Sage, 1990.

[48] The Coalition to Diversify Computing. *Resources.* http://www.cdc-computing.org/resources/.

[49] V. Tinto. *Leaving college: Rethinking the causes and cures of student attrition.* ERIC, 1987.

[50] N. Veilleux, R. Bates, C. Allendoerfer, D. Jones, J. Crawford, and T. Floyd Smith. The relationship between belonging and ability in computer science. In *Proceeding of the 44th ACM Technical Symposium on Computer Science Education*, SIGCSE '13, pages 65–70, New York, NY, USA, 2013. ACM.

[51] L. Williams, R. R. Kessler, W. Cunningham, and R. Jeffries. Strengthening the case for pair programming. *IEEE software*, 17(4):19, 2000.

[52] *Women In Computing Seminar.* http://courses.cs.washington.edu/courses/cse190a/.

[53] *Women In Computing Seminar Syllabus*, 2009. http://courses.cs.washington.edu/education/courses/cse190a/09au/190a_syllabus_au09.doc.

[54] D. Yeager, G. Walton, and G. L. Cohen. Addressing achievement gaps with psychological interventions. *Phi Delta Kappan*, 94(5):62–65, 2013.

[55] D. S. Yeager, R. Johnson, B. J. Spitzer, K. H. Trzesniewski, J. Powers, and C. S. Dweck. The far-reaching effects of believing people can change: Implicit theories of personality shape stress, health, and achievement during adolescence. *Journal of Personality and Social Psychology*, 106(6):867, 2014.

[56] *YesWeCode*, 2014. http://www.yeswecode.org/.

Evaluation of a Frame-based Programming Editor

Thomas W. Price
North Carolina State Univ.
Raleigh, NC, USA
twprice@ncsu.edu

Neil C. C. Brown
University of Kent
Canterbury, Kent, UK
nccb@kent.ac.uk

Dragan Lipovac
North Carolina State Univ.
Raleigh, NC, USA
dlipova@ncsu.edu

Tiffany Barnes
North Carolina State Univ.
Raleigh, NC, USA
tmbarnes@ncsu.edu

Michael Kölling
University of Kent
Canterbury, Kent, UK
mik@kent.ac.uk

ABSTRACT

Frame-based editing is a novel way to edit programs, which claims to combine the benefits of textual and block-based programming. It combines structured 'frames' of preformatted code, designed to reduce the burden of syntax, with 'slots' that allow for efficient textual entry of expressions. We present an empirical evaluation of Stride, a frame-based language used in the Greenfoot IDE. We compare two groups of middle school students who worked on a short programming activity in Greenfoot, one using the original Java editor, and one using the Stride editor. We found that the two groups reported similarly low levels of frustration and high levels of satisfaction, but students using Stride progressed through the activity more quickly and completed more objectives. The Stride group also spent significantly less time making purely syntactic edits to their code and significantly less time with non-compilable code.

Keywords

Frame-based editing, Syntax, Evaluation, Greenfoot, Novice programming

1. INTRODUCTION

Programming syntax and syntax errors represent a fundamental, common and difficult challenge for novices learning to program [5, 10, 30]. Programming environments and courses designed for novices often feature innovations to ease the burden of syntax, such as improved error messages [9, 11], more intuitive programming languages [23, 30] and block-based editors which avoid syntax errors altogether [8, 12, 29]. However, improved error messages are not always effective [9, 26], and block-based editors may have unforeseen consequences on programming behavior [25] and be perceived as less authentic by students [27, 33].

Frame-based editing is a novel way to edit code, which attempts to reduce the burden of syntax, while maintain-

ICER '16, September 8–12, 2016, Melbourne, VIC, Australia.

© 2016 Copyright held by the owner/author(s). Publication rights licensed to ACM.
ISBN 978-1-4503-4449-4/16/09...$15.00

DOI: http://dx.doi.org/10.1145/2960310.2960319

ing useful elements of textual programming [6]. It combines structured 'frames' of preformatted code, similar to code blocks, with 'slots' that allow for efficient textual entry of expressions. Previous work argues that frame-based editing can ease the transition from blocks to text [18] while leveraging the benefits of both [6] to reduce syntax errors and increase efficiency [3]. This paper seeks to evaluate some of these claims empirically by comparing two groups of novices working on a short programming activity in Greenfoot, an IDE designed to teach programming [17]. One group used Java with Greenfoot's original text editor, and the other used Stride, a new frame-based language offered by Greenfoot. All other aspects of the environment were identical for the two groups, allowing us to directly measure the impact of using the Stride editor. We investigated the following research questions: Compared with the original Java editor, how will the use of the Stride editor affect students':

RQ1 Frustration and satisfaction with the activity?

RQ2 Performance on the activity?

RQ3 Programming behavior during the activity?

RQ4 Incidence of syntax errors?

2. RELATED WORK

2.1 Syntax Errors

Syntax errors can be a very challenging [19] and time consuming [3] aspect of programming for novices. Programming syntax can be quite obtuse, and, as others have noted [26], programming languages and compilers are largely designed for professionals, not novices. Stefik and Siebert [30] compared novices' ability to comprehend and then reproduce a program in a variety of languages and found that some languages, such as Java, fared no better than one that used random ASCII characters as keywords. Researchers have attempted to identify the most problematic syntax errors made by novices in common programming languages such as Java [2, 10, 13, 14]. Though results only agree partially across data sources, some of the most common syntax errors in Java are missing semicolons; mismatched parentheses, quotes or brackets; and references to unidentified variables.

Difficulties with syntax may also impact students' ability to learn other, more fundamental principles of Computer Science. Lahtinen et al. [20] analyzed a survey of students' perceived difficulty with various aspects of computing and found that reported difficulty with syntax errors correlated with other, more complex tasks, such as understanding how to design a program and decomposing it into classes and procedures. Ahadi et al. [1] found that students' incidence of syntax errors was predictive of their overall success on a programming assignment. Jadud [14] defined the Error Quotient (EQ) as a measure of students' struggles with syntax errors, based on the incidence of repeated errors in consecutive compiles. Jadud found a weak but significant correlation between the EQ and both assignment and exam grades. Interestingly, Jadud and Dorn [15] later calculated the EQ for a much larger dataset of student work and found that a student's EQ only weakly correlated with the number of days that the student had spent programming.

Some systems have tried to reduce the challenges of syntax errors by providing better compiler messages. For example, Denny et al. identified common syntax errors [10] and then designed a system to enhance error messages with explanations and examples of correct code [9]. However, the authors found that these enhanced messages had no impact on students' ability to avoid or resolve errors, which is supported by other findings that more detailed messages are no better than shorter ones [26]. Traver [31] suggests a number of guiding principles for compiler messages, including clarity and brevity, specificity and locality, which also support this notion. Lee and Ko [21] found that personifying compiler feedback using a robot agent improved novices' completion of levels in a programming game, suggesting that some improvement of error messages is possible.

2.2 Comparing Blocks and Text

Block-based programming environments, including Alice [8], Scratch [29] and Snap! [12], address the challenges of syntax errors by attempting to reduce or eliminate them altogether. The effectiveness of block editors has been evaluated in a number of comparative studies. Lewis [22] compared Scratch and Logo in a 5th grade summer camp and found that students perceived exercises to be equally difficult with both languages. On assessment questions, Scratch students performed significantly better with conditionals, but not with loops. Booth and Stumpf [4] compared text and block interfaces for adults learning to program Arduino boards and found that the block group perceived the interface to be more friendly and experienced lower perceived workload. McKay and Kölling [24] used a cognitive modelling tool to predict the execution time of programming tasks in a variety of editors, including block, text and an early prototype of the Stride editor. They found that block and text editors were each more efficient at certain tasks, but the Stride editor outperformed both on most tasks.

Others have directly compared blocks and text within the same programming environment or assessment, similar to the work we present here. Price and Barnes [28] compared novices using a block-based and textual programming interface and found that the block group completed significantly more objectives in less time and spent significantly less time idle compared to the text group. Weintrop and Wilensky [33] compared the performance of students mostly familiar with both blocks and text on two versions of an assessment that presented questions using block and text modalities respectively. They found that while the block modality produced increased scores on most CS topics, the exact reasons for this are complex and merit further study. The authors also found that students perceived programming with blocks

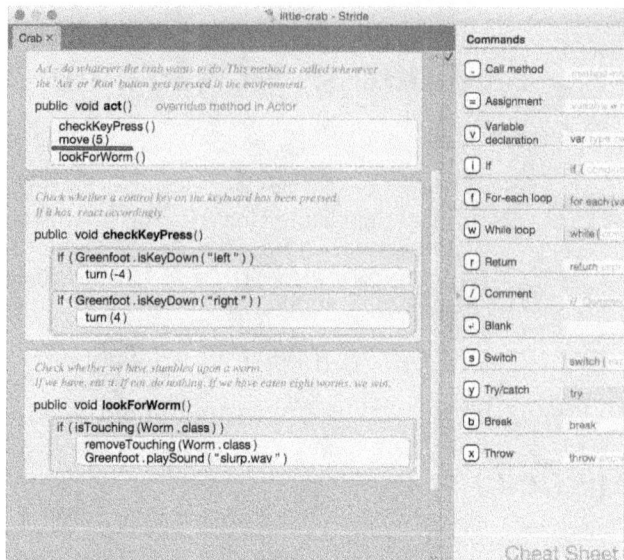

Figure 1: The Stride editor. Each large, yellow rectangle is a method *declaration* frame. Each method *call* (e.g. move(5)) is a separate frame, even though it does not have an explicitly drawn border. The frame cursor is the thin blue bar between the second and third method calls in the act method.

to be easier, in part due to their being easier to read, with better natural layout, but students also perceived blocks to be less powerful, authentic and efficient to work with [32].

2.3 Greenfoot and Stride

Greenfoot [17] is an integrated development environment (IDE) designed to allow beginners aged 14 and upwards to easily program games and simulations. Originally Greenfoot only allowed programming in Java, but since the release of Greenfoot 3 in late 2015, the Stride language is also provided (see Figure 1). Semantically, Stride is identical to Java: it is only the editing interactions and some syntax that differs. Specifically: Stride uses *frame-based editing*, which tries to merge block-based and text-based editing [6].

Stride frames are first-class interface elements which can be dragged, selected, created or deleted as a whole item. A frame cursor can be placed between frames (see Figure 1), much as a text cursor is placed between characters. The cursor can be moved via keys or placed with a mouse click. Frames can be created at the current frame cursor position by clicking in the sidebar (right-hand side of Figure 1), or more commonly by pressing the indicated command key. For example, pressing 'i' will create an if-frame.

Frames have unalterable structure and labels (e.g. the "while" of a while-loop), with editable *slots* where the user will enter code. There are two types of slots, as shown in Figure 2. Frame slots, like the body of a method or loop, are places where new frames can be entered. Like blocks, but unlike text, it is not possible to have an unterminated body of a method or if-statement. This enforces well-defined scopes, which are drawn as rectangles (see Figure 2). Indentation is drawn automatically according to the frame hierarchy and need not (indeed, cannot) be managed manually.

Text slots, such as the name of a variable declaration or

Figure 2: Slot types: text slots and frame slots.

the condition of a while loop, have a text cursor which allows names and expressions to be entered like in text-based editing. Unlike in block-based editing, expressions are text: it is not "frames all the way down." However, the expression editor also helps students, for example by balancing parentheses: adding an opening '(' always also inserts the closing ')',' and they are always deleted together.

Greenfoot automatically compiles student code whenever the user stops editing for more than one second. Errors are highlighted with a red underline similar to spell-checking errors in other software. If the user hovers over the error with the mouse or places the text cursor in the region, the error message will be shown with a pop-up. Java errors only originate from the Java compiler, whereas Stride errors can have two distinct sources. One is very similar to Java: syntactically valid Stride code is trivially transformed into Java and sent to the Java compiler, with any compilation errors shown on the original frames. However, Stride also performs syntax checking before generating Java code, which shows more targeted error messages. Most commonly, if a slot is left blank (e.g. an if condition, or the parameter in a method call) then an error is shown indicating that the slot "cannot be blank," rather than the consequent Java error "Illegal start of expression".

Stride offers a number of additional navigational features (e.g. a fold-out display of inherited superclass methods), as well as better context for code completion. However, the programming activity used in this study did not emphasize these features, so we focus here on the aspects of Stride which scaffold students' interaction with program syntax.

3. METHODS

To evaluate our research questions regarding the effectiveness of Stride's frame-based editor, we designed a controlled experiment in which we compared students working with Greenfoot's original Java editor to those working with the new Stride editor. All other aspects of programming activity and environment were kept constant, allowing us to directly measure Stride's impact.

3.1 Materials

We designed a Greenfoot tutorial and activity in which students create the Asteroids video game, adapted from a lesson in the Greenfoot textbook [16]. The core mechanics of the game were already implemented in a separate Java class file, and the students were tasked with responding to user input and calling existing methods to create game functionality. The activity was broken up into 9 steps, which introduced method calls, conditionals, parameters, variables, numeric comparisons and while-loops. We intentionally included a broad range of programming concepts with varying difficulty in the activity to avoid ceiling or floor effects.

Instructions for each step included an explanation of any new programming concepts and explicit objectives for the student. The instructions included pictures and analogous example code but never any code which could be directly used in a student's program. We created two versions of the activity and instructions, written in Java and Stride respectively. The instructions were identical across versions except for the programming language used in the example code and occasional language-specific explanations. For example, the Stride instructions identified which keyboard shortcuts would insert certain frames, and the Java instructions explained semicolons.

The instructions for the activity were provided on a website, and the website was instrumented to keep logs of how students progressed through the instructions. When students finished a step, they were required to click a button acknowledging its completion to proceed, which was logged to a database. Additionally, we instrumented the Greenfoot environment using the Blackbox logging framework [7] to keep detailed logs of student work over time, including regular snapshots of student source code and records of compilation errors.

Additionally, we designed a pre- and post-survey to give to students. The pre-survey contained four 5-point Likert items to assess students' self-efficacy and three to assess their interest with respect to computing, as well as a number of questions on past computing experience and demographic information. The post-survey repeated the self-efficacy and interest questions and additionally asked students to rate how much they enjoyed various aspects of the activity on a 5-point Likert-type scale. Additionally, it asked students to rate on a 5-point Likert-type scale how satisfying and frustrating they found four parts of the activity: creating the Asteroids game, figuring out what to do next, writing code in Greenfoot and figuring out what was wrong with their code when it had an error.

3.2 Procedure

The study took place during a middle school CS outreach program, which students attend voluntarily on Saturdays for 2-4 hours. We worked with three classes of students. The first two classes consisted of underserved students in a pre-college program. The first class ($n = 13$) was randomly assigned to the Java condition and the second was assigned to the Stride condition ($n = 9$). The third class consisted of students from local middle schools, and students were each randomly assigned to either the Java condition ($n = 5$) or the Stride condition ($n = 5$). Students in all three classes had been exposed to some block-based programming in 1 or 2 previous workshops but not textual programming. In total, we worked with 32 students (27 male; 5 female), with 18 in the Java condition and 14 in the Stride condition.

The Asteroids activity was led by the first author, though there was an unaffiliated graduate student in charge of each class as a whole. The whole activity lasted approximately 100 minutes. Students first took a pre-survey (5m), and then the instructor led them through setting up Greenfoot, loading the instructions and first two steps of the activity together (25m). During this time, students were encouraged not to work ahead, though a few did. Afterwards, students worked independently, using the instructions to complete as

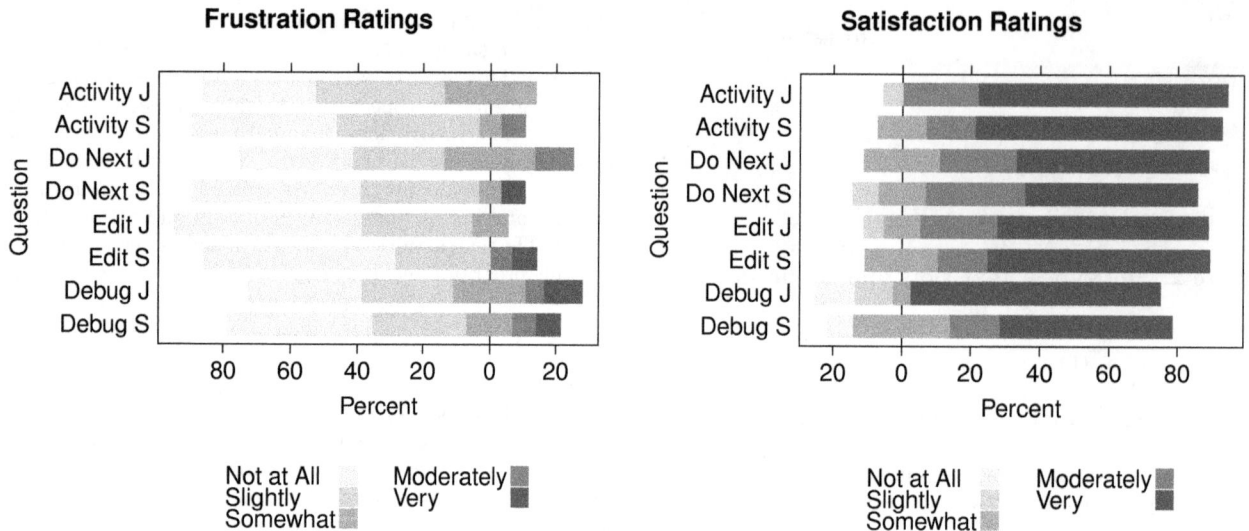

Figure 3: Post-survey ratings compared between the Java (J) and Stride (S) groups. The horizontal bars are aligned by the neutral "Somewhat" rating. Students rated how frustrating/satisfying they found "Creating the Asteroids game" (Activity), "Figuring out what to do next" (Do Next), "Writing code in Greenfoot" (Edit) and "Figuring out what was wrong with my code when it had an error" (Debug).

much of the activity as possible. Students worked for 60-70 minutes on the activity, with times varying among classes due to one class starting late (though the same amount of time is used from each class in the analysis). While students were not encouraged to work together, they were in close proximity and did discuss the activity. Afterwards, students stopped the activity and took a post-survey (5m).

The instructor led students through the first 2 of the activity's 9 steps because we wanted to provide adequate support for the challenging activity, while reducing possible bias from the instructor and allowing students to work independently as much as possible. For the Java-only and Stride-only classes, this introduction showed only that language during instruction. For the mixed class, the instructor demonstrated code using both Java and Stride. The first two steps, which were done together, are not included in our analysis, and all times are reported from the start of independent student work.

Along with the instructor, there were 3-4 additional student volunteers who were available to help students throughout the activity. Volunteers received training beforehand on how to handle student requests for help. When a student asked for help, volunteers directed them to look for an answer in the instructions. If the student was still confused, the volunteer then explained the relevant concept or problem with the student's code. Volunteers were instructed to avoid spending too much time with a given student, to avoid giving direct commands ("Now type X") and to never touch the mouse or keyboard. Volunteers were given a log sheet and instructed to record each interaction with a student, including that student's ID (to link to log files), the time and duration of help, and what type of help was given (explaining instructions, general programming concepts, language-specific concepts or debugging).

3.3 Data

We collected 4 sources of data for analysis:

1. Pre- and post-survey data
2. Log data from the instructions website
3. Log data from Greenfoot
4. Instructor logs of help requests

The Greenfoot logs contained the most verbose data. From these logs we extracted complete program traces for each student, showing how their code progressed over time. We also identified successful and unsuccessful compiles for each student and any resulting compiler messages. We used these program traces to determine when students successfully completed each of the objectives outlined in the 9 activity steps. Some steps had multiple objectives (e.g. an if statement with an else statement), and we evaluated these separately for a total of 13 objectives. Most objectives were independent, meaning a student could fail to complete one objective but succeed at the next. Two graders determined the time of completion for each student and each objective. The graders had an initial agreement of 87.8%, and after clarifying objective criteria and independently re-grading this rose to 94.5%. The remaining objectives were discussed to produce final times of completion for each student and each objective.

Due to technical problems, a number of students lost connection to the Greenfoot logging server during the activity. As a result, we only have complete Greenfoot log data for 24 of the 32 students for 50 minutes of programming (measured from the start of independent work), including 13 in the Java condition and 11 in the Stride condition. Of the 8 students with missing data, 3 came from the all-Java class, 1 from the all-Stride class and 2 from each condition of the mixed class. For analyses that involve the Greenfoot logs, we used only data from the first 50 minutes of the 24 students for whom

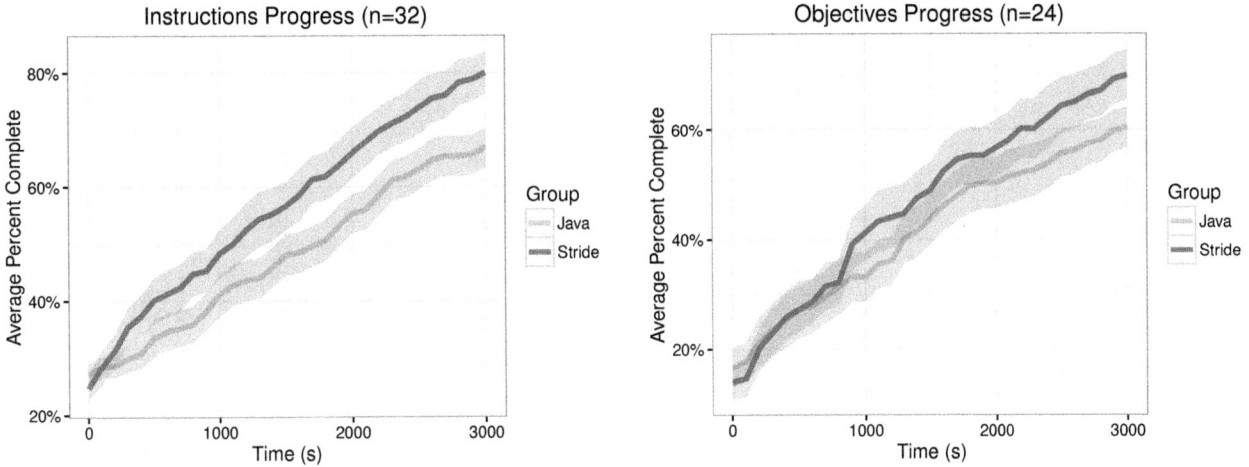

Figure 4: The mean percentage of instructions viewed (left) and activity objectives completed (right) by students in the Java and Stride conditions from the beginning of independent work (time = 0s) to the end of analyzed time (time = 3000s), with shading to indicate standard error.

we have full data. However, for other analyses we used all 32 students' data. Additionally, three students arrived 5-7 late minutes to the all-Stride class. All students arrived at least 10 minutes before independent work started, and the instructor waited for these students to catch up while working together. However, these students may have been slightly disadvantaged. All classes had between 24 and 26 minutes of group instruction before individual work.

4. ANALYSIS

4.1 Surveys

While student self-efficacy and interest with respect to CS are not directly addressed by our research questions, we included these questions in the pre- and post-surveys to assess the appropriateness of the Asteroids activity for CS outreach with our population. For both self-efficacy and interest questions, we averaged students' responses to each of the 3-4 questions in the category to produce a numerical value for both pre- and post-surveys. We performed a Wilcoxon signed-rank test[1] to compare pre- and post-survey response values. There was an improvement from pre to post, and this difference was significant[2] for both self-efficacy ($W = 28.5$; $p < 0.001$) and interest ($W = 22.5$; $p = 0.031$). This suggests that the activity was appropriate for our population and therefore an appropriate context in which to compare Stride and Java.

We also used pre-survey responses to look for potential differences between the Stride and Java groups before the activity. We tested for a difference in the groups' pre-survey self-efficacy and interest scores using a Mann-Whitney U test[1] and found no significant differences for self-efficacy ($U = 154$; $p = 0.293$) or interest ($U = 147.5$; $p = 0.413$). We asked students if they had had previous computing experiences, such as writing a computer program, creating a

website or make a video game. We summed the positive responses for each student to produce an experience score and found the difference between groups was not significant ($U = 84.5$, $p = 0.109$). There were more females in the Java group (4 out of 18) than the Stride group (1 out of 14), though there was an equal proportion of underrepresented minority students in the Java (9 out of 18) and Stride (7 of 14) groups. Given these similarities, we determined the two groups came from comparable populations. Additionally, there was no significant difference in the number of minutes volunteers spent helping students in the Java (M=12.4; SD=8.3) and Stride (M=14.0; SD=8.1) groups ($t(28.3) = -0.53$; $p = 0.599$; $d^3 = -0.189$).

To address RQ1, we compared students' post-survey responses to questions regarding their perceived frustration and satisfaction with specific parts of the Asteroids activity. Their responses are shown in Figure 3. The distributions are quite similar for both conditions and show evidence of floor and ceiling effects, with students generally showing low frustration and high satisfaction. Mann-Whitney U tests confirmed that there was no significant difference in frustration or satisfaction ratings between the two conditions.

4.2 Performance

To answer RQ2, we used a number of measures of performance. The most straightforward way to assess how students performed on the Asteroids activity is to compare how far they got in a given amount of time. Because we do not have Greenfoot log data for all 32 students, we can use progress in the instructions as a measure of self-reported progress on the activity. Figure 4 (left) shows the mean percentage of the instructions that each group had viewed, from the start of independent work to the end of the activity. By the end of the activity, the difference between the percentage of instructions viewed by the Java group (M=66.9%; SD=14.9%) and the Stride group (M=79.9%; SD=13.3%) was significant ($t(29.3) = -2.61$; $p = 0.014$; $d = -0.92$).

This self-reported progress is not as meaningful as the completion of assignment objectives, as determined by the

---

[1]The use of nonparametric tests, including the Wilcoxon signed-rank test and Mann-Whitney U test, indicates that data was either ordinal or not normally distributed as determined by a Shapiro-Wilk test.

[2]All tests were made at a 5% significance level.

[3]We report Cohen's d, an effect size measured in SDs.

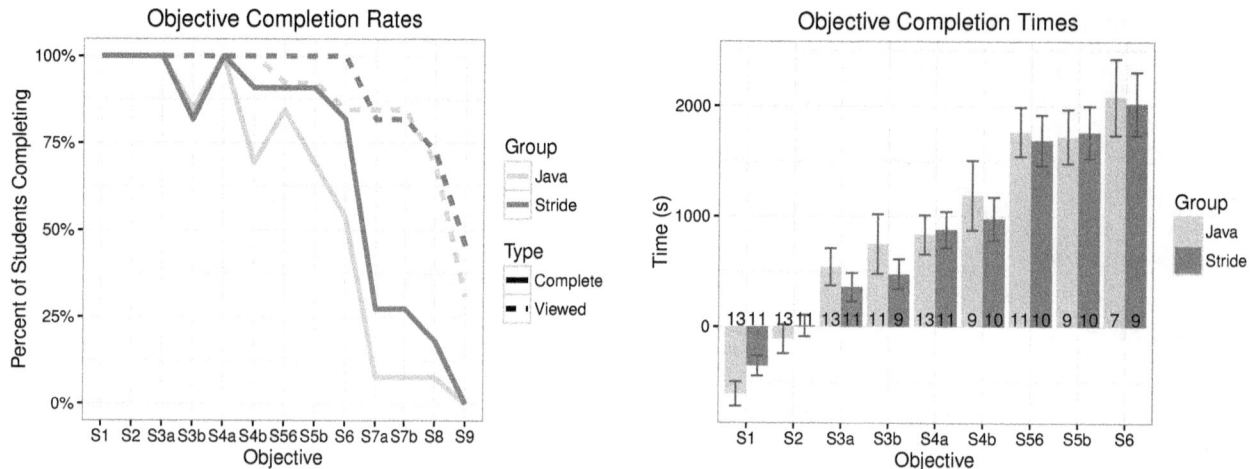

Figure 5: Left, the percent of students who completed and viewed instructions for each objective in each group during the first 50 minutes of independent work. Right, the mean time elapsed (with standard error) before Objectives S1-S6 were completed by students in each group. The number of students who completed the objective is shown below each bar.

graders, described in Section 3.3. Figure 4 (right) shows the percentage of objectives completed by students over time. This counts only objectives that were correctly completed by the student, as some students skipped or improperly completed objectives. This and all following analysis considers only the 24 students for whom we have complete data. Java students completed a mean 60.4% (SD=13.3%) of the 13 objectives, while Stride students completed a mean 69.9% (SD=14.5%). This difference was not significant ($t(20.4) = -1.66$; $p = 0.112$; $d = -0.69$), with a 95% confidence interval that the true difference between the Java and Stride means is between -21.6% and 2.5%.

We also analyzed students' performance on individual objectives, both in terms of the number of students completing the objective and the amount of time elapsed before the objective was completed. Figure 5 (left) shows the percent of students who completed and viewed instructions for each objective in each group. Objectives S1-S3b have almost identical completion rates for both groups, but the Stride group had a strictly higher completion rate for the next 7 objectives. The difference is especially stark for Objective S5b (Java = 69.2%; Stride = 90.9%) and Objective S6 (Java = 53.8%; Stride = 81.8%). These two objectives came at the end, so presumably fewer students in the Java group had time to complete them. Figure 5 (right) compares the mean amount of time that elapsed before students completed Objectives S1-S6 in each group. Note that some values are negative, as Objectives S1 and S2 were completed before independent work started (time 0). The Java group took slightly longer on most objectives (after time 0), but these differences were not large compared to the standard error. It is important to note that this time comparison considers only students who were able to complete a given objective in the first 50 minutes, so the later objectives have a strong selection bias to include the faster students in a group.

4.3 Programming Behavior

We used the detailed Greenfoot log data, along with the instructions log data, to categorize how users spent their

	Edit	Instr.	Run	Idle
Java	661 (235)	1088 (474)	562 (308)	686 (360)
Stride	585 (177)	1233 (221)	634 (262)	472 (311)

Table 1: The mean amount of time (with SD) spent on each category of action during the Asteroids activity.

time during the activity. We categorized time as editing code, viewing instructions, running the program or idle time. The first three categories each have specific actions associated with them, such as editing or compiling code, changing the instructions page or clicking the Run button. Each time one of these actions occurred, we labeled the time span until the next action occurred, or until 60 seconds elapsed, with that action's category. Any time beyond 60 seconds was labeled as idle, until the next action occurred. While this estimate is not perfect, it does give a reasonable picture of how students used their time. Table 1 shows the mean amount of time spent in each category for each group.

Two categories of particular interest are Edit and Idle time. A difference in editing time would show that one group spent longer interacting with the editor. A difference in idle time would indicate a possible difference in engagement between the two groups. Figure 6 shows the percentage of students' time spent idle and editing over 150 slices of time from 0 to 50 minutes, compared between the Java and Stride groups. While there is no apparent difference between the two groups for editing time, the Java group appears to spend much more time idle near the end of the activity, after 2000s have elapsed. The difference in total idle time per student, as shown in Table 1, was not significant ($t(22.0) = 1.57$; $p = 0.132$; $d = 0.63$), with a 95% confidence interval that the true difference between the Java and Stride means was between -70s and 499s. However, a Wilcoxon signed-rank test indicated that there was a significant difference between the proportion of time Java students spent idle before 2000s (Med=15.7%) and after (Med=28.6%) ($W = 15$; $p = 0.033$).

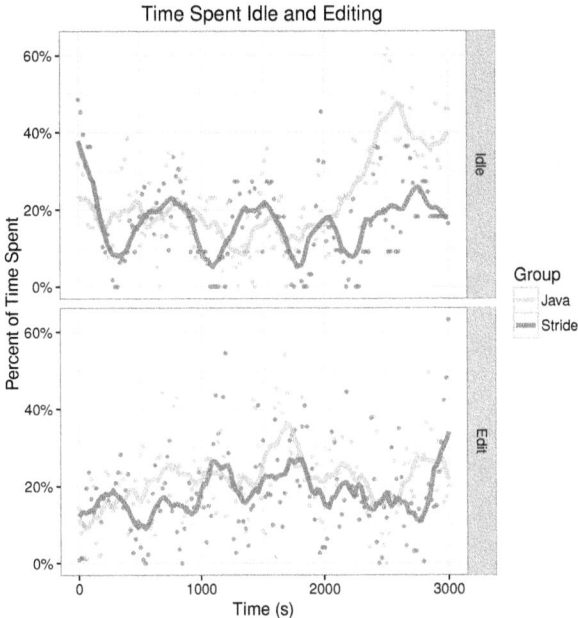

Figure 6: For 150 20-second slices throughout the activity, the average percent of time students in each condition spent Idle and Editing are shown as points. A kernel regression smoothing line is also plotted to show a rolling average.

For the Stride group, the difference between the proportion of time spent idle before 2000s (Med=12.5%) and after 2000s (Med=8.7%) was not significant ($W = 34$; $p = 0.966$).

Though students spent similar amounts of time editing their code in both conditions, we were also interested in the types of edits students made. One of the primary purported advantages of the Stride language is that it avoids the need for the purely syntactic elements of Java, such as brackets, semicolons and whitespace [6]. To investigate this claim, we analyzed each edit students made to their code to determine whether or not that edit changed only these purely syntactic elements (brackets, semicolons and whitespace). We then summed the time spent on these edits for each student, where each edit was assumed to have taken the time since the previous edit, to a maximum of 30s. A Mann-Whitney U test indicated that there was a significant difference between the amount of time spent on these syntactic edits between the Java group (Med=321s) and the Stride group (Med=94s) ($U = 134$, $p < 0.001$).

4.4 Syntax Errors

To get a basic understanding of whether the groups had different incidences of errors, we calculated the time each student spent with non-compilable code. This was done by summing the time between each unsuccessful compile and the next compile. The Java group spent a mean 1447s (SD=672.8s) with non-compilable code, while the Stride group spent a mean 1000s (SD=290.2s). The difference was significant ($t(16.8) = 2.16$, $p = 0.045$; $d = 0.84$). The Stride group spent on average 7.45 minutes less time with non-compilable code than the Java group, which spent on average almost half of the activity with non-compilable code.

We also counted the occurrences of each type of syntax

Group	Message	Mean
Java	';' expected	13.4 (9.53)
	illegal start of expression	6.31 (7.99)
	(or) expected	4.00 (2.42)
	reached end of file while parsing	2.77 (3.39)
	illegal start of type	2.38 (2.69)
Stride	*Invalid expression*	14.3 (11.3)
	Undeclared variable	13.7 (8.27)
	Expression cannot be empty	8.27 (5.08)
	cannot find symbol - method	4.73 (2.15)
	Method name cannot be blank	4.43 (4.52)

Table 2: The five most common syntax errors for the Java and Stride groups, with the mean (and SD) number of occurrences per student. Stride-specific errors are given in italics.

error viewed by students. While both Stride and Java compile automatically and flag errors with red underlines, we chose to analyze only errors which were actually displayed to the student, when their cursor or mouse enters this underlined code. Since Stride code is converted to Java before being compiled, both groups received errors from the Java compiler; however, Stride introduces a number of new error messages, which replace common Java errors with plain English. Table 2 gives the five most commonly viewed syntax errors for both groups. Many of the most common Stride errors were Stride-specific messages (denoted in italics). Additionally, each of the most common Java errors can be attributed to the presence of characters which Stride adds automatically: semicolons, brackets and parentheses. Notably, none of these top-5 errors are the same in the two groups. The difference between the total errors viewed by the Java group (M=42.3; SD=27.4) and the Stride group (M=55.5; SD=22.1) was not significant ($t(22.0) = -1.30$; $p = 0.208$; $d = -0.52$).

5. DISCUSSION

RQ1 *How did Stride affect frustration and satisfaction with the activity?* Students reported low frustration and high satisfaction with each aspect of the Asteroids activity, but there were no significant differences between the Java and Stride groups. It is possible that a real difference was masked by ceiling and floor effects (i.e. the activity was enjoyed enough that it overwhelmed any differences due to the editor). Previous comparisons between block and textual programming have similarly found no difference in students' perceived difficulty [22, 28], which mirrors our results with respect to frustration. Previous work on block-based programming has also suggested that it is perceived as less authentic than their textual counterparts [32]. While we did not assess perceived authenticity directly, if Stride was perceived as less authentic than Java, we have no evidence that it affected students' satisfaction with the activity.

RQ2 *How did Stride affect performance on the activity?* Taken together, our results suggest that Stride improved students' performance on the one-hour activity. The Stride group progressed through the instructions significantly faster and had a better completion rate than the Java group on the last 7 objectives. While there was no significant difference between the total number of objectives accomplished by the two groups, the first two results suggest that this may be due

39

to the small sample size (24), in part as a result of data loss. There was no significant difference in the amount of time taken to complete a given objective between the groups; however, it is important to remember that this compares only students who completed a given objective within the first 50 minutes of independent work. For example, on Objective 5b, 90.9% of Stride students completed the objective in time, while only 69.2% of Java students completed the objective. The time comparison on this objective possibly excludes the slowest 30% of Java students, compared to only 10% of Stride students. While positive, these results are not as strong overall as previous comparisons between textual and block editors [28], supporting the notion that frame-based editing may be best situated between learning blocks and text [18].

RQ3 *How did Stride affect programming behavior during the activity?* Students' programming behavior in each group offers some explanation of the improved performance observed in the Stride group. Students in both groups spent similar amounts of time idle for the first 30-35 minutes of the activity, after which the Java group's idle time significantly increases and the Stride group's does not. One explanation for this trend is that there comes a point at which some students start to lose interest in the activity (confirmed anecdotally by volunteers), but that this was less common in the Stride group. Additionally, though students in both groups spent similar amounts of time editing their code, Java students spent a median 321s making purely syntactic edits, compared to 94s for the Stride group. This amounts to almost half of the total time the Java group spent editing their code and is twice the proportion found in previous analyses [3]. It is also worth noting that Stride students encountered their own Stride-specific issues, such as accidentally inserting a frame by typing its hotkey, while intending to insert text. While the amount of time wasted as a result of these errors is more difficult to measure, graders report anecdotally that this was a frequent occurrence. Still, these difficulties did not seem to be enough to make up for the advantages that Stride offered.

RQ4 *How did Stride affect incidence of syntax errors?* Taken together, our results support the notion that Stride helps students with syntax errors, which may be another contributing factor to their efficiency. The Stride group spent significantly less time with non-compilable code. This may be due in part to the fact that many of the most common Stride error messages (including four of the top five) were custom messages designed to directly explain the problem in a novice-friendly way. These results contrast with previous work in which enhanced error messages failed to improve students' resolution of syntax errors [9, 26]. The five most common errors encountered by the Java group were somewhat consistent with results from previous work [5, 13, 14]. Each of these errors can be caused by a missing a semicolon, bracket or parenthesis. The Stride editor avoids the need for semicolons and brackets and automatically pairs parentheses, reducing the incidence of these errors. This is evidenced by the fact that none of these top five Java errors were represented in the top five Stride errors (in part because some were replaced by the new Stride messages).

6. CONCLUSIONS

In this paper we have presented a comparison of two groups of novices working on a short programming activity, one us-

ing the textual Java language and one using the frame-based Stride language. While we observed no differences between students' perceived frustration or satisfaction, the Stride group did progress through the activity quicker, spending less time with non-compilable code and less time on purely syntactic edits. This suggests that frame-based editing is a useful tool in reducing the burden of syntax for novice programmers and that it may lead to improved performance on programming tasks.

6.1 Limitations

This study took place in a voluntary after school outreach program, which is quite different from a controlled laboratory setting. We endeavored to control as many aspects of the study as possible, but real classrooms come with real confounds, such as interactions between students, possible instructor and volunteer bias and varying student ability. We chose to emphasize the ecological validity of the study, ensuring that it reflected a real-world setting, rather than a perfectly controlled laboratory. Unfortunately, our results also suffer from the loss of data due to technical errors. A number of the differences observed in the 24 students for whom we have full data were sizable but not significant. This only means the differences were not detectable, but not necessarily that they do not exist. For example, for the difference in the number of objectives completed by the Java and Stride groups, reported in Section 4.2, power analysis suggests we only had a 46.3% chance of detecting a large effect size (Cohen's d) of 0.8.

Additionally, this study is limited to a single population (middle school students) and a single, hour-long activity. Our findings with respect to programming performance and behavior will not necessarily generalize to longer, more complex activities, though it is unclear whether the differences observed would increase or decrease in magnitude with more time. These results are also limited to students' *performance* on the activity, which will not necessarily equate to learning gains. Our results with respect to specific syntax errors will likely not fully generalize to other activities, as syntax errors are highly dependent on the programming constructs being used. The activity was also quite popular with the students, who reported low frustration and high satisfaction, and this may have masked any effects that the editor had on student affect.

6.2 Future Work

Frame-based editing has been described as a way to ease the transition from blocks to text [18]. Our own findings support the notion that frame-based editing is more appropriate for novices than text but may not offer the same benefits as blocks. Future work should investigate the relationship between these three types of editors: blocks, frames and text. We can now move beyond the short-term, direct comparisons of student performance that have been presented in this and other work [28] to focus on the long-term effects of the editors, their impact on learning gains and the transitions from blocks to frames and frames to text. Further work on how these transitions might be mediated (e.g. [8]) is needed, along with more in-depth investigations of students' perceptions of these editors (e.g. [32]).

7. REFERENCES

[1] A. Ahadi, J. Prior, and R. Lister. Students' Syntactic Mistakes in Writing Seven Different Types of SQL Queries and its Application to Predicting Students' Success. In *Proceedings of the 47th ACM Technical Symposium on Computer Science Education*, pages 401–406, 2016.

[2] A. Altadmri and N. C. C. Brown. 37 Million Compilations: Investigating Novice Programming Mistakes in Large-Scale Student Data. *Proceedings of the 46th ACM Technical Symposium on Computer Science Education*, pages 522–527, 2015.

[3] A. Altadmri, M. Kölling, and N. C. C. Brown. The cost of syntax and how to avoid it: Text versus frame-based editing. In *CELT: COMPSAC Symposium on Computing Education & Learning Technologies; part of COMPSAC 2016: The 40th IEEE Computer Society International Conference on Computers, Software & Applications*, June 2016.

[4] T. Booth and S. Stumpf. End-user experiences of visual and textual programming environments for Arduino. In *Proceedings of the 4th International Symposium on End-User Development*, pages 25–39, 2013.

[5] N. C. C. Brown and A. Altadmri. Investigating Novice Programming Mistakes: Educator Beliefs vs Student Data. In *Proceedings of the Tenth International Computing Education Research Conference*, pages 43–50, 2014.

[6] N. C. C. Brown, A. Altadmri, and M. Kölling. Frame-Based Editing: Combining the Best of Blocks and Text Programming. In *Proceedings of the Fourth International Conference on Learning and Teaching in Computing and Engineering*, 2016.

[7] N. C. C. Brown, M. Kölling, D. McCall, and I. Utting. Blackbox: A Large Scale Repository of Novice Programmers' Activity. In *Proceedings of the 45th ACM Technical Symposium on Computer Science Education*, pages 223–228, 2014.

[8] W. Dann, D. Cosgrove, and D. Slater. Mediated Transfer: Alice 3 to Java. In *Proceedings of the 43rd ACM Technical Symposium on Computer Science Education*, pages 141–146, 2012.

[9] P. Denny, A. Luxton-Reilly, and D. Carpenter. Enhancing Syntax Error Messages Appears Ineffectual. In *Proceedings of the 19th ACM Conference on Innovation & Technology in Computer Science Education*, pages 273–278, 2014.

[10] P. Denny, A. Luxton-Reilly, and E. Tempero. All syntax errors are not equal. In *Proceedings of the 17th ACM Conference on Innovation and Technology in Computer Science Education*, page 75, New York, New York, USA, jul 2012. ACM Press.

[11] T. Flowers, C. Carver, and J. Jackson. Empowering students and building confidence in novice programmers through Gauntlet. In *34th Annual Frontiers in Education, 2004. FIE 2004.*, pages 10–13, 2004.

[12] D. Garcia, B. Harvey, and T. Barnes. The Beauty and Joy of Computing. *ACM Inroads*, 6(4):71–79, 2015.

[13] J. Jackson, M. Cobb, and C. Carver. Identifying Top Java Errors for Novice Programmers. *Proceedings*

Frontiers in Education 35th Annual Conference, pages 24–27, 2005.

[14] M. C. Jadud. Methods and tools for exploring novice compilation behaviour. In *Proceedings of the Third International Workshop on Computing Education Research*, pages 73–84, 2006.

[15] M. C. Jadud and B. Dorn. Aggregate Compilation Behavior: Findings and Implications from 27,698 Users. In *Proceedings of the 11th International Computing Education Research Conference*, pages 131–139, 2015.

[16] M. Kölling. *Introduction to programming with Greenfoot*. Pearson Education, Upper Saddle River, New Jersey, USA, 2009.

[17] M. Kölling. The Greenfoot Programming Environment. *Transactions on Computing Education*, 10(4):14:1—-14:21, nov 2010.

[18] M. Kölling, N. C. C. Brown, and A. Altadmri. Frame-Based Editing: Easing the Transition from Blocks to Text-Based Programming. In *Proceedings of the Workshop in Primary and Secondary Computing Education*, pages 29–38, 2015.

[19] S. K. Kummerfeld and J. Kay. The neglected battle fields of syntax errors. In *Proceedings of the Australasian Computing Education Conference*, pages 105–111, 2003.

[20] E. Lahtinen, K. Ala-Mutka, and H.-M. Järvinen. A Study of the Difficulties of Novice Programmers. In *Proceedings of the Tenth ACM Conference on Innovation and Technology in Computer Science Education*, volume 37, page 14, 2005.

[21] M. J. Lee and A. J. Ko. Personifying Programming Tool Feedback Improves Novice Programmers' Learning. In *Proceedings of the Seventh International Workshop on Computing Education Research*, pages 109–116, 2011.

[22] C. Lewis. How Programming Environment Shapes Perception, Learning and Goals: Logo vs. Scratch. In *Proceedings of the 41st ACM Technical Symposium on Computer Science Education*, pages 346–350, 2010.

[23] L. Mannila, M. Peltomäki, and T. Salakoski. What about a simple language? Analyzing the difficulties in learning to program. *Computer Science Education*, 2006.

[24] F. McKay and M. Kölling. Predictive modelling for HCI problems in novice program editors. In *Proceedings of the 27th International BCS Human Computer Interaction Conference*, pages 35–41, 2013.

[25] O. Meerbaum-Salant, M. Armoni, and M. Ben-Ari. Habits of programming in scratch. In *Proceedings of the 16th annual joint conference on Innovation and technology in computer science education.*, pages 168–172, 2011.

[26] M.-H. Nienaltowski, M. Pedroni, and B. Meyer. Compiler Error Messages: What Can Help Novices? In *Proceedings of the 39th ACM Technical Symposium on Computer Science Education*, pages 168–172, 2008.

[27] K. Powers, S. Ecott, and L. Hirshfield. Through the Looking Glass: Teaching CS0 with Alice. *ACM SIGCSE Bulletin*, 39(1):213–217, 2007.

[28] T. W. Price and T. Barnes. Comparing Textual and Block Interfaces in a Novice Programming

Environment. In *Proceedings of the 11th International Computing Education Research Conference*, 2015.

[29] M. Resnick, J. Maloney, H. Andrés, N. Rusk, E. Eastmond, K. Brennan, A. Millner, E. Rosenbaum, J. Silver, B. Silverman, and Y. Kafai. Scratch: Programming for All. *Communications of the ACM*, 52(11):60–67, 2009.

[30] A. Stefik and S. Siebert. An Empirical Investigation into Programming Language Syntax. *ACM Transactions on Computing Education*, 13(4), 2013.

[31] V. J. Traver. On Compiler Error Messages: What They Say and What They Mean. *Advances in Human-Computer Interaction*, 2010:1–26, 2010.

[32] D. Weintrop and U. Wilensky. To Block or not to Block, That is the Question: Students' Perceptions of Blocks-based Programming. In *Proceedings of the International Conference on Interaction Design and Children*, pages 199–208, 2015.

[33] D. Weintrop and U. Wilensky. Using Commutative Assessments to Compare Conceptual Understanding in Blocks-based and Text-based Programs. In *Proceedings of the 11th International Computing Education Research Conference*, pages 101–110, New York, New York, USA, 2015. ACM Press.

Flipping the Assessment of Cognitive Load: Why and How

Raina Mason
Southern Cross University
Australia
raina.mason@scu.edu.au

Simon
University of Newcastle
Australia
simon@newcastle.edu.au

Graham Cooper
Southern Cross University
Australia
graham.cooper@scu.edu.au

Barry Wilks
Southern Cross University
Australia
barry.wilks@scu.edu.au

ABSTRACT

Cognitive load theory is typically used to evaluate and improve learning materials, with the goal of optimising students' opportunity to acquire new knowledge and understanding. The cognitive load on a student is typically assessed either objectively, by taking physiological measurements while the student is learning, or subjectively, by asking the student to complete an appropriate questionnaire after the learning experience. However, there are circumstances in which a decision on learning materials must be made before those materials are developed and deployed, whereupon it is not helpful to measure the students during learning or to survey them after learning. Such circumstances necessitate a completely different approach, in which the assessment of the likely imposition of cognitive load is made by the instructors and informs the development of the learning materials.

This paper explores such a situation: the choice of a programming language and integrated development environment for an introductory programming course. The paper explains the impracticality of addressing this choice by way of the usual measures of cognitive load. It then presents the approach that was used, flipping the assessment of expected cognitive load from the students to the instructors. The paper explains how this was done, presents the findings, and concludes by suggesting possibilities for future work in the area.

1. INTRODUCTION

Learning computer programming is difficult [19, 27], and often yields low success rates [3, 42]. When learning programming it is often necessary to learn several things at once [4], which contributes to the inherent difficulty of the task. For example, beginners must simultaneously acquire knowledge of the tightly defined syntax of the programming language being used, the structure and organisation of the human-computer interface

ICER'16, September 8-12, 2016, Melbourne, Australia
© 2016 ACM. ISBN 978-1-4503-4449-4/16/09...$15.00
DOI: http://dx.doi.org/10.1145/2960310.2960321

(HCI) being used, and a set of generic programming concepts, rules, logic and algorithms. Generic programming concepts include variables, properties, functions/methods, arrays and other data structures, decision branching and loops [5, 31]. The inherently complex and interwoven nature of computer programming means that it is at best challenging to tease out the relatively many aspects of programming design and development into a sequence of isolated demonstrations and functionality [21].

For many, if not all, meaningful programming tasks, many elements of these distinct concept areas must be considered simultaneously, because the elements interact functionally with one another in the context of program design [21]. We propose that the high density of associations and interactions in the context of learning computer programming generates a high level of cognitive load [8] making programming inherently 'difficult' to learn. This issue is elaborated upon below in the section dealing with cognitive load theory.

Computer programming is often undertaken using an integrated development environment (IDE). The development of a working executable program entails the use of a number of distinct tools such as text editor, graphical user interface developer, code debugger, and often a compiler. An IDE provides a layer of user interface that integrates these tools so that users can learn to program using a single cohesive tool rather than a number of disparate tools.

Tertiary educators give a number of pedagogical reasons for using an IDE in preference to separate tools: "To reduce the amount that students had to learn in order to get to the heart of programming"; "it's really a smarter text editor with buttons for compiling and building ... so we can concentrate on language syntax" [23].

1.1 Comparing IDEs

There is a wide range of IDEs available, and in the context of introductory programming courses the reasons for choosing a particular environment over another can include [22]:

- support for a preferred programming language;
- low cost to students;
- ease of installation;
- ease of use;
- included graphical user interface; and
- increased student motivation.

Some IDEs are specific to particular programming languages, and are typically designed and developed to provide advanced users with 'shortcuts' to specific aspects of code development and algorithm deployment. Other IDEs are designed and developed specifically to help novice programmers learn either aspects of generic programming, aspects of a specific language, or both. For example, BlueJ [18] and Alice [17] were both designed specifically to aid learning objects-first and to motivate beginning students.

BlueJ [18] provides visual representations of the programming concept 'object', along with an interface in which objects and their methods and properties can be examined and manipulated. The Alice environment [17] uses a similar strategy of graphical depictions of objects. Alice additionally provides access to libraries of story characters to facilitate the construction of 3D worlds and aspects of storytelling through animations rendered on the basis of the properties and methods applied to the story characters.

Comparison between IDEs is complicated, as some are designed for professional use, some are designed to provide a gentler introduction to programming for novices by using visual languages or other features, and others attempt to address both audiences or are targeted specifically at intermediate users.

IDEs designed for use by novice programmers are typically intended to provide scaffolding for user support and/or to dispense with some aspects of unnecessary complexity. As an example, in many programming languages a program must be compiled before it can be run, but the mechanism for achieving compilation varies greatly with programming language and IDE. It might be achieved automatically, with a single button click, or with a sequence of steps that involve file manipulation and changing between windows. Most IDEs provide varying degrees of information about the likely success of compilation (syntax hints, detection of suspect code, auto-prompting of code, etc). Compiling as a process is logically distinct from the design and development of algorithms and code. For skilled programmers there may be benefits in being able to access and engineer aspects of compilation through mechanisms closer to first principles, as this may assist in fault detection and response; but for novice programmers this detour will tend to distract from the programming task at hand, possibly confusing and conflating these two tasks and leading to an overload of cognitive resources.

Although some IDEs have been designed to support novice programmers, they have often been based upon principles of human-computer interaction (HCI) [32] rather than explicitly from a cognitive processing perspective. However, there is some overlap between the two: for example, the principles of HCI include "reduce short-term memory load" [32 pp88] which is the basis of cognitive load theory.

When a change of programming language and/or IDE is being contemplated for an educational course, the people charged with the decision might set out to choose the language and/or IDE that will best assist its users to acquire the course content. However, it is difficult to overtly compare environments to determine their relative utility for novice or non-expert learners, given that some are provided with their own language, some support several languages, and particular tasks may be more or less complex in one environment than in another.

The work reported in this paper arises from discussion regarding a possible change of programming language and/or IDE at a particular university. One consideration in the decision is based on cognitive load theory: is there a combination of language and IDE that imposes substantially less cognitive load on novice users, thus leaving them better able to focus on learning the programming, the programming language, and its structures?

2. COGNITIVE LOAD THEORY

2.1 Human Cognitive Architecture

The limitations of working memory are well established. Working memory is of short duration, typically measured in seconds or minutes [2]. Perhaps more importantly, working memory is of limited capacity [12]: it is generally accepted that human working memory is limited to about seven (plus or minus two) elements of distinct, unrelated material [28]. Where the elements interact with one another, the interactions become additional elements to be attended to, and themselves occupy some of the working memory [12, 37].

Working memory is the hub of 'conscious attention'. It receives information presented to the senses via sensory memory [2], and draws information from long-term memory when seeking to interpret these sensory inputs. The interpretations are amalgamated within working memory structures to define our consciousness [11]. The limitations of working memory, in both duration and capacity, define an inherent bottleneck in aspects of human cognitive architecture. If working memory is tasked with more than it has the capacity to handle, processing will fail [39].

2.2 Sources of Cognitive Load

Cognitive load theory (CLT) distinguishes between two sources of cognitive load: intrinsic and extraneous [30].

Intrinsic cognitive load is associated directly with the nature of the information to be learnt. It derives primarily from the number and intensity of relationships between the individual elements of information that need simultaneous consideration. This relationship has been termed 'element interactivity', and helps to explain why some materials are difficult to learn [37]. Little can be done to reduce this load without changing the learning activity as it is effectively part of the content domain. We argue that computer programming as a content domain has a high level of element interactivity, and is thus difficult to learn.

Extraneous cognitive load is associated with the way in which the content to be learnt is presented to the learner. This incorporates all aspects of the format and synergies between reference materials with respect to the use of text, images, animations, audio, and other media [25]. It is also affected by the activities that learners are tasked with performing. Conventional problem solving, for example, is generally more taxing upon cognitive resources than study of similar worked examples [38]. In the context of learning computer programming, the programming language and the IDE act as intermediaries between user, content, and its manipulation, and necessarily contribute to extraneous cognitive load.

Intrinsic and extraneous cognitive load accumulate to define a total cognitive load, constantly varying at each point during a task performance or learning transaction [35]. If cognitive resources are overloaded at any point during an activity, the task performance and/or learning will falter.

In complex content domains, instructional materials and task performance can be designed to reduce the level of extraneous cognitive load, thus freeing cognitive resources to focus on intrinsic activities. In the computer programming domain, the interface and interaction design features of IDEs offer opportunities to reduce both intrinsic and extraneous cognitive load, as the design of the IDE can effectively contribute to simplifying or segmenting the problem itself.

2.3 Cognitive Load and Implications for Teaching and Learning

Schemas are cognitive constructs stored in long-term memory that hold knowledge and arrange it into well-defined hierarchically organised structures [39]. Although made up of multiple elements, schemas behave in working memory as individual elements. The development of schemas thus increases the capacity of working memory by increasing the complexity of the elements being handled. This provides a work-around to the natural limitations of working memory, but only once a person is sufficiently knowledgeable and holds developed schemas.

For example, the English alphabet may be processed as a single element, and reconstituted into a series of 26 letters starting at 'a' and ending with 'z'. Most readers will experience extreme difficulty in unpacking the concept of 'alphabet' into anything other than the sequence defined by alphabetic order, because we have automated this sequence [9]. That is, expert readers have a highly automated schema for 'alphabet'.

CLT incorporates a number of effects that focus on the role of working memory in processing information, hinging on the user's level of schema acquisition and automation. One important consideration is the split attention effect, which occurs when two or more sources of mutually referring information need to be identified and mentally integrated to enable performance [40]. IDEs, by their nature, offer many interactive tools, menus, windows, and objects as input mechanisms. Consideration needs to be given to the user's needs in searching, identifying, processing, coordinating, and manipulating elements of the interface while programming.

The most common strategy to avoid a split attention effect in hard-copy materials is to physically integrate the diverse sources of information, usually by integrating textual elements into graphical elements [7]. In the context of computer environments, additional strategies are available to mitigate unnecessary search, including features such as colour coding [15] and suitable hierarchical organisations of functionality aligned to users' schemas [8].

A programming IDE typically incorporates many separate elements of code, algorithm construction, and specific tool use, often needing to be deployed in conjunction with one another. Extraneous cognitive load in IDEs often stems from aspects of screen search and subsequent mental integration and coordination.

Search within a problem space typically uses means-ends analysis [35], which seeks a path from a current state to a specific goal state in a cognitive problem space. People typically work backward from the goal to their current position, before then taking the path forward to the goal [34]. Although this is an effective strategy for generating a solution path, it places very high impositions upon working memory, and so inhibits acquisition of the schemas associated with the successful forward-working solution path [34].

The cognitive load of means-ends analysis may be reduced by diverting attention from the goal state. Scaffolds that support the learner to move directly forward through a problem space assist in developing the forward chaining sequence of schemas for solution [1, 10].

The design and development of computer programs is analogous to determining a possible solution path. In this context there are likely benefits in deploying strategies that promote forward chaining through the problem space, rather than working backward. Two strategies that might assist in this regard are the provision of subgoals [6, 20] and segmentation of procedures [26].

2.4 Cognitive Load and Programming

A contributing factor to the difficulty of learning to program is that it inescapably combines aspects of logical concepts, algorithms, and programming language syntax. Each aspect needs to be implemented in the development of even the simplest of programs, and each interacts with the others in manifestations of element interactivity [4]. In having to deal simultaneously with all three and their interactions, programming novices are necessarily burdened with a very high level of load, so their success in learning is likely to depend upon aspects of extraneous cognitive load that might be subject to amelioration.

Furthermore, to a novice programmer the IDE is an integral and inescapable aspect of programming, and therefore imposes additional cognitive constraints that are not present in the learning of many other types of content. IDEs represent a primary source of extraneous cognitive load, as they integrate a number of distinct tools, each incorporating a substantial number of features. The design of the IDE will therefore embody many decisions regarding the organisation and presentation of those tools and their features, and different IDEs will impose different levels of extraneous cognitive load when used to address the same programming task.

3. FLIPPING THE ASSESSMENT OF COGNITIVE LOAD

Our goal in this project is to assess and compare a number of programming languages and IDEs to determine which, if any, impose the least extraneous cognitive load when undertaking typical novice computing tasks.

Assessment of cognitive load is typically performed by the students. At various stages during the learning experience they are asked to complete a series of Likert-style questions, asking about the mental effort that they felt they were expending, or perhaps about the perceived difficulty of the material [29, 36]. If different sets of learning materials are being assessed, different groups of students will be exposed to each, and the resulting subjective surveys compared.

Unfortunately, this approach is simply not feasible when choosing a programming language and IDE for a proposed future version of a course. It would be neither practical nor ethical to split the class into groups and teach a different programming language and IDE to each group. The programming language and IDE are absolutely integral to the course, are fixed before the course begins, and cannot simply be swapped in and out to assess each in turn. Consideration might be given to conducting an experiment on a group of novices before making the choice, giving different language/IDE combinations to different subgroups; but such an undertaking is generally infeasible, for example because of the difficulty of recruiting suitable participants before classes begin.

Instead what we needed was a way for the instructors themselves to assess the likely relative cognitive load on novice/semi-novice programmers of each of the combinations under consideration. Rather than assessing the mental effort or difficulty of various tasks, they would examine the tasks for evidence of the effects that are known to contribute to cognitive load. This is not guaranteed to produce the same results as surveying novice users about their mental effort; but when it is the only feasible option, and when it is conducted with a good awareness of CLT and its effects, it should still produce useful results.

It is in this spirit that we have flipped the assessment of cognitive load from the novices to the researchers in order to determine the cognitive loads imposed by a number of language/IDE combinations. This determination is of course relative: we are not trying to establish an absolute measure of cognitive load for each language/IDE pair; indeed, this is not a meaningful concept. Rather, we are seeking to discover which combinations appear to offer lighter cognitive load than others.

To compare different IDEs from a CLT perspective, we have devised a method of measuring the cognitive load impact imposed by an IDE in the performance of various programming tasks.

4. DEVELOPMENT OF THE COMPARISON PROCESS

Cognitive load is imposed by various factors in the programming environment and will change over the course of a programming task. For example, in one step of a programming task there may be a high extraneous load due to the split attention effect caused by physical separation of elements on the screen, while the next step may not have this imposition, and may even present prompts regarding how to proceed.

We have devised a set of directly observable factors that may increase or decrease cognitive load in the completion of steps in a programming task.

4.1 Cognitive Load Impact Factors

We identified eight factors that are expected to *increase* cognitive load while the user is carrying out a step.

Environment schema complexity (EC): complexity of aspects of the specific environment in performing this step. For example, one IDE requires users to know that a program is called a 'mainstack', and that to create a new program they need to choose 'New mainstack' from the File menu. In other environments one might 'Create new program', which is less environment-specific. Until this knowledge becomes automated, the attention given to this terminology will use working memory.

Programming schema complexity (PC): complexity of the general programming schemas required to perform this step. Programming schemas are re-usable programming concepts such as selection and iteration; they need to be acquired by programming novices, but are readily recalled by programming experts.

Think back (TB): number of elements from previous steps that must be kept in mind to perform this step.

Interactivity (I): complexity of the interactions between environment schemas, programming schemas, and think back required to perform this step.

Relevant physical elements (PE): number of relevant physical elements appearing on screen that may be chosen as part of performing this step; for example, a list of options in a menu, where one must be chosen to proceed.

Distractors (D): number of physical elements in view but irrelevant to performing this step, presenting tacit distraction.

Windows/palettes (WP): number of windows/palettes visible and active on screen and available to be manipulated while performing this step. For example, a particular environment may have a toolbox, compiler window, properties palette, and code window all open at one time, in addition to the common menus and buttons at the top of a screen.

Split attention (SA): extent of physical separation between elements of information or interaction that need to be mentally integrated to perform this step.

We then identified four factors that are expected to *reduce* cognitive load.

Prompts/hints (PH): instructions viewable in text or graphical form for performing this step, providing a subgoal and promoting working forward through the procedure.

Guiding search (GS): attention drawn to the next element required for performing this step. For example, highlighting text instructions or target entry field can mitigate screen search associated with the split attention effect.

Context-sensitive help (CS): help available as scaffold for performing this step. For example, tooltips, popup help or other prompts indicating the purpose of an element. This can support programmers in the use of schemas with which they are not fully conversant.

Groupings (G): clustering of elements into related functionality associated with performing this step. For example, automatic indentation, clustering of menu items. There are many alternative strategies for presenting various tools in an organised fashion consistent with schema hierarchies. These strategies act both as scaffolds for novices and as navigation pathways for more experienced users.

These cognitive load factors should not be considered as a complete list applicable to all IDEs or indeed to all software comparisons. They are factors that we have found useful in our assessment of a number of IDEs. We expect that other factors could emerge as computer hardware, software, and cognitive load theory continue to evolve.

4.2 Conducting the Comparison

We chose a small set of distinct tasks that would exercise a range of the IDE functions used by novice programmers. For each task, an expert user was recorded solving and narrating a typical student solution without errors. Experts versed in the cognitive load factors listed above then identified the steps involved in each recorded solution, and for each step they rated the extent of each of the cognitive load impact factors.

The comparison process has been used by the authors to assess the relative suitability of a number of language/IDE combinations for use in a class for teaching programming for mobile applications, commonly known as apps. After considering the prerequisite knowledge of the proposed users and the learning outcomes required, five candidate IDEs were chosen for comparison. Three of the environments are standalone, requiring installation on a computer before they can be used. The other two are cloud-based, accessed through a browser. The five candidates are as follows:

App Inventor: a web-based environment used to develop apps for Android phones. Code is built from jigsaw-like code-snippet blocks by dragging them to an editing area and fitting them together.

LiveCode: a standalone environment to produce mobile apps for Apple and Android devices. LiveCode has a text-based language, a little closer to English than most programming languages, with code entered via keyboard.

TouchDevelop: a web-based environment designed to develop apps for Windows and Android devices. The code is textual in form, with a number of special characters, but most of the text entry is carried out by tapping screen buttons rather than using a keyboard.

Visual Studio Express for Windows Phone: a standalone environment for the development of mobile apps for Windows phones, typically in C#. Code is text-based and entered via keyboard, and there is also some GUI development capability.

Xamarin Studio: a standalone environment for the development of mobile apps for Apple, Android and Windows devices, using the C# language in an IDE similar to Visual Studio. Xamarin has recently been incorporated into Visual Studio, but at the time this work was done it was a separate product.

Of these environments, App Inventor, LiveCode and TouchDevelop are marketed as simplified or learning environments that can also be used professionally, while Visual Studio and Xamarin are considered to be professional environments, although Visual Studio is used in many first programming courses [22].

Three programming tasks were selected to exercise different features of the environment. These were complete tasks that could be completed in all of the environments to be compared, and present three levels of complexity. Specifically the tasks were:

1) Hello world: create an app that displays a "Hello, world!" message when a button is clicked.

2) Animal display: create an app that loads and displays one of four animal images as chosen by a selection widget.

3) String permute: create an app that displays permuted versions of the string "Hello, world!" on the press of a button. The algorithm for this task is deliberately challenging for a novice programmer [13, 33].

Each of the three tasks was carried out in each environment, recorded by screen capture and overlaid with 'think-aloud' narrative. The programming tasks were carried out by relative experts (three of the authors) who have extensive experience in teaching programming languages. They solved the tasks in what they considered a straightforward way, without debugging, backtracking, or reworking. This ensured as far as possible that the comparisons were normalised and error-free, and that the evaluation was of the programming environment itself, not the tasks or the capability of the programmers.

We acknowledge that very few novice students produce an error-free implementation of a task in a single pass, and that novices will therefore be exposed to the error-reporting aspects of the IDE that were not included in our recordings. However, inclusion of errors would necessarily increase the differences between tasks that were already widely disparate, so for this stage we chose error-free implementations to enhance the comparability of the tasks.

The recordings were analysed by two authors working together. In a first pass, they identified the discrete steps in carrying out the task, noting that the same task will entail different steps in different environments. The two analysts, who are experienced both with teaching programming and with the 12 identified CL impact factors, then discussed each step to determine an agreed score for each of the impact factors. The 'load-adding' factors were scored as low, medium, or high, and the 'load-reducing' factors as present, not present, or not relevant. These measurements were consistently applied for each step of each task in each IDE, and were subsequently checked by the person who had carried out and recorded the task.

The application of these measurements was not intended to determine any absolute properties of the IDE/language combinations, but to give us a relative measurement that we could apply confidently over the set of recordings that we were analysing. When we decided, for example, that adding a button to a form in one IDE involved low interactivity, whereas customising the button involved medium interactivity, these measures are meaningful only in the context of our analysis of these particular tasks. Nevertheless, we believe that the process we have developed has strong potential to be used by other researchers in other contexts.

4.3 Analysis of Results

The scoring process described in the preceding subsection left us with many hundreds of steps, each with 14 distinct measures. We now required a means to reduce this data and transform it into information. We began by assigning numerical values to the measures. Table 1 shows the conversion scheme that we used.

The numeric values associated with scores in Table 1 have foundations within CLT. If an impact factor needs to be attended to, even minimally (for example, scanning a menu in search of a particular item), it must register as part of cognitive load, hence a score of 1. Factors requiring mindfulness of thought (for example, acting upon the chosen menu item) were given a score of 2. In the realm of cognitive load impact measures there is a clear recognition that the impositions of cognitive load are non-linear. Degradation of cognitive performance occurs only for relatively high levels of cognitive load, where there may be high levels of complex relationships in knowledge structures. Consequently, a high impact factor was given a score of 4, double the score for medium. While the selection of these numerical scores is undoubtedly discretionary, it is consistent

Table 1. Scoring scheme for IDE analysis

Impact Factor Measurement	Score
Low – minimal/no cognitive load impact	1
Medium – requires consideration	2
High – substantially present	4
Reduction factor present (subtracted)	2
Reduction factor not present	0
Reduction factor not relevant to this step	0

with the principles of CLT, and was used for comparison purposes in the subsequent analysis.

The IDEs also provide features that mitigate aspects of extraneous load. The availability of assistance as defined by prompts, guiding search, context help and groupings was deemed to warrant more than mere acknowledgment of presence, but of being cognitively meaningful, and so these items were attributed a score equal to medium.

Several useful aggregations of scores can be calculated after this allocation of numeric values to the impact measures. We will now define these and demonstrate their application.

4.3.1 Cognitive load impact score per step (CLISS)

CLISS is calculated by summing for each step the additive cognitive load impact factors and subtracting the scores for the supportive cognitive load impact factors:

$$CLISS = EC + PC + TB + I + PE + D + WP + SA - (PH + GS + CS + G).$$

An example calculation of CLISS is shown in Figure 1 for the Hello World task using the TouchDevelop IDE.

4.3.2 Threshold value

The CLISS values in Figure 1, which represents just part of one task in one environment, range from 3 to 9. A step that scores low on every load-adding impact factor, but has no load-reducing impact factors, will score 8. We define *a threshold value* to be a CLISS value denoting a step that will present many learners in a course with severe difficulty by exceeding the limits of their working memory. We chose 10 as the threshold for these tasks for our purpose, meaning that any step with a CLISS of 10 or more is likely to present a high degree of difficulty to *novice* users. Setting the threshold value as a constant allows comparison across tasks and across IDEs.

4.3.3 Number of steps

The number of steps required to complete a task makes no judgement of cognitive load impact, but may vary substantially between IDEs, and so should be considered in an overall evaluation. The number of steps is also used in the following measures.

4.3.4 Threshold score

The *threshold score* of a task in an environment is the proportion of its CLISS scores that are at or above the threshold value. Although the number of steps may vary significantly between the environments and tasks, the threshold score provides a normalised value for each environment-activity pair, enabling direct comparison between environments and tasks.

Figure 2 shows the number of steps, CLISS and threshold score for all fifteen environment-task combinations in our analysis.

While the threshold value provides a useful comparison of per-step difficulty, it does not indicate the influence introduced by a large number of steps. One environment may require many more steps than others for the same task, but the steps may all be cognitively less demanding. This can be seen in Figure 2 by comparing the measures for TouchDevelop and Visual Studio when performing the Permute task. Although Visual Studio involves far fewer steps than TouchDevelop, the cognitive load impact for each step is much higher, therefore so is the threshold score. Since Visual Studio is a professional development environment this is not an unexpected finding.

4.3.5 Average cognitive load impact per factor (ACLIF)

Average Cognitive Load Impact per Factor is a focused measure of the cognitive load impact due to particular effects. For example, the ACLIF for split attention (SA) for a particular environment can be calculated by ACLIFSA = sum(SA) / steps. The ACLIF results for the example analysis of mobile app development environments are shown in Figure 3, and the highest ACLIF for each factor for each activity is highlighted.

With just a few exceptions, which were principally in the simplest task, the maximum ACLIFs are found in Visual Studio and Xamarin, illustrating once more that these professional development environments have features that are likely to impose higher extraneous cognitive loads on beginners who have not yet internalised the required schemas.

ENVIRONMENT:	TouchDevelop				
TASK:	Hello World				
Step	6	7	8	9	10
Description	Choose 'wall'	Add button start	Custom-ise button	Add label	Finish editing button
EC	medium	low	medium	medium	medium
PC	low	low	medium	low	low
TB	low	low	low	low	low
I	low	low	medium	low	low
PE	medium	medium	medium	low	low
D	medium	medium	medium	low	low
WP	low	low	low	low	low
SA	medium	medium	medium	low	low
PH	yes	yes	yes	yes	no
GS	yes	yes	yes	yes	no
CS	no	yes	yes	no	no
G	yes	yes	yes	NA	no
CLISS	6	3	6	5	9

Figure 1. Example of portion of scoring spreadsheet

		CLISS				Threshold
1: Hello World	STEPS	Min	Max	Mode	Median	Score
App Inventor	18	2	10	9	8.5	6%
LiveCode	13	5	8	7	8	0%
TouchDevelop	22	2	13	8	7	14%
Visual Studio	18	4	13	8	8	28%
Xamarin	13	8	13	8	10	54%
2: Display Animals						
App Inventor	61	2	16	8	9	41%
LiveCode	54	5	16	8	8	20%
TouchDevelop	61	2	13	4	6	13%
Visual Studio	48	4	26	16	15	83%
Xamarin	50	6	26	11	11	64%
3: Permute						
App Inventor	60	2	16	9	10	52%
LiveCode	20	5	12	8	8	30%
TouchDevelop	88	2	17	8	8	22%
Visual Studio	36	4	23	15	15	83%
Xamarin	26	7	27	8	10	58%

Figure 2. Example comparison of CLISS and threshold scores

ACLIF (Average Cognitive Load per Factor)								
1: Hello World	EC	PC	TB	I	PE	D	WP	SA
App Inventor	1.33	1.11	1	1	*1.56*	1.5	*1.39*	1
LiveCode	1.23	1.08	1.08	1	1.08	1.54	1.31	1
TouchDevelop	*1.64*	1.27	1.14	1.18	1.41	1.41	1	*1.32*
Visual Studio	1.33	1.28	1.11	1.11	1.11	*1.72*	1.22	1.06
Xamarin	1.62	*1.62*	*1.23*	*1.31*	1.46	1.38	1.15	1.15
2: Display Animals								
App Inventor	1.56	1.44	1.46	1.51	1.57	1.2	1.16	1.07
LiveCode	1.54	1.28	1.24	1.26	1.35	1.59	1.35	1.19
TouchDevelop	1.49	1.46	1.3	1.36	1.74	1.05	1	1.15
Visual Studio	*1.96*	1.46	1.58	1.38	*2.6*	*3.29*	*3.19*	1.71
Xamarin	1.76	*2.34*	*2.14*	*2.1*	2.54	2.3	2.08	*1.74*
3: Permute								
App Inventor	1.37	1.85	1.48	1.68	1.48	1.32	1.18	1.17
LiveCode	*1.5*	1.3	1.25	1.4	1.5	1.6	1.65	1.05
TouchDevelop	1.4	1.77	1.53	1.67	1.59	1.65	1.01	1.43
Visual Studio	1.19	1.94	*2.06*	1.97	*2.64*	*3.44*	*3.11*	1.44
Xamarin	1.38	*2.19*	1.85	*2.04*	2.19	2	1.65	*1.5*

Figure 3. ACLIF comparison for tasks and environments

4.3.6 *Proportion of steps assisted (PSA)*

The PSA is the proportion of steps in a task that are assisted by individual cognitive load reduction factors (PH, GS, CS or G). PSA measures the cognitive load impact factors that contribute to reducing extraneous cognitive load, in contrast with ACLIF, which measures factors that increase cognitive load. The PSA for a factor is calculated by the count of the steps in which the reduction factor was present, divided by the number of steps. *PSA = count (reduction factor present) / steps.*

Figure 4 shows the PSA values in our analysis of mobile app development environments, highlighting the highest PSA for each reduction factor for each activity.

It can be seen from Figure 4 that TouchDevelop includes proportionally more prompts and hints, guided search, and context-sensitive help than the other environments examined.

4.4 Graphing

Some of the measures introduced above lend themselves to graphical presentations that can be useful for comparisons. In this section we will discuss one that we have found useful.

PSA (Proportion of Steps Assisted)			
1: Hello World	PH	GS	CS	G
App Inventor	11%	11%	6%	*78%*
LiveCode	54%	8%	8%	54%
TouchDevelop	*64%*	*50%*	*18%*	50%
Visual Studio	11%	17%	0%	50%
Xamarin	15%	0%	0%	38%
2: Display Animals				
App Inventor	23%	3%	5%	51%
LiveCode	19%	7%	22%	50%
TouchDevelop	*74%*	*38%*	38%	67%
Visual Studio	11%	17%	0%	50%
Xamarin	50%	10%	*48%*	*74%*
3: Permute				
App Inventor	30%	10%	2%	47%
LiveCode	30%	10%	45%	*75%*
TouchDevelop	*72%*	*31%*	*50%*	69%
Visual Studio	36%	3%	28%	67%
Xamarin	35%	0%	35%	69%

Figure 4. PSA comparisons for the mobile app development environments

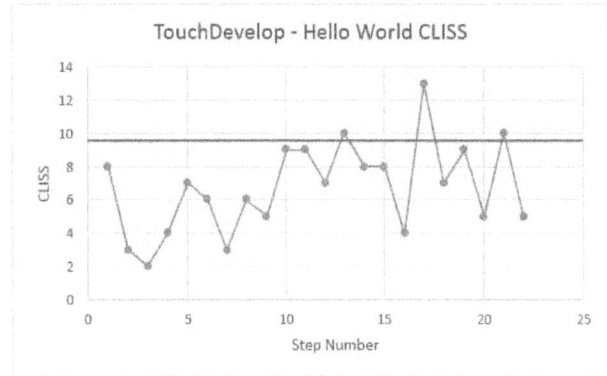

Figure 5. CLISS for "Hello World" in the TouchDevelop IDE

CLISS is a useful measure of the cognitive load impact of the environment at each step, and the threshold value is a CLISS value at or above which a step is likely to impose cognitive overload. It is informative to plot the CLISS of each step in a task, along with the threshold value. Figure 5 illustrates this for the simplest task in the TouchDevelop environment. The horizontal line is drawn at a value of 9.5: points below this line are below the threshold of 10, and points above the line are on or above the threshold. The figure clearly shows that three of the 21 steps have a CLISS at or above the threshold. Points above the threshold value represent 'pinch points' of high imposition of cognitive load, and may stall learning for students.

Examining the graphs for a single task across all five IDEs, we see differences in the number of steps, the number of spikes on or above the threshold value of 10, and the distribution of cognitive load during the performance of the task. Figure 6 illustrates this graphical comparison for the permute task.

We see from Figure 6 that TouchDevelop requires the greatest number of steps to complete the permute task, while Visual Studio and Xamarin have fewer steps but many exceeding the threshold. App Inventor distinguishes itself by having both a large number of steps and a large proportion of scores above the threshold. By contrast, LiveCode has the fewest steps, and the fewest above the threshold. LiveCode scaffolds tasks well using code skeletons, the code is more like English than in many programming languages, and there is extensive on-screen context-sensitive help, all of which contribute to this result.

5. DISCUSSION

The process described in this paper has been used to compare the relative cognitive loads imposed by several language/IDE combinations in performing a range of programming tasks. The objective is to enable normalised comparisons and contrasts between combinations, to assist in selecting a language and IDE for a course on programming mobile apps.

As novice learners progress toward expertise, they acquire increasingly well-organised schemas in programming concepts and programming language syntax. The expert reversal effect [16] suggests that instructional design strategies designed for novices should not be deployed for more expert users. Indeed, instructional strategies that are initially deployed for novices will impede their learning as their expertise increases [14]. In the context of computer programming, an IDE used as a learning and working environment for novices may need to be replaced by alternative IDEs as the users move towards expertise.

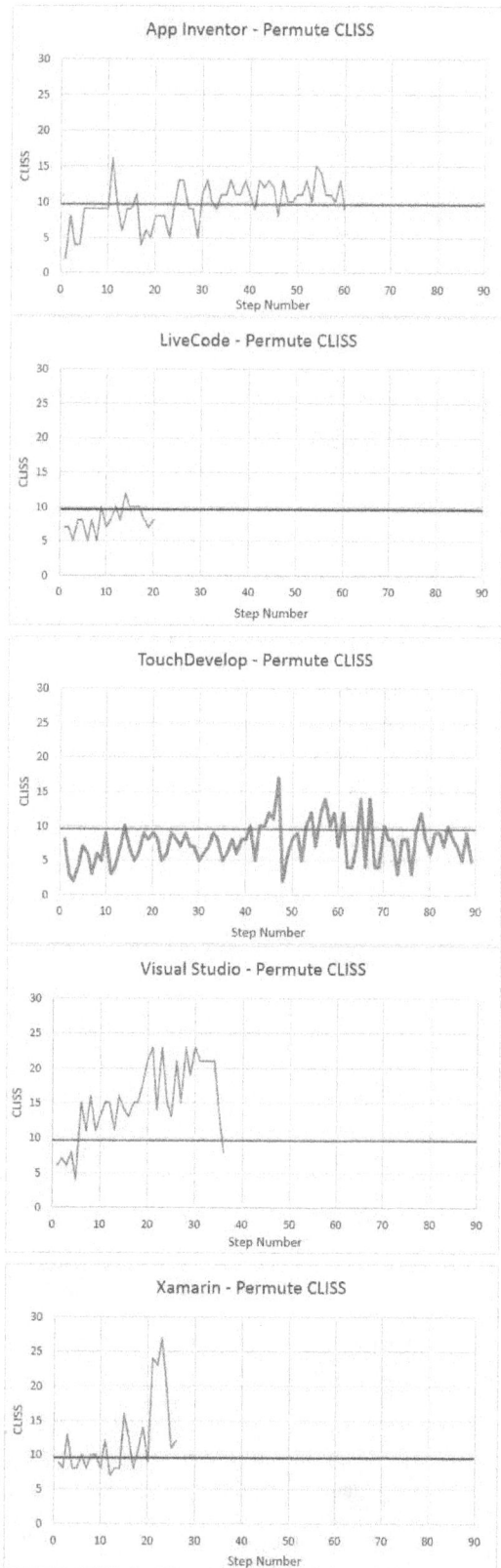

Figure 6. CLISS for the permute task for each IDE,
with a threshold value of 10

The process presented here can be used to assess and compare a variety of IDEs and determine where each might fit in the novice-expert sequence suggested above.

The process clearly involves elements of discretion and subjectivity. The assessment of the cognitive load impact factors for each step of each recording, the numerical scoring scheme following that assessment, the choice of a threshold value, and more, might well be done differently by different analysts. We do not see this as problematic, any more than we see it as problematic to assess the cognitive load of a teaching episode by surveying students about their experience of the episode. We have applied the method successfully, using it to assess and plot the relative impact of cognitive loads imposed by a number of different mobile apps development environments [24]. We believe that it could be used with different choices for the elements mentioned above and still produce similar relative findings. Therefore we argue that the method is sound as a means for enabling comparisons of extraneous cognitive load impositions arising from different programming tasks undertaken using different IDEs. That is, in situations where it is neither feasible nor ethical to have the students assess the cognitive load of an aspect of the teaching experience, it is possible to flip the assessment and have it carried out in advance by the instructors.

6. FUTURE WORK

The process described in this paper can immediately be applied to other development environments used in computer programming courses that do not focus on mobile apps. Environments for traditional programming languages (C, C#, LISP), scripting environments (HTML, XML), and domain-specific languages (SQL, Matlab) are widely used and can be evaluated by applying the method described in this paper. We suggest that the process could also be used to evaluate other user-oriented software.

Some IDEs offer multiple views, each intended for users at different levels. The Lego Mindstorms NXT IDE [40] is an example. The analysis and comparison process described in this paper may offer support in future designs of layered capability interfaces whereby additional levels of visibility and functionality are revealed in accordance with users' evolving levels of expertise.

The process presented here was opportunistic to our needs. As other aspects of CLT may become incorporated into IDEs, it can be enhanced to enable future application.

7. REFERENCES

[1] Paul Ayres and John Sweller. 1990. Locus of Difficulty in Multistage Mathematics Problems. Am. J. Psychol. 103, 2 (1990), 167. DOI:http://dx.doi.org/10.2307/1423141

[2] A. Baddeley. 1992. Working Memory. Science 255 (1992), 556–559.

[3] Jens Bennedsen and Michael E. Caspersen. 2007. Failure rates in introductory programming. SIGCSE Bulletin 39, 2 (2007), 32–36.

[4] Benedict du Boulay. 1986. Some difficulties of learning to program. J. Educ. Comput. Res. 2, 1 (1986), 57–73.

[5] Duane Buck and David J. Stucki. 2000. Design early considered harmful: graduated exposure to complexity and structure based on levels of cognitive development. (2000). http://doi.acm.org.ezproxy.scu.edu.au/10.1145/330908.331817

[6] Richard Catrambone. 1998. The subgoal learning model: Creating better examples so that students can solve novel problems. J. Exp. Psychol. Gen. 127, 4 (1998), 355–376. DOI:http://dx.doi.org/10.1037/0096-3445.127.4.355

[7] Paul Chandler and John Sweller. 1991. Cognitive Load Theory and the Format of Instruction. Cogn. Instr. 8 (1991), 293–332.

[8] Paul Chandler and John Sweller. 1996. Cognitive Load While Learning to Use a Computer Program. Appl. Cogn. Psychol. 10, 2 (April 1996), 151–170. DOI:http://dx.doi.org/10.1002/(SICI)1099-0720(199604)10:2<151::AID-ACP380>3.0.CO;2-U

[9] Graham Cooper. 1998. Research into Cognitive Load Theory and Instructional Design at UNSW. (1998). Retrieved October 12, 2000 from http://dwb4.unl.edu/Diss/Cooper/UNSW.htm

[10] Graham Cooper and John Sweller. 1987. Effects of schema acquisition and rule automation on mathematical problem-solving transfer. J. Educ. Psychol. 79 (1987), 347–362. DOI:http://dx.doi.org/10.1037/0022-0663.79.4.347

[11] Graham Cooper, Sharon Tindall-Ford, Paul Chandler, and John Sweller. 2001. Learning by imagining. J. Exp. Psychol. Appl. 7, 1 (2001), 68–82.

[12] N. Cowan. 2001. The magical number 4 in short-term memory: a reconsideration of mental storage capacity. Behav. Brain Sci. 24, 1 (February 2001), 87–114; discussion 114–185.

[13] Mark H. Goadrich and Michael P. Rogers. 2011. Smart smartphone development: iOS versus android. In ACM Press, 607. DOI:http://dx.doi.org/10.1145/1953163.1953330

[14] Slava Kalyuga. 2007. Expertise Reversal Effect and Its Implications for Learner-Tailored Instruction. Educ. Psychol. Rev. 19, 4 (October 2007), 509–539. DOI:http://dx.doi.org/10.1007/s10648-007-9054-3

[15] Slava Kalyuga, Paul Chandler, and John Sweller. 1999. Managing split-attention and redundancy in multimedia instruction. Appl. Cogn. Psychol. 13, 4 (August 1999), 351–371. DOI:http://dx.doi.org/10.1002/(SICI)1099-0720(199908)13:4<351::AID-ACP589>3.0.CO;2-6

[16] Slava Kalyuga, Paul Chandler, Juhani Tuovinen, and John Sweller. 2001. When problem solving is superior to studying worked examples. J. Educ. Psychol. 93, 3 (2001), 579–588. DOI:http://dx.doi.org/10.1037/0022-0663.93.3.579

[17] Caitlin Kelleher and Randy Pausch. 2007. Using storytelling to motivate programming. Commun. ACM 50, 7 (July 2007), 58. DOI:http://dx.doi.org/10.1145/1272516.1272540

[18] M. Kölling, B. Quig, A. Patterson, and J. Rosenberg. 2003. The BlueJ system and its pedagogy. J. Comput. Sci. Educ. Spec. Issue Learn. Teach. Object Technol. 13, 4 (2003).

[19] Raymond Lister et al. 2004. A Multi-National Study of Reading and Tracing Skills in Novice Programmers. ACM SIGCSE Bull. 36, 4 (2004), 119–150.

[20] Lauren E. Margulieux, Mark Guzdial, and Richard Catrambone. 2012. Subgoal-labeled instructional material improves performance and transfer in learning to develop mobile applications. In ICER '12 Proceedings of the ninth annual international conference on International computing education research. Auckland, New Zealand: ACM Press, 71–78. DOI:http://dx.doi.org/10.1145/2361276.2361291

[21] F. Marton and R. Säljö. 1976. On Qualitative Differences in Learning: I - Outcome and Process. Br. J. Educ. Psychol. 46, 1 (February 1976), 4–11. DOI:http://dx.doi.org/10.1111/j.2044-8279.1976.tb02980.x

[22] Raina Mason and Graham Cooper. 2014. Introductory Programming Courses in Australia and New Zealand in 2013 - trends and reasons. In Jacqueline Whalley & Daryl D'Souza, eds. Proceedings of the Sixteenth Australasian Computing Education Conference (ACE2014). CRPIT. Auckland, New Zealand: ACS, 139–147.

[23] Raina Mason, Graham Cooper, and Michael de Raadt. 2012. Trends in Introductory Programming Courses in Australian Universities – Languages, Environments and Pedagogy. In Michael de Raadt & Angela Carbone, eds. Proceedings of the Fourteenth Australasian Computing Education Conference (ACE2012). Melbourne, Australia: Australian Computer Society, Inc., 33–42.

[24] Raina Mason, Graham Cooper, Simon, and Barry Wilks. 2015. Using Cognitive Load Theory to select an environment for teaching mobile apps development. In Daryl D'Souza & Katrina Falkner, eds. Proceedings of the 17th Australasian Computing Education Conference (ACE2015). Sydney, Australia: ACS, 47–56.

[25] Richard E. Mayer. 2001. Multimedia Learning, New York, NY: Cambridge University Press.

[26] Richard E. Mayer and Paul Chandler. 2001. When learning is just a click away: Does simple user interaction foster deeper understanding of multimedia messages? J. Educ. Psychol. 93 (2001), 390–397.

[27] Michael McCracken et al. 2001. A multi-national, multi-institutional study of assessment of programming skills of first-year CS students. ACM SIGCSE Bull. 33, 4 (2001), 125–180. DOI:http://dx.doi.org/Working group report

[28] George Miller. 1956. The Magical Number Seven, Plus or Minus Two: Some Limits on Our Capacity for Processing

Information. Psychol. Rev. 63 (1956), 81–97. DOI:http://dx.doi.org/10.1037/h0043158

[29] Briana B. Morrison, Brian Dorn, and Mark Guzdial. 2014. Measuring cognitive load in introductory CS: adaptation of an instrument. In ACM Press, 131–138. DOI:http://dx.doi.org/10.1145/2632320.2632348

[30] Fred Paas, Alexander Renkl, and John Sweller. 2004. Cognitive Load Theory: Instructional implications of the interaction between information structures and cognitive architecture. Instr. Sci. 32 (2004), 1–8.

[31] C. Schulte and J. Bennedsen. 2006. Teachers & learners: which to study? What do teachers teach in introductory programming? (2006). http://doi.acm.org.ezproxy.scu.edu.au/10.1145/1151588.11 51593

[32] Ben Shneiderman and Catherine Plaisant. 2010. Designing the user interface: strategies for effective human-computer interaction 5th ed., Boston: Addison-Wesley.

[33] Simon, and David Conforth. 2014. Teaching Mobile Apps for Windows Devices Using TouchDevelop. In Proceedings of the 16th Australasian Computing Education Conference. Auckland, New Zealand: Australian Computer Society, Inc., 75–82.

[34] John Sweller. 1988. Cognitive Load During Problem Solving: Effects on Learning. Cogn. Sci. 12 (1988), 257–285.

[35] John Sweller. 1999. Instructional design in technical areas, Camberwell, VIC: The Australian Council for Educational Research Ltd.

[36] J. Sweller, P. Ayres, and S. Kalyuga. Cognitive Load Theory, volume 1. Springer, 2011.

[37] John Sweller and Paul Chandler. 1994. Why some material is difficult to learn. Cogn. Instr. 12 (1994), 185–233.

[38] John Sweller and Graham Cooper. 1985. The Use of Worked Examples as a Substitute for Problem Solving in Learning Algebra. Cogn. Instr. 2, 1 (1985), 59–89.

[39] John Sweller, J.J.G. Van Merriënboer, and Fred Paas. 1998. Cognitive Architecture and Instructional Design. Educ. Psychol. Rev. 10, 3 (1998), 251–296.

[40] Rohani A. Tarmizi and John Sweller. 1988. Guidance during mathematical problem solving. J. Educ. Psychol. 80, 4 (1988), 424–436. DOI:http://dx.doi.org/10.1037/0022-0663.80.4.424

[41] The LEGO Group. 2009. MINDSTORMS. (2009). Retrieved August 28, 2009 from http://mindstorms.lego.com/en-us/Default.aspx

[42] Christopher Watson and Frederick W.B. Li. 2014. Failure rates in introductory programming revisited. In ITiCSE '14 Proceedings of the 2014 conference on Innovation & Technology in Computer Science Education. Uppsala, Sweden: ACM Press, 39–44.

How Kids Code and How We Know:
An Exploratory Study on the Scratch Repository

Efthimia Aivaloglou
e.aivaloglou@tudelft.nl

Felienne Hermans
f.f.j.hermans@tudelft.nl

Software Engineering Research Group
Delft University of Technology
Mekelweg 4, 2628 CD, Delft, the Netherlands

ABSTRACT

Block-based programming languages like Scratch, Alice and Blockly are becoming increasingly common as introductory languages in programming education. There is substantial research showing that these visual programming environments are suitable for teaching programming concepts. But, what do people do when they use Scratch? In this paper we explore the characteristics of Scratch programs. To this end we have scraped the Scratch public repository and retrieved 250,000 projects. We present an analysis of these projects in three different dimensions. Initially, we look at the types of blocks used and the size of the projects. We then investigate complexity, used abstractions and programming concepts. Finally we detect *code smells* such as large scripts, dead code and duplicated code blocks. Our results show that 1) most Scratch programs are small, however Scratch programs consisting of over 100 sprites exist, 2) programming abstraction concepts like procedures are not commonly used and 3) Scratch programs do suffer from code smells including large scripts and unmatched broadcast signals.

Keywords

Scratch; block-based languages; programming practices; code smells; static analysis

1. INTRODUCTION

Scratch [20] is a programming language developed to teach children programming by enabling them to create games and interactive animations. The public repository of Scratch programs contains over 14 million projects. Scratch is a *block-based* language: users manipulate blocks to program.

Block-based languages have existed since the eighties [9], but have recently found adoption as tools for programming education. In addition to Scratch, also Alice [4], Blockly[1]

[1] https://developers.google.com/blockly/

ICER '16, September 08-12, 2016, Melbourne, VIC, Australia
© 2016 ACM. ISBN 978-1-4503-4449-4/16/09. . . $15.00
DOI: http://dx.doi.org/10.1145/2960310.2960325

and App Inventor [23] are block-based and aimed at novice programmers.

Several studies have shown that block-based languages are powerful as tools for teaching programming [15, 18, 5, 19]. Previous works involving static analysis of Scratch programs have evaluated the application of various programming concepts in Scratch projects [12, 16]. Recent works have focused on bad programming practices within Scratch programs [14], and automated quality assessment tools have been proposed for identifying code smells [8] and bad programming practices [2, 16]. In a recent controlled experiment we found that long scripts and code duplication decrease a novice programmer's ability to understand and modify Scratch programs [10].

The goal of this paper is to obtain an understanding of how people program in Scratch by analyzing their programming artifacts, i.e., the saved and shared Scratch projects. With this we aim to quantitatively evaluate the use of programming abstractions and concepts. Moreover, knowing that bad programming habits and code smells can be harmful [10], we also want to explore whether they are common. To address this goal, we answer the following research questions:

RQ1 What are the size and complexity characteristics of Scratch programs?

RQ2 Which coding abstractions and programming concepts and features are commonly used when programming in the Scratch environment?

RQ3 How common are code smells in Scratch programs?

Our study is based on data from the Scratch project repository. By scraping the list of recent projects[2], we have obtained 250,166 public Scratch projects and performed source code analysis on them. To the best of our knowledge, this is the first large-scale exploratory study of Scratch programs.

The contributions of this paper are as follows:

- A public data set of 233,491 non-empty Scratch projects (Section 3.1)

- An evaluation of the data set in terms of size, complexity, programming concepts and smells (Section 4)

- A discussion of the implications of our findings for educational programming language designers (Section 5)

[2] https://scratch.mit.edu/explore/projects/all/

2. RELEVANT SCRATCH CONCEPTS

Scratch is a block-based programming language aimed at children, developed by MIT. Scratch can be used to create games and interactive animations, and is available both as a stand-alone and as a web application. The main concepts in the Scratch programming environment are (we refer the reader to [3] for an extensive overview):

Sprites Scratch code is organized by 'sprites': two dimensional pictures each having their own associated code. Scratch allows users to bring their sprites to life in various ways, for example by moving them in the plane, having them say or think words or sentences via text balloons, but also by having them make sounds, grow, shrink and switch costumes.

Scripts Sprites can have multiple code blocks, called scripts. It is possible for a single sprite to have multiple scripts initiated by the same event. In that case, all scripts will be executed simultaneously.

Events Scratch is *event-driven*: all motions, sounds and changes in the looks of sprites are initiated by events called Hat blocks[3]). The canonical event is the `when Green Flag clicked`, activated by clicking the green flag at the top of the user interface. In addition to the green flag, there are a number of other events possible, including key presses, mouse clicks and input from a computer's microphone or webcam.

Signals Events within Scratch can be user-generated too: users can broadcast a message, for example when two sprites touch each other. All other sprites can then react by using the `when I receive` Hat block.

Custom blocks Scratch users can define their own blocks, which users can name themselves, called *custom blocks*. The creation of custom blocks in Scratch is the equivalent of defining procedures in other languages [16]. Because the term 'procedures' is common in related work, we will refer to custom blocks as 'procedures' in the remainder of this paper. Procedure parameters can be textual, numeric or boolean. When a user defines a procedure, a new Hat block called `define` appears, which users can fill with the implementation of their procedure.

3. RESEARCH DESIGN AND DATASET

The main focus of this study is to understand how people program in Scratch, by analyzing the characteristics of Scratch projects. To answer our three research questions, we conducted an empirical quantitative evaluation of project data we collected from the Scratch project repository. In the following paragraphs we describe the dataset, the process and the tools we used for analyzing it, and the methods we followed for detecting code smells.

3.1 Dataset

In order to collect the set of Scratch projects in the dataset we built a web scraping program. The scraping program, called Kragle, starts by reading the Scratch projects page[2] and thus obtains the project identifiers of projects that were

most recently shared. Subsequently, Kragle retrieves the JSON code for each of the listed projects.

We ran Kragle on March 2nd 2016 for 24 hours and, during that time, it obtained a little over 250,000 projects. Out of the 250,166, we failed to parse and further analyze 2,367 projects due to technical difficulties with the JSON files. Kragle, as well as all scraped projects and our analysis files are available.[4]

Once we obtained the Scratch projects, we parsed the JSON files according to the specification of the format[5]. This resulted in a list of used blocks per project, with the sprites and the stage of the project. We also cross referenced all blocks with the Scratch wiki to determine the shapes and the category of all blocks. For example, `When Green Flag Clicked` is a *Hat block* from the *Events category*.

3.2 Data analysis

All scraped project data, including the list of used blocks and parameters, were imported in a relational database. We used SQL queries, which are also made available,[4] for filtering, aggregating and extracting all statistical data required to address our three research questions. We also randomly sampled and manually inspected edge cases in the results, for example empty or overly complex projects. Data for these cases are provided as part of the dataset.[4]

To answer RQ1, we measured the size of projects based on the number of blocks in scripts and sprites and we calculated descriptive statistics, which are presented in Section 4.1. For measuring the complexity of the scripts we used the McCabe cyclomatic complexity metric [13], a quantitative measure of the number of independent paths through a program's source code. This is commonly calculated per script by counting the number of decision points in the script plus one. The decision points that Scratch supports are the `if` and the `if else` blocks.

For RQ2, we used the data on the code blocks and their categories to perform statistical analysis of applied programming abstractions and concepts. Similarly to [6] and [12], we consider the use of certain blocks to indicate that a programming abstraction or concept is being used in a certain project. In Section 4.2 we present the results related to the utilization of procedures, variables, loops, conditional statements, user interactivity and synchronization.

For RQ3, we focused on four types of code smells: duplicated code, dead code, large script and large sprite. In the duplicated code smell analysis, our first step was to define what we consider a code clone in the context of Scratch programming: a script that is composed of a set of blocks of the same type connected in the same way and is repeated within or across sprites of the same project. For the identification of clones we did not take into account the values of the parameters that may be used in the blocks, so that two blocks that only differ in the values of parameters are considered to be equal. We also investigated the case of clones with the same parameter values, and we refer to them as *exact clones*. The next step in the analysis was to determine the minimum size of the scripts that are considered clones instead of incidentally similar. We examined the number of detected clones for different script sizes and present the results in Figure 1. Based on this distribution, we opted to

---

[3]http://wiki.scratch.mit.edu/wiki/Hat_Block

[4]https://github.com/TUDelftScratchLab/ScratchDataset
[5]http://wiki.scratch.mit.edu/wiki/Scratch_File_Format_(2.0)

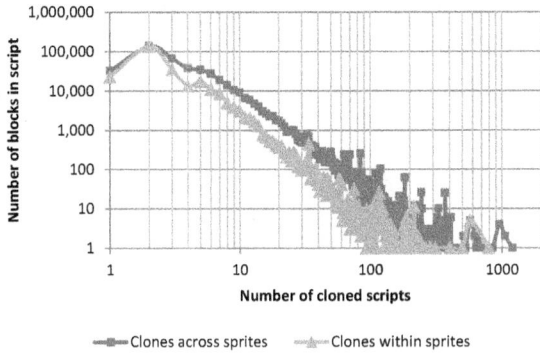

Figure 1: Number of cloned scripts of different block sizes across and within sprites

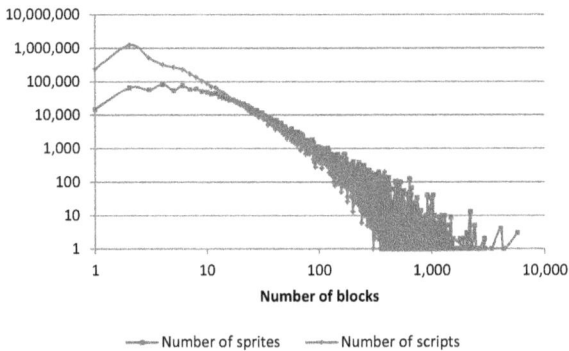

Figure 2: Size of sprites and scripts in number of blocks

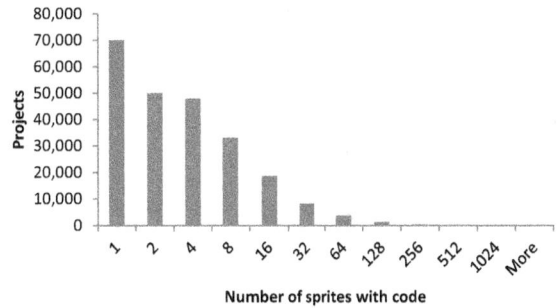

Figure 3: Number of sprites in the analyzed projects

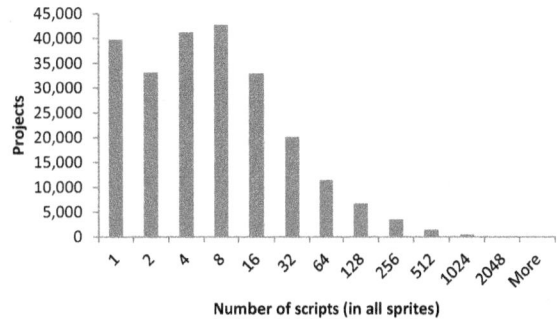

Figure 4: Number of scripts in the analyzed projects

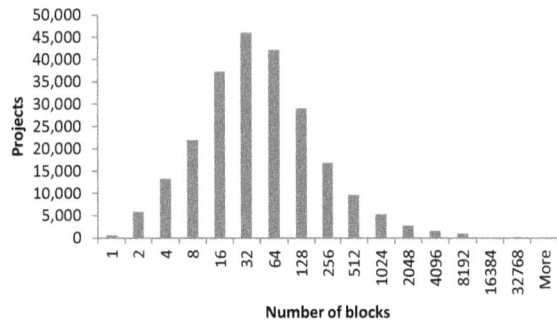

Figure 5: Number of blocks in the analyzed projects

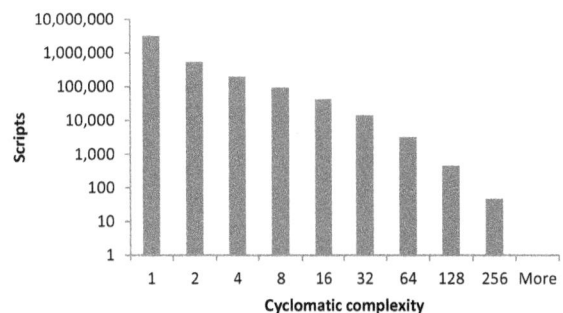

Figure 6: McCabe cyclomatic complexity of the 4,049,356 analyzed scripts

adopt the number also used by the authors in [16], which is a minimum size of five blocks per script.

In the context of Scratch, we consider the long method and the large class smells as large script and large sprite smells respectively. For these two smells we use the number of blocks as the size metric. Figure 2 presents the number of blocks in scripts and sprites of our dataset. We used these statistics to split the dataset and retrieve the top 10% largest scripts and sprites, as is commonly done in both source code analysis [1] and analysis of end-user programming artifacts like spreadsheets [11]. Using that strategy, we set the thresholds for the calculation of the large script and large sprite: 18 blocks and 59 blocks respectively. The results we obtained using these thresholds are presented in Section 4.3.

4. RESULTS

In the following sections, for each of the research questions, we describe the results obtained through the analysis of the 247,798 Scratch projects in our dataset.

4.1 Program Size and Complexity

The dataset contains a relatively small number of projects without any code: 14,307 (5.77%). Through random manual sampling we found that in some cases these projects contains only sprites and costumes, but no code, while other projects were entirely empty apart from the Scratch cat added by default. Since these projects are empty in terms of code, we excluded them from further analysis, leaving the final number of analyzed non-empty projects to 233,491.

55

		mean	min	Q1	median	Q3	max
Size	Sprites with code per project	5.68	1	1	2	5	525
	Scripts per project	17.35	1	2	5	12	3,038
	Number of blocks per project	154.55	1	12	29	76	34,622
	Blocks in Stage per project	4.80	0	0	0	3	2,613
	Blocks in Sprites per project	115.57	0	10	26	68	34,613
	Blocks in Procedures per project	34.17	0	0	0	0	20,552
Complexity	McCabe Cyclomatic Complexity (CC) per script	1.58	1	1	1	1	246
	McCabe CC per procedure script	3.75	1	1	2	4	183
Procedures	Procedures per project with procedures	11.50	1	1	2	6	847
	Arguments per Procedure	0.95	0	0	0	1	53
	Numerical arguments per procedure with arguments	1.73	0	1	1	2	22
	Text arguments per procedure with arguments	0.28	0	0	0	1	24
	Boolean arguments per procedure with arguments	0.13	0	0	0	0	14
	Calls per procedure	2.14	0	1	1	2	526
	Scripts with calls per procedure	1.13	0	1	1	1	59
Programming concepts	Variables per project	2.06	0	0	0	1	340
	Scripts utilizing variable	4.97	1	1	3	5	1,127
	Lists per project	0.55	0	0	0	0	319
	Conditional statements per project	10.02	0	0	0	3	5,950
	Loop statements per project	7.65	0	1	2	5	2,503
	User input blocks per project	4.77	0	0	1	4	1,889
	Broadcast-receive statements per project	8.57	0	0	0	2	2,460

Table 1: Summary statistics of the dataset of 233,491 non-empty Scratch projects

In Table 1 we summarize the statistics for the analyzed metrics. We use the mean value and the five-number summary to describe the dataset in terms of the number of sprites with code per project (including the stage sprite) and the number of scripts and blocks per project. Figures 3, 4 and 5 plot the distribution of these size metrics.

We find that the majority of Scratch projects are small; 75% of the projects have up to 5 sprites, 12 scripts and 76 blocks, while one fourth of the projects have up to 12 blocks. On the other end, 5% of the projects (11,712) have more than 18 sprites and 4.8% (11,214) consist of more than 500 blocks. The analysis also highlighted some surprisingly large projects: 135 with more than 300 sprites and even 30 projects with more than 20,000 blocks, whose Scratch identifiers are made available for further inspection.[4]

The number of blocks metric was further analyzed to understand code organization in more depth. The majority of Scratch code—74.78% out of 36,085,654 blocks—is written within sprites. An additional 3.1% of the total blocks are found in the stage class. More interestingly, the remaining 22.11% are blocks within defined procedures, which are found in only 7.7% (17,979) of the projects. The projects that contain procedures use them a lot; almost half of their total blocks (48.81%) are within procedures.

We further analyzed the utilization frequency of the different block shapes and categories, as defined in the Scratch documentation. Figures 7 and 8 present the results in terms of number of blocks from the total 36,085,654 blocks in the dataset projects. The most commonly used blocks are from the Control and Data categories. The Others category includes the blocks related to procedure calls and arguments.

To understand the complexity of the Scratch projects in our dataset, we use the McCabe cyclomatic complexity. The results of this metric per script are plotted in Figure 6. The majority (78.33%) of 4,049,356 scripts contain no decision points, while 13.08% have a cyclomatic complexity of 2, con-

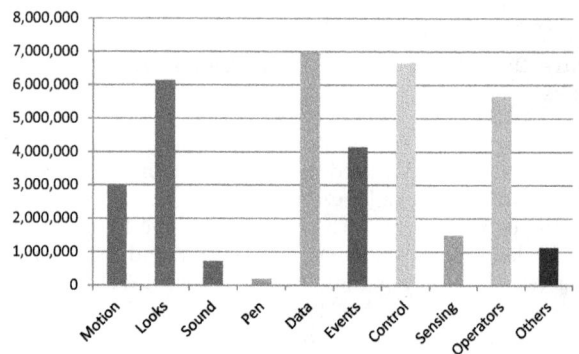

Figure 7: Number of blocks from each category in the analyzed projects

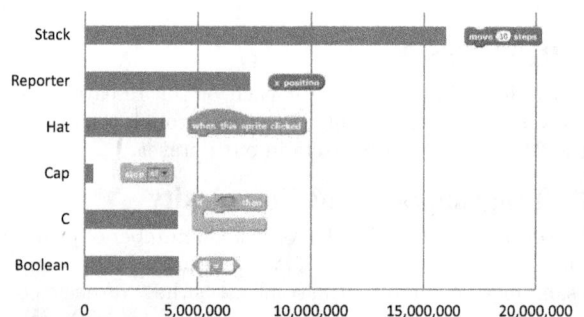

Figure 8: Number of blocks of each shape in the analyzed projects

	Number of projects	%
Retrieved	250,166	
Analyzed	247,798	
Non-empty (used for statistics)	**233,491**	
Projects with:		
Procedures	17,979	7.70%
Recursive procedures	1,052	0.45%
Variables	73,577	31.51%
Lists	9,358	4.01%
Conditional statements	92,959	39.81%
User input blocks	131,314	56.24%
Loop statements	180,210	77.18%
`repeat until <condition>`	31,739	13.59%
`broadcast - receive`	69,039	29.57%
Cloned scripts across sprites	59,634	25.54%
Cloned scripts within sprites	23,671	10.14%
Cloned procedures	4,945	2.12%
Cloned blocks across sprites	60,554	25.93%
Exact clones across sprites	27,574	11.81%
Exact clones within sprites	2,043	0.87%
Dead code	65,760	28.16%
Large scripts	69,521	29.77%
Large sprites	31,954	13.68%

Table 2: Elements and characteristics of the projects in the dataset

taining exactly one decision point. The complexity is higher, over 4, for 3.67% of the scripts. The analysis also highlighted 209 scripts with a cyclomatic complexity over 100 and up to 246.[4] Cyclomatic complexity was greater (mean value of 3.32) in defined procedures, with 56.46% of the procedures having at least one decision point.

> RQ1: The majority of Scratch projects are small and simple: 75% of the projects have up to 5 sprites, 12 scripts and 76 blocks. The majority (78%) of scripts contain no decision points. Most code is written in sprites. There exist surprisingly large and complex projects.

4.2 Programming Abstractions and Concepts

The first method for abstraction that we investigate are procedures. In the dataset we found 206,799 procedures in 17,979 (7.7%) projects. As summarized in Table 1, the projects that contain procedures have an average of 11.5 procedures, with 53.59% of these projects having up to 2. Figure 9 shows the distribution of procedures in projects. Regarding procedure arguments, we found that 55.57% have no arguments and 19.48% have only one (shown in Figure 10). The majority of procedure arguments (80.59%) are numeric, and the least used argument type is the boolean one—6.23% of the total procedure arguments, found in 5.32% of the procedures.

The use of procedures in projects was further investigated through the use of procedure calls, summarized in Figure 11. Most procedures are called exactly once (62.32% of them) or twice (14.30%) and from exactly one script (85.92% of them). Examining the origin of procedure calls, we observed that most of the calls (56.09%) originate from other procedures, and 1.06% even originate from the same procedure, making them recursive calls. These recursive proce-

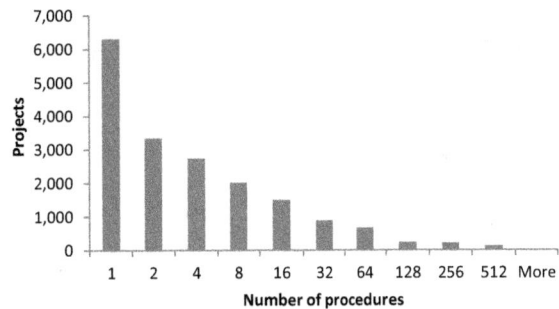

Figure 9: Number of procedures for the 17,979 projects that include at least one procedure

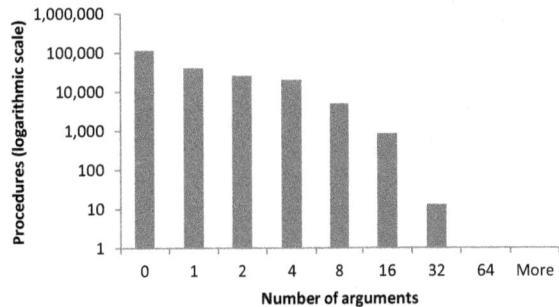

Figure 10: Number of arguments of the procedures in the dataset

dures are found in 1,052 projects, whose identifiers are made available.[4]

As shown in Table 2, almost one-third of the projects use variables and a small number (4.01%) use lists. The number of variables that is being used is also limited, with only 7.48% of the projects having five or more variables. The distribution of variable and list utilization is shown in Figure 12. Exceptional cases exist: the analysis highlighted 842 projects with more than 100 variables and with a maximum of 340. Examining the initialization of variables through the `set <variable> to <value>` blocks, we found that for 4.83% of all variables this was missing. While failing to initialize a variable in Scratch will not result in a runtime error as in some other programming languages, correctly setting the initial state of the program is important [2].

Regarding program control features, conditionals (`if <con-`

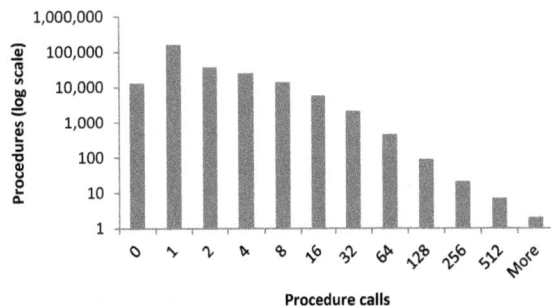

Figure 11: Number of calls of each procedure in the dataset

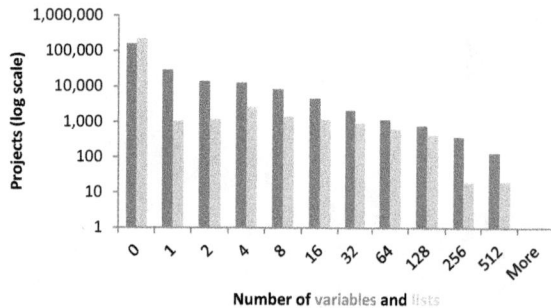

Figure 12: Number of used variables and lists

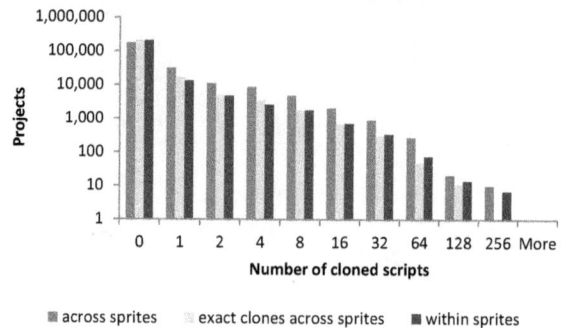

Figure 13: Cloned scripts in the dataset projects

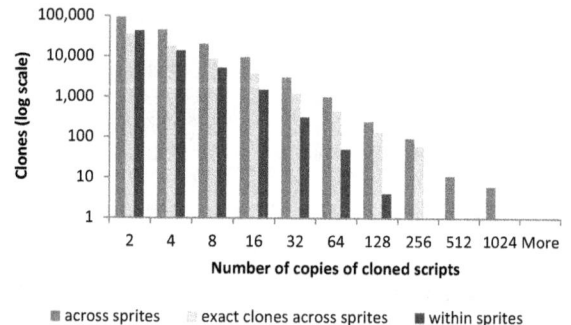

Figure 14: Number of copies of the identified clones

Block	Projects	Occurrences
when <> key pressed	71,096	294,771
when this sprite clicked	39,179	198,342
(Sensing) key <> pressed?	37,919	291,657
(Sensing) ask <> and wait	19,039	66,850
(Sensing) mouse down?	9,115	54,079
(Sensing) <attrib> of <>	9,068	155,468
(Sensing) mouse X	5,977	27,321
(Sensing) mouse Y	3,940	22,035
when <sensor> > <value>	705	1,570
(Sensing) video <> on <>	434	1,397

Table 3: Frequency of use of user input blocks in the 233,491 projects of the dataset

dition> then and if <condition> then else blocks) are used by 39.81% of the projects. Loops (blocks repeat <times>, forever and repeat until <condition>) are more common, used by 77.18% of the projects. The most common of the three is the forever block, accounting for 51.86% of all loops and the least common one is the repeat until <condition> block, accounting for 11.57% of all loops and used in 13.59% of the total projects.

Investigating user interactivity functionality, we found that 56.24% of the projects in the dataset contain user input blocks—an average of 8.48 blocks per such project. Table 3 lists the frequency of use of user input controls. We do not include the when Green flag pressed block here, as this is just used to start a Scratch program and hence cannot be considered input into the program. The most commonly used user input block is the when key pressed, found in 71,096 (30.45% of the total) projects. The most frequently used parameter for the key attribute is the space key, followed by the arrows and then the letters and numbers.

As detailed in Section 2, users can define their own events, using the blocks broadcast, broadcast and wait and when I receive. These blocks are used in 29.57% of the projects. broadcast and wait is rarely used, in 3.87% of the projects.

RQ2: A small number of projects (8%) use procedures, but they use them a lot and for more complex code. Most procedures are called once or twice, from a single script which, in more than half of the cases, is another procedure. Recursive procedure calls exist in 1,052 (0.5% of the total) projects. One third of the projects use variables, sometimes without initializing them. 40% of the projects contain conditional statements and 77% contain loops, but conditional loops are rarely used. More than half of the projects are interactive. 30% of the projects use broadcast and receive blocks.

4.3 Code smells

The duplicated code smell is the first smell that we examine. As explained in Section 3.2, we use 5 as the minimum number of blocks for the identified clones. In total, in the dataset we found 170,532 scripts cloned across sprites in 59,634 (25.54% of the total non-empty) projects. 726,316 copies of these scripts were found, making each clone being copied an average of 4.26 times. Figure 13 plots the distribution of clones across projects. The majority of projects contain up to two cloned scripts. Figure 14 plots the number of copies of the identified clones. It is of interest that 79,378 (46.55%) of the identified clones are copied three or more times, and even in 585 cases from 411 projects they are copied more than 50 times and up to 974.[4]

We further inspected which of the identified clones were duplicated within the same sprite: 63,682 (37.34% of the total) clones, in 10.14% of all projects. 2.12% of the projects contain cloned procedure definitions, which were measured to 12,878 (7.55% of the total) clones. Exact clones were found in 11.81% of the total projects. Their total number was 66,750 (39.14% of the total) clones. Exact clones in the same sprite were rare, found in 0.87% of the projects.

Apart from whole scripts, we also examined cases where scripts differ only in the first (Hat) block. This way we examine if Scratch programmers assign the same functionality to handle different types of events. Cloned functionality blocks are found to be rare: without considering the first block, only 2,243 additional clones were found in 920 projects.

The second smell that we examine is the dead code smell. We identify four types of dead code: (1) procedures that are not invoked, (2) unmatched broadcast-receive messages, (3) code that is not invoked and (4) empty event scripts, i.e., scripts that contain an event block alone. Investigating the first type, we find that a significant number of the defined procedures (13,036 or 5.06%) are not called in the projects. This is also shown in Figure 11 and it occurs in 2,079 projects. For the second type, we examined the broadcast-receive messages and found that they are not always synchronized: 3,33% of the `when I receive` blocks were found to wait for a message that is never being broadcasted, while 4,4% of the `broadcast` blocks broadcast a message that is not being received. This lack of syncronization occurs in 18,669 (7.99% of the total) projects.

The third and fourth cases are incomplete scripts. Those are either never invoked due to the lack of a starting `when <trigger>` block from the Scratch Events or Control category, or are comprised of only a `when <trigger>` block without any functionality. A total of 322,475 scripts like that were found in 56,890 (24.36% of the total) projects. The majority of these scripts (86.6%) are scripts missing a Hat block. Examining the size of these dead scripts, 72.34% are composed of a single block. However, some dead scripts are considerably large; 2,358 dead scripts in 1,553 different projects have more than 30 blocks and up to 2,610.[4]

The number of projects exhibiting the dead code smell, considering all four types of dead code combined, is 65,760 (28.16% of the total projects).

Finally, we examine the large script and the large sprite smells. The thresholds we use for the identification of large scripts and large sprites are 18 blocks and 59 blocks respectively, as explained in Section 3.2. The number of projects exhibiting the large script smell, i.e., containing at least one script with 18 or more blocks, is 69,521 (29.77% of the total projects) and the number of projects with the large sprite smell is 31,954 (13.68%).

> RQ3: Code clones are found in 26% of the projects, with almost half of the clones copied three or more times, in the same or across sprites. 28% of the projects contain code that is never invoked, and thus exhibit the dead code smell. In some cases these scripts are large. The large script smell is found in 30% of the projects and the large sprite one in 14%.

5. DISCUSSION

5.1 Implications

We believe a large scale study of programs like the current can help language designers to tailor their language. In this section we highlight directions in which our study could support language design. There are many other implications to be considered, which is why we have made our dataset public.

5.1.1 Popularity of different block types

Our analysis shows that some categories of blocks are rarely used, like the 'Pen' blocks, of which only 194,885 occur within 19,090 (8.17% of the total) programs. Hence, in future changes to the language, 'Pen' blocks might be less important to users to support or maintain.

5.1.2 Dead code

In our analysis, we find that more than one quarter of the Scratch projects contain dead scripts. In a sense, the dead scripts are harmless, as they are not executed. However, they do cause 'visual clutter' and might be distracting to novice programmers, as it might be hard to see which scripts are dead. In contrast to other visual educational languages, Scratch does not indicate scripts that are dead. LEGO Mindstorms, for example, does give the user feedback on dead blocks by making them gray.

Looking at the number of unconnected blocks, we hypothesize that Scratch programmers have a need for a separate workspace to store unconnected blocks temporarily. We envision that would be like the 'backpack', a Scratch feature meant to move scripts across sprites. In order to help novice programmers keep their code clean, the programming interface could actively encourage users to move unconnected blocks to that workspace when they exit the environment.

5.1.3 Exact clones between sprites

With occurrences in 11% of the Scratch projects in our dataset, the use of exactly identical clones between sprites is relatively common. In a sense, the Scratch users are not to blame for that, as Scratch does not support procedure calls between sprites, only within them. So in many cases there is no way to share the functionality other than by making a copy. We are not aware of the underlying rationale of the Scratch team that lead to this decision, however it seems that a large part of the Scratch users would use the functionality to call procedures between sprites.

5.1.4 Sharing of scripts and procedures

Investigating the use of clones between projects, we observe that there are 1,700 scripts that are used in multiple projects, sometimes as often as in 1,600 different projects. This seems to indicate that there are common patterns in Scratch projects, which means it might be very beneficial to Scratch programmers if they could not only share their projects, but also share some of their functionality, for others to use, like a library. An example of such a library could be: functions for platforming games, including the movement of sprites, collision detection and the implementation of 'lives'. This might empower new Scratch users to get started faster.

5.2 Insights for computing education

Our findings confirm that Scratch is mainly used for its intended purpose as a first-exposure programming environment for creating simple programs and interactive animations: the majority of programs are small and more than half are interactive and contain no conditional statements. The analysis also indicates that computational concepts like conditionals and variables are being applied —conditional statements are found in 40% of the projects and variables in 32%. The same does not hold for loops: even though 77% of the projects contain loops, only 14% contains conditional loops. We attribute the increased use of the `forever` loop to the Scratch language design and we are skeptical over whether it indicates an understanding of loop concepts.

Only 8% of the projects contain procedures, and those use them a lot and for more complex code, which is an indication of use by more experienced programmers. This very essential programming concept is therefore not sufficiently applied, which can be attributed both to limitations imposed by the Scratch environment, like the local scope of procedures, and to the difficulty for internalizing certain computational thinking concepts before a certain age [21].

The high occurrence of cloned scripts (in 26% of the projects) could be the result of the limited use of procedures. Other code smells are also frequently found: 28% of the projects include dead code and 30% have large scripts. Knowing from prior research that long scripts and code duplication decreases ability to understand and modify Scratch programs [10], and that Scratch programmers tend to exhibit certain bad programming habits [14], we believe educating novice programmers on code quality concepts is an issue that should be further researched.

It must be noted that the scope of this study includes the programming artifacts alone. Our findings are limited by the lack of (1) process data and (2) data on the age and other characteristics related to the programmers. However, the project data that is available in our dataset can facilitate further studies on computing education, and this is the reason that we are publishing it.

5.3 Threats to validity

A threat to the validity of this study is the fact that we did not scrape a random sample, but the most recent 250,000 projects. It could be the case that the programming habits of Scratch users are changing over time. However, we counterbalanced that by using a large dataset which comprises around 2% of all 14 million shared Scratch projects[6].

Furthermore we use the number of blocks in the Scratch projects as a measure for the length of a program, while this does not exactly correspond to the 'length' of a program in lines, and there can be multiple Scratch blocks on one line. We however believe that the number of blocks is a good proxy for size, and we plan a future experiment in which we will compare 'lines of Scratch code' to 'number of blocks'.

6. RELATED WORK

The evaluation of block-based languages in general, and Scratch in particular, as tools for programming education has received significant research attention during the past years. A number of studies have been carried out on the understanding of programming concepts and the programming practices of novice programmers in block-based environments, on the programming skills they develop, and on the quality of Scratch programs.

For example, a study on the internalization of programming concepts with Scratch with 46 students was presented in [15]. Concepts like loops, conditional loops, message passing, initialization, variables and concurrency were examined, and it was found that students had problems with the last three. In a later study with an equal set of subjects [14] the same authors identified two bad programming habits in Scratch, namely bottom-up development and extremely fine-grained programming. They connected the later to the

reduced use of if-blocks and finite loops and the increased use of infinite loops, a finding that is verified by our study. In [22], 29 projects created by 60 students working in groups were evaluated based on a list of criteria related to programming concepts, code organization and usability design.

Large-scale analyses of Scratch projects have been performed using the dataset made available by the Lifelong Kindergarten Group at the MIT Media Lab, which contains data for Scratch projects created until 2012, when the web-based programming environment was introduced. In [24], this dataset was used for exploring the learning patterns of programmers in terms of block use over their first 50 projects. Dasgupta et al. investigated how project remixing relates to the adoption of computational thinking concepts [6]. In [7], the use of programming concepts was examined in relation to the level of participation (commenting, remixing, etc), the gender, and the account age of 5,000 Scratch programmers.

Most related to our study for the second research question of programming abstractions and concepts is the work by Maloney et al. [12], who analyzed 536 Scratch projects for blocks that relate to programming concepts including loops, conditional statements, variables, user interaction, synchronization, and random numbers. Compared to their findings, our investigation reveals increased use of the first three concepts, and especially variables.

The Scratch automated quality analysis tools Hairball [2] and Dr. Scratch [17] are also related to our work on smell detection. The Hairball Scratch extension is a lint-like static analysis tool for Scratch that can detect initialization problems and unmatched broadcast and receive blocks. In their work [16], Moreno and Robles extended Hairball to detect two bad programming habits in Scratch: not changing the default object names and duplicating scripts, and apply them for evaluating 100 projects from the Scratch repository. The results on script duplication are substantially different from ours—we find projects with script clones to appear half as frequently. The Dr. Scratch tool [17] includes bad naming, code duplication and dead code identification functionality, and also evaluates Scratch projects in terms of abstraction, parallelism, logical thinking, synchronization, flow control, user interactivity and data representation.

7. CONCLUSIONS

In this paper we presented a large-scale study on 247,798 projects we scraped from the Scratch repository. We analyze these projects in terms of size, complexity, application of programming abstractions and utilization of programming concepts including procedures, variables, conditional statements, loops, and broadcast-receive functionality. We find that procedures and conditional loops are not commonly used. We further investigate the presence of code smells, including code duplication, dead code, long method and large class smells. Our findings indicate that Scratch programs suffer from code smells and especially from dead code and code duplication.

In addition to the findings presented in this paper, we provide as contributions the dataset that we used for our study, as well as the project identifiers and information on the edge cases that we found in the dataset in terms of size and number of procedures, variables, cyclomatic complexity, clones and dead code.[4]

---

[6]https://scratch.mit.edu/statistics/

8. REFERENCES

[1] T. L. Alves, C. Ypma, and J. Visser. Deriving metric thresholds from benchmark data. In *26th IEEE International Conference on Software Maintenance (ICSM 2010)*, pages 1–10. IEEE Computer Society, 2010.

[2] B. Boe, C. Hill, M. Len, G. Dreschler, P. Conrad, and D. Franklin. Hairball: Lint-inspired Static Analysis of Scratch Projects. In *Proceeding of the 44th ACM Technical Symposium on Computer Science Education*, SIGCSE '13, pages 215–220, New York, NY, USA, 2013. ACM.

[3] K. Brennan, C. Balch, and M. Chung. *Creative Computing*. Harvard Graduate School of Education, 2014.

[4] M. Conway, R. Pausch, R. Gossweiler, and T. Burnette. Alice: A Rapid Prototyping System for Building Virtual Environments. In *Conference Companion on Human Factors in Computing Systems*, CHI '94, pages 295–296, New York, NY, USA, 1994. ACM.

[5] S. Cooper, W. Dann, and R. Pausch. Teaching Objects-first in Introductory Computer Science. In *Proceedings of the 34th SIGCSE Technical Symposium on Computer Science Education*, SIGCSE '03, pages 191–195, New York, NY, USA, 2003. ACM.

[6] S. Dasgupta, W. Hale, A. Monroy-Hernández, and B. M. Hill. Remixing as a pathway to computational thinking. In *Proceedings of the 19th ACM Conference on Computer-Supported Cooperative Work & Social Computing*, CSCW '16, pages 1438–1449, New York, NY, USA, 2016. ACM.

[7] D. A. Fields, M. Giang, and Y. Kafai. Programming in the wild: Trends in youth computational participation in the online scratch community. In *Proceedings of the 9th Workshop in Primary and Secondary Computing Education*, WiPSCE '14, pages 2–11, New York, NY, USA, 2014. ACM.

[8] M. Fowler. *Refactoring: improving the design of existing code*. Addison-Wesley Longman Publishing Co., Inc., Boston, MA, USA, 1999.

[9] E. Glinert. Towards "Second Generation" Interactive, Graphical Programming Environments. In *Proceedings of the IEEE Workshop on Visual Languages*, pages 61—70, 1986.

[10] F. Hermans and E. Aivaloglou. Do code smells hamper novice programming? In *Proceedings of the International Conference on Program Comprehension*, 2016. to appear.

[11] F. Hermans, M. Pinzger, and A. van Deursen. Detecting and refactoring code smells in spreadsheet formulas. *Empirical Software Engineering*, 20(2):549–575, 2015.

[12] J. H. Maloney, K. Peppler, Y. Kafai, M. Resnick, and N. Rusk. Programming by choice: Urban youth learning programming with scratch. In *Proceedings of the 39th SIGCSE Technical Symposium on Computer Science Education*, SIGCSE '08, pages 367–371, New York, NY, USA, 2008. ACM.

[13] T. J. McCabe. A complexity measure. *IEEE Trans. Software Eng.*, 2(4):308–320, 1976.

[14] O. Meerbaum-Salant, M. Armoni, and M. Ben-Ari. Habits of programming in scratch. In *Proceedings of the 16th Annual Joint Conference on Innovation and Technology in Computer Science Education*, ITiCSE '11, pages 168–172, New York, NY, USA, 2011. ACM.

[15] O. Meerbaum-Salant, M. Armoni, and M. M. Ben-Ari. Learning Computer Science Concepts with Scratch. In *Proceedings of the Sixth International Workshop on Computing Education Research*, ICER '10, pages 69–76, New York, NY, USA, 2010. ACM.

[16] J. Moreno and G. Robles. Automatic detection of bad programming habits in scratch: A preliminary study. In *2014 IEEE Frontiers in Education Conference (FIE)*, pages 1–4, Oct. 2014.

[17] J. Moreno-León, G. Robles, and M. Román-González. Dr. Scratch: Automatic Analysis of Scratch Projects to Assess and Foster Computational Thinking. *RED : Revista de Educación a Distancia*, (46):1–23, Jan. 2015.

[18] B. Moskal, S. Cooper, and D. Lurie. Evaluating the Effectiveness of a New Instructional Approach. In *Proceedings of the SIGCSE technical symposium on Computer science education*, 2005.

[19] T. W. Price and T. Barnes. Comparing Textual and Block Interfaces in a Novice Programming Environment. In *Proceedings of the Eleventh Annual International Conference on International Computing Education Research*, ICER '15, pages 91–99, New York, NY, USA, 2015. ACM.

[20] M. Resnick, J. Maloney, A. Monroy-Hernãândez, N. Rusk, E. Eastmond, K. Brennan, A. Millner, E. Rosenbaum, J. Silver, B. Silverman, and Y. Kafai. Scratch: Programming for All. *Commun. ACM*, 52(11):60–67, Nov. 2009.

[21] L. Seiter and B. Foreman. Modeling the learning progressions of computational thinking of primary grade students. In *Proceedings of the Ninth Annual International ACM Conference on International Computing Education Research*, ICER '13, pages 59–66, New York, NY, USA, 2013. ACM.

[22] A. Wilson, T. Hainey, and T. Connolly. Evaluation of computer games developed by primary school children to gauge understanding of programming concepts. In *European Conference on Games Based Learning*, page 549. Academic Conferences International Limited, 2012.

[23] D. Wolber, H. Abelson, E. Spertus, and L. Looney. *App Inventor: Create Your Own Android Apps*. O'Reilly Media, Sebastopol, Calif, 1 edition edition, May 2011.

[24] S. Yang, C. Domeniconi, M. Revelle, M. Sweeney, B. U. Gelman, C. Beckley, and A. Johri. Uncovering trajectories of informal learning in large online communities of creators. In *Proceedings of the Second (2015) ACM Conference on Learning @ Scale*, L@S '15, pages 131–140, New York, NY, USA, 2015. ACM.

Control-Flow-Only Abstract Syntax Trees for Analyzing Students' Programming Progress

David Hovemeyer
York College of Pennsylvania
dhovemey@ycp.edu

Arto Hellas
University of Helsinki
avihavai@cs.helsinki.fi

Andrew Petersen
University of Toronto
Mississauga
petersen@cs.toronto.edu

Jaime Spacco
Knox College
jspacco@knox.edu

ABSTRACT

The abstraction of student code for use in automated analysis is a key challenge. The code must be processed in a manner that reveals interesting properties while reducing the "noise" introduced by less important details. In this work, we investigate the importance of control flow as a property in the analysis of students' programming processes.

We introduce the Control-Flow Abstract Syntax Tree (CFAST), a representation of source code that focuses on control structures, and apply it in an analysis of a large, multinational dataset of introductory programming exercises. We provide data on how many different control-flow designs are observed, how quickly students identify a "correct" control flow structure, and how much additional work is required to convert a correct structure to a correct program.

Our results indicate that while even simple problems yield a surprising number of CFASTs, the work of most students can be mapped to a small number of CFASTs. CFASTs that map to fewer submissions tend to be larger, and more complex, but they can still correspond to "correct" solutions to the problem.

1. INTRODUCTION

Modern learning environments are recording an increasingly detailed view of student working behaviours, resulting in a veritable gold mine for researchers. This is particularly true in courses such as introductory programming, where the emergence of easy-to-adopt automatic assessment systems and the need for students to spend considerable time working on practice assignments have combined to produce significant amounts of data about novice programmers. As a result, educational data mining and learning analytics in the context of computer science education has grown significantly over the last decade [19].

With the increase of both data granularity and quantity,

ICER '16, September 08-12, 2016, Melbourne, VIC, Australia
© 2016 ACM. ISBN 978-1-4503-4449-4/16/09... $15.00
DOI: http://dx.doi.org/10.1145/2960310.2960326

researchers face a question about what level of detail should be retained during analysis. Snapshots of programming exercises can, for example, be represented simply with numeric information (a timestamp and a score), as a string representing the submitted code, or in a format that encodes information about the structure of the solution, like an abstract syntax tree. In any case, the chosen granularity plays a large role in the quantity of explorable states [50], and it may even be the case that too fine-grained data simply introduces noise to the analysis process.

In this work, we explore the use of control-flow focused representations in analysis of novice programmer data. Our intuition is that control flow — conditions, decisions, and loops — forms the essential structure of any algorithm expressed in an imperative programming language. Selecting and interleaving appropriate plans to produce a workable control structure is a challenging task [43,44] and is necessary (although not sufficient) to solve any nontrivial programming problem [16, 26].

We introduce a variant of abstract syntax trees called a Control-Flow Abstract Syntax Tree (CFAST). A CFAST only includes control flow elements such as `while`, `if` and `for` and enclosing contexts sufficient to maintain sequence and nesting relationships between the control elements. Our goal, then, is to assess the usefulness of control flow structure in categorizing novice programmer submissions to programming exercises. In particular:

RQ 1. Do CFASTs encode useful information about student programming behaviour?

    1.1 Do the solutions map to a small number of CFASTs?

    1.2 How do students add control elements to code?

    1.3 If the control structure in a submission is correct, does it remain correct in subsequent submissions?

RQ 2. Can CFASTs be used to identify students in difficulty?

    2.1 At what point in their programming process do students reach a CFAST that corresponds with a correct solution?

    2.2 Do sequences of CFASTs encode evidence of ineffective programming behaviours?

This article is organized as follows. In Section 2 we review the body of work related to how students construct computer programs and focus on work related to schemas, plans and plan composition. In Section 3, we describe the data sources used in our analysis and discuss the CFAST structure in more detail. We outline the results from our evaluation of CFAST structures in Section 4 and highlight key findings in more detail in Section 5. Finally, in Section 6, we conclude the article and outline potential future work.

2. RELATED WORK

In their influential review of computer science education research, Robins et al. suggest that "the distinction between effective and ineffective novices" is of central importance [34]. Our work adds to the body of knowledge in this area by exploring whether control-flow representations of novice programmer code provide insights into programming ability or evidence that a student is in difficulty.

2.1 Schemas and Plans

In the mid 1980's, Spohrer and Soloway identified several common errors, several of which involved control structures, and argued that these errors were caused by issues with selecting appropriate *plans* (or *schemas*) for solving problems and interleaving such plans [43, 44]. Bellamy and Gilmore, in contrast, argue that programmers frequently use other representations, including control-flow based representations, when solving problems [3]. Regardless, work on schema acquisition suggests that programmers demonstrate "backwards development" as plans are being formulated and "forward development" when previously stored plan schema are accessed and implemented [12, 29]. More recent work on problem solving techniques used by a small number of high school aged students found a similar preference for bottom-up strategies of problem solving [21]. This work suggests that an analysis of a sequence of control flow representations of programs, if the data is sufficiently fine-grained, may be able to identify when a student is formulating a new plan, rather than implementing a previously observed plan.

Soloway introduced the Rainfall problem as an example of a simple problem that required interleaving of plans [40]. A successful solution to Rainfall reads integers from standard input and, after all integers have been entered, outputs the average, with some variants also requiring that negative numbers be identified as errors or that additional output be generated. In particular, since the number of integers to be entered is not pre-defined, the problem requires interleaving plans that involve control (sentries and repetition).

There has been a recent resurgence of research on Rainfall and, more generally, in plan composition [14, 15, 23, 37, 38]. In 2013, Simon noted that the Rainfall problem appeared to have become more difficult and suggested that unfamiliarity with input-based loop control patterns may be the cause [38]. Some later researchers found that the problem was no more difficult, with Fisler arguing that the method of instruction, including teaching certain control-based patterns, might explain the difference in results [14]. Seppala et al. argued that differences in observed difficulty could be attributed to varying formulations of the problem and levels of experience in participants [37]. Lakanen et al. did not comment on difficulty but found that most students could design a program with a viable high-level control structure — one that reflected the control flow taught in class to deal with data from an array — but often failed to deal with edge cases [23].

Other modern research on plans and plan composition

have proposed a shift away from Rainfall and other IO-driven problems [15], but control flow structures remain an important feature of the problems being studied. Many errors in plan composition resulting in malformed or inappropriately structured control [16, 26], and analysis of control flow will be able to some, but not all of these, invalid programs. For example, errors that introduce (or omit) control structures could be identified with an analysis of control structures in a program, but errors that result in a different condition (but the same structure) require a more precise analysis.

Building on this potential to differentiate between correct and invalid program designs, Luxton-Reilly et al. proposed using control flow as the first level of a taxonomy designed to categorize student solutions to coding problems [24]. They used control flow graphs (CFGs) to represent control in programs. The taxonomy was evaluated by asking CS1 students to provide solutions to a set of ten problems (five with conditionals and five with loops). They found that even submissions to the simplest problems exhibited large numbers of CFGs (6-58, with half containing more than 50), including a large number of "correct" CFGs. For many problems, there was a clear "most popular answer", but several exercises featured a number of CFGs with comparable numbers of correct submissions, and several bins contained only a single, "correct" submission. These observations demonstrate significant variation in the complexity of student submissions, even for simple problems, and suggest that there might be value in evaluating the "quality" of a control flow representation, such as a CFG, by comparing it to a reference solution.

2.2 Novice Programmers and Control

Researchers have also examined control structures separate from schemas and plans to identify the roots of misconceptions commonly held by novice programmers. In the early 1980's, Soloway et al. identified student strategies for solving loop problems [41], and related studies by Bonar and Soloway suggested that misconceptions of the "while" loop were based on natural language interpretations of the word "while" [4, 5]. They suggested that novice programmers have less problems with post-test loops, since the natural interpretation of "until" better matches the actual execution of such loops.

This result has been confirmed by several independent groups. As part of the "commonsense computing" series, Simon et al. investigated what students with no experience programming know about programming concepts and found that they prefer post-test loops [39], and VanDeGrift et al. found that students performed better when both sides of a conditional were explicitly defined [49]. Separately, Craig et al. looked for evidence of "natural" representations of programming concepts in knitting patterns [9]. They confirmed a preference for post-test loops and identified a preference for terminating ("stop when"), rather than continuing ("continue while"), conditions in loops. Stefik et al. focused on word choice and noted that non-programmers rated the most common keywords for loops (including "for" and "while") as the most unintuitive and the word "repeat" as the most intuitive [45, 46].

Loop problems feature prominently in research on student understanding of programming concepts, since they are a major, challenging component of CS1 courses [18, 48] and are a common source of errors [36]. Robins et al. reviewed questions asked by students during a lab and noted that while conditionals and loops generated many questions, students improved in their ability to solve such problems over time [33]. This contrasts with questions about reference types and scope, which remained at a high volume throughout the course. In contrast, later work by Cherenkova et al. mined student submissions to programming exercises and found control structures — both conditionals and loops — to be particularly challenging and to remain challenging relative to other course topics [8]. However, since the exercises were featured in a Python course that taught objects late, it is possible that the topics identified by Robins et al. as being more difficult were simply not encountered.

2.3 Code Mining and Analytics

Ihantola et al., an ITiCSE working group, surveyed the state of educational data mining in 2015 and concluded that there has been a significant increase, over the past decade, in the number of papers that use data mining techniques to study computer science education [19]. Their work contains a comprehensive survey of papers from 2005–2015 that, like this paper, mine large sets of programming data to better understand novice programmers.

One thread of research in this area is focused on finding heuristics to identify students who are frustrated [35] or to predict novice programmer performance [20, 27, 47, 52]. Watson et al. claimed in 2014 that programming behaviour is an effective predictor of student performance in CS1 and showed that their algorithm outperformed various traditional predictors of performance [51].

Much of the early work in this area relies on the insight that syntactic errors are a significant issue for novice programmers [10, 11, 25, 46]. The most prominent early work in this area was performed by Jadud, who suggested that sequential submissions featuring syntactic errors was an indicator of a student in need of assistance [20]. Later work, by Spacco et al., examined submission traces and identified evidence of students *flailing* and increased ability, over the course of the term, in producing syntactically correct programs [42].

However, other recent work has expanded the set of features in an attempt to model the student programming process. Carter et al. explicitly extended previous work to model programming process as a state machine [6, 7]. Others have started to incorporate semantic correctness, as evaluated by tests: Koprinska et al. used submission times as well as improvement over a sequence of submissions [22], and Ahadi et al. identified students at risk after just one week of the term using the number of steps required to reach a correct solution and the the number of tests passed, among other non-programming exercise factors [1]. Pettit et al. used traditional software metrics like cyclomatic complexity to describe how student submissions to coding exercises evolved over time [28]. In total, these projects suggest that other features, like control-flow structure, must be integrated into our models of student behaviour and performance.

Another thread of research examines methods for using student submissions to provide feedback. Glassman et al. clusters submissions and proposes providing examples from other clusters [17]. The proposed clustering relies on a number of features, including structural (control-based) features. Other groups provide hints by comparing a novice's current submission to a reference solution [2], by transforming submissions into a canonical abstract syntax tree (AST) form and comparing to other student submissions [30–32], and finding related questions and study material based on pat-

Course	Total # activities	Concepts addressed		
		if	loops	both
1	9	0	4	5
2	9	5	2	2
3	9	4	5	0

Table 1: Summary of activities analyzed in each course

Function template and PyDoc

```
def insert(lst, v):
    """(list of int, int) -> NoneType
    Insert v into lst just before the rightmost
    item greater than v, or at index 0 if no
    items are greater than v.

    >>> my_list = [3, 10, 4, 2]
    >>> insert(my_list, 5)
    >>> my_list
    [3, 5, 10, 4, 2]
    >>> my_list = [5, 4, 2, 10]
    >>> insert(my_list, 20)
    >>> my_list
    [20, 5, 4, 2, 10]
    """
```

Python source code   *CFAST*

```
def insert(lst, v):          FunctionDef
    if v > max(lst):             If
        lst.insert(0, v)         Else
    else:                          For
        lst.reverse()                If
        for i in range(len(lst)):      Break
            if (v < lst[i]):
                lst.insert(i, v)
                break
```

Figure 1: Example exercise consisting of a Python function template and its PyDoc, source code from a sample student submission, and the corresponding CFAST

terns in submitted problems [13]. These efforts are examples of potential applications of control-focused mining of student submissions.

3. METHODOLOGY

3.1 Data Sources

We have prepared data from CS1 courses taught at three very different institutions. Course 1 was taught at the University of Toronto and Course 2 was taught at the University of Helsinki, both large research universities. Course 3 was taught at York College of Pennsylvania, a small, undergraduate focused college. The first course was taught in Python, the second in Java, and the third in C. All three courses assumed students were entering with little to no programming experience and explicitly taught conditionals and loops in the first half of the course.

Each data set consists of student submissions to a number of programming activities, which range from short exercises

Course/ Activity	Avg. # lines	# distinct (w/ correct)	Avg. subs per student	% in top 20% CFASTs	% in CFAST w/ most correct subs	# CFASTs for 90%	Total correct submissions
1/37	6.9	341 (101)	4.6	89.3	47.7	24	960
1/39	5.6	40 (9)	3.1	98.3	86.1	2	826
1/45	6.8	190 (43)	5.9	95.0	79.9	4	927
1/47	11.5	979 (207)	6.3	75.4	07.9	121	866
1/48	5.9	86 (14)	3.8	97.1	82.1	1	1044
1/59	9.7	239 (45)	5.2	95.1	63.9	6	787
1/63	8.4	491 (143)	8.0	83.2	26.1	73	704
1/64	5.8	180 (69)	3.9	90.2	35.9	16	850
1/84	21.4	232 (97)	2.8	88.1	10.8	35	876
2/018	13.3	7 (3)	6.8	98.9	93.1	4	414
2/021	20.8	12 (5)	6.3	96.6	49.4	6	402
2/023	12.7	5 (3)	6.5	95.6	95.6	3	399
2/024	15.5	17 (8)	16.9	85.7	36.9	9	405
2/026	18.1	15 (7)	7	94.1	57.6	7	376
2/027	17.5	36 (7)	10	93.4	86.8	8	293
2/029	44.5	142 (25)	29.5	78.6	33.9	25	356
2/035	15.0	27 (6)	13.8	94.4	88.9	6	149
2/041	22.7	96 (26)	29.7	69.6	17.4	28	226
3/111222333444	13.0	39 (5)	8.5	93.9	78.8	2	76
3/bananana	9.3	9 (3)	4.3	98.6	98.6	1	87
3/checkinput	12.2	32 (8)	7.4	90.9	78.8	2	72
3/doublecoupon	11.7	9 (4)	3.9	36.0	53.5	2	110
3/keepdoubling	12.5	22 (10)	10.6	89.2	74.3	4	87
3/memberdiscount	19.4	31 (12)	5.4	84.4	37.7	6	92
3/restaurant	12.3	18 (7)	3.6	80.7	74.7	4	101
3/squares	13.3	22 (9)	11.8	87.3	69.8	4	70
3/triplecoupon	16.0	12 (7)	4.2	71.8	47.1	4	105

Table 2: Summary statistics for CFASTs in each activity: average number of lines of non-blank/non-comment lines of code submitted by students for each exercise, number of distinct CFASTs (and size of subset containing any correct submissions), avg. number of submissions per student, percentage of students whose final CFAST was in the top 20% most frequently observed CFASTs, percentage of students whose final submission was in the single CFAST with the most correct submissions, number of CFASTs needed to account for 90% of all submissions, and total number of correct submissions

to more substantial programming problems. All of the activities were presented to students using integrated programming environments in which students are able to submit answers to coding problems an unlimited number of times and receive feedback from a suite of automated tests after each submission. Therefore, each submission represents an explicit decision by the student to submit her code for automated testing, and encodes the time of submission, code submitted, and results of the tests.

The data sets do not include all of the problems presented to students. We selected the required exercises that focus on control-flow topics, omitting optional exercises, exercises with no control flow, and exercises that focused on more advanced topics such as classes or reference parameters. Table 1 summarizes the activities that were selected.

It's clear, from the topics addressed, that the programming exercises were very different, and these differences reflect the intended use of the exercises. In Course 1, the activities were intended to be challenging, formative feedback, with integration of concepts highlighted. In contrast, in Course 2 assignments were typically first introduced as isolated practice assignments, and then integrated together, and in Course 3, the exercises were designed to evaluate basic proficiency in individual concepts in the course, without integration.

3.2 Constructing CFASTs

For each student code submission, we construct a *CFAST*, meaning "Control-Flow only Abstract Syntax Tree". Prior work has focused on control flow graphs (CFGs) [24], which are typically constructed for individual functions and encode all possible control paths through the function. In contrast, CFASTs can be easily constructed over entire programs, and rather than encoding control paths, they reflect *control structure*: the specific syntactic elements chosen to implement the control and how they are sequenced and nested.

To construct a CFAST, we use a standard library to parse a program and generate a full abstract syntax tree (AST). Submissions which cannot be parsed (for example, because of a syntax error) cannot be analyzed. Then, we walk the resulting AST, pruning nodes that do not represent control-flow structures. Note that, for this analysis, the conditions used to direct control are also discarded. They could be retained in future work, but for the purposes of this study, we chose to focus solely on control structure.

For example, when constructing a CFAST for a C language submission, the only AST nodes retained are if and else statements; loop statements; and break, continue, and return. Block nodes are used to contain a sequence of statements nested in a function definition, loop, or if, and are retained only when they contain control structures. The resulting structure maintains structural relationships (sequences and nesting) as well as the specific keywords chosen to implement control in the program. Figure 1 shows an example of a Python program and its corresponding CFAST. Indentation is used to indicate the tree structure of the CFAST.

Table 2 lists summary statistics about the CFASTs of student submissions in each activity.

3.3 Threats to Validity

This study is necessarily limited by the type of data used and the methods applied. We selected data from a range of institutions, but the topics and formats of questions that generated the data are limited. Our programming assignments are typically small exercises from the early weeks of CS1 courses that feature an imperative programming approach. In addition, the exercises selected were built to focus on control topics and do not contain structures introduced later, like classes.

As we rely on quantitative methods applied to anonymous submissions, our analyses are blind to the individual contexts of the students represented in the data set. In particular, we cannot know the thought processes that lead to the events we have observed. Our hypotheses on individuals struggling with specific constructs are *interpretations* based on experience, rather than evidence-based observations. Similarly, we do not know why students submitted their code. While we expect that the majority of submissions were attempts to obtain feedback or to submit a potentially complete solution, it's possible that the student was choosing, for example, to store the solution on the server for future work or unknowingly submitted several times due to an unresponsive network connection.

Finally, when contrasting the CFAST path lengths to course outcomes, we chose to use exam scores as a proxy of knowledge or skill despite knowing that it is a rather poor metric. It was selected as being the only supervised evaluation of student ability that was available from all three institutions.

4. RESULTS

4.1 Evaluating RQ 1

In RQ 1, we were interested in finding out whether CFASTs were a useful lens through which to understand student code, both statically and over time. To make this question more concrete, we identified three specific components, 1.1–1.3.

4.1.1 RQ 1.1

RQ 1.1 asks "Do student solutions converge on similar or identical CFASTs?" We approached this question in two ways.

For each activity, we counted the percentage of students whose last submission was (a) in the top 20% of most frequently observed CFASTs, and (b) in the single CFAST with the most correct submissions. The fifth and sixth columns of Table 2 show the results.

From this data, it is clear that for all activities, a large majority of all submissions fall under a relatively small number of CFASTs. This confirms the hypothesis that most students will use similar or identical control flow structures when solving the same problem. We also see that for *many* activities, the CFAST with the most correct submissions contains a

Course/Activity	(a)	(b)	(c)	(d)	(e)
1/37	54.1	43.5	43.5	45.9	82.2
1/39	76.2	52.5	52.5	23.8	88.5
1/45	79.6	42.9	42.9	20.4	83.0
1/47	38.1	27.1	27.1	61.9	82.0
1/48	81.4	56.1	56.1	18.6	80.5
1/59	57.7	45.0	45.0	42.3	88.3
1/63	57.6	31.3	31.3	42.4	89.8
1/64	34.2	25.4	25.4	65.8	87.9
1/84	44.7	40.7	40.7	55.3	89.0
2/018	99.7	99.7	38.8	0.3	61.4
2/021	80.0	79.4	28.7	20.0	63.2
2/023	91.9	91.9	28.9	8.1	77.8
2/024	82.4	80.0	9.1	17.6	40.0
2/026	81.3	76.2	29.3	18.7	68.5
2/027	79.6	78.6	25.5	20.4	22.5
2/029	82.4	80.2	6.2	17.6	9.2
2/035	95.5	92.6	17.2	4.5	5.7
2/041	87.7	84.6	7.9	12.3	2.5
3/111222333444	79.5	76.4	12.1	20.5	16.7
3/bananana	91.4	80.2	42.0	08.6	56.2
3/checkinput	82.1	68.5	15.3	17.9	34.8
3/doublecoupon	80.6	75.6	32.5	19.4	41.9
3/keepdoubling	86.5	71.6	07.6	13.5	35.1
3/memberdiscount	75.7	73.3	19.8	24.3	40.3
3/restaurant	80.6	77.4	23.9	19.4	45.8
3/squares	90.1	67.6	11.0	09.9	30.2
3/triplecoupon	79.8	78.8	23.2	20.2	44.7

Table 3: **For all partially-correct submissions, the percentage of the time the next submission was observed to be (a) in the same CFAST, (b) at least partially correct and in the same CFAST, (c) fully correct and in the same CFAST, and (d) in a different CFAST. In addition, (e) indicates the percentage of students without successive submissions from a partially correct submission.**

substantial percentage of all correct submissions. Anecdotally, we found that the single CFAST with the most correct submissions tended to correspond to the "obvious" control structure. However, we do see some notable exceptions: for example, activities 1/47, 2/041, and 3/memberdiscount all had a significant degree of variation in the CFASTs of correct solutions. Significantly, all of these exercises included chained or independent decisions.

To further investigate the amount of variation in correct solutions, we counted how many CFASTs were required to account for 90% of all correct solutions for each programming activity. This data is shown in the seventh column of Table 2. Again, in general a relatively small number of control-flow structures accounts for most correct submissions, but we do see certain activities leading to a greater than usual variety of correct solutions, such as 1/47.

4.1.2 RQ 1.2

RQ 1.2 asks, "How do students add control flow elements to their code?" We conducted two analyses to address this question.

As a way of tracking changes in control flow over student work histories, we computed the tree edit distance [53] between the CFASTs of successive pairs of submissions in each

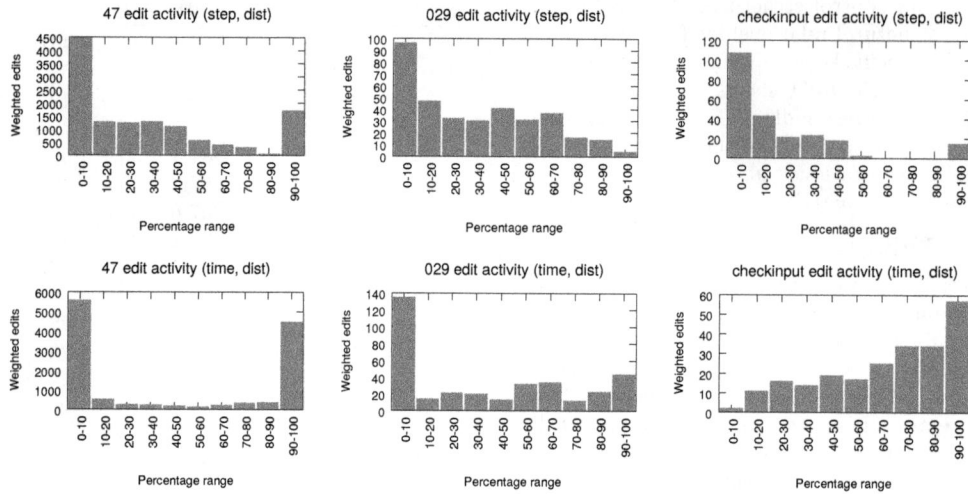

Figure 2: Step- and time- accumulated edit distance for three activities (1/47, 2/029, and 3/checkinput)

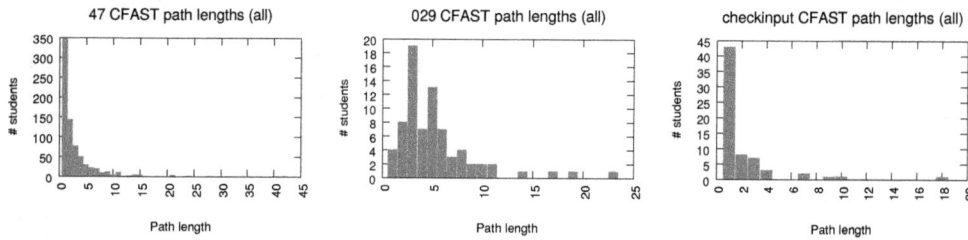

Figure 3: Histograms of CFAST path lengths for three selected activities (1/47, 2/029, and 3/checkinput)

student's work history, assigning a weight of 1 to each deletion, insertion, and replacement. Note that this metric takes only changes to the CFAST into account, and ignores code changes which do not affect the CFAST. To visualize the resulting data, we constructed histograms showing the accumulated edit distance over all adjacent pairs of submissions. We analyzed both step-wise and time-wise[1] chronology, using percentages to represent step or time, with 0% being the first step or the start of work, and 100% being the last step or the end of work. Figure 2 shows examples of accumulated edit distance for three activities.

We can see some interesting patterns in these histograms. The CFAST edits (which represent changes in the control structure) tend to occur early in the sequence of submissions (steps), which we interpret as indicating that students tend not to submit their work for testing until they arrive at something approximating their final control structure, although subsequent fine-tuning does occur at least some of the time. The time data for courses 1 and 2 is somewhat similar, showing changes occurring early. (The surge in edits at the end

---

[1]Note that the time-based chronology is computed differently for the three courses. For courses 1 and 2, time is based on absolute submission timestamps. For course 3, in which fine-grained edit events are available, time is relative to the time the student actually spent working, under the assumption that any interval of 5 minutes or more between edit events represents a break in the student's work.

of the steps in activity 1/47 is largely due to students who completed the activity with a single submission, which we treated as occurring at the end of the timeline.) The time-wise histogram for 3/checkinput looks quite different because we were able to track student work sessions more precisely, and could account for the student work which preceded the first submission.

Another way to understand control-flow changes is to examine the paths — sequences of CFASTs — by which students arrive at either a correct solution or their last submission. A path whose length is 1 indicates a student who did not make any changes to the control-flow structure of her program over time. A longer path indicates a student who tried different control-flow structures over time. Figure 3 summarizes the CFAST paths as a histogram of path lengths for three selected activities. One interesting phenomenon we can observe from the path histograms is that most paths are fairly short, meaning few or no changes in control structure over time. We also observe that there is a long tail in each histogram showing a few students who tried a variety of control structures, possibly returning to previously-tried structures. We will have more to say about this phenomenon in Section 4.2.2.

4.1.3 RQ 1.3

RQ 1.3 asks, "Once a student has control flow correct in code, does it remain correct?"

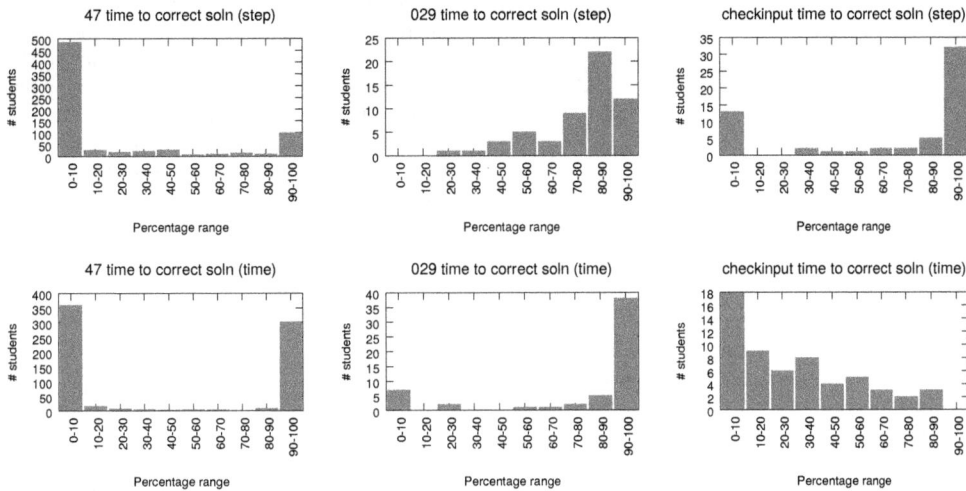

Figure 4: Histogram of time required to complete a correct solution after first reaching the final CFAST form, expressed as a percentage of total steps/duration, for three selected activities (1/47, 2/029, and 3/checkinput)

To address this question, we examined all consecutive pairs of submissions in all student work histories where the first submission was at least partially correct, and counted how often the next submission (a) had the same CFAST, (b) had the same CFAST and was at least partially correct, (c) had the same CFAST and was completely correct, and (d) used a different CFAST. In addition, (e) indicates the percentage of students *without* consecutive submissions, which is important for interpreting the other columns. Table 3 presents the results of this analysis.

One observation regarding the data in Table 3 is that there are significant variations by course. Courses 2 and 3 both exhibit a fairly strong tendency for subsequent submissions to stay in the same CFAST, and a fairly low percentage of students who have only a single submission. These courses tend to support the hypothesis that students arrive at an intended control flow pattern earlier rather than later, and tend to stick with it. In contrast, in Course 1, the probability of a subsequent submission remaining in the same CFAST is lower, and the probability of students not having subsequent submissions is higher. We believe that because the activities in Course 1 are, in general, harder than those in Courses 2 and 3, there is a higher percentage of students in course 1 who give up, and also a higher incidence of plan changes for the students who persist.

4.2 RQ 2

In RQ 2, we were interested in whether CFASTs would shed any light on whether students are working productively or struggling. We identified two concrete component questions, RQ 2.1 and RQ 2.2.

4.2.1 RQ 2.1

RQ 2.1 asks, "At what point in their programming process do students reach a CFAST that corresponds with a correct solution?"

We assessed this question somewhat indirectly. Figure 4 shows step-wise and time-wise histograms of time to reach a correct solution as a percentage of the total time (number of steps or elapsed time), for three selected activities.

Shorter time to correct solution corresponds to later emergence of control structure. We observe that there is some tendency for the "final" CFAST form to appear either early or late in a student's work history.[2] Activity 2/029 is an interesting exception, with different students' final control structures appearing at many different points in the students' work histories. One explanation for this difference is that this activity included a visualization, encouraging experimentation with different control structures, and also included intermediate milestones, encouraging submissions with partial functionality to a greater degree than most of the other activities.

4.2.2 RQ 2.2

RQ 2.2 asks, "Do sequences of CFASTs encode evidence of ineffective programming behaviours?" We identified one metric which we supposed might be correlated with academic performance: CFAST path length, meaning the extent to which student work histories were observed to exhibit changes in control structure from submission to submission. Specifically, we surmised that students who had greater mastery of control structures would change them less often, and thus we would see a negative correlation between path lengths and academic performance.

To test this hypothesis, we computed the sum of the lengths of the observed CFAST paths for each student, and computed the correlation with exam scores. For Courses 1 and 2, we used the course's written final exam score, and for Course 3, we used the programming question scores for the second midterm exam (which was the exam focusing the most on control structures.) Table 4 shows the results.

For Course 1, there was a significant but weak negative correlation between cumulative path lengths and exam scores. For Course 2, we see no statistically significant correlation. For Course 3, we see a significant moderate negative correla-

---

[2]Note that because students who have a single submission (of which there are a substantial number in activities 1/47 and 3/checkinput) are considered to reach the final CFAST form at the end of the history, these plots may exaggerate the "late" appearance of control structure to some degree.

Course	Exam type	Correlation rho	p-value
1	Final written exam	-0.11	0.008
2	Final written exam	-0.17	0.34
3	*Programming, 2nd midterm*	*-0.40*	*0.003*

Table 4: Correlations between accumulated CFAST path lengths and exam scores

tion. One possible explanation for the significant result for Course 3 but not Courses 1 and 2 is the type of activities used. The activities in Course 3 cover control flow concepts at a relatively basic "application" level, so students who have difficulty constructing a correct control-flow form for such exercises are likely to have important deficits in their concept knowledge. In contrast, Courses 1 and 2 include some more sophisticated "synthesis" activities, where some amount of exploration is expected. In addition, there are other possible confounding factors. For example, students who plagiarize their solutions will have low path length, but may fare poorly on an exam. Another issue is that students who give up early will have low path lengths.

5. DISCUSSION AND CONCLUSIONS

In this study, we explored the applicability of Control-Flow only Abstract Syntax Trees (CFAST) for source code snapshot analysis. We studied whether students' solutions converge to specific CFASTs and how students work with their code through the CFAST representations. We also explored the extent to which CFASTs can be used to identify students in difficulty.

Our findings agree with those of Luxton-Reilly et al. [24]. We confirmed that for *most* exercises, most of the student submissions could be categorized under a relatively small number of control structures. We did notice some interesting exceptions to their findings, however. For a few activities in our study, for example 1/47, there were a very large number of attempted (979) and correct (207) control forms. We posit that additional requirements for conditional logic (if/else) can lead to exponential increase in the number of reasonable solutions to a programming problem.

Here, the order of the assignments and practice likely plays a large role. If the students have already practiced the individual constructs before attempting to construct larger programs – by merging existing plans together — they are likely more successful in the process. At the same time, if the students have not practiced sufficiently the individual constructs beforehand, students may enter a trial-and-error problem solving mode, where their attempts in constructing working solutions to the problems may be rather wild. The data showed a handful of students who show a high degree of trial-and-error behavior, which merits further study. Such behavior — when encoded through the accumulated distinct CFAST path lengths — was not indicative of the performance in a written exam, but had a modest negative correlation with a programming-related midterm.

Overall, changes in control structures, as indicated by CFAST changes, provide some useful insights into students' programming strategies. However, we noticed some phenomena in our data that impeded analysis. For example, it was more common than we anticipated for students to only submit one potential solution for an activity. Often, this was the correct solution for the problem, which means that the students work through the problem (or plagiarize it) on their own, and do not need the feedback from the submission system. It would be meaningful to have access to CFAST changes on the client system even if the students choose to not submit their solutions at every step.

We have several ideas for future work. Use of fine-grained edit information can help to overcome the issue of infrequent student submissions. We would like to conduct more detailed analyses of *how* student code changes over time: for example, do we see implementation of control structures bottom-up or top-down? We think that it may be helpful to introduce some details about non-control-flow constructs into our analysis: for example, upper and lower bounds might be interesting as a way of characterizing loop structures, and might help tease out important correctness requirements within the set of submissions in a single CFAST. Based on our observations that frequently vs. infrequently observed CFASTs tend to correspond to "obvious" vs. "idiosyncratic" control structures, CFASTs may be useful in selecting example solutions (as suggested by Luxton-Reilly et al. [24]) or to automate construction of peer instruction questions.

6. REFERENCES

[1] A. Ahadi, R. Lister, H. Haapala, and A. Vihavainen. Exploring machine learning methods to automatically identify students in need of assistance. In *Proceedings of the Eleventh Annual International Conference on International Computing Education Research*, pages 121–130, 2015.

[2] P. Antonucci, C. Estler, D. Nikolić, M. Piccioni, and B. Meyer. An incremental hint system for automated programming assignments. In *Proceedings of the 2015 ACM Conference on Innovation and Technology in Computer Science Education*, pages 320–325, 2015.

[3] R. Bellamy and D. Gilmore. Programming plans: Internal or external structures. *Lines of thinking: Reflections on the psychology of thought*, 2:59–72, 1990.

[4] J. Bonar and E. Soloway. Uncovering principles of novice programming. In *Proc. 10th ACM SIGACT-SIGPLAN Symposium on Principles of Programming Languages*, pages 10–13, 1983.

[5] J. Bonar and E. Soloway. Preprogramming knowledge: a major source of misconceptions in novice programmers. *Human-Computer Interaction*, 1:133–161, June 1985.

[6] A. S. Carter, C. D. Hundhausen, and O. Adesope. The normalized programming state model: Predicting student performance in computing courses based on programming behavior. In *Proceedings of the Eleventh Annual International Conference on International Computing Education Research*, pages 141–150, 2015.

[7] J. Carter, P. Dewan, and M. Pichiliani. Towards incremental separation of surmountable and insurmountable programming difficulties. In *Proceedings of the 46th ACM Technical Symposium on Computer Science Education*, pages 241–246, 2015.

[8] Y. Cherenkova, D. Zingaro, and A. Petersen. Identifying challenging cs1 concepts in a large problem dataset. In *Proceedings of the 45th ACM Technical*

Symposium on Computer Science Education, pages 695–700, 2014.

[9] M. Craig, S. Petersen, and A. Petersen. Following a thread: Knitting patterns and program tracing. In *Proceedings of the 43rd ACM Technical Symposium on Computer Science Education*, pages 233–238, 2012.

[10] P. Denny, A. Luxton-Reilly, and E. Tempero. All syntax errors are not equal. In *Proceedings of the 17th Conference on Innovation and Technology in Computer Science Education*, pages 75–80, 2012.

[11] P. Denny, A. Luxton-Reilly, E. Tempero, and J. Hendrickx. Understanding the syntax barrier for novices. In *Proceedings of the 16th Annual Joint Conference on Innovation and Technology in Computer Science Education*, pages 208–212, 2011.

[12] F. Détienne. Design strategies and knowledge in object-oriented programming: Effects of experience. *Hum.-Comput. Interact.*, 10(2):129–169, Sept. 1995.

[13] A. K. Dominguez, K. Yacef, and J. R. Curran. Data Mining for Individualised Hints in e-Learning. In *Proceedings of the International Conference on Educational Data Mining*, pages 91–100, 2010.

[14] K. Fisler. The recurring rainfall problem. In *Proceedings of the Tenth Annual Conference on International Computing Education Research*, pages 35–42, 2014.

[15] K. Fisler, S. Krishnamurthi, and J. Siegmund. Modernizing plan-composition studies. In *Proceedings of the 47th ACM Technical Symposium on Computing Science Education*, pages 211–216, 2016.

[16] D. Ginat, E. Menashe, and A. Taya. Novice difficulties with interleaved pattern composition. In *Proceedings of the 6th International Conference on Informatics in Schools: Situation, Evolution, and Perspectives*, pages 57–67, 2013.

[17] E. L. Glassman, J. Scott, R. Singh, P. J. Guo, and R. C. Miller. Overcode: Visualizing variation in student solutions to programming problems at scale. *ACM Trans. Comput.-Hum. Interact.*, 22(2):7:1–7:35, Mar. 2015.

[18] K. Goldman, P. Gross, C. Heeren, G. Herman, L. Kaczmarczyk, M. C. Loui, and C. Zilles. Identifying important and difficult concepts in introductory computing courses using a delphi process. *SIGCSE Bull.*, 40(1):256–260, Mar. 2008.

[19] P. Ihantola, A. Vihavainen, A. Ahadi, M. Butler, J. Börstler, S. H. Edwards, E. Isohanni, A. Korhonen, A. Petersen, K. Rivers, M. A. Rubio, J. Sheard, B. Skupas, J. Spacco, C. Szabo, and D. Toll. Educational data mining and learning analytics in programming: Literature review and case studies. In *Proceedings of the 2015 ITiCSE on Working Group Reports*, pages 41–63, 2015.

[20] M. C. Jadud. Methods and Tools for Exploring Novice Compilation Behaviour. In *Proc. of the 2nd International Workshop on Computing Education Research*, pages 73–84, 2006.

[21] U. Kiesmueller, S. Sossalla, T. Brinda, and K. Riedhammer. Online Identification of Learner Problem Solving Strategies Using Pattern Recognition Methods. In *Proceedings of the Fifteenth Annual Conference on Innovation and Technology in Computer Science Education*, pages 274–278, New York, NY, USA, 2010.

[22] I. Koprinska, J. Stretton, and K. Yacef. Students at Risk: Detection and Remediation. In *Educational Data Mining*, 2015.

[23] A.-J. Lakanen, V. Lappalainen, and V. Isomöttönen. Revisiting rainfall to explore exam questions and performance on cs1. In *Proceedings of the 15th Koli Calling Conference on Computing Education Research*, Koli Calling '15, pages 40–49, New York, NY, USA, 2015. ACM.

[24] A. Luxton-Reilly, P. Denny, D. Kirk, E. Tempero, and S.-Y. Yu. On the differences between correct student solutions. In *Proceedings of the 18th ACM Conference on Innovation and Technology in Computer Science Education*, pages 177–182, 2013.

[25] D. Moore, A. Parrish, and D. Cordes. Analyzing syntax error patterns among novice programmers. In *Proceedings of the 35th Annual Southeast Regional Conference*, pages 188–190, 1997.

[26] O. Muller, D. Ginat, and B. Haberman. Pattern-oriented instruction and its influence on problem decomposition and solution construction. *SIGCSE Bull.*, 39(3):151–155, June 2007.

[27] A. Petersen, J. Spacco, and A. Vihavainen. An exploration of error quotient in multiple contexts. In *Proceedings of the 15th Koli Calling Conference on Computing Education Research*, pages 77–86, 2015.

[28] R. Pettit, J. Homer, R. Gee, S. Mengel, and A. Starbuck. An empirical study of iterative improvement in programming assignments. In *Proceedings of the 46th ACM Technical Symposium on Computer Science Education*, pages 410–415, 2015.

[29] R. S. Rist. Schema creation in programming. *Cognitive Science*, 13:389–414, 1989.

[30] K. Rivers and K. R. Koedinger. Automatic generation of programming feedback: A data-driven approach. In *The First Workshop on AI-supported Education for Computer Science (AIEDCS 2013)*, page 50, 2013.

[31] K. Rivers and K. R. Koedinger. Automating hint generation with solution space path construction. In *Intelligent Tutoring Systems*, pages 329–339. Springer, 2014.

[32] K. Rivers and K. R. Koedinger. Data-driven hint generation in vast solution spaces: a self-improving python programming tutor. *International Journal of Artificial Intelligence in Education*, pages 1–28, 2015.

[33] A. Robins, P. Haden, and S. Garner. Problem distributions in a CS1 course. In *Proc. 8th Australian Conference on Computing Education*, pages 165–173, 2006.

[34] A. Robins, J. Rountree, and N. Rountree. Learning and teaching programming: A review and discussion. *Computer Science Education*, 13:137–172, 2003.

[35] M. M. T. Rodrigo and R. S. Baker. Coarse-grained detection of student frustration in an introductory programming course. In *Proceedings of the Fifth International Workshop on Computing Education Research Workshop*, pages 75–80, 2009.

[36] M. Satratzemi, V. Dagdilelis, and G. Evagelidis. A System for Program Visualization and Problem-solving Path Assessment of Novice Programmers. In

Proceedings of the 6th Annual Conference on Innovation and Technology in Computer Science Education, pages 137–140, New York, NY, USA, 2001.

[37] O. Seppälä, P. Ihantola, E. Isohanni, J. Sorva, and A. Vihavainen. Do we know how difficult the rainfall problem is? In *Proceedings of the 15th Koli Calling Conference on Computing Education Research*, pages 87–96, 2015.

[38] Simon. Soloway's rainfall problem has become harder. In *Proceedings of the 2013 Learning and Teaching in Computing and Engineering*, LATICE '13, pages 130–135, Washington, DC, USA, 2013.

[39] B. Simon, T.-Y. Chen, G. Lewandowski, R. McCartney, and K. Sanders. Commonsense computing: what students know before we teach (episode 1: sorting). In *Proc. 2nd International Workshop on Computing Education Research*, pages 29–40, 2006.

[40] E. Soloway. Learning to program = learning to construct mechanisms and explanations. *Commun. ACM*, 29(9):850–858, Sept. 1986.

[41] E. Soloway, J. Bonar, and K. Ehrlich. Cognitive strategies and looping constructs: an empirical study. *Comm. of the ACM*, 26:853–860, November 1983.

[42] J. Spacco, P. Denny, B. Richards, D. Babcock, D. Hovemeyer, J. Moscola, and R. Duvall. Analyzing student work patterns using programming exercise data. In *Proc. of the 46th ACM Technical Symposium on Computer Science Education*, pages 18–23, 2015.

[43] J. C. Spohrer and E. Soloway. Novice mistakes: Are the folk wisdoms correct? *Commun. ACM*, 29(7):624–632, July 1986.

[44] J. C. Spohrer, E. Soloway, and E. Pope. A goal/plan analysis of buggy pascal programs. *Hum.-Comput. Interact.*, 1(2):163–207, June 1985.

[45] A. Stefik and E. Gellenbeck. Empirical studies on programming language stimuli. *Software Quality Journal*, 19(1):65–99, 2011.

[46] A. Stefik and S. Siebert. An empirical investigation into programming language syntax. *Trans. Comput. Educ.*, 13(4):19:1–19:40, Nov. 2013.

[47] E. S. Tabanao, Ma, and M. C. Jadud. Predicting At-risk Novice Java Programmers Through the Analysis of Online Protocols. In *Proceedings of the Seventh International Workshop on Computing Education Research*, pages 85–92, 2011.

[48] A. E. Tew and M. Guzdial. Developing a validated assessment of fundamental cs1 concepts. In *Proceedings of the 41st ACM Technical Symposium on Computer Science Education*, SIGCSE '10, pages 97–101, 2010.

[49] T. VanDeGrift, D. Bouvier, T.-Y. Chen, G. Lewandowski, R. McCartney, and B. Simon. Commonsense computing (episode 6): logic is harder than pie. In *Proc. 10th Koli Calling International Conference on Computing Education Research*, pages 76–85, 2010.

[50] A. Vihavainen, M. Luukkainen, and P. Ihantola. Analysis of source code snapshot granularity levels. In *Proceedings of the 15th Annual Conference on Information Technology Education*, SIGITE '14, pages 21–26, New York, NY, USA, 2014. ACM.

[51] C. Watson, F. W. Li, and J. L. Godwin. No tests required: Comparing traditional and dynamic predictors of programming success. In *Proceedings of the 45th ACM Technical Symposium on Computer Science Education*, pages 469–474, 2014.

[52] C. Watson, F. W. B. Li, and J. L. Godwin. Predicting performance in an introductory programming course by logging and analyzing student programming behavior. In *Proceedings of the 2013 IEEE 13th International Conference on Advanced Learning Technologies*, pages 319–323, Washington, DC, USA, 2013.

[53] K. Zhang and D. Shasha. Simple fast algorithms for the editing distance between trees and related problems. *SIAM J. Comput.*, 18(6):1245–1262, Dec. 1989.

Analyzing Student Practices in Theory of Computation in Light of Distributed Cognition Theory

Maria Knobelsdorf

Universität Hamburg
Department of Informatics
Vogt-Kölln-Straße 30

22527 Hamburg, Germany
+49 40 42883 2307

knobelsdorf@informatik.uni-hamburg.de

Christiane Frede

Universität Hamburg
Department of Informatics
Vogt-Kölln-Straße 30

22527 Hamburg, Germany
+49 40 42883 2079

frede@informatik.uni-hamburg.de

ABSTRACT

This paper describes a qualitative study investigating how undergraduate CS majors solved assignments from a Theory of Computation (ToC) course in individually-formed study groups. We use Distributed Cognition Theory as the underlying theoretical framework and ask two research questions: 1) How do students use mathematical notations to work on their assignment, and 2) how and by which means do students assure themselves that their approach is correct? We observed 12 undergraduate CS majors tasked with developing a proof for NP-completeness working in three study groups. Data collected in this study points to students' lack of working proficiency, especially with regard to creating mathematical inscriptions, as a key aspect in their difficulties in solving ToC assignments. This result is significant because it highlights the need to reexamine widely used assumptions about reasons for students' difficulties with ToC, e.g., lack of interest due to abstract and theoretical nature of ToC.

General Terms

Human Factors

Keywords

CS Ed, students, theory of computation, distributed cognition theory, qualitative research, NP-completeness proofs, ethnographical approach, observational study.

ICER '16, September 08-12, 2016, Melbourne, VIC, Australia © 2016 ACM.

ISBN 978-1-4503-4449-4/16/09...$15.00 [SEP]

DOI: http://dx.doi.org/10.1145/2960310.2960331

1. INTRODUCTION

In the course of their undergraduate program, CS majors usually are required to take several courses in Theory of Computation (ToC). However, this has never been a great relationship as many of the students fail or perform poorly on final exams which can even cause students to drop CS as a major. To address the problem and improve the situation, a variety of pedagogical approaches have been introduced in the past decade. For example, Chesñevar et al. introduced the course content within the historical context in which ToC emerged as a new discipline [3], Habiballa et al. contextualized ToC topics with practical examples from professional life [12], Sigman [29] applied discovery learning techniques, Hämäläinen [13] used problem-based learning, Korte et al. [20] developed a constructionist approach with game-building, Wermelinger and Dias [33] and Zingaro [35] offered programming assignments, and Crescenzi et al. [6] build connections to algorithm construction. Another line of research in this field has been tools and environments which were suggested as part of the course's pedagogy, for example [2], [4], [9], [10], [14], [27], [31].

All these suggested approaches present intelligent ideas of how to convey ToC in a more coherent, lively, interactive, and meaningful way to students. At the same time, all of these approaches and tools have been developed with the assumption that students' difficulties with ToC are mainly caused by a lack of interest and ability to understand the abstract concepts and theorems. Unfortunately, none of these assumptions has been empirically validated in advance in order to inform pedagogical considerations by detailed insights about the nature of students' difficulties. We found only two studies focusing precisely on this matter [22], [26] and therefore read the lack of additional studies as a call to action for CS Ed research in this field. We argue that a student-oriented research approach that conducts a detailed investigation into students' difficulties with ToC will provide more sustainable information than general assumptions current pedagogy is based on so far, e.g. [1], [11]. These insights will help creating pedagogy that better addresses the student perspective.

Based on Distributed Cognition Theory as a theoretical framework (see section 2), we have designed a qualitative study investigating how undergraduate CS majors develop proofs to show NP-completeness while working in individually-formed small-sized study groups (sections 3 and 4). The results contain a category system capturing students' activities observed during their study sessions, a detailed report about how three groups developed their proof solution, and a discussion with further interpretations (section 5). The paper concludes by reviewing contributions and outlining further research (section 6).

2. THEORETICAL BACKGROUND

We have built our research on an understanding of teaching and learning shaped by Distributed Cognition Theory (DCog). This theoretical framework has been introduced extensively before, e.g., [8], [30], and thus we will only review key elements of this theory here.

DCog is a theoretical framework that offers a conceptualization of human cognitive processes. This framework is based on Activity Theory which has its roots in Russian cultural-historical psychology [32]. *Activity*, the main concept in Activity Theory, denotes the interaction of people with the world in which they live. Activities of people are assumed to be mediated by material and representational systems (e.g., symbols, inscriptions, visuals), which are often metaphorically referred to as *tools* or *mediational means* [34]. These tools are provided to individuals by their surrounding culture and are passed from one generation to the next. Being socially distributed cultural entities, "tools and the practices of the user community that accompany them are major carriers of patterns of previous reasoning" ([24], p. 53).

Traditional cognitive science research locates cognitive processes solely within the skin and skull of individuals. Taking humans as the unit of analysis, educational research focuses on individuals acquiring, constructing, or processing knowledge. Extending on Activity Theory, DCog argues that cognitive processes are not just individual and mental, but are constituted through a cognitive system as the interplay between one or several human beings, their activities and particular resources, materials or tools used in these activities [17]. The cognition process is understood to be distributed between, several agents, between agents and tools, and/or through time and space ([15], p. 176). "This has the important implication that when understanding learning, we have to consider that the unit that we are studying is people in action using tools of some kind (see Wertsch, 1991, 1998; Säljö 1996). The learning is not only inside the person, but in his or her ability to use a particular set of tools in productive ways and for particular purposes." ([28], p. 147).

Shifting the unit of analysis towards the tight integration between mediational means and cognition opens a new perspective on educational research in ToC [25], [30]. When investigating students' difficulties with learning ToC, we shift the unit of analysis towards the whole cognitive system of which our students are part. This includes other students, especially their individually-formed study groups where collaboration between several agents takes place. It specifically involves mathematical inscriptions, i.e., symbols, visuals and notations specifically designed to conceive theoretical objects and to mediate mental and collaborative processes of human agents that lead to these objects, see also [18]. The traditional cognitive science model would regard lecture notes and slides and their presentation during lecture as a form of repository that is used to convey knowledge to the student's mind. From that perspective, a student needs to acquire or construct a mental representation of this deposited knowledge, and once understood and correctly stored within his or her mind, to apply it in different context and related tasks (for example when solving a particular assignment building on that knowledge). In contrast, from the perspective of DCog, the inscriptions and visualizations used in lecture notes embody not

only the factual knowledge that is usually paid attention to, but also knowledge for how to use these *tools* in order to create further factual knowledge, e.g. when working on an assignment. This shift of analysis focuses therefore not just on the outcome of students learning but on the process itself and the relevant mediational means. A comparable approach was used by Cutts et al. (2012) suggesting an abstraction transition taxonomy of students' ability to transfer domain knowledge in a programming course [7]. Following DCog as a theoretical framework, this study will pay particular attention to mathematical inscriptions as mediational means, i.e. formal, symbolic notation and visualizations, to communicate in student activities with ToC.

3. RESEARCH DESIGN AND METHODS

Because we are interested in how students work on typical assignments from ToC in regular classroom environments, we approach the research field following the *Natural Inquiry* paradigm as explained by Guba and Lincoln ([21], p. 36ff). In this section we will present and justify the chosen research design and related methods used to accomplish our study.

3.1 Course Setup

For our study, we chose the ToC course "Algorithms and Data Structures" (AD) that is offered annually each summer semester in the CS department of Universität Hamburg, Germany, as part of the undergraduate CS programs. The course is usually attended by approx. 300 undergraduate CS students. It starts in mid-April and is 13 weeks long covering the following topics: Algorithm Design, Data Structures, and Complexity Theory. The course is meant to be taken in the second year of students' CS major. In their first year, students are recommended to take an introductory course to ToC, covering Automata Theory and Languages as well as logic, Turing Machines and in parts NP completeness. Most students have taken this course before attending AD. In addition, the majority of students has also taken an introductory Math course during their first year.

The course setup of AD consists of three components:

- 90 minutes of lecture per week given by a faculty member who presents the course topics, central concepts, algorithms, and their proofs and illustrates them with examples using slides and blackboard in a lecture hall. Slides and additional lecture notes are available online through the whole course period.

- Every second week, a homework sheet with 4-8 assignments are handed out based on the current lecture topics, which students are expected to solve in self-chosen study groups of 4 students and submit in writing for reviewing and grading by teaching assistants two weeks later. Most assignments require developing formal proofs.

- Every second week a 90-minute tutorial session attended by approximately 20 students and led by teaching assistants, during which students are expected to present their solutions to last weeks' homework assignment. Here, students have the opportunity to check the correctness of their solutions and discuss them with the group.

At the end of the course, a final exam is to be solved in written form. Within this pedagogical approach, it is expected that students can follow and understand the presented algorithms, concepts, theorems, and corresponding proofs during the lectures.

For their homework, students are expected to work in study groups but without any further support by teaching assistants or the teacher of the course. The tutorial sessions are supposed to serve students as verification and improvement of their self-directed work and learning processes. But, many students report having difficulties with this pedagogical approach and the dropout rate tends to be very high. This was also the case during summer semester 2016, when our study took place.

In 2016, the teacher of the course used the textbook by Cormen et al. [5]. He started the course with defining an Algorithm and introduced then successively Correctness, Runtime Analysis, the Divide-and-Conquer-Principle, several Data Structures and Sorting Algorithms before presenting Computational Complexity. For the homework he used comparable assignments to [5] requiring constructions and mathematical proofs. The final exam assignments were aligned to the course assignments. With 285 students starting the course, 211 attended final exams, and 154 students passed among which 20 students got an A.

3.2 Research Questions

We decided to focus our study on NP-completeness assignments for three reasons: 1) This topic is regarded as an important theoretical concept, 2) studies investigating how students work with this concept are particularly lacking, and 3) this topic was introduced in week 5 of the course which was advantageous for our data collection. Based on the chosen theoretical framework (see section 2), the setup of the course AD (section 3.1), and the chosen topic of NP-completeness, we decided to focus on assignments where students are tasked to develop formal proofs. Within this scope, we conclude previous reasoning and our research interest to the following research questions:

- *How do students use mathematical inscriptions and related visualizations as mediational means in the course of working on their NP-completeness proof assignment?*
- *How and by which means do they assure themselves that their approach is correct?*

3.3 Data Collection

Parker and Lewis [23] conducted a study about students' difficulties with the big-O Notation similarly focused and motivated as our study. They interviewed students about their difficulties with big-O Notation, also asking them related domain-specific questions. As we were interested in how students *work*, and not in how they *reflect on their own work*, we decided for an ethnographically oriented observational study instead without participating in students' activities. For this observational study, we relied on the homework assignments from the AD course that students were required to work on while attending lecture.

Although having a background in CS and ToC, we were not involved in teaching the AD course and had no influence on the design of students' homework. However, the teacher of the course supported our study and provided us with the assignment sheet about complexity classes and NP-completeness proofs two weeks earlier. This way, we had more time to decide which of the assignments we would observe students working on. Here, we chose one of the shorter and easier assignments that did not require particularly creative ideas or complicated constructions, so that we were able to observe students following the given method using involved inscriptions and visualizations. We will introduce the chosen assignment and related proof detail in section 4.

The teacher encouraged students during the lecture to volunteer for our study. In addition, he encouraged teaching assistants to provide information on student performance on the chosen assignment. In the week before the study, we were also allowed to attend all 20 tutorial sessions and ask students permission to attend, observe, and record their individually-organized study group sessions. Four study groups volunteered and we attended all four sessions of these groups. Because the first group's session took place one week earlier than the other three groups' sessions and also before NP-completeness was introduced in the lecture, we decided not to use it for the data analysis.

The data collection took place early November 2015. Students invited us to join their regular session in one of the seminar rooms on the campus of the CS department. The room was of an average size with a whiteboard, table, and chairs. We attended the session but did not participate in student activities. In the beginning, we explained the purpose of our study, emphasized that we were not involved in grading or any other teaching activities of the course, and that this was not meant to test students but to better understand how they work, and that the insights gained would be useful for future pedagogical innovations. After a while, when students started running into problems, they repeatedly asked us for hints and support, but we remained silent. Because students worked in groups, their dialogues evoked think-a-loud sessions without any interference from our side. Because of data recording restrictions, we were not able to video tape the whole session. But, we were allowed to record the speech and took photographs of students' created inscriptions or visualizations on paper and whiteboard. In addition, we took individual notes during the session.

3.4 Data Analysis

The observed and recorded sessions were transcribed together with the taped material. The data analysis was based on qualitative content analysis [22] using a summarizing technique. As the smallest data unit, we defined one statement per person not longer than one sentence. The abstraction level was relatively low, and we kept paraphrasing close to the original statements. Categories were derived from these generalizations.

As a first step, we worked with just one session by paraphrasing and generalizing the transcript. We summarized the codes, looking for similarities and differences, and explicating them to categories. We used the category system to code the transcript again with coding software. Next, we coded the remaining sessions with our category system, adding new codes where needed. The result of this data-driven analysis was a system of categories and subcategories that evolved during the multi-phase creation process. The category system structured the transcripts and provided a content-related overview of students' working processes. We used this to scaffold our interpretations of students' activities in single case studies of each group's session.

In addition, we used the categories to analyze how much time each group spent on each activity. For that matter, we split the written transcript in ten minute blocks and counted first the overall number of lines within one block creating a benchmark for a time frame of each line. Next, we counted the number of lines belonging to one category within the block in order to determine how much time students spent on that activity. Activites where students remained silent could not be included further. But there were only few moments where students remained silent, therefore not significantly changing the overall result of this numerical analysis.

4. NP-COMPLETENESS ASSIGNMENT

In this section, we will introduce the NP-completeness assignment students were observed working on, what the solution to this assignment can look like and what is needed to produce it. We will conduct this analysis using DCog as theoretical lenses.

4.1.1 The Assignment

Show that every $L \in P$, except $L = \emptyset$ and $L = \Sigma^*$, is NP-complete if $P = NP$. Why is this not true for the excluded cases?

In the weekly lecture one week before the assignment was handed out, the teacher of the course presented and explained all relevant concepts underlying this assignment, i.e., complexity classes and their relationship, NP-completeness and reducibility. The teacher used slides and relied mostly on the textbook by Cormen et al. [5]. For NP-completeness proofs, all relevant theorems and definitions were introduced concluding in a five-step-method (ibid., p. 1078) for proving that a language L is NP-complete:

1. Prove $L \in NP$
2. Select a known NP-complete language L'
3. Describe an algorithm that computes a function f mapping every instance w of L' to an instance of f(w) of L
4. Prove that the function f satisfies $w \in L'$ if and only if $f(x) \in L$ for all $w \in \Sigma^*$
5. Prove that the algorithm computing f runs in polynomial time

In addition, an illustration of the reduction (ibid., p. 1067, see also Figure 1) was provided with a concept of "yes"- and "no"-instances referring to the mapping of f.

4.1.2 The Requested Proof

Following the five-steps-method, we already know that L is in NP because $L \in P = NP$. We choose L' to be a NP-complete language. Following step 3 and 4, we choose k_1 and k_2 to be a fixed element in L and $\Sigma^* - L$, respectively. We can do this because neither L nor $\Sigma^* - L$ are empty (the excluded cases). We construct the reduction function f, reducing L' to L, as follows. For a given word w:

- $f(w) := k_1$, if w is a word of L' (yes-instances)
- $f(w) := k_2$, if w is not a word of L' (no instances)

Testing whether w is a word of L' takes polynomial time because P is equivalent to NP. Mapping w to a constant requires constant time, which is less than polynomial. If L is empty, a reduction would be only possible if L' is empty as well, but then L' wouldn't be NP-complete. If L is the language of all strings over an alphabet sigma, than $\Sigma^* - L$ is empty and we don't find any satisfiable mapping for w when it is not a word of L'. QED.

Besides the five-steps-method, this solution uses the following mediational means in order to be created:

- Characteristics of complexity classes, the five-step method with polynomial time reduction
- The formal-language framework with related inscriptions, especially the two symbols $\emptyset$ and Σ^* denoting the empty language and the language of all strings over an alphabet sigma, respectively
- Function framework with related mathematical inscriptions
- Relation between algorithms and functions as well as growth of a function
- Visualizations of function mapping between two sets
- Venn diagrams for sets

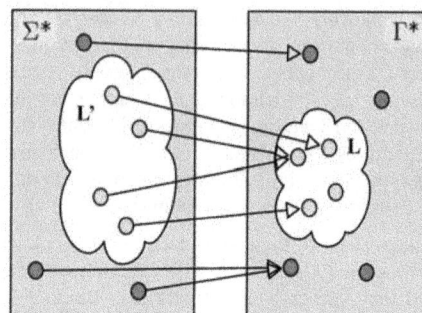

Figure 1: Illustration of the reduction function $f: \Sigma^* \to \Gamma^*$ ([5], p. 1068) with yes-instances (in green) and no-instances (in red).

With these tools and concepts, the solution is created by assuming that the complexity classes P and NP are equal and, therefore, solvable in polynomial time. This relationship can be captured by a Venn diagram. The given language L has three characteristic: 1) it is a member of P, 2) it is not empty, and 3) it is a subset of Σ^*. This relationship can be captured by illustrating a set and subset and naming them respectively. Both visualizations then embody two important pieces of information relevant to proceeding with the proof. The written form of the five-step instruction embodies the procedure needed to create the proof. Creating the mapping of the function f can be also done with an illustration like Figure 1. Developing the proof means precisely following the five-step method and creating a satisfiable mapping of f according to step 4 with the polynomial runtime of the corresponding algorithm.

When able to use all the provided concepts and tools, the proof itself is rather simple and does not require any particularly creative idea or complicated construction. This was also reflected in the amount of points that students could obtain with a correct solution (2 out of 16 of the entire homework sheet set of that week). In the next session we will discuss how it worked out for students.

5. RESULTS

This section presents the categories we developed and the summary of three groups' working processes. The section ends with a comparison of the sessions and a discussion about our observations in light of the research questions presented in Section 3.2.

5.1 The Category System

1. Clarifying the assignment
Reading the assignment text out loud or silently Discussing the assignment Returning back to the assignment Discussing tasks, problems and challenges related to the assignment Exchanging different opinions about the task and its difficulty

2. Clarifying concepts and inscriptions
Clarifying concepts Clarifying inscriptions

3. Requesting group members to act
Requesting to solve the problem Requesting to write the solution down Requesting to take notes on the white board

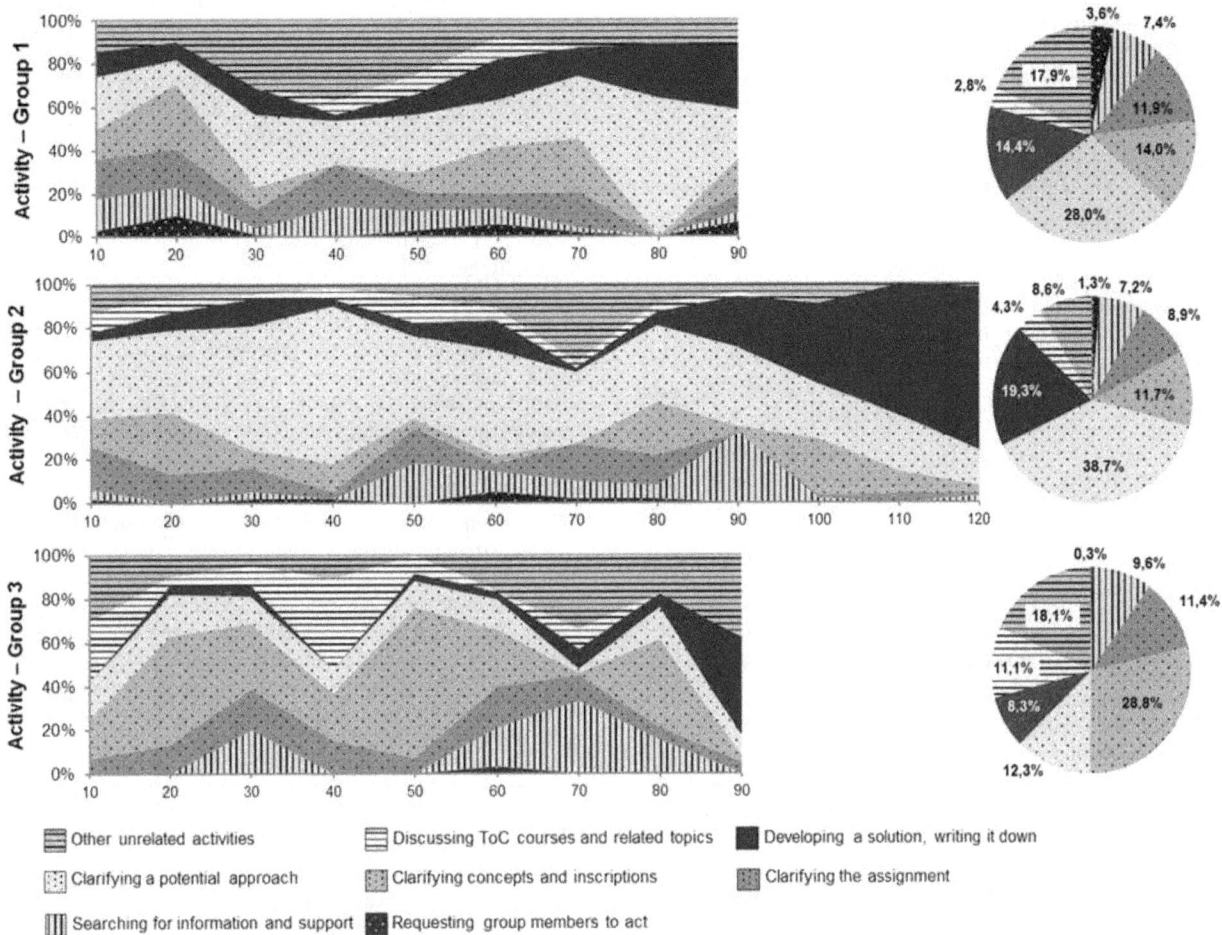

Figure 2 Working Process of Groups A, B and C relating time spent with categories

Legend:
- Other unrelated activities
- Clarifying a potential approach
- Searching for information and support
- Discussing ToC courses and related topics
- Clarifying concepts and inscriptions
- Requesting group members to act
- Developing a solution, writing it down
- Clarifying the assignment

4. Clarifying an approach for a potential solution
Suggesting a given or known approach
Applying an approach
Discussing an approach and its appropriateness to solve the assignment
Discussing the reduction and its direction
Rejecting an approach

5. Developing a solution and writing it down
Discussing a solution
Applying a solution from another assignment
Checking the correctness of the solution
Writing down the solution
Running into writing problems with formal notation
Rejecting a solution

6. Discussing ToC courses and related topics
Discussing courses and related literature or assignments

7. Searching for information and support
Searching for information on the internet or in books
Searching for information in the lecture notes and slides
Asking friends or other students for help
Discussing the usefulness/trustworthiness of found information

8. Other unrelated activities
Talking about different topics (people, hobbies, private life etc.), leaving the room, having phone calls or texting

5.2 Working Sessions of the Study Groups

5.2.1 Summarizing the Group Work Activities

Figure 2 summarizes which activities each of the student groups undertook as part of solving this assignment. The line charts on the left-hand side show in ten minute increments how much time students spent on the activities as captured by the categories. On the right-hand side, a pie chart for each group illustrates how much time was spent proportionally on each of the categories. As all groups routinely switched between single activities within a ten minute block, these charts give a summary of what happened. The collected data reveals a number of interesting insights: First and foremost, it can be observed that only for group B, the overall pattern of first clarifying items and then developing the solution – which a teacher might have expected – becomes apparent. Across all groups it can be observed that students spent more than half of their time on clarification issues rather than developing the solution and writing it down indicating their lack of working proficiency in this field of CS.

More in detail, group A spent 90 minutes on this session, working on the assignment for about 71 minutes (see Group A, Figure 2). Most of this time was spent on *clarifying an approach for a potential solution* (25 minutes). Almost 11 minutes were spent on *clarifying the assignment* and almost 13 minutes on *clarifying concepts and inscriptions*. Only 13 minutes were spent in total on *developing a solution and writing it down*. As can be seen in the graph of group A, they started from the begging to solve the assignment.

Group B spent almost 117 minutes on this session working on the assignment for about 102 minutes (see Group B, Figure 2). They spent most of their time on *clarifying an approach for a potential solution* (45 minutes). In comparison to that, they spent just 11 minutes on *clarifying the assignment* and almost 14 minutes on *clarifying concepts and inscriptions*. In contrast to that, they spent 22 minutes on *developing a solution and writing it down*.

Group C spent 90 minutes on this session working on the assignment for about 64 minutes (see Group C, Figure 2). They spent most of their time on *clarifying concepts and inscriptions (26 minutes)*. In comparison to that, they spent just 11 minutes on *clarifying an approach for a potential solution* and 10 minutes on *clarifying the assignment*. In contrast to that, they spent only 7 minutes on *developing a solution and writing it down*.

5.2.2 Process of Developing the Proof in Group A

Group A consisted of three students (A1, A2, and A3), while a fourth member (A4) joined the session in the end. The whole session was dominated by a constant dialogue between A1 and A2, while A3 said little and spent most of the time looking for information on the internet or being distracted. A1 was constantly asking questions which A2 would answer. In between, they would sometimes alternate these roles. In the last 15 minutes, A4 appeared but did not say much. Therefore, A1 and A2 together concluded the session. Next, we will summarize how the group processed in developing the required proof for the assignment.

The working process started with the group reading the assignment. A1 and A2 had a short discussion about the relationship of P, NP, and NPC as it was defined in the assignment. A1 was not sure about this, but remembered the five-steps-method from the lecture and looked for it in the lecture material. A1 requested the others use this as a pattern for their approach:

A1: No, this is really a todo-list, what one has to do, when one wants to prove NP-completeness.

A2 discussed the first step of the method and concluded that it was easy because P=NP was already given. Next they read step two and three and tried to apply it to their assignment. Here, A1 started to reflect on how they could create a reduction for L' when it is empty:

A2: That's what we have. We have a L from P
A1: Then, we need to choose L' from NPC. So. We assume that in this case it [pointing to L in the script] is the empty set. Therefore, we agree that our L' is empty.
A2: Can't do that. [...]
A1: But we are supposed to show that it is not, hence we need to include it in our proof and then show that it is not working [...]
A2: True [...] right, we can't map to anything because we have nothing.

Next A1 and A2 read step four and this was when they get confused about the properties f needed to satisfy. They started reflecting about the reduction and how it needed to be applied

correctly. They decided to look on the internet for explanations but instead found other methods for how NP-completeness could be proved as well, and this made them more confused. In between, they switched to a conversation about the symbols $\emptyset$ and Σ^*, clarifying their meanings. They were uncertain about whether $\emptyset$ was the empty language or the empty string. They also did not know what Σ^* meant exactly. In order to clarify this, they asked another student via text messages for help and also started looking again for information on the internet until they found an explanation. They returned back to create a reduction for L being the empty language. They believed they had found an argument for why L could not be empty. However, they did not know how to write it down using mathematical inscriptions. For example, they reflected on which symbol needed to be used for the mapping of the function and what the right order of all symbols and inscriptions should be. Hence, they decided to write their idea down in natural language (they spend the first 20 minutes for this part).

Next they tried to prove that L could not be Σ^*. Here, A1 started reflecting on how the reduction functions in general. For this, A1 created different cases with L (e.g., being a subset of NP or NP being empty or Σ^*), asking A2 how the reduction would work in these circumstances. A1 read the lecture slides looking for an explanation. A3 looked for information in the internet and from time to time suggested additional information which was not helpful. A1's thoughts continued circulating around the reduction and why the defined mapping between L and L' would prove NP-completeness. A1 regularly questioned the direction of the definition of f (what is given and what must hold). Apparently, A1 did not understanding that step three and four described an equivalence. In this working phase, they became distracted many times by receiving text messages from third parties. A3 was not participating in the discussion at this point. A2 tried to answer A1's questions, but was not able to do this fully. A4 joined the group but would not participate in this discussion fully. They kept trying to create a contradiction when constructing a satisfiable function f for the case that L equals Σ^*. During this discussion, A1 and A2 noticed that in addition f needed to run in polynomial time. They started computing the runtime of f and concluded that it was exponential and therefore could not work (by then, 80 minutes had passed).

Feeling uncertain, they kept looking for additional information and found the concept of "yes"- and "no"-instances and the illustration of the reduction (see Figure 1) provided in the lecture slides. With these tools they managed to create an argumentation for why L could not be the empty language or Σ^*:

A1: Sigma star always says yes and the empty language says always no.
A2: So, it's okay when sigma star says yes, isn't it?
A1: Yes, but not when we have a no-instance [...]. Well, it only gets damaged, when you have a yes on one side but an empty set on the other side because you can't map to a no-instance. And the other way it breaks because when you have a no and you have sigma star, there are only yes-instances, then it breaks.

A1 wrote this argument down with natural language. They kept discussing because they were uncertain about their argument's correctness. After another short discussion, the students decided to submit what they had and finish the session. Their reviewed solution received 0.5 out of 2 possible points.

5.2.3 Process of Developing the Proof in Group B

Group B consisted of four students (B1, B2, B3, B4). The first 60 minutes of the session were dominated by a dialogue between B1,

B2, and B3 while B4 said little. In the second half of the session, B4 started asking questions and then also contributing more. No one in the group dominated the dialogue as this was the case in group A. Each group member was asking questions, suggesting answers, and next steps.

Group B started their session by discussing the assignment and moved on to the definition of NP-completeness. They drew a Venn diagram on the whiteboard for successfully clarifying the new relationship of classes P and NP. Next, they remembered the reduction concepts from the lecture and tried to define it without using the lecture slides. Instead, they started to discuss the direction of the reduction in detail, switching their decision about what was right several times. Afterwards, they began talking about Turing machines and tried to use them for a potential solution, but they were not quite satisfied with their approach. Apparently, they did not know or remembered the five-step-method presented in the lecture. Next, they discussed whether their Venn diagram would be accepted as a solution but were uncertain about this as well. As they reflected on what they had done already, they recognized that they were just discussing the givens of the proof. They went on with looking for additional information and developed new approaches and ideas for the solution. Like group A, they did not know how to write down their solution and ideas in a correct formal way and decided to use natural language instead. Not confident with their result so far, they kept looking for information and finally found the five-steps-method, the "yes"- and "no"-instances, and the visualized reduction in the lecture material. With these tools and the detailed clarification of the givens in the first half of their session, they were able to solve the whole assignment correctly, but kept discussing how to write it down in a formal way. After another short discussion, they decided that they had accomplished the task and they would write down the solution properly later on at home. Their reviewed solution received 2 out of 2 possible points.

5.2.4 *Process of Developing the Proof in Group C*

Group C consisted of four students (C1, C2, C3, C4). In Group C, only students C3 and C4 had attended the introductory ToC course in the semester before. After a discussion whether the ToC course is a precondition for the AD course, the students started with solving the assignment by discussing the relation between Σ^* and $\emptyset$, the term of reduction and the definition of NP-completeness. Shortly after that C1 and C2 explained that they did not understand this approach and C3 and C4 started explaining topics from the previous ToC course. Afterwards, they continued with defining NP-completeness while using the reduction, and later on, they defined the empty set and Σ^*. The students also used the term "polynomial time." Unlike the sample solution, they tried to use a specific L to prove NP-completeness. The students solved the first part but were not sure how to prove that the empty set and Σ^* are excluded. The students did not know the five-step-method and tried to develop their own approach. One idea they tried was to visualize everything they knew so far, but they did not write the definitions for the excluded cases on the whiteboard assuming that they were clear. As they did not proceed, they asked a teaching assistant for help. They received a hint and concluded wrongly that they can use the concept of decidability. In the end, they argued that the empty set and Σ^* are excluded because they were not decidable cases. Their reviewed solution received 0 out of 2 possible points.

5.3 Discussion

5.3.1 *Students' Approaches to Develop the Proof*

Groups A and B spent more than half of their session time clarifying the approach for how to prove the statement. Group A spent the time working to understand the five-steps-method, while Group B spent their time developing an approach on their own until they found the five-steps-method as well. Group C spent most of time clarifying concepts and inscriptions and then a noteworthy amount of time discussing topics from a previous ToC course, believing that this was relevant for the assignment. They created a proof using Turing machines, a concept they remembered from the ToC course they attended the semester before.

In all sessions, student activities constantly changed, and they did not manage to accomplish systematically one working phase after the other. Instead, it was a constant back-and-forth between several activities. Students' search for relevant information resembled an investigation, looking for clues and hints. In between, there were some "Deus ex machina"-like moments, where students' friends or teaching assistants provided helpful clues or some explanations via text messaging.

Students seemed unaware that they could and also should organize their working processes more systematically, e.g., by clarifying first if they lacked understanding about relevant concepts and approaches and agreeing on a method to create understanding first before turning to the assignment's proof. Because of students' fundamental lack of organizing the work, we have reason to believe that the way students worked could be also observed with another proof assignment from ToC and was not particularly related to NP-completeness.

5.3.2 *Students' Missing Working Proficiency and Methods in ToC*

Group A did not develop the correct proof. They made the mistake of trying to prove what was already given (L is not empty or Σ^*). In addition, they got lost in a longer discussion about how the reduction functions and why. A1 tried to figure out what was given and what needed to hold, when in fact it was an equivalence (x element L <u>if and only if</u> f(x) in L'). In conclusion, they lacked basic techniques of reading a given statement, decoding the givens, and what needed to be proved. Group B ran into problems, but managed to develop the right idea of the proof. However, they were not able to write it precisely down. Given their discussion, our impression was that they did not fully understood the mechanism of the proof but rather used the provided tools to grasp the correct idea. Group C did not develop the correct proof because they did not work with the lecture material and also lacked an approach for developing the proof.

This overall result was particularly unexpected because we chose the second ToC course that CS students at our department are supposed to attend in their second year of the undergraduate CS program. It is expected that students would, by that time, already be familiar with developing proofs within ToC and also be able to master proofing techniques. Apparently, the observed students did not manage to develop the relevant competencies of ToC in the past semesters and require here additional help.

5.3.3 *RQ1: How do students use mathematical inscriptions in the course of working on their assignment?*

We observed two aspects that answer the first research question: 1) Students used given mathematical inscriptions and related visualizations to mediate the clarification process, but 2) they did not create their own inscriptions and visualizations to mediate the proof development.

All observed groups read the assignment text and interacted with the mathematical inscriptions used in the text. Specifically, they repeatedly discussed the meaning of the symbols ∅ and Σ^* during the course of the session, but none of them used the whiteboard or paper to create inscriptions and visualizations that would have captured their own understanding. So, they kept returning to discuss the symbols' meaning, creating different versions of them. Consequentially, students' understandings differed slightly among the group, and they could not work out together an argument for why both cases were excluded from NP. The only exception was when students created a Venn diagram for clarifying the relationship between P, NP and NPC using the whiteboard. With that, the students did recognize that within the assumption of the assignment, a language from P was also a member from NP and, therefore, computable in polynomial time. Every time they returned to this question, they could point to their diagram and remember their previously created answer. By doing so, they created a shared understanding among the group and captured an important aspect of their cognitive process visible for everybody on the whiteboard.

For their working process, students used lecture material and additional information from the internet. Because the material was using mathematical inscriptions, they used them as well by reading and pointing to symbols and elements when discussing the approach. However, they only used spoken language to create a shared understanding about this part. Therefore, students' solutions were not fully elaborated and missed the precision in argumentation expected. Students were aware that it was important to write down their solution, and they repeatedly asked themselves to do this. But, as they observed themselves, they lacked the ability to do it. The crucial point was that students understood the "writing down" as capturing the outcome of their work, the piece of paper they were required to submit for review. They seemed to be unaware that "writing down" could have been also part of their working process, an externalization of their thoughts helping them to elaborate on their first ideas. This absence of creating mathematical inscriptions and related visualizations within the working process emphasized their relevance for capturing verbalized thoughts and elaborating them further as interplay between the inside and the outside in a shared distributed cognitive process.

5.3.4 RQ2: How and by which means do students assure themselves that their approach is correct?

It seemed to be very important for all groups to create certainty regarding all aspects of the working process and, in particular, the developed proof. They assured themselves that their approach was correct by…

- …looking for comparable approaches on the internet in order to compare them with their own approach. In most of the cases this was not successful because it provided additional approaches and inscriptions, they were not able to understand fully.
- …questioning each others' approaches and explaining them to the group. In many cases this approach was successful.

Another source for certainty could have been the five-step-method. Using it as a blueprint for their proof, students would not

have needed to develop an approach at all. This would have been the best possibility to determine whether the first part of their solution was correct. However, students were not able to understand the method fully. So, instead of being able to use it to create certainty, they required additional means to create certainty of their understanding of the method.

5.3.5 Additional Data Gathering

Because all three groups were challenged by the NP-completeness assignment and especially with writing their proofs down, we wondered if the other study groups performed the same way. Since the week in which all groups had worked on that assignment already passed at the time of our analysis, we asked the teaching assistants to provide us with relevant information about students' submitted results of that assignment. We received information about 52 groups (corresponds to approximately 125 students) out of approximately 90 groups. Out of these 52 groups, the following scoring was the result regarding the NP-completeness assignment:

Groups	Points	Using mathematical inscriptions
15%	0	n/a (no submission)
6%	0	only natural language
29%	0.5	only natural language
31%	1	only natural language
8%	1.5	yes but with mistakes
11%	2.0	yes, with only little natural language use

Concluding, the three observed groups A, B, and C are spread around this overall result representing high, low, and mediocre scorings. These results also strongly indicate that the majority of the students attending the course seemed to be having problems developing a correct final solution and using mathematical inscriptions to capture their proof development.

6. CONCLUSION

This paper introduced Distributed Cognition Theory to the research field of Education in Theory of Computation (ToC). It did so by showing how an observational research study based on this theoretical framework can be designed to investigate collaborative cognitive processes of CS students studying ToC. The methodology, novel in this field, yielded insights into how CS students worked on an assignment from ToC to proof NP-completeness. The examination of collected qualitative and quantitative data revealed that observed CS students lacked the working proficiency and methods for completing the task at hand. This result is significant because a common assumption in the related work in this field up until now is that students are lacking in interest to ToC or abilities to understand the field's body of knowledge. The implication of this result is that ToC Ed research may need to consider to refocus towards pedagogies focused on teaching students how to practice ToC besides introducing the body of factual knowledge of that discipline.

This study was a first step towards a bigger research project. As a next step, we will further validate this result for the whole cohort and also investigate CS students working on proof assignments using other ToC concepts, e.g., Turing machines. Then, we will compare those approaches with an investigation of how theoretical computer scientists solve such assignments. The outcome of these future studies will provide us with insights for continuing student-oriented pedagogy fostering working proficiency in this field of education, see also [19].

REFERENCES

[1] Armoni, M., Rodgers, S., Vardi, M., and Verma, R. 2006. Automata theory - its relevance to computer science students and course content. *SIGCSE Bulletin.* 38, 1, 197-198.

[2] Berque, D., Johnson, D., and Jovanovic, L. 2001. Teaching theory of computation using pen-based computers and an electronic whiteboard. *ACM SIGCSE Bulletin,* 33, 3, 169-172.

[3] Chesñevar, C., González, M., and Maguitman, A. 2004. Didactic strategies for promoting significant learning in formal languages and automata theory. In *Proceedings of the 9th annual SIGCSE conference on Innovation and technology in computer science education.* ITiCSE '04. ACM, 7-11.

[4] Chudá, D. 2007. Visualization in Education of Theoretical Computer Science. In *Proceedings of the 2007 international conference on Computer systems and technologies.* CompSysTech '07. 84.

[5] Cormen, T., Stein, C., Rivest, R., and Leiserson, C. 2009. Introduction to Algorithms. McGraw-Hill Higher Education, 3rd edition.

[6] Crescenzi, P., Enström, E., and Kann, V. 2013. From theory to practice: NP-completeness for every CS student. In *Proceedings of the 18th ACM conference on Innovation and technology in computer science education.* ITiCSE '13. ACM, 16-21.

[7] Cutts, Q., Esper, S., Fecho, M., Foster, S., Simon, B. 2012. The Abstraction Transition Taxonomy: Developing Desired Learning Outcomes through the Lens of Situated Cognition. In *Proceedings of the ninth annual International Conference on International Computing Education Research.* ICER '12. ACM, 63-70.

[8] Deitrick, E., Shapiro, B., Ahrens, M., Fiebrink, R., Lehrman, P., and Farooq, S. 2015. Using Distributed Cognition Theory to Analyze Collaborative Computer Science Learning. In *Proceedings of the eleventh annual International Conference on Computing Education Research.* ICER '15. ACM, 51-60.

[9] Devedzic, V., Debenham, J., and Popvic D. 2000. Teaching Formal Languages by an Intelligent Tutoring System. Educational Technology and Society 3, 2, ISSN 1436-4522.

[10] García-Osorio, C., Mediavilla-Sáiz, I., Jimeno-Visitación, J., and García-Pedrajas, N. 2008. Teaching push-down automata and turing machines. *ACM SIGCSE Bulletin*, 40, 3.

[11] Goldreich, O. 2006. *On teaching the basics of complexity theory, Theoretical Computer Science: Essays in Memory of Shimon Even.* Springer-Verlag, Berlin.

[12] Habiballa, H. and Kmet, T. 2004. Theoretical branches in teaching computer science. *International Journal of Mathematical Education in Science and Technology.* 35, 6, 829-841

[13] Hämäläinen, W. 2004. Problem-based learning of theoretical computer science. In *Proceedings of the 34th ASEE/IEEE Frontiers in Education Conference.* S1H/1 -S1H/6 Vol. 3.

[14] Hielscher, M. and Wagenknecht. C. 2006. AtoCC: learning environment for teaching theory of automata and formal languages. In *Proceedings of the 11th annual SIGCSE conference on Innovation and technology in computer science education.* ITICSE '06. ACM, 306-306.

[15] Hollan, J., Hutchins, E., & Kirsh, D. 2001. Distributed Cognition: Toward a New Foundation for Human-Computer Interaction Research. *Human-Computer Interaction in the New Millennium.* Carroll, M., Eds., ACM Press, New York, 75-94.

[16] Hopcroft, J., Motwani, R., and Ullman, J. 2006. *Introduction to Automata Theory, Languages, and Computation.* 3rd Edition, Pearson.

[17] Hutchins, E. 1995. *Cognition in the wild.* Bradford: MIT Press.

[18] Knobelsdorf, M. 2015. The Theory Behind Theory - Computer Science Education Research Through the Lenses of Situated Learning. In Proceedings of the 8th International Conference on Informatics in Schools: Situation, Evolution, and Perspectives (ISSEP), Lecture Notes in Computer Science, Volume 9378, Springer, 21-21.

[19] Knobelsdorf, M., Kreitz, C., and Böhne, S. 2014. Teaching theoretical computer science using a cognitive apprenticeship approach. In *Proceedings of the 45th ACM technical symposium on Computer science education.* SIGCSE '45. ACM, New York, 67-72.

[20] Korte, L., Anderson, S., Pain, H., and Good, J. 2007. Learning by game-building: a novel approach to theoretical computer science education. In *Proceedings of the 12th annual SIGCSE conference on Innovation and technology in computer science education.* ITiCSE '07. ACM, 53-57.

[21] Lincoln, Y., and Guba, E. 1985. *Naturalistic Inquiry.* Sage Publications. Newbury Park, California.

[22] Mayring. P. 2000. Qualitative Content Analysis. Forum: Qualitative Social Research [Online Journal], 1, 2, Art. 20.

[23] Parker, M. and Lewis, C. 2014. What makes big-O analysis difficult: understanding how students understand runtime analysis. *Journal of Computing Sciences in Colleges.*29, 4, 164-174.

[24] Pea, R. 1993. Practices of distributed intelligence and designs for education. In *Distributed cognitions: Psychological and educational considerations.* G. Salomon, Ed. Cambridge: Cambridge University Press, 47-87.

[25] Perkins, D. 1993. Person-plus: A distributed view of thinking and learning. In *Distributed cognitions: Psychological and educational considerations.* G. Salomon, Ed. Cambridge: Cambridge University Press, p. 88-110.

[26] Pillay, N. 2009. Learning Difficulties Experienced by Students in a Course on Formal Languages and Automata Theory. *SIGCSE Bulletin.* 41, 4, 48-52.

[27] Rodger, S. H., Bressler, B., Finley, T., and Reading, S. 2006. Turning automata theory into a hands-on course. In *Proceedings of the 37th SIGCSE technical symposium on Computer science education.* SIGCSE '06. ACM, 379-383.

[28] Säljö, R. 1998. Learning as the use of tools: a sociocultural perspective on the human-technology link. *In Learning with computers.* Littleton, K. and Light, P., Ed. Routledge, New York, 144-161.

[29] Sigman, S. 2007. Engaging students in formal language theory and theory of computation. *SIGCSE Bulletin.* 39, 1, 450-453.

[30] Tenenberg, J. and Knobelsdorf, M. 2013. Out of our minds: a review of sociocultural cognition theory. *Computer Science Education.* 24, 1, 1-24.

[31] Verma, R. 2005. A visual and interactive automata theory course emphasizing breadth of automata. In *Proceedings of the 10th Annual SIGCSE Conference on innovation and Technology in Computer Science Education.* ITiCSE '05. ACM, 325-329.

[32] Vygotsky, L. S. 1978. *Mind in Society: The Development of Higher Psychological Processes*: Harvard University Press.

[33] Wermelinger, M. and Dias, A. 2005. A prolog toolkit for formal languages and automata, *ACM SIGCSE Bulletin.* 37, 3.

[34] Wertsch, J. V. 1993. *Voices of the Mind: Sociocultural Approach to Mediated Action.* Harvard University Press.

[35] Zingaro, Z. 2008. Another approach for resisting student resistance to formal methods, *ACM SIGCSE Bulletin*, 40, 4.

The Role of Self-Regulation in Programming Problem Solving Process and Success

Dastyni Loksa and Andrew J. Ko
The Information School · DUB
University of Washington
{dloksa, ajko}@uw.edu

ABSTRACT

While prior work has investigated many aspects of programming problem solving, the role of self-regulation in problem solving success has received little attention. In this paper we contribute a framework for reasoning about self-regulation in programming problem solving. We then use this framework to investigate how 37 novice programmers of varying experience used self-regulation during a sequence of programming problems. We analyzed the extent to which novices engaged in five kinds of self-regulation during their problem solving, how this self-regulation varied between students enrolled in CS1 and CS2, and how self-regulation played a role in structuring problem solving. We then investigated the relationship between self-regulation and programming errors. Our results indicate that while most novices engage in self-regulation to navigate and inform their problem solving efforts, these self-regulation efforts are only effective when accompanied by programming knowledge adequate to succeed at solving a given problem, and only some types of self-regulation appeared related to errors. We discuss the implications of these findings on problem solving pedagogy in computing education.

CCS Concepts

• **Social and professional topics~Computer science education** • **Social and professional topics~CS1**

Keywords

Programming, Problem Solving, Self-Regulation, Think-Aloud.

1. INTRODUCTION

Programming problem solving is a complex activity that poses many diverse cognitive demands on learners. As Elliot Soloway argued thirty years ago, expert programmers "have built up large libraries of stereotypical solutions to problems as well as strategies for coordinating and composing them. Students should be taught explicitly about these libraries and strategies for using them." [30]. Students are often left to develop these strategies on their own, and when they fail to do so, they quit [2].

Prior work has investigated a wide range of materials, pedagogies, and techniques for teaching programming problem solving strategies. For example, recent studies have explored worked examples and the effect of sub-goal labels, finding that examples

and sub-goal labels can promote greater problem solving success [20,22,23]. Other efforts such as the Idea Garden have investigated strategy hints, giving learners suggestions about how to approach a problem (e.g., divide and conquer), finding that hints can promote independence and self-efficacy [5]. Similarly, Linn & Clancy found that case studies including code and expert explanations can lead to a more integrated understanding of programming process and some gains in problem solving success [18].

While these pedagogies and materials improve learner's *content* knowledge for programming, prior work in the learning sciences literature suggests *process* skills, and in particular *self-regulation*, are equally critical. Self-regulation is the ability to be aware of one's thoughts and actions and evaluate how well they are moving one closer towards a goal [28]. Several studies have investigated self-regulation in learning, finding, for example, that successful learners generate self-explanations of material and use self-explanations to monitor for misconceptions [21]; that self-explanation prompts can improve problem-solving skill and self-efficacy [8]; that high performing CS students use more metacognitive and resource management strategies [3]; and that general metacognitive training can promote improvements in domain-specific skills such as listening and science inquiry [10].

Only a handful of studies have explicitly investigated self-regulation in the context of programming. One of the earliest was conducted by Clements & Gullo, investigating the effect of teaching programming problem solving [7]. They found that teaching programming via Logo, relative to teaching computer use, subjectively promoted greater "reflectivity." Pea and Kurland reviewed this and other work on the effects of learning to code, finding little evidence that learning to code promoted self-regulation or metacognition. However, they they did draw upon learning sciences literature to argue that programming itself *requires* self-regulation for planning programming solutions [24]. This is consistent with more recent work, identifying self-regulated learning strategies [11,12], and showing that programming expertise demands a high degree of self-awareness and self-monitoring [9,17].

Acknowledging that programming requires self-regulation, more recent studies have investigated ways of teaching self-regulation for programming. Bielaczyc et al. investigated the impact of teaching self-explanation, finding that students who received explicit training on self-explanation strategies used these strategies more than those without the training, increasing problem solving success [4]. More recently, Loksa et al. found that combining similar self-regulation instruction with a framework for programming problem solving activities promoted not only greater problem solving success, but also gains in productivity, self-efficacy and growth mindset [19].

While prior work provides compelling evidence that self-regulation is key to successful programming, it leaves several open questions:

- To what extent do novices self-regulate when programming?
- To what extent does programming experience in CS1 and CS2 promote self-regulation in programming?
- To what extent is self-regulation related to successful programming problem solving?

In this paper, we investigate these questions, first proposing a theoretical framework for self-regulation in the context of programming. We then present an empirical analysis of novice programmers' self-regulation activities and explore how variation in self-regulation was associated with problem solving success. We end with a discussion our findings on computing education, with several ideas for how to promote self-regulation through teaching.

2. THEORETICAL FRAMEWORK

Lacking an existing theoretical framework of self-regulation in computing, we derive our framework from key self-regulation elements which are common across prior work. Prior work frames self-regulation as the ability to monitor and control one's behaviors, thoughts, and emotions for the demands of the moment, and monitoring progress toward goals [16]. In the context of learning, self-regulation involves *metacognition* (thinking about one's thoughts) [10], *planning* (evaluating progress toward a learning goal), and *motivation* (manipulating one's intrinsic and extrinsic goals to make progress toward learning) [31].

In the context of programming, we propose that self-regulation helps plan and evaluate progress toward writing a program that solves some computational problem. Our hypothesis is that the more a participant self-regulates their programming activities, the more successful they will be at solving the problem.

This hypothesis, however, demands a more granular view of what "progress" means in programming, and how self-regulation is related to progress. Loksa et al. recently defined progress in programming problem solving as six distinct and nominally sequential but iterative activities [19]; we propose these are related to self-regulation as follows:

- *Reinterpreting the problem prompt.* Programming tasks begin with some problem that programmers must interpret and clarify. As with any problem solving, this understanding is a cognitive representation of the problem used to organize one's "continuing work" [13]. The more explicitly one engages in regulating this understanding (e.g., by reflecting on whether their understanding is correct), the more likely they will correct misconceptions of it.
- *Searching for analogous problems.* Programmers draw upon problems they have encountered in the past, either in past programming efforts or even in algorithmic activities from everyday life [14,30]. By reusing knowledge of related problems, programmers can better conceptualize a problem's computational nuances. Learners may self-regulate by being aware of limitations in their knowledge of related problems.
- *Searching for solutions.* With some understanding of a problem, programmers seek solutions that will solve the problem by adapting solutions to related problems or by finding solutions in textbooks, online, or from classmates or teachers [15]. During solution search, learners may monitor the extent to which they have searched and the degree to which the search was satisfactory.
- *Evaluating a potential solution.* With a solution in mind, programmers must evaluate how well it will address the problem. This includes feasibility assessments, mental simulations of algorithm behavior, or other techniques of prototyping before implementation. Self-regulation may help

learners to decide whether their evaluation of a potential solution is adequate, or whether they need to more certainty.
- *Implementing a solution.* With a solution in mind, programmers must translate the solution into code using their programming languages and tools. Learners may self-regulate their awareness of working memory limitations and manage prospective memory for future tasks.
- *Evaluating an implemented solution.* After implementing a solution programmers iteratively converge toward correctness, evaluating how well their implementation solves the problem, usually by testing and debugging. Learners may self-regulate their certainty in an implementation's correctness to prevent overconfidence.

Based on these six stages, and prior work on the elements of self-regulation in learning, we identify five types of self-regulation that support programming problem solving:

- *Planning.* Learners should reflect on what their next step in a problem solving process should be (e.g., *did new information reveal a gap in understanding? What tasks remains for an implementation?*) [29]. The more a learner engages in explicit planning, the more successful they should be.
- *Process monitoring.* Programmers who explicitly monitor their progress toward solving a problem are more successful (e.g., *is a sub-goal complete? Is the code sufficiently tested?*) [4,15,17,19]. The more learners monitor when a task is complete, the more successful they should be.
- *Comprehension monitoring.* Learners should monitor their understanding of computational concepts in problems and solutions [19,29] (e.g., *am I confused? Is my understanding of this failure accurate?*). The more aware learners are of their misconceptions, the more successful they should be at correcting them.
- *Reflection on cognition.* Learners should make judgments about the qualities and limitations of their memory and reasoning [31] (e.g., *am I forgetting something? Am I making any assumptions?*). The more aware learners are of their cognitive biases, the more likely they are to correct for them.
- *Self-explanation.* Learners should explain to themselves why they have come to a conclusion or decision, and then use that rationale to monitor their progress [4,21,30] (e.g., *this was the right loop condition because it halts at the end of the list*). The more learners engage in self-explanation, the more they will find flaws in their reasoning.

While all five of these self-regulation activities are likely critical to any kind of problem solving, we suspect that they are particularly useful in programming. This is for two reasons: 1) programming problems are often about abstract computational processes, requiring additional cognitive load to reason about abstract ideas in working memory, and 2) programming languages require precision and completeness, demanding repeated interpretation of the code one has written. Self-regulation may play a key executive control role, facilitating more logical, precise and systematic reasoning about abstract computational ideas, helping a learner to manage their cognition as they navigate a largely invisible solution space.

While self-regulation may be essential some prior work suggesting that teaching it improves problem solving success [4,9,17,19], to what extent do novice programmers engage in self-regulation without explicit instruction? Do these self-regulation skills, however undeveloped, contribute to problem solving success? In the coming sections, we investigate this questions directly.

	CS1 (21 students)	CS2 (16 students)
Gender	F=11, M=10	F=8, M=8
Age	[18, 18, 27]	[18, 20, 24]
Self-Efficacy	[-3, 2, 8]	[-2, 2, 6]

Table 1. Sample size, gender, age and self-efficacy for each experience group, showing [min, median, max].

3. METHOD

Our target population was students who had enrolled in up to two introductory programming courses (which we will call CS1 and CS2). This ensured exposure to the syntax and semantics of at least one programming language, but minimal experience with problem solving. We recruited participants from lower-division CS and information science classes via email and flyers, ultimately recruiting 37 students. Because CS1 was required for many degrees, but CS2 for only for CS and a few, we viewed these as two separate populations, dividing participants into those who had enrolled in or completed CS1 and those who and enrolled in or completed CS2. Table 1 shows that the groups were balanced across gender, age, and self-efficacy (-8 to 8 on our scale).

When participants arrived, we gathered age, gender, CS course enrollment, and programming self-efficacy, which we adapted from [1] to be language agnostic. Then, to help participants practice thinking-aloud [6], we provided participants with a worked example of a problem consisting of a problem and solution in pseudo-code. We instructed participants to say everything that went through their mind as they read the example and solved problems. If at any point they remained silent for 1-minute they were prompted "remember to think out loud." After participants had time to read and understand the example, they solved a problem that was isomorphic in structure and context. After completing the 1st problem, participants received a 2nd and 3rd problem for practice.

Finally, we gave participants three additional problems to solve one at a time, each without examples. We adapted our problems from prior work that focused on while loop usage [22]. The final three problems consisted of one problem isomorphic to the practice problems, and two context-shifted problems, where the structure of the problem was consistent with prior problems, but the domain was different. Our intent was to provide both familiar and novel problems to investigate variation in self-regulation. Figure 1 shows the final three problems. We instructed participants to write in pseudo-code, focusing on logic over syntax.

ISOMORPHIC PROBLEM

Problem 4: The instructor has now given you a collection of test grades and asked you to calculate the class average for passing grades (those that are 70 or above). Here are all the test grades for the class.

CONTEXT SHIFTED PROBLEMS

Problem 5: Your best friend is a golfer, but is not very good at math. They continue to make errors when adding up scores. You volunteer to write a program that will add up the golf scores and print out the scores for the first nine holes, the second nine holes, and total for the round.

Problem 6: Suppose that a certain group's population grows at a rate of 10% every year. Write a program that will determine how many years it will take for the population to double.

Figure 1. Problem prompts 4-6.

We collected two forms of data. The first was audio recordings of participants' think aloud. We transcribed the recordings and then coded them for 9 types of verbalizations: 4 of the 6 problem solving activities from Section 2 and all 5 of the self-regulation types from Section 2. We based this data collection on best practices of verbal data [6], measures of self-regulation [4,26,28], and theories of problem solving process [19,25]. Table 2 shows our coding scheme for each verbalization type. We merged two problem solving activities—*searching for a solution* and *evaluating a solution*—into *adapting a solution* because they were not observable in our think aloud data and adapting requires finding a solution, and evaluating it. We excluded *implementation* because we did not track participants' editing which are difficult to identify through audio. The 1st author developed the codebook and trained with another researcher, iteratively refining the the coding scheme until reaching consensus. To verify the validity of the scheme each researcher independently coded 10% of the transcripts and then compared each sentence in the transcripts, coming to an 83% agreement across all sentences. The 1st author then completed the remainder of the coding.

The second form of data was the participants' programming solutions. We analyzed solutions for errors by identifying lines of code that would need to be added, removed, or changed in order for the participants' solutions to produce the correct output. We treated lines of code that were unnecessary for a working solution as errors. This analysis was performed only on problems 4-6 because solutions to problems 1-3 were provided in the examples.

Code	Definition	Examples
Reinterpret problem	Questioning details of the problem prompt or problem requirements.	*"I only need to find the sum?"* *"...it says those that are 70 or above. Does that mean 70% or the number of points?"*
Analogous problem search	Identifying similarities between the current problem and other problems or solutions.	*"It seems like a similar structure of the problem example."* *"So this is like the first question I had."*
Adapt solution	Identifying what needs to change about a prior solution to solve the current problem.	*"This was also like the first one except without the last step of finding the average."* *"This one is a bit different because this time, we have to only calculate the average."*
Evaluate solution	Judging the correctness of code.	*"All right. I'm just going to check the solution."; "So let me just check the for loop."*
Planning	Expressing intent to perform some task, or description of a task participants is doing.	*"I'm going to initialize variables first"* *"I'm just copying the code from the example."*
Process monitoring	Declaring that a programming sub-goal is complete.	*"So that's the end of the for-loop."* *"So I got the first part. Going on to the second. "*
Comprehension monitoring	Reflection about the understanding of code or problem prompts.	*"I don't know, end while means..."* *"And so actually, I don't know how this golf scoring works,"*
Reflection on cognition	Judgments about mental processes, mistakes, assumptions, or biases.	*"I was refreshed from earlier about how to do logical operations within while loop."* *"I read the question wrong."*
Self-explanation	An account of why a decision was correct.	*"So I don't need LCV because, probably because we don't have a list."* *"The average will be zero at first because we didn't add anything."*

Table 2. The 4 problem solving activity codes and 5 self-regulation codes analyzed in participants' think-aloud data, along with definitions and representative quotes from transcripts.

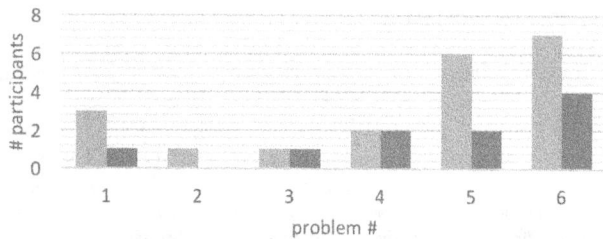

Figure 2. The number of participants who verbalized at least one problem reinterpretation, by problem and experience (CS1→light, CS2→dark).

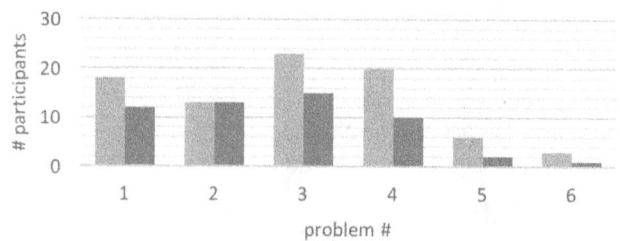

Figure 3. The number of participants who verbalized at least one search for analogous problems, by problem and experience (CS1→light, CS2→dark).

4. RESULTS

In this section, we first discuss the extent to which participants verbalized their problem solving and self-regulation, mirroring the framework in Section 2. Then, we investigate the relationship between self-regulation and errors in participants' solutions. Throughout, we compare the behaviors of participants in the CS1 and CS2 groups. All between group statistical hypothesis tests reported were Kruskal-Wallis tests.

4.1 Problem Solving Process

Here we discuss the four problem solving activities observable in the transcripts, discussing the extent to which participants engaged in them and how they were influenced by self-regulation.

4.1.1 Reinterpreting the problem prompt

Reinterpretation is critical to understanding the nuances and ambiguities in problems [13]. We expected participants to use process and comprehension monitoring to identify knowledge gaps, leading them to reinterpret the problem prompt. Our data showed, however, that very few participants engaged in problem reinterpretation. Of all 37 participants, only 15 verbalized about reinterpreting the prompt. This lack of reinterpretation was consistent across both experience groups: 8 (of 21) CS1 and 7 (of 16) CS2 participants verbalized reinterpreting.

As shown in Figure 2, CS1 participants primarily reinterpreted the context shifted problems, 5 and 6, where they demonstrated difficulty conceptualizing the problem they were attempting to solve. In contrast, the CS2 participants that reinterpreted did so across most of the problems. This suggested a pattern of self-regulation related to experience, but the frequency of reinterpretation verbalizations across all problems was not different between groups (p=0.59, H=2.57).

Participants often began coding without fully understanding the problem, leaving them with knowledge gaps in the problem requirements and causing them to later stop implementation to address the gaps. For example, while implementing a loop for problem 6, P4 (CS1) stopped to question, *"Should I do less than 200? ...doubles? [Should it be] While 100 is less than or equal to 200?"* Only after deciding what logic to use were they able to continue coding. Similarly, P3 (CS1) questioned requirements while coding the output for their solution, realizing that a small detail may invalidate their work: *"do you want me to give you this decimal years, how many years it would take? Because this is a whole different math, I think."* After resolving this concern, they completed the output and started on the next problem. During this process, comprehension monitoring helped participants identify gaps (e.g., should they use less than, or less than and equal to?) Process monitoring spurred participants into reinterpreting the problem. Stronger self-regulation at the beginning of problem solving may have prevented these disruptive task switches.

4.1.2 Searching for analogous problems

Programmers draw upon knowledge of previously encountered problems to provide insight into new problems [14,30]. We expected that participants would engage in process monitoring and self-explanation to identify when they had found a past problem that might help them build a solution.

Our results showed that participants frequently searched for analogous problems and solutions. Of the 37 participants, 29 verbalized a search for analogous solutions at least once across all problems. Figure 3 shows that this varied by problem and was more prevalent for problems 1-4, where there were prior examples to leverage. Of all search verbalizations, 83% (316 of 380) occurred in this context. Participants may have perceived problems 5 and 6 as entirely new problems, unable to see the deeper structural similarities due to their inexperience.

CS1 participants verbalized searches for analogous problems across many problems, while CS2 participants did not. While the frequency of search verbalizations across all problems was not significantly different (p=0.89, H=0.29), the CS1 participants searched in up to 5 of the 6 problems, relying on prior solutions to solve the problem. In contrast, CS2 participants verbalized searching for only 3 of the 6 problems, with many verbalizing none. This indicates that those with less experience were self-regulating *more*, perhaps due to the problems being more novel to them.

The content of participants' search verbalizations differed by experience. First, CS1 participants tended to explicitly reference examples (e.g. *"...which means I have to combine example one and example two."* (P26)) while CS2 participants referenced problem details (e.g. *"So it's sort of like the last problem where you need to be keeping track of certain scores."* (P10)). Another difference was the scope of the analogy identified. CS1 participants often identified similarities about surface features of the solution; for example, P33 identified that their loop should be the same as the one in the example, *"So I think you would just do the same, except you take out everything that's under 70 for this one."* Similarly, P44 said, *"So the loop termination condition is very similar to the first example."* CS2 participants indicated the entire solution as being analogous: *"Okay, so this is like the exact same [problem] pretty much with different values."* (P37). This difference reveals that CS1 participants were self-regulating at a structural granularity, while CS2 self-regulated at a computational level.

4.1.3 Adapting previous solutions

Just as programmers rely on prior knowledge to conceptualize novel problems, they also rely on previous [15]. Self-regulation is integral to this, requiring comprehension monitoring to understand the previous solution and the current problem, while planning the adaptations necessary, all while monitoring their adaptation progress.

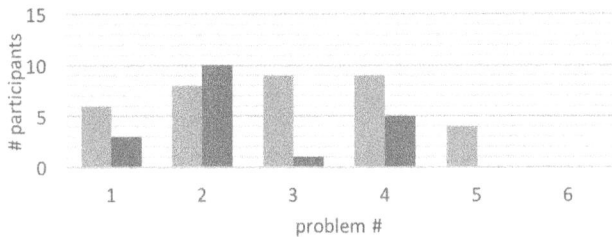

Figure 4. The number of participants who verbalized at least one solution adaption, by problem and experience (CS1→light, CS2→dark).

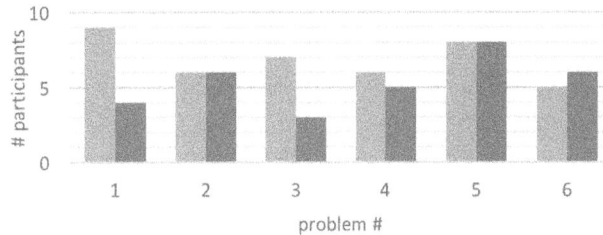

Figure 5. The number of participants who verbalized at least one solution evaluation, by problem and experience (CS1→light, CS2→dark).

Our data shows that although many *searched* for previous problems, only half verbalized *adapting* a previous solution (10 of 21 CS1 and 9 of 16 CS2). However, as Figure 4 shows, frequency varied by experience. CS1 participants tended to verbalize adaptation for more of the six problems, but did not verbalize more frequently (CS1 and CS2 groups had a median of 1 verbalization across all problems, p=0.88, H=0.02).

CS2 participants also appeared to be more confident, suggesting less need for comprehension monitoring. To illustrate, consider P18 (CS1), who said: "*So this one is a bit different because this time, we have to only calculate the average for those students who have passed.*" In contrast, the much shorter, and arguably more confident comment made by P4 (CS2), "*So it's the same problem as example one, it's just the values are different.*"

While the length and tone of the verbalizations for adapting previous solutions varied slightly, the content varied little, with most providing a single high level detail about how the previous solution would need to be changed. Examples include P15 (CS1), who said "*So basically, it's the same thing but now, we're just counting two instead of the sevens*" and P6 (CS2), "*So this time, instead of sevens, we should count the twos.*"

4.1.4 Evaluating solutions
Evaluation of a solution, including analysis and testing, are critical to successfully solving programming problems [17]. We expected participants to engage in comprehension monitoring and process regulation to determine whether to engage in evaluation and determine the quality and level of detail of the evaluation.

Figure 5 shows only about half of participants verbalized evaluation. Overall, 42% (9 of 21) of CS1 participants did compared to 62% (10 of 16) of CS2 participants. However, this difference was not statistically significant (p=0.27, H=1.20).

There were two types of evaluations. Many were short statements that occurred before or just after the mental simulation of code. Those that occurred before announced the *intent* to evaluate. For example, P10 (CS1) completed their solution and said, "*All right. I'm just going to check the solution.*" Similarly, P22 (CS2) finished initializing variables but wanted to verify that they listed the correct values in their array stating, "*Let me to double check*" before reading off each of the values in the problem prompt, verifying they exist in the array. Statements that occurred after evaluation focused on the *result* of evaluation. For example, P10 (CS1) said, "*All right. I am satisfied with this solution*" after tracing their completed solution. P5 (CS2) said, "*I think that's fine*" after briefly looking over their code. These verbalizations likely represented their decision that their evaluation was adequate.

Most evaluations were on entire solutions but some participants evaluated smaller portions of code. For example, P26 (CS1) evaluated the initialization of their grades array: "*I'll just double check to make sure I put them all in correctly*" ensuring that the

data was correct. P3 (CS2) verbalized intent to evaluate their loop, "*So let me just check the for loop*", after which they returned to implementing their output. Some participants verbalized their tracing. For instance, P39 (CS1) traced their completed solution while saying, "*Awesome, that should be good. First nine holes zero, second nine holes zero, total score, go through it each time. Print it the first time, print the second time, add them up for a total... Awesome.*" While there were differences between participants, there were no systematic differences between the groups.

Evaluation impacted problem solving by exposing misconceptions and errors and by helping participants gain confidence. For example, P22 (CS2) identified an error: "*Double checking. Yep. Oh, I think we need a print line. Yeah.*" In these cases, participants returned to either reinterpreting the problem to clarify ambiguities, or they returned to code having located a defect. The second outcome was an increase in confidence allowing the participant to continue onto the next sub-problem or problem. For example, after evaluating, P19 said: "*All right. I am satisfied with this solution.*"

4.2 The Role of Self-Regulation
Having discussed the problem solving behaviors that rely upon, and thus indirectly indicate self-regulation, in this section we describe our findings on the role of self-regulation.

4.2.1 Planning
Planning is pervasive throughout programming problem solving, guiding the direction that programmers take and driving the choices of both what to do and when to do it [30]. We expected that few participants would exhibit planning given their inexperience.

In fact, as you can see in Figure 6 the *majority* of participants verbalized planning. Only two did not, both of whom were CS1 participants. For context, one of these participants had slightly fewer errors than the average participant while the other had the 3rd most errors in their solutions among all participants. CS1 participants had a median of 5 planning verbalizations while the CS2 group had a median of 6. However, this was not a significant difference (p=0.17, H=1.88).

When participants verbalized planning, they focused on two topics. First, they spoke about intent to evaluate such as when P10 stated,

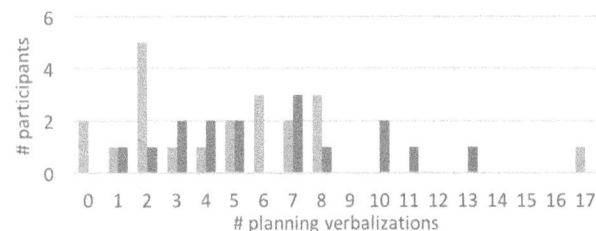

Figure 6. Frequency of participants' planning verbalizations across all problems, by experience (CS1→light, CS2→dark).

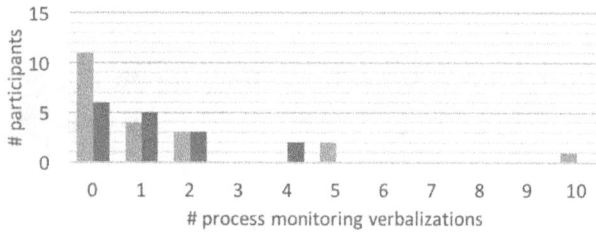

Figure 7. Frequency of participants' process monitoring across all problems, by experience (CS1→light, CS2→dark).

"*I'm just going to check the solutions*" or while already evaluating P16 said, "*Let's go through this one more time.*" Second, they spoke about plans for implementation, primarily for a specific line of code. Examples include P6, who said, "*I'm gonna print out the result*" or P30's realization, "*...and we can do a sum for sum1 right here.*" The more abstract and less granular plans for code included larger sections of code as in P31's comment, "*So after reading this, I think a good first step would be to initialize the variables*" or when P5 decided to write the structure of their if-statement block, "*so first I'm just going to write it.*" There were no discernable differences in the types of planning between the CS1 and CS2 participants.

4.2.2 Process monitoring
Our framework suggests that programmers engage in process monitoring to track their progress through their problem solving process, identifying when goals have been completed, then utilizing planning to identify necessary next steps.

Our data showed that only half of participants verbalized process monitoring and those that did, did it rarely. Figure 7 shows that only 10 of 21 CS1 participants verbalized process monitoring, averaging just 1 verbalization per participant over all six problems. There was one outlier in this group, a 22-year old female, who verbalized about process a total of 10 times across all problems. There were no indications as to why she verbalized process as much as she did and her other self-regulation behaviors were unremarkable, however, she made fewer errors than 63% of participants. CS2 participants had a median of 1 verbalization; not significantly different from CS1 which had a median of 0 (p=0.61, H=0.26).

We observed two types of process monitoring. The most prevalent was a declaration of having completed an implementation sub-goal. This was often verification of completing the initialization of all needed variables, or completion of a loop. For example, P29 said: "*Okay, so I've got the list. I've got the count. I've got LCV. I've got sum.*" or P6's comment about completing the content of a loop: "*So I got the total and the count, so that's the end of the for-loop.*" The second type of process monitoring was when participants declared a solution complete. Examples of this include, "*And printed. I'm on the next task.*" (P1), and "*Yay I'm done (maybe).*" (P22). Both types appeared to help participants segment their process, marking the end of a task and the beginning of planning the next one.

4.2.3 Comprehension monitoring
Our framework suggests that programmers engage in comprehension monitoring to identify knowledge gaps. The more a programmer is aware of their misunderstandings about a problem or a piece of code, or of their own confidence of some given code being correct, the more likely they will make better decisions.

Surprisingly, we found that CS2 participants were much less likely to verbalize comprehension monitoring than CS1 participants. Only 6 of 16 (37%) CS2 participants verbalized comprehension monitoring, compared to the 14 of 21 (66%) CS1 participants. Moreover, Figure 8 shows CS2 participants verbalized significantly

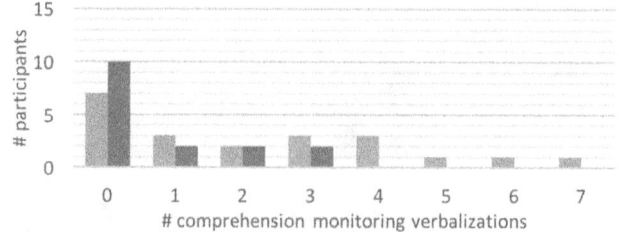

Figure 8. Frequency of participants' comprehension monitoring across all problems, by experience (CS1→light, CS2→dark).

less (p=0.03, H=4.70) than CS1 participants with a median of 0 verbalizations per participant to CS1's 2.

There were two types of comprehension monitoring. First, many statements involved participants realizing they did not understand something. For instance, CS1 participant P8 commented, "*I don't know what end while means...*" while reading example pseudo-code, and then proceeded to self-explain, finally coming to an understanding. Similarly, P25 (CS1) acknowledged their confusion after reading an example, "*So I'm a little bit confused.*" Rather than just continuing, their process monitoring facilitated the realization of something that was unclear and they decided to re-reading the example. The other type of comprehension monitoring involved participants absorbing information, often from examples or when attempting to understand a problem. For instance, while reading example code P11 (CS1) said, "*So I think I will say, I 90% understand this method.*" While they acknowledged they did not fully understand the example, they felt their comprehension was sufficient to begin work on a similar programming problem. There was no different in the type of comprehension monitoring made by CS1 and CS2 participants; CS1 participants just verbalized more.

The role of comprehension monitoring was primarily to understand examples or a problem. The majority of verbalizations occurred while reading example solutions, including indicators of understanding (e.g. "*It's very simple and I think people can understand it really well*", P10, CS2) and confusion ("*I'm not sure what the length means?*" (P11, CS1). When participants monitored problem comprehension, they indicated statements of confusion, as in P18 (CS1)'s need for domain knowledge: "*And so actually, I don't know how this golf scoring works. How does the golf scoring works?*" We found no differences in the content of CS1 and CS2 participants' comprehension monitoring.

4.2.4 Reflection on cognition
Our framework proposes that metacognitive reflection helps programmers to be aware of their own thought processes and the limits and biases in their memory and reasoning. Because prior studies characterize metacognition among novices as being rare, we expected few participants to verbalize it during problem solving activities.

Reflection was more common than we expected. Figure 9 shows that CS2 participants tended to reflect (9 of 16, or 56% vs. 9 of 21, or 42% of CS1 participants). CS2 participants had a median of 1 verbalization compared to a median of 0 for the CS1 participants. However, the frequency difference between groups, across all problems, was not significant (p=0.18, H=1.80).

The content of participants' reflections was similar across groups. Some reflections were on process, such as "*I could calculate it by hand, but I don't want to do that*", when P25 (CS1) was contemplating how find the number of 7s rolled on a pair of dice. Another example was P10 (CS2)'s comment, "*I'm thinking about*

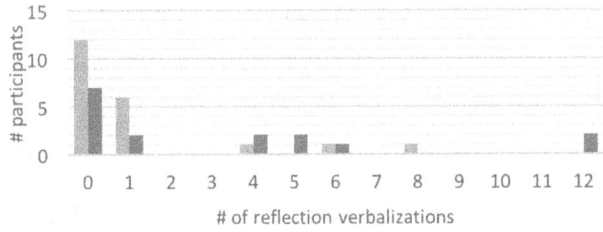

Figure 9. Frequency of participants' metacognitive reflection across all problems, by experience (CS1→light, CS2→dark).

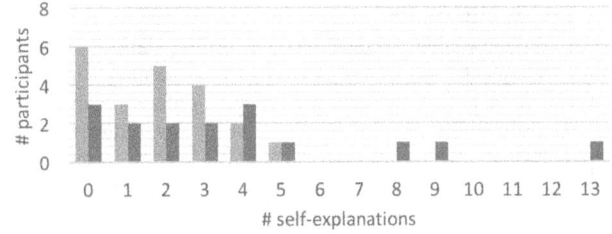

Figure 10. Frequency of participants' self-explanations across all problems, by experience (CS1→light, CS2→dark).

the best way to approach the problem", pausing to consider how to approach solving a problem after reading the prompt. Other reflections concerned confidence. For example, "*And I'm not so sure if this is right*" (P25, CS1), and "*I feel like it's not correct but I'm just going to roll with it*" (P38, CS1). A third type of reflection was when participants identified mistakes, as in "*oh, I forgot to set the rolls.*" (P28, CS2), and "*I feel like I'm wasting mental energy trying to see what scenario is going on when I should be focusing on the essentials*" (P38, CS1). The final type of reflection consisted of reminders, as when P10 (CS2) was trying to establish a process, "*Always need to remember to increment the loop control variable.*"

4.2.5 Self-explanation

In our framework, we suggest that programmers use self-explanation to rationalize decisions they have made and to develop understanding that will influence future decisions. We expected to see participants engage in self-explanation to resolve confusion.

Figure 10 shows that most participants did engage in self-explanation. Overall, 75% (28 of 37) self-explained at some point, with 81% (13 of 16) of CS2 participants self-explaining while only 71% (15 of 21) CS1 participants did. Despite the variation, the frequency of self-explanations across all problems between groups was not significant (p=0.108, H=2.57).

There were three types of self-explanations. Many aimed to increase code comprehension, as in "*Oh wait, no, then it can't be length, because I get to count, all right, count equal zero.*" (P19, CS1), or tracing code for clarification as in, "*And it will not go in two again, which means it will run exactly five times.*" (P28, CS2). Other self-explanations identified participants deciding what code to write. For example, P25 (CS1) was deciding which variables to initialize: "*So I don't need LCV because, probably because we don't have a list.*" P28 (CS2) rationalized about what to write for their loop conditional and said, "*...while loop can use the length, right? Yeah. Because, you have to go through all the items and check it.*"

4.3 Self-Regulation and Errors

In the prior sections we investigated the extent to which participants engaged in self-regulation during problem solving, finding several variations, particularly by experience. In this section, we investigate the extent this variation explained participants' errors.

As we described in Section 2, we measured errors as the smallest number of lines that needed to be added, removed, or changed for a solution to produce correct output. We expected participants with less experience to have more errors in their solutions. Across problems 4-6 (the problems analyzed for errors) CS1 participants' median errors was 6 (with 2 perfect scores on all problems). CS2 participants had a median of 3 errors (with 3 participants receiving perfect scores). For the easier questions, a lack of complexity in the problems, as well as the provided examples, likely contributed to the CS1 participants' ability to craft suitable solutions. On these questions they did not make many more errors than the CS2 group

(p=0.34, H=0.88). On the most difficult problem (problem 5 in Table 1), however, the CS1 group made significantly more errors than CS2 (p<.001, H=8.35). This was true despite the problem being only slightly more complex than previous problems.

To investigate the relationship between self-regulation and errors, we built a multiple linear regression model based on several variables. We included gender, programming experience, and self-efficacy, as each tend to effect programming success. We then included frequencies of all five self-regulation types across all problems. This model assumed that verbalizations of each type of self-regulation are indicators of overall self-regulation skill, as opposed to being specific to a problem.

Table 3 shows the resulting model for all participants. We found a significant model ($F(8,28) = 2.66$, p=0.26), with an R^2 of 0.43, with gender a significant factor (p<0.05), with women having more errors in their solutions. Because we found significant disparities in the behavior of participants by experience groups, we also built two separate regression models, one for participants in CS1 (n=21), and one for CS2 (n=16). We included the same factors in these models, excluding programming experience. Table 3 shows the two resulting models for each group. The model was significant for CS1 ($F(7,13)=3.11$, p<0.05), with an R^2 of 0.62, but none of the factors had a individually significant relationship with errors. The CS2 model was *not* significant overall ($F(7,8)=2.232$, p>0.05)—likely due to a small sample size of 16—but there were several large and significant effect sizes in the coefficients that we hypothesized would effect errors (a common rule for judging whether to interpret significant coefficients of a non-significant model). These included a ~3 error *decrease* for each verbalization of comprehension monitoring (p<0.05), a ~1 error *decrease* for each verbalization of planning (p<0.05) and ~1 error *increase* of for each verbalization of self-explanation (p<0.05).

Variable	All participants			CS1 participants			CS2 participants		
	B	SE B	β	B	SE B	β	B	SE B	β
Gender (M=0, F=1)	3.62	1.58	**0.36***	5.99	2.88	0.52	0.55	1.50	0.09
# CS Courses	-1.49	0.90	-0.30	–	–	–	–	–	–
Self-Efficacy	0.29	0.37	0.12	0.93	0.57	0.31	-0.15	0.29	-0.12
Planning	-0.06	0.23	-0.05	-0.44	0.34	-0.29	-0.79	0.29	**-0.91***
Process Monitoring	-0.64	0.37	-0.26	-0.59	0.45	-0.25	0.26	0.60	0.11
Comp. Monitoring	0.61	0.51	0.23	0.62	0.63	0.23	-2.90	0.99	**-1.09***
Reflection	0.20	0.32	0.13	1.10	0.54	0.41	0.02	0.26	0.03
Self-explanation	0.01	0.42	-0.01	0.11	1.07	0.03	0.98	0.34	**1.19***
R^2		0.43			0.62			0.66	
F		**2.66***			**3.11***			2.23	

*p < 0.05

Table 3. Three models predicting errors from demographic and self-regulation variables. Unstandardized coefficients (B), standard errors (SE B), and standardized coefficients (β).

5. DISCUSSION

Our results show a few trends. First, most self-regulation behaviors were infrequent, inconsistently verbalized, shallow in their application, and often ineffective at reducing programming errors. Among those with more experience, the frequency of planning and comprehension monitoring was related to fewer errors, while more frequent self-explanation predicted more errors. In this section we interpret these results and discuss implications.

The infrequency of self-regulation was quite visible among CS1 participants. They engaged in *searching for analogous problems*, *adapting previous solutions* and *planning*, but showed little depth in reasoning. The infrequency of *reinterpreting the problem prompt* and *evaluation* by CS1 participants was consistent with prior work [27] and their infrequent *comprehension monitoring* and *planning*: they rarely reflected on their understanding of the problem or their code. Table 3 shows the self-regulation they exhibited had little relationship to the errors they made, suggesting that their efforts to self-regulate were simply ineffective.

Similarly, the CS2 group exhibited infrequent and shallow self-regulation. Even the most frequent self-regulation behavior, planning, only occurred about once per problem (Section 4.2.1). CS2 participants also reinterpreted the problem prompt throughout the problem solving process rather than at the beginning, suggesting shallow or absent comprehension monitoring. The lack of process monitoring also plagued CS2 participants. Despite increased experience, they were not very aware of what they are doing or why. That said, the more that CS2 participants engaged in planning and comprehension monitoring, the fewer errors they created (Table 3). This suggests that as learners acquire the necessary knowledge to write programs, self-regulation skills begin to account for differences in success.

It was surprising that self-explanation was not related to success, and in the case of CS2 participants, was associated with *more* errors. This is in direct contrast to prior work, which has shown that self-explanation is a key strategy in problem solving success [4,21,30]. One interpretation is that *verbalizations* of self-explanations are simply more prevalent when participants are struggling: successful participants may have internally self-explained, and done so in a more disciplined manner.

Although we did not study the progression from CS1 to CS2 directly, our results suggest that something is leading to more effective self-regulation. This is in line with Falkner et al.'s work [12] which found that, compared to novices, CS students in their final year of college used more successful self-regulation strategies such as design, testing and problem decomposition. One explanation for this is that CS1 courses are somehow teaching self-regulation and programming problem solving—this is not the case at our institution, but it may arise indirectly through lab sections, TAs, or classroom discussions. Another explanation might be that students who decide to continue to CS2 have independently developed more effective self-regulation strategies.

Interestingly, gender was associated with errors, but only for students CS1 participants. Moreover, this was not explained by differences in self-efficacy. One possibility is that there is some other gender-related factor not in our model; another is that the women who responded to our recruiting were systematically different from the men (we noticed that many women expressed wanting to help future students struggle less than they did).

One implication of these results is on the prior work on self-regulation in computing education. Despite prior studies showing that self-regulation is key in programming expertise [9, 17], and that it can be productivity taught to novices [4,19], our study demonstrates that novices *do* self-regulate, albeit infrequently and poorly. This suggests that efforts to teach self-regulation in CS have a foundation to build upon, but that they may also need to address flaws in students' existing self-regulation behaviors. Our results suggest that these flaws are a lack of *consistent, disciplined* self-regulation during problem solving and few reflections on cognition.

Another implication is that, because self-regulation is only effective with adequate prior knowledge, it may be that the *timing* of teaching self-regulation skills is important. Having disciplined self-regulation skills but lacking adequate programming knowledge may only serve to exhaust and frustrate learners. However, disciplined self-regulation skills may facilitate learners using newly acquired programming knowledge sooner, and more productively.

Our results have several implications for teaching. If self-regulation behaviors are critical to programming success as prior work suggests [9,17], it should be explicitly taught. Prior work has shown that self-explanation [4], and problem solving frameworks [19] can promote success. Our work suggests targeted instruction on specific types of self-regulation—planning and comprehension monitoring—may need further investigation. There are many questions about how these might be taught (e.g., when, how to interleave with syntax and semantics, what pedagogy to use). While only planning and comprehension monitoring had a relationship with errors in our study, other forms of self-regulation might also be taught explicitly. For instance, is instruction on metacognitive reflection [10] beneficial for programmers? How might teaching problem decomposition and reinterpretation effect success? These remain open areas for computing education research.

As with any empirical study, ours had many limitations. First, all studies of this kind could benefit from more data. With a sample size of 37 it was difficult to achieve the power needed to precisely identify effects so many important relationships may have been masked. Also, linear regressions show correlation and not causation; thus, our interpretations may be missing important unseen factors, meaning self-regulation may not cause programmers to craft more successful solutions. Due to typically high variation in programming knowledge, our results were also noisy, further compounding the small sample. While think-aloud protocol is well established for studying self-regulation [6,16], and one of the only mechanisms allowing us to observe cognitive processes, its robustness as a signal varies due to participants' comfort thinking aloud to a stranger. Finally, because participants' knowledge is difficult to measure, our choice of programming problems from prior work led to a slight ceiling effect on errors, hindering our ability to more precisely identify relationships to errors.

Despite these and many other limitations to the validity and generalizability of our results, we view our findings as an important first step in understanding the relationship between self-regulation and programming problem solving. With further research, better instruments, and refined theories, we hope for a future in which teachers not only understand the importance of self-regulation in computing education, but can teach it too.

6. ACKNOWLEDGMENTS

This work was supported in part by the National Science Foundation (NSF) under grants 1314399, 1240786, 1153625, 1240957, and 1314384. Any opinions, findings, conclusions or recommendations are those of the authors and do not necessarily reflect the views of the NSF.

7. REFERENCES

[1] Askar, P. and Davenport, D. 2009. An investigation of factors related to self-efficacy for Java programming among engineering students. *TOJET: The Turkish Online Journal of Educational Technology* 8.1. http://eric.ed.gov/?id=ED503900.

[2] Beaubouef, T., and Mason, J. 2005. Why the high attrition rate for computer science students: some thoughts and observations. *ACM SIGCSE Bulletin*, 37(2), 103-106.

[3] Bergin, S, Reilly, R and Traynor, D. 2005. Examining the Role of Self-Regulated Learning on Introductory Programming Performance. *Proceedings of the First International Workshop on Computing Education Research*, 81–86.

[4] Bielaczyc, K., Pirolli, P. L., and Brown, A. L. 1995. Training in self-explanation and self-regulation strategies: Investigating the effects of knowledge acquisition activities on problem solving. *Cognition and instruction*, 13(2), 221-252.

[5] Cao, J., Fleming, S., Burnett, M. M., and Scaffidi, C. 2015. Idea Garden: Situated support for problem solving by end-user programmers. *Interacting with Computers* 27(6), 640-660.

[6] Chi, M. T. 1997. Quantifying qualitative analyses of verbal data: A practical guide. *The journal of the learning sciences*, 6(3), 271-315.

[7] Clements, D. H., and Gullo, D. F. 1984. Effects of computer programming on young children's cognition. *Journal of Educational Psychology*, 76(6), 1051.

[8] Crippen, K. J., and Earl, B.L. 2007 The impact of web-based worked examples and self-explanation on performance, problem solving, and self-efficacy. *Computers & Education* 49, no. 3: 809–21.

[9] Eteläpelto, A. 1993. Metacognition and the expertise of computer program comprehension. *Scandinavian Journal of Educational Research*, 37(3), 243-254.

[10] Fahim, M, and Fakhri Alamdari, E. Maximizing Learners' 2014. Metacognitive awareness in listening through metacognitive instruction: An empirical study. *International Journal of Research Studies in Education* 3, no.3.

[11] Falkner, K, Vivian, R and Falkner, N.J.G. 2014 Identifying Computer Science Self-Regulated Learning Strategies. *Proceedings of the 2014 Conference on Innovation & Technology in Computer Science Education*, 291–96.

[12] Falkner, K, Szabo, C, Vivian, R and Falkner, N.J.G. 2015. Evolution of Software Development Strategies. *Proceedings of the 37th International Conference on Software Engineering - Volume 2*, 243–52.

[13] Greeno, J.G. and Hall, R.P. 1997. Practicing representation. *Phi Delta Kappan* 78(5), 361.

[14] Hoc, J, and Nguyen-Xuan, A. 1990. Language semantics, mental models and analogy. *Psychology of programming*, 10, 139-156.

[15] Ko, A.J., Myers, B. and Aung, H.H. 2004. Six learning barriers in end-user programming systems. *Proceedings of the IEEE Symposium on Visual Languages and Human Centric Computing,* 199-206.

[16] Koriat, A. 2016. Processes in Self-monitoring and Self-regulation. *The Wiley Blackwell Handbook of Judgment and Decision Making*, 2 Volume Set.

[17] Li, P. L., Ko, A. J., & Zhu, J. 2015. What makes a great software engineer?. *International Conference on Software Engineering-Volume 1*

[18] Linn, M. C., and Clancy, M. J. 1992. Can experts' explanations help students develop program design skills? *International Journal of Man-Machine Studies*, 36(4), 511-551.

[19] Loksa, D., Ko, A. J., Jernigan, W., Oleson, A., Mendez, C. J., and Burnett, M. M. Programming, Problem Solving, and Self-Awareness: Effects of Explicit Guidance. ACM Conference on Human Factors in Computing (CHI), to appear.

[20] Margulieux, L.E., Guzdial, M., and Catrambone, R. 2012. Subgoal-labeled instructional material improves performance and transfer in learning to develop mobile applications. *ACM International Conference on Computing Education Research*, 71–78.

[21] Michelene T. H. Chi, M. B. 1989. Self-Explanations: How Students Study and Use Examples in Learning to Solve Problems. *Cognitive Science* 13(2), 145–82.

[22] Morrison, B. B., Margulieux, L. E., and Guzdial, M. 2015. Subgoals, context, and worked examples in learning computing problem solving. *ACM International Conference on Computing Education Research*, 21-29.

[23] Morrison, B.B., Margulieux, L.E., Ericson, B., Guzdial M. 2016. Subgoals help Students Solve Parsons Problems. *ACM Technical Symposium on Computing Science Education*, 42-47.

[24] Pea, R. D., and Kurland, D. M. 1984. On the cognitive effects of learning computer programming. *New ideas in psychology*, 2(2), 137-168.

[25] Pennington, N. and Grabowski, B., 1990. The tasks of programming. *Psychology of programming*, 307, 45-62.

[26] Pintrich, P. R., Wolters, C. A., and Baxter, G. P. 2000. Assessing metacognition and self-regulated learning. In *G. Schraw, & J. C. Impara (Eds.), Issues in the measurement of metacognition*. NE: University of Nebraska-Lincoln.

[27] Ido, R., Holmes, N. G., Day, J., and Bonn, D. 2012. Evaluating Metacognitive Scaffolding in Guided Invention Activities. *Instructional Science* 40(4). 691–710.

[28] Sawyer, K. R. 2006. Introduction: The new science of learning. In R. K. Sawyer (Ed.) *The Cambridge handbook of learning sciences* (1-18). New York: Cambridge University Press.

[29] Soloway, E., and Spohrer, J. C. 2013. *Studying the novice programmer*. Psychology Press.

[30] Soloway, E. 1986. Learning to program = learning to construct mechanisms and explanations. *Communications of the ACM*, 29(9), 850-858.

[31] Winne, P.H. and Perry, N.E. 2000. Measuring self-regulated learning. In P. Pintrich, M. Boekaerts, & M. Seidner (Eds.), *Handbook of self-regulation*. 531-566. Orlando, FL: Academic Press.

Replication, Validation, and Use of a Language Independent CS1 Knowledge Assessment

Miranda C. Parker, Mark Guzdial
Georgia Institute of Technology
85 5th Street NW
Atlanta, GA 30308
miranda.parker@gatech.edu,
guzdial@cc.gatech.edu

Shelly Engleman
SageFox Consulting Group
675 Seminole Ave NE Suite 303
Atlanta, GA 30307
+1-404-633-9005
sengelman@sagefoxgroup.com

ABSTRACT

Computing education lags other discipline-based education research in the number and range of validated assessments available to the research community. Validated assessments are important for researchers to reduce experimental error due to flawed assessments and to allow for comparisons between different experiments. Although the need is great, building assessments from scratch is difficult. Once an assessment is built, it's important to be able to replicate it, in order to address problems within it, or to extend it. We developed the Second CS1 Assessment (SCS1) as an isomorphic version of a previously validated language-independent assessment for introductory computer science, the FCS1. Replicating the FCS1 is important to enable free use by a broader research community. This paper is documentation of our process for replicating an existing validated assessment and validating the success of our replication. We present initial use of SCS1 by other research groups, to serve as examples of where it might be used in the future. SCS1 is useful for researchers, but care must be taken to avoid undermining the validity argument.

CCS Concepts

• Social and Professional topics ➔ Student assessment

Keywords

Assessment; CS1; validity; replication

1. ROLE OF VALIDATED ASSESSMENTS IN EDUCATION RESEARCH

All discipline-based education research communities need assessments of learning. At least some of these assessments should be validated to create an argument that they are actually measuring the concepts they are intended to measure. If the community accepts the argument, the instrument can be a useful tool for the research community.

We use *assessments* to mean instruments and methods for evaluating and documenting the nature, quality, or ability of

ICER '16, September 8–12, 2016, Melbourne, VIC, Australia.
© 2016 ACM. ISBN 978-1-4503-4449-4/16/09…$15.00.
DOI: http://dx.doi.org/10.1145/2960310.2960316

students [1]. In our context, assessments are used to measure a student's understanding, learning, or ability within a course or subject area. We will focus on multiple-choice assessments of learning made of a series of questions, composed of a stem followed by response options [18]. The stem is the question, which may also be referred to as an item. The response options are comprised of correct and incorrect options, and the latter can also be referred to as distractors or foils. Assessments are abundant in discipline-based education fields older than computing, such as physics, mathematics, and engineering education [15, 19]. However, computing education has few validated assessments [41].

Concept inventories are a class of assessment instruments with some of the features discussed above. They are standardized, multiple-choice, assessment tools to identify misconceptions, investigate learning, measure student understanding of core concepts, and, if desired, ascertain the pedagogical impact on the student's achievement towards expert-level thinking [1, 10, 18]. Concept inventories are not final exams, but include broader topics more central to the subject and can inform instructional or curricular changes [34]. Advanced topics in computing have concept inventories, including algorithms and architecture [16, 26, 28]. Similar to the broader area of assessments, CS1 has few concept inventories.

1.1 History of Assessments and Concept Inventories

We briefly summarize here the history of standardized exams. Standardized, objective tests of learning originated in the early 1900s [30]. Previously, most learning assessments were essay-based. Objective testing presented a more efficient and reliable way to test a student's learning than to have (for example) essay questions that need to be interpreted and which different graders might interpret differently. The first large-scale use of objective tests was the Pennsylvania Study in 1928, which tested no less than 70 percent of all Pennsylvanian college seniors and approximately 75 percent of Pennsylvanian high school seniors [30]. Besides being 12 hours and 3,200 questions long, what marked the Pennsylvania Study was the focus on *learning* rather than *achievement*. Students were tested in their senior year of high school, and then again in their sophomore and senior years of college. The distinction between *achievement assessment* and *assessment of learning* is important, as achievement is the accumulation of learning up to a certain time and learning is a change in student's knowledge over time [30]. For example, achievement assessments such as assignments, quizzes, and exams are not in and of themselves measurements of learning. Rather, they serve as a method to evaluate performance in the form of a grade for a course. Also, these instruments are not validated and tend to be based on the instructor's perception of the subject [1]. On the other hand, assessments of learning are integral parts of course design. These learning instruments allow instructors to reflect on what learning outcomes they want for their students and also decide which assessment devices might be best suited for those outcomes [32].

Validated, broadly applicable learning assessment instruments are essential for growth of the research discipline. Validation is an argument that the assessment measures what it purports to measure [36]. Validated assessment instruments can be used, for example, to compare different instructional approaches [10]. They can be used to measure a student's understanding of the material, which may not be reflected in their grades, since grades could be influenced by factors other than learning, e.g., class attendance. With the recent proliferation of introductory computing curricula across the globe, validated assessment instruments are needed to explicitly compare approaches for learning.

Concept inventories, as a type of validated assessment, were first developed in the 1980s within the physics education community, beginning with the Force Concept Inventory (FCI) [15, 19]. This concept inventory assessed students' conceptions of Newtonian physics. The FCI was used in understanding and identifying where students and instructors conceptions differed [34]. Even conventionally high performing students failed simple conceptual FCI questions, which is indicative of the difference between concept inventories and final exams. The FCI was validated and shown to be a reliable assessment by a study with 6,000 students and their scores on the FCI [12]. The results of using the FCI helped support the shift within the physics community to teach with a more active, student-engagement approach rather than lecture-based teaching.

The FCI showed that concept inventories can be effective instruments for supporting education reform [41]. When used with valid and reliable assessments, concept inventories can help match instruction to what the students need to learn [10]. This is achieved by providing a before and after view of student learning, based on different teaching strategies. Additionally, concept inventories can evaluate student understanding relative to the goals of the course, further promoting the use of assessments in curriculum development [1]. All of the benefits of a concept inventory are not held to a specific class or institution. Concept inventories can compare students' learning outcomes across instructors, institutions, curricula, and pedagogical practices [34].

Concept inventories as assessments of learning have been adapted for and promoted change within STEM fields beyond just physics and the FCI. However, within computing, concept inventories are in their infancy. There are validated concept inventories in the subfields of digital logic and discrete math [1, 14]. The AP CS A exam is a prime example of a valid concept inventory in computing that is used across institutions [34]. However, it is not useful as a research instrument because its questions were not designed to test individual learning objectives or concepts, but instead to achieve psychometric goals of having a normal distribution of student scores [35]. Core concepts in different computing areas have been identified, as well as common misconceptions [34], but there are not many valid concept inventories for CS1.

1.2 Motivation for Replication

In 2010, Allison Elliott Tew created the first validated language-independent content knowledge assessment for introductory computer science at an undergraduate level (a course commonly referred to as "CS1"), the Foundational CS1 Assessment (FCS1) [35, 38]. Tew followed an intensive procedure for the creation of FCS1. First, she defined a minimal content for the course by doing an analysis of the most popular CS1 textbooks [37]. She developed a test specification that was reviewed by a panel of experts [37]. She defined a pseudocode language to be used, and then generated four isomorphic tests: One in her pseudocode, and one in each of MATLAB, Python, and Java. She piloted the questions in an open-ended format, to test readability and generate distractors [38]. Finally, she validated the whole assessment by having participants take two tests (counter-balanced) one week apart: one in their "native" CS1 language, and one in the pseudocode.

The FCS1 was validated through a multi-step argument including expert panel review of the content, large-scale comparison between the FCS1 and language-dependent isomorphic tests, and comparison between performance on the FCS1 and on the students' final CS1 exams. As previously noted, there is a distinct difference between concept inventories and course exams. However, the course exams can be used as a part of a validity argument, and the argument is made stronger by different pieces of evidence working together.

FCS1 has been used by the computing education research community in various contexts, and has been useful in providing insights into student learning. For example, the assessment was used by the ITiCSE 2013 McCracken Working Group in comparison with a novice programmer's ability to solve a practical programming task [39]. The FCS1 was used to measure students' performance, which was then compared to teachers' expectations of the students' performance. The group found that teachers' expectations did not match student performance, and tended to be too optimistic in comparison with the anticipated score. The McCracken Working Group use of FCS1 and their results serve as an example of using FCS1 to answer a research question.

In the case of multiple-question assessments, such as the FCS1, an openly accessible assessment can easily reach a point of *saturation*. We define *saturation* in this context to be where the test or its answers could be easily found (e.g., with an Internet search engine), reducing the effectiveness of the exam. If answers can be found and memorized (or looked up dynamically during the test), then the test is measuring memorization or ability, not understanding. Saturation would weaken the argument for validity of the assessment. If there is a dearth of learning assessments, as in computer science education research, saturation might leave the community without a valid way of measuring learning. However, the existence of multiple assessments dampens the negative consequences of an assessment reaching saturation. As a community, we need to replicate valid knowledge assessments to prevent loss of information and research potential due to saturation.

In order to avoid saturation of the assessment, only a few people have had access to FCS1. For this paper, one author helped with the development of FCS1 and thus had legal access to the assessment. The FCS1 remains the intellectual property of the original author, and we do not have permission to distribute it. We developed a process to iterate on the FCS1 questions to create the Second CS1 Assessment (SCS1), which we followed by a validation process.

```
Given the following code segment.
array = [5, 2, 1, 3, 4, 6, 0, 8, 9]
i = 0
even = 0
WHILE (i < length(array)) AND (array[i] != 0)
DO
        IF (array[i] % 2) == 0 THEN
                even = even + 1
        ENDIF
                i = i + 1
        ENDWHILE
```

What are the values of the variables i and even after the while loop completes its execution?

    A.   i = 1; even = 0

    B.   i = 5; even = 3

    C.   i = 5; even = 4

    D.   i = 6; even = 3

    E.   i = 6; even = 4

```
Given the following code segment.
array = [3, 6, 8, 1, 2, 0, 7, 2, 9]
i = 0
odd = 0
WHILE (i < length(array)) AND (array[i] != 0)
DO
        IF (array[i] % 2) == 1 THEN
                odd = odd + 1
        ENDIF
                i = i + 1
        ENDWHILE
```

What are the values of the variables i and odd after the while loop completes its execution?

    A.   i = 1; odd = 0

    B.   i = 5; odd = 2

    C.   i = 5; odd = 3

    D.   i = 8; odd = 4

    E.   i = 8; odd = 5

Figure 1. Example of an isomorphic mapping. The top box includes the original question from FCS1, and the bottom box has the isomorphic mapping we created for SCS1. The content area of indefinite loops and question style of tracing were maintained, but the problem and variables were altered.

Table 1. Areas considered when creating an isomorphic mapping of FCS1.

Isomorphic area	Area Choices
Content areas	<ul><li>fundamentals</li><li>logical operators</li><li>conditionals</li><li>definite loops</li><li>indefinite loops</li><li>arrays</li><li>function/method parameters</li><li>function/method return values</li><li>recursion</li><li>object oriented basics</li></ul>
Question Types	<ul><li>definitional</li><li>tracing</li><li>code completion</li></ul>

measure of CS1 learning more accessible. Uses of the SCS1 exemplify how it might be used in making research arguments, and where the validity argument for SCS1 is undermined.

2. REPLICATING A VALID ASSESSMENT

We created an isomorphic version of the FCS1 Assessment to create the SCS1 Assessment. Our methods are described here so that they may be used in future replications of valid content knowledge assessments. Like FCS1, SCS1 was designed to measure understanding of introductory computer science concepts at the undergraduate level in a language-independent manner. SCS1 problems are all in a pseudocode language invented by Tew [35] which has been used successfully in other instruments [17]. The replication process is the same as in any education domain [3] but we know that education findings do not always map directly from one domain to another, especially in computing [23]. Therefore it is worth demonstrating the effectiveness of an approach in a new domain. This section details our application of proven replication techniques to a computer science assessment, FCS1.

We created the questions for SCS1 by creating isomorphic copies of the questions in the FCS1. An isomorphic question is created by maintaining the content area for a question as well as the style used to ask the question, but altering the word problem, variables, and answer choices (see examples in Figure 1). The original FCS1 covered nine content areas with three different question types (described in Table 1). Each question in the SCS1 maps to a question in the FCS1 with the same content area and question style, but with different question text and distractors. The difficulty level of each question was not directly addressed when creating an isomorphic mapping, but was assessed in our validation studies outlined in Section 4.

We created isomorphic copies instead of writing completely new questions in order to maintain the validity of FCS1 for SCS1. When replicating valid content knowledge assessments, it can be wise to make small, iterative changes to strengthen the validity argument of the replicated assessment. Arguments for validity are addressed in Section 3.

Tew and Dorn explained the importance of validated assessments for computing education and described the process of developing two validated assessments [36]. We build on their work to highlight the importance of replicating those assessments, present a process for replicating and validating, and start a discussion for how validated assessments can be used most effectively for our community. The more assessments there are—made by replicating previously validated assessments—the more chances the community has to measure learning gains accurately and to determine the effectiveness of teaching approaches. By creating the SCS1, we have made a language-independent, validated

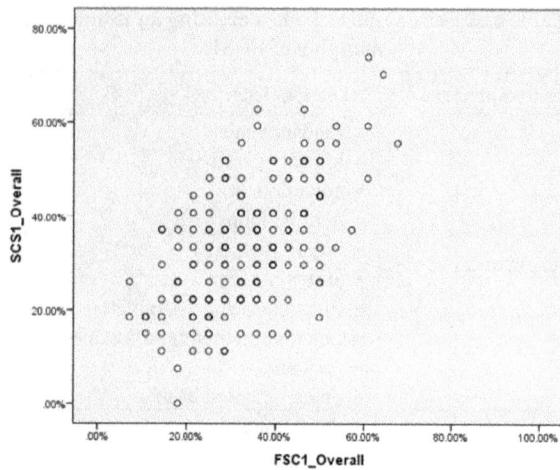

Figure 2. Scatterplot of scores for correlation of FCS1 and SCS1

2.1 Think-Aloud Interviews

While the underlying content remained the same, we changed the questions to create SCS1. The resulting questions might not be read as we intended. We might also have made mistakes in generating distractors. It was important to hear people interpret the questions and answers to ensure that students understood the assessment as we intended. One author conducted these interviews and took notes throughout. The notes of the interview were discussed with another author to analyze where issues were occurring and what needed to change.

We interviewed three students with think-aloud interviews. These students were from our target population: undergraduate students enrolled in introductory computing classes. These interviews were 90 minutes in length, which gave the participants enough time to finish approximately half of the exam. The interviews consisted of a student reading and solving each question aloud, with occasional questioning by the interviewer. The first two students completed the first and second half of SCS1 respectively. The third student was given questions that the first two interviews indicated needed further review, in order of criticality (e.g., problems that needed the most changes after an interview were more critical to review in the next interview). As anticipated, there were typos (the use of the wrong word in a problem) and wording issues (such as vague pronouns, or subject-verb agreements) where the questions were not clear. One question was found to be too easy during the think-aloud interviews so the problem and answers were changed accordingly to increase the difficulty level. All other errors found in the assessment were "sanity check" changes, where the think-aloud interviews revealed that a question might have no right answer, multiple right answers, or nonsensical answers.

2.2 Validation Study

After the test was created, we set out to show construct validity. That is, we wanted to show that the SCS1 measured what it was intended to measure. Tew has created a construct validity argument for FCS1. We aimed to show that SCS1 had construct validity by showing that SCS1 measured the same content as FCS1. Validity arguments are not transitive, so we cannot claim that SCS1 would correlate (for example) with CS1 final exam scores. FCS1 did, but we did not explicitly validate that SCS1 measured the same constructs as the CS1 final exam scores. We

Table 2. Overall correlation between FCS1 and SCS1

Course	FCS1	
	Pearson's Correlation Coefficient	p-value
All (n=183)	0.566	p=0.000**

Table 3. Overall correlations by course, where 1301 is traditional CS in Python, 1315 is Computational Media in Python, and 1371 is CS for Engineers in MATLAB

Course Descriptions	FCS1	
	Pearson's Correlation Coefficient	p-value
Python for CS Majors (n=140)	0.483	$p = 0.000$**
Media Computation (n=30)	0.298	$p = 0.110$
MATLAB for Engineering Majors(n=13)	0.509	$p = 0.076$

have a more limited validity argument, as is typical for an instrument replication study.

To validate the SCS1 against the FCS1, we administered FCS1 and SCS1 to a group of students (n=183), one week apart and counterbalanced. Half of the group took the FCS1 in Week 1 and the SCS1 in Week 2, where the other half of the group took the SCS1 in Week 1 and the FCS1 in Week 2. These students took the assessments near the end of an introductory computing course. There were three courses from which students were recruited— two courses taught CS using Python and one course using MATLAB. The three courses had different computer science emphases. One of the Python courses was a fairly common CS1 approach (e.g., using the *How to Think Like a Computer Scientist* text [6]). The second Python course used a media computation context [11]. The MATLAB course was focused on engineering problem solving. The range of kinds of classes is desirable when validating an assessment of this type.

Students were given one hour to take the exam. Each student was provided with a pseudocode overview to use as reference throughout the assessment. Students were compensated for their participation according to their instructor's discretion, though typically they were given some form of extra credit. Their participation in the study served as practice for their final exam, which was a couple of weeks away from being administered at the time of the study.

It should be noted that the two groups did not take identical versions of the SCS1 Assessments. There was a slight change to one of the questions on the SCS1 between the administrations of the exams due to a typo that was not found during the think-aloud interviews. Analysis on the effect of the typo can be found in the next section.

3. VALIDATING A REPLICATION

A replicated assessment is validated to ensure that the assessment is measuring what the creator or user thinks it is measuring. The use of a non-validated assessment could result in incorrect inferences being drawn about learning and knowledge. The replication can be validated against the original, validated assessment.

In this section, we present our detailed argument for the *construct* and *content* validity of the SCS1. *Construct validity* considers the extent to which performance on an assessment can be interpreted in terms of one or more constructs. *Content validity* considers the extent to which assessment questions provide an adequate and appropriate sample of the domain tasks. We maintained *content validity* from the FCS1 by constructing questions on the exact same content. We only need to argue for *construct validity,* as that is the only thing that changed in the new instrument. Construct and content validity work together to provide evidence that an assessment is working as intended. Since construct validation is dependent on inferences drawn from a variety of data [3, 22], we present a quantitative analysis of the questions on the SCS1 assessment, as well as discuss the correlation between the scores on the FCS1 and SCS1 assessments.

It should be noted that the counter-balanced structure of our validation study could have resulted in unintended priming effects [7]. However, we dismiss the possibility of a priming effect by considering that the students were already primed for the first test by being enrolled in an introductory computing course for almost a full semester before taking our test [27]. In addition, as the tests served as practice final exams, students were motivated to perform on both tests. While it is possible that students explicitly studied concepts they were unfamiliar with on the first test, it is likely that they studied most content from the course in preparation for their final exams during this period.

3.1 Correlation with FCS1

An important step in validation is to correlate scores on the new assessment with other measures of CS1 learning, such as a previously validated assessment. Concurrent validity describes the characteristic of an assessment correlating with a previously validated assessment [22]. Correlating the scores on the FCS1 assessment with final exam scores showed concurrent validity with FCS1. In the development of SCS1, we did not access final exam scores, and so we do not have a direct relation between SCS1 and final exam or course scores. Instead, Pearson's correlation analysis was used to investigate whether student scores on the SCS1 can be positively correlated with their scores on the FCS1.

A Pearson correlation coefficient was computed to assess the relationship between the score on the FCS1 and SCS1 Assessments (see Table 2). There was a strong positive correlation between the two variables, Pearson's $r(183) = .566$, $p = 0.000$. A scatterplot summarizes the results in Figure 2. This is key to our argument that SCS1 is a validated replication of the FCS1.

After finding a positive correlation between the FCS1 and SCS1 scores, we analyzed the correlation based on the course the student participant was enrolled in. Pearson correlation coefficients were computed to assess the relationship between the course and the scores on the FCS1 and SCS1 Assessments (see Table 3). There was a strong, positive correlation for one course, Pearson's $r(140) = .483$, $p = 0.000$. This course was taught in Python and is the one required of computer science majors. The other two courses did not show statistically significant correlations between the scores. The lack of statistically significant correlations by course means that SCS1 is valid for CS1 students *in general*, but may be less accurate for

subpopulations. If a CS1 course does not cover object-oriented programming or recursion, for example, it would not match the minimal model that Tew defined, and SCS1 (and FCS1) would probably be less accurate for measuring knowledge for the specific course. The course differences do suggest the need for further research to understand where the SCS1 is most accurate and where it is not.

One possible explanation for the lack of statistical significance is the number of participants in the two classes, both of which are significantly smaller than the computer science majors' class. Overall, our number of participants is much smaller than Tew's. It is possible that the classes could reach statistical significance if more students were sampled from the two classes. Another possible explanation is that the students in those sections without statistical significance were for non-computer science majors. Tew found that correlation with the pseudocode test was strongest for the higher-performing students, and weaker for lower-performing students [35]. As our IRT analysis (see Section 3.2) suggests, SCS1 shows better discrimination among student participants with higher ability. The computer science majors may have greater internal motivation for learning for the subject and would be more successful at demonstrating their knowledge on an unfamiliar assessment.

Our results with SCS1 may be pointing to possible limitations of any pseudocode-based assessment. A pseudocode test may always bias in favor of students with greater understanding. We know that greater knowledge results in better transfer of cognitive skill [31]. High performance on a pseudocode test demands greater knowledge of the original material for the student to successfully transfer knowledge to pseudocode.

Overall, our results demonstrate a strong positive correlation between the scores on the SCS1 and FCS1 assessments. In addition there is a strong positive correlation between the assessments for traditional approaches to CS1 taught in Python. This suggests that the SCS1 has concurrent validity as it corresponds to an established measure, the FCS1.

3.2 Quantitative Analysis using IRT

The data gathered during our study provides a quantitative argument towards construct validity. Item response theory (IRT) is an important method for assessing the validity of measurement scales [13]. In particular, IRT measures the *difficulty* and *discrimination* of each question. In this context, *difficulty* measures the percentage of the test-takers that answered a given question correctly. *Discrimination* measures how well a student's performance on a given question predicts their performance on the overall test. If a question has good discrimination then a student that answers that question correctly is very likely to do well on the test. An ideal assessment using a multiple choice format with five options should have a difficulty of 70-74% on the overall assessment [20] and discrimination levels should be in the "good" range. Overall, if the questions have appropriate difficulty and discrimination and the scores between the two assessments are correlated, then the argument can be made that the assessment shows evidence of validity [13].

While the FCS1 and SCS1 assessments are positively correlated, both are considered very difficult assessments. In our IRT analysis of both assessments on one sample of students, the difficulty of problems was skewed towards a "hard" difficulty level where less than fifty percent of students answered a given problem correctly (see Table 4). The majority of problems were "fair" discriminators rather than "good." "Fair" is defined as having a point-biserial correlation of .1 to .3 [8]. Point-biserial correlation is a correlation

Table 4. Item response theory classifications of SCS1 questions.

		Difficulty (0-100%)			
		Hard (0-50%)	Moderate (50-85%)	Easy (85-100%)	Total
Discrimination	Poor (<0.1)	5, 8, 15, 18, 20, 24, 27	--	--	**7 items**
	Fair (0.1-0.3)	4,6,7,9,10,11,12,13,16,17,21,22,25,26	23	--	**15 items**
	Good (>0.3)	14	1, 2, 3, 19	--	**5 items**
	Total	**22 items**	**5 items**	**0 items**	**27 items**

between student performance on an item (right or wrong) and test score. We would like to note that these results differ from what was previously found regarding the FCS1 assessment. More questions were "hard" and "fair" than was determined in the original FCS1 work, though this is to be expected given the different population of participants between studies. Cronbach's alpha is a measurement of reliability, or the internal consistency based on correlations between different items an assessment. A Cronbach's alpha of 0.65 is considered acceptable [8]. For FCS1 Cronbach's alpha was 0.53; for SCS1 Cronbach's alpha was 0.59. The results imply that the internal consistency for these assessments is slightly below an acceptable level. Taken together, this suggests that there is a need to iteratively refine both instruments and re-test using a larger, more diverse sample of students.

As mentioned previously, there was a typo in one question that was found in between test administrations. Upon detection of this typo, we fixed this item to more accurately measure understanding with half of our test population. After analyzing the results, the typo in the question did matter. Students performed worse on the question with the typo (25% of students received the correct answer) than without it (59% of students received the correct answer). This was later than we would have liked to be still catching typos, but the statistical analysis suggests that SCS1 is still considered to have concurrent validity with FCS1.

4. EXAMPLE USES OF SCS1
Validated assessments offer us well-defined yardsticks for comparing populations, e.g., between experimental conditions or over time. We welcome the CS Education research community to use the SCS1 to measure performance or learning gains (e.g., by using the SCS1 as a pre-test and post-test). We include three of the first uses of SCS1 outside of its initial development.

4.1 Measuring Teachers' Knowledge
Our group used the SCS1 to measure knowledge of teachers during a professional development workshop. Assessments are necessary during these sessions to show effectiveness and impact [5]. We asked teachers (n=18) in a weeklong professional development workshop on Computer Science Principles [2] to complete the SCS1. Half of the teachers had taught computer science or programming for two or more years and all of the teachers were teaching CS at the high school and undergraduate level.

The teachers, on average, got one more question correct compared to the students in the validation study. The average student score on SCS1 in our validation study was 9.68 (σ=3.5), or 35% (σ=13.1%) and the average teacher score on SCS1 was 10.72 (σ=6.1) or 39% (σ=22.4%). This is likely the first measurement of

a high school CS teacher population with a validated instrument that can be compared to an undergraduate student population.

We have little information about the quality of high school computer science teachers, at least in the United States. What we do know suggests great variability in teacher knowledge, with most teachers we have interviewed saying that they know too little and would like to know more [4, 25]. We don't know enough about the teachers who took the workshop to make any claims about high school CS teacher knowledge more broadly. We do see potential in using SCS1 to compare CS in-service teachers to undergraduate computing students, and in order to consider the relative strengths of computing knowledge learned as a student in a classroom versus as a teacher in a classroom.

4.2 Comparing CS1 Approaches
A team in the Philippines used the SCS1 as an achievement assessment within a pilot class for introductory computing at their institution. They wanted a method to assess progress with the changes they were implementing, such as a shift in programming language used. The Philippine team wanted to use the scores on the SCS1, as well as grades from within the class and past courses, as a way to compare different approaches taken in the introductory course.

The Philippines team's use of SCS1 points to how instructors might use a validated assessment to inform their instructional practices. The single use of the SCS1 does not provide enough information to support any hypotheses. If there were two comparable populations enrolled in two different classes, then the SCS1 might be used to compare the post-class students understanding. If it was used both as a pre-test and post-test, the SCS1 could be used to make an argument about learning, much as how Hake used the FCI [12]. The Philippines' team's use of SCS1 points to potential hypothesis testing in the future.

4.3 Translation and Adaptation
A group in Germany translated and adapted the SCS1 to fit their needs of measuring learning in their CS1 course. We present their story here to highlight the challenges of replicating a validated assessment.

The first stage of the German process was replication, as in our approach described in this paper—a careful creation of an isomorphic test from the SCS1. The research group in Germany translated the SCS1 assessment into German over two versions. The first version was created by translating the SCS1 from English into German, which we will refer to as SCS1-G. SCS1-G was translated back to English (SCS1-E) by a second individual and compared with the original English version. Differences between the SCS1-E and the original SCS1 assessment were discussed and collaboratively adjusted in the German translation when needed. Two more individuals looked at SCS1-G and SCS1-E to look for any differences or inconsistencies, which were primarily in variable names and formatting. The second German version of SCS1 was created after the last round of revisions of the first version, when the two individuals noticed an overall inconsistency in wording of questions. The translation team addressed inconsistencies such as phrases preceding code segments that did not previously precede all code segments. There were also cultural differences that fed into the second German version of SCS1, including how questions were worded and how words are connoted (versus denoted) between the languages.

At this point, the process could continue the way that we validated the SCS1 against the FCS1. SCS1-German could be validated against our SCS1, given enough students who understood both German and English. However, the German team wanted to extend SCS1 to meet their special needs.

The German team was concerned that the students might be able to guess at the answer if the student had even a small amount of previous CS knowledge. They created a sixth answer choice for every multiple-choice question so that students could state, "I am unsure." This option was present in both German versions of SCS1. Although this addition reduces comparability with the original SCS1, the German team felt the lack of such an answer choice would not be fair to the students and might introduce a lot of false positive answers or blank answers. A blank answer is difficult to interpret – did the student run out of time or just not know the answer?

Even without the extension, we cannot make a validation argument that SCS1-G is equivalent to SCS1 in terms of the constructs it tests. Translation weakens the validity argument. Changing an assessment by adding questions or distractors *always* weakens the validity argument. The German example does point to the need for more validated assessments, like the SCS1. It also serves as an example of how we can use the replication and validation process that we describe in this paper as a template for viewing other attempts, e.g., we can see how the SCS1-G process mapped to our replication process but not the validation process.

5. PARAMETERS OF FUTURE WORK WITH SCS1

As with any validated assessment of learning, the use of SCS1 is complex. It holds significant research potential in serving as a tool to measure student learning and answer hypotheses we could not before. However, SCS1 also has limited support for different use-cases.

5.1 Following Hake's Lead

The SCS1 assessment can also be used like other validated concept inventories from other subjects, especially following the lead in Physics Education Research. The Force Concept Inventory [15] was used by Hake to measure learning interventions in Physics classrooms, with $n=6542$ students [12]. Hake found that interactive-engagement methods correlate to better problem-solving abilities. This was an important first step in making the argument for active learning approaches [9].

As with the Force Concept Inventory, the SCS1 might be used with large sample sizes to demonstrate the effectiveness of learning interventions. We could gather metadata from the test takers, such as demographics, tools used in their class, and their perceptions and attitudes towards computing. This metadata and the scores on the assessment could be analyzed for interesting correlations between achievement and the metadata points.

The SCS1 could be used to further the work in discipline-based computing education research by comparing student scores on the assessment in comparable, but different, approaches to introductory computing. For example, we might compare students in and not in interdisciplinary computing courses [21]. Furthermore, the SCS1 might be used to measure differences in courses taught using different programming languages. To make useful comparisons we would need to use SCS1 as a pre-test and a post-test so that we measure learning *gains* and not just achievement, as discussed earlier [11, 33]. We believe that many researchers in the computing education community could productively use the SCS1 to quantitatively measure student understanding, though only on the content areas represented in the test.

5.2 The Fragility of a Validated Assessment

Validation is an argument that an assessment measures what it purports to measure [36]. We have presented an argument here that SCS1 measures knowledge related to CS1 (as defined by [37]) across students who learned CS using Java, MATLAB, and Python. The argument is fragile, though. It does not withstand changes to SCS1.

While portions of the SCS1 focus on different parts of CS1 (e.g., conditionals, assignments, or loops), we cannot easily construct an argument that subsets of the SCS1 are equally valid. We have shown that SCS1 is equivalent to FCS1. We have not shown that portions of SCS1 are equivalent to portions of FCS1. The developers of FCS1 did not show that portions of FCS1 measure portions of CS1 knowledge.

Consider a possible example: the conditional questions in SCS1 only cover *parts* of students' understanding of conditionals. The gap between what the questions cover and what students understand may not be significant when we are considering the whole test (e.g., the assignment and loops sections may be so effective that they mask the weaknesses in conditionals). However, if the questions were pulled out separately, the gap may make the questions a poor assessment of knowledge of conditionals. Similarly, reporting just the conditionals section when students take the whole SCS1 does not constitute a valid measurement. Although it is easy to look only at how students performed on the conditional questions, the analysis does not represent a valid measurement of the student's understanding of conditionals since our validation argument only extends to the *whole* test.

Similarly, adding additional questions, additional question choices, or changing the order of questions invalidates the instrument. Additional questions may be more difficult, or may measure something different than CS1 knowledge. Changing the order of questions means that questions are not primed the way that they were when we validated SCS1. For example, if assignment questions came before loops questions, students might do better on loops because they were reminded how variables worked by the assignment questions. Reversing the order might lead to worse performance on the loops questions because students didn't have the priming effect first. It *might* not make any difference, but we did not test for different orderings, so we cannot make the argument for validity if the ordering is changed.

The SCS1 validity argument suggests a wealth of opportunities for improvement with future iterations of CS1 content knowledge assessments. The SCS1 is the first, albeit fragile, step towards future development of these critical concept inventories.

6. CONCLUSION: A CALL FOR MORE ASSESSMENTS

The SCS1 assessment was replicated from the FCS1 and demonstrates concurrent validity. However, there are many aspects of SCS1 that can be improved to better gauge students' CS1 content knowledge. Due to the replication and validation processes, SCS1 inherits any limitations of the FCS1 assessment. Thus, any issues with the FCS1 still hold true with SCS1. Additionally, the IRT analysis and the Cronbach's alpha suggest that the current SCS1 questions should be improved. That is, additional adjustments should include moderating difficulty level of questions on the SCS1 assessment and improving the discrimination of each question to make them more useful in influencing the overall result on the assessment. Each question can be improved in terms of difficulty and discrimination in order to make an objectively better assessment.

Similar to looking to other fields for information about replication and validation, we can look to other concept inventories and work done to improve them. FCI, although central to the research of concept inventories, is not without its flaws either. Rebello and Zollman have worked on the distractors on the FCI could be improved by gathering open-ended responses to questions and inserting the common responses as answer choices [29]. Additionally, Mühling et al. have created tests of basic programming ability by iterating on the assessment until the assessment had appropriate difficulty [24]. These processes can be used with the SCS1 assessment to create a revised version of the test with revised distractors and until appropriate IRT results are reached.

More assessments could be created using the SCS1 and the process for replication and validation described here. For example, we do not know if the SCS1 is useful for measuring understanding of blocks-based languages. Assessments are beginning to emerge for these languages, but a stronger claim for their validity can be made if scores on these assessments are correlated with SCS1 [40]. A blocks-based assessment could be created for content using the process defined for the FCS1 and SCS1 assessments. Performance on the SCS1 could be correlated with the blocks-based assessment to make an argument for the validity of the blocks-based assessment. Even though students who studied blocks might not perform as well on the pseudocode-based SCS1, the SCS1 could be used to measure understanding separated from the medium students use to program. Weintrop and Wilensky used a similar development process to create their blocks-and-text commutative assessment [40], but did not validate against an existing instrument. The SCS1 could provide that validation comparison.

These recommendations for the future improvement of the SCS1 assessment are not an exhaustive list. The community of computer science educators and researchers will decide which assessment to use, to validate, and to replicate, and we hope that SCS1 plays a role in that work. By engaging the community, the SCS1 may be considered an open source assessment—freely available for use, for replication, and for extension or modification.

As is, the SCS1 assessment can provide insight to differences in instructional approaches, effectiveness of interventions, and how the students and teachers, or different subsets of those groups, differ in their knowledge of CS1. As with any assessment, there are caveats. The argument for validity is fragile, and thus the assessment can only be used as-is or else it needs to be re-validated. As the use and re-validation of this instrument grows, it

and its counterparts can provide an important resource for the ICER community.

Information will be made available on how researchers can get access to SCS1 at the presentation of this paper and upon request to the authors.

7. ACKNOWLEDGMENTS

We would like to thank the students who participated in the study and their instructors who graciously gave us the time.

This material is based on work supported by the National Science Foundation under Grant No. 1432300 and the National Science Foundation Graduate Research Fellowship under Grant No. DGC-1148903. Any opinions, findings, and conclusions or recommendations expressed in this material are those of the authors and do not necessarily reflect the views of the National Science Foundation.

8. REFERENCES

[1] Almstrum, V.L., Henderson, P.B., Harvey, V., Heeren, C., Marion, W., Riedesel, C., Soh, L.-K. and Tew, A.E. 2006. Concept inventories in computer science for the topic discrete mathematics. *ACM SIGCSE Bulletin*. 38, 4 (2006), 132.

[2] Astrachan, O. and Briggs, A. 2012. The CS Principles Project.

[3] Brennan, R.L. 2006. *Educational measurement*.

[4] Bruckman, A., Biggers, M., Ericson, B., Mcklin, T., Dimond, J., Disalvo, B., Hewner, M., Ni, L. and Yardi, S. 2009. "Georgia Computes !": Improving the Computing Education Pipeline. *Proceedings of the Special Interest Group on Computer Science Education (SIGCSE'09)*. (2009), 86–90.

[5] Cooper, S., Grover, S. and Simon, B. 2014. Building a virtual community of practice for K-12 CS teachers. *Communications of the ACM*. 57, 5 (2014), 39–41.

[6] Downey, A.B. 2014. Think Python: How To Think Like a Computer Scientist. *Green Tea Press Think X series*. June (2014), 300.

[7] Fazio, R.H., Sherman, S.J. and Herr, P.M. 1982. The feature-positive effect in the self-perception process: Does not doing matter as much as doing? *Journal of Personality and Social Psychology*. 42, 3 (1982), 404–411.

[8] Field, A. 2005. *Discovering Statistics Using SPSS*.

[9] Freeman, S., Eddy, S.L., McDonough, M., Smith, M.K., Okoroafor, N., Jordt, H. and Wenderoth, M.P. 2014. Active learning increases student performance in science, engineering, and mathematics. *PNAS Proceedings of the National Academy of Sciences of the United States of America*. 111, 23 (2014), 8410–8415.

[10] Goldman, K., Gross, P., Heeren, C., Herman, G.L., Kaczmarczyk, L., Loui, M.C. and Zilles, C. 2010. Setting the Scope of Concept Inventories for Introductory Computing Subjects. *ACM Transactions on Computing Education*. 10, 2 (2010), 1–29.

[11] Guzdial, M. 2013. Exploring hypotheses about media computation. *Proceedings of the ninth annual international ACM conference on International computing education research - ICER '13* (2013), 19.

[12] Hake, R.R. 1998. Interactive-engagement versus traditional methods: A six-thousand-student survey of mechanics test

data for introductory physics courses. *American Journal of Physics*. 66, 1 (1998), 64.

[13] Hambleton, R.K., Swaminathan, H. and Rogers, H.J. 1991. *Fundamentals of item response theory*.

[14] Herman, G. 2011. *The Development of a Digital Logic Concept Inventory*.

[15] Hestenes, D., Wells, M. and Swackhamer, G. 1992. Force Concept Inventory. *The Physics Teacher*.

[16] Karpierz, K. and Wolfman, S. a. 2014. Misconceptions and concept inventory questions for binary search trees and hash tables. *Proceedings of the 45th ACM technical symposium on Computer science education - SIGCSE '14*. (2014), 109–114.

[17] Lee, M.J. and Ko, A.J. 2015. Comparing the Effectiveness of Online Learning Approaches on CS1 Learning Outcomes. *ICER*. (2015), 237–246.

[18] Libarkin, J. 2008. Concept Inventories in Higher Education Science. *STEM Education Workshop 2*. (2008), 1–13.

[19] Libarkin, J.C. and Anderson, S.W. 2005. Assessment of Learning in Entry-Level Geoscience Courses : Results from the Geoscience Concept Inventory. *Journal of Geoscience Education*. 53, 4 (2005), 394–401.

[20] Lord, F.M. 1952. The relation of the reliability of multiple-choice tests to the distribution of item difficulties. *Psychometrika*.

[21] Magana, A.J., Falk, M.L. and Reese, M.J. 2013. Introducing Discipline-Based Computing in Undergraduate Engineering Education. *ACM Transactions on Computing Education*. 13, 4 (2013), 1–22.

[22] Miller, M.D., Linn, R.L. and Gronlund, N.E. 2012. Validity. *Measurement and assessment in teaching*. Pearson Higher Ed.

[23] Morrison, B.B., Margulieux, L.E. and Guzdial, M. 2015. Subgoals, Context, and Worked Examples in Learning Computing Problem Solving. *ICER*. (2015), 21–29.

[24] Mühling, A., Ruf, A. and Hubwieser, P. 2015. Design and First Results of a Psychometric Test for Measuring Basic Programming Abilities. *WiPSCE '15*. (2015).

[25] Ni, L., Guzdial, M., Tew, A.E., Morrison, B. and Galanos, R. 2011. Building a Community to Support HS CS Teachers: the Disciplinary Commons for Computing Educators. *Proceedings of the 42th ACM technical symposium on Computer Science Education - SIGCSE '11*. (2011), 553–558.

[26] Paul, W. and Vahrenhold, J. 2013. Hunting High and Low: Instruments to Detect Misconceptions Related to Algorithms and Data Structures. *Proceedings of the 44th ACM technical symposium on Computer Science Education - SIGCSE '13*. (2013), 29.

[27] Pollatsek, A. and Well, A.D. 1995. On the use of counterbalanced designs in cognitive research: a suggestion for a better and more powerful analysis. *Journal of Experimental Psychology: Learning, Memory, and Cognition*. 21, 3 (1995), 785–794.

[28] Porter, L., Garcia, S., Tseng, H.-W. and Zingaro, D. 2013. Evaluating student understanding of core concepts in computer architecture. *Proceedings of the 18th ACM conference on Innovation and technology in computer science education - ITiCSE '13*. (2013), 279.

[29] Rebello, N.S. and Zollman, D. a. 2004. The effect of distracters on student performance on the force concept inventory. *American Journal of Physics*. 72, 1 (2004), 116.

[30] Shavelson, R.J. 2007. *A Brief History of Student Learning Assessment: How We Got Where We Are and a Proposal for Where to Go Next*.

[31] Singley, M. and Anderson, J.R. 1989. *The Transfer of Cognitive Skill*. Harvard University Press.

[32] Stefani, L. 2004. Assessment of Student Learning: promoting a scholarly approach. 1 (2004).

[33] Stefik, A. and Siebert, S. 2013. An Empirical Investigation into Programming Language Syntax. *ACM Transactions on Computing Education*. 13, 4 (2013), 1–40.

[34] Taylor, C., Zingaro, D., Porter, L., Webb, K.C., Lee, C.B. and Clancy, M. 2014. Computer science concept inventories: Past and future. *Computer Science Education*. 24, 4 (2014), 253–276.

[35] Tew, A.E. 2010. *Assessing Fundamental Introductory Computing Concept Knowledge in a Language Independent Manner Assessing Fundamental Introductory Computing Concept Knowledge*. Georgia Institute of Technology.

[36] Tew, A.E. and Dorn, B. 2013. The Case for Validated Tools in Computing Education Research. *Computer*. 46, 9 (2013), 60–66.

[37] Tew, A.E. and Guzdial, M. 2010. Developing a validated assessment of fundamental CS1 concepts. *Proceedings of the 41st ACM technical symposium on Computer science education - SIGCSE '10*. (2010), 97.

[38] Tew, A.E. and Guzdial, M. 2011. The FCS1 : A Language Independent Assessment of CS1 Knowledge. *Proceedings of the 42nd ACM technical symposium on computer science education* (2011), 111–116.

[39] Utting, I., Tew, A.E., McCracken, M., Thomas, L., Bouvier, D., Frye, R., Paterson, J., Caspersen, M., Kolikant, Y.B.-D., Sorva, J. and Wilusz, T. 2013. A Fresh Look at Novice Programmers' Performance and Their Teachers' Expectations. *Proceedings of the {ITiCSE} Working Group Reports Conference on Innovation and Technology in Computer Science Education-working Group Reports*. (2013), 15–32.

[40] Weintrop, D. and Drive, C. 2015. Using Commutative Assessments to Compare Conceptual Understanding in Blocks-based and Text-based Programs. (2015), 101–110.

[41] Yadav, A., Burkhart, D., Moix, D., Snow, E., Bandaru, P. and Clayborn, L. 2015. *Sowing the Seeds: A Landscape Study on Assessment in Secondary Computer Science Education*.

Benchmarking Introductory Programming Exams: Some Preliminary Results

Simon
University of Newcastle
Australia
simon@newcastle.edu.au

Judy Sheard
Monash University
Australia
judy.sheard@monash.edu

Daryl D'Souza
RMIT University
Australia
daryl.dsouza@rmit.edu.au

Peter Klemperer
Mount Holyoke College
United States of America
pklemper@mtholyoke.edu

Leo Porter
University of California, San Diego
United States of America
leporter@eng.ucsd.edu

Juha Sorva
Aalto University
Finland
juha.sorva@aalto.fi

Martijn Stegeman
University of Amsterdam / Open University of the Netherlands
Netherlands
martijn@stgm.nl

Daniel Zingaro
University of Toronto Mississauga
Canada
daniel.zingaro@utoronto.ca

ABSTRACT

The programming education literature includes many observations that pass rates are low in introductory programming courses, but few or no comparisons of student performance across courses. This paper addresses that shortcoming. Having included a small set of identical questions in the final examinations of a number of introductory programming courses, we illustrate the use of these questions to examine the relative performance of the students both across multiple institutions and within some institutions. We also use the questions to quantify the size and overall difficulty of each exam. We find substantial differences across the courses, and venture some possible explanations of the differences. We conclude by explaining the potential benefits to instructors of using the same questions in their own exams.

1. INTRODUCTION

Computing education research is dominated by papers about programming courses [11], and many of these papers address the difficulty faced by some students in learning to program. Analysis of pass rates in introductory programming courses worldwide [1, 18] confirms that students fail or withdraw from these courses at higher rates than are deemed acceptable by their institutions.

While a number of research projects [4, 6] have established that many students completing introductory courses are effectively

ICER'16, September 8-12, 2016, Melbourne, Vic, Australia
© 2016 ACM. ISBN 978-1-4503-4449-4/16/09...$15.00
DOI: http://dx.doi.org/10.1145/2960310.2960337

unable to program, we are not aware of any research into the consistency or reliability of assessment across multiple courses. If a student earns a bare pass in a course, what grade would that same student have earned in a comparable course at another institution, perhaps in another country? This is not an idle question. One purpose of assessment is to certify students as fit for practice, and this certification is questionable if it conveys different meanings in different contexts.

Assessment of a programming course often culminates with an end-of-semester exam. There has been some analysis of exams from multiple institutions, for example in data structures [16] and in programming [7, 9, 12]. However, this has generally not been paired with analysis of student performance, and consequently has not addressed the comparability of results across the institutions.

One approach to comparison of courses is benchmarking: explicitly measuring outcomes at different institutions and comparing them against one another or against an established benchmark. But these outcomes cannot simply be student grades or pass rates, because there is no assurance that the assessments or the marking are comparable. On this point, Lister [3] expresses "surprise at the confidence most academics have in their respective grading schemes".

It is highly unlikely that the instructors at multiple institutions could agree to use exactly the same assessment items in their courses. Each course is taught differently, according to its particular learning objectives and the preferences of its instructor, and the assessments will necessarily reflect those differences.

However, final examinations, when they are used, often consist of reasonably large numbers of small questions, and we reasoned that it might be easier to gain agreement on a subset of those questions. In previous work [14] some of the authors established a set of questions that were likely to be accepted into multiple exams. A new group was then formed to implement the proposal, incorporating the questions in exams and gathering the data for analysis. In a recent paper [13] we explored the reasoning behind benchmarking and explained how the results might be used. In this paper we detail the findings of our analysis.

2. METHOD

Ten benchmarking questions were used in 13 final written examinations at seven institutions in five countries: Australia, Canada, Finland, Netherlands, and USA.

Each instructor was able to choose what proportion of the exam was taken up by these questions, and for their own assessment purposes each instructor was free to mark the questions according to whatever scheme they chose. In some cases the courses were taught and assessed by members of the research group; in other cases by colleagues of group members.

For the benchmarking analysis the ten questions were marked according to a specific scheme, which was not necessarily the same as those used for assessment purposes. Therefore in some exams, once the assessment mark had been determined some of the questions were marked again for our analysis, possibly by a different marker. As this applied only to some exams, and then only to some questions, no attempt was made to compare the marks from these two different sources.

For each question we formed an average mark for the students in each institution, and then the average of these institutional marks. It would not have been appropriate to form an average of all the students who took the exams, as such an average would be skewed towards the performance of the larger classes. The institutional average was then considered as the benchmark against which each institution in turn could be compared.

For questions with a simple answer that is either right or wrong, the average for an institution is the proportion of students who gave the right answer. For more complex questions, where a mark was applied according to a specified scheme, the average is the average mark of the students at the institution, normalised to a percentage.

No measure of inter-rater reliability was applied to the marking. By its nature, a benchmark of this sort will be applied by many people who have not been trained or tested in its use. Effort therefore focused on making the marking scheme as clear and unambiguous as possible rather than on subsequently testing whether it had been applied consistently.

As will be explained in section 4, one institution was not included in the average, and the average at another institution was formed from only one of the two exams for which we collected data.

Further details of the analysis are presented in section 4.

3. QUESTIONS

In this section we present and discuss the benchmarking questions that were used in this study. The questions are intended for use in procedural or object-oriented programming languages, and together we used versions in Java, Python, and C. When using the questions, instructors may change braces and indentation to conform to the style used in their course, and may add type prefixes to variable names if appropriate, but are otherwise expected to use the questions in the form provided. The questions presented in this section are the Java versions. After each question we present the average over institutions of the students' average marks on that question, which we are calling the benchmark result for the question.

The mark given with each question indicates the question's contribution to the benchmarking total of 27. For example, question 1 contributed 1 mark to the 27, whereas question 10 contributed 6 marks to the 27.

3.1 Question 1 (1 mark)

If a dependent child is a person under 18 years of age who does not earn $10,000 or more a year, which expression would define a dependent child?
(a) `age < 18 && salary < 10000`
(b) `age < 18 || salary < 10000`
(c) `age <= 18 && salary <= 10000`
(d) `age <= 18 || salary <= 10000`

This question tests knowledge of relational and boolean operators to form boolean expressions. It also tests students' understanding of the correspondence between a natural-language description and a programmed expression.

The benchmark result for question 1 is 90%.

3.2 Question 2 (1 mark)

What are the values of *girls*, *boys*, and *children* after the following code has been executed?
```
int girls = 0;
int boys = 0;
int children = 0;
children = girls + boys;
girls = 15;
boys = 12;
```
(a) 0, 0, 0
(b) 0, 0, 27
(c) 15, 12, 0
(d) 15, 12, 27

This question [10] tests the combination of assignment and sequence: do students understand that the fourth statement is an action carried out halfway through a sequence of actions, or do they see it as a statement of truth that holds regardless of where it appears?

The benchmark result for question 2 is 89%.

3.3 Question 3 (3 marks)

There are three integer variables, *a*, *b* and *c*, which have been initialised. Write code to shift the values in these variables around so that *a* is given *b*'s original value, *b* is given *c*'s original value, and *c* is given *a*'s original value. The following diagram illustrates the direction of the shifts:

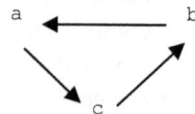

It seems likely that all students in a procedural or object-oriented introductory programming course are exposed to the standard swap of two variables that uses a third variable to temporarily hold one of the values. Extension to an exchange of three variables invites students to show that they can apply a familiar process to an unfamiliar context.

The benchmark result for question 3 is 70%.

3.4 Question 4 (1 mark)

What will be the value of the variable *z* after the following code is executed?

```
int x = 1; int y = 2; int z = 3;
if (x < y) {
    if (y > 4) {
        z = 5;
    } else {
        z = 6;
    }
}
```

The Leeds ITiCSE working group [4] established that many students are unable to trace or hand-execute simple pieces of code. Question 4 tests students' ability to trace a nested pair of *if* statements.

The benchmark result for question 4 is 96%, the highest of the benchmark results.

3.5 Question 5 (1 mark)

Consider the following block of code, where variables *a*, *b*, *c*, and *answer* each store integer values:

```
if (a > b) {
    if (b > c) {
        answer = c;
    } else {
        answer = b;
    }
} else if (a > c) {
    answer = c;
} else {
    answer = a;
}
```

Which of the following sets of values for *a*, *b*, and *c* will cause *answer* to be assigned the value in variable *b*?

(a) a = 1, b = 2, c = 3
(b) a = 1, b = 3, c = 2
(c) a = 2, b = 1, c = 3
(d) a = 3, b = 2, c = 1

Question 5, like question 4, tests students' ability to trace nested *if* statements, but with two added levels of complexity. First, the outer statement has an *else if* and an *else* that are not present in question 4. Second, the students are effectively asked to trace the code four times, once for each of the answer options. However, it is possible to bypass this process by working out what the code actually does [3], in which case selection of the correct option is trivial.

The benchmark result for question 5 is 89%.

3.6 Question 6 (1 mark)

What will be the value of *result* after the following code statements are executed?

```
int[] nums1 = { 1, -5, 2, 0, 4, 2, -3 };
int[] nums2 = { 1, -5, 2, 4, 4, 2, 7 };
int result = 0;
int j = 0;
while (j < nums1.length)
{
    if (nums1[j] != nums2[j])
    {
        result = result + 1;
    }
    j = j + 1;
}
```

This third code-tracing question adds the further complexities of a *while* loop used to traverse two arrays. This question is based on one used by the Leeds ITiCSE working group [4]. As with question 5, the question is possibly easier to answer if students can begin by working out what the code does [3].

The benchmark result for question 6 is 80%.

3.7 Question 7 (1 mark)

What is the outcome or likely purpose of the following piece of code?

```
int result = 0;
for (int j = 0; j < number.length; j++)
{
    if (number[j] < 0)
    {
        result = result + 1;
    }
}
```

(a) to find the smallest number in the array
(b) to count the negative numbers in the array
(c) to sum the negative numbers in the array
(d) to add 1 to each of the negative numbers in the array
(e) to find the index of the first negative number in the array

The BRACElet project [8, 19] established among other things that students have great difficulty discerning the purpose or outcome of small pieces of code. Question 7 is a simple example of this form of code-reading question.

The benchmark result for question 7 is 85%.

3.8 Question 8 (6 marks)

What is the outcome or likely purpose of the following piece of code? Express your answer as a short phrase, like the phrases provided as possible answers in question 7.

```
int result = 0;
for (int count = 1; count <= num; count++)
{
    result = result + count;
}
```

A further BRACElet finding [15] is that students find it easier to select the purpose of a piece of code from a list of options than to discern it from scratch. Question 8 helps to test this finding by posing a counterpoint to question 7.

Some students at one participating institution answered that in this piece of code, *num* is undefined. Yet the code was presented as a piece of code, not as a complete program or method, so this should not be seen as a serious problem – especially as students were far more successful in question 7, where *number* is similarly undefined.

The benchmark result for question 8 is 44%, by far the lowest of the ten questions.

3.9 Question 9 (6 marks)

We can represent an array of integers as a sequence of elements arranged from left to right, with the first element at the left and the last element at the right. Using this representation, a programmer wishes to move all elements of an array one place to the right, with the rightmost element being 'wrapped around' to the leftmost position, as shown in this diagram.

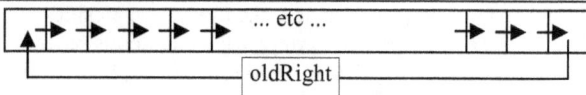

Here is the code that performs that shift for an array referred to by the name *values*:

```
int oldRight = values[values.length - 1];
for (int j = values.length - 1; j > 0; j--)
    values[j] = values[j - 1];
values[0] = oldRight;
```

For example, if *values* initially contains the integers [1, 2, 3, 4, 5], once the code has executed it would contain [5, 1, 2, 3, 4].

Write code that will undo the effect of the above code. That is, write code that will move all the elements of the array one place to the left, with the leftmost element being wrapped around to the rightmost position.

The BABELnot project [5] proposed three tests to assess whether student programmers had progressed from the neo-Piagetian preoperational stage to the concrete operational stage. Question 9 [3] tests the students' concept of reversibility: given code to perform a certain iterative operation, can students write the code to reverse that operation?

One problem observed with this question is that with certain data structures such as lists and arraylists the question has a trivial solution: remove the first item from the list and append it to the end. While the code provided for the initial operation suggests that an explicitly iterative solution is expected, it makes sense for students to apply the higher-level solution if they are able. Our detailed marking scheme, based on the individual steps of the explicit solution, coped poorly with such higher-level solutions.

The benchmark result for question 9 is 66%. It would presumably have been different if all students had attempted explicit iterative solutions.

3.10 Question 10 (6 marks)

Write a method that will be given an array of integers and will calculate and return (as a double) the mean (average) of all the integers in the array.

Question 10 is based on Soloway's classic rainfall problem [17], but is far simpler. It is designed to test whether students can write a method that returns a value; whether they can iterate through an array; whether they know how to calculate an average; and whether they can find a double quotient of two integer numbers.

Like question 9, this question proved to have higher-level solutions that subverted some of the intended design. In particular, some languages provide built-in methods to average, or at least to sum, the numbers in a list or an array. A method that correctly calls such a built-in method can avoid explicit iteration and explicit integer division. Further, not all languages give an integer result when two integers are divided, so not all students had to explicitly ensure that the result is a double.

While the marking scheme provided was expressed in terms of integers, giving one mark for each of six criteria, one participant gave half marks for components of this question, possibly inflating the results at that institution.

The benchmark result for question 10 is 64%. As with question 9, we suspect that it might have been different if all students had attempted explicit iterative solutions.

4. RESULTS

In this section we present the results of our benchmarking, at the same time illustrating a number of questions that the benchmarking questions might help to explore.

The principal data summary for each institution will be a plot of the students' marks for each question against the benchmark average that we have calculated, with all marks normalised to 100%. This will give a view of how the students at that institution performed relative to the complete student set.

Considering the benchmark value for a question as the population mean, we tested the marks for that question at each institution to determine whether they were significantly different from the benchmark. For the binary questions we applied a test of population proportions, and for the multi-mark questions, a one-sample two-tailed t-test.

Where it appears to shed further light, we will show a scatter plot of individual students' marks for the benchmarking questions against their mark for the remainder of the exam. This will illustrate the spread of student performance on both subsets of the exam questions, and also give an idea of the difficulty of the rest of the exam compared with that of the benchmarking questions.

Our final measure is the notional 'size' of the exam, measured relative to the benchmarking questions. We first posit that every exam question has a 'size', which might be some sort of composite of its difficulty and the time a student would take to answer it. An exam would then have a size that is the sum of the sizes of its questions. We further assume that the marks allocated to questions are more or less proportional to their sizes. With these assumptions, the ratio of the marks possible in the exam to the marks possible in the benchmarking questions gives us a rough measure of the size of the exam. To illustrate, an exam in which 50% of the marks were allocated for the benchmarking questions would be twice the size of those questions, while an exam in which 25% of the marks were allocated for the benchmarking question would be four times the size of those questions.

4.1 Institution A

Institution A is a metropolitan university in Australia. The benchmarking questions were used in the final exam for the introductory programming course, which is taught in Java, and is typically taken by students in the first year of a computer science degree. The final exam contributes 40% of the students' final mark in the course. The benchmarking questions make up only 25% of the exam, which is therefore four times the 'size' of the benchmarking questions, and one of the biggest exams in our study. Figure 1 shows the performance of the students in this course, both as a plot of the average class mark against the benchmark, and as a scatter plot of marks on the benchmarking questions, out of 27, against marks on the remainder of the exam, normalised to a percentage.

Figure 1a shows that students in this course performed below the benchmark. Question 8 was significantly below the benchmark with $p < 0.05$, and questions 1, 5, 7, 9, and 10 with minuscule p values. The course instructor might now focus on questions 7, 9, and 10, which display the biggest differences; decide whether they are integral to the learning goals of the course; and if necessary

Figure 1a: performance by question at institution A (dashed line) compared with the benchmark (solid line)

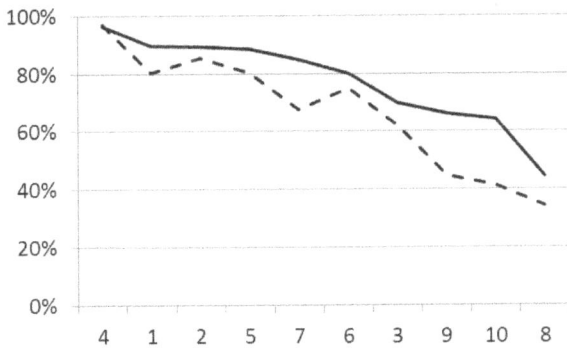

Figure 1b: students' marks for the benchmarking questions (out of 27) against their marks for the rest of the exam (out of 100); the solid diagonal indicates comparable performance on both

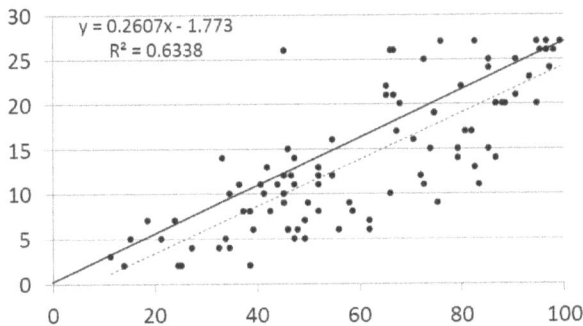

$y = 0.2607x - 1.773$
$R^2 = 0.6338$

plan how to address the indicated shortcomings in the students' learning.

On the scatter plot, the marks have a tendency to lie beneath the diagonal, meaning that students tended to perform better on the rest of the exam than on the benchmarking questions. This means that, relative to the benchmarking questions, this exam is not particularly challenging. Nevertheless the spread of marks on both axes indicates a wide range of achievement among the students.

4.2 Institution B

Institution B is a metropolitan university in Australia, where the benchmarking questions were used in the introductory programming course in a coursework masters degree, which is typically taken by graduates seeking a qualification in an area unrelated to their first degree. The introductory programming course is taught in Java, and the final exam contributes 60% of the students' final mark in the course. The benchmarking questions make up 29% of this exam, giving it a size of 3.4 times the benchmarking questions. Figure 2 shows the performance of the students in this course.

The students' performance is significantly above the benchmark on questions 3 (p minuscule) and 8 (p<0.05), and otherwise close to the benchmark except for questions 4 and 9. The instructor for this exam had declined to use question 9 because it was perceived to be too difficult for the students in the course, so marks of 0 were entered for all students for this question. This left question 4 as an unexplained anomaly.

Figure 2: performance by question at institution B compared with the benchmark (solid line)

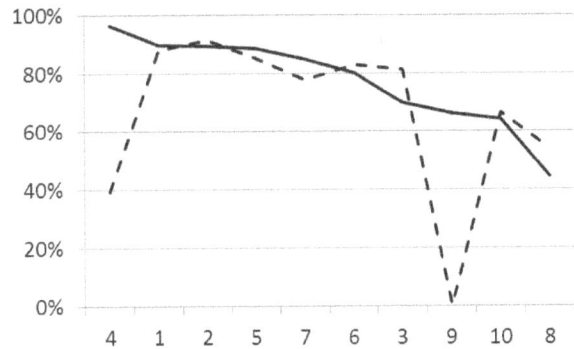

Once the anomaly was discovered in the course of this analysis, question 4 was checked again. The instructor had, as invited, altered the braces to match the style used in that class, leaving the code as follows:

```
int x = 1; int y = 2; int z = 3;
if (x < y)
    if (y > 4)
        z = 5;
else
    z = 6;
```

The code is functionally identical to that in the original benchmarking question. However, the *else* now aligns with the first *if*, even though structurally it belongs with the second. It seems clear that this misleading indentation changed the nature of this question, so that it can no longer be considered the same question that was used by the other institutions.

For institution B it is not meaningful to scatter-plot students' benchmarking marks against their marks for the rest of the exam, as the two anomalous results would skew the benchmarking marks downward. For the same reason, none of the marks from institution B were included in the averages that are being used as a benchmark.

4.3 Institution C

Institution C is a major Finnish university that has a number of introductory programming courses for different student cohorts. The course used in this study is designed for engineering students and uses Python. The exam makes up 50% of the students' final mark, and yet is a small exam, with the benchmarking questions taking up 45% of the exam.

Performance at institution C is comparable with the benchmark for questions 2, 3, and 4, and significantly above it for every other question, with $p < 0.05$ for question 1, $p < 0.01$ for questions 6 and 9, and p minuscule for the remaining questions.

The spike for question 10 is interesting. Question 10 asks students to write a method to find the average of the elements in an array. The course at institution C is taught in Python, which offers inbuilt methods to do either the task itself or a useful subtask. It seems plausible that the spike represents the students who made use of these inbuilt methods.

The scatter plot suggests that the exam is challenging, with many students performing better on the benchmarking questions than on the rest of the exam. Nevertheless, the clustering in the top right

Figure 3a: performance by question at institution C compared with the benchmark (solid line)

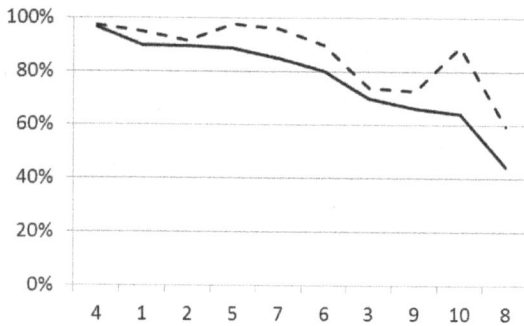

Figure 3b: students' marks for the benchmarking questions against their marks for the rest of the exam

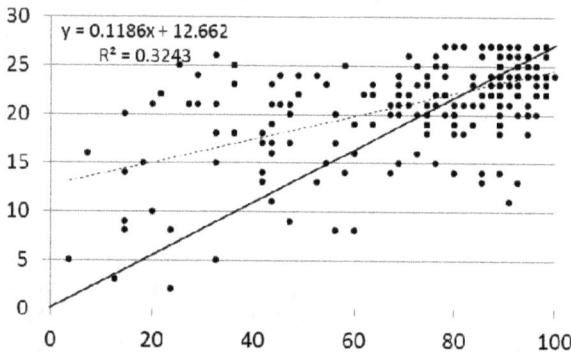

$y = 0.1186x + 12.662$
$R^2 = 0.3243$

Figure 4a: performance in a two-course sequence at institution D compared with the benchmark (solid line)

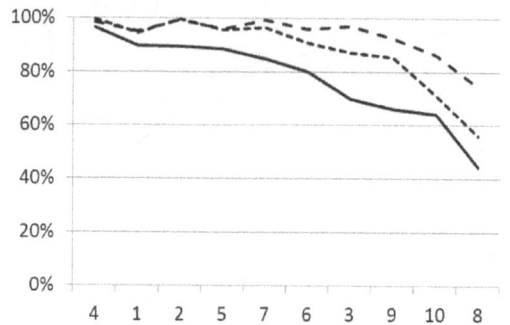

Figure 4b: students' marks for the benchmarking questions against their marks for the rest of the exam in the 'CS1' quarter

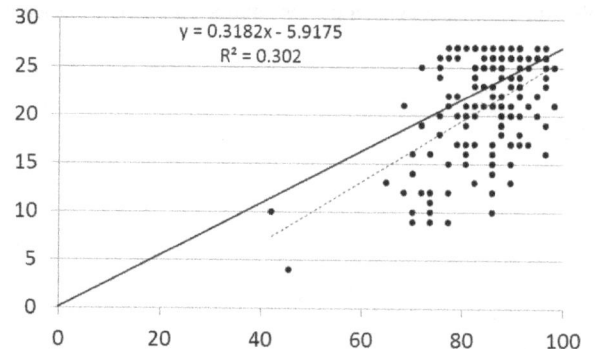

$y = 0.3182x - 5.9175$
$R^2 = 0.302$

quadrant indicates that many students were able to handle both sets of questions with little difficulty. Students at universities in Finland are able to drop courses without major consequences; if some students who expected to do poorly dropped the course before the final exam, this could have skewed the results upward.

4.4 Institution D

Institution D is a major university in the USA. The results from this university are particularly interesting because they come from both parts of a two-quarter sequence, which the instructors describe as being like a CS1 and a CS1.5. Both courses use Java. The exams are worth 25% and 30% respectively of the overall marks in the first and second courses. The benchmarking questions make up 43% of the final exam in the first course, making it quite a small exam; and 16% in the second, making it the biggest exam in our study.

Performance is significantly above the benchmark for every question in both courses, with most p values minuscule. In figure 4a, the CS1.5 course is represented by the uppermost line, indicating a better performance than the CS1 course on the benchmarking questions. The results presented here are from the same quarter, so they show a progression not of the same students but of the cohorts in general.

As shown in figure 4b, the students in the CS1 course tended to perform better on the rest of the exam than on the benchmarking questions, which means that the exam was not particularly challenging. This is reinforced by the fact that only two students scored less than 50% on the exam. In the CS1.5 course, as shown in figure 4c, the students scored very well on the benchmarking questions, with only three scoring less than 18/27. However, the

Figure 4c: students' marks for the benchmarking questions against their marks for the rest of the exam in the 'CS1.5' quarter

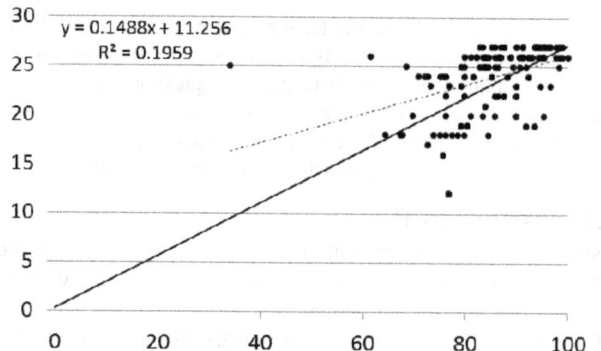

$y = 0.1488x + 11.256$
$R^2 = 0.1959$

fact that very few scored less than 70% on the exam suggests that notwithstanding its size, the exam was not a serious challenge for these students at this stage of their study. A top mark in this course is required for entry to the CS major, which is highly competitive. As a consequence, many of the weaker students withdraw from the course, which helps to explain the high performance.

An issue for consideration with the second of these courses is that the exam included 10 bonus marks alongside the 190 'normal' marks. Bonus marks always raise questions of implementation: for example, can a student get an exam mark higher than 100%, and if so, will that contribute more than the specified percentage to the student's overall mark in the course? Likewise, can a student get

Figure 5a: performance by question at institution E compared with the benchmark (solid line)

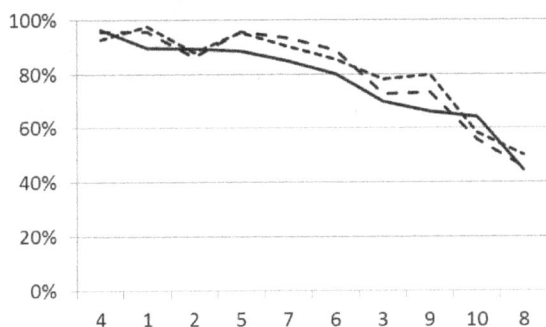

100% in the exam despite answering some questions incorrectly, by virtue of the bonus marks? Each of these can raise conceptual problems. For our analysis we had to decide whether to calculate the exam's size on the basis of 190 marks or 200 marks. Our decision was to ignore the bonus nature of the final 10 marks and to regard the exam as consisting of 200 marks, as a consequence of which we would no longer have to deal with student scores of more than 100% in the exam.

It was decided not to include the result from the CS1.5 course in the average for Institution D or in the benchmark, as this was the only course in our data set that is clearly not an introductory course.

4.5 Institution E

Institution E is a university in the Netherlands. The introductory programming course is a purely elective course, taken typically by students in the third year of their study. About a third of the students are taking technical degrees such as science, and about two-thirds are taking non-technical degrees such as social science. The course at Institution E is taught in C, and begins with the first half of an online Harvard introductory programming course. It is taught in two versions: one full-time (40 hours a week) for four weeks, and one half-time (20 hours a week) for eight weeks. In each version the exam contributes nothing to the students' final mark, but is a hurdle that they must clear in order to pass. The benchmarking questions make up 47% of the exam.

Performance in both courses is significantly below the benchmark for question 10 ($p < 0.05$) but significantly above the benchmark for questions 6 and 7 ($p < 0.05$) and questions 1, 5, and 9 ($p < 0.01$). This is possibly due in part to the fact that the course is entirely elective for the students, and is therefore taken only by students who have some reason to believe that they will do well in it.

Performance is very similar on the two offerings. This appears to suggest that students taking the course at twice the intensity in half the time are neither advantaged nor disadvantaged by so doing.

4.6 Institution F

Institution F is a regional university in Australia. The introductory programming course used in this study uses the Python version of the media computation approach [2]. The course is offered in the first year of the information technology degree, at two campuses in Australia and a third campus in another country. The course is notionally identical at all three campuses, using the same material and the same assessment items. The exam contributes 50% to

Figure 6a: performance by question at three campuses of institution F compared with the benchmark (solid line)

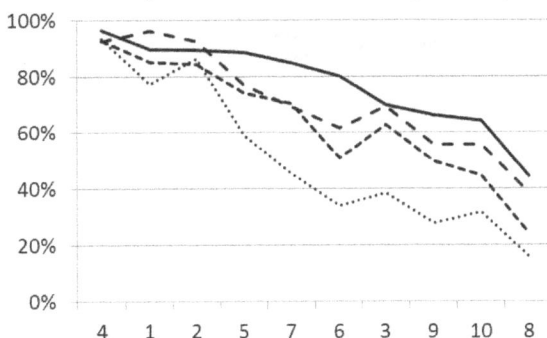

Figure 6b: students' marks for the benchmarking questions against their marks for the rest of the exam at the overseas campus

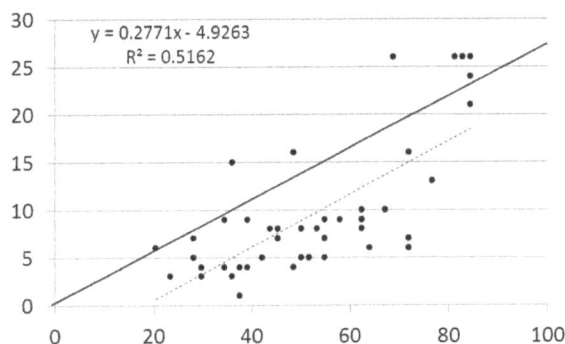

students' overall mark in the course, and the benchmarking questions make up 36% of the exam.

In the competition for good students in Australia, regional universities fare poorly in comparison with metropolitan universities. Furthermore, at institution F the information technology degree has a lower entry requirement than the computer science degree. For both of these reasons, the students might be expected to perform more poorly than most others in the study. This expectation is borne out in Figure 6a, which shows all three campuses performing below the benchmark. Combining the campuses, the scores are significantly below the benchmark, generally with minuscule p values, on every question except question 2.

Figure 6b shows a scatter plot of student performance at the overseas campus, the worst-performing of the three. While the number of students at this campus is not high, there is a clear tendency for them to perform worse on the benchmarking questions than on the remainder of the exam, suggesting that it is not a challenging exam; and yet the main cluster of students has scored between 20% and 65% on the latter, suggesting that these students are struggling even with this relatively easy exam. The instructor at institution F is exploring factors that might have contributed to a performance so far below the benchmark.

4.7 Institution G

Institution G is a suburban campus (not the main research campus) of a metropolitan university in Canada. The introductory programming course is taught in Python, the exam contributes

Figure 7a: performance by question in three sections at institution G compared with the benchmark (solid line)

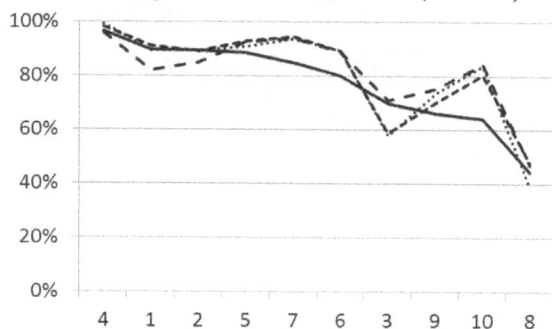

Figure 7b: students' marks for the benchmarking questions against their marks for the rest of the exam; this plot is just of one section; the other two sections are highly comparable

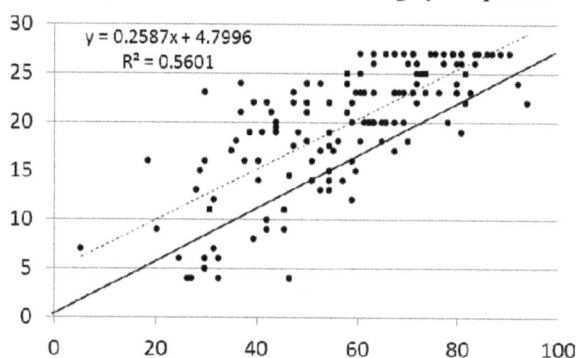

$y = 0.2587x + 4.7996$
$R^2 = 0.5601$

45% to a student's final mark for the course, and the benchmarking questions make up 29% of the exam. All three sections of the course use the same teaching material, but they do not all use the same approach: when we collected the data, two sections made substantial use of peer instruction, while the third section did not.

Figure 7a shows that performance was generally above the benchmark, and very similar in all three sections. The combined performance is significantly below the benchmark on question 3 ($p<0.01$), and significantly above it on questions 6 and 7 ($p<0.01$) and questions 9 and 10 (p minuscule).

As at institution C, the course is taught in Python and shows a spike at question 10. Again, this is possibly attributable to students who used Python's inbuilt methods to bypass the explicit detail expected in the answer.

Figure 7b is a scatter plot of students in one of the three sections; the plots for the other two sections are virtually identical to this one. Results tend to lie above the diagonal, meaning that students performed better on the benchmarking questions than on the rest of the exam; that is, the exam is fairly challenging. We also note a good spread of results both on the benchmarking questions and on the rest of the exam, showing that this exam does a good job of discriminating among its students.

5. DISCUSSION AND CONCLUSION

Instructors wishing to include these ten questions in the final exams of their introductory programming courses should contact the lead author, who will provide the marking scheme and, if required, versions of the questions in other programming languages. When they (re)mark their students' answers according to our marking scheme, instructors will be able to determine:

- the performance of their students relative to the benchmark established here, using plots like those in part *a* of our figures;
- student issues with any of the programming concepts covered by the individual benchmarking questions (see section 4.1);
- the relative performance of students taught using different approaches (see sections 4.5 and 4.7);
- the size of their exam compared with those in our study, using the proportion of their exam that the benchmarking questions occupy;
- the difficulty of their exam relative to the benchmarking questions, by noting whether the points on their scatter plot tend to lie above the diagonal, below it, or neither;
- the difficulty of their exam for their own students, by observing the spread of scatter points on each axis (see sections 4.4 and 4.7).

We hope that many instructors will perceive the usefulness of these measures, and will use the benchmarking questions in their own exams to avail themselves of the information.

To use the questions, instructors need to be sure that their students are familiar with all of the question types. In particular, students are known to struggle with code-reading questions (questions 7 and 8) when they first encounter them [19], so it would not be reasonable to examine students on such questions without prior exposure.

After using the questions, instructors will need to give careful consideration as to their interpretation. There are many factors involved in the performance of students in a course at an institution, and every finding must be interpreted in its own context. We do not believe that it would be valid or productive to use the benchmark to establish relative rankings of institutions in programming education.

This is not, and will never be, a global benchmark for introductory programming. It cannot be used with courses taught using functional or logical programming languages. It cannot be used in all courses that use procedural or object-oriented languages, because not all will cover the same material. At present the benchmark is based only upon a small number of institutions, although if others use the questions and notify us of their results, we will adjust the benchmark figures accordingly. And finally, it is likely that the questions themselves will need to change over time, to accommodate advances in computing education and in assessment practices; if and when that happens, a distinctly new version of the benchmark questions will be issued, so that users can be clear on which version they are using and comparing their results with.

Nevertheless, we believe that at this juncture the benchmarking questions and process could be extremely useful and informative to many educators, and we will be pleased to assist others in their use.

6. ACKNOWLEDGEMENTS

We are grateful to Kerttu Pollari-Malmi and Andy Cheng for including the benchmarking questions in their introductory programming examinations, and to Susan Snowdon for assistance with the statistics.

REFERENCES

[1] J Bennedsen and ME Caspersen (2007). Failure rates in introductory programming. SIGCSE Bulletin, 39:2, 32-36.

[2] MJ Guzdial and B Ericson (2013). Introduction to computing and programming in Python: a multimedia approach. Pearson Education.

[3] R Lister (2011). Concrete and other neo-Piagetian forms of reasoning in the novice programmer. 13th Australasian Computing Education Conference (ACE 2011), 9-18.

[4] R Lister, ES Adams S Fitzgerald, W Fone, J Hamer, M Lindholm, R McCartney, JE Moström, K Sanders, O Seppälä, B Simon, and L Thomas (2004). A multi-national study of reading and tracing skills in novice programmers. SIGCSE Bulletin, 36:4, 119-150.

[5] R Lister, M Corney, J Curran, D D'Souza, C Fidge, R Gluga, M Hamilton, J Harland, J Hogan, J Kay, T Murphy, M Roggenkamp, J Sheard, Simon, and D Teague (2012). Toward a shared understanding of competency in programming: An invitation to the BABELnot project. 14th Australasian Computing Education Conference (ACE 2012), 53-60.

[6] M McCracken, V Almstrum, D Diaz, M Guzdial, D Hagan, Y Ben-David Kolikant, C Laxer, L Thomas, I Utting, and T Wilusz (2001). A multi-national, multi-institutional study assessment of programming skills of first-year CS students. SIGCSE Bulletin - Working Group reports: Making inroads to improve computing education, 33:4, 125-140.

[7] A Petersen, M Craig, and D Zingaro (2011). Reviewing CS1 exam question content. 42nd ACM Technical Symposium on Computer Science Education (SIGCSE'11), 631-636.

[8] J Sheard, A Carbone, R Lister, B Simon, E Thompson, and JL Whalley (2008). Going SOLO to access novice programmers. 13th Annual Conference on Innovation and Technology in Computer Science Education (ITiCSE 2008), 209-213.

[9] J Sheard, Simon, A Carbone, D Chinn, T Clear, M Corney, D D'Souza, J Fenwick, J Harland, M-J Laakso, and D Teague (2013). How difficult are exams? A framework for assessing the complexity of introductory programming exams. 15th Australasian Computing Education Conference (ACE 2013), 145-154.

[10] Simon (2011). Assignment and sequence: why some students can't recognise a simple swap. 11th Koli Calling International Conference on Computing Education Research, 21-30.

[11] Simon, A Carbone, M de Raadt, R Lister. M Hamilton, and J Sheard (2008). Classifying computing education papers: process and results. Fourth International Computing Education Research Workshop (ICER 2008), 161-171.

[12] Simon, J Sheard, A Carbone, D D'Souza, J Harland, and M-J Laakso (2012). Can computing academics assess the difficulty of programming examination questions? 11th Koli Calling International Conference on Computing Education Research, 160-163.

[13] Simon, J Sheard, D D'Souza, P Klemperer, L Porter, J Sorva, M Stegeman, and D Zingaro (2016). Benchmarking introductory programming exams: how and why. 21st ACM Conference on Innovation and Technology in Computer Science Education (ITiCSE '16).

[14] Simon, J Sheard, D D'Souza, M Lopez, A Luxton-Reilly, IH Putro, P Robbins, D Teague, and J Whalley (2015). How (not) to write an introductory programming exam. 17th Australasian Computing Education Conference (ACE 2015), 137-146.

[15] Simon and S Snowdon (2014). Multiple-choice vs free-text code-explaining examination questions. 14th Koli Calling International Conference on Computing Education Research, 91-97.

[16] B Simon, M Clancy, R McCartney, B Morrison, B Richards, and K Sanders (2010). Making sense of data structures exams. Sixth International Computing Education Research workshop (ICER 2010), 97-105.

[17] E Soloway (1986). Learning to program = learning to construct mechanisms and explanations. Communications of the ACM, 29:9, 850-858.

[18] C Watson and FW Li (2014). Failure rates in introductory programming revisited. 19th ACM Conference on Innovation and Technology in Computer Science Education (ITiCSE '14), 39-44.

[19] J Whalley, R Lister, E Thompson, T Clear, P Robbins, PKA Kumar, and C Prasad (2006). An Australasian study of reading and comprehension skills in novice programmers, using the Bloom and SOLO taxonomies. Eighth Australasian Computing Education conference (ACE 2006), 243-251.

Evidence That Computer Science Grades Are Not Bimodal

Elizabeth Patitsas, Jesse Berlin, Michelle Craig, and Steve Easterbrook
Department of Computer Science
University of Toronto
Toronto, Ontario, Canada
patitsas,mcraig,sme@cs.toronto.edu and jesse.berlin@mail.utoronto.ca

ABSTRACT

Although it has never been rigorously demonstrated, there is a common belief that CS grades are bimodal. We statistically analyzed 778 distributions of final course grades from a large research university, and found only 5.8% of the distributions passed tests of multimodality. We then devised a psychology experiment to understand why CS educators believe their grades to be bimodal. We showed 53 CS professors a series of histograms displaying ambiguous distributions and asked them to categorize the distributions. A random half of participants were primed to think about the fact that CS grades are commonly thought to be bimodal; these participants were more likely to label ambiguous distributions as "bimodal". Participants were also more likely to label distributions as bimodal if they believed that some students are innately predisposed to do better at CS. These results suggest that bimodal grades are instructional folklore in CS, caused by confirmation bias and instructor beliefs about their students.

1. INTRODUCTION

It is a prevailing belief in the computer science education community that CS grades are bimodal, and much time has been spent speculating and exploring why that could be (for a review, see [1]). But these discussions do not include statistical testing of whether the CS grades are bimodal in the first place.

From what we've seen, people take a quick visual look at their grade distributions, and then if they see two peaks, they say it's bimodal. But eyeballing a distribution is unreliable; for example, if you expect the data to have a certain distribution, you're more likely to see it.

Anecdotally, we've seen new instructors and TAs (and students) shown histograms of grades and told the grades were "bimodal." The bimodality perception hence becomes an organizational belief, and those who enter the community of practice of CS educators are taught this belief. Every community of practice has a knowledge base of beliefs that

inform their practice [13], and these beliefs may or may not be based on empirical evidence.

1.1 Explanations of Bimodality

A number of explanations have been presented for why CS grades are bimodal, all of which begin with the assumption that this is the case.

1.1.1 Prior Experience

A bimodal distribution generally indicates that two distinct populations have been sampled together [5]. One explanation for bimodal grades is that CS1 classes have two populations of students: those with experience, and those without it [1].

High school CS is not common in many countries, and so students enter university CS with a range of prior experience. However, this explanation fits students into two bins. Prior experience is not as simple as "have it" vs. not – there is a large range on how much prior experience students can have programming, and practice with non-programming languages like HTML/CSS could also be beneficial [21].

1.1.2 Learning Edge Momentum, Stumbling Points, and Threshold Concepts

One family of explanations could be summarized as that some CS concepts are more difficult for students to learn, and if they miss these concepts, they fall behind while their peers advance ahead of them [1]. Because CS1 as it is typically taught builds on itself heavily, once a student falls behind, they continue to fall further and further behind [1].

One might think of this explanation as a variant of the prior experience explanation, where the students who succeed have better study skills, and those who fall behind do not.

1.1.3 The Geek Gene Hypothesis

Some would instead argue that the two populations in CS1 classes are those who have some "natural talent," giftedness, or predisposition to succeed at computing. Guzdial has referred to this belief as the "Geek Gene Hypothesis" in his writing [6].

This belief appears to be quite prevalent. In a survey of CS faculty, Lewis found that 77% of them strongly disagree with the statement "Nearly everyone is capable of succeeding in the computer science curriculum if they work at it." [15].

However, there seems to be little evidence that there is indeed a "Geek Gene", and that plenty of evidence that effective pedagogy allows for all students to succeed [8].

ICER '16 September 08-12, 2016, Melbourne, VIC, Australia

© 2016 Copyright held by the owner/author(s).

ACM ISBN 978-1-4503-4449-4/16/09.

DOI: http://dx.doi.org/10.1145/2960310.2960312

1.1.4 Lousy Assessment

Another line of explanation implicates instructors' assessment tools as the source of bimodally distributed grades [33, 23]. A common trend on CS exams is to ask a series of long-answer coding questions. Zingaro et al. found that these questions are coarse in terms of the information given to instructors: students either put all the pieces together, or fail to. Instructors do not adequately identify when a student has partial understanding nor quantify how much understanding this student has of a concept.

As an alternative, Zingaro et al. experimentally compared using short answer questions which build upon each other to having one isomorphic long-answer question. When the different conceptual parts of the question were broken up, the resulting grades were normally distributed, whereas the long-answer questions led to grades that the authors described as bimodal [33].

1.1.5 Or perhaps CS grades are not bimodal?

A competing view of CS grades argued by Lister is that the grades are not, in fact, bimodal [17]. Lister observed that CS grades distributions are generally noisy, and in line with what statisticians would accept as normally distributed. Lister argued that the perception of bimodal grades results from instructors' beliefs in the Geek Gene Hypothesis, and hence see bimodality where there is none [17]. Lister's argument was theoretical, and based on statistical theory; in our paper we will test his argument by statistically analysing real world grades distributions.

2. WHAT IS A BIMODAL DISTRIBUTION?

To properly tackle the question of "are CS grades bimodal?", we should first clearly establish what bimodality means.

Most standard continuous probability distributions have a mean, a median, a mode, and some measure of the distribution's width (variance). Standard distributions most people might be familiar with include the normal (Gaussian), Pareto, Poisson, Cauchy, Student's t, and logistic distributions. When we plot them with a histogram, we see what's called their probability density.

All of these distributions have a single mode, and have a probability density that can be modelled with a function that has a single term. For example, the normal distribution's PDF is:

$$f(x) = a e^{-\frac{(x-b)^2}{2c^2}}$$

In this function, a represents the height of the curve's peak, b is the position of the centre of the peak, and c represents the width of the curve [31].

In contrast, a bimodal distribution has two *distinct* modes. A 'multimodal' distribution is any distribution with multiple distinct modes (two or more).

For an example, consider these examples from [28]. Both are created by the equal mixture of two triangular distributions (solid lines). The sums are shown with dashed lines:

As we can see, when the two sub-distributions are far away (example **a**), we get a distribution with two peaks. But when the two sub-distributions are close together (example **b**), they add together to form a plateau, with a single peak. Example a is considered bimodal; example **b** is not.

The same can be seen for normal distributions (also from [28]):

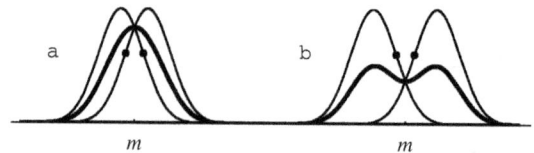

For a distribution to be bimodal, the sub-distributions can't overlap too much. As shown in [28], for the two distributions to be sufficiently far apart, the distance between the means of the two distributions needs to exceed 2σ. This, however, assumes the two distributions have the same variance.

More formally, if the two sub-distributions do not have the same variance, then for their sum to be bimodal, the following must hold [30]:

$$2^{\frac{1}{2}} \frac{|\mu_1 - \mu_2|}{\sqrt{(\sigma_1^2 + \sigma_2^2)}} > 2$$

2.1 Real World Data

Consider this histogram of sepal widths for the Iris species *versicolor*, taken from the Wikipedia page on "normal distribution" [31]:

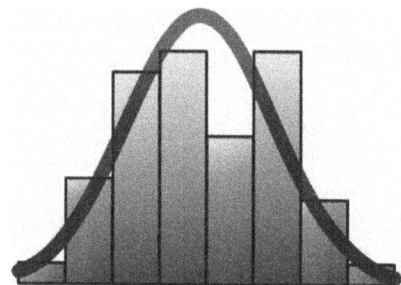

These data have two peaks, but it is considered a normal distribution. If we were to try and model these data as the mixture of two normal distributions, the two sub-distributions would be too close together to produce two distinct peaks. The simplest way to model these data is as a normal distribution.

Finally, it must be stressed that what we see in a histogram is a result of how we bin the data. It is possible to bin these data in a way which do not have two 'peaks' (for example, using larger intervals for the bins, or shifting the intervals).

2.2 Skewness and Kurtosis

By definition, a normal distribution is symmetric around its mode (which is also its mean and median). However, many real world data which produce a bell curve when graphed as a histogram do not fit these properties.

2.2.1 Skewness

Skewness is a measure of how asymmetric the data are. A distribution with a skewness of zero is perfectly symmetric. In comparison, a distribution with a negative skewness will have a longer 'tail' on the left side than on the right side; the opposite is true of positive skewness [32]:

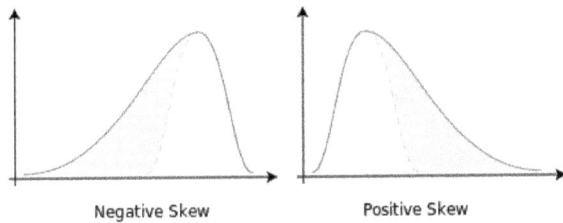

Negative Skew   Positive Skew

One may expect grades distributions to be skewed. One cause of skewness is the ceiling effect: if students are performing well (and this is normally distributed), and we set a maximum grade of 100%, this will cause the students at the top of the class to be bunched together.

By convention, if the absolute value of the skewness is greater than 1, a distribution is considered highly skewed; an absolute value of skewness between 0.5 and 1 is considered moderately skewed; less than 0.5 is considered approximately symmetric [32].

2.2.2 Kurtosis

Kurtosis is a measure of how 'tailed' the data is. A distribution with high kurtosis has a sharp peak and short tails. A distribution with low/negative kurtosis has a low peak and long tails. The normal distribution has a kurtosis of 3. A distribution with a kurtosis greater than this cannot be bimodal [30].

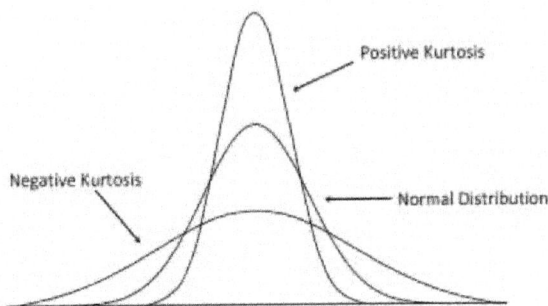

If you look back at the illustration of adding two normal distributions together, for the bimodal example, the distribution winds up being rather spread out horizontally. That distribution has low kurtosis. Indeed, for a distribution to be spread out far enough horizontally to allow for multi-modality, it necessarily will have low kurtosis.

3. STUDY 1: STATISTICAL ANALYSIS OF GRADES

Are CS grades bimodal, or unimodal? To test this, we acquired the final grades distributions for every undergraduate CS class at the University of British Columbia (UBC), from 1996 to 2013. This represents 778 different lecture sections, containing a total of 30,214 final grades (average class size: 75).

3.1 Testing for normality vs. bimodality

There are a number of ways to test whether some data are consistent with a particular statistical distribution.

One way is to fit your data to whatever formula describes that distribution. You can then eyeball whether your resulting curve matches the data, or you could look at the residuals, or even do a goodness-of-fit test.

Another is to use a pre-established statistical test which will allow you to reject/accept a null hypothesis on the nature of your data. We used this approach, for the ease of checking hundreds of different distributions and comparing them.

There are a large variety of tests for whether a distribution is normal, such as Anderson-Darling and Pearson's chi-squared test. We chose Shapiro-Wilk, since it has been found to have the highest statistical power [25].

There are few tests for whether a distribution is bimodal. Most of them essentially work by trying to capture the difference in means in the two distributions that are in the bimodal model, and testing whether the means are sufficiently separate. We used Hartigan's Dip Test, because it was the only one available in GNU R at the time of analysis.

We also computed the kurtosis for every distribution due to the necessary (but not sufficient) condition of kurtosis < 3 for bimodality [30]. To minimize false positives, we only performed Hartigan's Dip Test on distributions where the kurtosis was less than 3.

We chose the standard alpha value of 0.05. Given that we performed thousands of statistical tests, false positives are inevitable – we expect 5% of our tests will yield a false positive.

3.2 Test results

3.2.1 Unimodality vs. Multimodality

Beginning with kurtosis, 323 of the 778 lecture sections had a kurtosis less than 3. This means that 455 (58%) of the classes were definitely not bimodal, and that at most 323 (42%) classes could be bimodal.

Next we applied Hartigan's Dip Test to the 323 classes which had a kurtosis less than 3. For this test, the null hypothesis is that the population is unimodal. As a result, if $p < \alpha$, then we may reject the null hypothesis and conclude we have a multimodal distribution. This was the case for 45 classes (13.9% of those tested, 5.8% of all the classes).

Of the 45 classes which were multimodal, 16 were 100-level classes (35%), 5 were 200-level (11%), 12 were 300-level (27%), and 12 were 400-level (27%). For comparison, in the full set of 778 classes, 171 were 100-level (22%), 165 were 200-level (21%), 243 were 300-level (31%), and 199 were 400-level (26%).

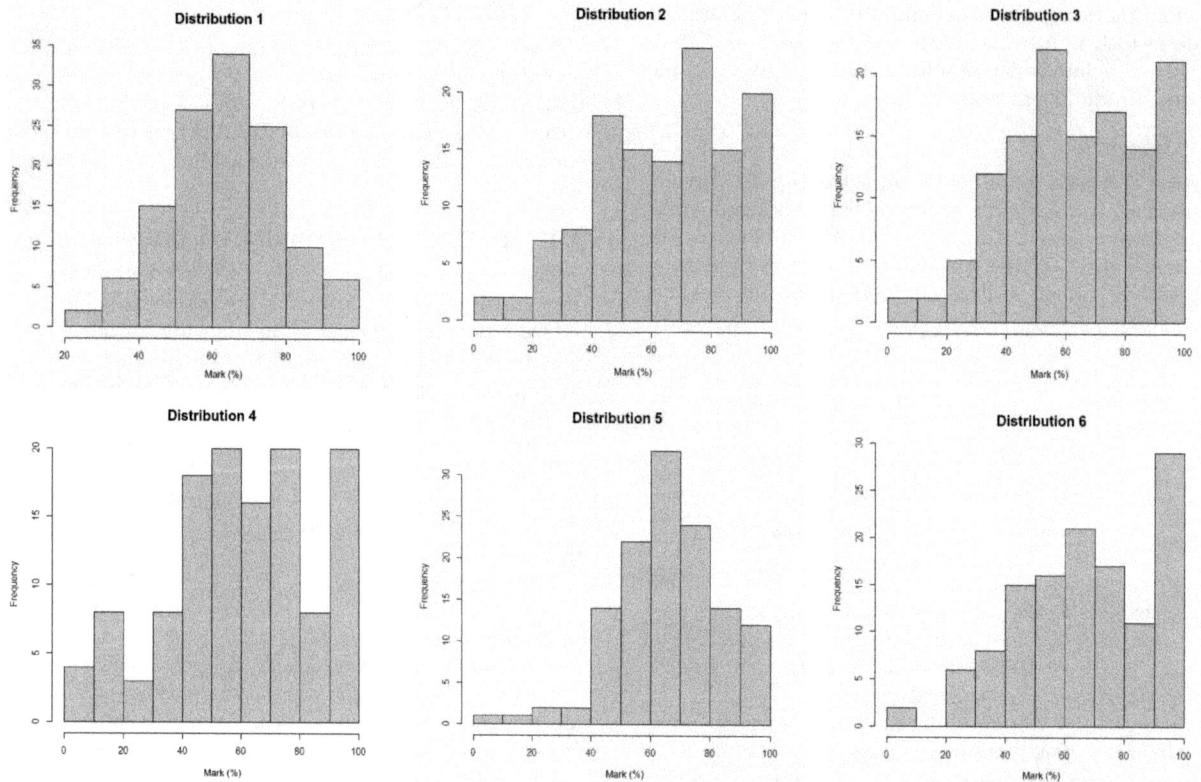

Figure 1: The six histograms shown to participants, all of which were generated using GNU R's `rnorm` function. A ceiling of 100% was used, which is most evident in Distribution 6. Each generated distribution had 100 points, and was generated with an average of 60 and standard deviation of 5.

1. Questions about how large their typical class was ("class-size") and how long they had been teaching ("years-experience").

2. A priming question: 'It is a commonly-held belief that CS grades distributions are bimodal. Do you find this to be the case in your teaching?' ("have-bimodal")

3. Questions on how often they look at their grades distributions:
   - 'When teaching, how often do you look at histograms of your students' grades? (This applies both to term work and final grades.)' ("look-histo")
   - 'How often do you look at how many students fall into each letter category (A, B, etc)? (This applies both to term work and final grades.)' ("look-letter")

4. Six histograms, all generated with GNU R's `rnorm`, shown in Figure 1. For each histogram, we asked two questions:
   - 'How often do you see the shape of [this distribution] in your classes?'
   - 'What sort of distribution would you describe [this distribution] as?'

5. Questions on the 'Geek Gene':
   - Nearly everyone is capable of succeeding in computer science if they work at it. ("all-succeed")
   - Some students are innately predisposed to do better at CS than others. ("innately-predisposed")

Table 1: The pages of the survey. Pages 2 and 5 were swapped for a random half of the participants. We chose the all-succeed question because it had been used in [16].

3.2.2 Normality

For the Shapiro-Wilk test, the null hypothesis is that the population is normally distributed. So, if $p < \alpha$, we can reject the null hypothesis and say the population is not normally distributed. This was the case for 106 classes.

44 of the 45 classes which were previously determined to be multimodal were among the 106 classes which the Shapiro-Wilk test indicated weren't normally distributed. In short, 13.6% of the classes aren't normally distributed, many of which are known to be multimodal.

For the 86.4% of classes where we failed to reject the null hypothesis, we can't guarantee that they are actually normal, because of type II error. Fortunately, we have a large sample size and good statistical power. We bootstrapped a likely beta value, providing an estimated false negative rate of 1.48%.

In short, an estimated 85.1% of the final grades in UBC's undergrad CS classes are normally distributed. If CS grades were typically bimodal, we would expect far more than 5.8% of classes to test as bimodal.

3.2.3 Skewness

While most of the distributions appear to be normally-distributed, it is worth noting that the average skewness of all the distributions was -0.33, ranging from -2.30 to 1.02. For just the distributions we'd determined to be normal, the average skewness was -0.13, ranging from -1.11 to 0.84. It is therefore likely that for many of the distributions which are unimodal but not normal, their non-normality is because they are too skewed to pass a test of normality. This may be a result of the ceiling effect in grade distributions.

3.3 Discussion

It is worth noting that we only examined final grades: our analysis did not include term grades.

As grades only came from one institution, one may wonder about the generalizability. We tried to get access to grades distributions from other institutions but generally found it difficult to gather the same scale of data. Analyzing five grades distributions from the University of Toronto, we found them to be normally-distributed.

While we can't assert that every university has the same grades distributions as UBC, the large scale of data both in numbers and time-span gives does give us a great deal of information. More work should be done to replicate our findings at other institutions.

What stood out for us is that at both UBC and UToronto, the CS faculty would routinely assert that their CS grades are bimodal – and we now had evidence to the contrary.

Our results support Lister's argument that CS grades are generally not bimodal, and that the perception of bimodality comes from instructors expecting their grades to be [17].

4. STUDY 2: HUMAN INTERPRETATION OF DISTRIBUTIONS

So if CS grades are rarely bimodal, why does the belief in bimodality persist? An insight came one day when generating some random normal distributions in R: with only 100 data points, there's often more than one peak. The multiple peaks may be erroneously perceived as "bimodal". A typical "large class" does not have a large enough sample size to consistently provide a smooth bell curve. Indeed, many of the distributions produced by R's `rnorm` looked very much like the grade distributions we'd seen in our own classes and called "bimodal."[1]

Interested in whether instructor perceptions affect the interpretation of noisy distributions, we designed an experiment wherein participants are presented with histograms of distributions produced by R's `rnorm` function, and asked to categorize the distribution (normal, bimodal, uniform, etc). We initially had two research questions:

1. Do CS instructors who believe in the Geek Gene categorize more noisy distributions as bimodal?

2. If we prime participants that CS distributions are commonly thought to be bimodal, are they then more likely to see bimodal distributions in the noise?

Once we'd analysed our data for those two research questions, a third research question arose:

3. If instructors label noisy distributions as bimodal, are they more likely to agree with the Geek Gene hypothesis? (i.e., is there a possible feedback loop between looking at distributions and instructors' beliefs?)

4.1 Experimental design

A difficulty in studies looking at priming effects is that you cannot state the purpose of the study in the consent form. If you do, then you are priming participants, even the participants you want in your control group. To disguise our study, we presented it as one asking people how often they saw various distribution shapes in their own classes.

We presented each participant with the six histograms shown in Figure 1, all of which we'd generated using R's `rnorm` function. We generated a few dozen histograms and selected the six histograms from that pool: one to be clearly normal (distribution 1), one that was mildly skewed (distribution 5) as though students who were failing were pushed up to 50%, one where the ceiling effect was visible (distribution 6), and three noisy distributions which had multiple peaks (distributions 2-4).

We asked each participant whether they saw this shape of distribution in their own classes (very often to never on a Likert scale), and then how they would categorize the distribution (normal, bimodal, multimodal, uniform, other).

We randomly assigned participants to one of two treatments:

Treatment 0: participants were asked whether they agreed with the Geek Gene Hypothesis, then asked to categorize the distributions, and were not being primed to think about bimodality.

Treatment 1: participants were primed to think about the common-held belief about CS grades distributions, before they saw the distributions; after that we asked them whether they agreed with the the Geek Gene Hypothesis.

The survey had five pages, which are described in Table 1. For each question we created a shorthand, in bold, for use in our analysis.

---

[1]One may wonder how many of the distributions generated by `rnorm` will test as bimodal per Hargigan's Dip Test. We generated 100,000 distributions with $n=100$, $\mu=60$, $\sigma=5$ and only 133 distributions (1.3%) tested as multimodal per the Dip Test.

Parameter	Treatment 0				Treatment 1			
	2	3	4	5	2	3	4	5
innately-pred		-2.2 (1.2)	-22 (4.5e-2)*		0.2 (1.8)	2.8 (1.8)	5.6 (2.3)*	
all-succeed	-37 (14)*	-35 (14)*	-39 (14)*		3.5 (2.6)	4.6 (2.8)	6.9 (3.2)*	
look-histo	7.0 (57)	6.0 (57)	7.8 (57)	-22 (3.1e-6)*		-2.6 (2.4)*	-3.8 (2.1)*	-6.4 (3.1)*
look-letter	32 (2.7)	1.4 (2.1)	1.0 (2.1)	-4.1 (3.2)		27 (1.9)	29 (0.9)	32 (1.8)

Table 2: Coefficients from the `polr` regression on seeing-bimodality for each treatment; standard errors are in parentheses; * denotes statistical significance.

	LR Chisq	Df	signif?
innately-predisposed	11.0	2	yes
all-succeed	14.8	3	yes
look-histo	4.1	4	no
look-letter	6.1	4	no

Table 3: Results of the `Anova` of the regressions on the two treatments; i.e., does the relationship between a given factor and seeing-bimodality differ between the two treatments?

Because so many of the potential participants were our colleagues, we deliberately did not collect names and identifying information about the participants in the survey. We did not want to know who was or was not a participant, nor how they responded to the survey.

As a courtesy, we offered to participants the option of having their email recorded on a separate platform if they wanted us to follow up with them about the results of the study[2]. We did not look at this email list until after our analysis was complete.

4.2 Participants

We recruited 60 CS instructors, mostly from the SIGCSE members' list. Some participants were recruited from other online CS education communities, and some were recruited at ICER 2015. 53 participants completed every question on the survey; 28 were in Treatment 0 (the non-primed group), and 25 were in Treatment 1 (the primed group).

The participants who had provided their emails for follow-up purposes were debriefed. Since fewer than half of the participants had provided their email, we posted open letters to the online communities where we had recruited participants.

4.3 Results

For each participant, we computed a value we'll call "seeing-bimodality," which is the number of distributions they had categorized as bimodal/multimodal. In our data, seeing-bimodality ranged from 0 to 5.

4.3.1 Regresion on seeing-bimodality

We wanted to see if seeing-bimodality could be predicted by participants' responses to the questions we'd asked. The regression we performed was to model seeing-bimodality as a function of innately-predisposed, all-succeed, look-histo, and look-letter, using the shorthands from subsection 4.1.

When visualizing the results, we noticed that the relationship between seeing-bimodality and the Likert questions varied between the two treatments. To perform a non-parametric equivalent of ANCOVA, we performed an ordinal

[2]The survey was on SurveyMonkey; signing up for follow-up emails was via Google Forms.

logistic regression on the two treatments separately using the `polr` function from R's `MASS` library, and then used the `Anova` function from the `car` package to compare the two.

In doing so we expected to compute 28 p values. Applying a Šidák correction to the standard alpha level of 0.05, we used 0.002 as our alpha level for this section of our analysis.

We found a statistically significant relationship between seeing-bimodality and participants' responses to the questions relating to the Geek Gene hypothesis (all-succeed and innately-predisposed), as shown in Table 2. Furthermore, when it came to all-succeed, the effect was statistically significantly stronger in the treatment which was primed to think about CS grades being bimodal, as shown in Table 3. We also observed there was a strong negative correlation between all-succeed and innately-predisposed.

We also found a statistically significant relationship between seeing-bimodality and how often participants reported looking at histograms of their grades (look-histo). This relationship was not statistically significantly different between the two treatment groups.

4.3.2 Regression on all-succeed

After finding a one-way relationship between grade perceptions and the Geek Gene Hypothesis, we wanted to see if there was any evidence of a feedback loop between the two. Because all-succeed and innately-predisposed correlated so highly, we found they were interchangeable as measures of belief in the Geek Gene. Since logistic regression involves only one dependent variable, we had to pick one of the two to use. We chose to do this analysis with all-succeed because the question item had been used in another study [16].

Recall that our study was set up so that a random half of the participants categorized distributions then were asked about the Geek Gene (Treatment 1), and the other half were asked about the Geek Gene and then categorized the distributions (Treatment 0). If there's a feedback loop here, we would expect that seeing-bimodality would predict all-succeed in Treatment 1, but not in Treatment 0.

Guidelines for statistical power in logistic regression are that for an alpha level of 0.05, you need 10–20 data points per independent variable in your model [18]. Because this part of the analysis requires the statistical power to reject a null hypothesis, we modelled all-succeed as only a function of seeing-bimodality, and set $\alpha = 0.05$.

For Treatment 1, we found that seeing-bimodality was a statistically significant predictor of all-succeed, as shown in Table 4. In Treatment 0, we found that it was not. This indicates that there is a feedback loop between categorizing distributions as bimodal and agreement with the Geek Gene Hypothesis.

We hence have observed evidence for the feedback loops illustrated in Figure 2.

Parameter	Treatment 0			Parameter	Treatment 1			
	1	2	3		1	2	3	5
seeing-bimodality	-0.2 (0.9)	-1.1 (1.0)	-0.7 (1.1)	seeing-bimodality	0.6 (1.0)	0.9 (1.2)	1.4 (1.0)	1.7 (3.2e-7)*
intercepts	-3.8 (1.2)	-2.0 (0.8)	-0.3 (0.6)	intercepts	-2.6 (1.1)	0.2 (0.7)	1.5 (0.8)	

Table 4: Coefficients from the `polr` regression on `all-succeed` for each treatment; standard errors are in parentheses; * denotes statistical significance. p values were calculated from z values using `coeftest`.

4.4 Discussion

We were initially surprised that regularly looking at histograms of grades was associated with a higher score for seeing-bimodality. This led us to add our third research question, based on the idea that it could be that the more often you look at your grades, the more it solidifies your conception of what your grades are like. This supports our observation that categorizing distributions as bimodal increases belief in the Geek Gene Hypothesis.

Our approach to priming may have led participants to believe more that grades are bimodal. Because the survey presents us, the researchers, as authority figures, and we imply that grades are thought to be bimodal, some participants could assume it to be true since we said so.

When we piloted our survey, some participants opined that they believed that some students were predisposed because of prior experience, rather than inherent brilliance.

We had hoped to recruit a larger number of participants; however, recruiting a large number of CS educators to fill out the survey turned out to be infeasible with our resources. It must be noted that we did not have a representative sample of CS educators. The educators who participate in CS education communities are generally much more invested in their teaching than their peers who do not. Furthermore, some of our participants may be familiar with Ahadi and Lister [2], which could have influenced their responses.

But we would expect the SIGCSE community to be *less* inclined to believe in the Geek Gene hypothesis than their non-SIGCSE peers. We still had enough participants who agreed with the hypothesis for us to conduct our analysis. Future work is needed to replicate our findings with a more representative sample of CS educators.

4.4.1 Supporting Literature

Our findings agree with the psychology literature: people's biases affect their decision-making more when they are judging more ambiguous information [10]. For example, Heilman et al. found that resumes of extremely qualified candidates were likely to be judged worthy of a salary increase regardless of the gender listed on the resume—but for resumes of ambiguously qualified candidates, resumes with male names were more likely to be viewed positively than those with female names [10]. As another example, Eyesnck et al. studied the interpretation of sentences as either threatening or non-threatening by people who have anxiety and by a control group [4]. They found that unambiguously threatening/non-threatening sentences were interpreted similarly between groups, but participants with anxiety were more likely to label ambiguous sentences as threatening than participants in the control group. Visual information is subject to this phenomenon also: Payne et al. showed participants a series of photos of black and white people holding either guns or ambiguous objects, and participants were more likely to identify the ambiguous object as a gun if it was held by a black person [22].

Furthermore, belief can affect judgment regardless of ambiguity. For example, Kahan et al. found that participants were more likely to get a math problem incorrect if the correct result would disagree with their political beliefs [12]. It is hence plausible that a computer scientist who believes in the Geek Gene Hypothesis could look at an unambiguously unimodal distribution and still view it as bimodal.

As for our evidence that looking at histograms reinforces belief in the Geek Gene Hypothesis, *systems justification theory* explains that once you are forced to take a position on a subject, you're more likely to believe and defend it [11].

5. THE GEEK GENE HYPOTHESIS AS A SOCIAL DEFENSE

Once again, our findings support Lister's hypothesis that CS grades are generally not bimodal and this perception stems from instructors expecting to find bimodal grades due to a belief in the Geek Gene Hypothesis. We would go a step further and argue that the perception of bimodality is a *social defense* in the CS education community.

5.1 What is a Social Defense?

In sociology and social psychology, a "social defense is a set of organizational arrangements, including structures, work routines, and narratives, that functions to protect members from having to confront disturbing emotions stemming from internal psychological conflicts produced by the nature of the work" [20].

For example, Padavic et al. [20] found that the "work-family" narrative in business is an example of a social defense: people will say that women leave the workplace because of "family", despite the large amount of evidence that women leave their jobs because of inadequate pay or opportunities for advancement [20], particularly when they see male co-workers promoted ahead of them. The "work-family" narrative is a more palatable explanation rather than to confront sexual discrimination in the workplace, and so the narrative continues.

5.2 Teacher Self-Efficacy

Guzdial reported that, per Fives [9], teachers generally have a high level of self-efficacy (great confidence in their teaching ability) at the start of their career. This then plummets as they face the realities of classroom teaching. With time, their self-efficacy slowly increases again. [9]

Teacher self-efficacy is not necessarily tied to how well they can teach: university educators often get little meaningful feedback on how their students are learning, given their large class sizes and lecture-based pedagogies. [9]

Guzdial reasoned that if an individual university-level CS educator has high self-efficacy, and sees evidence of students not learning, then it's rational for them to believe that the problem lies with the students and that the problem is innate to them—i.e., beyond the ability of the teacher to improve it [9]. Compounding this, Sahami and Piech have observed that CS educators are more aware of their top and bottom students than they are of their average students, giving educators a biased perception of their students' abilities [27].

Relatedly, Guzdial noted that CS educators have poor results, because we so frequently use ineffective teaching methods [7]. Indeed, Porter et al. recently found that performance on early assessments in CS1 correlate highly with final grades, indicating that surprisingly little learning goes on in CS1 [24]. The results of Zingaro, Petersen, and Craig would add that not only do CS educators frequently use ineffective pedagogies, they also frequently use ineffective assessment tools [33, 23].

We theorize that the Geek Gene Hypothesis is a social defense: it is easier for computer science educators to blame innate qualities of their students for a lack of learning than it is for the educators to come to terms with the ineffectiveness of their teaching.

A social defense is a phenomenon on a social scale, in contrast to Guzdial's observation about individual teachers. When numerous educators bond over how their students just "don't have it," it allows for the Geek Gene hypothesis to go from one individual's suspicion to a social narrative. And as bimodal grade distributions sometimes do occur, those cases are used to argue that this is a common and inherent phenomena in CS classes. When administrators accept this narrative and do not mandate professors to improve their teaching, the narrative can continue unchallenged.

The perception of bimodal grades provides evidence to the Geek Gene narrative that some students "have it" and some do not. And when new educators begin teaching, do not see all their students learning, and have been primed by colleagues to see bimodality, the new educator can then see this as evidence of the Geek Gene. The reproduction of the Geek Gene Hypothesis is hence social in nature.

Recent studies have found that academic disciplines in which "brilliance" is seen as necessary for success have less demographic diversity [14]. Looking at the history of science, women and people of colour were long denied entry and acknowledgment in science because they were seen as lacking the "brilliance" needed to do science [26].

If computing ability is viewed as being the result of a "Geek Gene", then educators may use this as an reason not to teach students who lack this "gene". Similarly they could lower expectations of these groups and encourage them less. Research on implicit biases consistently find that implicit biases against seeing women and people of colour as being brilliant scientists [29]. Students with disabilities or attention disorders could also be affected, or whoever else a particular educator might see as lacking the "gene". The "Geek Gene" narrative can also contribute to how women and minorities feel they do not belong in CS classes. It has been documented that underrepresented groups feel demotivated when their more experience peers boast that CS is "easy", and this could trigger stereotype threat [3].

6. CONCLUSIONS

Our analysis of UBC's grades indicates that while bimodal grade distributions can be found, they are far from typical (at most 5.8% of cases given type I error). Much more commonly, grade distributions are normal (85.1%) or skewed.

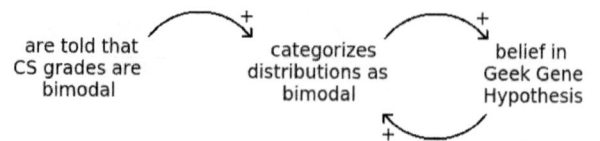

Figure 2: Individual-level feedback loops leading individuals to categorize ambiguous distributions as bimodal.

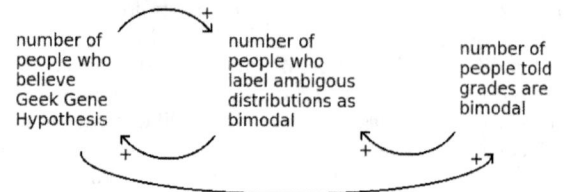

Figure 3: Social-level feedback loops leading individuals to categorize ambiguous distributions as bimodal.

Our psychology experiment found that priming participants to think about the common perception of bimodal grades leads to participants being more likely to label ambiguous distributions as bimodal. This indicates confirmation bias plays a role in the belief that bimodal grades are typical, when our (more rigourous, less anecdotal) evidence is that they are uncommon.

We also found that participants who reported beliefs consistent with the Geek Gene Hypothesis were more likely to label ambiguous distributions as bimodal. This indicates instructor beliefs play a role in perception of bimodality.

We observed that instructors who report looking at histograms of their grades were more likely to label ambiguous distributions as bimodal. As well, the random half of participants who labelled distributions as bimodal and then were asked about the Geek Gene Hypothesis were more likely to agree with it than the random half of participants who had been asked about the Geek Gene first.

Both our analysis of UBC's grades and our psychology experiment provide evidence for Lister's hypothesis that CS grades are not typically bimodal.

We theorized that the perception of bimodal grades in CS is a social defense. It is easier for the CS education community to believe that some students "have it" and others do not than it is for the community to come to terms with the shortfalls of our pedagogical approaches and assessment tools. A belief in the Geek Gene gives educators an easy way out from confronting these issues and being pushed to do better. In order for efforts to have CS taught "for all" to succeed, the CS education community needs to develop and use pedagogical approaches and assessment tools that will benefit all students.

7. ACKNOWLEDGMENTS

The first author received funding from the Social Science and Humanities Research Council of Canada. We would also like to thank our anonymous reviewers for their feedback, as well as Andrew Petersen, Jeff Forbes, and Aditya Bhargava for their suggestions.

8. REFERENCES

[1] A. Ahadi and R. Lister. Geek genes, prior knowledge, stumbling points and learning edge momentum: parts of the one elephant? In *Proceedings of the ninth annual international ACM conference on International computing education research*, pages 123–128. ACM, 2013.

[2] A. Ahadi and R. Lister. Geek genes, prior knowledge, stumbling points and learning edge momentum: parts of the one elephant? In *Proceedings of the ninth annual international ACM conference on International computing education research*, pages 123–128. ACM, 2013.

[3] C. Ashcraft, E. Eger, and M. Friend. *Girls in IT: The Facts*. National Center for Women & Information Technology, 2012.

[4] M. W. Eysenck, K. Mogg, J. May, A. Richards, and A. Mathews. Bias in interpretation of ambiguous sentences related to threat in anxiety. *Journal of abnormal psychology*, 100(2):144, 1991.

[5] S. J. Gould. *The mismeasure of man*. WW Norton & Company, 1996.

[6] M. Guzdial. Anyone can learn programming: Teaching > genetics, 2014.

[7] M. Guzdial. Teaching computer science better to get better results, 2014.

[8] M. Guzdial. Learner-centered design of computing education: Research on computing for everyone. *Synthesis Lectures on Human-Centered Informatics*, 8(6):1–165, 2015.

[9] M. Guzdial. Source of the "geek gene"? teacher beliefs: Reading on lijun ni, learning from helenrose fives on teacher self-efficacy, 2015.

[10] M. E. Heilman, C. J. Block, and P. Stathatos. The affirmative action stigma of incompetence: Effects of performance information ambiguity. *Acad. of Mgmnt. J.*, 40(3):603–625, 1997.

[11] J. T. Jost, M. R. Banaji, and B. A. Nosek. A decade of system justification theory: Accumulated evidence of conscious and unconscious bolstering of the status quo. *Political psychology*, 25(6):881–919, 2004.

[12] D. M. Kahan, E. Peters, E. C. Dawson, and P. Slovic. Motivated numeracy and enlightened self-government. *Yale Law School, Public Law Working Paper*, (307), 2013.

[13] J. Lave and E. Wenger. *Situated learning: Legitimate peripheral participation*. Cambridge university press, 1991.

[14] S.-J. Leslie, A. Cimpian, M. Meyer, and E. Freeland. Expectations of brilliance underlie gender distributions across academic disciplines. *Science*, 347(6219):262–265, 2015.

[15] C. Lewis. Attitudes and beliefs about computer science among students and faculty. *SIGCSE Bull.*, 39(2):37–41, June 2007.

[16] C. Lewis. Attitudes and beliefs about computer science among students and faculty. *SIGCSE Bull.*, 39(2):37–41, June 2007.

[17] R. Lister. Computing education research geek genes and bimodal grades. *ACM Inroads*, 1(3):16–17, 2010.

[18] J. H. McDonald. *Handbook of biological statistics*, volume 2. Sparky House Publishing Baltimore, MD, 2009.

[19] D. H. Meadows. *Thinking in systems: A primer*. Chelsea Green Publishing, 2008.

[20] I. Padavic and R. J. Ely. The work-family narrative as a social defense, 2013.

[21] T. H. Park, A. Saxena, S. Jagannath, S. Wiedenbeck, and A. Forte. Towards a taxonomy of errors in HTML and CSS. In *Proceedings of the ninth annual international ACM conference on International computing education research*, pages 75–82. ACM, 2013.

[22] B. K. Payne, Y. Shimizu, and L. L. Jacoby. Mental control and visual illusions: Toward explaining race-biased weapon misidentifications. *Journal of Experimental Social Psychology*, 41(1):36–47, 2005.

[23] A. Petersen, M. Craig, and D. Zingaro. Reviewing CS1 exam question content. In *Proceedings of the 42Nd ACM Technical Symposium on Computer Science Education*, SIGCSE '11, pages 631–636, New York, NY, USA, 2011. ACM.

[24] L. Porter, D. Zingaro, and R. Lister. Predicting student success using fine grain clicker data. In *Proceedings of the Tenth Annual Conference on International Computing Education Research*, ICER '14, pages 51–58, New York, NY, USA, 2014. ACM.

[25] N. M. Razali and Y. B. Wah. Power comparisons of Shapiro-Wilk, Kolmogorov-Smirnov, Lilliefors and Anderson-Darling tests. *Journal of Statistical Modeling and Analytics*, 2(1):21–33, 2011.

[26] M. W. Rossiter. *Women scientists in America: Struggles and strategies to 1940*, volume 1. JHU Press, 1982.

[27] M. Sahami and C. Piech. As CS enrollments grow, are we attracting weaker students? In *Proceedings of the 47th ACM Technical Symposium on Computing Science Education*, SIGCSE '16, pages 54–59, New York, NY, USA, 2016. ACM.

[28] M. F. Schilling, A. E. Watkins, and W. Watkins. Is human height bimodal? *The American Statistician*, 56(3):223–229, 2002.

[29] J. G. Stout, N. Dasgupta, M. Hunsinger, and M. A. McManus. Steming the tide: using ingroup experts to inoculate women's self-concept in science, technology, engineering, and mathematics (stem). *Journal of personality and social psychology*, 100(2):255, 2011.

[30] Wikipedia. Multimodal distribution — wikipedia, the free encyclopedia, 2016. [Online; accessed 6-April-2016].

[31] Wikipedia. Normal distribution — wikipedia, the free encyclopedia, 2016. [Online; accessed 6-April-2016].

[32] Wikipedia. Skewness — wikipedia, the free encyclopedia, 2016. [Online; accessed 6-April-2016].

[33] D. Zingaro, A. Petersen, and M. Craig. Stepping up to integrative questions on cs1 exams. In *Proceedings of the 43rd ACM technical symposium on Computer Science Education*, pages 253–258. ACM, 2012.

Lightweight, Early Identification of At-Risk CS1 Students

Soohyun Nam Liao[1], Daniel Zingaro[2], Michael A. Laurenzano[3], William G. Griswold[1], Leo Porter[1]

[1]University of California, San Diego

[2]University of Toronto, Mississauga

[3]University of Michigan

ABSTRACT

Being able to identify low-performing students early in the term may help instructors intervene or differently allocate course resources. Prior work in CS1 has demonstrated that clicker correctness in Peer Instruction courses correlates with exam outcomes and, separately, that machine learning models can be built based on early-term programming assessments. This work aims to combine the best elements of each of these approaches. We offer a methodology for creating models, based on in-class clicker questions, to predict cross-term student performance. In as early as week 3 in a 12-week CS1 course, this model is capable of correctly predicting students as being in danger of failing, or not, for 70% of the students, with only 17% of students misclassified as not at-risk when at-risk. Additional measures to ensure more broad applicability of the methodology, along with possible limitations, are explored.

Categories and Subject Descriptors

K.3.2 [**Computer Science Education**]: Computer and Information Science Education

Keywords

Peer Instruction; CS1; clickers; prediction

1. INTRODUCTION

Early identification of struggling students could be highly valuable for instructors and students alike. Instructors could explore possible intervention strategies to help struggling students, and students who are made aware that they are likely struggling may be spurred to change study habits or seek additional assistance. Moreover, communicating with students about their performance may play a role in the general effort to better personalize education in small and large classrooms and online learning environments.

To identify struggling students, research from the 1970s through the 1990s focused primarily on static personal features (GPA, gender, etc.). Recent work has begun using dynamic data, such as assignments [2] and in-class performance [12] to identify these students.

Porter et al. provided promising results that easy-to-obtain, in-class clicker data is correlated with final exam scores; however, that analysis was limited to a single term [12]. Next, Ahadi et al. demonstrated that machine learning models based on a combination of static and assignment submission data could be used to predict students in the bottom half of final exam scores; however, that analysis was done in a CS1 course with a very large number of assignments [2]. That latter work focused on modeling a single term, although the authors did show the potential to use machine learning to perform cross-term predictions.

The present work aims to build upon the strengths of both of these works by using easy-to-obtain, in-class clicker results to predict student outcomes across terms. By doing so, we aim to provide modeling practices whose data is easy to generate (requiring little course change), and where the time-consuming collection of sensitive student demographics or background information is not required.

The modeling is performed on a Peer Instruction (PI) CS1 course in Python. Our goal is to predict a final exam score using in-class clicker question data, after which classification decisions ("struggling" or "not struggling") can be made. This two-step process gives flexibility to the instructor, as they can choose the threshold at which to intervene.

In addition, recognizing that not all CS1 courses employ PI, we explore the use of the same questions as quiz questions rather than in-class clicker questions. We find that model accuracy declines only slightly, suggesting that our approach may be applicable to lecture-based courses as well.

We offer the following in this work:

- Despite confounding factors between terms (different students, different assignments, different topic ordering, and different exams), we demonstrate that naturally-collected clicker data from one term can be used to create a statistical model capable of identifying struggling students early in the other term (week 3 of 12).

- We provide details on building a model for a course and offer guidance on selecting thresholds based on instructor need. For those not using PI, we provide evidence that the use of questions as quizzes can provide similar prediction accuracy.

- Our model for the studied CS1 course accurately predicts 22% of students as struggling and 48% as not struggling. Only 17% of students are miscategorized as not needing assistance when assistance was needed.

ICER '16, September 08-12, 2016, Melbourne, VIC, Australia

© 2016 ACM. ISBN 978-1-4503-4449-4/16/09...$15.00

DOI: http://dx.doi.org/10.1145/2960310.2960315

2. BACKGROUND

Many researchers over the last several decades have reported correlations between early-term predictors and late-term outcomes (see Robins [13] for a review). These kinds of relationships are of interest for at least two reasons: in terms of teaching, they help us determine who is likely to succeed or fail in a particular CS course; in terms of the discipline at large, they can inform research that seeks to increase representation or performance of particular student subgroups.

Much of the early work used static student factors that cannot change or are difficult to change through the duration of the course. A typical such study is that of Wilson and Shrock [18], in which the authors report relationships between 12 student factors and midterm exam score. These factors include gender, programming experience, non-programming computing experience, comfort level, and attributions of success and failure.

These kinds of factors, existing before the course starts, are called presage factors [5]. Process (or dynamic) factors, on the other hand, capture aspects of learning and the interaction between student, context, and content. Recent availability of educational technology such as clickers and instrumented programming IDEs means that we have a wealth of process data at our disposal [7]. Process factors are often more powerful predictors than are presage factors [2, 17]. In addition, we see process factors, moreso than presage factors, as under our purview to influence. With early detection of concerning process data (low class attendance, maladaptive programming patterns, incorrect responses to formative feedback), we may be able to intervene and set a new path for these students. A prerequisite for such intervention, of course, is our ability to use process data to make accurate, early predictions of student success.

Much of the relevant literature in this area concerns predicting performance in CS1 [2, 3, 12, 16, 17]. For example, one study [16] collected data on assignment submission time to deadline, time elapsed between snapshots, edit distance between snapshots, and other features of the programming process, and used this data to predict whether each student would fail, pass, or excel in a CS1 course. Two weeks into the six-week course, the authors could make this prediction with 64% accuracy.

Research on the early prediction of students' CS performance in courses other than CS1 is sparse. In one work, the authors study the predictive power of weekly multiple-choice tests, homework grades, and previous CS1 performance on CS2 exam grades [4]. Student data was anonymized in such a way that weekly test scores could not be linked with exam scores. Instead, comparisons of grade distributions suggest, two-thirds of the way through the course, that test scores could be used to predict exam scores. Other significant predictors of exam score include scores on all team-based assignments (16-25% of variance explained) and CS1 grade (41-60% of variance explained).

The two prior papers most closely aligned to the present work are those of Porter, Zingaro and Lister [12] and Ahadi, Lister, Haapala and Vihavainen [2].

In the earlier of these papers, the authors leverage Peer Instruction (PI) clicker data as a naturally-occurring source of what students know [12]. The authors found significant correlations between clicker question correctness and final exam scores. The case is made that one can predict exam scores using only the first three weeks of course clicker data. While the work suggests as much, it does not follow through

by predicting student success in a future offering of the course. While correlations within one semester are interesting in themselves, such correlations do not tell us whether we really could predict and potentially intervene on students who will be at-risk as a course progresses.

In the latter paper, the authors report on a 6-week CS1 course [2]. The interest is in what can be predicted after the first week of class, rather than after the first three weeks of class. This was a traditional lecture-based course, not a PI course. As such, the PI fine-grained clicker data was not available. In lieu of clicker data, the authors use age, gender, grade average, major, prior experience, number of steps (total keypresses) taken on each assignment, and correctness scores on each assignment. There were 24 assignments given in the first week of class. Using machine learning techniques, the authors built a well-performing model on the training data (first term) and applied it to the test data (second term). Interestingly, the features with highest information-gain — and therefore those selected for the model — are largely the process predictors (e.g., number of steps taken on various assignments), not the presage predictors. The best-performing model was correct for 86-90% of the training data students and 71-80% of the test data students.

One concern with the process predictors from Ahadi et al. [2] is that some of the assignments asked in the first week resemble end-of-term outcomes. For example, one assignment has students write a program that repeatedly asks for and plots numbers within a given range; this requires integrative knowledge of variables, conditionals, and loops. Although the predictive value is clear, there are concerns that the nature and number of these early-term assignments may dissuade students without considerable prior programming experience.

The present paper draws ideas from and extends both of these papers. First, from Porter et al. [12], we use PI clicker data; no sensitive student data is collected or required. In contrast, the data used by Ahadi et al. [2] includes student surveys, student records' access, instrumented IDEs, and a large number of early programming assignments, all of which complicate data collection and course administration. Second, we leverage the idea of using the model built in one term to make predictions in a subsequent term [2, 17]. Such prediction across terms serves as evidence of a model that generalizes outside of its immediate context.

3. METHOD

The data are collected from a CS1 course taught in Python at a large North American research university during two consecutive fall terms ($n = 171$ and $n = 142$, respectively). Each offering was 12 weeks long and had three weekly 50-minute lectures. Student work included two term tests, weekly pair-programming labs, two large programming assignments, and a final exam. The second term, but not the first, also included short, weekly programming exercises. Both terms were taught by the same instructor using the PI pedagogy [10, 11, 19]. As further explained below, PI focuses on students discussing conceptual questions and responding with electronic clickers. The PI materials used in this study are based on those of a prior study [12].

The course content and lecture materials between the two terms are quite comparable as they were taught by the same instructor. We examined the PI clicker questions used in each course offering and found that 88% of all clicker questions appeared in both terms. Student responses to early matched questions (first three weeks), along with final exam scores, were used as the training and test data. Throughout the analysis, the former term is used as training data and the latter as test data.

3.1 Peer Instruction Format

PI is an increasingly popular active learning pedagogy in computer science courses [9, 11]. For clarity, we outline the core components of a PI class, the different votes we collect from students, and possible interpretations of these votes.

In a PI course, instruction is centered around a series of questions that students solve in class. Although the number of questions varies, the courses studied here had 3-5 questions per lecture. As part of the process, students are asked to select their answer, often using in-class electronic response systems (clickers). An individual PI cycle follows a well defined process:

Individual Vote: Students are shown the question and asked to solve it individually. They then record their answer using the clicker, the results of which are transmitted to the instructor. As an approximation, this vote can be viewed as student understanding prior to in-class instruction.

Group Vote: Students are then asked to discuss the problem in small groups and come to a consensus. They then respond again using the clicker. As an approximation, this vote can be viewed as student understanding after discussion. While it is possible that students could vote the same as their peers without understanding the chosen response, prior research suggests that this is not a major concern [10].

Classwide Discussion: Based on student responses, the instructor leads a classwide discussion about the question, aiming to both engage students in a discussion of why particular response choices were made and clarify to the class why certain responses are correct or incorrect.

(Optional) Isomorphic Vote: For some questions deemed to be particularly important for learning, the instructor asks a follow-on question after the classwide discussion. This isomorphic question is a different question on the same concept just discussed. The students respond to this question individually. As an approximation, the isomorphic vote can be viewed as student understanding at the conclusion of the PI process on that concept.

Through a participation grade, students are rewarded for attending class and participating in PI questions, not on providing correct responses.

3.2 Data Analysis and Modeling

In this section, we describe the process for creating and applying the model. The steps include: partitioning the data, preprocessing the data, using Principal Components Analysis to reduce data dimensionality, building the model, using the validation set to determine a classification threshold, and applying that model and threshold on the test set. Details are provided to encourage replication.

Defining Struggling Students: This decision depends on the course and the instructor. For our study, we spoke with the course instructor and defined "struggling" to be those students who score in the bottom 40% of students on the final exam. This threshold could be modified based on instructor preferences.

Data Set Partitioning: The data from the first term was split into two subsets: training set and validation set. The validation set is used to optimize the number of predictors in the trained model and to determine thresholds to best classify students. Only after the model is fully constructed

Table 1: Data Set Size After Preprocessing

Term 1		Term 2
Training Set	Validation Set	Test Set
117	54	142

and appropriate thresholds determined is it applied to the test set (students in the second term). Table 1 illustrates the size of each set for our model. The size ratio of the training set to the validation set is 2:1.

Data Preprocessing: Two standard steps are conducted to prepare the data for analysis. First, to account for differences in difficulty of exams across terms, we convert raw final exam scores to scaled scores. The scaling is done by first determining each exam score's z-score, then scaling all z-scores between the maximum and minimum z-score. Final exam scores of the training set, validation set, and test set are thereby scaled to the range $[0,1]$.

The second step addresses clicker responses that are missing. A student may fail to answer some clicker questions (e.g., by being absent, arriving late, forgetting to click, or leaving early), but our modeling approach does not handle missing data. If we simply omit students who fail to answer one or more questions, then we would lose the data of the vast majority of students in the class. We therefore use data imputation. Data imputation is essentially informed guessing: we guess how the student would have responded based on their responses and the responses of other students. The accuracy of such guesses is impacted by the number of questions that the student legitimately answered. (We investigate the impact of students who commonly miss class in Section 4.4.) Data imputation is performed using the well-established R mi package [15].

Dimensionality Reduction: As many clicker questions were asked each week, using all responses would lead to a model that overfits the data. To prevent this overfitting, we use Principal Components Analysis (PCA) to reduce the number of dimensions in the data using the R Caret package [8]. PCA extracts a given number of predictors (i.e., composites of clicker questions) that best represent the data. We explore using different numbers of predictors to determine the best number for our data by optimizing the model accuracy with regard to the validation set (the test set is not used in this process).

Building the Linear Regression Model: We create a linear regression model using the principal components chosen by PCA and predict a scaled final exam score for each student. The prediction model was created and tested using the R Caret package [8]. In the training phase, we use k-fold cross-validation (k=10) to optimize the regression model parameters. The trained model also provides variable importance information, which describes the predictive power of each clicker question.

Classifying Students: The output of the model, when applied to either the training or test data, is a predicted final exam score. This prediction can then be used to classify students. The following are the possible student classifications:

- **Correct Non-Intervention.** Our model correctly predicts that a student will be in the top 60% on the final exam.

- **Correct Intervention.** Our model correctly predicts that a student will be in the bottom 40% on the final exam.

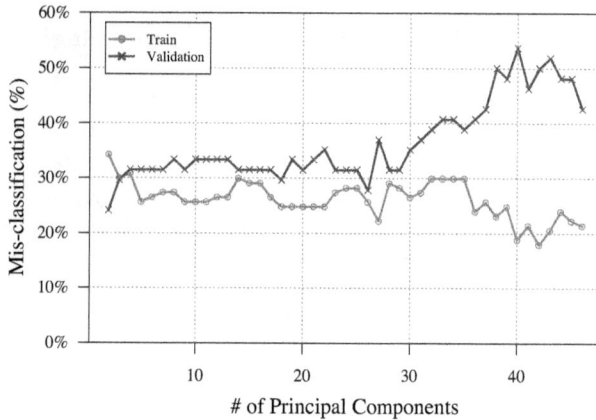

Figure 1: Impact on Accuracy of the Number of Principle Components

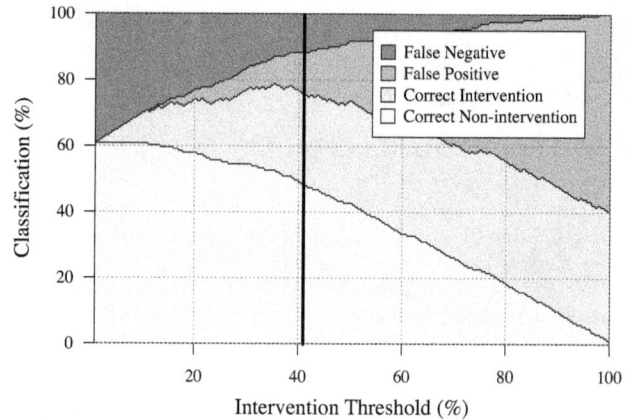

Figure 2: Intervention Threshold for Training and Validation Set

- **False Negative.** Our model predicts that a student will be in the top 60% on the final exam, but they end up in the bottom 40%.
- **False Positive.** Our model predicts that a student will be in the bottom 40% on the final exam, but they end up in the top 60%.

Given that we have predicted final exam scores, we could simply apply the original threshold that defines struggling students (in our case, the bottom 40%) to the predicted final exam results. However, due to error variance in predicted scores, this choice may not be ideal in that it could result in a large number of false positives or false negatives. As such, we instead use the validation set (again, not the test set) to determine an appropriate threshold for classifying students. We refer to this second threshold as the classification threshold or intervention threshold. We explore tradeoffs inherent in determining this threshold in Section 4.1.2.

To summarize, there are two relevant thresholds in our modeling approach. The first is the percentage of students that should be classified as struggling (this can be based on common exam outcomes and final grades). The second is the threshold that we use to classify students as in need of assistance, taking into account the likelihood of misclassifying students.

4. RESULTS

In this section, we model student performance across terms. We describe steps taken to build the model and apply it to identify struggling students. We then explore the model further to learn about influential PI votes, class attendance, and applicability to lecture classes.

4.1 Constructing the Model

4.1.1 PCA Variable Selection

We use the training and validation set to determine the appropriate number of principal components to use in building the model. We define model accuracy as the correct classification rate. Figure 1 illustrates the misclassification rate of the training set and the validation set with respect to the number of principal components. The misclassification rate is the proportion of students for whom a prediction of being in the top 60% or bottom 40% would be incorrect. This figure demonstrates that fewer than 30 principal

components provides good validation set accuracy. Additional components may improve the accuracy of the model for the training set, but at the potential expense of the validation and test sets. With a view toward choosing fewer rather than more components, and a desire to optimize performance on the training and validation sets, we chose nine principal components for our model.

4.1.2 Intervention Threshold

We next set the threshold for the percentage of the class on which to intervene. This intervening score could simply be set to the same point at which we consider students to be struggling (e.g., the bottom 40%). However, the choice of intervention threshold has a large impact both on model accuracy and on the number of students who are identified as potentially needing help. The higher the threshold, the more false positives (students receiving help who do not need it) and the more instructor resources are spent helping those students. In turn, the lower the threshold, the more false negatives (students not getting help who need it).

One can consider the two threshold extremes to better understand the tradeoffs present in selecting an intervention threshold. First, one might choose a threshold of 0%. This threshold would cause no students to be identified for an intervention, meaning that we never help a student who does not need help (zero false positives), but also never help students who do need help (maximum false negatives). Second, one might choose a threshold of 100%, in which case we help everyone that needs help (zero false negatives), but also help everyone else (maximum false positives). The question then becomes: how should we balance these tradeoffs? The answer ultimately comes down to instructor discretion based on available resources and the cost of intervention.

As an instructor cannot know the results for their present class, they can use student data from the prior term to help choose an appropriate intervention threshold. To help visualize the impact of the instructor's threshold decision, Figure 2 shows the impact of the intervention threshold for the first term data (training set and validation set combined). In this figure, we see that as we increase the threshold from 0% to 40%, our method tends to more accurately predict poor performers. However, as we continue to raise the threshold, we introduce false positives at an increasing rate.

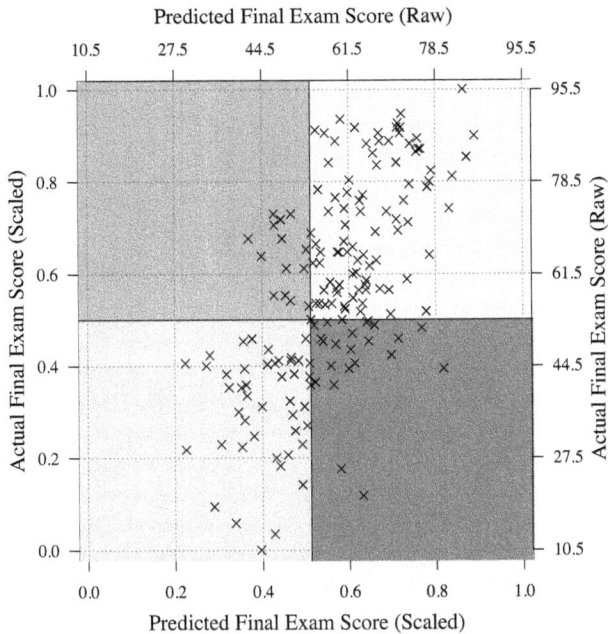

Figure 3: Model Accuracy for Training Data

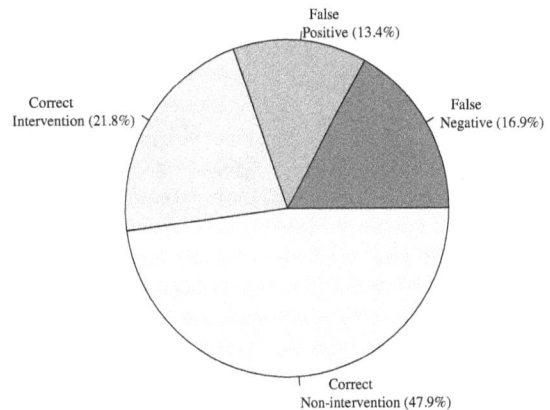

Figure 4: Model Accuracy for Test Data

For the remainder of this analysis, we chose the intervention threshold with the highest accuracy (i.e, that minimized the misclassification rate). Other threshold decisions to minimize false positives or false negatives would be possible and would be at the instructor's discretion.

We use the validation set alone (not with the training set) to determine the intervention threshold with the highest accuracy; that threshold is 41%. This means that to identify students who are in the bottom 40% of the class, we will conclude that students whose predicted final exam score is in the bottom 41% will struggle. Although the small difference between 40% and 41% may suggest that the alternative threshold is unnecessary, when we use different model parameters we found larger thresholds (e.g. 55%). We next examine our model for the training data in the context of this threshold and then apply this threshold to the test data.

4.1.3 Model Accuracy for Training Set

Although the ultimate goal of developing this model is to examine its accuracy on the test set, here we begin by examining the model's accuracy for the training set. Figure 3 plots the model's predicted final exam score per student (x-axis) against their actual final exam score (y-axis). There are two labels per axis. The "Raw" scores are the actual scores on the exam out of 105 points. The "Scaled" scores are scaled by the students' z-scores and are hence between 0 and 1. Recall that the reason for the scaled scores is that exams across multiple terms may have different difficulty.

The linear model in this figure, built using nine principal components, is fairly accurate ($rho : 0.628, R^2 : 0.395$). To examine the prediction accuracy, we focus on the four colored quadrants. Keeping with the color convention from Figure 2, we can identify the regions of correct predictions (intervention, no intervention, false positive, and false negative) for the threshold chosen above.

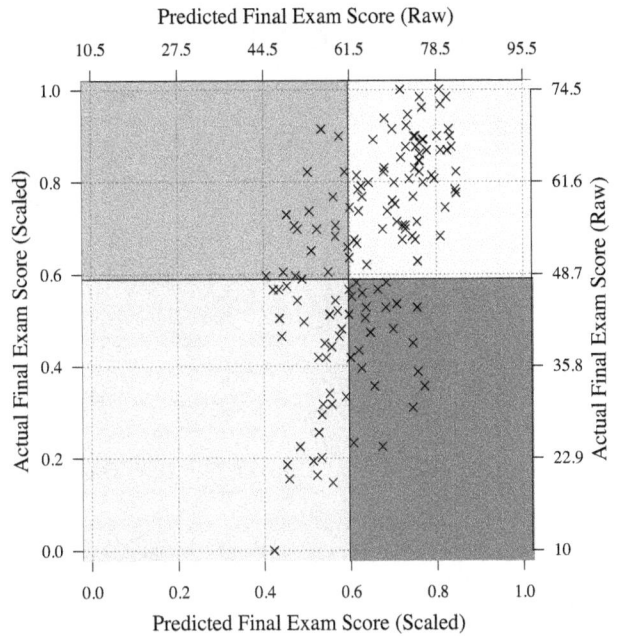

Figure 5: Classification Accuracy for Test Data

4.2 Applying the Model

4.2.1 Model Accuracy for Test Set

Figure 4 provides the plot of predicted versus actual final exam score for the test data. The model is again reasonably accurate ($rho : 0.574, R^2 : 0.329$) despite the differences between terms (ordering of topics, different students, different exams, etc.). We revisit these differences in Section 5.

4.2.2 Student intervention accuracy

While the model provides a predicted final exam score, our intended use is to apply the 41% threshold to determine students who are likely to fall into the bottom 40% of exam scores. Figure 5 provides the accuracy of our student classifications. 70% of students are accurately predicted. 13% of predictions are false positives and 17% are false negatives. Recall that one can increase the intervention threshold to

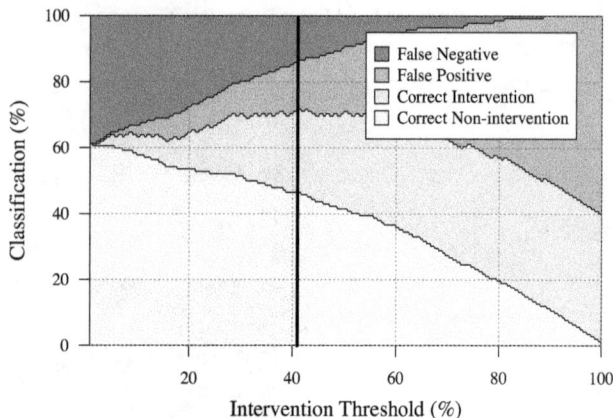

Figure 6: Threshold Impact for Test Data

decrease the number of false negatives, but at the expense of increasing false positives.

As mentioned above, an instructor's choice of intervention threshold impacts false negatives and false positives. Figure 6 demonstrates the impact of the intervention threshold on the test set. This figure is shown only to demonstrate the tradeoffs in the context of the test set results; recall that the threshold was determined using the validation set. Such a figure of the test set results would not be available until the end of the later term, too late for intervention to be useful.

4.3 Model Influences

Figure 7 provides the importance scores for the early-term clicker questions as determined by the model. In the top half of the figure, the questions are labeled by the relevant vote in the PI process: individual (solo), group, or isomorphic (iso). The key take-away here is that both isomorphic and individual votes play a larger role, particularly among the very top predictors, than group votes. This corresponds with prior findings that group votes can be noisy due to confounds between actual learning and copying perceived correct answers [10].

In the bottom half of the figure, the questions are organized by the time they occurred in the term.[1] Here we see that questions from week 2 are among the very top predictors. Week 2 content includes functions, particularly return types, and boolean expressions and conditionals. As expected, questions from week 1 and week 3 also appear among the top 15 predictors.

4.4 Impact of Student Attendance

The results above include all students in the test set, regardless of their class participation. Is it reasonable to expect the model to predict a student's final exam score when they have only attended a small number of classes? To study this question, we examined the model's accuracy on only students who answered 70% or more of the clicker questions. For this large subset of students, the model predicting final exam scores for the test set remains similarly accurate ($rho : 0.556, R^2 : 0.309$).

The classification of poorly-performing students is more accurate than when all students are included. Figure 8 provides the resulting classification accuracy. The model's ac-

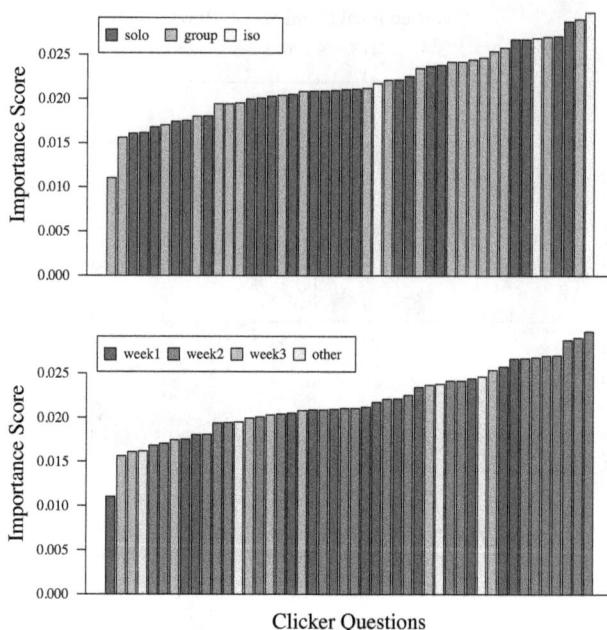

Figure 7: Question Importance for the Model

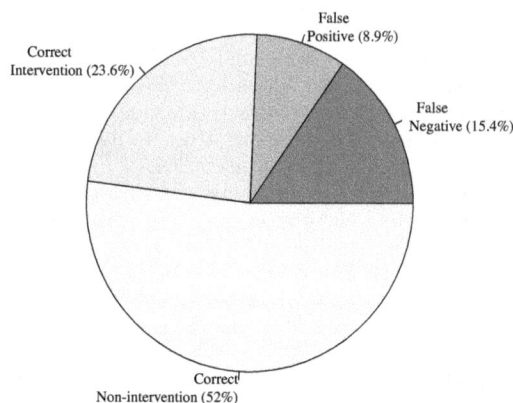

Figure 8: Model Classification Accuracy for Only Frequently-Responding Students in Test Data

curacy for student classification has increased from 70% to 76%, demonstrating the importance of class attendance for model accuracy.

4.5 Applicability to Non-PI Classes

One core aim of this effort is to ensure that the modeling is made more accessible to other instructors who wish to benefit from predictions in their classes. Although PI has gained considerable traction in computing [11], a large number of instructors may not wish to adopt PI and/or clickers. In this section, we examine the possibility of using the PI clicker questions as either before-class quizzes or brief start/end-of-class quizzes. The questions are available at [1].

To explore this idea, we built a new model using only individual clicker votes. These votes may be representative of student thinking before class as they occur before the group and classwide discussion. One confound, however, is

---

[1] "Other" occurs because some questions that appeared in the first 3 weeks of the test set were in later weeks in the training set due to minor reorganization of topics in the course.

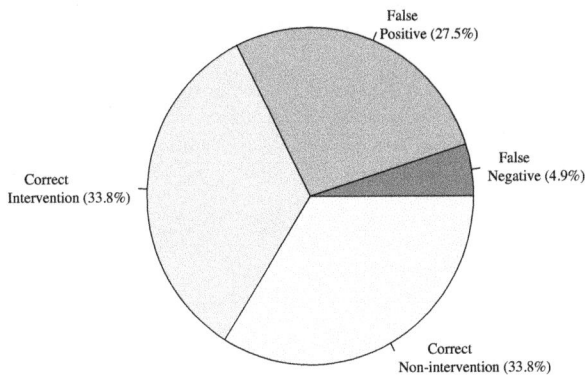

False Positive (27.5%)

False Negative (4.9%)

Correct Intervention (33.8%)

Correct Non-intervention (33.8%)

Figure 9: Classification Accuracy for Test Data When Limited to Only Using Individual Votes

that they may occur mid-way through a class and students may have learned from prior class content. Alternatively, one might ask these questions after the class, in which case the results may more closely resemble the isomorphic votes. As the isomorphic votes were highly predictive in our model, the results in this section may understate the expected modelling ability of questions used at the end of class.

Compared to the full model, this new model is only marginally worse at predicting student final exam scores in the test set ($rho : 0.546, R^2 : 0.299$) and at classifying poor performers. Figure 9 shows that the classification accuracy is 68% for all students, compared to 70% accuracy when we included the group and isomorphic votes. Although false negatives have been reduced significantly, this is simply due to selecting a higher intervention threshold for maximum accuracy, which, in turn, increased the number of false positives. The overall accuracy suggests that instructors who wish to adopt this approach with lightweight multiple-choice quizzes may be able to successfully predict low performing students without the requirement of adopting PI.

5. DISCUSSION

This work demonstrates the potential to use student clicker data to predict low-performing students across terms. The requirement on instructors is lightweight as they can either use the same clicker questions across terms or, potentially, quizzes including these multiple choice questions. After building the linear model, instructors can then make their own decisions about how to identify poor performers based on the two threshold values: the percentile on the final exam that is considered low-performing and how to optimize their classification threshold.

5.1 Revisiting Results

Cross-Term Differences: The ability to predict student outcomes across terms may seem straightforward given that the clicker questions changed little from the first term to the second. However, a number of differences are evident even though the same instructor taught both terms. The differences include: different students, different in-class student inquiries and resultant discussion, different assignments, different topic ordering (topics were rearranged slightly to address assignment changes), and most critically, different ex-

ams. An additional confound is the noise and missing data inherent in clicker responses graded on participation. Although the modeling approach outlined here may help mitigate some of these effects (e.g., using student percentiles to reduce the impact of differing exam difficulties), the robustness of the modeling technique is all the more surprising when these differences and confounds are recognized.

Question Quality: The quality of the model is implicitly based on the quality of the clicker questions and their utility for identifying student misconceptions across a variety of topics. Two major factors contributed to the quality of the questions in this course. The first is that CS1 has been widely studied by the computer science education research community and the design of these questions was informed by that research. The second is that the instructor has taught the course for a number of years and has refined the questions over this time period. As a result, we provide these questions to those wishing to adopt this approach [1].

Helping Poor Performers: This paper is not the first to recognize the inherent benefits of identifying low-performing students early in the term [2, 12], but the approach outlined here vastly reduces barriers to adoption (e.g., large number of coding assignments in the first week). Once it is easy to identify these students, instructors will be tasked with acting on these results. Interventions to improve students' outcomes deserve further attention and are the focus of ongoing work.

Low-Performing Threshold: The thresholds for poor performers have a large impact on the classification accuracy and, potentially, instructor resources dedicated to intervention plans. We chose a bottom 40% threshold based on cut-offs chosen by the instructor, but other values could be chosen. We caution, however, that the modeling technique outlined here is more effective at classifying large groups than small groups. As such, this particular model may struggle to identify small subsets of students (e.g., the bottom 5%) as identifying such outliers is both difficult in general and ill-suited for this model.

As mentioned previously, an instructor's choice of intervention threshold impacts the number of students for whom intervention is offered. An instructor can optimize this threshold to maximize accuracy, minimize false negatives, or perform an intervention for some particular number of students. Resource requirements may, at least partially, constrain the instructor. For example, should the instructor wish to e-mail students in jeopardy, they may optimize for a fairly low false negative rate (accepting more false positives) because the intervention is inexpensive. In contrast, if the instructor aimed to have a special in-person session for struggling students, they may optimize based on room sizes or the availability of instructional staff.

5.2 Comprehensive Picture of Early CS1

Prior work suggests fruitful links between early identification of students and informing what we know about CS concepts that are challenging to students [2, 12]. Porter et al. [12] focus on individual clicker questions and their relationship to exam outcomes. However, due to the type of modeling used, a number of highly correlated clicker questions on the same topic may all appear important. Ahadi et al. [2] study predictors in the larger context of a machine-learning model, but the predictors are scores on code-writing assignments that do not isolate individual concepts.

Our method allows us to again benefit from the best features of each of these prior works. By examining highly-predictive clicker questions in the context of a comprehen-

Table 2: Topics among top 10 predictive questions, ordered by importance rank. Questions whose votes appeared multiple times include the importance rank and corresponding vote categories, respectively.

Rank(s)	Week	Vote	Topic
1,5,7	2	iso, gr, ind	Code tracing through nested function calls where variables used are in or out of scope
2,3	2	ind,gr	Logic/ Boolean expression evaluation and boolean variable assignment
4	2	ind	The difference between a function printing a value versus returning a value
6	2	iso	Given a boolean expression with variables, determine what values those variables would need to have to evaluate as false
8	1	ind	Code tracing through a single function call where the function has multiple arguments
9	1	gr	Variable types (integer versus double)
10	3	gr	Code Tracing through nested conditionals

sive model, we gain a more complete picture of the critical topics and concepts in the first three weeks of the course.

To do this, we examined the top ten questions in terms of importance from Figure 7. As each question may be answered multiple times through the individual, group, and optional isomorphic vote, a single question may appear multiple times among the top predictors. Although this may seem contradictory to the notion that highly-correlated results should be pruned from the model, recall that each of these votes represents a different point in student understanding: before discussion, after discussion, and after instructor explanation, respectively. Indeed, two questions appeared for multiple votes, resulting in eight unique questions.

The topics of these questions appear in Table 2. Critical topics from the beginning of CS1 appear in the top predictors, including variables, types, boolean expressions, function calls, parameters, scope, and conditionals. Loops are absent from this list because they do not appear in the course until Week 4. None of these topics, nor their ranking, appears particularly contradictory to what one might expect as top predictors from an introductory course [6, 14].

5.3 Threats to Validity

There are two categories of threats to validity. The first is with regard to the building of the model while the second focuses on the course itself.

5.3.1 Model Construction

Class size: The construction of this model required a fairly large class as we partition the training data into a 2/3 training set and 1/3 validation set. Moreover, among the remaining training set, k-fold cross validation (k=10) is necessary to avoid overfitting. As such, the applicability of our technique to smaller classes is unknown.

Model Robustness and Overfitting: In exploring successful model construction on the training set, a number of parameters were explored and the resultant models had similar degrees of correctness. Use of the test set was limited in order to avoid overfitting to the test set. However, in the research process, the test set was queried more than once. The robustness and similarity of results (e.g., classification accuracy between 68%-73%) across these queries suggest that overfitting did not occur, however whenever a test set is examined more than once, overfitting/overtuning becomes a concern.

5.3.2 Cross-Term Course Repetition

Questions: As mentioned, the clicker questions in this study had a basis in the literature and have been used in multiple courses. As the model is based on the question results, modeling for different questions may yield different results. **Exam**: The questions on the final exams across the two terms are completely different because exams are made public at the instructor's institution. As previously mentioned, the differences between the exams (both in terms of question difficulty and conceptual coverage) may lead to lower model accuracy. By contrast, reusing significant portions of exams could yield increased modeling accuracy. **Instructor**: The same instructor taught both terms of the course. Whether the model applies to another instructor using the same questions is unknown and is part of ongoing work.

6. CONCLUSION

This work proposes a lightweight modeling technique based on prior-term data to identify low performers in a course. The approach relies solely on the naturally-occurring student responses to clicker questions in a Peer Instruction classroom. Should an instructor not use Peer Instruction, our results suggest that simply asking the same multiple-choice questions before or after class could produce similarly accurate results.

At the heart of the prediction methodology is the instructor's goals for identifying poor performers. As such, they can choose to trade off overestimating the number of poor performers to ensure they reach everyone in need or underestimating the number of poor performers to avoid spending course resources on those who may not need help. For our CS1 course in python, our approach results in a model that accurately predicts 70% of students in the test set as either needing or not needing assistance. We also show that we are able to more accurately predict students who attend class more frequently and that the important topics identified by the model can inform our view of the early weeks of CS1.

7. ACKNOWLEDGMENTS

Thank you to the anonymous reviewers for their helpful feedback on this work. This work was supported by NSF grant 1140731.

8. REFERENCES

[1] Peer instruction for computer science. peerinstruction4cs.org, 2013.

[2] A. Ahadi, R. Lister, H. Haapala, and A. Vihavainen. Exploring machine learning methods to automatically identify students in need of assistance. In *Proceedings of the Eleventh international Conference on Computing Education Research*, pages 121–130, 2015.

[3] S. Bergin, A. Mooney, J. Ghent, and K. Quille. Using machine learning techniques to predict introductory programming performance. *International Journal of Computer Science and Software*, 4(12):323–328, 2015.

[4] H. Danielsiek and J. Vahrenhold. Stay on these roads: Potential factors indicating students' performance in a CS2 course. In *Proceedings of the 47th ACM Technical Symposium on Computer Science Education*, pages 12–17, 2016.

[5] M. de Raadt, M. Hamilton, R. Lister, J. Tutty, B. Baker, I. Box, Q. Cutts, S. Fincher, J. Hamer, P. Haden, M. Petre, A. Robins, Simon, K. Sutton, and D. Tolhurst. Approaches to learning in computer programming students and their effect on success. *Higher Education in a changing world: Research and Development in Higher Education*, 28:407–414, 2005.

[6] K. Goldman, P. Gross, C. Heeren, G. L. Herman, L. Kaczmarczyk, M. C. Loui, and C. Zilles. Setting the scope of concept inventories for introductory computing subjects. *Transactions on Computing Education*, 10(2):1–29, 2010.

[7] P. Ihantola, A. Vihavainen, A. Ahadi, M. Butler, J. Börstler, S. H. Edwards, E. Isohanni, A. Korhonen, A. Petersen, K. Rivers, M. A. Rubio, J. Sheard, B. Skupas, J. Spacco, C. Szabo, and D. Toll. Educational data mining and learning analytics in programming: Literature review and case studies. In *Working group report of the 20th annual conference on Innovation and technology in computer science education*, pages 41–63, 2015.

[8] M. Kuhn. Building predictive models in R using the caret package. *Journal of Statistical Software*, 28(1), 2008.

[9] C. Lee, S. Garcia, and L. Porter. Can peer instruction be effective in upper-division computer science courses? *Transactions on Computing Education*, pages 12–22, 2013.

[10] L. Porter, C. Bailey-Lee, B. Simon, and D. Zingaro. Peer instruction: Do students really learn from peer discussion in computing? In *Proceedings of the Seventh international Conference on Computing Education Research*, pages 45–52, 2011.

[11] L. Porter, D. Bouvier, Q. Cutts, S. Grissom, C. Lee, R. McCartney, D. Zingaro, and B. Simon. A multi-institutional study of peer instruction in introductory computing. In *Proceedings of the 47th ACM Technical Symposium on Computing Science Education*, pages 358–363, 2016.

[12] L. Porter, D. Zingaro, and R. Lister. Predicting student success using fine grain clicker data. In *Proceedings of the tenth annual conference on International computing education research*, pages 51–58, 2014.

[13] A. Robins. Learning edge momentum: A new account of outcomes. *Computer Science Education*, 20(1):37–71, 2010.

[14] A. Robins, P. Haden, and S. Garner. Problem distributions in a CS1 course. In *Proceedings of the 8th Australian conference on Computing education*, pages 165–173, 2006.

[15] Y.-S. Su, A. Gelman, J. Hill, and M. Yajima. Multiple imputation with diagnostics (mi) in R: Opening windows into the black box. *Journal of Statistical Software*, 45(1):1–31, 2011.

[16] A. Vihavainen. Predicting students' performance in an introductory programming course using data from students' own programming process. In *IEEE 13th International Conference on Advanced Learning Technologies*, pages 498–499, 2013.

[17] C. Watson, F. W. Li, and J. L. Godwin. No tests required: Comparing traditional and dynamic predictors of programming success. In *Proceedings of the 45th ACM Technical Symposium on Computer Science Education*, pages 469–474, 2014.

[18] B. C. Wilson and S. Shrock. Contributing to success in an introductory computer science course: a study of twelve factors. *SIGCSE Bulletin*, 33:184–188, 2001.

[19] D. Zingaro. Peer instruction contributes to self-efficacy in CS1. In *Proceedings of the 45th ACM technical symposium on Computer Science Education*, pages 373–378, 2014.

Some Trouble with Transparency: An Analysis of Student Errors with Object-oriented Python

Craig S. Miller
DePaul University
243 S. Wabash Ave.
Chicago, IL 60604
cmiller@cdm.depaul.edu

Amber Settle
DePaul University
243 S. Wabash Ave.
Chicago, IL 60604
asettle@cdm.depaul.edu

ABSTRACT

We investigated implications of transparent mechanisms in the context of an introductory object-oriented programming course using Python. Here transparent mechanisms are those that reveal how the instance object in Python relates to its instance data. We asked students to write a new method for a provided Python class in an attempt to answer two research questions: 1) to what extent do Python's transparent OO mechanisms lead to student difficulties? and 2) what are common pitfalls in OO programming using Python that instructors should address? Our methodology also presented the correct answer to the students and solicited their comments on their submission. We conducted a content analysis to classify errors in the student submissions. We find that most students had difficulty with the instance (self) object, either by omitting the parameter in the method definition, by failing to use the instance object when referencing attributes of the object, or both. Reference errors in general were more common than other errors, including misplaced returns and indentation errors. These issues may be connected to problems with parameter passing and using dot-notation, which we argue are prerequisites for OO development in Python.

Keywords

abstraction; object-oriented programming; Python

1. INTRODUCTION

For perhaps as long as software has existed, computing practitioners have worked to create useful abstractions in order to develop software that is understandable, reliable and manageable. When designing programming languages and their development environments, both academics (e.g. [12]) and industry professionals (e.g. [27]) tout the benefits of abstraction while also acknowledging its potential pitfalls and trade-offs with transparency.

Given the importance and centrality of abstraction in computing, educators have strongly advocated for its inclusion

in computing curricula [29, 3] and have studied how students learn abstraction [13, 21, 15, 19]. Less studied is the role of abstraction in the software environment and its consequences on learning. Clean abstractions in programming languages and environments minimize implementation details and arguably reduce cognitive load. High cognitive load has been theoretically and empirically linked to reduced learning [28].

One research effort that connected abstraction and cognitive load was a study comparing how abstraction is used in scenario-based programming versus object-oriented programming [2]. Here scenario-based learning made use of a visual language called *live sequence charts* (LSC) that abstracts out procedural details with the specification of declarative action sequences. The results suggested that scenario-based programming reduced cognitive load by separating integration and implementation of new features, something that object-oriented languages blurred. The authors argue that OOP requires, rather than develops, abstract thinking [2]. However, this study was limited in several ways. First, it relied on findings from two different samples (9 graduate students vs. 19 high school students). Second, as a relatively small qualitative study, it did not seek to identify how frequently various difficulties emerge from making underlying implementation details visible.

Of course, other research has extensively studied student programming errors, often with the goal of identifying the factors that cause them. For example, a recent survey and study of student errors on the commonly studied Rainfall programming problem revealed large variation in student performance [24]. While the authors discussed possible factors that might account for the variation, they did not consider the level of abstraction in the programming environment. A second study that appeared at the same time considered the frequency of particular errors in an exam situation and categorizations of student solutions to the problem [14]. Like the other study, the authors did not consider the role of abstraction in their categorization of submissions or errors, hypothesizing instead on whether the exam format (paper vs. computer) might affect student performance [14].

The goal of this paper is to explore some consequences of having underlying mechanisms visible to students as they learn computing concepts. On the one hand, as Alexandron et al. determined, presenting students with a clean abstraction reduces cognitive load and thus supports their learning of targeted concepts [28]. On the other hand, providing some transparency to underlying implementation might also support learning as it provides elements from which

ICER '16, September 08-12, 2016, Melbourne, VIC, Australia

© 2016 ACM. ISBN 978-1-4503-4449-4/16/09. . . $15.00

DOI: http://dx.doi.org/10.1145/2960310.2960327

students may construct an understanding of how object-oriented mechanisms operate. We characterize transparency as having two properties:

1. The transparent construct provides some underlying explanation of the system's operation.

2. The transparent construct demands some mental effort and notational understanding.

These two properties depict the trade-off of transparency for learning. The first characteristic provides a benefit of understanding, uncovering the operational elements of the system, what computing education researchers have termed the notional machine [5, 25]. The second property provides a cost that, if significant, could detract from the learning benefit.

This trade-off may have implications that extend beyond the properties of the programming language. For example, it arguably plays a role in whether visualization systems are effective instructional aids for students. On one hand, they potentially uncover the inner workings of the notional machine [26]. Yet the cognitive load of transforming the visual component in terms of the student's mental model of the notional machine may impede learning.

The trade-off between abstraction and transparency can also play a role in how scaffolding supports learning (see [2, 10] for discussion). Abstraction can appear in the form of "black box" modules that minimize complexity to improve student performance [10]. Alternatively, glass-box scaffolding [10] reveals underlying mechanisms with the goal of supporting learning. Of course, as with visualization tools, the effectiveness of glass-box scaffolding depends on the students' ability to interpret the inner workings and successfully integrate their understanding of them with their model of the notional machine.

Here we explore the apparent trade-off between abstraction and transparency in the context of teaching object-oriented concepts using the Python programming language. Python is increasingly used to teach introductory programming and OO concepts [4, 7, 1, 20, 6]. Compared to other OO languages such as Java, the OO model of Python is arguably less abstract in that some implementation details are visible and require explicit handling by the programmer. Most notably, the instance (self) object must be explicitly stated as a parameter in the definition of instance methods. Moreover, all instance data is explicitly referenced as attributes to the instance object.

To make these points explicit, let us consider a simple method declaration in Python and an example call to it. Drawing upon the problem that we will use in our study, the following method adds an object to a collection of objects, whose underlying data structure is a Python list:

```
def add(self, item):
    'add an item to the catalog'
    self.items.append(item)
```

Here is an example statement that might call the method:

```
store.add(obj1)
```

Note that the Python interpreter takes the instance object and passes it as the first parameter when calling the method.

The method definition illustrates how both the self parameter and the reference to the instance data address our properties for transparency. For the self parameter, students can see how the instance object is passed to the method (property 1), but knowledge of parameter passing is needed and the student must mentally transpose the object in the method call to its position as the first parameter in the method definition (property 2). For the reference to the instance data, the student can see how the data relates to the instance object (property 1), but knowledge of dot-notation is required to see how access is provided (property 2).

Goldwasser and Letscher [7] argue that this transparency facilitates learning by providing students with the underlying mechanism. This uncovers properties of the notional machine [25] addressing noted misunderstandings regarding a unique state for each object [9, 23, 22].

In contrast to the Goldwasser and Letscher interpretation, one of our previous studies revealed student difficulty with the explicit references to the instance (self) object and its instance data [17]. However, our previous study was limited by its small sample and did not reveal the extent to which these transparent elements give students difficulties. The goal of this work is to better establish how these transparent mechanisms produce difficulty for students as they work out a solution. Consequently, we expect to address these questions:

- To what extent does Python's transparent OO mechanisms lead to student difficulties?

- What are common pitfalls that instructors should address?

As we will see, the visible elements of Python's OO mechanisms produce some difficulties for students. We caution that the methodology of this paper will not necessarily indicate if immediate difficulties with the transparent mechanisms nevertheless yield long-term learning advantages. Nor will the findings necessarily argue against Python as an introductory language. The OO handling is only one element of the language and its overall simplicity may still be an advantage to learners. Nevertheless, our study does alert instructors to potential pitfalls of Python's OO implementation and suggests which elements should receive more practice before OO modeling is introduced. It also offers us directions for further exploring the trade-off between abstraction and transparency in learning environments, which we hope are applicable to other areas in computing.

2. STUDY OF STUDENT DIFFICULTIES

Here we present a study that explores how the transparent elements of Python's OO implementation leads to student difficulties. Using an exercise problem where students are asked to define a method, we will see the relative frequency of errors that result from the visible elements and compare them to problems that can occur with other languages. The remainder of this section provides an overview and the next section provides operational details of how the study was conducted.

2.1 Design and Context

In order to establish frequency of errors, our study asks students in introductory programming courses to define a method that requires references to the object's instance data. As a basis of comparison, this programming exercise also includes elements that pose difficulty to students across a variety of languages. Presented in detail in the next section, the study addresses these elements by asking students to write a new method to an already defined class. This 'lookup' method has a list as instance data, which is necessarily accessed using dot-notation on the instance object (e.g. 'self.items'). The solution also requires a sequential search, an equality test that accesses object attributes, and a return statement that needs to be appropriately placed and include a reference to an object attribute.

Because the study accesses object attributes, it allows us to explore the extent of difficulty that students experience with the dot-notation. Any observed difficulty with the notation reveals a cost to the transparency (property 2), that is, an explicit link between the instance object and its instance data.

Our study further explores where difficulties with dot-notation are likely to occur. In addition to accessing the list data, the solution requires attribute references in the equality condition and the return statement. The more complex context of the equality condition may yield more difficulty than the relatively simple, isolated expression in the return statement.

We also consider how various attribute names influence the construction of a reference. Previous research [16, 11] indicates that students are more likely to construct an incorrect reference involving attributes with identifying labels (e.g. **name**, **id**, **title**) than with descriptive labels (e.g. **color**, **texture**, **shape**). For example, a student is more likely to just reference an object (e.g. **obj**) when the intention is to reference an identifying attribute that belongs to the object (e.g. **obj.title**). To verify this effect, the study randomly selects attributes from a set of identifying and descriptive attributes for the problem exercise.

3. METHOD

3.1 Participants

The students were recruited from two different classes. The first, of which there were several sections, is a second-quarter Python class in a sequence designed for novice programmers. The class follows a first-quarter Python class in which students spend ten weeks learning basic programming constructs including branching, loops, function definitions, file I/O, and collection classes. In the first Python course students utilize built-in methods for objects using dot notation from the second week of the quarter and define functions starting in the second or third week of the quarter. The first course takes a procedural approach to problem solving, and students generally write three to six functions per weekly assignment. The second course begins with defining classes, and then covers multiple application domains for which classes are useful including GUI development and the creation of a web crawler. The definition of classes is covered in the first three weeks of a ten-week quarter.

The second class is an accelerated Python course for students who have already taken at least one programming course. It covers most of the material in the first- and second-quarter courses for novices but in a single ten-week period. In particular all the material from the first Python course is covered in an accelerated fashion in the first six weeks of the quarter. The remaining four weeks are spent on recursion, defining classes, and creating a web crawler. The development of GUIs is omitted in the accelerated course,

and only a week is spent on defining classes rather than three weeks in the novice course sequence. Generally students in the accelerated course have programmed in Java or another object-oriented language so that the development of classes is not new to them.

If advised correctly, students in the second-quarter Python class and the accelerated Python class should have no more than one previous programming course at the time of the study. However, many students in these courses may also have had prior programming experiences from their secondary school. Transfer students may also have had prior programming experiences at their previous institution.

3.2 Programming Exercise

Students were presented a programming exercise through an online web application. The online presentation provided students with two class definitions: an **Item** class and a **Catalog** class. The exercise then instructed students to add a simple "lookup" method to the Catalog class. The code for these classes is given below.

```
class Item:
    'an Item class for the catalog'
    internal_id = 100
    def __init__(self):
        Item.internal_id += 1
        self.id = Item.internal_id
        self.quantity = 0

class Catalog:
    'a simple Catalog class'
    def __init__(self):
        'the constructor'
        self.items = []

    def add(self, item):
        'add an item to the catalog'
        return self.items.append(item)

    def has_style(self, desired_style):
        '''returns true if catalog has an
            item of the given style'''
        for obj in self.items:
            if obj.style == desired_style:
                return True
        return False

    def size(self):
        '''return the number of items
            in the catalog'''
        return len(self.items)
```

The Item class implements simple objects with attributes and values (e.g. name: 'apple', texture: 'smooth') and the Catalog class represents a list of these items and includes methods for adding an item and obtaining the number of items in the list. The Catalog class also provides a method (has_style), whose structure is similar to the method that they are asked to write (lookup).

The lookup method involves searching the catalog list for an object with a particular attribute and then returning another specified attribute for the matching object. The complete instructions for the programming task are presented in Section 3.3.

The web application systematically varied, and thus randomly assigned, the targeted attribute and returned attribute. The set of attributes (e.g. 'name', 'texture') were chosen to invoke a grocery domain and used example values accordingly (e.g. 'apple', 'smooth'). The complete set of possible attributes are calories, color, label, name, shape, status and texture. Below is a correct solution for the **lookup** method given **shape** as the targeted attribute and **name** as the returned attribute.

```
def lookup(self, target):
    'returns needed attribute'
    for obj in self.items:
        if obj.shape == target:
            return obj.name
    return None
```

To further verify correctness and that the instructions were understandable, the web application was pilot-tested with former students from the courses.

3.3 Problem Wording for Exercise

Below is an example set of instructions that were presented to students for the programming problem. This particular set asked the student to find the targeted **shape** attribute and return the **name** attribute of the matching object.

Exercise Problem

The following is a short programming problem. Since we are interested in learning about initial strategies and difficulties, we ask that you do not try to run your code when providing your solution. After you submit your untested code, you will see a correct solution and will be able to compare it to your code.

For this problem, Item and Catalog classes have been defined.

The code for both the Item and the Catalog class can be viewed in **this page**. *Note: 'This page' links to the code presented in Section 3.2.*

The Item class creates objects consisting of attributes (e.g. "style") and values (e.g. "flat"). When a new Item object is created, an id attribute is automatically assigned. Here's an example of interacting with the class in a console:

```
>>> obj = Item()
>>> obj.id
102
>>> obj.style = "flat"
>>> obj.style
'flat'
>>>
```

Note that Python allows attributes to be assigned values with an assignment statement. In addition to id and style, possible attributes for the Item class include calories, color, label, name, shape, status and texture.

The Catalog class produces objects that contain a collection of items. Here's an example of interacting with the Item and Catalog class:

```
>>> listing = Catalog()
>>> listing.add(obj)
>>> listing.has_style("flat")
```

```
True
>>> listing.has_style("twisted")
False
>>> listing.size()
1
```

Problem: Write a method for the Catalog class called **lookup**. This method should take a string as an argument to find the first object that matches its shape attribute. The method should then return the name of the matching Item object.

For example, consider that listing is a Catalog object that has an Item with shape of 'round' and name of 'apple'. Then, this call:

```
listing.lookup('round')
```

would return

```
'apple'
```

If there is no matching object, the method should return the Python keyword **None**.

Using just the editing space below, write your definition of the **lookup** method so that it works as described above. When you have finished, click on the submit button below the editor.

3.4 Procedure

The lead author visited the labs of relevant Python classes to give a brief explanation of the project and invite students to participate. Students were provided with a URL for the pages containing the code written by the authors and the programming exercise. Students who wished to participate completed the consent form on the first page. A second page collected demographic information including age, gender and the number of prior programming courses. A subsequent page presented the exercise instructions and related code. This page included an embedded editor with syntax-aware formatting for Python. Students used this editor to submit their definition of the lookup method. The online application recorded the time each student took to read the instructions to the programming task and submit their solution. After submitting their solution they were provided with the correct solution and asked to comment on their submission.

4. RESULTS

Thirty-six students (6 females and 30 males) provided valid submissions. By this we mean submissions that contained Python code and had a plausible submission time. In particular, one response with a submission time of 7 seconds was dropped from the analysis. The median number of reported prior programming courses was 2 (mean=2.6) and the median age was 20 (mean=21.2). The median submission time was 9.3 minutes (mean=9.8).

Table 1: Frequent Programming Difficulties

Label	Location	Description	Example	Freq
Missing self parameter	Parameters	Required self parameter is missing in function header	```def lookup(string):``` ```# body omitted```	53%

Incorrect reference to self list	Loop	Code uses an incorrect name for the list of Item objects	```def lookup(self, aStr):```
			``` if self.Item == aStr:```
			``` return self.id```
			``` else:```
			``` return None```
				36%

Missing loop	Loop	There is no loop to check the list of Items objects	```def lookup(self, item):```
			``` if item in self.items:```
			``` return self.id```
			``` else:```
			``` return None```
				31%

Incorrect conditional operator	Equality condition	Code uses an operator other than == to test the object attribute and the function parameter	```def lookup(self, string):```
			``` for obj in self.items:```
			``` if string in self.items:```
			``` return obj.style```
			``` else:```
			``` return None```
				31%

Incorrect reference to param	Equality condition	Code incorrectly references the parameter for the desired test value	```def lookup(self, catalogNumber):```
			``` for item in self.items:```
			``` if item == self.item.id:```
			``` return self.item.style```
			``` else:```
			``` return None```
				17%

Test object with no attribute	Equality condition	The variable representing the Item object is missing the attribute	```def lookup(desired):```
			``` for item in self.items:```
			``` if item == desired:```
			``` return item.id```
			``` return None```
				50%

Test object with wrong attribute	Equality condition	The variable representing the Item object has the wrong attribute	```def lookup(x):```
			``` if Catalog.has_style(x) == True:```
			``` return self.id```
			``` else:```
			``` return None```
				19%

Bad object reference	Return	Return statement does not reference the matching object	```def lookup(self)```
			``` for obj in self.items:```
			``` if obj == calories:```
			``` return color```
			``` return None```
				39%

Returned object with no attribute	Return	The object returned does not have an attribute referenced	```def lookup(str, atr):```
			``` for obj in self.items:```
			``` if obj.has_style(self, atr):```
			``` return obj```
				17%

Returned object with wrong attribute	Return	The returned value has the wrong attribute	```def lookup(desired):```
			``` for item in self.items:```
			``` if item == desired:```
			``` return item.id```
			``` return None```
				28%

Premature return	Return	A return of None is added before the end of the loop, typically in an else statement	```def lookup(self, ID):```
			``` for item in self.items:```
			``` if item.id == ID:```
			``` return item.calories```
			``` else:```
			``` return None```
				19%

4.1 Analysis of Errors and Comments

The 36 submissions were coded in a multi-step process. First, both authors read the student responses and independently devised codes for the submitted Python code and the reflective comments. The two sets of codes were discussed and merged into a single set, yielding 26 codes, 18 for programming mistakes and 8 for the comments. Both authors then independently coded the submissions using the agreed-upon code definitions, which produced a 90% agreement rate. The remaining points of disagreement were discussed until consensus on the coding of all submissions was achieved.

4.2 Frequency of Errors

Table 1 shows the coded errors of the student responses. Only errors that appeared in at least 10% of submissions are listed.[1] The last column presents the frequency of the error as a percentage. Given the sample of 36 valid responses, the standard error for the presented frequencies is approximately 8%.

The first two entries in the table correspond to difficulties particular to Python's OO implementation, namely omitting the self object in the parameter list (53%) or failing to successfully reference the list data from the self object (36%). Most of the other difficulties concern references, either with the matching attribute or the returned attribute. As a point of comparison, a smaller number of students (19%) placed the **return None** statement so that the method would incorrectly finish before the exhaustive search was completed (see last entry in the table).

In addition to incorrect indentation of the loop, we counted other indentation problems and noted only 11% (standard error 5%).

4.3 Summary of student comments

The application solicited student comments after they saw a correct solution. Here we highlight common issues related to frequent problems. Of the 19 (53%) students who omitted the self parameter, 9 (25%) noted their mistake in the comments after seeing the solution. In the next section, we provide examples of these comments when we discuss the issue.

With respect to the instructions, 8 (22%) students commented on having difficulty understanding the instructions and 7 (19%) wished that more information was provided. Here are some examples of these comments:

> The coding was not explained enough, needs more comments to understand each method.

> The solution makes perfect sense, it's just hard for me to visualize using two classes and how to refer to everything. It wasn't explicitly clear we can use the obj object to do so, maybe I skimmed over it too fast.

Only 2 (6%) students indicated that they wished that they could have tested the code. For example, one student wrote the following:

---

[1]The table does not indicate cases where students added unnecessary statements, which occurred in 19% of the responses.

> Not being able to test it is a pain, because that is usually where I have Eurika [sic] moments and am able to see the problems/how it is working so far.

4.4 Errors with instance object and data

Here we focus on student errors involving the instance (self) object and its data. As already noted, 19 (53%) students did not include the instance object, identified with the name 'self', in the parameter list. Of these students, 9 (25%) made no reference to self in their code. An additional student used a variable named 'self' but initially assigned one of its properties in the code:

```
def lookup(style):
    self.style = style
    for obj in self.items:
        if obj.style = style:
            return obj.id
    return None
```

Of the remaining self omissions, 7 students provided correct references to the instance data (i.e. self.items), assuming they had listed the self object in the parameter list.

Of the 9 students who noted their omission of self in their comments, the comments ranged from having 'simply forgot' to those suggesting greater difficulty:

> I simply forgot to pass in the 'self' parameter for the method

> oh and I missed the self in the class function

> I did not expect to need self for this program.

> I forgot to include the 'self' argument, in spite of using it in the body of the function. The only reason I knew to do that, however, is by constantly reminding myself that I have to write it like that by looking at how earlier classes and functions were defined.

> Primarily, I found it a bit difficult to identify the main points of interest in creating the parameters. ... but I could not quite figure out ... how to write the parameter for lookup.

4.5 Attribute reference errors

When referencing object attributes, students often omitted the attribute name. This omission occurred more frequently in the equality test (18 of 36) than in the return statement (6 of 36). The difference in proportions is statistically significant (p=0.003 using Fisher's Exact Test).

To explore the effect of attribute type, the attributes of **name**, **id** and **label** were classified as identifying attributes and the remaining attributes were classified as descriptive attributes. Consistent with previous studies [16, 11] identifying attributes were more likely to be missing from the object: 25% more likely for targeting attributes and 8% more likely for returned attributes. However, these differences were not statistically significant (Fisher's Exact Test produces respective p-values of 0.14 and 0.43). Below is an example where a student omitted an identifying attribute (**label**) in the equality condition:

```
def lookup(desired):
    for item in self.items:
        if item == desired:
            return item.id
    return None
```

This mistake was noted in the student's comment:

> I forgot to add 'self' from the parent class. I also forgot '.label'

Additional student comments expressed difficulty using the dot-notation include the following:

> The whole obj.something thing is confusing still. So is comparing an object to a string.

> I found it difficult to locate where the initial item was set up and which variable it was stored in.

> Was not sure how to pull from the list.

5. DISCUSSION

In this section, we compare the results to previous studies and make some recommendations to instructors.

5.1 Problems with transparent elements

Consistent with the Miller et al. [17] findings, most student answers showed problems with the explicit use of the instance (self) object. The prevalence is remarkable in that the given methods provided examples of listing self as a parameter and accessing its instance data. Part of the difficulty may be due to the mismatch between the typical way of calling the method (e.g. **obj.lookup('blue')**) and way one is required to define the method with the instance object (e.g. **def lookup(self, color)**).

Comments and subsequent errors in the student answers indicate that the causes of the omissions range from being a significant conceptual misunderstanding to a simple oversight. When an omission occurred, most students then showed little evidence of referencing an object. On the other hand, a sizable minority of students successfully referenced the instance data with the 'self.items' expression and many of their comments indicated that they 'simply forgot' to add the instance object to the parameters.

Even a minor oversight could have learning implications given the feedback that the Python interpreter provides. Below is the error message students see when they omit the self parameter:

> TypeError: lookup() takes 1 positional argument but 2 were given

Because the error message does not mention 'self' or refer to the instance object placed before the calling method, students who simply forgot the instance object among the parameters may have difficulty interpreting this message to correct their omission.

More than a third of the students (13 of 36) incorrectly constructed the reference to the instance data, even though correct references were presented in the method examples. Referencing instance data may be difficult because the students were not well practiced with using dot-notation to access a data object as an attribute. We consider this point in the next section, which addresses difficulties constructing references elsewhere in the code.

Despite student difficulty with the dot-notation, student facility with the notation is arguably a critical component of learning how the instance object is related to its data. Moreover, its relative simplicity may be the best approach for showing its relationship. If so, it affords successful glass-box scaffolding as described by Hmelo and Guzdial [10].

5.2 Reference-point errors

Reference difficulties were not just reserved to the instance object. They were also prevalent with objects from the list data. Perhaps most interesting is that the reference-point errors were more likely to occur in the equality construction than in the return statement. We note that a similar result was obtained in the prior Miller study on reference-point errors [16]. In that study, students were less likely to make reference-point errors in a standalone expression than in the context of a larger, more complex statement. A possible reason that more complex expressions incur a greater cognitive load and thus detract from successfully constructing the reference.

While not statistically significant in our study, we did see that students were more likely to make reference-point errors when working with identifying attributes than with descriptive attributes. Moreover, the proportion of observed differences (0.25 for the attribute reference in the equality condition and 0.08 for the attribute in the return statement) was comparable to that observed in the Miller study [16], where differences in proportion ranged from 0.11 to 0.49. The failure to produce a statistically reliable difference may be due to the relatively small sample sizes using identifiable attribute names (N=12 for the equality reference and N=14 for the return statement). Some of the so-called identifying attribute names (e.g. **label**) may also have a reduced effect.

Regardless of the contributing causes to student difficulty in constructing references, the demonstrated difficulty indicates a potential cost in explicitly linking the self instance object and its instance data. Here the substantial difficulty with the attribute references lends doubt as to whether these students are benefiting from Python's transparent (i.e. explicit) handling of the instance object and its instance data. Missing this connection may make it difficult to see how each instance object has its own individual state, a commonly reported misconception [9, 23, 22].

If the difficulties students had with constructing references is a sign of problems understanding the connection between the instance object and the object data, this supports assertions made in previous work. Alexandron et al. [2] observed that the way a programming language deals with abstraction is connected to the programming paradigm underlying the language. For example, "procedural languages separate the abstraction of control from the abstraction of data" (pg. 311), whereas "object-oriented languages focus on decomposing the system into objects that abstract data and control." (pg. 311). Even if the decomposition of the system into objects has been done for students, as it was in this exercise, it may be that the cognitive load of understanding that structure interferes with students' ability to integrate new functionality into the class.

5.3 Limitations

Our study identifies difficulties with the transparent elements of Python's object-oriented notation. The findings are helpful for identifying prerequisite knowledge for successfully understanding how the instance object and its data are connected. Without that knowledge, the difficulties lend doubt as to whether the students in this study were able to benefit from seeing the connection made explicit by the Python environment. Less certain is how these transparent elements affect long-term learning. Our study is not a controlled experiment where the level of transparency is manipulated and learning outcomes are measured. While difficult to implement, such an experimental design would provide stronger empirical findings on how transparency affects student learning. Without that, we rely on our interpretation of how the language features lead to difficulties and compare them to problems that ostensibly occur across languages (e.g. reaching a return statement before the search is complete). Our conclusion is thus predicated on whether these difficulties incur a cognitive load that inhibits learning of OO concepts. Of course, as we have advised, proficiency in parameter passing and dot-notation may avoid added cognitive load. Moreover, as Goldwasser and Letscher argue, the explicit reference to the instance object and its members may produce other positive learning outcomes, such as "the distinction between instance scope versus local scope." [7](p. 44).

Another consideration is that our particular findings may be subject to known factors that affect student performance. They include student preparation, approach of instruction, student motivation, and programming environment. Perhaps the most important factor is how the problem is presented to the students. We provide the full set of instructions in Section 3.3 so that readers can consider how they may affect student performance.

5.4 Guidance for Instructors

Given these difficulties, instructors are advised to have students practice the fundamentals of parameter passing and dot-notation as a prerequisite to class definitions. For students to see how Python transforms the method call by adding the instance object as one of the parameters, student understanding of parameter passing needs to be effortless. Similarly, effortless facility of object-attribute references enables students to focus on the whole construction of the expression.

The study also reveals when students have greater difficulty constructing references. Most notably, they express less difficulty constructing references in simple expressions. Initially instructors may want to have students practice attribute references in the context of simple expressions, then more complex expressions and finally their use in object-based methods. With sufficient practice, the student's cognitive resources could be used to understand the link between instance object and instance data.

6. CONCLUSION

In this paper, we identified transparent elements in Python's OO implementation and observed consequent problems in student code. We suggest that these transparent mechanisms add to cognitive load and thus detract from learning unless students are proficient with the underlying concepts. Instructors are advised to have students practice these concepts, namely parameter passing and dot-notation, before they cover class definitions.

This finding also suggests future work that could be broadly conducted in computing education. To the extent that cognitive load and transparency are related, researchers may want to adopt measures for programming languages and environments (such as those based on Green's cognitive dimensions [8]) similar to those that have been applied to measure cognitive load in learning activities (e.g. see [18]). With such measures in place, experiments could provide better insight on learning trade-offs between abstraction and transparency.

We also explored where students had difficulty constructing references. Consistent with prior research [16], students were more likely to omit the attribute name in the context of a complex expression. Also consistent with prior study [11, 16], we observed some effect of attribute name on omitting attributes, although our analysis did not find the effect to be statistically reliably in the context of this study. Drawing upon the previous studies, difficulty with reference constructions appears to be easily manipulated. The recurring difficulty may not reflect a fundamental misconception on how objects are composed and their constituent parts accessed. Competence with reference construction is nevertheless a prerequisite for conceptually linking objects and their instance data in the Python environment.

7. REFERENCES

[1] K. K. Agarwal and A. Agarwal. Python for CS1, CS2 and beyond. *J. Comput. Sci. Coll.*, 20(4):262–270, Apr. 2005.

[2] G. Alexandron, M. Armoni, M. Gordon, and D. Harel. Scenario-based programming: Reducing the cognitive load, fostering abstract thinking. In *Companion Proceedings of the 36th International Conference on Software Engineering*, ICSE Companion 2014, pages 311–320, New York, NY, USA, 2014. ACM.

[3] J. Boustedt, A. Eckerdal, R. McCartney, J. E. Moström, M. Ratcliffe, K. Sanders, and C. Zander. Threshold concepts in computer science: Do they exist and are they useful? In *Proceedings of the 38th SIGCSE Technical Symposium on Computer Science Education*, SIGCSE '07, pages 504–508, New York, NY, USA, 2007. ACM.

[4] C. Dierbach. Python as a first programming language. *J. Comput. Sci. Coll.*, 29(6):153–154, June 2014.

[5] B. Du Boulay. Some difficulties of learning to program. *Journal of Educational Computing Research*, 2(1):57–73, 1986.

[6] R. J. Enbody and W. F. Punch. Performance of Python CS1 students in mid-level non-Python CS courses. In *Proceedings of the 41st ACM Technical Symposium on Computer Science Education*, SIGCSE '10, pages 520–523, New York, NY, USA, 2010. ACM.

[7] M. H. Goldwasser and D. Letscher. Teaching an object-oriented CS1 — with Python. In *ACM SIGCSE Bulletin*, volume 40, pages 42–46. ACM, 2008.

[8] T. R. Green. Cognitive dimensions of notations. In A. Sutcliffe and L. Macaulay, editors, *People and Computers V*, pages 443–460. Cambridge University Press, Cambridge, UK, 1989.

[9] M. Guzdial. Centralized mindset: A student problem with object-oriented programming. In *Proceedings of*

the *Twenty-sixth SIGCSE Technical Symposium on Computer Science Education*, SIGCSE '95, pages 182–185, New York, NY, USA, 1995. ACM.

[10] C. E. Hmelo and M. Guzdial. Of black and glass boxes: Scaffolding for doing and learning. In *Proceedings of the 1996 international conference on Learning sciences*, pages 128–134. International Society of the Learning Sciences, 1996.

[11] S. Holland, R. Griffiths, and M. Woodman. Avoiding object misconceptions. *SIGCSE Bull.*, 29(1):131–134, 1997.

[12] G. Kiczales. Towards a new model of abstraction in the engineering of software. *International Workshop on Reflection and Meta-Level Architecture*, pages 67–76, 1992.

[13] H. Koppelman and B. van Dijk. Teaching abstraction in introductory courses. In *Proceedings of the Fifteenth Annual Conference on Innovation and Technology in Computer Science Education*, ITiCSE '10, pages 174–178, New York, NY, USA, 2010. ACM.

[14] A.-J. Lakanen, V. Lappalainen, and V. Isomöttönen. Revisiting rainfall to explore exam questions and performance on cs1. In *Proceedings of the 15th Koli Calling Conference on Computing Education Research*, Koli Calling '15, pages 40–49, New York, NY, USA, 2015. ACM.

[15] K. Malan and K. Halland. Examples that can do harm in learning programming. In *Companion to the 19th Annual ACM SIGPLAN Conference on Object-oriented Programming Systems, Languages, and Applications*, OOPSLA '04, pages 83–87, New York, NY, USA, 2004. ACM.

[16] C. S. Miller. Metonymy and reference-point errors in novice programming. *Computer Science Education*, 24(3):123–152, 2014.

[17] C. S. Miller, A. Settle, and J. Lalor. Learning object-oriented programming in python: Towards an inventory of difficulties and testing pitfalls. In *Proceedings of the 16th Annual Conference on Information Technology Education*, SIGITE '15, pages 59–64, New York, NY, USA, 2015. ACM.

[18] B. B. Morrison, B. Dorn, and M. Guzdial. Measuring cognitive load in introductory cs: Adaptation of an instrument. In *Proceedings of the Tenth Annual Conference on International Computing Education Research*, ICER '14, pages 131–138, New York, NY, USA, 2014. ACM.

[19] J. E. Moström, J. Boustedt, A. Eckerdal, R. McCartney, K. Sanders, L. Thomas, and C. Zander. Concrete examples of abstraction as manifested in students' transformative experiences. In *Proceedings of the Fourth International Workshop on Computing Education Research*, ICER '08, pages 125–136, New York, NY, USA, 2008. ACM.

[20] T. Newhall, L. Meeden, A. Danner, A. Soni, F. Ruiz, and R. Wicentowski. A support program for introductory CS courses that improves student performance and retains students from underrepresented groups. In *Proceedings of the 45th ACM Technical Symposium on Computer Science Education*, SIGCSE '14, pages 433–438, New York, NY, USA, 2014. ACM.

[21] R. Or-Bach and I. Lavy. Cognitive activities of abstraction in object orientation: an empirical study. *ACM SIGCSE Bulletin*, 36(2):82–86, 2004.

[22] J. Sajaniemi, M. Kuittinen, and T. Tikansalo. A study of the development of students' visualizations of program state during an elementary object-oriented programming course. *J. Educ. Resour. Comput.*, 7(4):3:1–3:31, Jan. 2008.

[23] K. Sanders and L. Thomas. Checklists for grading object-oriented CS1 programs: Concepts and misconceptions. In *Proceedings of the 12th Annual SIGCSE Conference on Innovation and Technology in Computer Science Education*, ITiCSE '07, pages 166–170, New York, NY, USA, 2007. ACM.

[24] O. Seppälä, P. Ihantola, E. Isohanni, J. Sorva, and A. Vihavainen. Do we know how difficult the rainfall problem is? In *Proceedings of the 15th Koli Calling Conference on Computing Education Research*, Koli Calling '15, pages 87–96, New York, NY, USA, 2015. ACM.

[25] J. Sorva. Notional machines and introductory programming education. *ACM Transactions on Computing Education (TOCE)*, 13(2):8, 2013.

[26] J. Sorva, V. Karavirta, and L. Malmi. A review of generic program visualization systems for introductory programming education. *ACM Transactions on Computing Education (TOCE)*, 13(4):15, 2013.

[27] J. Spolsky. The law of leaky abstractions. In *Joel on Software*, pages 197–202. Apress, 2004.

[28] J. Sweller. Cognitive load during problem solving: Effects on learning. *Cognitive science*, 12(2):257–285, 1988.

[29] J. M. Wing. Computational thinking. *Commun. ACM*, 49(3):33–35, Mar. 2006.

Learning Curve Analysis for Programming: Which Concepts do Students Struggle With?

Kelly Rivers, Erik Harpstead, Ken Koedinger
Human-Computer Interaction Institute, Carnegie Mellon University
5000 Forbes Ave
Pittsburgh, PA 15232
{krivers, eharpste, koedinger}@cs.cmu.edu

Abstract

The recent surge in interest in using educational data mining on student written programs has led to discoveries about which compiler errors students encounter while they are learning how to program. However, less attention has been paid to the actual code that students produce. In this paper, we investigate programming data by using learning curve analysis to determine which programming elements students struggle with the most when learning in Python. Our analysis extends the traditional use of learning curve analysis to include less structured data, and also reveals new possibilities for when to teach students new programming concepts. One particular discovery is that while we find evidence of student learning in some cases (for example, in function definitions and comparisons), there are other programming elements which do not demonstrate typical learning. In those cases, we discuss how further changes to the model could affect both demonstrated learning and our understanding of the different concepts that students learn.

Keywords

learning curve analysis; educational data mining; programming syntax; knowledge components

1. Introduction

In recent years there has been growing interest in using large collections of logged programming data to understand how students learn, what they struggle with, and what we can do to improve computer science education. This trend is occurring at the same time as a rise in the use of Educational Data Mining (EDM) [2], a field of study which has developed many useful new approaches for analyzing and interpreting collected student data. However, the majority of research done on programming data has only used metric approaches that cover easily measurable content, such as the compiler errors students encounter and their typical working behaviors [10]. These studies have taught us a great deal about how students write code, but they have mostly examined the output of code, instead of investigating how the code that students write changes over time. It is possible that, by ignoring the written code that students produce, we are missing out on a great deal of useful information.

The broader field of EDM investigates how details of student work can be used to determine what and how students are learning. Leveraging theories about the ideal shape of learning [14] and the structure of student knowledge [13], researchers in this space have developed methods for tracking student learning of knowledge components across multiple problems [4, 6], to see if students' ability to solve problem steps associated with particular concepts matches what theory would predict. Discrepancies between theory's predictions and students' behaviors can be used to suggest improvements to instruction that result in demonstrably better student learning [20]. These techniques have been successful in structured environments such as intelligent tutoring systems and have demonstrated applicability to many fields such as mathematics, vocabulary, and chemistry; however, with a few notable exceptions [1], they have seen less application in domains like programming.

In this work, we present a preliminary exploration of the application of knowledge-based learning curve analysis on programming data with the goal of extending the promise of educational data mining to programming. As this is, to our knowledge, the first attempt to apply learning curve analysis to programming data, our research questions are the following: can we successfully apply the methods of knowledge component modeling and learning curve analysis to code-writing programming data, and can we use the resulting models to evaluate student learning? In order to address these goals, we must first determine which individual concepts students might be struggling with. In this paper, we discuss multiple possible models of programming knowledge components, describe how we modified the traditional modeling process to be compatible with programming data, and analyze the resulting models, sharing our thoughts on the process along the way.

The contributions of this paper are:

- A modification to the traditional method of knowledge component modeling, to be used with code-writing data.

- Learning curves computed using real student data and categorizations of different syntax-based programming concepts based on these curves.

- Recommendations on future directions for knowledge modeling and learning curve analysis in the domain of programming.

2. Background

The work we present in this paper is rooted in the context of the Knowledge-Learning-Instruction (KLI) framework [13]. The KLI framework is concerned with providing a vocabulary for exploring how different types of knowledge constrain learning processes and in turn how different learning processes constrain which instructional choices will be optimal for robust student learning. Central to the broader theory of KLI is the concept of a Knowledge Component (KC) which is defined as "an acquired unit of cognitive function or structure that can be inferred from performance on a set of related tasks." As learners are provided with instructional events for a particular KC it becomes more likely that they will demonstrate mastery of that KC when later assessed. This might seem straightforward, but it can be challenging to rigorously define what the KCs in a given domain are, and from there decide how best to structure the instructional environment to support those particular KCs.

On the other hand, most EDM research into programming data so far has focused on high level performance metrics and errors, instead of looking at how student code changes over time. However, there have been some exceptions. Several researchers have investigated the use of interaction networks as a way to interpret student work on a programming problem over time. This includes work on Parsons problems [7], Karel programs [16], and Java assignments [8]. These approaches tell us a great deal about how students develop their programs over time, but they do not separate out different knowledge concepts that can be investigated individually.

Some researchers have applied other EDM methods to programming data. Berges and Hubweiser used Item Response Theory (IRT) to compare the difficulty of different programming concepts, using concepts tagged on source code written by the students [3]. Kasurinen and Nikula applied Bayesian Knowledge Tracing (BKT) to programming data by predicting whether students would apply the correct structure to their code answers across sets of questions and found that about half of their students were predicted to have reached mastery on five central concepts by the end of their course [11].

In work closer to our own, Cherenkova et al. mapped problems to the concepts they were designed to test and used student success (on first attempt) to determine which concepts students were most challenged by [5]. They identified conditionals and loops as being particularly challenging for students. Yudelson et al. built student models based on code submissions over time, using the Rasch model and variations on the Additive Factors Model (AFM) [22]. Their process has many similarities to ours, but focuses on the question of how best to model students instead of investigating which specific concepts students are struggling with.

2.1 Learning Curve Analysis

Inspired by the power law of practice [14], learning curve analysis is an approach from broader EDM research that focuses on estimating learners' performance over time [4]. The learning theory behind the approach is that the probability that a learner would make an error in exercising a given skill should decrease over time as they get more opportunities to practice the skill. Traditionally, skills in this context are formalized as KCs, with a given task exercising one or more KCs. Students who possess a mastery of those KCs are more likely to perform the task correctly.

From a statistical perspective, learning curves are fit to student performance data using the Additive Factors Model (AFM) [4]. AFM is a specialized form of logistic regression that uses information about a student's prior practice opportunities with a set of KCs to predict the probability that they will perform correctly on a given opportunity. The mathematical formulation of AFM's regression equation takes the following form:

$$\ln \frac{p_{ij}}{1 - p_{ij}} = \theta_i + \sum_k \beta_k Q_{kj} + \sum_k Q_{kj}(\gamma_k N_{ik})$$

This equation says that the log odds of a given student i performing step j, which exercises KC k, correctly can be predicted by a combination of an intercept for the student θ_i, an intercept for the KC β_k, and a KC slope γ_k, where N_{ik} represents a count of how many prior opportunities student i has had to practice KC k and Q_{kj} is a binary Q-matrix defining the mapping between KCs and steps.

The general assumptions of the AFM model are that every student possesses individual differences in initial ability, represented by the student intercept; every KC has a different initial difficulty, represented by the KC intercept; and that everyone tends to master a given KC at the same rate, represented by a single KC slope for all learners. In the most commonly used implementation of AFM [12] there is a fourth constraint imposed, not noted in the regression equation, where KC slopes cannot be negative (meaning that people do not unlearn or forget KCs).

3. Methodology

Before applying learning curve analysis to programming data we must first answer a few questions about how to adapt the usual methods to the unique properties of the programming domain. This is more difficult than it may at first sound, due to differences in the format of data traditionally used in learning curve analysis and the kind of data generated by programming tasks.

In the tutoring systems traditionally evaluated with learning curves, problems are broken down into individual steps, where a step is conventionally defined as the smallest unit of action that a student can perform correctly [21]. In programming data, there is no such definition of what a step should be. Programming data can be collected at as low a level as every keystroke made by students, but it is unclear how correctness could be measured for these low-level edits. Alternatively, data can be collected on student submissions and help requests; these submissions can be measured for correctness (using suites of test cases), but they also encompass many individual edits that have been made to the code.

In intelligent tutors, each problem's steps are tagged with one or more KCs at time of analysis. Since each step can be individually measured for correctness, each of the KCs can be analyzed for changes in correctness over time, to see whether students are learning. The analogy between tutor steps and submissions breaks down here, as failing test cases in a programming submission does not mean that every component of the code is wrong; it only means that a subset of the components are wrong. Therefore, we need to define a way to represent steps in programming problems that allows us to do useful data analysis.

To accomplish this, we address the following questions in the next sections:

- What are the KCs of programming?

- What are the steps and opportunities in a programming problem?

- How should correctness be measured for each of these steps?

3.1 Programming KCs

In order to model learners' acquisition of programming KCs, we first need to determine what the KCs of programming are, so that we can construct a KC model that will accurately reflect student performance on programming tasks. In a broader sense this question has been a point of interest in the Computer Science Education Research community for many years, as many researchers have attempted to discover what the low-level concepts students are learning actually are.

First, one could view a programming problem as a set of constraints that the program needs to fulfill. These constraints can take the form of subproblems and/or test cases, which can all be individually assessed to see whether their requirements have been met. This model is a direct analogy to the step model typically used in tutoring systems. However, the subproblems and test cases are not themselves KCs, as we do not want students to learn how to solve specific test cases; we want them to learn how to write code that can be used to solve test cases like the ones assigned. Therefore, we still need to map these subproblems to sets of KCs.

Instead of using constraints, one could view programs through a broader algorithmic lens. From this perspective, students combine programming plans (common code substructures) in order to solve problems [19]. This approach has great potential as an accurate measure of student knowledge, but it assumes that students already understand the syntax of the programs they are writing, which is not always the case with novices. As we are investigating the work of new programmers in this paper, we leave algorithmic KC models for future work.

When considering the structure of knowledge in the programming domain, programming skill could be characterized as learning to choose the right program constructs (or combinations of constructs) in the appropriate circumstances for a specific goal. These can be represented as condition-and-response pairs, where a condition is the action that needs to be done and the response is the program token (or tokens) that can be used to execute that action. For example, if a student needs to store a value, they have to use the variable assignment operation. As a simplifying assumption, we could use the different textual tokens that appear in programs as indicators of construct use; additionally, if we can parse student code into Abstract Syntax Trees (ASTs), we can identify exactly when and where specific constructs are being used by walking the tree to find different node types. In this paper we utilize these AST node types to test whether this theory of programming knowledge as the ability to identify the correct conditions and provide the correct responses is an accurate model of programming KCs.

This approach still leaves some questions about implementation; for example, should each AST node type be treated as an individual KC, or should some tokens be collapsed together into broader categories? As a first step towards exploring this approach we decided to use a strategy that would include every token type in the built-in Python AST library. Once an initial candidate KC model has been created, it is common practice in learning curve analysis to explore various model refinements of merging more fine grained models, using both automated [4] and manual [20] methods; we plan to undertake this refinement in future work. These methods may help us determine how to change the original AST node types into KCs that are closer to the true knowledge that students are learning.

3.2 Programming Steps and Opportunities

A 'step' is hard to define in a generative context where students can do a lot of typing at once. For now, we choose to define a step at the level of a student's deliberate action, whenever they submit a program or ask for a hint. However, we cannot use the submission process as a single opportunity for all of the problem's KCs, since it implies that all KCs are required to be concurrently present in order for a student to solve a given submission correctly. While this is an accurate description of how the programming tutor provides feedback to students, it makes it difficult to tease apart which KCs students are struggling with most when they get a submission incorrect. Therefore, we say instead that each submission/hint request can be viewed as a single step that encompasses a sequence of opportunities in parallel, where each opportunity corresponds to an individual KC.

In traditional learning curve analysis, only the first attempt at each KC opportunity is used to measure student learning. This is done because traditional systems give students immediate feedback on each individual step. This means that after the first attempt, correctly solving a step does not necessarily mean that a student understands how to perform the step correctly; it could be that they are only doing what the feedback told them to, with no further comprehension. Programming problems seem different, as students are given feedback on the whole problem, not the individual tokens they're writing. Still, it is possible that student might be applying the feedback to individual tokens. Therefore, we test two different kinds of KC step models: one which includes only data from the first attempt to each problem (where only the first submission of each session with a problem is counted in fitting learning curves), and one which includes all student submissions to the same problem. We call these two step-models First-Attempt and All-Attempts.

3.3 Step Correctness

The final question we must answer is how to determine if a particular application of a programming KC was done correctly. Since we are using AST node types as KCs, we can evaluate the correctness of each KC opportunity by determining whether that node has been used correctly in the student's code. We define 'correct use' as follows: a) that the node occurs in the program, and b) that the node does not occur in the computed difference between the program and a correct version of the program, as generated by the ITAP algorithm [17]. In other words, an AST node type must be included in the correct portion of a student's code to be measured as correct. For a given opportunity, we explore two alternative approaches to measuring correctness. First, we could say that every KC opportunity must be evaluated in every attempt. In that case:

- If the KC occurs in the edit between the student's solution and the goal solution, it is INCORRECT

- If the KC is missing from the student's solution and this is the student's last (measured) attempt at that problem, it is INCORRECT

- Otherwise, it is CORRECT

Alternatively, we can say that all KC opportunities are evaluated in the first attempt, but in following submissions we only look at opportunities which changed after the previous attempt. Then:

- If the KC occurs in the edit between the student's solution and the goal solution, it is INCORRECT

- If the KC occurs in the edit between previous and current state (or if this is the first attempt), it is CORRECT

- If the KC is missing from the student's solution and this is the student's last attempt at the problem, it is INCORRECT

- Otherwise, it is skipped for this step

Overall, we have a 2x2 variation structure with four KC models which we propose to build, as is shown in Table 1. We can think of the First-Attempts/Modified-Steps model as being closest to traditional KC models, and the All-Attempts/All-Steps model as providing the most data possible. We can compare these KC models to determine which provides the best learning curves, which we can then use to analyze student work and see what they understand and what they struggle with.

Table 1: The four KC models proposed in method modification.

First-Attempt/Modified-Steps	All-Attempts/Modified-Steps
First-Attempt/All-Steps	All-Attempts/All-Steps

4. Analysis

Now that we've hypothesized possible KC models, we need to test them with real student data to see whether they can produce viable learning curves. In the following sections, we describe how we generated the four models and prepared them for statistical analysis.

4.1 Dataset

The data we use comes from a study run in Spring 2016 on two introductory programming courses at Carnegie Mellon University. In this study, students were given access to an instance of Cloudcoder [15], an online IDE, which contained 40 Python programming practice problems covering a range of topics, including basic function structure, expression operations, conditionals, loops, lists, dictionaries, and recursion. Each practice problem had a Submit button which could be used to test the student's work against a collection of test cases, which would immediately showing the student the results. Students also sometimes had access to a Hint button which, when pressed, would generate a next-step hint for them based on the ITAP algorithm [18]. The study design randomized when students had access to the hint button, so that half of the students had access from weeks 1-3 of the study and the other half had access from weeks 4-6. All students could access the Hint button from weeks 7+.

We have not yet described how hint attempts would be included in the model, as they are not a typical component of programming log data. In traditional intelligent tutoring systems, hints are conventionally counted as an incorrect attempt at whatever KC the hint would have pointed the student toward. Therefore, we find the edit that was used to construct the hint (where the edit is composed of an old code snippet and a new code snippet), and for each KC opportunity determine whether the given node type occurred in the edit. Nodes which did occur are included as a HINT opportunity, while the other nodes are ignored. This process can be used across all four KC Model types, as it is a direct analogy from traditional ITS models.

All student use of the practice problems was optional, though students were told in class that completing practice problems could help them learn more. Out of 692 students in both classes, 89 agreed to having their data collected and chose to submit an answer for at least one programming problem. These 89 students made 2907 submissions and 380 hint requests over the course of the semester, resulting in a total of 3287 states over all 40 problems.

4.2 Model Generation Process

For each problem, we used Python's AST library to automatically identify all node types that occurred in the exemplar solution of the problem. For example, the problem *helloWorld* (which asked students to return the string 'Hello World!') contained five main AST node types: Module, Function Definition, Arguments, Return, and String. This is similar to the approach used in JavaParser to identify concepts occurring in Java programs [9]. 48 unique tokens were identified across all problems, with an average of about 11 tokens per problem.

We sorted the states by timestamp, then generated a solution space from all of the states using ITAP's path construction methodology [17]. For each state, we then used the solution space to identify the set of edits between the state and the closest goal state (for attempt states), or the specific edit that would be provided in a hint (for the hint request states). We identified the nodes that occurred in these edits and the original states, and the edits between original states and previous states by traversing the given ASTs.

For the Modified-Steps method, we generated a set of opportunities where opportunity names corresponded to node types and correctness depended on the method mentioned above (incorrect if node was not in the state or the goal-edit, correct if the node was in the state-edit, not included otherwise). For the All-Steps model, we used the same process, except that all KCs not marked as incorrect were marked as correct. The two models generated this way were both First-Attempt models; to generate the corresponding All-Attempts models, we went back through the steps and re-named them to include the step's iteration, as was described above. This resulted in all four models that we wished to test.

4.3 DataShop

At this point, we were ready to perform learning curve analysis on the KC models. To accomplish this we used DataShop, an online data analysis service [12]. In order to upload the models to DataShop, we generated files which included the following properties: Student ID, Timestamp, Student Response Type, Problem Name, Step Name, Outcome, and KC. (KC corresponded to the node type for each step, regardless of the used step name; the rest of the data was already available). DataShop automatically performed AFM on the datasets and generated learning curves for the KCs, making it possible for us to move directly to analysis of the results.

5. Results

Now we can examine the learning curves that resulted from this data in order to determine how well our models fit the traditional idea of a learning curve, and which KCs students struggle with the most. In all of the learning curves that follow, we cut off the graphs once the number of students included in each data point drops below 9, in order to make sure that at least 10% of our population is always represented (and to avoid strange outlier behavior).

First, we want to see what the whole-data-set learning curve (which averages the learning curves of all the KCs) looks like for each model. If the KC model is accurate, these curves should start with a high error intercept and then curve downwards, eventually

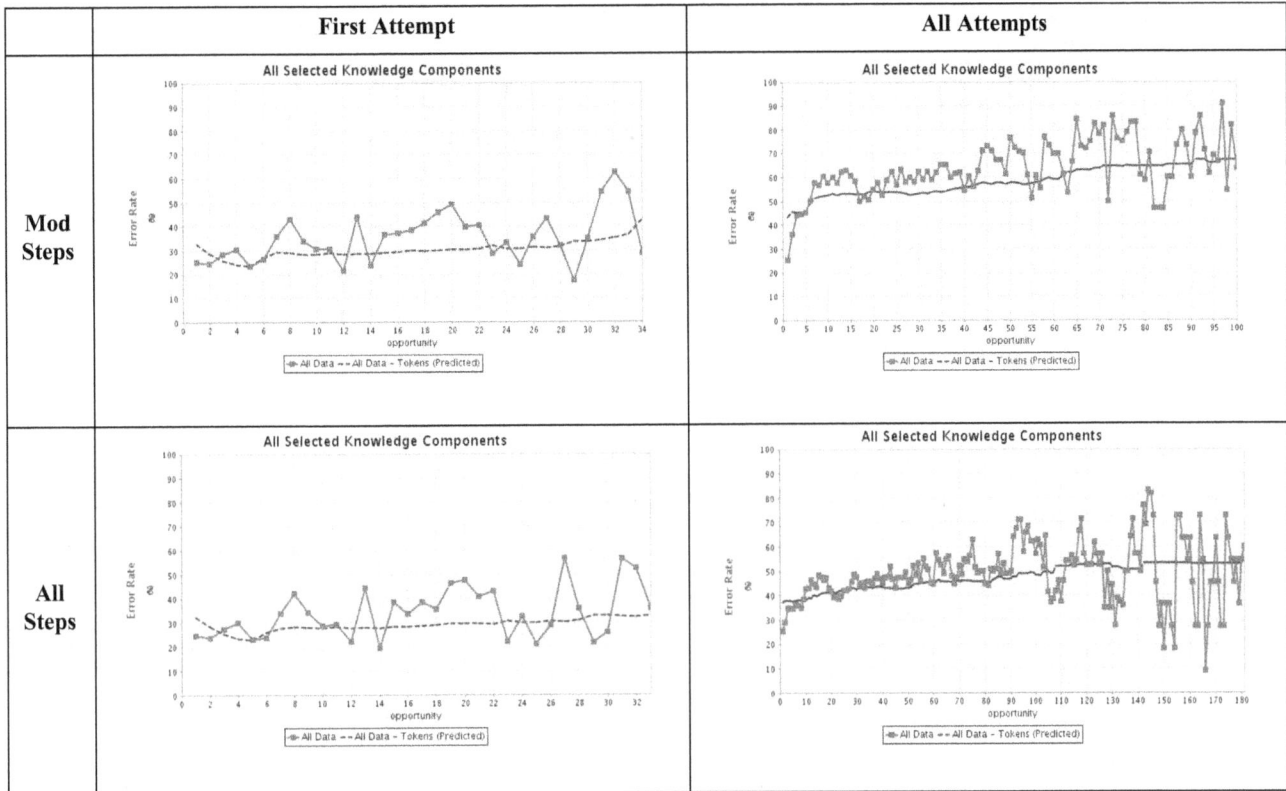

Figure 1: Full-model learning curves for all four types of models.

plateauing near an error rate of zero (as students achieve mastery of all the individual KCs). As is shown in Figure 1, our KC models clearly do not match our expectations. The two All-Attempts curves actually increase over time, showing the opposite effect of what we expect based on theory. The two First-Attempt curves show more promise; they start with a declining curve over the first five states, then plateau at about 30% error rate afterwards. The data itself is jagged, but that does not necessarily invalidate our model as the curves for individual KCs can still have the expected downwards curve.

Comparing these results makes it clear that the First-Attempt model is a better fit than the All-Attempts model (which supports the traditional method of counting student attempts in tutoring systems). The Modified-Step and All-Step models, on the other hand, turned out to be almost identical in structure (due to the

high overlap in their data), to the point that they could be used interchangeably. The Modified-Step model is closer to the traditional ITS model, so we will use it for the following analysis.

Next, we can examine the learning curves for each individual KC to determine where learning is happening. In DataShop, individual learning curves can be sorted into five categories: curves where there is not enough data for solid analysis (little-data), curves that start and end with low error rates (already-learned), curves that start and end with high error rates and show no downward trend (no-learning), curves that start and end with high error rates but do show a downwards trend (still-learning), and curves that start high but end low, demonstrating student mastery (good-learning). Optimally we'd like to see lots of good-learning curves, as they indicate that students are learning the concepts as expected, but the other curves are informative as well; already-learned concepts do not need to be covered as much, no-

learning curves indicate problematic KCs, and still-learning curves demonstrate where extra practice is needed.

We examined the individual KC learning curves within the First-Attempt Modified-Step model, and found the following categorizations for our set of all AST node KCs:

- Little-data: !=, <=, >=, Alias, Dictionary, Divide, Expression, Import, In, List, Not, Not In, Or, Slice, Subtract, Tuple, Unary Operation, Unsigned Subtract, While

- Already-learned: If, Module

- No-learning: <, >, Add, And, Assign, Attribute, Binary Operation, Boolean Operation, For, Index, Integer Divide, Load, Modulo, Multiply, Name, Number, Parameter, Power, Return, Store, String, Subscript

- Still-learning: ==, Call

- Good-learning: Arguments, Compare, Function Definition

At first glance, this categorization only suggests that there are many KCs which are not being practiced enough (in the Little-data category) and many KCs which are not being learned (in the No-learning category). However, it's possible to glean much more information by investigating the individual learning curves and seeing what they show about the data. To demonstrate this, we share examples of the different kinds of learning curves (excepting little-data, which is usually non-informative), and we discuss what they might mean.

5.1 Good Learning Curves

First, we'll look at a successful learning curve for the Function Definition KC (as shown in Figure 2). This is an unusual KC as it only applied to the first six problems of the dataset that students had access to; these problems were presented with no starter code, while all future problems were given with a function header (to help standardize student responses).

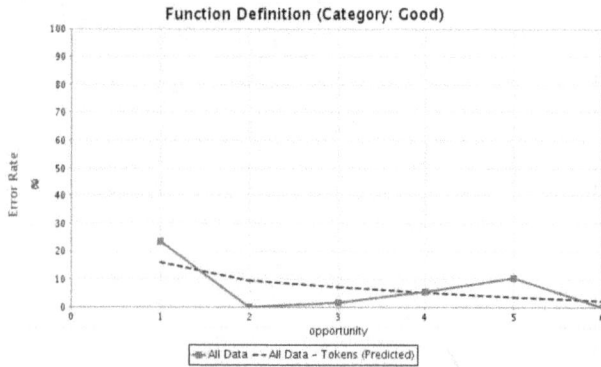

Figure 2: The good learning curve generated for the Function Definition KC. Starts at 23% error and approaches 0%.

In this learning curve, the error rate starts at an average of 23.4%; not as high as many other KCs, but high enough to indicate that around one out of five of students are struggling with the KC at their first attempt. In this model each new attempt is (usually) associated with a new problem; therefore, this graph shows that students struggled with the function definition in the first problem (helloWorld), but quickly mastered it in the following problems. We investigated the uptick at opportunity 5 and found that it was due to three of the twenty-five students asking for a hint before submitting anything to the associated problem (isPunctuation); as hints are counted as incorrect states by AFM, this resulted in an increase in the error rate.

The Arguments learning curve is very similar to Function Definition, which is sensible as the two occur together. However, the Compare learning curve (shown in Figure 3) demonstrates a different learning effect. The data in this model mostly progresses slowly downwards, but it has a blip at opportunity 5, where it hits 0 only to jump back up again. This seems to be due to a problem which used comparison very simply (to check if a value was less than 0, an edge case) that is surrounded by problems which use multiple comparisons that must be combined. This might be a sign that the skill required to use a single comparison operation is different from the skill of combining multiple comparisons, and that the two should be separated into different KCs (and taught as separate concepts as well).

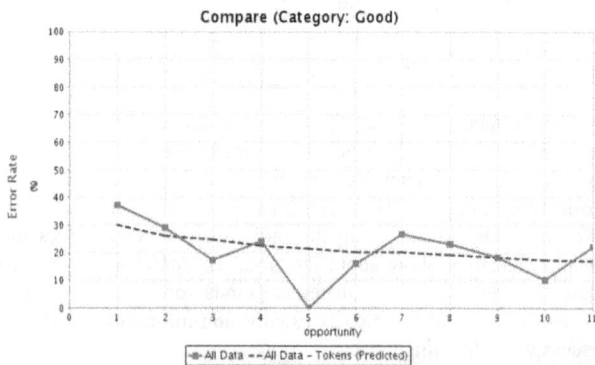

Figure 3: The learning curve generated for the Compare KC. The model trends downwards, from 30% to below 20%, and the data shows a similar trend.

5.2 Still-Learning Curves

Next we'll look at a learning curve which seems to be trending downwards (as we'd expect), but does not reach a low enough error rate to say that the student has truly learned the concept. The Call KC occurs every time the student uses any function call in their code; therefore, it is surprising to see that this data is mostly consistent (albeit with a jagged appearance) and steadily heading downwards. This suggests that students are not learning new concepts for every new function they have to call; instead, they are learning a single concept, how to use *any* function call successfully. With more opportunities, we would expect this model to reach mastery. Therefore, we may wish to include more problems that let students practice using function calls.

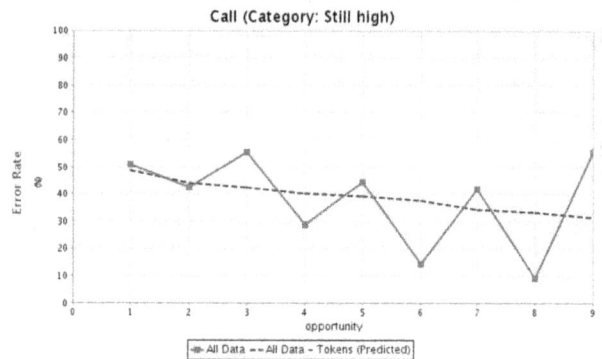

Figure 4: A learning curve that has not yet demonstrated mastery, showing student progress in the Call KC. The model starts at around 50% error rate and reaches 30% error rate before running out of opportunities.

5.3 Already-Learned KCs

One of the learning curves generated by our method was quite surprising to us; we did not expect to find that If statements would be classified as already-learned (as is shown in Figure 5)! This classification could be due to several reasons; perhaps the students are using if statements correctly but making errors in the tests and bodies of the statements, or perhaps the concept of a conditional is intuitive enough that students truly do solve the problems with no trouble. To investigate this, we looked more closely at the data associated with this learning curve, and we quickly determined that the real cause might be the method used to generate KC models at the beginning.

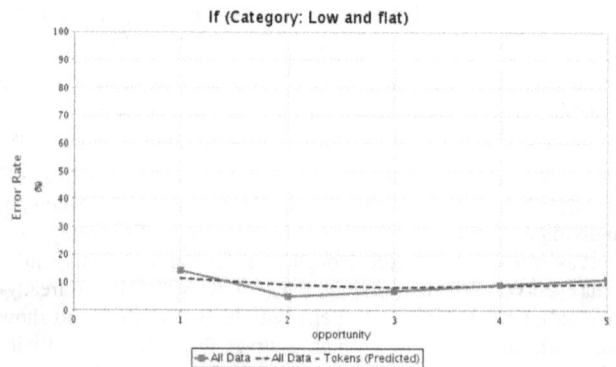

Figure 5: The learning curve for the If Statement KC, which seemingly demonstrates that students have mastered using if statements from the very beginning. The curve remains below 20% error for all opportunities.

For each problem, we had generated a set of KCs to be measured based on the teacher solution to the problem. In the teacher view of the problems, many of the early problems could be solved by returning simple boolean expressions. However, students who solved these problems often opted to use conditionals instead, often writing code of the form *if (boolean expr): return True else: return False*. This means that students often got a great deal of practice at writing conditionals that was not actually measured. If these problems included If statements in their KC models, we would expect a more accurate learning curve for those students; however, this would also unfairly penalize the students who did not use If statements but succeeded in solving the problem. This could possibly be remedied by basing the KC model for each problem and each student off of the student's eventual correct state, instead of the teacher's goal state; however, this would provide less overlap between student models, and would provide less connection to the teacher's intended problem design.

5.4 No-Learning Curves

Now that we have covered what the successful KC's learning curves look like, we can start examining what might be happening with the curves that show no learning at all. Upon examination, these fall into two categories: data which has a flat error rate, and data with more jagged error rates.

The first category (flat error rate) is demonstrated by Boolean Operation, For, Index, and Subscript. We'll use the For KC as an example here (shown in Figure 6). This curve is exactly what we'd expect: it demonstrates a consistent error rate, which, though low, is not good enough to reach mastery. Investigation into the individual opportunities did not show a consistent reason for this; some error states were due to missing for loops, while others were caused by for loops being used in the wrong place.

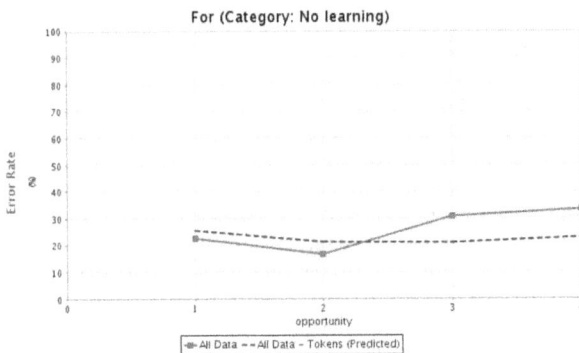

Figure 6: The learning curve for the For Loop KC, which shows a flat error rate. The error rate stays consistently between 20 and 30%.

The data with jagged error rates is more interesting to examine. Attribute, Binary Operation, and Return give us this effect; we'll examine the Binary Operation KC (which encompasses all non-comparison or boolean operations with two operands), shown in Figure 7. By investigating the incorrect states that are represented by each of the opportunities, we can determine why students do so well at some states and so poorly at others.

First, we looked into the low error rate opportunities (1, 2, 3, 5, 9, and 12). The first four were all problems where the only goal was to perform mathematical operations which were provided by the prompts, and it seems that most students had already mastered these mathematical skills (which is not surprising, as these are similar to basic calculator operations). The other opportunities,

with higher error rates, have a range of causes: some used non-mathematical operations (like concatenating strings), and some combined multiple operations in non-intuitive ways. Furthermore, binary operations such as x+1 were often treated as basic values in the more complex programs, and thus could often be marked incorrect when the real blame fell on higher-order constructs. This also occurred with the Name, Number, and String KCs; all had wildly inconsistent learning curves due to their prolific use throughout programs.

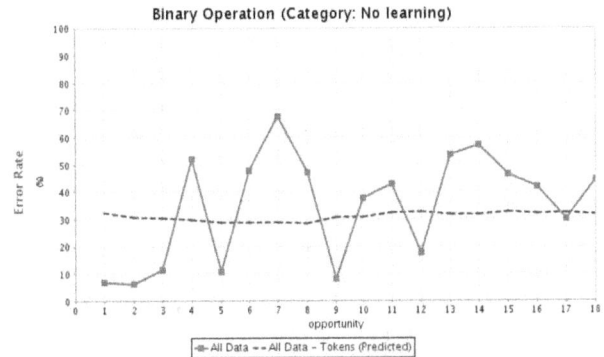

Figure 7: A learning curve generated for the Binary Operation KC. The jagged pattern indicates potential problems with the KC.

It may be possible to improve the fit of binary operations by splitting them up based on the operator type; however, the learning curves generated for the operators themselves either have too little data to identify learning or exhibit no learning at all. We might meet more success if we group up the operators into sub-categories and separate out the different purposes that some of the overloaded operators (like addition) have.

6. Discussion

In this paper, we've attempted to automatically generate KC models for programming out of the AST components used in program solutions. We've investigated whether these models should be generated using all attempts vs the first attempt only, and whether only modified nodes should be included in each opportunity vs all KC nodes. Our results show that the first attempt model tends to produce cleaner learning curves, and the two step models perform equally well. However, the general learning curves produced do not show the expected reduction in error rate. To determine why, we looked into the individual KC learning curves.

In investigating these individual learning curves, we found wide-ranging results. First, we found that several KCs did not contain enough data to demonstrate learning; in other words, the students weren't getting enough practice to master those concepts. This can be remedied by producing more problems that cover the neglected KCs. Many KCs did not exhibit any learning (possibly due to bad KC modeling), but some did show learning, either complete or partial. Investigating the erroneous states that led to these learning curves helped us identify several unexpected occurrences, such as the fact that students had already mastered If statements by the time they reached the problems where they were first supposed to use them, and the fact that function calls seem to be learned independently of different function types. Findings such as these, if they are validated in future work, could be used to inform the teaching of programming (for example, by including the instruction of conditionals much earlier in the curriculum, as students will apparently use them regardless of instructor intent).

In future work, we plan to modify the KCs used in the models we've generated to see if we can improve the modeling of the student data. Several possible modifications were mentioned in the Results section; for example, we might group similar AST nodes (such as the comparison operators <, >, <=, and >=) together into joint KCs, as they can all be used for semantically equivalent purposes. We might also try to identify when a single KC is actually representing several different concepts; for example, we can split the Add operator into its different types (string concatenation and numeric addition), and we can try to identify simple edge-case comparisons and separate them from more complex comparisons. Modifying these KC models may lead to better-fitting learning curves that better model how students are learning.

We've also considered additional approaches that could be used in defining programming step opportunities and correctness in the processing stages of model construction. First, we could generate KC models for each problem based on the student's individual goal state, instead of the teacher goal state; this would allow us to capture learning on all the AST nodes that a student used, instead of just measuring learning on the originally intended concepts. This approach might remedy the problem shown in the If statement KC. Alternatively, instead of using path construction to identify the correctness of KCs, we could use the test cases assigned to the program, where each test case could be mapped to the set of nodes which that test case is supposed to cover. This would require more advanced program analysis, but could yield more accurate results without relying on the creation of goal states for correctness measurement. We also considered using the provided teacher solution for comparing student solutions to a goal state instead of computing goal states via algorithm; however, attempting this quickly revealed that it was a useless approach, as the multitude of possible solutions led to an artificially high error rate in all KCs.

In this paper we demonstrated how DataShop could be used to examine learning curves and investigate erroneous states; however, there are other DataShop features which we did not utilize. For example, the Performance Profiler feature can be used to identify the error rates for different KCs across different problems/steps/etc. Using this system, we could look more deeply into the data to determine whether some KCs are being used in different contexts at different times (for example, if the Add node has different error rates when adding numbers when compared to adding strings or lists). This could help us start building up more semantic KC models which may have a greater chance at successful modeling.

There are several limitations to our work. First, we are using learning curve analysis and AFM in ways that they were not originally designed for; it is possible that the results we have gotten from them may not be indicative of actual student learning. Additionally, our decision to define KC correctness based on the edits between the state and a chosen goal state is a very rough approximation of true KC correctness. It's possible that the optimal goal for the student's current state will not have been chosen, resulting in more edits than are necessary; it's also possible that a node could be correctly used, but would still need to be changed in order to get to a correct code state. Future work in hand-coding the states might be used to see how accurate this automated approach is at estimating KC correctness.

Furthermore, our method of representing steps as simultaneously-executed actions is very different from the traditional implementation of steps in intelligent tutoring systems and other educational technology. Compounding this is the fact that there may be many other invisible steps that we are not measuring at all, such as students' design decisions, which occur before they even start to write code. We welcome suggestions on how this step model could be modified to better represent the reality of student work.

In traditional intelligent tutoring systems, it is assumed that problem sequencing is handled with a mastery paradigm [6]; once a student has mastered a concept the system can move on to a new topic. However, in a conventional programming task, this is impossible, since old KCs must be used to build up new ones as more advanced concepts are learned. Therefore, it's possible that the behavior of learning curves will be different in this context than in other, less construction-based contexts.

Finally, we were unable to construct a validation strategy for the models at the time of writing, as we did not yet have student performance data outside of the system to compare the models to. Therefore, we must rely on the success of AFM in other domains as evidence that the models can truly emulate student learning. If student data was available, we could check for similarity between the produced model's student intercepts (which are supposed to simulate the incoming ability of individual students) and the pretest scores of students in the class; this at least could be used to determine whether the model as a whole mirrors reality accurately. Additionally, we could design test items to target specific KCs, then have the students complete these items after practicing, in order to see whether students perform better on items that are shown as mastered in the model. We hope to use these approaches and others in future work.

7. Conclusion

We hope that, overall, this work can serve as evidence of the fact that programming data can be evaluated using approaches that more closely examine the code that students produce and the learning that students do over time. Approaches such as KC modeling and learning curve analysis can help us understand the precise concepts that students are struggling with, which may inform the future design of programming curricula in order to better enable learning. There are many modifications that could be made to the models presented here in order to more accurately represent programming knowledge, and we hope that others will use and adjust some of the method presented in this paper to test these modifications in future work.

8. Acknowledgements

Thanks to Jason Imbrogno for his help with an early version of this project. This work was supported in part by Graduate Training Grant awarded to Carnegie Mellon University by the Department of Education (# R305B090023).

9. References

[1] Anderson, J.R. and Reiser, B.J. 1985. The LISP Tutor. *BYTE.* 10, 4 (1985), 159–175.

[2] Baker, R.S.J.D. and Yacef, K. 2009. The State of Educational Data Mining in 2009 : A Review and Future Visions. *Journal of Educational Data Mining.* 1, 1 (2009), 3–16.

[3] Berges, M. and Hubwieser, P. 2015. Evaluation of Source

Code with Item Response Theory. *ITiCSE '15* (2015), 51–56.

[4] Cen, H. et al. 2006. Learning Factors Analysis – A General Method for Cognitive Model Evaluation and Improvement. *ITS '06* (2006), 164–175.

[5] Cherenkova, Y. et al. 2014. Identifying Challenging CS1 Concepts in a Large Problem Dataset. *SIGCSE '14* (2014), 695–700.

[6] Corbett, A.T. and Anderson, J.R. 1995. Knowledge Tracing: Modeling the Acquisition of Procedural Knowledge. *User Modeling and User-Adapted Interaction*. 4, 4 (1995), 253–278.

[7] Helminen, J. et al. 2012. How Do Students Solve Parsons Programming Problems? — An Analysis of Interaction Traces. *ICER '12* (2012), 119–126.

[8] Hosseini, R. et al. 2014. Exploring Problem Solving Paths in a Java Programming Course. *PPIG '14* (2014).

[9] Hosseini, R. and Brusilovsky, P. 2013. JavaParser: A Fine-Grain Concept Indexing Tool for Java Problems. *AIEDCS '13* (2013), 60–63.

[10] Ihantola, P. et al. 2015. Educational Data Mining and Learning Analytics in Programming: Literature Review and Case Studies. *ITiCSE WG '15* (2015), 41–63.

[11] Kasurinen, J. and Nikula, U. 2009. Estimating Programming Knowledge with Bayesian Knowledge Tracing. *ITiCSE '09* (Aug. 2009), 313–317.

[12] Koedinger, K.R. et al. 2010. A data repository for the EDM community: The PSLC DataShop. *Handbook of educational data mining*. 43.

[13] Koedinger, K.R. et al. 2012. The Knowledge-Learning-Instruction Framework: Bridging the Science-Practice Chasm to Enhance Robust Student Learning. *Cognitive Science*. 36, 5 (Jul. 2012), 757–798.

[14] Newell, A. and Rosenbloom, P.S. 1981. Mechanisms of skill acquisition and the law of practice. *Cognitive skills and their acquisition*. 1–56.

[15] Papancea, A. et al. 2013. An Open Platform for Managing Short Programming Exercises. *ICER '13* (2013), 47–51.

[16] Piech, C. et al. 2012. Modeling How Students Learn to Program. *SIGCSE '12* (2012), 153–158.

[17] Rivers, K. and Koedinger, K.R. 2014. Automating Hint Generation with Solution Space Path Construction. *ITS '14* (2014), 329–339.

[18] Rivers, K. and Koedinger, K.R. 2015. Data-Driven Hint Generation in Vast Solution Spaces: a Self-Improving Python Programming Tutor. *International Journal of Artificial Intelligence in Education [pre-release]*. (2015).

[19] Soloway, E.M. 1986. Learning to Program = Learning to Construct Mechanisms and Explanations. *Communications of the ACM*. 29, 9 (Sep. 1986), 850–858.

[20] Stamper, J.C. and Koedinger, K.R. 2011. Human-Machine Student Model Discovery and Improvement Using DataShop. *AIED '11* (2011), 353–360.

[21] VanLehn, K. et al. 2007. What's in a Step? Toward General, Abstract Representations of Tutoring System Log Data. *UMAP '07* (2007), 455–459.

[22] Yudelson, M. V. et al. 2014. Investigating Automated Student Modeling in a Java MOOC. *EDM '14* (2014), 261–264.

A Picture of the Growing ICER Community

Simon
University of Newcastle
Australia
simon@newcastle.edu.au

ABSTRACT

This bibliometric study examines the authorship of the papers presented at ICER since the conference began in 2005. It finds that the pattern of authorship complies well with Lotka's law, an accepted model of author distribution within a discipline. ICER's most prolific authors are identified and their contributions quantified, along with measures of the collaborations between authors. New authors are found to be joining the community at a steady rate, some beginning as co-authors with established community members and some joining alone or with other new authors. The analysis extends to the contributions from different countries. The conclusion is that the community of ICER authors is truly international, has a solid core around which excellent growth is evident, displays strong collaboration, and has at least one of the characteristics of a full-fledged discipline.

1. INTRODUCTION

Where do ICER's authors come from? How many papers do individual authors write? How many authors contribute to individual papers? What are the patterns of collaboration? To answer these and related questions, a brief bibliometric study has been conducted of all the papers accepted to ICER over its eleven-year history.

Bibliometric analysis of this sort is fairly common in the library sciences but not particularly widespread in other areas. Nevertheless, it has been applied to publications in discipline-based educational research, such as science education [11] and engineering education [13, 14]. Within computing education it has featured briefly in papers by Simon and colleagues [8, 10], but there do not appear to be any papers dedicated to the topic. It is therefore unusual and perhaps quirky, but it has merit as the computing education conference equivalent of genealogical research – it helps us to understand who we are ('we' in this case being the ICER authors) and where we have come from. It thus strengthens the notion of the computing education community as a community and not just a set of authors who happen to publish in the same journals and conferences.

ICER'16, September 8-12, 2016, Melbourne, Vic, Australia
© 2016 ACM. ISBN 978-1-4503-4449-4/16/09...$15.00
DOI: http://dx.doi.org/10.1145/2960310.2960323

Bibliometrics is the mathematical and/or statistical study of publications. There have been at least three other bibliometric studies of ICER, examining very different aspects of the conference.

Lister and Box [2] conducted a citation analysis of the papers from the first three years of ICER; that is, an analysis of the books, journals, and conferences that are cited in ICER papers. Having already conducted similar analysis of both the SIGCSE Technical Symposium and the Australasian Computing Education Conference, they were able to discern a number of ways in which ICER differed from these other conferences. ICER papers tended to cite a greater variety of conferences and a greater variety of journals, and to focus more on the literature of students and learning rather than on syllabic content.

Malmi et al [3] classified papers according to a system previously applied to papers in various areas of computing, and concluded that ICER papers have "more in common with research in information systems than with that in computer science or software engineering".

Miró Juliá et al [4] studied the collaboration networks among authors in ICER, in six computing research conferences, and in six computing education conferences. They concluded that ICER did not sit easily with either the computing research conferences or the computing education conferences, but displayed some of the characteristics of each.

All three of these studies conclude that ICER is unlike whichever other publication venues they looked at. This leads inevitably to the question of just what ICER *is* like. This paper sets out to answer that question by examining the authorship patterns of ICER over its first eleven years.

2. A BRIEF HISTORY OF ICER

SIGCSE, the ACM's Special Interest Group on Computer Science Education, has a long history of running computing education conferences. In 2005 ICER became the third SIGCSE conference, joining the SIGCSE Technical Symposium, which is held in the US early each year, and ITiCSE, which is held in various other countries in the middle of each year. Both SIGCSE and ITiCSE are computing education conferences, but ICER was designed to be something different: a computing education *research* conference. Perhaps the most common type of paper at SIGCSE and ITiCSE [9] is the experience report, also known as the Marco Polo paper ('I went there and I saw this') [12] or Genesis paper ('and he saw what he had made, and it was good') [9]: a report on a technique that has been tried in the classroom, or a piece of software that has been developed for classroom use, but with no clear research component. ICER was intended to be a venue at which only clear and unequivocal research was presented.

Table 1: Summary of the eleven offerings of ICER

ICER	Location	Program chairs	Submitted	Accepted	Accept rate
2005	Seattle, USA	Richard Anderson, Sally Fincher, Mark Guzdial	35	16	46%
2006	Canterbury, UK	Richard Anderson, Sally Fincher, Mark Guzdial	23	13	57%
2007	Atlanta, USA	Richard Anderson, Sally Fincher, Mark Guzdial	24	14	58%
2008	Sydney, Australia	Raymond Lister, Michael Caspersen, Mike Clancy	46	16	35%
2009	Berkeley, USA	Mike Clancy, Michael Caspersen, Raymond Lister	24	13	54%
2010	Aarhus, Denmark	Michael Caspersen, Mike Clancy, Kathryn Sanders	38	12	32%
2011	Providence, USA	Michael Caspersen, Alison Clear, Kate Sanders	47	18	38%
2012	Auckland, NZ	Alison Clear, Kate Sanders, Beth Simon	54	21	39%
2013	San Diego, USA	Beth Simon, Alison Clear, Quintin Cutts	70	22	31%
2014	Glasgow, UK	Quintin Cutts, Beth Simon, Brian Dorn	69	17	25%
2015	Omaha, USA	Brian Dorn, Quintin Cutts, Judy Sheard	96	25	26%

The locations of the ICER conferences currently form a clear repeating pattern: USA, Europe, USA, Australasia.

From the outset, ICER has had three program chairs each year. The first three offerings were led by the 'triumvirate' of Richard Anderson, Sally Fincher, and Mark Guzdial. Three years later their place was taken by a second triumvirate of Raymond Lister, Michael Caspersen, and Mike Clancy; but during their term a change was made to a rolling system whereby each year one chair would depart and one would be appointed. This system, which has persisted since 2010, has the advantage that every year there are experienced chairs to guide the new one. An interesting consequence of the change from fixed to rolling chairs is that one chair, Michael Caspersen, served for four years rather than three. As he is likely to be the only person ever to chair ICER for four consecutive years, on his retirement from the position he was symbolically presented with an engraved (window) de-icer.

In its second and third years, and again in its fifth, ICER had substantially fewer paper submissions than in the first and intervening years. In those years the paper acceptance rate was over 50%. In more recent years submission numbers have been consistently higher, and the acceptance rate has ranged between 25% and 40%. From 2013 onward, two associate chairs have been appointed each year to help with the load of making decisions on each paper.

Table 1 summarises the eleven ICER conferences that have been held to date, listing for each conference its location, program chairs, number of submissions, number of accepted papers, and acceptance rate.

For its first six years ICER called for and accepted only a single type of paper, the *research paper*. From 2011 to 2013 the conference also accepted *discussion papers*, shorter papers that were in some respect not full research papers, but that were considered to be worth airing and discussing at the conference. In addition, workshops on various research topics have often been co-located with ICER, and there has been a co-located doctoral consortium since 2008.

ICER's program committee has grown steadily, if not monotonically, from 19 members in 2005 to 61 in 2015. Only ten of the original 19 were on the committee in 2015, so there have clearly been many new members over the years.

3. PAPERS
In the eleven years since ICER began, the conference has accepted and published 170 research papers and 17 discussion papers. The number of discussion papers is so small that they cannot be usefully analysed as a group, so for the purposes of this analysis the research and discussion papers will be considered together, a total of 187 papers.

4. AUTHORS AND CONTRIBUTIONS
Counting the names immediately below the titles of all of the 187 papers gives a total of 598 authors. However, this is not the same as the number of distinct authors, as many authors have contributed to more than a single ICER paper. We shall instead refer to this quantity as the number of *author contributions*, defining an author contribution as one author's contribution to one paper. The total of 598 author contributions to 187 papers means that the papers have an average of about 3.2 authors each.

In determining the number of distinct authors, one must be aware that authors can change their names between papers, or can use different forms of the same name; and that it is possible for different authors to have the same name. By way of illustration one need look no further than Table 1: the program chairs included Kathryn Sanders in 2010 and Kate Sanders, the same person, in 2011. A simple text comparison of author names must therefore be informed by additional information such as the authors' institutions and the groups, if any, in which they tend to work. Such a count of the ICER authors finds that the 187 papers have 312 distinct authors.

4.1 Persistent authors
Only two authors, Robert McCartney and Kate Sanders, have had papers at every ICER since 2005. Mark Guzdial has had papers at ten, Beth Simon at nine, and Raymond Lister at eight. Table 2 shows the 31 authors who have had papers at four or more ICERs.

Table 2: authors with papers accepted at specified number of ICERs

ICERs	Authors	Names
11	2	Robert McCartney, Kate Sanders
10	1	Mark Guzdial
9	1	Beth Simon
8	1	Raymond Lister
7	4	Anna Eckerdal, Sally Fincher, Lynda Thomas, Carol Zander
6	5	Brian Dorn, Brian Hanks, Päivi Kinnunen, Briana Morrison, Carsten Schulte
5	7	Jonas Boustedt, Colleen Lewis, Lauri Malmi, Jan Erik Moström, Laurie Murphy, Judy Sheard, Simon
4	10	Jens Bennedsen, Neil Brown, Stephen H Edwards, Sue Fitzgerald, Michael Hewner, Christopher D Hundhausen, Matthew C Jadud, Gary Lewandowski, Renée McCauley, Josh Tenenberg
3	21	…
2	45	…
1	215	…

Table 3: High-contributing authors ranked by complete count (CC), also showing complete-normalised count (CNC) and rank according to CNC

CC	Author	Country	CNC	CNC rank
18	Beth Simon	USA	5.3	2
16	Robert McCartney	USA	3.2	4
14	Mark Guzdial	USA	6.3	1
	Kate Sanders	USA	2.6	9
10	Raymond Lister	Australia	2.6	10
	Lynda Thomas	UK	1.8	18
9	Carol Zander	USA	1.5	28
8	Sally Fincher	UK	2.8	8
	Simon	Australia	1.5	24
7	Brian Hanks	USA	2.4	12
	Briana Morrison	USA	1.7	19
	Anna Eckerdal	Sweden	1.5	27
6	Colleen Lewis	USA	3.5	3
	Brian Dorn	USA	3.2	5
	Carsten Schulte	Germany	3.1	6
	Päivi Kinnunen	Finland	2.6	10
	Jonas Boustedt	Sweden	1.8	16
	Lauri Malmi	Finland	1.8	17
	Judy Sheard	Australia	0.9	51
	Jan Erik Moström	Sweden	0.9	53

4.2 Prolific authors

Which authors have had most papers published at ICER? The authors listed in the preceding section are clearly in consideration, but the number of ICERs at which an author has had papers is not the same as the number of ICER papers by that author. More than 20 authors have had two papers at the same ICER; Robert McCartney, Mark Guzdial, Lynda Thomas, and Simon have each had three papers at a single ICER; and Beth Simon co-authored three papers at ICER 2008 and four at ICER 2011.

There are a number of different ways of quantifying an author's contribution to a paper [1]. With *complete counting*, each author of a paper is given a count of 1 for that paper, regardless of the number of authors. If a paper has four authors, each of the four will be given a count of 1, and the paper will register four contributions. In *complete-normalised counting*, on the other hand, the paper itself is given a count of 1, which is then divided equally among the authors. If a paper has four authors, each of the four will be given a count of 0.25.

Each system has its merits and its drawbacks. Complete-normalised counting acknowledges the shared load of a joint paper, but at the same time it could be seen as devaluing collaboration by giving the authors of a two-author paper only half the credit that either would have earned by writing the paper alone. I have previously argued the importance of collaboration in computing education research [7], suggesting that broader collaboration "might indicate a greater engagement with the computing education community, and will often give more confidence in the generalisability of results". The analysis in this paper will therefore place more emphasis on complete counting, but will acknowledge the differences between it and complete-normalised counting.

Table 3 identifies the 20 authors who have contributed six or more papers to ICER, ranked by complete count. With 18 papers, Beth Simon from the USA is the clear leader.

The rightmost two columns of table 3 show the complete-normalised counts of these high-contributing authors and their ranks according to that count. In the CNC ranking, Mark Guzdial takes the lead from Beth Simon, because his 14 papers were shared among fewer authors than her 18 papers. Kate Sanders, ranked equal third by CC with 14 papers, drops with CNC to ninth place – displaced by authors who have contributed fewer papers, but with fewer co-authors, such as Colleen Lewis (6 papers, CNC 3.5), Brian Dorn (6 papers, CNC 3.2), and Michael Hewner (4 papers, CNC 3.0). Other substantial differences in ranking can be found by examining the rightmost column of table 3.

It is important to repeat that each of these counting systems has its merits and its drawbacks. A high complete count clearly indicates involvement in a large number of papers, whereas a high complete-normalised count indicates a smaller number of co-authors, and thus possibly a greater contribution to each paper. But of course it is a worthy achievement to be ranked in the top couple of dozen by either system.

4.3 Lotka's law

Lotka's law of author productivity [5] encapsulates the empirical observation that in a sufficiently large list of published papers within a discipline, 60% of authors will contribute to only one paper, 15% to two papers, 7% to three papers, and so on. More precisely, given a total pool of A authors, the number of authors A_n contributing to n papers will be CA/n^p, where C and p are constants that vary according to the discipline but are generally expected to be close to 60% and 2 respectively. Although this is not the most rigorous approach, C can be trivially estimated from the case where n=1, that is, the proportion of authors contributing to just one paper; for ICER this estimate gives a value of 68.6%, quite close to the generally quoted 60%. Nicholls [5], having validated Lotka's law on multiple diverse data sets, suggests that

Table 4: Observed and predicted numbers of authors contributing to specified numbers of papers, using Lotka's law with C=68.6% and p=2.2

Contributions	Authors Observed	Authors Predicted
1	214	214
2	42	47
3	22	19
4	12	10
5	2	6
6	8	4
7	3	3
8	2	2
9	1	2
10	2	1
11	0	1
12	0	1
13	0	1
14	2	1
15	0	1
16	1	0
17	0	0
18	1	0

Table 5: ICER authors with 20 or more ICER co-authors

Raymond Lister, Simon	32
Robert McCartney	28
Sally Fincher	25
Kate Sanders	24
Beth Simon, Briana Morrison	23
Judy Sheard, Stephen H Edwards	22
Lynda Thomas	21
Brian Hanks	20

values of 71% to 81% are more realistic than 60%, in which case ICER is very much at the low end of the range. The conclusion is that ICER has about the expected number of authors who have contributed only one paper, and perhaps even fewer than expected: authors tend to come back to ICER.

Table 4 shows the observed numbers of authors contributing to specified numbers of papers, alongside the numbers predicted by Lotka's law with the power constant p set at 2.2 to give a reasonable match with the observed counts for two, three, and four contributions.

What table 4 tells us is that the authors of ICER form a good fit with the power law proposed by Lotka for a sufficiently large list of published papers within a discipline. That is, the eleven years of ICER appear to constitute a sufficiently large list of published papers, and the ICER community displays the publishing hallmarks of a research discipline. This is not a given: a similar analysis of the ITiCSE conference [9] shows a very poor fit with Lotka's law, with 79.5% of authors contributing to just one paper each.

4.4 Sociable authors

Section 4.2 mentions some authors who have a high complete count, having contributed to a large number of papers, but a relatively low complete-normalised count, having shared those papers with many co-authors. It is possible to discern multiple papers with effectively the same set of authors, groups of researchers who follow an initial paper with more work and subsequent papers. At the same time there are authors who become involved in multiple projects with different co-researchers, and subsequently accumulate larger sets of co-authors.

Table 5 shows the authors with the greatest number of ICER co-authors. It is interesting that the two highest-ranked, with 32 co-authors each, both come from Australia. However, these authors have not achieved this high collaboration level by working

together all of the time: they have only eleven co-authors in common.

4.5 New authors

Particularly in its early years, ICER was perceived by some as a fairly closed club. How easy is it to join this club, or indeed to break into it?

There are two ways for a new author to join the ICER community: to co-author a paper with one or more continuing authors, authors who have previously had papers accepted to ICER; or to contribute to a paper with no continuing co-authors. If most new authors took the former path, it could be considered that they were joining the community by invitation, which would support the view of the community as closed. Invitation of new members is to be expected – as, for example, when a postgraduate adviser writes a paper in collaboration with a new student – but it should not be the only means of entry to the community.

The situation can be examined by observing, for each year, the number of continuing authors, the number of new authors who have co-authored with continuing authors, and the number of new authors who have not co-authored with continuing authors. These counts are shown in figure 1.

The figure shows that while there is a steady number of continuing authors, some 20-35 each year, they do not form the bulk of the authors. Only in 2009, 2011, and 2014 have the continuing authors outnumbered the new authors, and in those years the margin was small. In all of the other years the new authors have been in the majority; and in all years there is a

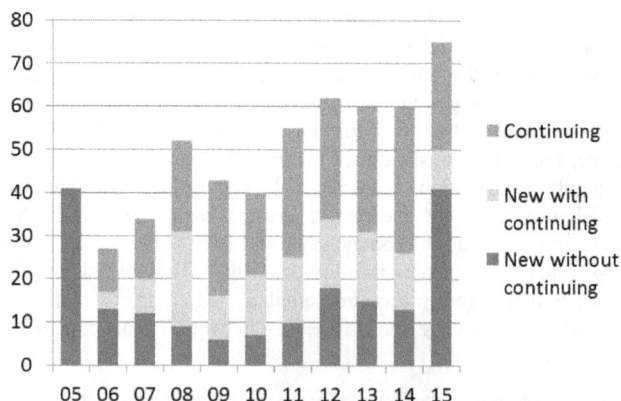

Figure 1: Counts of continuing authors and of new authors with and without continuing authors

reasonable proportion of new authors not accompanied by continuing authors.

The papers themselves display a similar trend, following the first three years which were naturally dominated by papers from new authors. In the subsequent eight years, about 40% of ICER papers have had a mix of continuing and new authors, about 30% have had only continuing authors, and about 30% have had only new authors.

These results together show that ICER is by no means a closed club: that a steady stream of new authors join it, both in collaboration with continuing authors and alone or with other new authors.

4.6 Collaboration clusters

In 2012, Miró Juliá et al [4] studied the collaboration networks among authors in six computing education conferences, six computing research conferences, and ICER. They observed the expected clusters of authors formed by adding transitivity to co-authorship: if A has written a paper with B and a paper with C and D, and C has written another paper with E, F, and G, then all seven of these authors will be in the same cluster. They noted further that every collaboration network will include one 'giant component' comprising a large percentage of its members.

In 2012, ICER's giant component comprised just 49% of its authors, which is above the 14%-46% seen in computing education conferences and at the low end of the 43%-83% seen in computing research conferences [4]. When the ICER analysis is extended to include the subsequent four years, the giant component becomes 55%, which fits more comfortably in the range for computing research conferences. It clearly takes some years to grow a giant component to the point where it is reasonably stable. The 2012 analysis incorporated all seven years of ICER to that point, but 12-16 years of the other conferences; perhaps the analysis was conducted too early in the life of ICER, and perhaps ICER's network characteristics are still stabilising.

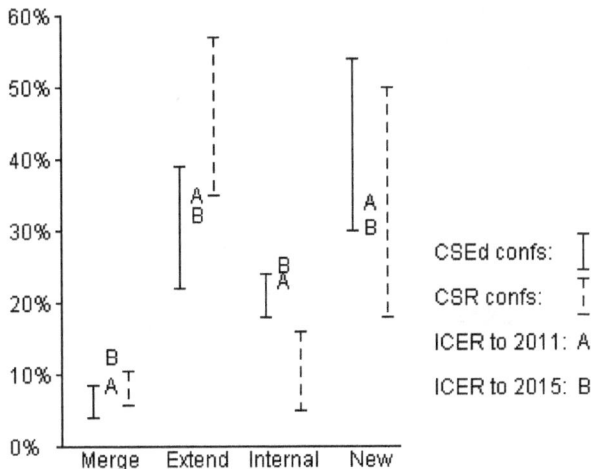

Figure 2: Percentages of Merge, Extend, Internal, and New papers for computing education conferences, computing research conferences, ICER to 2011, and ICER to 2015. All values except those represented by B are from Miró Juliá et al [4].

Miró Juliá et al [4] defined four groups of papers according to the effect the papers have on the collaboration network. *Merge* papers include authors from two distinct clusters, and so merge those two into a single cluster. If there are also co-authors who are new to the network, they are added to the merged cluster. In *Extend* papers, existing authors from a single cluster join with new authors, thus adding new members to the cluster of the existing authors. *Internal* papers are written by existing authors who are already in the same cluster, and so change nothing in the network. *New* papers are written by authors all of whom are new to the network, and so generate a new cluster.

The 2012 analysis includes the proportions of Merge, Extend, Internal, and New papers in the conferences under consideration. Figure 2 shows the ranges of these values for computing education conferences, for computing research conferences, and for ICER to 2011 [4]. The values for ICER have been recomputed to incorporate the subsequent four years, and are shown on the figure as the points marked B. Most noteworthy is that since 2012 the proportions of Merge and Internal papers at ICER have moved beyond the range of those proportions at computing education conferences and at computing research conferences. This means that existing ICER authors are more likely to have further papers accepted to ICER, either with the same co-authors (Internal papers) or with new co-authors who are already in the network (Merge papers). This persistence of ICER authors is what ensures the good fit with Lotka's law discussed in section 4.3.

5. PAPERS AND COUNTRIES OF ORIGIN

If all of a paper's authors come from the same country, that can be designated as the country of origin of the paper. If the authors come from two or more countries, the paper can be called multinational. Of the 187 papers being examined, 47 are multinational: 34 with authors from two countries, nine spanning three countries, two spanning four countries, and two papers with authors from five countries.

There are at least four ways to count a country's share of a multinational paper [1]. This analysis uses *whole-normalised counting*, in which each distinct country found in a paper's author list takes an equal share of the unit count for that paper. A paper with three authors from Denmark and one from New Zealand will count as 0.5 for each country, not 0.75 for Denmark and 0.25 for New Zealand. While the different schemes produce somewhat different counts, this one was chosen for its relative simplicity.

Table 6 shows the number of papers from each country. Note that with rounding of the fractional counts, the sum of the counts in table 6 is slightly less than the actual number of papers.

Table 6: Number of papers from each country (rounding errors from fractional papers are significant)

USA	106.5	Ireland	4.0
UK	17.2	Denmark	3.5
Finland	12.8	New Zealand	3.3
Australia	12.0	India	1.0
Germany	8.2	Italy	1.0
Israel	5.5	Philippines	1.0
Canada	5.1	Spain	1.0
Sweden	4.8	Russia	0.2

Far more papers have come from the USA than from any other country. From Europe the standouts are the UK, Finland, and Germany. Away from North America and Europe, Australia has produced the highest number of papers.

There are many factors that would influence a country's contribution to ICER, among them being the proportion of academics who readily speak and write English, the proportion of the population who undertake post-secondary education, and the availability of funding for travel to conferences. These factors are not easy to quantify, but one that is relatively easy is the country's population. Table 7 displays the same paper numbers as table 6, but ranked by the number of ICER papers per hundred thousand of population.

Finland is the outstanding leader by this criterion, with Ireland, Israel, and New Zealand leading the remaining countries.

6. BREADTH OF COLLABORATION

The average of 3.2 authors per paper, mentioned at the beginning of section 4, suggests a great deal of collaboration. In this section we shall consider aspects of that collaboration.

A paper from 2008, the fourth year of ICER, holds the record for the greatest number of authors. Entitled *DCER: Sharing empirical computer science education data*, it was written by 14 authors from the USA, Sweden, the UK, and Canada [6].

Collaboration in academic publishing is generally reckoned to be a good thing, and collaboration on ICER papers could be regarded as one measure of the strength of the computing education research community. No collaboration at all can be inferred from a paper with a single author. Several authors at the same institution form a next level of collaboration, and it is probably fair to say that several authors at different institutions constitute a greater depth of involvement with the computing education research community. Perhaps arbitrarily, this analysis ranks multinational contributions higher still, regardless of the number of institutions involved. Collaborations between educational institutions and industry are also counted as multi-institutional or multinational as appropriate.

Table 7: Papers per 100 thousand of population

Country	Papers	Pop (million)	Papers/100K
Finland	12.8	5.5	23.2
Ireland	4.0	4.7	8.5
New Zealand	3.3	4.6	7.2
Israel	5.5	8.2	6.7
Denmark	3.5	5.7	6.1
Australia	12.0	24.3	5.0
Sweden	4.8	9.9	4.8
USA	106.5	324.1	3.3
UK	17.2	65.1	2.6
Canada	5.1	36.3	1.4
Germany	8.2	80.7	1.0
Spain	1.0	46.1	0.2
Italy	1.0	59.8	0.2
Philippines	1.0	102.3	0.1
Russia	0.2	143.4	0.01
India	1.0	1326.8	0.01

Figure 3 shows the number of papers in each of the categories of collaboration mentioned above. It is pleasing that the biggest single category is not single authors, as might be expected, but multiple authors within a single institution, which has more than three times as many papers as the single-author category. However, half of the papers entail collaborations between institutions, and half of those are multinational collaborations. Collaboration is strongly in evidence, and a great deal of that collaboration is between researchers at multiple institutions.

One figure measured by Miró Juliá et al [4] is the average number of collaborators per author. In 2012 this average was 3.31 for ICER, above the 1.59-3.11 found in computing education conferences and near the top of the range of 1.7-3.6 for computing research conferences. When the subsequent four years of ICER are included, the average climbs to 4.73, well above all of the 2012 measures [4]. This is further confirmation that ICER authors are a highly collaborative group.

7. DISCUSSION

This analysis contributes to a picture of the ICER authorship, a picture that will help members of the computing education community to better know and understand that community.

The community of ICER authors appears to conform well to Lotka's empirical description of publication within a discipline. The proportion of authors contributing to just one paper is at the low end of the scale, and the exponent of the power law is reasonably low, indicating that many authors contribute to high numbers of papers. ICER appears to be in a reasonable steady state, with authorship patterns very much like those that would be expected of a complete research discipline.

There is evidence of strong collaboration among ICER authors, both within and between institutions, adding to the perception that the authors of ICER papers are a community rather than a collection of individuals with a shared interest.

The steady influx of new authors is also an excellent sign, showing clear growth in the community. The fact that these new authors appear in more or less equal numbers with established ICER authors on the one hand, and in papers written completely by new authors on the other, illustrates that many of the existing

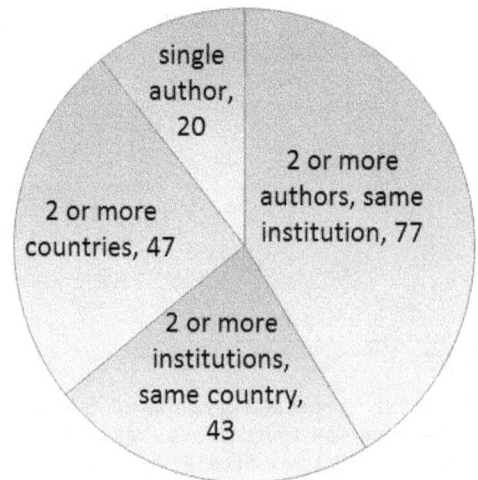

Figure 3: Papers at each level of collaboration

authors are doing a good job of bringing new members to the community, but that this is by no means the only way for a new author to enter the community.

In conclusion, ICER papers display an authorship pattern that has been described as characterising a complete discipline. There is a steady flow of new authors, whether mentored by continuing authors or in papers with only new authors. There is strong evidence of collaboration, both within and between institutions. Taken together, these findings portray the ICER authorship as a vibrant international community with strong bonds, good collaboration, and welcoming of new membership.

8. REFERENCES

[1] PO Larsen (2008). The state of the art in publication counting. Scientometrics 77:2, 235-251.

[2] R Lister and I Box (2009). A citation analysis of the ICER 2005-07 proceedings. Eleventh Australasian Computing Education Conference, Wellington, New Zealand. Conferences in Research and Practice in Information Technology 95, 119-128.

[3] L Malmi, J Sheard, Simon, R Bednarik, J Helminen, A Korhonen, N Myller, J Sorva, and A Taherkhani (2010). Characterizing research in computing education: a preliminary analysis of the literature. Sixth International Computing Education research Workshop (ICER 2010), 3-11.

[4] J Miró Juliá, D López, and R Alberich (2012). Education and research: evidence of a dual life. Eighth International Computing Education research Workshop (ICER 2012), 17-22.

[5] PT Nicholls (1989). Bibliometric modeling processes and the empirical validity of Lotka's law. Journal of the American Society for Information Science 40:6, 379-385.

[6] K Sanders, B Richards, JE Moström, V Almstrum, S Edwards, S Fincher, K Gunion, M Hall, B Hanks, S Lonergan, R McCartney, B Morrison, J Spacco, and L Thomas (2008). DCER: sharing empirical computer science education data. Fourth International Computing Education research Workshop (ICER 2008), 137-148.

[7] Simon (2007). A classification of recent Australasian computing education publications. Computer Science Education 17:3, 155-169

[8] Simon (2008). Koli Calling comes of age: an analysis. Seventh Baltic Sea Conference on Computing Education Research (Koli Calling 2007), Koli National Park, Finland, November 2007. Conferences in Research and Practice in Information Technology 88, 119-126.

[9] Simon (2015). Emergence of computing education as a research discipline. Doctoral dissertation, Aalto University, Finland.

[10] Simon, A Carbone, M de Raadt, M Hamilton, R Lister, and J Sheard (2008). Classifying computing education papers: process and results. Fourth International Computing Education research Workshop (ICER 2008), 161-171.

[11] C-C Tsai and ML Wen (2005). Research and trends in science education from 1998 to 2002: a content analysis of publication in selected journals. International Journal of Science Education 27:1, 3-14.

[12] D Valentine (2004). CS educational research: a meta-analysis of SIGCSE Technical Symposium proceedings. 35th SIGCSE Technical Symposium on Computer Science Education, ACM SIGCSE Bulletin 36:1, 255-259.

[13] P Wankat (2004). Analysis of the first ten years of the Journal of Engineering Education. Journal of Engineering Education 93:1, 13-21.

[14] B Williams and P Neto (2012). Tracking engineering education research and development – contributions from bibliometric analysis. International Journal of Engineering Pedagogy 2:2, 37-44.

Methodological Rigor and Theoretical Foundations of CS Education Research

Alex Lishinski
Michigan State University
College of Education
East Lansing, MI
lishinsk@msu.edu

Jon Good
Michigan State University
College of Education
East Lansing, MI
goodjona@msu.edu

Phil Sands
Michigan State University
College of Education
East Lansing, MI
Phil.sands@gmail.com

Aman Yadav
Michigan State University
College of Education
East Lansing, MI
ayadav@msu.edu

ABSTRACT

The problem of the lack of rigor in CS education research has frequently been discussed and examined. Previous reviews of the literature have examined rigor on both theoretical and methodological dimensions, among others. These reviews have also looked at differences in indicators of rigor between conference proceedings and journal publications. However, to date there is no comprehensive review that has examined the intersection of methodological and theoretical quality.

This paper reports results from a literature review in which we analyzed both the use of theory and methodological rigor of four years of CS education research from the Computer Science Education (CSE) journal and the proceedings of the International Computing Education Research (ICER) conference. The goal was to provide an updated and expanded picture of the methodological quality and use of theory in the most rigorous CS education publications, as well as to compare between conference proceedings and journal publications on these dimensions. Our focus was on research that draws upon learning theory from education, psychology and other disciplines outside CS education.

The results of our review show a different picture than earlier reviews. Focus on empirical results in conference proceedings articles has surpassed that of journal publications, and empirical studies are significantly more likely to make use of theory from outside CS education. Overall, our analysis shows a significant increase in the proportion of articles drawing on theory from outside CS education, compared to earlier literature reviews, whereas indicators of methodological quality show no such change.

Keywords

computing education, research methods, literature review, theoretical grounding

1. INTRODUCTION

Computer science education is an education field, but by and large it does not have the same mature and independent status of other content area education fields. Computer science education research is largely done by practitioners, computer scientists who teach and computer science teachers, rather than dedicated education researchers with specialized training in social science research methods and theory [17]. For this reason, there is much concern about the rigor of computer science education research. The field, although decades old, can be considered young in terms of scholarly development [17]. As a practitioner driven field, rather than a researcher driven field, there are a few major areas for improvement in CS education research.

The rigor of CS education research has been previously examined on a number of dimensions. The degree to which research relies on empirical results [1], the methodological rigor of those empirical studies [16], the diversity of research methods employed [2], and the degree to which relevant theory from the behavioral sciences and other education fields is used to ground and guide research [6]. With respect to the last of these dimensions, Mark Guzdial made the statement at a 2005 SIGCSE panel that "Too much of the research in computing education ignores the hundreds of years of education, cognitive science, and learning sciences research that have gone before us" [2]. In an editorial for a 2015 special issue of Computer Science Education, Anthony Robins quoted Guzdial and argued that his assessment of CS education research remained true 10 years later.

Fincher and Petre (2004) gave six broad principles for CS education research. They are:

- Pose significant questions that can be answered empirically

- Link research to relevant theory

- Use methods that permit direct investigation of the question

- Provide a coherent and explicit chain of reasoning

- Replicate and generalize across studies

- Disclose research to encourage professional scrutiny and critique

The present study sought to investigate the degree to which CS education research addresses the first three of these principles. To that end, we present the details of a literature review of recent publications in *Computer Science Education* (CSE) and the *Proceedings of the International Computing Education Research conference* (ICER) in which we sought to answer the following research questions:

- To what extent do CS education research articles make use of previous theory from outside CS, and how does this compare to the results of previous reviews?

- To what extent do CS education research articles present empirical results, what level of methodological rigor is used, and how do these results compare to those of previous reviews?

- To what extent do CS education research studies make explicit their research questions, and how does this compare to the results of previous reviews?

- Is there any connection between the methodological and theoretical quality of research?

2. THE ROLE OF THEORY IN EDUCATION RESEARCH

Theory plays an essential role in education research. Suppes argued that education research as a field initially grew as a result of embracing empiricism, but later faltered as a result of inattention to theory [19]. Theory provides the deeper and enduring foundation for the importance and significance of education research [19]. Suppes argued that the importance of theory to education research can be seen by analogy to the role played by theory in the successes of the hard sciences and other social sciences like psychology and economics. The role of theory in the hard sciences lies in its power to organize experience in more deep and rigorous ways, and only through such rigorous organization of experiences is it possible to address the underlying complexity of the phenomena being studied. This is only more true in the behavioral sciences. Superficial empiricism misses essential elements of any subject of scientific study, and in its most extreme form, provides no generalizable principles whatsoever [19].

In scientific fields, by 'theory' is meant a certain kind of explanation, that offers a 'how' and a 'why' something works the way it does [8]. To build theory is to construct a connected set of ideas that form an organized way of explaining particular phenomena [8]. McMillian and Schumacher argued that theory can be seen as beholden to the following criteria: provide parsimonious explanations of observed phenomena, be consistent with the existing body of knowledge, provide a mechanism for verification and revision, and stimulate further research [11]. Thus conceived, theory protects against unscientific approaches to inquiry [8]. Underlying assumptions are made explicit, predictions and explanations for observed phenomena are provided, and perspectives for

understanding some class of phenomena are provided by theory [8]. Furthermore, given the societal importance of the phenomena studied in education and behavioral sciences, particularly the fact that social policy is often informed by behavioral science research. Therefore, Tellings argued, solid, grounded, generalizable theoretical models are needed to guide research in the behavioral sciences [20].

2.1 Theory in Computer Science Education Research

The second principle for CS education research is to link research to appropriate theory. Fincher and Petre characterized CS education as an essentially interdisciplinary field. This characterization comes both from the essential fact that computer science education is rooted in both a behavioral science field and a STEM field, as well as the more contingent fact that computer science education is among the more immature education fields. CS education has traditionally borrowed methods and concepts from other fields, including mathematical content areas like physics, as well as other behavioral sciences like psychology. Fincher and Petre described interdisciplinary fields as a 'trading zone' where disciplines come together and ideas, theories and methods are exchanged [6]. General guidance on the study of learning can come directly from theory, as well as indirectly, by means of analogy to educational research done in other similar disciplines [6]. Computer science education borrows a number of different types of research tools from the broader field of education, such as theories, models, and instruments [6]. Examples of theories include Bruner's work on cognitive development, which emphasized the relationship between cognitive process and how well structured disciplinary content is, Vygotsky's work on the Zone of Proximal Development (ZPD), which conceptualizes limits to the amount of learning that can be expected given the student's current developmental state, and Lave's work on how learning must be conceptualized as inextricably situated in authentic contexts, both concrete and social. Models of educational processes include Bloom's Taxonomy, which conceptualizes assessment in education by reference to a hierarchical set of cognitive behaviors that serve to indicate what has been learned, as well as Kolb's learning cycle, which describes the cyclical process by which concrete experiences are turned into abstract representations [6]. Instruments include the Motivated Strategies for Learning Questionnaire (MSLQ) [13], a set of motivational scales, and the Wechsler Adult Intelligence Scale, an intelligence test.

3. METHODOLOGICAL QUALITY IN CS EDUCATION RESEARCH

As in all research fields, methodological quality is a very significant concern for CS education research. The third principle of CS education research is to use methods appropriate to the research questions being investigated. Fincher and Petre framed the relationship between research methodology and rigor in terms of bias-reduction. All studies should provide evidence for their claims, but the strength of the evidence provided by any given study is a function of bias-reduction, which is achieved through appropriately rigorous methodology, among other things (e.g., operationalization of constructs, interpretation of results) [6]. Fincher and Petre detailed the bias reducing properties of different research designs and methods. For example, a within-subjects design (pre/post) reduces bias due to individual differences over a between-subjects design (post only) [6]. Likewise, an experimental design reduces bias more so than a quasi-experimental design, because random assignment eliminates selection bias.

Research questions are likewise an important part of CS education research. Fincher and Petre warned against the backwards approach of designing your study to explain an already observed result. Experiments designed without a specified research question can lead to bias in a number of ways, because the research questions guide the use of theory and development of methods and interpretation of results. For this reason, research questions should be identified before specifying the methods of the study [5]. Research questions in quantitative studies make explicit the variables of interest and the relationships between them which are to be tested, which in turn suggests the methods that should be used [4]. Research questions in qualitative studies, on the other hand, should specify the main concept of interest and connect to a particular strategy of qualitative investigation, but the questions should be expected to evolve and be refined through the course of investigation [4]. Research questions differ in the degree to which they fit the theory and methods used, but in this study we limit our analysis to whether or not research questions are specified.

4. PREVIOUS LITERATURE REVIEWS IN CS EDUCATION

Literature reviews in CS education are not uncommon, and they often focus on areas where the literature lacks rigor. One common theme in past reviews has been empiricism. A series of reviews has looked at the degree to which research presented at SIGCSE, the largest CS education conference, presents empirical results. The investigation of lack of empirical rigor has shown a consistently improving trend. A review of SIGCSE studies from 1984-2003 found that 21% of studies were 'experimental' (their definition of this term is explained further below) [21], a similar review of studies from multiple CS education research venues found 40% to be experimental [16], whereas a later review of SIGCSE research from 2014-2015 found over 70% of studies to be empirical [1]. This increasing trend is heartening to those concerned about rigor in CS education research, but it is not without caveats. In the most recent review, although 70% of studies were classified as empirical, the quality of such empirical evidence was questionable. Of the 70% of studies classified as empirical, the most common source of data was student feedback surveys [1].

Randolph et al. looked at methodological quality in CS education research across several publication venues [16]. The focus of this literature review was to compare journal publications with conference proceedings publications with respect to 5 indicators of methodological rigor. The indicators of methodological quality were attitudes-only outcome variables, one group posttest-only designs, experimental designs, use of qualitative methods, and reporting only anecdotal evidence. The authors found no statistically significant differences between journal and proceedings publications on these indicators, suggesting that both types are equally rigorous.

Malmi et al. reviewed the use of theory in computer science education research articles from Computer Science Education, the proceedings of ICER, and Transactions of Computing Education [10]. Using their theories, models, and frameworks (TMF) construct, the authors found that about half of all papers published in these outlets did not use any sort of TMF. Looking just at CSE and ICER papers, there was an equal use of TMFs, with articles from both publications using some TMF 57% of the time. The authors further classified the identified TMFs by reference discipline, finding that TMFs came from CS education research in 16% of cases, Computing in 24% of cases, education in 29% and psychology in 19%. Specific TMFs were also counted, but the authors found such diversity in TMFs (314 instances of 226 distinct TMFs; 200 TMFs mentioned only once) that this analysis was not particularly informative.

Previous literature reviews have also looked at categories of CS education research. Joy et al. examined research across many different outlets for CS education research in order to create a taxonomy of research [7]. The basis for their analysis was the notion of a continuum running from a purely technical perspective to a purely educational perspective, comprising four major categories. These were (a) system, which were studies on educational software focusing on the technical, (b) technology, studies on educational software focusing more on the educational but lacking implementation, (c) practical pedagogy, which were educational studies that report results not connected to substantial educational theory, and (d) theoretical pedagogy, studies that were substantially grounded in education theory. Joy et al.'s study provides a taxonomy of the types of studies that are prevalent in different CS education journals, but what has not been looked at heretofore in reviews of the CS education literature is the degree to which CS education research draws theory from the behavioral sciences themselves and from outside CS by analogy, as well the sorts of theoretical themes that are prevalent in the research, and shifts over time in this composition [7]. Other literature reviews have created similar categorizations of different types of computer science education research [9, 18].

5. FOCUS, NEED AND PURPOSE OF STUDY

Our focus in this study was investigating the rigor of research in computer science education research, on both the methodological and theoretical dimensions. It is these two dimensions that we thought were most relevant to assessing the degree to which CS education research is becoming a more mature education discipline along the lines of mathematics or science education. We chose to focus our attention on articles from ICER and CSE, because the previous studies on rigor in CS education research suggest that among journals, CSE is likely to contain the most rigorous work, and among conference proceedings, ICER is likely to contain the most rigorous work [7].

Our investigation of the methodological rigor of CS education research follows from that of Randolph et al. [16]. We examined articles for methodological quality along the 5 dimensions chosen by the authors in that study. However, we felt that the dimensions examined in Randolph et al. [16] were not extensive enough, so we expanded our framework to contain several additional dimensions.

Our investigation of the theoretical rigor of CS education research is a continuation of the work done by Malmi et al. [10]. However, our focus differed from that work, in that we chose to focus our investigation on the use of theory drawn specifically from work in psychology, education and other social science disciplines that seek to explain the processes by which learning takes place, to give a rough definition. Our reason for restricting our focus in this manner comes from the arguments made in Fincher and Petre [6] and Almstrum et al. [2]. Fincher and Petre argued that computer science education is an inherently interdisciplinary field, and so we thought that an important measure of how mature the discipline has become is the degree to which it reaches for guiding theory from outside itself [6]. The focus on learning theory is similarly motivated by the point made in Almstrum et al. and Robins, that CS education has tended to not make use of previous research from the learning sciences (broadly construed) [2, 17].

The purpose of our study was to examine the theoretical and methodological dimensions of rigor in the same group of papers. We were interested to find out whether the two dimensions of rigor were related in any quantifiable sense. We also thought that the previous work on methodological rigor [16] could be expanded upon. Our goal was to improve the analysis of methodological rigor by using a more detailed set of indicators. We also shifted focus in our analysis of theoretical rigor compared to previous work [10], focusing on the use of theory from outside computer science.

The need for our study is to both provide updated and improved data on these two dimensions of rigor. Randolph et al. looked at articles up to 2005, whereas Malmi et al. looked at articles up to 2011 [10], so the last four years of articles have not been examined on these dimensions of rigor. Our study provides more current data on the rigor of CS education research, which can be compared with that reported in previous studies, and from which more conclusions about the trajectory of rigor in computer science education research can be drawn [7].

6. METHODOLOGY

6.1 Selection of Articles

Articles reviewed for this study include selections from 4 years (2012-2015) of Computer Science Education (CSE), and the proceedings from ICER. There are other outlets for CS education research that could have been included as well, but these 2 were selected because they cover 2 primary venues where rigorous, theory based empirical articles are likely to be published. ICER is a research conference that places a far greater emphasis on both empiricism and theoretical grounding than other conferences, and CSE is a journal that features work that is both empirical and theoretical in nature. We coded all articles from both publications in the years 2012-2015. The rationale for the range of years used was that the most recent year examined in Malmi et al. was 2011 and we wanted to have continuity and comparability with the results of that study.

6.2 Categories of Methodological Quality

Drawing from Randolph et al.'s study [16] on methodological quality in CS education research, we looked at several methodological dimensions. Randolph et al. used 5 indicators of methodological quality to examine all CS education research studies that had human subjects. They were:

- *Attitudes Only*: These studies measured only students'

or teachers' attitudes toward the intervention studied. This is distinct from studies where the sole outcome measure is some form of attitudes that are not related to the intervention, such as attitudes toward CS, or self-beliefs.

- *Anecdotal Only*: These studies reported only subjective accounts from the author about the quality of an intervention or instructional approach. This is distinct from rigorous qualitative research, in which subjective observations are coded and accounted for within some kind of rigorous framework

- *Single Group: Posttest Only*: These studies reported quantitative data, but only for one group (no control group) and only after the intervention (no pretest control). This is distinct from experimental and quasi-experimental designs that use posttest only data to do a multiple group comparison.

- *Experimental Designs*: Randolph's definition of experimental included essentially all studies in which quantitative data was collected [15]. This includes all manners of quantitative research design (true experiment, quasi-experiment, single group) and data collection plans (posttest only, pretest and posttest). We collected data on this category for comparability of results, but we also collected data on studies that were experiments in the technical sense of the word, with randomly assigned treatment and control groups.

- *Qualitative Research*: These studies involved non quantitative data that was rigorously analyzed or coded for themes. The data can include coded interviews with students, coded samples of student work, coded transcripts of classroom discourse, or any other type of data that is not quantitative in nature. This is distinct from anecdotal data in which qualitative observations may be reported, but they are not done in a rigorous, thoroughgoing manner.

We modified the coding framework from Randolph et al. [16]. We coded all articles for these original 5 dimensions so that our results would be comparable, but the framework was adjusted and expanded to capture elements of methodological quality not captured by the original framework to add additional levels of nuance to the original framework beyond the simple good/bad division used by Randolph et al. [16]. The expanded framework was structured as follows:

- *Qualitative Data*: The qualitative data category comprised all studies that reported non-quantitative data. Of these studies, we coded them into two groups, Qualitative and Anecdotal, corresponding to the categories from Randolph et al.'s [16] original framework described above. We coded those studies as qualitative that had a systematic protocol or framework for analysis, and as anecdotal those studies that simply reported subjective results.

- *Quantitative Data*: This quantitative data category comprised all studies with any sort of quantitative data. Of those studies, we coded them into three groups: Experimental, Quasi-experimental, and Single Group. Experimental studies were those which used multiple groups with completely random assignment. Quasi-experimental studies were those which used multiple groups without completely random assignment. Single Group studies were those which used just a single group for evaluation. All of these categories were given distinct codes.

- *Data Collection Procedure*: Of all quantitative studies, we further characterized them on the basis of their data collection procedure. We coded studies into two groups, posttest only, and pre/post. Posttest only studies collected data only after an intervention, whereas pre/post studies collected data before and after an intervention.

- *Mixed Methods*: If the study in question used both quantitative and qualitative measures, we coded the study as mixed methods in addition to the coding for the quantitative and qualitative methods.

The quantitative studies were also coded for the type of outcomes they measured. The categories were attitudes only, psychological, data mining, overall grade, and other. We coded for the type of outcome measure as a way of expanding on the coding of studies that used an 'attitudes only' outcome. In addition to counting those studies, we wanted to get a sense of what other types of outcomes CS education studies are using, which should be a very rough proxy for the type of conclusions that these studies lend themselves to drawing.

- *Attitudes only* corresponds to the original category from Randolph et al. [16] described above, corresponding to studies in which the only outcome was the attitudes of participants toward the study intervention.

- *Psychological* refers to all broadly psychological measurement instruments, for example, surveys on self-efficacy, surveys on attitudes towards computing, and cognitive tests of psychological constructs like problem solving.

- *Data Mining* refers to outcomes that were the result of an automatic data collection process such as data from compilers, IDEs or LMSs.

- *Overall Grade* refers to outcomes based on overall course grades or final exam grades in the course where the intervention took place.

- *Other* refers to any outcomes not falling in one of the above categories.

These revised categories correspond to more detailed levels of methodological rigor. In addition to these levels, we also decided to code articles for whether or not explicit research questions appear in them. We thought that the inclusion of explicit research questions is also an indicator of methodological rigor, as authors must formulate a substantive question that their results can answer, rather than simply presenting a series of results that, while perhaps significant and interesting, may not substantively add to the theoretical knowledge of the topic. For that reason we coded all articles as a yes/no for whether they included explicit research questions.

6.3 Qualitative Coding for the Use of External Theory from the Learning Sciences

Similar to Malmi et al., we examined all articles as well for their use of theory from the learning sciences, with a particular focus on just studies from outside computer science education. We classified particular studies as making use of outside theory if they contained at least one citation to a reference on learning theory from outside CS education. We considered learning theory studies to be theoretical and/or empirical papers/books from psychology, cognitive science, etc. In other words, anything that derives from some abstract model of how students learn or understand. This can be direct references to psychological theory pieces (e.g. Constructivism in Education), Empirical psychology pieces (e.g. An Empirical Examination of Motivational Issues in Problem Solving in Middle School Students), or articles from other disciplines that explicitly invoke such theory (e.g. Self-Efficacy and Essay Revision Process in High School Writing Students). Broadly, theoretical studies describe specific mental and behavioral processes that underlie learning, and they are not studies in a computer science context, even if these studies have a learning theory bent (e.g. Constructivism in Computer Science Education).

Following Fincher and Petre's distinction between the direct and indirect use of theory, we further divided theoretical references into two categories:

- *Broad Theoretical*: The reference is to general literature in the learning sciences that has no subject specific reference point. This includes purely theoretical (e.g. Robbins (2004) Revision of achievement goal theory: Necessary and illuminating) as well as empirical studies, so long as they are general and not specific to an academic subject area (e.g. Green et al. (1989) Training in creative problem solving: Effects on ideation and problem finding and solving in an industrial research organization).

- *Analogy to Another Content Area*: The reference is used to bring some theoretical basis for understanding students' learning and behavior by analogy to a study from a specific content area outside computer science (e.g. Math Education). The purpose of the reference should be to posit an explanation or model for understanding student learning, but the content of the reference is a study that examines these processes or models in a specific non-CS content area (e.g. "Smith, Pasero, and McKenna [6] used data from Trends in International Mathematics and Science Study (TIMSS) and found that in fourth and eighth grade, boys had higher confidence than girls in science and were more likely to like science than girls.") This category is intended to refer to contexts in which authors make a general point about learning theory that is applied to their own CS context, but they do so using a study from another content area.

We also coded all articles for the presence of research questions. If we located within the article one or more questions that framed the purpose and scope of the study, whether or not they were explicitly labeled as research questions, the article was coded as containing research questions. Broader statements of research topic and aims that were not phrased as questions were not counted as research questions.

The articles were analyzed individually by three researchers. Each researcher coded a third of the articles from years 2013 through 2015, and 18% of the articles were used for inter-rater reliability pilot testing. For each pilot paper, two raters out of the three were chosen to code the paper independently for inter-rater analysis. The third rater coded the paper for inclusion in the data, after inter-rater reliability had been established. An iterative process of coding, revising the codebook, recoding, and discussion was used until the independent coders could consistently apply codes with an acceptable level of agreement on the pilot papers. The pilot papers were a subsample of the 2015 and 2014 articles. The 2012 articles were split between two of the researchers for coding, but were not made part of the inter-rater coding.

For subsequent coding rounds, codes were discussed and codes altered when one or more of the researchers believe they had miscoded their own work. When required codes (e.g. 'theory / no theory') were missing due to human error, these were flagged and recoded to ensure a complete data set. The most reliable results for inter-rater reliability were for the identifying the presence of learning theory code ($\kappa = 0.69$), whether or not a study was empirical code ($\kappa = 0.88$), and the presence of research questions code($\kappa = 0.70$). Due to the relatively low occurrences of the indicators of outcomes and methodologies, the respective κ values were biased towards larger confidence intervals, making them inappropriate for inclusion [22] [3].

7. RESULTS

The results of coding the articles are shown below. First, descriptive statistics are shown for all of the theoretical and methodological indicators used. Next, the results of comparison tests are shown for differences between CSE and ICER, differences between articles using theory and those not using theory, and differences between our results and the results of previous literature reviews. The test statistic refers to the independent samples z test for 2 proportions [12].

7.1 Use of outside Theory

The majority of the studies examined in both CSE and ICER made use of external theory. Descriptive statistics on the proportion of articles making use of outside theory are in Table 1. The majority of studies making use of theory used just direct references to theory while a smaller number used both direct references and references through another discipline, and almost no studies referenced external theory only through another discipline.

Table 1: Use of theory by publication

	Number of Articles	Yes Theory	No Theory
CSE	53	41	12
ICER	83	55	28

7.2 Methodological Quality

7.2.1 Randolph et al. Methodological Indicators

The results of the methodological analysis of the articles are in the tables below. The descriptive statistics for the methodological indicators, as defined in Randolph et al. [16] are shown first in tables 2 & 3, for CSE and ICER respectively, followed by the expanded set of indicators used in

our expansion of the coding framework in tables 4 & 5, for CSE and ICER respectively. Note that Randolph et al. [16] used a specific definition of experimental to refer to any attempt to manipulate a variable and draw causal conclusions. Randolph et al.'s [16] definition encompasses all quantitative studies, regardless of whether they use a design that meets the strict definition of 'experimental', including studies from the single group posttest only. For this reason the first set of descriptive statistics provide a different value for experimental than the subsequent set, because for our coding scheme, we restricted use of the category empirical to its strict definition in which a variable is manipulated by random assignment of participants.

Table 2: Randolph et al. methodological indicators: CSE (empirical studies only)

	Num. Articles	Total	Prop.
Anecdotal	4	38	0.11
Attitudes Only	4	38	0.11
Sing. Group Posttest	8	38	0.21
Experimental	10	38	0.26
Qualitative	11	38	0.29

Table 3: Randolph et al. methodological indicators: ICER (empirical studies only)

	Num. Articles	Total	Prop.
Anecdotal	4	72	0.06
Attitudes Only	3	72	0.04
Sing. Group Posttest	20	72	0.28
Experimental	14	72	0.19
Qualitative	19	72	0.26

7.2.2 Additional Methodological Indicators

Descriptive statistics for the variables unique to our coding scheme are shown below, broken out by publication. Our indicators of type of research design and outcomes are shown in Table 4 and Table 5. Articles using quantitative research designs were coded for type of outcome, and a given study may have more than one outcome.

Table 4: CSE: Additional Methodological quality indicators and outcomes

	Num Articles	Total	Prop.
Research Questions	18	38	0.47
Mixed Methods	5	38	0.13
Single Group	15	38	0.39
Quasi-Experiment	10	38	0.39
Experimental	1	38	0.03
Attitudes	5	38	0.13
Psychological	9	38	0.24
Overall Grade	5	38	0.13
Data Mining	2	38	0.05
Other Outcome	17	38	0.45
Qualitative	11	38	0.29
Anecdotal	4	38	0.11

Table 5: ICER: Additional Methodological quality indicators and outcomes

	Num Articles	Total	Prop.
Research Questions	40.00	72.00	0.56
Mixed Methods	7.00	72.00	0.10
Single Group	30.00	72.00	0.42
Quasi-Experiment	14.00	72.00	0.42
Experimental	6.00	72.00	0.08
Attitudes	6.00	72.00	0.08
Psychological	11.00	72.00	0.15
Overall Grade	10.00	72.00	0.14
Data Mining	10.00	72.00	0.14
Other Outcome	23.00	72.00	0.32
Qualitative	19.00	72.00	0.26
Anecdotal	4.00	72.00	0.06

7.3 Comparisons between CSE and ICER

Results from our analysis were compared between CSE and ICER, to test the hypothesis examined in Randolph et al. [16], that articles from journals and conference proceedings differ in their rigor, using the five indicators as defined in that analysis. Also included are our indicators for the use of theory and the proportion of articles that describe an empirical study. The results of these comparisons are in table 6. These results show that CSE and ICER articles are no different in terms of methodological quality, confirming results reported in Randolph et al. [16]. However, the results of our analysis showed that ICER had a significantly higher proportion of articles describing empirical studies.

7.4 Comparisons between Theory and non Theory groups

After initial analysis, papers were grouped by whether or not they contained theory for the purpose of comparing these groups on other indicators. The intent was to examine whether rigorous use of theory correlated with rigorous methodological practices. The results of these comparisons are in table 7. These results show that articles making use of theory are significantly more likely to describe empirical studies, but all other comparisons show no relationship between theory use and methodological rigor.

7.5 Comparisons between current and previous results

Results of our article analysis were compared to those reported by previous literature reviews. However, a couple of caveats are necessary about how the data was equated between our study and the previous reviews. From Malmi et al. [10], we did not use the total proportion of articles they report as using a TMF, but rather, their reported proportion of articles using a TMF from education and psychology only. The results are in table 8.

For the comparisons with the Randolph et al. results, we calculated the proportions relative to the same reference groups as described in that study, which were different for each indicator. Contrast this to the descriptive results above, which were reported using the whole sample as a reference group. Furthermore, the comparisons to Randolph et al.'s results come with the limitation that our comparison was not identical to theirs. Whereas we focused on the most rigorous CS education journal and conference, Randolph et

al. [16] used a cross section of CS education literature and did not provide results broken out by specific publications. For this reason, the reported differences can be attributed to the effects of differential rigor between publications, as well as changes in the field in the ten years separating our data from the previous study. These results are in table 9.

Lastly, we compared our results to those described in Al-Zubidy et al. [1], which categorized articles from the proceedings of SIGCSE with respect to whether or not they reported on an empirical study. Al-Zubidy et al.'s analysis used the same definition of experimental as used by Randolph et al. [16], so the comparison between our results and theirs are shown as well. These results are in table 10.

With the foregoing qualifications in mind, the results of our comparisons show some areas in which CS education research has changed in recent years. A significantly higher proportion of articles in our sample made use of outside theory than in the results presented by Malmi et al, suggesting that the field is increasingly reaching into other disciplines to frame and interpret studies with respect to previous research in learning theory. The comparison with Randolph et al.'s results shows that significantly fewer articles in our sample presented anecdotal or attitudes only results [16]. This could be the result of our limited breadth of analysis relative to Randolph et al., but results reported in Al-Zubidy, comparing their categorization SIGCSE papers to earlier reviews of SIGCSE papers, support the conclusion that CS education research is moving away from superficial results and more towards empirical results [1]. However, the results on the 'positive' methodological indicators (experimental and qualitative), as well as the 'negative' indicator of single group posttest only designs, show no change from Randolph et al.'s analysis. Furthermore, the prevalence of explicit research questions has increased significantly from the proportion reported in Randolph et al. [14]. One way to interpret these results is that while CS education is moving away from the superficial forms of research that it has been criticized for in the past, researchers have not yet moved towards toward significantly greater use of the more rigorous forms of non-superficial research. The comparison with the SIGCSE results give an interesting indication of the progress of the field as well. Al-Zubidy et al. noted that the proportion of SIGCSE papers reporting empirical results has increased dramatically over time [1]. Our results show that this progress has been substantial enough that the level of empiricism in SIGCSE papers has caught up to that of CSE and ICER. Nevertheless, the comparison of the proportion of experimental articles shows that there is still a gap in at least one indicator of methodological rigor between SIGCSE and the other publications.

8. DISCUSSION AND CONCLUSIONS

This literature review has attempted to give both a current picture of the rigor in CS education research as well as an idea of the trends across previous reviews and the current one. We also wanted to investigate the connections between use of theory and methodological rigor. Our review provides a description of the CS education literature showing that most research being published currently (in the venues we examined) is using theoretical constructs and frameworks drawn from general learning sciences research outside of CS education. This review also shows that a large majority of studies published are empirical. There are no benchmarks

Table 6: Methodological quality comparisons: CSE vs ICER

	test stat	p-value	prop CSE	prop ICER
Articles using Theory	1.92	0.17	0.77	0.66
Empirical articles	4.74	0.03	0.72	0.87
Experimental (Randolph sense) articles	0.69	0.41	0.26	0.19
Qualitative (Randolph sense) articles	0.08	0.77	0.29	0.26
Anecdotal (Randolph sense) articles	0.91	0.34	0.11	0.06
Attitudes only (Randolph sense) articles	1.69	0.19	0.11	0.04
Posttest only (Randolph sense) articles	0.59	0.44	0.21	0.28

Table 7: Methodological quality comparions: Theory vs no-Theory

	test stat	p-value	prop. Theory	prop. no-Theory
Empirical articles	4.34	0.04	0.85	0.70
Experimental (Randolph sense) articles	0.22	0.64	0.21	0.25
Qualitative (Randolph sense) articles	1.68	0.20	0.30	0.18
Anecdotal (Randolph sense) articles	0.00	0.98	0.07	0.07
Attitudes only (Randolph sense) articles	0.04	0.84	0.06	0.07
Posttest only (Randolph sense) articles	0.32	0.57	0.27	0.21

Table 8: Sample vs Malmi et al. (2014)

	Test Stat.	p-val	Sample	Malmi
CSE	27.07	0.00	0.77	0.33
ICER	15.11	0.00	0.66	0.36

Table 9: Sample vs Randolph (2007)

	Test Stat.	p-val	Sample	Randolph
anecdotal	35.23	0.00	0.07	0.38
attitudes	14.64	0.00	0.08	0.31
1 group post	2.48	0.12	0.37	0.49
experimental	2.21	0.14	0.74	0.65
qualitative	0.27	0.60	0.29	0.26
Research Qs	54.41	0.00	0.70	0.19
Empirical	10.14	0.00	0.81	0.66

Table 10: Sample vs Al-Zubidy et al. (2016) SIGCSE results

	Test Stat.	p-val	Sample	SIGCSE
Empirical	1.29	0.26	0.81	0.76
Experimental	9.12	0.00	0.55	0.38

for how much of CS education research should be empirical, but presumably, the greater the number of articles drawing from theory outside the field, the better.

Comparison of our results to the results of previous reviews gives cause for both optimism and further concern about the rigor of research in CS education. The increase in the use of theory from the learning sciences over the past few years is dramatic and demonstrates how quickly the field is developing. The reduction in the number of studies based on anecdotal reports or attitudes only data is a positive indicator of progress as well, as is the observed result that papers published in SIGCSE are also moving in this direction. However, the data on the other methodological indicators suggests that there is still work to be done to advance the rigor of research in CS education. While the superficial forms of CS education research have declined, the move of researchers towards more rigorous qualitative and quantitative designs has not been significant. These results are consistent with the notion that the field is in a gradual evolution. The first step in this evolution was to incorporate more theory from the learning sciences and move away from the less rigorous forms of research. These shifts in the research have served to partially answer the call made in

Almstrum et al [2] for greater use of theory and rigorous methods. Nevertheless, the problem described by Robins [17], that most CS education researchers do not have the formal methodological training for rigorous behavioral science research, explains why the next step in the evolution has not occurred yet. Therefore, the next step in the development of CS education research should be a refinement of methodological approaches towards more rigor.

CS education research has long had concerns about rigor. This review has suggested that progress is being made. There are also important questions that go beyond the scope of this review. Questions raised by Malmi et al. [10] about the development of endemic theoretical constructs and frameworks in CS education remain unanswered. The question of how CS education compares in its rigor to other content area education fields, both now and historically, is also an interesting question for future research. Overall, however, CS education can be expected to continue to evolve methodologically as interest in the field continues to grow and researchers continue to gain more methodological training. Robins' [17] diagnosis of the field appears correct, and his advice for current doctoral students doing CS education work to pursue breadth in reading and methodological training seems to be an appropriate way forward to advance CS education as an increasingly well-developed field.

9. ACKNOWLEDGMENT

Part of this work was supported by the National Science Foundation under grant number 1502462. Any opinions, findings, and conclusions or recommendations expressed in this material are those of the author(s) and do not necessarily reflect the views of the National Science Foundation.

10. REFERENCES

[1] A. Al-zubidy, J. C. Carver, S. Heckman, and M. Sherriff. A (Updated) Review of Empiricism at the SIGCSE Technical Symposium. *Proceedings of the 47th ACM Technical Symposium on Computer Science Education (SIGCSE '16)*, pages 120–125, 2016.

[2] V. L. Almstrum, O. Hazzan, M. Petre, and M. Guzdial. Challenges to Computer Science Education Research. *Computer Science Education*, pages 191–192, 2005.

[3] T. Byrt, J. Bishop, and J. B. Carlin. Bias, prevalence and kappa. *Journal of Clinical Epidemiology*, 46(5):423–429, 1993.

[4] J. W. Creswell. *Research Design Qualitative, Quantitative, and Mixed Approaches*. Sage, Los Angeles, 3rd edition, 2009.

[5] J. W. Creswell. *Educational research: Planning, conducting, and evaluating quantitative and qualitative research*. Pearson, Boston, 4th edition, 2012.

[6] S. Fincher and M. Petre. *Computer Science Education Research*. Taylor and Francis, 1st edition, 2004.

[7] M. Joy, J. Sinclair, S. Sun, J. Sitthiworachart, and J. Lopez-Gonzales. Categorising computer science education research. *Education and Information Technologies*, 14(2):105–126, 2009.

[8] Kirsti Klette. The Role of Theory in Educational Research. In *Norwegian Educational Research towards 2020 - UTDANNING2020*, pages 3–7, 2011.

[9] L. Malmi, J. Sheard, R. Bednarik, A. Korhonen, N. Myller, and A. Taherkhani. Characterizing Research in Computing Education : A preliminary analysis of the literature. *Sixth international workshop on Computing education research*, pages 3–11, 2010.

[10] L. Malmi, J. Sheard, Simon, R. Bednarik, J. Helminen, P. Kinnunen, A. Korhonen, N. Myller, J. Sorva, and A. Taherkhani. Theoretical underpinnings of computing education research. *Proceedings of the tenth annual conference on International computing education research - ICER '14*, pages 27–34, 2014.

[11] J. McMillian and S. Schumacher. *Research in Education: A Conceptual Introduction*. Longman, London, 2000.

[12] R. L. Ott and M. Longnecker. *Ott, R. L., & Longnecker, M. T. (2008). An introduction to statistical methods and data analysis*. Cengage Learning, Chicago, 6th edition, 2008.

[13] P. R. Pintrich and E. V. de Groot. Motivational and self-regulated learning components of classroom academic performance. *Journal of Educational Psychology*, 82(1):33–40, 1990.

[14] J. Randolph, G. Julnes, S. Erkki, and S. Lehman. A methodological review of Computer Science Education research. *Journal of Information Technology Education*, 7:135–162, 2008.

[15] J. J. Randolph. *Computer Science Education Research at the Crossroads: A Methodological Review of Computer Science Education Research: 2000-2005*. PhD thesis, 2007.

[16] J. J. Randolph, G. Julnes, R. Bednarik, and E. Sutinen. A comparison of the methodological quality of articles in computer science education journals and conference proceedings. *Computer Science Education*, 17(4):263–274, 2007.

[17] A. Robins. The ongoing challenges of computer science education research. *Computer Science Education*, 25(2):115–119, 2015.

[18] J. Sheard, S. Simon, M. Hamilton, and J. Lönnberg. Analysis of research into the teaching and learning of programming. *Proceedings of the fifth international workshop on Computing education research workshop - ICER '09*, pages 93–104, 2009.

[19] P. Suppes. The Place of Theory in Educational Research. *Educational Researcher*, 3(6):3–10, 1974.

[20] A. Tellings. Eclecticism and Integration in Educational Theories: A Metatheoretical Analysis. *Educational Theory*, 51(3):277–292, 2001.

[21] D. W. Valentine. CS educational research: a meta-analysis of SIGCSE technical symposium proceedings. *ACM SIGCSE Bulletin*, 36(1):255–259, 2004.

[22] A. J. Viera and J. M. Garrett. Understanding interobserver agreement: The kappa statistic. *Family Medicine*, 37(5):360–363, 2005.

Computer Science Principles: Impacting Student Motivation & Learning Within and Beyond the Classroom

Kara A. Behnke
University of Colorado Boulder
ATLAS Institute, 1125 18th Street
320 UCB, Boulder, CO 80309
Kara.Consigli@Colorado.edu

Brittany Ann Kos
University of Colorado Boulder
ATLAS Institute, 1125 18th Street
320 UCB, Boulder, CO 80309
Brittany.Kos@Colorado.edu

John K. Bennett
University of Colorado Denver
inWorks, 1380 Lawrence St.
Suite 1400, Denver, CO 80204
JKB@UCDenver.edu

ABSTRACT

The Computer Science (CS) Principles framework seeks to broaden student participation and diversity in the field by focusing on the creative and social aspects of computing. As the pilot effort undergoes its early execution phases, this research contributes to the theoretical and practical application of CS Principles. We investigated the impact of CS Principles on student motivation and learning outcomes and sought to determine if the pedagogy created any lasting change on student perceptions of CS as a field of practice.

We report a case study of how CS Principles created an effective framework for introducing undergraduate students to the fundamentals of computer science. We discuss how Self-Determination Theory instantiates Self-Directed Learning, Constructionist, and Connectivist learning theories, which can be used to inform the pedagogical framework. Quantitative and qualitative measures were used to assess the impact of CS Principles on student motivation and learning outcomes, followed by an additional surveying of students one year after the completion of the course.

Results indicate that CS Principles facilitated positive programming experiences for students, helped increase learning interest and improve attitudes of CS as a field of study, positively changed perceptions of CS as a creative practice, and also encouraged students to continue learning CS after the course had finished. In particular, many non-majority students in the course self-reported to having positive changes and attitudes about CS explicitly because of the course. These finding suggest that CS Principles is a step in the right direction for creating more engaging and compelling curricula to diverse groups of students, especially those with minimal experience and exposure in the field. We discuss opportunities for future work using the selected theoretical framework for CS Principles.

Keywords

Computer Science Principles; computational thinking; self-determination theory; self-directed learning; constructionism; connectivism; motivation; learning outcomes.

1. INTRODUCTION

As educators, we want to create meaningful and engaging learning experiences for computer science (CS) students. As researchers, we want to find empirical evidence for what *exactly* fosters meaningful and engaging experiences in the learning process. How should we teach effective and foundational CS skills that students need to succeed in the 21st century, yet provide a meaningful and engaging curricula that appeals to them?

Although the computer science community has labored to increase participation in K-12 education [28, 7] and to create intellectually rich and engaging courses [29, 19, 38, 17, 23, 24, 18, 28, 6], many students, particularly females and students of color, find traditional approaches for learning computer science off-putting, asocial, and boring [25, 4, 16]. Some consider Advanced Placement[1] examinations as a bridge to help students engage and enroll into CS courses in higher education [16]. Although the number of students taking Advanced Placement (AP) CS courses has increased in recent years, the number of students taking this examination is much smaller compared to other science, technology, engineering and mathematics (STEM) AP Examinations [16]. These efforts show that teaching introductory CS on a broad level and in an engaging way, particularly for those with limited exposure or no previous experience in CS, remains a significant pedagogical challenge.

Computer Science Principles is a new AP computer science course designed to introduce students to the central ideas of CS, to instill ideas and practices of computational thinking [40], promote programming literacy and creativity, and to engage students in activities that show how CS impacts and changes the world [5, 3]. CS Principles is intended to help students gain competencies similar to those gained by students completing a university CS course for non-majors [3].

The Computer Science Teachers Association (CSTA) Standards form a basis by which educators can begin to implement a coherent CS curriculum that is available to all students [5], but more work needs to be done in designing, implementing, and evaluating these standards in real-world classrooms [3]. For example, although pilot projects have tested how CS Principles could support different teaching learning approaches and portfolio-based assessments for the AP examination [3], research remains limited on whether students who have taken CS Principles continue to pursue computing by taking additional CS courses, or if they pursue computing in other venues after course completion. In addition, we have limited understanding how different populations undertake and perform in CS Principles, despite its primary goal to broaden participation and diversity in computing [35, 3].

ICER '16, September 08-12, 2016, Melbourne, VIC, Australia.
© 2016 ACM. ISBN 978-1-4503-4449-4/16/09…$15.00.
DOI: http://dx.doi.org/10.1145/2960310.2960336

---

[1] The Advanced Placement (AP) program is a rigorous academic program in the United States that allows high school students to take college-level courses and exams and to potentially earn college credit while still in high school.

Previous work suggests the CS Principles framework can potentially influence student engagement for learning introductory computer science [5, 3]. This research extends prior work by examining the impact of CS Principles on student motivation and learning outcomes while in the classroom and after one-year of course completion. The research questions to be addressed through the study were: (1) *Does Computer Science Principles improve student motivation in learning CS?* (2) *Does Computer Science Principles meet the intended learning objectives of the framework?* (3) *Do these results differ across differing student populations?*

We begin introducing the relevant literature related to CS Principles and learning engagement, detail the theoretical framework and case-study of measuring student motivation and learning outcomes in a CS Principles undergraduate course in the United States, and conclude with a discussion of future opportunities in CS Principles pedagogy.

2. BACKGROUND

In this section we review the current literature on CS Principles pedagogy and its connection to human motivation research and educational research. We explore the application of Self-Directed Learning, Constructionism, and Connectivism into both the design and facilitation of the CS Principles framework.

2.1 Computer Science Principles

Computational thinking [41] captures many important aspects of the work in which computer scientists engage, including using algorithmic approaches to solve challenging problems. Therefore, CS Principles is organized into seven *Big Ideas*[2] with six correlating *Computational Thinking Practices*[3] [5]. The *Big Ideas* represent the fundamental CS skills that are essential to succeed in future college courses and in a variety of computing and STEM careers [5]. The *Computational Thinking Practices* represent foundational computer science theories and practices [5]. The CS Principles framework constructs thirty-five curriculum learning objectives by matching the seven big ideas with the six computational thinking practices [9].

Pilot implementations of CS Principles courses [35, 3], taught at both high school and collegiate levels appear to have positively impacted females and underrepresented students [3], but these pilots differed in structure, breadth, and focus [35]. One possible reason for this is that the CS Principles content, represented by the framework's list of topics and objectives and its broad assertions of desired outcomes, resulted in multiple interpretations by instructors to achieve the learning outcomes [35].

The vision for CS Principles is not a packaged curriculum ready to be taught and administered, but rather a curriculum framework specified by the seven loosely defined big ideas and the six computational thinking practices. Therefore, pilot CS Principles efforts reflect a broad interpretation of the big ideas and computational thinking practices, resulting in substantially different courses [35]. Even though most of the pilot sites reported that students found the curriculum engaging [35], more

evaluation is needed to determine whether students achieved the desired learning outcomes intended for CS Principles.

Pilot efforts have also shown how CS Principles can support different teaching and learning approaches and portfolio-based assessments for the AP examination [3], yet there is limited research on whether students who have taken CS Principles continue to pursue computing by taking additional CS courses, or if they pursue computing in other venues after course completion. Broadening participation and diversity in computer science is a key objective and helped initiate the creation of the CS Principles framework [5, 9], yet more work is needed to determine if there is a meaningful impact on students, particularly for non-majority populations, beyond the course itself. Thus, prior work leaves considerable room to explore other approaches to teaching introductory CS to diverse groups of students and to assess how these approaches may potentially impact their motivation and continued pursuit of CS education.

The primary goal of this research is to examine whether CS Principles impacts student motivation and intended learning outcomes for teaching the fundamentals of computer science. The secondary goal of this work is to explore any potential lasting effects on student learning after course completion. In order to conduct this work, a theoretical lens is needed that brings into focus the disparate ideas of effective CS pedagogy and human motivation research. The conceptual framework needs to (1) frame the pedagogical outcomes that are desirable by the CS education community, and (2) use a theory that is appropriate for the design and implementation of effective motivational learning techniques. As explained below, the conceptual and theoretical framework chosen for this work is Self-Determination Theory [32].

2.2 Self-Determination Theory

Self-Determination Theory (SDT) is an empirically derived theory of human motivation that distinguishes different types of motivation based on the reasons or goals that give rise to an action. The most basic distinction of human motivation is between *intrinsic motivation*, which refers to doing something because it is inherently enjoyable or interesting, and *extrinsic motivation*, which refers to doing something because it leads to a desired outcome [31]. Much theoretical discussion has postulated whether extrinsic or intrinsic motivation is better for learning [31]. SDT postulates there are three universal psychological needs that are essential for optimal human development and functioning—competency, autonomy, and relatedness [31]—and that these can arise due to both intrinsic and extrinsic factors [33].

SDT has shown that people learn more effectively and creatively when they feel competent, autonomous, and related to something bigger than themselves [31]. We present a novel instantiation of autonomy, competency, and relatedness that build upon other learning theories: Self-Directed Learning [20], Constructionism [29], and Connectivism [34]. In the spirit of computational thinking, we present Self-Directed Learning, Constructionism, and Connectivism as a subclass of SDT that inherit *autonomy*, *competency*, and *relatedness*. The relationship of this connection to CS Principles is discussed further in the remainder of this section.

2.2.1 Self-Directed Learning—Autonomy

Autonomy is our innate desire to be self-directed. Autonomy within SDT concerns a sense of volition or willingness when doing a task [31, 21, 32]. When activities are done for interest or

---

[2] Big Ideas: Creativity, Algorithms, Programming, Abstraction, Data and Information, The Internet, and Global Impact

[3] Computational Thinking Practices: Connecting Computing, Analyzing Problems & Artifacts, Developing Computational Artifacts, Abstracting, Communicating Collaborating

personal value, perceived autonomy is high. Ryan et al. [33] argue that, "Provisions for choice, use of rewards as informational feedback (rather than to control behavior), and non-controlling instructions have all been shown to enhance autonomy and, in turn, intrinsic motivation" [33]. SDT thus shows how learning can enhance autonomy when learning provides students with flexibility, choices in how to select tasks and complete goals, and use reward structures to provide meaningful feedback [33]. Self-Directed Learning [20] may also inform ways to design motivational structures into pedagogy.

In this research, we incorporate self-directed learning into the CS Principles framework. We attempt to implement the six principles of self-directed learning into the curriculum and content design. In the case study, students are encouraged to (1) *take initiative* regarding the specific content on which to focus their efforts so that they can (2) take responsibility for their learning by *selecting and assessing* their own learning activities, which can potentially (3) sustain their *motivation* and *volition* because of the emphasis on individual creative interests, and (4) by *setting their own goals*, which are framed carefully in the learning environment in order to (5) help *scaffold* these objectives and skills for students, so that they can (6) create peer-to-peer *collaboration* within their learning communities. In this work, course curriculum is built around these principles in an effort to teach the process of computational thinking by encouraging and facilitating students with "self-directed autonomy" throughout the CS Principles framework.

2.2.2 Constructionism—Mastery

In SDT, competency refers to our innate desire to gain *mastery*[4] of an activity over time, i.e., to get better and better at what we do [31, 10, 32]. SDT further contends that mastery, or the process of gaining competency in self-ability, is essential for education and motivation [31, 32]. Mastery of an activity is challenging, hard work [14, 15], but gratifying through induced flow [10]. Mastery creates the sense of accomplishment and efficacy, which is facilitated by the exercise of one's capacities under conditions of optimal challenge [32]. These elements promote flow [10] by allowing learners to overcome failures and master the material. This work also leads CS educators to employ "learning by doing" pedagogy, particularly through the lens of constructionism.

Constructionism [29], a subclass of constructivist theory [28], posits that learners construct mental models to understand the world around them. In contrast to constructivism, constructionism argues that learning happens most effectively when students are also active in making tangible artifacts in the real world to reflect their understanding of the learned material. Therefore, constructionism has often been used to teach computer science [19, 29]. By actively constructing tangible artifacts to demonstrate understanding, students learn the material through mastery and persistence. Constructionism facilitates computational thinking [8] and computational artifacts through the recursive learning [25] of mastering a challenge.

This research posits that CS Principles incorporate constructionism when students actively construct models, computational artifacts, and computer programs. We use constructionism in this model to facilitate "learning-by-making" [19] in an effort to make CS more personally engaging,

motivating, and meaningful for introductory students [23, 24, 3]. This appears to be an effective approach, since Brown [8] and Wagner [39] argue that innovation-creation and computational thinking can only be effectively learned within iterative constructionism. Having the desire to master something because one finds it deeply satisfying and personally challenging inspires the highest levels of creativity [2], which is a direct goal of the CS Principles [3].

2.2.3 Connectivism—Purpose

Feelings of relatedness to community, or *purpose*[5], is essential for optimal human development and well-being [31]. Relatedness and purpose concern the emotional and personal bonds between individuals. It reflects our strivings for contact, support, and community with others [32]. Purposeful needs are not antithetical to autonomy or mastery; in fact, one often feels most related and purposefully driven to those who are responsive to one's autonomous expressions [31, 32]. When students experience support of their autonomy and feel connected to and supported by others, they are more likely to be highly motivated in the learning process [33]. Students are engaged and motivated in domains where they feel purposefully connected [31, 33], which gives rise to learning theories that enable learning experiences to be conducive toward interrelation and purpose.

Connectivism [34] guides the development of learning materials for the networked world. Connectivist theory asserts that individuals learn and work in a networked environment [34]. As a result, learners do not have control over what they learn since others in the network continually and actively change information, requiring new learning, the unlearning of old information, and relearning current information [1]. However, this "loss of control" does not indicate a loss of autonomy for the learner— rather, connectivists advocate for enabling learners to become autonomous and independent so that they can retroactively acquire information to build a valid, accurate, and current knowledge base [1]. Some of the key intellectual ideas behind digital learning includes connectivism (learning is the connection of people to knowledge), distributed representation (knowledge exists in the network of learners) and negotiated meaning (the meaning of knowledge is negotiated in the network) [12, 13]. Connectivism is fundamentally driven by individuals creating purpose and communal meaning within a network. Therefore, connectivist communities of purpose increasingly play an important role for human motivation and learning.

In summary, under conditions conducive to autonomy, mastery, and purpose, people will likely express their inherent tendency to learn, to do, and to grow. People are engaged and motivated in domains where their basic psychological needs can be fulfilled [32]. These interpersonal processes are fundamental to learning and personal motivation. Self-directed autonomy, constructing mastery, and connectivist purpose thus inform the design and application of this instantiation of Computer Science Principles.

3. METHOD OF STUDY

3.1 Purpose

To answer the three research questions, we conducted a case study [36] within an introductory computer science undergraduate

---

[4] We use "mastery" nomenclature over Ryan & Deci's [31] "competency"; mastery underscores an ongoing process of learning, whereas competency suggests a completed state of experience or being [10].

[5] We use "purpose" as a term for Ryan and Deci's [31] "relatedness"—*purpose* can refer to multifaceted forms of relatedness, rather than just interpersonal connection [32, 11].

course. We used a mixed methods approach that examined both quantitative and qualitative data. We then examined whether results differed across student demographics, gender, etc., and if so, the way in which the results differed. We investigated how CS Principles pedagogy can support self-directed learning, constructionism, and connectivism, while also exploring whether there was a lasting impact of the course on students one-year after the completion of the material.

3.2 Research Design

3.2.1 Site Selection

An introductory CS course intended for undergraduate non-majors was chosen as the site of this case study. This course was historically taught in an interdisciplinary department at a public four-year university in the United States. The course's reputation from previous years—many different majoring students taking the course, and a higher representation of women compared to other introductory CS courses—provided a favorable demographical representation, which matches the theoretical objectives for the CS Principles pilot curricula and the intended research objectives. This introductory CS course was not a required course for any degree or major, although it did offer elective credit for departments in liberal arts and CS programs at the university.

3.2.2 Duration of Study

The duration of the case study was one academic semester (sixteen weeks). One year after the class took place, a follow-up survey was issued to students to measure any lasting effects or impact of the course.

3.2.3 Description of Population

A total of ninety-four students enrolled into the course. Twenty-seven people identified as female (29%). Although the representation of women in the course is not ideal, it is more than double the U.S. national average (12%) of undergraduate CS degree recipients who are women [4].

The ethnic distribution of students enrolled in the course were predominately White (77%). However, non-majority populations were also present, including American Indian or Alaska Native (4%), East Asian or Pacific Islander (11%), Middle Eastern or Central Asian (2%), Latino or Hispanic (4%), and Black or African American (2%). This diversity spectrum of non-majority students is generally similar to those who take AP CS courses in high school [16].

Thirty-four different majors were represented in the course, including majors in dance, film, psychology, mathematics, physics, engineering, biochemistry, neuroscience, political science, architecture, environmental design, among others. Twenty-five students (27%) were undeclared, open-option, or pre-engineering majors. Eleven students (12%) were declared CS majors. Most of the students taking this course were freshman (41%); however, a range of other students also took the course including sophomores to fifth-year seniors.

3.2.4 Implementation

3.2.4.1 Course Website

To facilitate the CS Principles framework, the course had a website with a carefully designed learning-management system (LMS) for the students to use throughout the semester. The course website served as the main platform for students to retrieve lesson materials and to upload their coursework. The course

website was built using WordPress, an open-source content management system that uses HTML, CSS, PHP, and MySQL to manage Web content. The LMS also implemented user-experience mechanics to provide "self-directed learning," "constructionist," and "connectivist" mechanisms through the website. This topic is discussed further below.

3.2.4.2 Course Structure

The undergraduate course used CS Principles to structure the course [9]. A review of the computational thinking practices and their associating big ideas leads to an association of *Connecting Computing* and *Analyzing Problems and Artifacts* with self-directed learning mechanisms, *Developing Computational Artifacts* and *Abstracting* with constructionist-learning methods, and that *Communicating* and *Collaboration* practices with connectivist connections.

Connecting Computing and *Analyzing Problems & Artifacts* encourage self-directed learning, or student autonomy, by encouraging students to "learn to draw connections," to be "creative" in their learning, to "evaluate and analyze their own computational work," and "develop and express their own solutions" to computational problems [5, 9]. The focus on self-development and the freedom of creative expression underscores autonomy. *Developing Computational Artifacts* and *Abstracting* support constructionist learning or help students gain mastery of skills through "learning-by-making." For these computational thinking practices, students learn by "designing and developing interesting computational artifacts," and "develop models and simulations of natural and artificial phenomena," which leads to the "[facilitation of] the creation of knowledge" [5]. Students engage in constructionist learning by modeling and building artifacts, which encourages the student into the construction of knowledge. Finally, the *Communicating* and *Collaborating* practices support connectivist learning by requiring students to "describe computation and the impact of technology and computation" [5]. Students contemplate and communicate purpose, "collaborate on a number of activities" with other students, and promote a sense of relatedness by expressing how "computing has global impact" [5]. The connection and communication with others to create knowledge employs the foundation of connectivism. We used these computational thinking practices, theoretically framed by SDT, to structure the course objectives and intended learning outcomes for the course. These objectives were reflected in the course syllabus, course website, and learning objectives via assigned homework.

3.2.4.3 Course Learning Objectives

The course learning objectives directly correlate to the CS Principles computational thinking practices and big ideas. The computational thinking practices frame the "policy" or larger theoretical implications of the course, whereas the big ideas implement the "mechanisms" to facilitate these practices. Therefore, the curriculum required students to complete six CS Principles by finishing thirty-five laboratory assignments, six online quizzes, a midterm examination, self-reflections on their learning each week, and a final semester project. Each assignment for the course was grounded in self-directed learning, constructionism, or connectivism, and designed to reflect the core affordances of the relevant big idea and computational thinking practice. Students had to complete all laboratory assignments and online quizzes for each computational thinking practice in order to complete that learning objective for the course.

In addition to completing all six computational thinking practices, students had to take a midterm examination, post self-reflections about their learning progress, and complete a semester-long project. Rather than take a final examination, students were required to plan, develop, and submit a semester-long project by the end of the course. The semester project was intended to be broad enough to allow students to express individual creativity, and structured enough so that students produced approximately the same amount of work. The semester project required students to submit a Project Proposal, Digital Artifact (construction of a computational artifact), and Written Report (communicating purpose) of their work. Students also had opportunities to receive extra credit toward their grade by completing extra Labs.

3.3 Theoretical Framework

3.3.1 Self-Directed Autonomy

Self-directed learning was implemented into the curriculum by employing a "self-paced" structure for the course. Each of the six requirements enumerated by [20] was realized in a particular aspect of the course.

Students could choose where to put their efforts, within a hard deadline for all coursework at the end of the semester. In order to facilitate curriculum objectives in a self-paced course, all the course materials and assignments were available on the LMS website during the first week of class. We also implemented *scaffolding* techniques [20] to support student autonomy. This included setting semester-long goals for the students, but allowing enough flexibility for them to focus their efforts onto their own interests. The official learning objectives for the course were: (1) Demonstrate your mastery of six CS Principles, with each Principle requiring you to take an online Quiz for completion; (2) Research and develop a Semester Project; (3) Complete the Midterm Examination; (4) Write self-reflections about your learning experiences throughout the semester on the website Forums or submit privately on the course website.

For example, the semester project was open-ended so that students could focus on a particular topic that was of interest to them. In addition, the requirement for students to self-reflect about their learning experiences by writing about them was a mechanism designed to assess students' individual learning activities, a critical component to self-directed learning. Finally, students were given an opportunity to receive extra for completing additional assignments. Students could independently choose whether or not to complete these additional assignments, just as they could set their own goals by choosing which assignments to focus on first, last, etc.

The course website offered several ways to scaffold and guide student work, while preserving student autonomy.

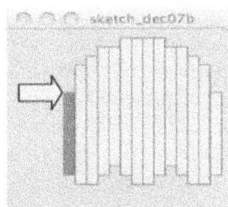

Figure 1. Step-by-step Scaffolding in a Programming Lab.

One of these scaffolding mechanisms was a class schedule with recommended deadlines and objectives on a week-to-week basis. Labs also provided appropriate scaffolding mechanisms to guide the student through the content. This was done by explicitly listing the objectives for that particular assignment, offering step-by-step guidance when appropriate, and by providing hints for the more complex or challenging lessons.

Figure 1 exemplifies how the LMS scaffolds students to complete the "Blinky *Programming* Lab," in which students draw the *Pac-Man©* character, Blinky, using the Processing programming language. Even though the "helpful hints" were provided at the end of the Lab, students could not simply look up the answer or write the code from what they saw on the lesson page. They had to analyze the information given to them, use that information to construct knowledge, and "think computationally" to solve the problem at hand. This scaffolding structure was implemented into every available Lab to help guide the students into taking responsibility for their own learning.

3.3.2 Constructing Mastery

Receiving frequent and relevant feedback on performance is an important process towards mastery. Therefore, we focused on providing students with feedback on the *progress* they made in completing the coursework. When students completed an assignment, they were not given a conventional grade (i.e., a student receiving an "A" or a 3.5 on a 4.0 scale or a 90% mark) but rather were given visual feedback on their progress through the website's user interface (see Figure 2). The website user interface incorporated a "progress bar" that highlighted the student's standing in the completion of course objectives. Figure 2 is a screenshot of the user interface depicting one way that students receive feedback on course progress.

Figure 2. Mastery Feedback for Student Progress.

We chose to provide feedback on course progress so that students can adjust their behavior as needed and know what they need to do next to complete course objectives.

In an effort to prevent cheating, student feedback via the "progress bar" was updated only after the instructor or teaching assistant reviewed and "approved" the lesson submission. This practice allowed the instructor or teaching assistant the ability to "grade" student work, ensuring that students aren't cheating by submitting irrelevant or poor quality work. If student work was not up to standards, they could resubmit until they had mastered the material. This feedback employs the constructionist learning principle of "learning through effort." In addition, many Labs required learners to construct digital artifacts through code or tooling technologies, thus enabling the "constructionist mastery."

3.3.3 Connectivist Purpose

In an effort to create a sense of purpose and social engagement for students, the course website implemented a connectivist framework similar to conventional social media. Students had the ability to create avatars (upload a picture to their profile), update status on an "activity stream," the ability to "friend" other students or make peer-to-peer connections, communicate through private messaging and public chat forums, and even form "groups" to collaborate with specific sets of users.

Bulletin-board systems (BBS), more commonly known as forums, were also implemented into the course website to promote connectivism. BBS functionalities were implemented into the LMS to provide a mechanism for students to collaborate and share. Forums allowed students to post to specific "threads" to organize content. Students could also create private or public "groups" that invited specific people to that microcosm. We chose to implement these social media-like features in an effort to support and facilitate connectivist networks, which may potentially create a sense of purpose for students in the learning environment.

3.4 Instrumentation & Evaluation

3.4.1 Procedures

This case study implemented proxy pre-test and post-test design [30] to test the research questions. Primary data was collected in the form of quantitative and qualitative surveying, student course grades, website metadata, and content analysis. Proxy pre-tests and post-test responses measuring overall student interest in CS were analyzed, and triangulated by qualitative data survey responses.

3.4.1.1 Student Course Grades

Discrete evaluation in the form of course grades[6] were used as one source of quantitative data for analyzing learning outcomes. Student grades resulted in a non-normal distribution, which was skewed in a positive direction. Therefore, non-parametric tests were used to evaluate and analyze the grades as quantitative data. We triangulated student course grades to other qualitative data, since course grades themselves are often too coarse to give meaningful data regarding students' learning.

3.4.1.2 Proxy Pre-Test & Post-Test

Using the Intrinsic Motivation Inventory (IMI) is an established methodological practice for measuring motivation in Self-Determination Theory research [11]. The pre-test and post-test survey used the IMI questions and employed a five-point Likert scale to compute the dependent variable of "student motivation" into an ordinal, interval, and nominal data scales.

The survey instrument also included additional questions beyond the IMI scale in an effort to measure students' familiarity with technology, whether they had studied programming or computer science prior to the course, if they considered CS a creative practice, how they rated their pre- and post-programming skills, etc. These questions were theoretically aligned with IMI and

computational thinking questions in order to determine overall interest, attitudes, and pursuits of computer science. Open and axial coding procedures were used to analyze open-ended questions. Summative and inferential statistics were used to analyze the quantitative questionnaire data.

3.4.1.3 One-Year Follow-up Survey

We conducted a one-year follow-up survey for students who participated in the undergraduate course. This survey was used to assess whether the findings in the pre-test and post-test were reflected in the students' actions or perceptions after the course had completed. For example, itemized questions asked if students continued to learn CS in traditional undergraduate courses, through free online tutorials, in non-traditional forms such as hack-a-thons, etc. The survey was emailed directly to students who had participated in the course the previous year. A total of twenty-six participants responded to the one-year follow-up study (28% response-rate of students whom participated in the course). The evaluation procedures for the follow-up survey were similar to the pre-test and post-test survey, including open and axial coding, and the use of summative and inferential statistics.

3.4.1.4 Content Analysis

Web analytics were collected as a primary metric of quantitative and qualitative observation. Information provided by participants through the website, such as user names, profile avatars, number of visits, number of comments, lesson submissions and time-stamps, among others, were represented through descriptive summaries. In addition, website information was included as part of the qualitative content analysis procedures, which included open coding and axial coding techniques.

3.4.1.5 Threats to Internal Validity

The principal researcher of this work was also the lead instructor for the course. Although the role of a *teacher researcher* [22] is a common methodological process in education research, we recognize that is less common in other fields of research, such as computer science education. Previous work [22] indicates that teacher research offers an opportunity to shape educational practice and to validate, affirm, and improve teachers' personal practice. In addition, the role of a teacher-researcher is arguably less problematic in the context of a case study, since case studies are, by definition, situationally subjective and bounded by time and activity, which is directly dependent on the context of its environment [36]. In this context, the role as teacher-researcher aligns with the case study research strategy.

Because the research site was an undergraduate course, students were not required to participate in the research. As part of the informed consent procedures, we emphasized that students' participation or lack of participation in the research would not affect their course grade. In addition, we did not analyze any research data until after the course had concluded for the semester. We incentivized students to participate in the research by providing them with extra credit towards their final grade for completing any research procedures. Students also had other opportunities to obtain extra credit that were not related to any research procedures (such as completing additional Labs and coursework).

Another potential threat to validity is that the one-year follow-up survey had a low response rate of 27%. Therefore, we recognize that these respondents might be biased, in that students who kept some connection with computing were also more motivated to

---

[6] Although students were not traditionally graded while enrolled in the course, the instructor needed to "convert" students' progress into course grades into the university system at the end of the semester. Final grades were calculated according to how many learning objectives they completed in the course total.

complete the survey. We discuss this in more detail in the Future Work section.

4. ANALYSIS & FINDINGS

Findings from this case study show that CS Principles is an effective framework for introducing students to the fundamentals of computer science. Results from the post-test and the one-year follow-up survey show that many students went on to pursue CS in some capacity. In addition, CS Principles positively influenced student perception of CS and attitudes about the field as a whole. Both quantitative and qualitative data showed that students perceive CS as a creative, socially relevant, and important field of practice.

4.1 Impact on Learning Outcomes

Course grades were used as a measure for the dependent variable "learning outcomes." The majority of students did well in the course, where forty-two students (45%) received A's[7] and 18% of students received B's. Since the CS Principles curriculum seeks to appeal to a broad audience, we used a Spearman's Rho test to measure if there was any correlation between student gender and student grades in the course. The association between grade and gender was found to not be statistically significant; therefore, students in the variable group did not fare better or worse in the course strictly because of gender. This result is received positively, because the CS Principles is intended to appeal to both men and women.

4.1.1 Positive Programming Experiences

Students indicated a "low confidence" score in their programming skills at the beginning of the semester. This was measured by students rating their overall programming experience on a 1-5 Likert scale. 88% indicated they had "no experience" or "little experience" in programming ($\sigma=0.8$); only 12% of students indicated "some experience," and only one student in each course indicated a moderate or high confidence in their programming skills. However, after taking the course, a majority of students moved from "no experience" to "some experience." The value of p is 0.015, which is significant at ≤ 0.05. Therefore, students in the variable group had a meaningful increase in their level of experience for programming after the course, which is a direct goal for the CS Principles framework.

4.1.2 Continuation of Learning CS

The one-year follow-up survey was used to measure whether students would pursue (or did pursue) computing after the course ended. A total of 25 students participated in the one-year post-survey (27%). Of the survey takers, 12 were female and 13 were male. Six students (24%) reported that they had taking additional CS or programming courses at the university in the past year. Without being asked, one student reported that they switched into a CS major specifically because the case study course helped motivated them to do so. Surprisingly, more students reported that they had taken online courses or website tutorials than formal courses at the university. Nine students (36%) reported that they had taken some kind of online learning to continue their pursuit of CS. Students had varying purposes for using the online resources, whether to learn a specific skill or to reach a specific objective,

such as learning how to build a website, learning code to enhance their job skills or future career, or to help supplement their studies for other courses. Lastly, seven students (28%) reported that they continued their pursuit of CS by participating in hands-on learning activities during a workshop, summer internship, etc. This suggests that many students pursue their study of CS but not necessarily through a formal continuation in higher education, even if some did actively choose to change their major as a result of the course.

4.2 Impact on Student Motivation

Our findings indicate that CS Principles positively impacted student motivation in learning computer science. CS Principles increased interest in CS as a field of study, helped students consider CS as a field of practice, facilitated positive programming experiences, and helped encourage students to continue learning CS after the course concluded.

4.2.1 CS Principles Improve Attitude about CS

Emergent categories and themes indicated that students had shifting attitudes about CS as a result of the course. The dominant category most frequently referred to in student open-ended questions were attitudes, knowledge, and definitions of CS. Analysis after coding indicated that 77.3% of students had a positive *attitude* towards CS (either a changed-to-positive or stayed-positive). 57.5% of students had a positive *definition* of CS. In addition, 47% of students had a *positive knowledge identifier* about CS—an example of a positive knowledge identifier would be "I like to build websites." Presumably this student would expect to be good at CS because of this interest and experience in web development. Nevertheless, 53% of students had a *negative knowledge identifier*, a student who assumes that one has to be good at hardware in order to be good at CS, leading to a negative knowledge identifier. There were nearly twice as many students who had a *positive change in definition* of CS than the students who had a *positive same*, or *negative* attitude about CS. Overall, the definition of "computer science" by students was often closely tied with specific knowledge identifiers and student perceptions and attitudes about their own ability and skill level in that knowledge.

4.2.2 Increased Interest in CS as a Field of Study

Students not only improved in their attitude about CS, their interests in CS as a field of study also increased. In the proxy pre-test and post-test survey, IMI survey items sought to measure whether the course increased their interest in CS. To determine if there was an increase in student interest in CS as a result of the course, a Student t-test was conducted between the pre-test and post-test measure of student interest used as part of the IMI scale. The two-tailed p=0.012, indicating a statistically significant difference. Qualitative findings also supported the quantitative data; for example, a female student reported that *"this course made me more interested in computer science and... start doing some computer science in my everyday life. My way of thinking has changed."*

4.2.3 CS as a Creative Field of Practice

One of the key themes of CS Principles is to show students that CS is a creative practice. Students in CS Principles are also expected to demonstrate that creativity through practice. Survey questions sought to measure student's preconceptions about whether they considered CS as a creative practice and whether their exposure to the course changed this perception in some way.

---

[7] The university for this case study uses a five-point grade lettering system, where an A=92-100%, B=83-91%, C=74-82%, D=65-73%, and F=0-64%.

During the pre-test, a majority of students thought that CS was a creative practice (55%), where 12% thought CS was not a creative practice, and 33% were unsure. After taking the class, almost no students were unsure about whether CS was a creative practice or not. The post-test showed a significant increase of students' positive perception, where 96% considered CS to be a creative practice. These data suggest that the content of the course helped shift student perceptions about CS as a creative field of practice. Another t-test was used, where $p=2.52E-05$, which is significant at ≤ 0.05, indicating a significant increase in students' perception of CS as a creative practice. A male student of color reported: *"I realized that my creative approach is actually beneficial to the sciences...it was a class that truly left a lasting impression on me."*

5. DISCUSSION

Findings show that CS Principles had a positive impact on students, indicating that the CS Principles curriculum framework supports student interest and motivation to learn introductory computing. In addition, CS Principles enabled students to consider CS as a creative field of practice, fostered more positive attitudes about CS as a field of practice, and increased the level of interest for students to pursue learning computer science in multifaceted ways. The findings from the follow-up survey also suggest that CS Principles established a strong foundation for students to pursue CS as a tool to support other academic interests. Although some students did change their major, most pursued non-traditional avenues to continue their learning. How they pursued their continuation of learning is nuanced yet persistent; to this end, the course accomplished the overarching goals of the framework. Therefore, CS Principles as a curricular framework for introductory students was observed to be a success in this case study.

5.1 Relevance of Self-Determination Theory

Generally, we found that Self-Determination Theory matched well with the overlying CS Principles framework. Lessons were also learned about the practical application of the subclass theories.

5.1.1 Self-Directed Autonomy

Students' attitudes toward the self-paced nature of the course were bimodal, either strongly positive or strongly negative. Students with positive views appeared to benefit from the self-directed learning, showed a higher degree of autonomy, and performed better (had higher final grades in the course). Students with negative views about the self-directed autonomy argued they needed more extrinsic motivation to keep them on track, such as having a hard deadline for assignments. Students also reported a dislike for the reading and reflection assignments the most, suggesting that the building of artifacts were viewed as more positive learning experiences. Although students reported the scaffolding mechanisms in assignments helped their learning, this suggests that too-much self-direction may not necessarily be beneficial to learning; some constraints can aid in creativity and productivity [2]. Therefore, removing course deadlines does not inherently support self-directed learning or autonomy. We recommend that practical applications of CS Principles incorporate "creative freedom with guidelines."

5.1.2 Constructing Mastery

Overall, constructionist elements in the course were found to enhance the CS Principles curriculum. The course structure also supported constructionism. Most of the students reported that their "best" experiences in the course happened when they were programming and building computational artifacts. Moreover, students appeared to experience aspects of mastery when overcoming challenges and solving difficult learning problems. Some students reported disliking the reading or "textbook" assignments, and commented that these assignments did not align with their goals and expectations for the course, again pointing toward constructionism as an appropriate model for facilitating introductory computing. Other qualitative data indicated constructionist methodologies allowed students the freedom to fail, and demonstrated the importance of feedback, which promoted learning. As one student noted: *"I liked the lack of tests a lot. I also liked how the emphasis of the quest grading was on effort because it made me feel more free to experiment with the coding and make mistakes."* Web-analytics from the course website also show that many students took advantage of redemption. Overall, constructionist elements of the course theoretically and practically matched CS Principles.

5.1.3 Connectivist Purpose

In terms of the more explicit technological connectivist portions of the course—specifically the social media features on the site—the students continuously utilized these options throughout the semester. For example, eight different forums were created by students, with over thirty-five topics in the forum, totaling 318 posts by students. In addition, seven student "groups" were created, averaging eight people per group. These interactions thereby support both the theoretical and practical application of the connectivist community purpose.

Students also reported a positive shift in their attitudes about CS, but more significantly, many students reported the importance and purpose that CS has on society. Most students viewed the course content as valuable and meaningful, beyond the context of the course itself. One student reported: *"This course has made me much more interested in and motivated to continue with CS. I feel like I already know so much more about technology in general, and how crucial it is to global development."*

5.2 Future Work

One limitation in this work is the methodological approach. Implementing the same curriculum within a high school course or additional undergraduate courses would confirm the replicability of CS Principles instantiating Self-Determination Theory. However, similarly to other CS Principles pilots, it is difficult to precisely replicate course curriculum when CS Principles is a broad framework rather. Studies that attempt to replicate previous pilots rather than reimagining them is a recommended next-step.

In addition, since all coursework and student interactions occurred on a website, replicating these efforts into a "distance learning" or online context is a practical extension to this work. Distance learning literature and research, whether it is Massively Online Open Courses (MOOCs) or an online undergraduate course, are often concerned about motivating and sustaining students to complete all of the online learning objectives [34, 1]. The core objectives of CS Principles, as well as the pedagogical flexibility offered by the framework, denote that this course could potentially scale to MOOCs and other distance-learning initiatives. We encourage research and teaching efforts focused on assessing self-directed creative constraints and scaffolding materials in distance learning within CS Principles. In addition, there needs to be more consideration in how to apply situated learning techniques into the context of an online course, particularly in the realm of constructionism and connectivism.

6. REFERENCES

[1] Ally, M. 2008. Foundations of educational theory for online learning. In T. Anderson (Ed.), *The Theory and Practice of Online Learning* (Fifth Edit.). AU Press, Athabasca University.

[2] Amabile, T. M. 1996. *Creativity in Context.* Boulder, CO: Westview Press.

[3] Arpaci-Dusseau, A., Astrachan, O., Barnett, D., Bauer, M., Carrell, M., Dovi, R., … Uche, C. 2013. Computer science principles: analysis of a proposed advanced placement course. In *Proceeding of the 44th ACM technical symposium on Computer science education (SIGCSE '13)* (pp. 251–256). Denver, CO: ACM New York.

[4] Ashcraft, C., Eger, E., & Friend, M. 2012. Girls in IT: The facts. *National Center for Women and Information Technology.* Boulder: University Press of Colorado. Retrieved from NCWIT: https://www.ncwit.org/sites/default/files/resources/girlsinit_t hefacts_fullreport2012.pdf

[5] Astrachan, O., & Briggs, A. 2012. The CS principles project. *ACM Inroads*, 3(June), 38–42.

[6] Behrens, A., Atorf, L., Schneider, D., & Aach, T. 2011. Key factors for freshmen education using MATLAB and LEGO mindstorms. In *ICIRA'11 Proceedings of the 4th international conference on Intelligent Robotics and Applications - Volume Part I* (pp. 553–562). Springer-Verlag Berlin, Heidelberg. Retrieved from http://link.springer.com/chapter/10.1007/978-3-642-25486-4_55

[7] Briggs, A., & Snyder, L. 2012. Computer Science Principles and the CS 10K Initiative. *ACM Inroads*, 3(2), 30–31.

[8] Brown, T. 2008. Design thinking. *Harvard Business Review*, 86(6), 84–92, 141. Retrieved from http://www.ncbi.nlm.nih.gov/pubmed/18605031

[9] College Board. 2014. *AP Computer Science Principles Draft Curriculum Framework.*

[10] Csikszentmihalyi, M. 1990. *Flow: The Psychology of Optimal Experience.* New York: Harper and Row.

[11] Deci, E. L., & Ryan, R. M. 1991. A motivational approach to self: Integration in personality. In R. Dienstbier (Ed.), *Nebraska symposium on motivation*, 38(1), 237-288. Lincoln, NE: University of Nebraska Press.

[12] Downes, S. 2006. *An Introduction to Connective Knowledge.* Creative Commons License. Retrieved from http://www.downes.ca/post/33034

[13] Downes, S. 2012. *Connectivism and Connective Knowledge: Essays on Meaning and Learning Networks.* Creative Commons License. Retrieved from http://www.downes.ca/files/Connective_Knowledge-19May2012.pdf

[14] Duckworth, A. L., Peterson, C., Matthews, M. D., & Kelly, D. R. 2007. Grit: perseverance and passion for long-term goals. *Journal of Personality and Social Psychology*, 92, 1087–1101.

[15] Dweck, C. 2006. *Mindset: The New Psychology of Success.* New York: Ballantine Books.

[16] Ericson, B., & Guzdial, M. 2014. Measuring demographics and performance in computer science education at a nationwide scale using AP CS data. *Proceedings of the 45th ACM Technical Symposium on Computer Science Education (SIGCSE '14)*, 217–222.

[17] Ericson, B., Guzdial, M., & Biggers, M. 2007. Improving secondary CS education: Progress and problems. In *SIGCSE '07 Proceedings of the 38th SIGCSE technical symposium on Computer science education* (pp. 298–301). New York, NY: ACM.

[18] Furst, M., Isbell, C., & Guzdial, M. 2007. Threads™: How to restructure a computer science curriculum for a flat world. In *SIGCSE '07 Proceedings of the 38th SIGCSE technical symposium on Computer science education* (pp. 420–424). New York: ACM.

[19] Kafai, Y. & Resnick, M., Eds. 1996. *Constructionism in Practice: Designing, Thinking, and Learning in a Digital World.* Mahwah, NJ: Lawrence Erlbaum Associates, Inc.

[20] Knowles, M. 1975. *Self-directed Learning: A Guide for Teachers and Learners.* New York: Association Press.

[21] Locke, E. a., & Latham, G. P. 2002. Building a practically useful theory of goal setting and task motivation: A 35-year odyssey. *American Psychologist*, 57(9), 705–717. doi:10.1037//0003-066X.57.9.705

[22] MacLean, M. S., Mohr, M. M., Mohr, M. M., & National Writing Project (U.S.). 1999. *Teacher-researchers at work.* Berkeley, Calif: National Writing Project

[23] Malan, D. J., & Leitner, H. H. 2007. Scratch for budding computer scientists. In *SIGCSE '07: Proceedings of the 38th SIGCSE technical symposium on Computer science education* (Vol. 39, pp. 223–227). New York, NY: ACM. doi:10.1145/1227504.1227388

[24] Maloney, J. H., Peppler, K., Kafai, Y., Resnick, M., & Rusk, N. 2008. Programming by choice: urban youth learning programming with scratch. In *SIGCSE '08: Proceedings of the 39th SIGCSE technical symposium on Computer science education* (pp. 367–371). New York, NY: ACM.

[25] Margolis, J., & Fisher, A. 2002. *Unlocking the computer clubhouse: Women in computing.* Cambridge, MA: MIT Press.

[26] Mitgutsch, K. 2012. Learning through play - A delicate matter: Experience-based recursive learning computer games. In J. Fromme & A. Unger (Eds.), *Computer Games and New Media Cultures* (pp. 571–584). Dordrecht: Springer Netherlands. doi:10.1007/978-94-007-2777-9

[27] Owens, B. B., & Stephenson, C. 2011. *CSTA K – 12 Computer Science Standards.* New York, NY. Retrieved from http://dl.acm.org/citation.cfm?id=2325380

[28] Papert, S. 1980. *Mindstorms: Children, computers, and powerful ideas.* New York, NY: Basic Books.

[29] Papert, S. & Harel, I. 1991. *Constructionism.* Ablex Publishing Corporation.

[30] Rovai, A. P., Baker, J. D., & Ponton, M. K. 2014. *Social Science Research Design and Statistics: A Practitioner's Guide to Research Methods and IBM SPSS Analysis.* Chesapeake, VA: Watertree Press.

[31] Ryan, R. M. & Deci, E. L. 2000. Self-determination theory and the facilitation of intrinsic motivation, social

development, and well-being. *American Psychologist, 55,* 68–78.

[32] Ryan, R. M., & Powelson, C. L. 1991. Autonomy and relatedness as fundamental to motivation and education. *The Journal of Experimental Educational: Unraveling Motivation, 60*(1), 49–66.

[33] Ryan, R. M., Connell, J. P., & Grolnick, W. S. 1993. When achievement is *not* intrinsically motivated: A theory of self-regulation in school. In A. K. Boggiano & T. S. Pittman (Eds.), *Achievement and Motivation: A Social-developmental Perspective.* New York: Cambridge University Press.

[34] Siemens, G. 2005. Connectivism: A learning theory for the digital age. *International Journal of Instructional Technology and Distance Learning, 2*(1), 3–10.

[35] Snyder, L., Barnes, T., Garcia, D., Paul, J., & B. Simon 2012. The first five computer science principles pilots: Summary and comparisons. *ACM Inroads, 3*(2), 54–57.

[36] Stake, R. E. 1995. *The Art of Case Study Research.* Thousand Oaks, CA: SAGE Publications.

[37] Tew, A. E., Fowler, C., & Guzdial, M. 2005. *Tracking an Innovation in Introductory CS Education from a Research University to a Two-Year College.* In SIGCSE '05: Proceedings of the 36th SIGCSE technical symposium on Computer science education (pp. 416–420).

[38] Utting, I., Cooper, S., & Kölling, M. 2010. Alice, Greenfoot, and Scratch – A discussion. *ACM Transactions on Computing Education (TOCE), 10*(4), 1–11. doi:10.1145/1868358.1868364.http

[39] Wagner, T. 2012. *Creating Innovators: The Making of Young People Who Will Change the World.* New York, NY: Scribner.

[40] Wing, J. M. (2006). Computational thinking. *Communications of the ACM, 49*(3), 33–35.

Aspects of Graduateness in Computing Students' Narratives

Sebastian Dziallas
School of Computing
University of Kent
Canterbury, CT2 7NF, England
+44 1227 827684
sd485@kent.ac.uk

Sally Fincher
School of Computing
University of Kent
Canterbury, CT2 7NF, England
+44 1227 824061
S.A.Fincher@kent.ac.uk

ABSTRACT

In this paper, we explore graduates' characterisations of their learning experiences at university and beyond. Using a narrative methodology, we elicited life stories from graduates of the School of Computing at the University of Kent. We initially review and situate our approach within the wide variety of existing narrative approaches. Then, we turn to an aspect of the student experience that struck us as particularly significant: the "year in industry". We discuss the accounts of ten participants who completed a year in industry and highlight their perspectives of the effect it had on them. Finally, we propose a narrative construction of the concept of graduateness – of what it means to complete a university degree.

Categories and Subject Descriptors

K.3.2 [**Computers and Education**]: Computer and Information Science Education – *curriculum, computer science education.*

General Terms

Human Factors

Keywords

Narrative Methods, Qualitative Research, Graduateness, Year in Industry, Turning Points, Boundary Objects

1. INTRODUCTION & GRADUATENESS

"The past and the present live alongside each other in our working lives, overlapping and intertwining, until it is sometimes hard to know where one ends and the other starts." [51]

University reflects a profound time of individual development for people not only in terms of disciplinary knowledge and skills, but also in terms of their personal growth. Research on the specific effects of college has filled volumes; many of these studies are

quantitative in nature and follow a positivist research tradition. [47] Some reports, such as the *Browne review*, have focused on the benefits of higher education in terms of employment opportunities, income, and health outcomes. [9] Other studies have explored claims of university as a means for social mobility. [25, 41, 60]

In the UK, the discussion about the effect of university is often framed in terms of "graduateness". According to Glover et al., graduateness can be "defined as the effect on knowledge, skills and attitudes, of having undertaken an undergraduate degree...." [20] However, the question of *which* attributes should be considered for graduateness has been the subject of many debates. When the UK Higher Education Quality Council released a discussion paper to determine the "attributes of 'graduateness'" in 1996, a particularly exasperated response in the *Times Higher Education* noted: "This is sheer speciousness. ...there are good reasons for challenging the assumption of one immutable model of higher education to which all institutions should aspire." [24] Yet, existing research has largely focussed on an aspirational list of generic capabilities to be achieved by students regardless of discipline. [20] Students are held to have more or less graduateness when measured by generic instruments such as the *Reflective Thinking Questionnaire* and *Motivated Strategies for Learning Questionnaire*. [58] In contrast, for this study, we are interested in students' own conception of their education to capture their characterisations of what it means to undertake a computing degree.

2. METHODOLOGY

2.1 Characteristics of Narratives

In this study, we adopt a narrative methodology. Narrative approaches represent a wide range of practices across different disciplines, and are commonly used in psychology, sociology, anthropology, and oral history. [27, 42] As well as disciplinary diversity, narrative methodologies also reflect different methods: some approaches elicit narratives through interviews (e.g. [39]), while others examine individual speech acts (e.g. [7]), and others again focus on century-old folklore and tales (e.g. [29]). As different approaches conceptualise the terms *narrative* and *story* differently, we first look at existing definitions and establish how we use the terms in our research and throughout this paper.

Although there is little agreement on a canonical definition of the term *narrative* [48], the central feature of a narrative as a series of events being recounted, remains characteristic across domains. Labov, from a sociolinguistic perspective, defines a *minimal narrative* as "as a sequence of two clauses which are *temporally ordered.*" [30] Sarbin, a psychologist, highlights the role of narrative in organizing "episodes, actions, and accounts of actions." [52] And Adler points to an emerging psychological consensus that narratives are "composed of structured reconstructions of events that describe characters and their shifting intentions over the course of time." [1]

The term *story* is sometimes used synonymously with narrative, but there are important differences between the two: a story is a specific form of narrative. Its major events form a *plot* and it generally has a setting and characters, as well as a narrative arc with beginning, middle, and ending. [48] A story can also deploy literary devices, like climax or *dénouement*. The focus of a story lies with the actors, their actions, and the consequences. As Cheryl Mattingly observes, stories "are about someone trying to do something, and what happens to her and to others as a result". [33]

However, certain forms of narrative, whilst chronologically arranged, do not or cannot draw on elements of story in their construction. For example, when writing a diary, the author cannot know what is going to happen next, cannot give additional significance to an event than it has at the time it occurs, and so cannot place events in a dramatic arc. [18] We call such narratives *non-storied*.

2.2 Narrative Analysis

The wide range of narrative approaches and their application in different disciplinary traditions has resulted in an equally wide range of analytic strategies. Figure 1 represents different structural characteristics and analytic approaches to narrative, and situates our work within them. Figure 1 is structured to position narrative artefacts as data and is constructed from the researchers' point of view. We believe this is a useful framing, but also recognize that it necessarily simplifies the considerable variety of work in this area. The approaches mapped in figure 1 do not, for instance, represent categories such as the content and structures of narratives, the act of telling stories, or societal and cultural influences on the stories being told; three axes identified by Holstein and Gubrium that are orthogonal to our mapping. [27]

In figure 1 the horizontal axis delineates characteristics of the narrative artefact itself, from storied to non-storied. At the storied end of the axis are accounts for which interpretive elements such as "the journey" or "turning points" are integral. One example here is the life story (which we discuss in detail below). On the non-storied end of the axis are narrative forms such as diaries.

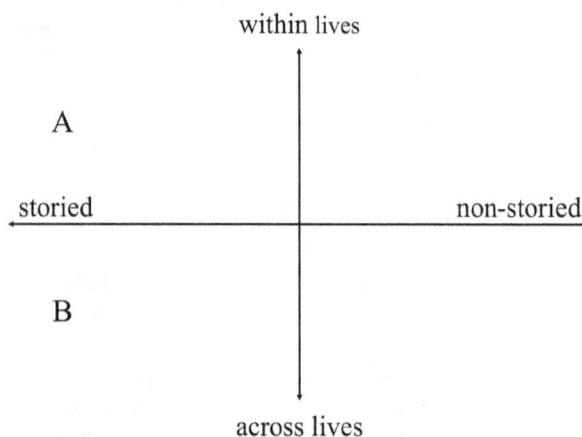

Figure 1. Different Narrative Approaches

The vertical axis does not describe characteristics of narrative accounts, but of their analysis (and so also has epistemological implications). On the one end, analysis is concerned with preserving the individual, specific nature of the material even if researchers may set it in a wider thematic or theoretical context. At the other end, analysis is concerned with finding similar elements across many accounts (lives) which then become data for an argument, a thesis.

We illustrate the quadrants of figure one with examples of different narrative approaches, although the fact that we locate an example in one quadrant does not mean that a researcher is confined there: they may have taken different approaches in other work.

In the top-left quadrant research is concerned with the stories people construct and the larger trajectories those stories contain. For instance, in his work on narratives of craft workers, Elliot Mishler adopts a case-centered approach to explore similarities and differences in individual narratives while maintaining their integrity. [44] He writes:

> "The distinctive feature of this approach, and its fundamental requirement, is that individual trajectories of change are retained through all stages of analyses. Findings, therefore, do not refer to measures of variables aggregated across groups of individuals but to similarities and differences among intra-individual or intra-case patterns of change...." [44]

McCartney and Sanders have employed a similar approach in their report of a longitudinal study of computing undergraduates. They justify their use of the approach by quoting Reed Stevens.

> "Stevens et al. explain their choice of a similarly narrative approach by saying that they want to "get at the whole person's experience ... to recover engineering students moving through their undergraduate educations" and capture "their individual pathways and experiences as engineers-in-the-making." [59, pp. 355-356]" [40]

In contrast, the top-right quadrant focuses on authentic details without necessarily being concerned with larger trajectories. Research in this quadrant is exemplified by the 1940's UK Mass Observation project which, for decades, sent questionnaires to its participants and regularly elicited responses to "day surveys" (in which respondents detailed their activities on the 12th day of each month). The Mass Observation reports provide insight into the individual circumstances of the respondents' lives. Annebella Pollen quotes historian James Hinton, who observes:

> "The more you try to use the writing of individual respondents as a basis for generalisation, the more you are forced to put to one side precisely what it is that MO [Mass Observation] can best reveal: individuals struggling to make sense of their lives. ... Individual subjectivity is always more complex than generalisations about the life of the group. Every person does it differently; and the more one knows about any particular individual, the less they can be used to illustrate some more general experience or theme." [50]

Much of CSEd is engaged with teachers and learners making sense of learning. Colleen Lewis in her microgenetic analysis of student debugging focuses on the individual narrative of one student's engagement with debugging. [31] Rather than following a particular individual, some researchers choose a narrative incident as their focus. Deitrick et al. describe the learning of a pair of middle school students through their non-storied discursive engagement with programming. [15]

In the bottom-left quadrant are approaches that deal with multiple accounts, but accounts which concern themselves with storied reports, made meaningful by the contributor. For instance, Dan McAdams discovered an overarching theme across many life story interviews with adults who showed particular concern for the well-being of the next generation (as described by psychological measures). These adults often told stories containing *redemptive sequences* in which "bad" scenes - that describe negative circumstances - turn out well in the end. [39] As part of this work, McAdams and colleagues operationalised a definition of redemption sequences into a coding scheme which they used to develop more generalizable findings. Yet, as Adler and colleagues observe, work in this quadrant is not removed from the original narratives.

> "Although researchers have developed approaches for streamlining the work, conducting narrative research fundamentally involves a deep immersion in participants' stories, working to tease out their meaning in a valid and reliable way." [2]

Storied approaches are not common in CSEd, but Guzdial and Tew made an explicit examination of storied construction of pedagogic design in their early work on Media Comp classrooms. [21] And Mike Hewner's work investigating how students make course choices relies on the expression of personal and curricula trajectories. [26]

In the bottom right-hand quadrant, researchers gather data from many sources, in a variety of ways, and work to find meaning across them that may not be evident from any single account. Beatrice Webb details this sort of analysis as central to investigation in social science "The simplest (and usually the least fertile) way of expressing the results of an investigation is to follow the strictly chronological order in which the events occur." [61] She describes the necessary work of breaking down narrative data "... to isolate and examine ... its various component parts, and to recombine them in new and experimental groupings." [61] More recently, Teresa Amabile and others gathered and broke apart responses to 12,000 daily questionnaires to predict what events affect the experience and performance of members on project teams. [4] And while Amabile and her colleagues acknowledge differences in how individual study participants experience events at work, their approach relies on collecting a broad sample of "frequent brief reports from many individuals across time." [5] An example of work in CSEd in this quadrant is an extensive study by Lister et al. examining novice programmers' reading and tracing skills. In interviews for that study, students were given a set of multiple choice questions and asked to "think out loud" as they worked to answer the questions. [32] This resulted in a collection of spoken and textual narratives, as Lister and colleagues also captured students' code traces (which they call "doodles"). These narrative fragments are temporally ordered accounts and describe students' actions; but they are, of course, non-storied.

There is an additional aspect to figure 1, which draws on the epistemological element of the vertical axis. Those researchers who work *across lives* (in the bottom half of figure 1) aim to make decontextualized and generalizable statements to establish an objective truth. Methodologically they work to seek, describe and compare quantifiable elements (such as affective, motivational, or integrative themes [2]) across many narratives – and in doing so, habitually devise and apply coding systems and aim for high inter-rater reliability ratings in testing their hypotheses. At the other end of the scale (in the top half) researchers focus on the idiosyncrasies of a life in context in analysis that "deals in human or human-like intention and action and the vicissitudes and consequences that mark their course." [11] Researchers here engage with the individual and particular and are not concerned with an objective "truth" of events, but rather with the sense people make of them. Methodologically, they often rely on the relationship of researcher and subject, the identification of emergent themes, and frequently explore individual cases in detail. Alongside these differences of method and approach, the form that researchers choose to report their work also differs. Researchers in the top half of figure one most often use a *narrative mode* of presentation such as case studies and comparisons. Researchers in the bottom half typically use numeric, or statistical presentations in a *logico-paradigmatic mode*. [11, 49]

2.3 Narrative Identity

In this work, we are concerned with storied narratives. A number of researchers connected the notion of storied narratives to the concept of identity. Hammack, for instance, draws on aspects of cultural psychology and writes:

> "Identity is defined as ideology cognized through the individual engagement with discourse, made manifest in a personal narrative constructed and reconstructed across the life course and scripted in and through social interaction and social practice." [23]

In another model, Sfard and Prusak "equate identities with stories about persons" and write that these stories that form one's identity must be "reifying, endorsable, and significant". [53] In a commentary on their work, Mary Juzwik distinguishes the terms narrative and story and draws on previous research establishing a connection between *identity* and *story* through the concept of the *life story*. The life story reflects who a person thinks they really are and includes narratives from across contexts of their lifetime. [28] Juzwik incorporates this concept into Sfard and Prusak's framework. Rather than viewing a person's identity as a collection of undifferentiated stories, she argues that "reifying, endorsable, and significant" stories become part of a person's life story, which in turn forms one's identity. [28]

The approach we take in this work also focuses on the *life story* (situating it on the storied end of figure 1). However, as with narrative, the term life story also encapsulates different approaches. According to Plummer, a life story is broadly an "account of one person's life in his or her own words." [48] (He describes different kinds of life stories in [48].) In our work, we follow McAdams, who argues that people construct stories to make sense of their lives and integrate these stories into their life story, which is part of their personality. McAdams describes differences in personality through a three-level framework. [38] Broad dispositional traits, such as conscientiousness and neuroticism, form the first level and remain relatively stable over the course of a lifetime. [14] These, however, only provide what McAdams calls a "psychology of the stranger" – a rather generic view of a person. The second level consists of personal concerns, motivations, and goals which are contextualized within time and place and thus change over time. Finally, the third level is the life story. For McAdams, we continually revise the life story as we "weave together the reconstructed past, the perceived present, and the anticipated future". [3] These stories are at the core of who we are and provide the self with unity and purpose. [35]

The emergence of a person's life story is linked to their identity development: younger children between the ages of 5 and 10 – whilst capable of telling coherent stories of single events – do not construct life stories that integrate past, present, and future. [22] By the time they reach high school, however, this has changed. McAdams et al. interviewed college students and found that they were able to tell coherent life stories. In fact, when they interviewed the same students again, they discovered that their life stories exhibited thematic continuity over time. [34]

3. THIS STUDY
We collected life stories from graduates of the School of Computing at the University of Kent (a medium-size public research-focussed, PhD-granting university in the UK) to explore how they make sense of their learning experiences. We recruited participants via email through the alumni office at the University of Kent and invited them to indicate their interest in reflecting on their learning experiences. We then conducted interviews with 35 people who had attended the School of Computing. We used the following prompt, which was originally developed by Dan McAdams as part of his own work on life stories and which we adapted to elicit participants' reflections on their learning experiences. [36] The interviews were then professionally transcribed and pseudonymised.[1]

> I'd like you to think about your learning career, your learning 'life', as if it were a book. Each part of your learning composes a chapter in the book. Certainly the book is unfinished at this point: still, it probably contains a few interesting and well-defined chapters. Please divide your learning 'life' into its major chapters and briefly describe each chapter. You may have as many or as few as you like, but I'd suggest at least 2 or 3 and at most 7 or 8. Think of this as a general table of contents for your book. Please give each chapter a name and describe its overall contents.

These interviews form the basis of a larger study that aims to characterise graduateness in computing education by exploring graduates' individual narratives (located at point A in figure 1). In this paper, however, we chose to explore the experiences of a subset of our participants, as we were struck by a common element in their narratives. For these students the "year in industry" played a significant role in their story. In terms of analysis, in this paper, we aim to make some generalisable statements about graduates' narrative construction of graduateness (located at point B in figure 1). Methodologically, Elliot Mishler notes that working in the positivist tradition loses "… the pattern, form, and structure of trajectories of development" which we are particularly interested to preserve in this work. [44] Pascarella and Terenzini similarly observe that "rendering tone, tint, texture, and nuance [of the college experience] may require the finer brushstrokes characteristic of qualitative approaches." [47] The work we present is here is then distinctly qualitative.

---

[1] We use pseudonyms throughout this paper for both the names of our participants and the companies they worked at. For each participant, we also denote their graduation year next to their name the first time we quote from their interview transcript.

4. CONTEXT: KENT & YEAR IN INDUSTRY
All practice-facing disciplines share educational challenges of how – and how much – to incorporate professional practices into the curriculum, and they vary in their approaches. Medicine (and associated subjects with clinical components, such as Nursing and Dental Studies) will incorporate "clinical rotations", where students go out into hospitals and work within a variety of specialities. Law departments often establish in-house "law clinics" where students work *pro bono* on cases alongside practicing lawyers. Computing's approach has tended to be to interleave industry experience into the curriculum through "fully immersive" experiences [17] where the student leaves the educational environment entirely and works within a professional environment for a period of time. Cooperative placements (a semester in University, a semester in work), internships (a limited-time placement, often during the Summer vacation), or "sandwich" years (the third of four years spent working in industry) are all common models. During these times, students work for and are employed by an external company. In the UK, placement programmes commonly follow the sandwich model.

The placement year program at the School of Computing at the University of Kent was initially established in the mid-1980s. By the early 1990s the "year in industry" was reflected in graduates' degree titles. Changes in the structure of the year in industry program in the late 1990s, when a new head of school hired dedicated staff, led to an increased number of participating students. As a result of these changes, the placement program within the school is unusually strongly structured. [19] The school's dedicated placement office works with students on an individual basis and helps with the preparation of CVs, applications, and with interview practice, gives talks and presentations throughout the curriculum, and visits students during their time on placement. Upon returning from their placement year, students deliver a poster presentation about their work experience to faculty and students in the school. Today, 70% of all students pursuing an undergraduate degree in computing at the university complete a year in industry. [19] The high number of students and the dedicated support mean that there is an expectation from the beginning for students consider a year in industry.

5. CHAPTERS & SELF-SIGNIFICATION
In a comprehensive review of existing studies, Habermas and Bluck identify four types of coherence that provide unity within the psychological construct of the life story: temporal, causal, and thematic coherence, and the cultural concept of biography. [22] The latter accounts for differences in how members of different cultures recall autobiographical memory (e.g. with a focus on the individual or the community). [13] Habermas and Bluck write:

> "Temporal coherence and the cultural concept of biography are used to form a basic, skeletal life narrative consisting of an ordered sequence of culturally defined, major life events. Causal and thematic coherence express the unique interpretative stance of the individual." [22]

That is to say, regardless of the chronological sequencing of events, the way a person constructs connections in their narrative reflects their own perspective and the sense they make of the events being recounted.

Our method of elicitation foregrounds temporal and thematic coherence. Temporally, almost all of the participants divided their "learning life" chronologically into chapters according to the schools and university they attended and the jobs they held. One of them noted explicitly: "So I really saw my chapters just as kind of like stages of school." (Alex Barlow, 2013) For them, each new chapter coincides with, and indeed describes, a transition to a new environment. Others followed a largely chronological order, but include chapters with a particular thematic focus. Table 1, for example, contains the chapter titles from our interview with David Bruce.

Table 1. Chapter Titles for David Bruce

1. Early Experiments	8. The Kindness of Strangers
2. Secondary School	9. Yaveo
3. The Computer Science Degree	10. Going Independent
4. Volunteering with the Student Union	11. Contractor Roles I've Known and Loved
5. Working at Jalia	12. Things I've Learned from Teaching
6. Stuff I Picked Up from the Internet	13. Mistakes I Have Made
7. Little Life Lessons	14. The Future

Summarizing and interpreting stories are two cognitive skills central to the development of thematic coherence. [22] In inviting participants to name the chapters we invite them to express their own interpretation through a form of *self-signification*. David Snowden observes: "I often talk about self-signification as adding layers of meaning for good reason. The content of the narrative is only a part of the meaning that the contributor can supply, the way they interpret is also key." [54] The act of naming then reflects the interpretive stance of the narrator, rather than that of the researcher. [55]

In our study, one participant described his early foray into electronics in one chapter:

> Then ... the next one is going to be, possibly GCSE [secondary education certificate examinations in year 11] and possibly a little bit later where I actually diverged away from computing again. I went into electronics. Because I'd done computing [in school], I couldn't then carry on with it so I went into electronics and really enjoyed that for the next couple of years. ... We just happened to have a teacher [who] ...offered a GCSE. There were about 20 of us that did that. (Joe Stewart, 2012)

Which is easy to read as a positive and productive experience. But when asked to name the chapter, he responded:

> That's ... the diverge away from computing so ... maybe *"a distraction"* or something, I don't know. I went on a slightly different course. (Joe Stewart)

This form of self-signification can reveal meaning participants attribute to an experience beyond its mere description: unlike the term diverge, a "distraction" suggests a negative connotation that was not previously apparent to us as researchers.

As we reviewed the chapter titles, we noted that almost all of the graduates who had completed a year in industry had separated it into a new chapter.[2] In many cases, they were entitled "the placement year" or "working at Jalia". These titles reflect the next step in the temporal sequence of stages during university. But for some graduates, they also indicate the type of experience they had: the kind of company they worked at (for instance, a startup or a small business), the geographic location, or the fact that they returned to the same company post-graduation (in the case of "Jalia Part One or USA").

Table 2. Year in Industry Chapter Titles

The Placement Year	Working at Jalia
The Placement Year of the Startup	Year in Industry
Working for a Small Business	Welcome to the Real World
Applying Computing to Industry	Jalia Part One or USA

Indeed, the terms *placement year* and *year in industry* serve as a catch-all for many different kinds of experiences: the people we interviewed worked at large consulting firms, smaller IT businesses, start-ups, and open source companies – and some of them spent time working in foreign countries. Of course, each of these experiences is different in its own way, but there are also similarities. A year in industry is a transition for everyone who undertakes it. But for some, it forms a more significant part of their life story.

6. EFFECTS & PERSPECTIVES

The effect of the year in industry experience emerged in our interviews with participants, rather than in the individual chapter titles.

> I think to be honest, that the placement year is pretty fundamental for where I am now in my life.... (Nathan Baker, 2013)

For some students, it provided insight into the kinds of work they wanted to do after they graduated.

> Well, it showed me what I *didn't* want to do after I graduated. I was a tester for a small Java company, and although I found it interesting finding the bugs, it wasn't really something that I wanted to go into. (Alice Hayes, 2007)

> People always say, don't they, "A year in industry, that made me decide I definitely wanted to [do x]." ... For me it was, "Yes, I *don't* want to go into industry, certainly not yet." (Joe Stewart)

> It made me realise that start-ups are crazy and that it's a problem when you have no money. You have to go and chase money and what you do doesn't really matter. (Joel Bailey, 2012)

---

[2] Of the two participants who did not do so, one had deliberately not sought new work, but continued previous freelance work during his placement year. And the other spoke more generally in terms of his chapters: "I guess each chapter is marked by a clear end, but in my case, that would be the graduation. So like the beginning of the summer and going into the next, taking a break and then going into the next stage." (Alex Barlow)

There was also a sense that most students returning from their year in industry (though not all, as we discuss below) approached the final year at university in a different manner.

> … and if I hadn't have done that [the year in industry] I dare say I would probably gone down a very different path. Just in terms of how seriously I took that final year and how hard I worked…. (Nathan Baker)

This transformation of attitude was apparent even to students who did not complete a year in industry themselves.

> Quite a few classmates did do that [a year in industry]. In hindsight, now, I wish I had done it. I wish I had done it. The people that you saw, you met them in what would have been their fourth year, my third year, they work *differently*. (Emily Briggs, 2009)

In their study of recent college graduates in their first jobs in software development, Begel and Simon found that "many of the social and communication problems … were rooted in the anxieties of working on a large team with a large, legacy codebase." [8] Our participants spoke vividly of their interactions with these large codebases.

> … having to get to grips with the monstrosities that they have come up with. Because some of this stuff was just insane. Design decisions that no one could agree with. It was just out of this world. (Jake Mason, 2015)

> … then you go to something like this where there's this mess of other people's code, and it *kind of* works, and there are bugs, and you've got to make it do this thing. Yes, overwhelming I guess, was a word that I'd use. (John Warren, 2012)

At the same time, the work they were doing was often under tight deadline. Students were keenly aware of the differences between academic and workplace deadlines and the consequences of missing deadlines in their new context.

> Your time management is so much better. Because if you don't deliver something for your boss on time, then he's going to be fucking pissed. (John Warren)

Part of the experience that participants commented on was their adaptation to the workplace and the development of time management skills which they then employed upon returning to university.

> The first few times it happened – "Oh shit I've got two hours to fix this." And then towards the end you approach it very differently. You don't go into this blind panic of, "Aaargh. Deadlines. Deadlines." No, you sit there, you break it down, you manage your time and you get the job done. (Nathan Baker)

> And so by third year, coming back after a year of working, it just completely changed my mentality. I was like, yes, this just needs to get done. I just need to set out a plan. Work out a weekly schedule, make sure I do the coursework early, and I worked out how much I needed to get in each piece of work to get the grade. (Alex Barlow)

Students also returned to university with newly developed presentation skills and experience of working with others on teams.

> So, after your sandwich year, you give a presentation. I gave a good presentation, because Jalia had trained me in presentation skills. (Nicholas Bradley, 2002)

One graduate, David Bruce, described his good experience of working on a team and how he realised the importance of team roles and good leadership.

> So that was something that I appreciated. The value of a good project manager, as a result of that year in industry and what they can do. (David Bruce, 2006)

He also reflected on the importance of communication skills when working on teams.

> [Before] it was like, "That doesn't matter. I'm a shit-hot programmer. I don't need to care about what people feel." It turns out if you do, and you communicate nicely and respectfully with people, …you get on a lot better in the world. It's a lot easier. Everything goes a lot more smoothly. (David Bruce)

In their work, Begel and Simon observe that "many of the problems they [new college graduates] have typically have a root cause in poor communication skills and social naïveté." [8] The experience David Bruce describes indicates that the year in industry helped him realise the importance of these skills before entering the workforce upon graduating from university.

7. DISCUSSION

7.1 Name & Frame

In reviewing the stories of participants who completed a year in industry, two aspects of their experience claimed our attention. One was the year in industry as a turning point, which marked a significant change in the narrator's life direction. The other was the notion of boundary objects bridging the academic and work environments.

As is often the case in qualitative work of this nature, these were not aspects we were specifically seeking at the outset of our work. Indeed, we noticed them in the interview transcripts before we fully understood them. Star vividly captures a researcher's sense of growing awareness that a particular phenomenon is important:

> "It is a little irritating feeling, kind of a pre-sneeze sensation – and it is also exciting. Learning to trust this message is the toughest lesson I have to teach my students – no less than myself." [56]

Having noticed, we then worked to name the phenomena; this in turn allowed us to locate each within a theoretical frame that provided additional explanatory power. We use them here to discuss graduateness and the year in industry.

7.2 Transitions & Turning Points

In their work, Enz and Talarico describe the difference between *transitions* and *turning points*. [16] The former involve changes in external circumstances; in the words of Brown et al., they "alter the fabric of daily life." [10] For example, relocating to a different city or even country would be considered a transition. In contrast, turning points describe a change in the trajectory of a person's life – they are the "turns in the road". [37] So while, for example, going to university marks a transition for everyone, it only becomes a turning point for some.

Turning points depend on a person's perception of change and the meaning they attribute to an event after it occurred. Thus, turning points only emerge in retrospective reflection. Elliot Mishler calls this the "double arrow of time" which, he writes, "is an inherent and intractable feature of how we remember and continually restory our pasts, shifting the relative significance of different events for whom we have become...." [43] This means turning points are individually constructed and personally meaningful. They may not be reliably identifiable from the outside: identifying a turning point requires the narrator to explicitly establish causal connections between an event and a change in the direction of their life. (As a corollary, if the narrator does not view an event as contributing to a turning point in their life, we may never learn of its effect.)

Other studies have also used transitions as a lens into students' experiences. For instance, O'Shea explores transitions and turning points in the experiences of female first-generation students at university. [45] Palmer, O'Kane, and Owens focus on students' sense of "not belonging" as they transition from home to university. [46] And in a study with psychology students who completed a placement year, Auburn identified two *linguistic repertories*, one referring to the skills they had developed on placement, the other on how academic staff subsequently perceived and valued those skills. [6]

In this study, we coded the interviews for turning points using the two-part definition proposed by Enz and Talarico. [16] First, turning points require a change in a person's life direction. Second, they must refer to a specific episode, rather than an overall period of time.

> "Although perceived turning points may consist of several linked events within a temporally extended unit of time (e.g., college or a trip to another country), one must cite specific episodic experiences within the larger time frame in order to create causal links between the turning point and one's current life direction." [16]

Not everybody experienced the year in industry as a turning point, in fact, using this strict definition, we only found two turning points relating to the year in industry. We did not code several cases where participants described events as turning points, but did not specify a single episodic experience. Some participants for whom the year in industry was a transition identified limited immediate effects for themselves upon returning to their final year in university.

> Interviewer: Did the year in industry at Jalia influence the way, or change the way, you approached university when you came back?

> Respondent: A little. Not much. ... it did influence in ways, but it's a fairly rigid final year, so not so much. (Nicholas Bradley)

> I think in terms of learning, the final year at university was really more of the same.... The final year of uni was the same again, really. (Melissa Bryan, 2006)

For participants for whom the year in industry was a turning point the effect was considerable. For instance, Nathan Baker spoke elaborately of the effect the year in industry had on him. He realized that the practices and theories he had learned at university provided the foundation for the work he was doing on large-scale software applications.

> And that is when I really started to enjoy my programming. Because at uni I was by no means one of the good programmers. Like you have got those few

guys who have been writing code since they could type, and the first year projects for them are just a joke. But that [during the year in industry] is when I started to see myself as an actual programmer who could actually code in Java.... (Nathan Baker)

He also approached his final year differently:

> So I came back to uni and approached it in a very, very different way. Not only would I go to the lectures, I would sit at the front in the lectures. I would sit there making notes in the lectures. I would also go out and actually do that further reading that they recommended, each week whatever we did in the lectures regardless of the module, I would actually go and read the chapters and all the course books. (Nathan Baker)

Both of these excerpts reflect turning points: they each refer to a specific episode in time and describe a significant change in Nathan's life – towards viewing himself as a programmer and in engaging differently with his course at university. More than that, these turning points are connected to the transition of beginning and returning from his year in industry. Enz and Talarico found that these kinds of *transition-linked turning points* are often central to a person's life story. [16] Indeed, Nathan even used the term "turning point" to describe his experience.

> I think it is quite obvious that the big turnaround point is doing that placement year. (Nathan Baker)

7.3 Boundary Objects

We first noticed boundary objects in our interview with David Bruce in which he describes his experience at university before discussing his year in industry. With the exception of a brief reference earlier in the conversation, this is the first time he mentions his placement year in detail.

> ... [at the university] there was a room ... that was the Unix lab. You could get your Unix login and go and log in up there. [There was] this thing which was actually really cool. It was like a thin client thing where you just had this little box.... It would sit vertically next to the desk and there was a keyboard and a display, but it didn't really have any computing power in it itself. All of it was running on a big server somewhere.

> The university didn't issue smart cards, but Jalia did, and I worked at Jalia for a year as a Year in Industry. You had your ID badge which would let you into the building and so on. It had your picture on it, but you put it into the machine and it would bring up your session. You could move it around. ... If you need to go and see somebody over the other side of the building, you can pull out your card and walk over there. (David Bruce)

The smart card here is the object that moves between university and year in industry with different, but related, meanings in the different situations.

> With your smart card, if you're going to London the next day, you pull it out ...and you get on the train in the morning and go up to London and put it in the machine in the London office and your session comes back. You can use all of that there. The smart cards would [all] work in the same way. When you got back

from your year in industry I could do that, and it obviously wouldn't bring back your Jalia session but you could have it in the university. So you could suspend your session and put it back in. (David Bruce)

For David Bruce the talismanic "smart card" does not do the same work in both environments: on returning to university he is not able to use the smart card in the same way, yet it still carries meaning for him, although it is differently expressed in the academic environment. As a boundary object, it accompanies him in both environments and acts as an anchor for one kind of experience within another. His exposure to the infrastructure in the Unix Lab anticipates his experience at Jalia, where he receives his smart card. On his return, he brings his smart card with him: now it does not do the same work, but it echoes his experience on placement year.

Boundary objects do not have to be concrete "things". [57] While David Bruce's smart card is an artefact, we observed an abstract boundary object in the daily routine students establish during their year in industry.

> We worked in different companies, different environments. One of the guys worked in San Francisco in America. We all came back with the same idea. We want the structure so we can enjoy our weekends and we can enjoy the weeknights because we know we have dedicated time to do it in. (Jake Mason)

Upon returning to university, they retained the work patterns from their industrial placements.

> We sat and worked nine until five on our project every weekday. We took weekends off like you would in a real job. It was kind of not wanting to break that routine. (Jake Mason)

For Jake Mason the work ethic he and his team mates bring back from the year in industry is, as they recognise, out of place. After their year in industry, they do not return to student work patterns, but maintain the more highly structured timetable of the work environment.

> The next part would be about my final year, group projects, working in a team of people where we have all come back from placement. We have all got this kind of structure that we want to put in. We don't just want to be typical lazy students that will just sit down and work a bit, watch some telly and work a bit. (Jake Mason)

In this way, the time-management practices become a boundary object that the students carry between the two communities.

According to Star, there are three components to boundary objects: (1) Interpretive flexibility; (2) the structure of informatics and work process needs and arrangements; and (3) the dynamic between ill-structured and more tailored uses of the objects. [56]

For Star and Griesemer boundary objects mark the intersection of communities and mediate meaning between them. [57] In their example, animal skins act as a bridge between the world of fur trappers and the world of museum curators. By examining the object - the animal skin - the curators can be explicit about the things that they value in it (specific named species, undamaged skins). Looking at the skins with them, the curators' values are made apparent to the trappers, who usually work to different ends (monetary reward, ease of hunting, edibility).

Rather than boundary objects sitting between communities, in our work we see boundary objects carried between communities and carrying meaning with them. However, in both our constructions, boundary objects are central to the development of coherence across multiple social worlds. [57] In the stories we collected from graduates, these social worlds are the academic and professional workplace; the boundary objects integrate the experiences of one community within another.

8. CONCLUSION

In their longitudinal study of student transitions at university, Christie and colleagues write that "learning is not just about how students meet the requirements demanded of them at specific points in their academic career, but is embedded in the totality of their prior learning experiences." [12] Graduateness, then, as part of a person's life story, is constantly reconstructed and incorporates learning experiences from the past and present, and beliefs and expectations about the future. In this paper, we propose a narrative construction of graduateness that centres on students' individual experiences and the sense they make of them.

This sort of construction is significant because the value and purpose of an education is not just in the moment, but emerges over time. One of our study participants, Nathan Baker, noted:

> I think the thing that is quite common is that you are always, always learning. … Your vision of what you want to learn can only come from you. What you learned two years ago is probably going to mean nothing to you now but at the same time what you did learn serves... It is like layers isn't it? Where each thing is like a foundation layer for the next thing. And I guess that is something that I think if you look back at everything I have done, each thing provides the underlying layer for the next thing. (Nathan Baker)

In this paper, in the context of using a life story approach as a lens to examine graduateness, we focussed on students' experience of a year in industry. In doing so, two features emerged that illuminate both students' own conceptions of their education and the construction of graduateness more broadly. The first, turning points, indicate a major shift in a person's life. They feature prominently in the life story. Indeed, it would be hard to identify - or experience - turning points outside of storied narrative. The year in industry is a transition for everyone, but a turning point for some. The second feature, boundary objects, promote coherence across social worlds. [57] And as Habermas and Bluck established, coherence (with its four components) is central to the concept of the life story. [22] The year in industry exposes boundary objects as participants' carry meaning between the academic and professional workplace.

For students, the year in industry with its inherent change in external circumstances marks a stark contrast to the university experience. Yet, students return to university after their year in industry, carrying with them their work experiences and the sense they have made of them. This return to the academic world may be a significant quality of the year in industry. From the preliminary work we present here, the year in industry then seems to be a fertile location for the emergence of turning points and boundary objects. Having identified these constructs in this study, it may sensitise us (and other researchers) to see them in wider work to characterise graduateness in computing education.

9. ACKNOWLEDGEMENTS
We are grateful to the anonymous reviewers for their helpful comments.

10. REFERENCES

[1] Adler, J.M. 2012. Living into the story: Agency and coherence in a longitudinal study of narrative identity development and mental health over the course of psychotherapy. *Journal of Personality and Social Psychology*. 102, 2 (2012), 367–389.

[2] Adler, J.M. et al. 2015. The Incremental Validity of Narrative Identity in Predicting Well-Being: A Review of the Field and Recommendations for the Future. *Personality and Social Psychology Review*. (May 2015), 1088868315585068.

[3] Adler, J.M. and McAdams, D.P. 2007. Time, Culture, and Stories of the Self. *Psychological Inquiry*. 18, 2 (Jun. 2007), 97–99.

[4] Amabile, T. and Kramer, S. 2011. *The Progress Principle: Using Small Wins to Ignite Joy, Engagement, and Creativity at Work*. Harvard Business Review Press.

[5] Amabile, T.M. and Kramer, S.J. 2011. Meeting the Challenges of a Person-Centric Work Psychology. *Industrial and Organizational Psychology*. 4, 1 (Mar. 2011), 116–121.

[6] Auburn, T. 2007. Identity and placement learning: student accounts of the transition back to university following a placement year. *Studies in Higher Education*. 32, 1 (Feb. 2007), 117–133.

[7] Bamberg, M. 2004. Form and Functions of "Slut Bashing" in Male Identity Constructions in 15-Year-Olds. *Human Development*. 47, 6 (2004), 331–353.

[8] Begel, A. and Simon, B. 2008. Novice Software Developers, All over Again. *Proceedings of the Fourth International Workshop on Computing Education Research* (New York, NY, USA, 2008), 3–14.

[9] Browne, J. 2010. *Securing a sustainable future for higher education: an independent review of higher education funding and student finance*. Department for Business, Innovation & Skills.

[10] Brown, N.R. et al. 2012. Historically defined autobiographical periods: their origins and implications. *Understanding Autobiographical Memory: Theories and Approaches*. D. Berntsen and D.C. Rubin, eds. Cambridge University Press. 160–180.

[11] Bruner, J. 1986. *Actual minds, possible worlds*. Harvard University Press.

[12] Christie, H. et al. 2016. "It all just clicked": a longitudinal perspective on transitions within university. *Studies in Higher Education*. 41, 3 (Mar. 2016), 478–490.

[13] Conway, M.A. et al. 2005. A Cross-Cultural Investigation of Autobiographical Memory On the Universality and Cultural Variation of the Reminiscence Bump. *Journal of Cross-Cultural Psychology*. 36, 6 (Nov. 2005), 739–749.

[14] Costa Jr, P.T. and McCrae, R.R. 1992. Four ways five factors are basic. *Personality and Individual Differences*. 13, 6 (Jun. 1992), 653–665.

[15] Deitrick, E. et al. 2015. Using Distributed Cognition Theory to Analyze Collaborative Computer Science Learning. *Proceedings of the Eleventh Annual International Conference on International Computing Education Research* (New York, NY, USA, 2015), 51–60.

[16] Enz, K.F. and Talarico, J.M. 2016. Forks in the Road: Memories of Turning Points and Transitions. *Applied Cognitive Psychology*. 30, 2 (Mar. 2016), 188–195.

[17] Fincher, S. et al. 2004. Cooperative education in information technology. *International Handbook for Cooperative Education*. R. Coll and C. Eames, eds. WACE. 111–123.

[18] Fincher, S. 2013. The Diarists' Audience. *Documents of Life Revisited: Narrative and Biographical Methodology for a 21st Century Critical Humanism*. P.L. Stanley, ed. Ashgate Publishing, Ltd. 77–92.

[19] Fincher, S. and Finlay, J. 2016. *Computing Graduate Employability: Sharing Practice*. Council of Professors and Heads of Computing.

[20] Glover, D. et al. 2002. Graduateness and Employability: student perceptions of the personal outcomes of university education. *Research in Post-Compulsory Education*. 7, 3 (Oct. 2002), 293–306.

[21] Guzdial, M. and Tew, A.E. 2006. Imagineering Inauthentic Legitimate Peripheral Participation: An Instructional Design Approach for Motivating Computing Education. *Proceedings of the Second International Workshop on Computing Education Research* (New York, NY, USA, 2006), 51–58.

[22] Habermas, T. and Bluck, S. 2000. Getting a life: The emergence of the life story in adolescence. *Psychological Bulletin*. 126, 5 (2000), 748–769.

[23] Hammack, P.L. 2008. Narrative and the Cultural Psychology of Identity. *Personality and Social Psychology Review*. 12, 3 (Aug. 2008), 222–247.

[24] Harris, R. 1996. Misleading talk of what is a graduate. *Times Higher Education*.

[25] Haveman, R. and Smeeding, T. 2006. The Role of Higher Education in Social Mobility. *Future of Children*. 16, 2 (Fall 2006), 125–150.

[26] Hewner, M. 2014. How CS Undergraduates Make Course Choices. *Proceedings of the Tenth Annual Conference on International Computing Education Research* (New York, NY, USA, 2014), 115–122.

[27] Holstein, J.A. and Gubrium, J.F. eds. 2011. *Varieties of Narrative Analysis*. SAGE Publications, Inc.

[28] Juzwik, M.M. 2006. Situating Narrative-Minded Research: A Commentary on Anna Sfard and Anna Prusak's "Telling Identities." *Educational Researcher*. 35, 9 (2006), 13–21.

[29] Klapproth, D.M. 2004. *Narrative as Social Practice: Anglo-Western and Australian Aboriginal Oral Traditions*. Walter de Gruyter.

[30] Labov, W. 1972. *Language in the Inner City: Studies in the Black English Vernacular*. University of Pennsylvania Press.

[31] Lewis, C.M. 2012. The Importance of Students' Attention to Program State: A Case Study of Debugging Behavior. *Proceedings of the Ninth Annual International Conference on International Computing Education Research* (New York, NY, USA, 2012), 127–134.

[32] Lister, R. et al. 2004. A Multi-national Study of Reading and Tracing Skills in Novice Programmers. *Working Group Reports from ITiCSE on Innovation and Technology in Computer Science Education* (New York, NY, USA, 2004), 119–150.

[33] Mattingly, C. 1998. *Healing Dramas and Clinical Plots: The Narrative Structure of Experience*. Cambridge University Press.

[34] McAdams, D.P. et al. 2006. Continuity and Change in the Life Story: A Longitudinal Study of Autobiographical Memories in Emerging Adulthood. *Journal of Personality*. 74, 5 (Oct. 2006), 1371–1400.

[35] McAdams, D.P. 2001. The psychology of life stories. *Review of General Psychology*. 5, 2 (2001), 100–122.

[36] McAdams, D.P. 1997. *The stories we live by: personal myths and the making of the self*. Guilford Press.

[37] McAdams, D.P. et al. 2001. *Turns in the Road: Narrative Studies of Lives in Transition*. American Psychological Association.

[38] McAdams, D.P. 1995. What Do We Know When We Know a Person? *Journal of Personality*. 63, 3 (Sep. 1995), 365–396.

[39] McAdams, D.P. et al. 2001. When Bad Things Turn Good and Good Things Turn Bad: Sequences of Redemption and Contamination in Life Narrative and their Relation to Psychosocial Adaptation in Midlife Adults and in Students. *Personality and Social Psychology Bulletin*. 27, 4 (Apr. 2001), 474–485.

[40] McCartney, R. and Sanders, K. 2015. School/Work: Development of Computing Students' Professional Identity at University. *Proceedings of the Eleventh Annual International Conference on International Computing Education Research* (New York, NY, USA, 2015), 151–159.

[41] Milburn, A. 2012. *University challenge: how higher education can advance social mobility*. Cabinet Office.

[42] Mishler, E.G. 1995. Models of narrative analysis: A typology. *Journal of Narrative & Life History*. 5, 2 (1995), 87–123.

[43] Mishler, E.G. 2006. Narrative and identity: the double arrow of time. *Discourse and Identity*. Cambridge University Press.

[44] Mishler, E.G. 2004. *Storylines: Craftartists' Narratives of Identity*. Harvard University Press.

[45] O'Shea, S. 2014. Transitions and turning points: exploring how first-in-family female students story their transition to university and student identity formation. *International Journal of Qualitative Studies in Education*. 27, 2 (Feb. 2014), 135–158.

[46] Palmer, M. et al. 2009. Betwixt spaces: student accounts of turning point experiences in the first-year transition. *Studies in Higher Education*. 34, 1 (Feb. 2009), 37–54.

[47] Pascarella, E.T. and Terenzini, P.T. 2005. *How College Affects Students: A Third Decade of Research*. Jossey-Bass.

[48] Plummer, K. 2001. *Documents of Life 2: An Invitation to A Critical Humanism*. SAGE Publications Ltd.

[49] Polkinghorne, D.E. 1995. Narrative configuration in qualitative analysis. *International Journal of Qualitative Studies in Education*. 8, 1 (Jan. 1995), 5–23.

[50] Pollen, A. 2014. Shared Ownership and Mutual Imaginaries: Researching Research in Mass Observation. *Sociological Research Online*. 19, 3 (Aug. 2014).

[51] Rebanks, J. 2015. *The Shepherd's Life: Modern Dispatches from an Ancient Landscape*. Flatiron Books.

[52] Sarbin, T.R. 1986. *Narrative Psychology: The Storied Nature of Human Conduct*. Praeger.

[53] Sfard, A. and Prusak, A. 2005. Telling Identities: In Search of an Analytic Tool for Investigating Learning as a Culturally Shaped Activity. *Educational Researcher*. 34, 4 (May 2005), 14–22.

[54] Snowden, D. 2011. Meaning & the content heresy. *Cognitive Edge*.

[55] Snowden, D. 2011. Naturalizing Sensemaking. *Informed by Knowledge: Expert Performance in Complex Situations*. K.L. Mosier and U.M. Fischer, eds. Psychology Press. 223–234.

[56] Star, S.L. 2010. This is Not a Boundary Object: Reflections on the Origin of a Concept. *Science, Technology & Human Values*. 35, 5 (Sep. 2010), 601–617.

[57] Star, S.L. and Griesemer, J.R. 1989. Institutional Ecology, `Translations' and Boundary Objects: Amateurs and Professionals in Berkeley's Museum of Vertebrate Zoology, 1907-39. *Social Studies of Science*. 19, 3 (Aug. 1989), 387–420.

[58] Steur, J.M. et al. 2012. Graduateness: an empirical examination of the formative function of university education. *Higher Education*. 64, 6 (May 2012), 861–874.

[59] Stevens, R. et al. 2008. Becoming an Engineer: Toward a Three Dimensional View of Engineering Learning. *Journal of Engineering Education*. 97, 3 (2008), 355–368.

[60] Urahn, S.K. et al. 2012. *Pursuing the American Dream: Economic Mobility Across Generations*. The Pew Charitable Trusts.

[61] Webb, B. 1938. *My Apprenticeship (Volume 2)*. Penguin.

Identifying Design Principles for CS Teacher Ebooks through Design-Based Research

Barbara Ericson, Kantwon Rogers, Miranda Parker, Briana Morrison, Mark Guzdial
Georgia Institute of Technology College of Computing
801 Atlantic Drive
Atlanta, GA 30332
ericson@cc.gatech.edu

ABSTRACT

Several countries are trying to provide access to computing education for all secondary students. However, there are not enough teachers who are prepared to teach computer science. Interactive electronic books (ebooks) are a promising approach for providing low-cost professional development in computer science. Over the last four years, our research group has been conducting design-based research by iteratively developing and testing versions of a teacher ebook to help secondary teachers with no programming experience learn to teach an introductory programming course. The interactive elements in the ebook were designed based on research results from educational psychology and are intended to make learning more efficient and effective. Our goals for this effort are to increase teachers' knowledge of computer science concepts and to improve teachers' confidence in their ability to teach computer science. In this paper we summarize our previous work and report on a large-scale study of version two of the teacher ebook. We also recommend several design principles for interactive ebooks for computing teachers based on feedback from teachers, log file analyses, and randomized controlled studies.

Categories and Subject Descriptors

Social and professional topics ~ Computing education

General Terms

Measurement; Design; Experimentation

Keywords

high school teacher professional development; ebooks; electronic books; design-based research

1. GOAL: MORE CS TEACHERS

The United States president, Barack Obama, announced a new initiative in January, 2016, *Computer Science for All [33]*. President Obama declared that computer science "is a new basic skill." In his 2016 State of the Union address, he said that we should offer every student computer science classes. There are similar initiatives in the United Kingdom [8; 9], New Zealand [4; 5] Denmark [10], and other countries around the globe.

The challenge in all of these efforts is to find enough teachers to staff computer science classrooms. Since computer science is not

ICER '16, September 08-12, 2016, Melbourne, VIC, Australia
© 2016 ACM. ISBN 978-1-4503-4449-4/16/09...$15.00
DOI: http://dx.doi.org/10.1145/2960310.2960335

currently considered a core subject in most states in the US, we do not have accurate national records about the availability of introductory computer science courses. We do know that fewer than 10% of high schools in the United States offer the Advanced Placement Computer Science A course, which is equivalent to a college level CS1 course [13]. In New York City, the largest school system in the United States, less than 10% of the high schools have any computer science teacher at all [39].

An effective computer science high school teacher has content knowledge about computer science as well as pedagogical content knowledge (PCK) about how to teach computer science [30]. Our goal for professional development is to increase teacher self-confidence, in addition to increasing content knowledge and PCK. Ni found that teacher self-confidence is a critical factor in getting teachers to pursue further learning in computer science [28]. We know that CS teacher self-confidence about teaching depends greatly on their confidence that they can do the programming needed in their course [30].

In the United States, a new Advanced Placement course and exam is in development, *CS Principles*. A goal for this course (AP CSP) is to broaden participation in computing [1]. In support of that project, we provide free on-line professional development to teachers learning the programming part of CSP. We chose programming because we knew that it was critical for developing teacher self-confidence. We chose to build an electronic book (*ebook*) to provide that professional development freely at scale.

The most important outcome of our project is the design principles that can inform future ebooks for CS teacher professional development. To develop the design principles, we adopted a *design-based research* (DBR) approach. We started with hypotheses based on learning theories, developed the book based on those hypotheses, tested the ebook with real teachers, analyzed the data from the tests, then modified our hypotheses. We used our modified hypotheses to inform re-development of the book, and iterated the cycle. In parallel, we conducted laboratory experiments to test our hypotheses using randomized controlled studies.

In this paper, we describe our process and the design principles that we have generated from our iterations and experiments. We present our arguments for our ebook approach and describe how the features of our ebook are informed by theory about learning and teacher professional development. This paper summarizes the results from our prior studies and presents the new results from a large-scale study of version 2 of the teacher ebook, which was conducted during the spring and summer of 2015.

2. METHODS

We use a *design-based research* methodology to frame our work. Design-based research is an iterative approach to educational research that grew out of the work of Ann Brown, an educational psychologist, and Alan Collins, a learning scientist [7]. The goal of design-based research is to both improve practice and generate or advance theories that transcend the particular context [3]. We are drawing on theories from educational psychology and trying to advance those theories by testing them in actual learning environments. However, we also conduct randomized controlled experiments to validate the hypotheses we generate.

2.1 Why Ebooks

The general problem we are addressing is how to provide professional development opportunities to working (*in-service*) secondary school teachers to prepare them to teach CS. We started our work by asking two questions: (1) what do expert computer science high school teachers do and (2) how do we teach CS within the time limitations of a working teacher.

In our studies of expert CS teachers [15; 28], we realized that the tasks and skills of a high school CS teacher are unlike those of a professional software developer. We found that CS teachers rarely write code. They often help students debug code, and they teach students how to evaluate their own and peer's code [19]. Expert teachers know what students get wrong, how to diagnose those misconceptions, and what activities help students develop a better understanding [32], i.e., pedagogical content knowledge (PCK) [21].

In an interview study of working professionals taking post-graduate CS classes on-line, we found that many learners did not succeed, and for reasons that had little to do with the course itself [6]. We found that learners dropped out of the course because of events in their lives outside of the class, which made it impossible for them to keep up with the pace of the course. The pedagogy of typical CS classes, with a focus on apprenticeship via programming activities, led to unpredictably long work sessions dealing with mundane issues (e.g., "hours because one comma was out of place"). The working professionals from that study are similar to the working teachers we are studying.

Another scalable way to deliver low-cost professional development to teachers is through Massive Open Online Courses (MOOCs). However, MOOCs have had low completion rates, which is problematic when the goal is to prepare teachers to teach a complete curriculum [36]. Effective teacher professional development requires at least 50 hours of effort by a teacher [11]. We need on-line classes that support that much time investment in a structure and pace that allows teachers to fit the learning into their busy lives.

We decided to focus on ebooks as a medium because they can be self-paced. They can also be designed to provide low cognitive-load activities, which are easy to schedule in a busy life (e.g., few confounding syntax errors). We can also provide content to meet the unique needs of teachers, such as pedagogical content knowledge (PCK). Another difference between our ebooks and MOOCs is that our ebooks feature active learning using an *Examples+Practice* approach, which is explained in the next section. Much of the content in MOOCs is delivered via video lectures. A meta-analysis of 225 studies found that active learning lead to better student performance than lecture in STEM fields [17]. Active learning also had a larger effect on female students in male-dominated fields and on disadvantaged students.

2.2 Ebook Features and Educational Psychology Principles

We have presented the design of our ebook in other papers [14; 16], so we present the features at a higher-level here, with a focus on how they relate to the design principles later. The general structure of our ebooks is *Examples+Practice*. We use worked examples to teach computer science and problem solving [38], and we interleave one or two practice activities per worked example as recommended by Trafton & Reiser [40] to focus attention on the worked examples.

Our goal with the Examples+Practice format is to offer efficient and effective instruction that leads to learning across many small chunks of time. We expect the Examples+Practices sets to have lower cognitive load than traditional code writing activities, and that this lower cognitive load will lead to more learning with less time and effort [37]. A frustrating syntax error that takes hours to fix (as we know happens [6; 22]) is inefficient – there is too little learning from a large investment of time. Our hypothesis is that our ebooks will lead to high completion rates with small learning sessions (20 minutes to one hour), which will increase teachers' content knowledge and confidence.

Worked Examples: Most of our examples are in the form of *active code* segments, which are editable, executable code segments. Learners[1] are encouraged to edit these code segments, e.g., to answer a question in a practice problem. Our active code examples include *audio tours* that describe the program using audio narration. Audio tours build on the dual modality principle, that moving explanation from visual text to auditory narration can reduce cognitive load and improve learning [25; 29]. Some of our examples are in the form of a *code lens*, which is an executable code segment that uses Guo's visualization tool [18].

Practice: We have four forms of practice. Two are fairly typical: *multiple-choice* and *fill-in-the-blank questions*. The multiple-choice and fill-in-the-blank questions both offer immediate feedback tailored to the response, i.e., the learner is told more than just "right" and "wrong."

A third form of practice is a *Parsons problem* where learners are given a problem to solve and given a correct program to solve it, but the lines of the program are spread across "refrigerator magnets" which have to be dragged into the right order with the right indentation [12; 16; 20; 31]. Prior research on Parsons problems has shown a notable correlation between scores on Parsons problems and scores on code writing problems [12]. Also, the lowest quartile of students did better on Parsons problems than on code writing or code tracing problem [12], which may mean that solving Parsons problems is easier than writing code. Parsons problems provide feedback by highlighting blocks that are in the wrong place or have the incorrect indentation.

The fourth form of practice is *editing active code* segments. The feedback from this type of practice is Python error messages or the output from execution of the code.

Teacher Notes: The teacher ebook also includes pedagogical content knowledge (PCK) notes to help teachers diagnose student's misunderstandings and learn how to teach the

---

[1] In the ebooks described in this paper, our users are teachers, but in the role of students. We use the generic "learners" when speaking of the teachers learning through our ebook.

programming concepts. For example, one teacher note is a video that explains the student misconception that assigning one variable to another creates a relationship between the two variables, such that any change to one will automatically change the other.

Videos: Unlike MOOCs there aren't very many videos in the teacher ebook. Most of the videos demonstrate student misconceptions.

3. EBOOK ITERATIONS

All design-based research studies involve iterations of development, data gathering, and analysis. In this section, we present summaries from our previous studies and the new results of a large-scale study with teachers using version 2 of the teacher ebook. We also report on the changes we made to version 3 based on the teacher feedback from version 2.

3.1 Early Studies: Teacher Observations

We added interactive content to the ebook "How to Think Like a Computer Scientist – Interactive Edition" and observed teachers working through a chapter of that ebook. We found that the teachers didn't do all of the interactive activities. For example, they rarely watched the videos or listened to the audio tours. One of the teachers mentioned that he had watched some of the videos, but found that they covered the same content as the ebook, so he didn't feel that he needed to watch them. Some of the teachers hadn't even noticed the audio tour button and the book text never mentioned them. This study was described previously [16].

3.2 Early Studies: Log File Analysis of Student Use

A log file analysis of high school and undergraduate student use of the "How to Think Like a Computer Scientist – Interactive Edition" ebook found that most students ran the code, solved Parsons problems and answered multiple-choice questions. Fewer students edited the code, watched the videos, or listened to audio tours. While the teachers that we had observed found the Parsons problems a bit too easy, some students clearly struggled to solve them. This study was also described previously [16].

3.3 Early Studies: Usability Study

Another of our early studies concerned the usability of some of the interactive features of the ebook, which we reported on previously [14]. We tested the usability of the interactive features, active code, code lens, Parsons problems, and multiple-choice questions against those of similar ebooks (Zyante and CS Circles). Most of the teachers in the study preferred the Runestone user interface for all but one of the interactive features (the code lens).

3.4 Version 1: Teacher CSP Ebook

We conducted a pilot study with ten teachers during the spring of 2015 which we reported on in [14]. They worked through the first eight chapters of the first version of the teacher ebook at their own pace. These chapters covered variables, math operators, and assignment. The ebook introduced these concepts in several contexts: numbers, manipulating strings, making a virtual robot turtle move and draw, and modifying the colors of images. This version also contained teacher notes about common misconceptions and other pedagogical content knowledge.

The study participants were asked to take post-tests after every two chapters. They were also asked to answer feedback questions after every two chapters. Most of the teachers reported that they enjoyed the interactive features of the ebook. One teacher wrote, *"I feel like this would be an effective and beneficial tool for*

students and teachers." However, a few of the teachers didn't use the interactive features very much. One of the teachers mostly answered multiple-choice questions (usually incorrectly) – she may have been rushing through the ebook to make the deadline in order to receive compensation for completing the study. Teachers who used more of the interactive features and spent more time in the chapters reported higher confidence in their ability to teach the material. Of the ten participants, five (50%) "completed" the ebook (took all of the post exams) which is a higher completion rate than is typical for MOOCs. However, this was only a small pilot study with only ten teachers, and the compensation likely influenced completion behavior.

3.5 Version 2: Teacher CSP Ebook

We made modifications based on feedback from the pilot study, such as adding a video to show how to solve a Parsons problem, asking the reader to listen to an audio tour, and breaking the chapters into smaller sections. We completed writing the ebook in the early spring of 2015. This version of the ebook contained five parts: computer abilities (chapters 1-2), naming (chapters 3-6), repeating (chapters 7-11), decisions (chapters 12-15), and data (chapters 16-19).

We evaluated this new content in several ways.

- We conducted a large scale study of teachers using the ebook on-line,
- paid a pilot CSP teacher to give us detailed feedback, and
- had a pilot CSP teacher use the ebook with her high school students and both the teacher and her students gave us written feedback.
- We used the ebook in our blended learning (partly on-line and partly face-to-face) professional development. We also made the ebook freely available to other groups offering face-to-face professional development such as the *CS Matters* group in Maryland and *Project Lead the Way.* Two of the teachers who we interviewed were part of blended learning cohorts, and that context seemed to have an influence on their use of the ebook (as seen in section 3.6.4).

3.6 Large-scale Teacher study of Version 2

We recruited teachers by sending email to our list of over 500 teachers who had attending professional development at Georgia Tech in the past. Guzdial announced the availability of the teacher ebook on his blog on April 1, 2015, with a link to more information about the study.

To qualify for the study, participants had to be at least 18 years old, hold a Bachelors degree, and could not have taught Python. Over 200 teachers applied to be part of the study from April to August 2015. While the majority of the teachers were from the United States (75%), teachers also applied from the UK, Spain, Mexico, Australia, England, Scotland, Thailand, Germany, Greece, New Zealand, Canada, France, Russia, The Netherlands, Finland, China, Pakistan, Belgium, Brazil, and the Philippines.

To qualify for the study the teachers also had to score less than 70% correct on the pretest (7 or less questions correct out of 11). The pretest consisted of multiple-choice questions on variables, assignment, conditionals, functions, lists, strings, loops, and mathematical operations. These questions were from a thesis by Juha Sorva that compiled a list of common misconceptions [35]. All multiple-choice questions included the answer "I don't know". Interestingly, several teachers registered for the study multiple times and some of them failed the pretest after passing it the first time. It appears that the teachers were deliberately failing the pretest to gain access to the ebook.

Of the 229 teachers who applied for the study, 130 teachers qualified for the study by scoring less than 70% on the pretest. Of these only 45 (35%) took the first end-of-chapter test (after chapter two) and only five people took the test after chapter 17 as shown in Figure 1.

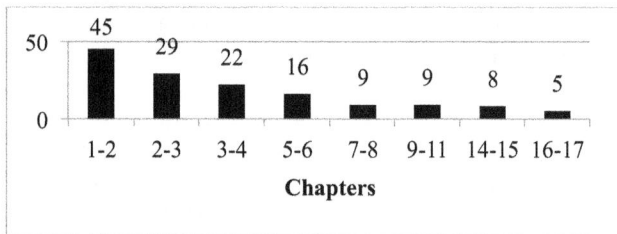

Figure 1 – The number of people who took each of the approximately every two chapter post-tests.

The completion rate for those who took the first post-test (45) to the last post-test (5) is only 11%, which is about the same completion rate as most MOOCs. However, our actual completion rate may have been higher since logging was accidentally turned off during the summer (in late June) when many teachers reported working through the ebook. Several teachers provided feedback via an external website for the later chapters, so we do think the actual completion rate was higher than 11%.

Design-based research recommends mixed methods to evaluate educational interventions and works closely with educators on the design and evaluation of educational interventions. One difficulty we faced was gathering feedback from all of the remote teachers in the study. We prompted teachers to fill out a feedback survey approximately every other chapter. The survey asked what features the teachers found most valuable, what they would change to make the readings more effective, and whether the chapter covered the content well. We initially sent email to teachers who were part of the ebook study to request that they provide feedback when the log file showed that they had completed about every other chapter. In late June we added links to the external feedback surveys directly in the ebook at the end of about every other chapter. Even though we are missing the log file data from late June to fall, we do have teacher feedback on what the teachers found valuable and what should be improved.

3.6.1 Teacher Feedback

Thirty-eight teachers filled out a total of 74 feedback forms during the study. A count of the number of times each feature was mentioned as valuable is shown in Figure 2 below.

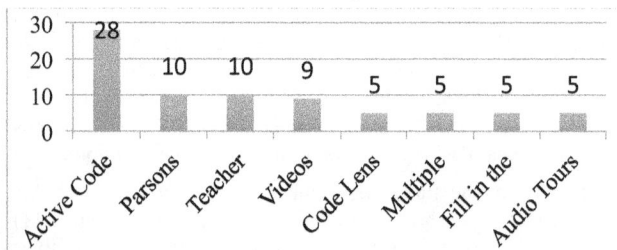

Figure 2– The number of times each feature was mentioned as valuable in the feedback

We computed the number of times each feature was mentioned. Some of the comments mentioned more than one feature. Some comments were vague such as simply mentioning "practice" which we interpreted as all the types of practice problems: multiple-choice, Parsons problems, and fill in the blank.

3.6.1.1 Feedback on the Content

Some teachers commented on the content of the ebook. *"I liked the pace and the quick introduction of turtle and images. Several teachers give general comments: "So far I love the ebook. It is well organized, [has] appropriate links, [and is] not too overwhelming for a new coder."* Another teacher wrote, *"I think the explanations are very clear and easy to understand."*

3.6.1.2 Feedback on the Worked Examples

The active code feature was the feature that was most often mentioned as valuable (28 times) as shown in Figure 2. One teacher commented, *"The interactive code sections (active code) were very helpful. I think my students would benefit from using this format because they are able to see immediately whether their code works and get feedback."* Teachers also appreciated being able to edit the code in the active code feature. *"I really enjoy being able to manipulate the code. I do have some programming experience and it's fun to play with the numbers and watch the outputs change."* Audio tours were mentioned five times. One teacher wrote, *"The audio tours are a great idea. Students hear the vocab being used correctly and can repeat it if necessary."* The code lens, which gave them the ability to step through code and see the values of the variables change, was also mentioned 5 time with one teacher writing, *"Using the code lens tool for tracing was absolutely fantastic."*

3.6.1.3 Feedback on the Practice Problems

One teacher wrote that the most valuable feature was *"The questions that examine your understanding."* Parsons problems were mentioned 10 times, while multiple choice and fill in the blank questions were each mentioned 5 times. Teachers also liked that some of the practice problems required them to modify the example code such as changing the "if" statements to "if "and "else".

3.6.1.4 Feedback on Teacher-Focused Features

The teacher notes were mentioned 10 times. *"It was helpful that you showed the common misconceptions students have with variables. That should help me address those directly as I teach."* Another teacher wrote *"I appreciated the note about the rainfall problem -- anticipating students' struggles and giving us real data about how student perform on the task."* Several teachers mentioned the short videos in the ebook as being valuable. *"Videos are great."* Some teachers appreciated the end of chapter summaries. One teacher wrote, *"I like the key terms provided at the end in the form of a summary review."*

Not all teachers were happy with the ebook. One teacher commented, *"None of it [was valuable]. I already know this stuff."* While we intended this ebook for teachers with no textual programming experience, several teachers had much more experience than we expected of participants in the study.

3.6.1.5 Teacher Suggestions for Changes

Several teachers wanted the ability to write more code in the ebook and thought that some of the examples would be too difficult for beginners. *"Perhaps have the reader write some very simple code along with the examples you already have. If this is for true beginners, some of your examples are going to be total 'Greek' to them, even with the explanations. The current examples may be a bit intimidating."* Some people found errors in the ebook, *"there were a few typos"* or in the user interface, *"Sometimes the audio did not work."* Some teachers found the order of the first two chapters strange. *"The sequence seemed a little goofy to start with coding [in chapter 1] and then go into what a computer can do in chapter 2]."*

Some teachers found particular chapters and/or concepts difficult. One teacher wrote after chapters 7 and 8, *"I think at this point I would like to see MORE examples. This was the first chapter that I felt in over my head. I would have liked to also see examples of a FOR loop and a WHILE loop that does the same thing side by side – so that I could compare the two and see what the differences are. I would like to see a list of CODES LEARNED and what they do, and the proper syntax, after each chapter. That way I would be constantly reviewing both the CODES (Python commands) and the CONCEPTS (vocabulary)."* One teacher suggested that we, *"elaborate [more on the] explanation of functions."* Another teacher wrote *"Chapter 16 [the chapter introducing data analysis] was very difficult."*

Teachers also wanted more *"more quiz questions"* and *"more examples"*, and they wanted more answers to the practice questions to check themselves. *"It would be great if we were given a way to access the answers to different exercises we've done. That way, when we've finished, we can check our work. Or, if we have no idea how to start, we can get an idea of how to begin."* Teachers also asked for hints to help them when they were stuck, especially for the Parsons problems. *"Maybe give more hints when you get things wrong in a drag and drop or a program construction task. I got stuck, didn't know what was wrong - and there was nothing to direct me."*

Teachers also wanted the ebook to cover more of the content of the CS Principles course. It currently covers only two of the big ideas from the CS Principles course: programming and data.

3.6.1.6 Teacher Confidence

Since one of our goals was to increase teacher confidence in his or her ability to teach the content, we were particularly pleased to find evidence of increased confidence. *"I have been told that I will teach Computer Science next year – and I am completely overwhelmed and intimidated – but this course is helping to put my mind at ease."* In a later chapter the same teacher said, *"I feel as if I am slowing adding on to my knowledge of the Python language. It is helpful to 'build' my knowledge."*

3.6.2 Feedback from the Non-Completers

In the fall of 2015 we asked those who hadn't completed the ebook why they did not complete it. Seven of the nine (78%) teachers said that they didn't have time due to other commitments or family issues, as expected from Benda's study [6].

Two of the nine (22%) gave answers based on the content of the ebook. One teacher wrote, *"I found the later lessons/exercises were less relevant to the sort of teaching I deliver in programming."* Another teacher listed the reasons as *"the user interface of the book; redundancy of activities; too much jumbled info on the screen; did not pick up where I left off."* When asked what most needed to be changed two teachers mentioned some way to keep track of where you were, *"It wasn't at first apparent which lessons I had completed, although I know that later this functionality was added."* This functionality was added during the summer of 2015 in response to this feedback.

Other teachers were concerned about the interface. *"I would like to see it look more like an e-zine. Would give it a more professional feel."* Another teacher was frustrated by the lack of help, *"Sometimes if I was stuck I didn't know how to complete a task and there was no help."* Some of the feedback was contradictory with one teacher asking for more videos and another suggested that we *"lose the videos."*

Teachers reported working on the ebook afterschool, in the evenings, and in the summer. The amount of time they reported spending in a session ranged from 20 minutes to 1.5 hours. When asked what would have encouraged them to finish the ebook most of them said more time. They also suggested face-to-face professional development, continuing-education credit, financial incentives, certificates, and feedback on their performance on the assessments.

3.6.3 Feedback from the Completers

In the fall of 2015 we also asked those who had completed the ebook to fill out a survey. We asked how much total time they spent on working through the ebook, and the answers ranged from six to 30 hours with most answering around 10-20 hours. As we mentioned earlier logging was accidently turned off in late June so we can't determine the total time spent from the log files. The reasons for completing the ebook included it being required, wanting to learn the material, trying to prepare for teaching CSP in the fall, and *"I like to finish things."*

When asked what should be added one teacher wanted *"supporting lesson plans."* This teacher was clearly interested in the ebook as a resource for *students*, not for teacher development. *"The ebook is designed so that students can independently work on activities. There needs to be a way for a teacher to hold students accountable for completing the ebook. Are there assignments? Are there quizzes?"* Another teacher wrote, *"Enjoyable. Work[ed] at my own pace. Thought provoking and engaging. I understand CSP and Python better than I did when I began. I could use this to teach in my class if it was possible."* Another teacher wanted, *"more questions in each section and more opportunities to write code."* Asked about the overall experience one teacher reported, *"I thought it was a good experience overall. But I did get very frustrated at certain points because I was not understanding it."*

3.6.4 Interviews with Teachers

To gather more in-depth feedback from the study participants our evaluators interviewed three of the teachers from the United States during the winter of 2016. Each interview was conducted over the phone, lasted between 50-60 minutes, and was audio recorded and transcribed.

Teachers' responses were first sorted into broad coding categories. The coding categories and themes were guided by a set of interview questions and also emerged iteratively from the data. Data analysis proceeded by moving back and forth between individual cases and the more general view across cases. The individual cases were then used as examples of the more general coding categories (similar to the approach used in [30]).

Table 1. Teacher id, experience, motivation, and number of completed chapters

ID	Experience	Motivation	Completed
A	First time teaching CS	May teach CSP in the fall	13 chapters
B	Teaching AP CS A for 10 years	Students want to learn Python for robotics competition	3 chapters
C	Taught an introductory computing course using Scratch	May teach CSP in the fall	8 chapters

Teacher A, had been told to complete a certain number of chapters before her in-person professional development started "I took a Computer Science training class this summer. Before the class started, they asked that we go through this book. They asked us to get to a certain point in the book. I got actually a little bit past where they had asked us to go."

Teacher B was evaluating the ebook as a possible resource. "I tried to sign up for every single course that I possibly could to get me familiarized with the material. So, basically, I've used [the] eBook for more of a resource for me. I'm really still in the process of trying to kind of just figure out what I need for this unit, or whatever it is I need to do for my courses."

Teacher C reported that she had signed up for several professional development opportunities at the same time and stopped working with the ebook when the workload became too much, "I thought I could do both... the CSP Mobile [and] CSP Python. So, I was also in the CSP Mobile Course while I was doing the Python. Then I stopped taking the Python [eBook] course."

Interestingly, all three teachers used the eBook at school. They worked between 30 and 60 minutes at a time. When asked how they used the ebook, all three of the interviewed teachers mentioned reading the text, completing the practice items (multiple choice, fill-in-the-blank, and Parsons problems), and completing the end of chapter tests. One teacher said that even though she was asked to edit the code and use the code lens to step through code, she didn't do that. "I would do all the questions just to make sure I understood it. I didn't really play around with the code that much, which in retrospect, I think ... would have been better if I did. Like... you could run the code. Then they said you could change things and play with the code. But I really didn't. That was more of a time thing. ... I did not use the code lens that often... I understood what I was doing and I didn't need it".

Teacher B mentioned using the metaphors from the eBook in her computing class and that the eBook helped her generalize computing concepts. "I found the different metaphors for a variable that I can use for teaching for Python or for any other language. The computer's contents are taught in such a way that it's not just I'm learning Python. I'm also learning computer concepts and how to teach them and apply them to any language." She also said, "I think everything was useful. I really do. I really like this eBook."

All three teachers reported that the ebook contributed to their knowledge of and confidence in teaching CS. Teacher C was asked how much the ebook contributed to her confidence and she replied, "Quite a bit really. I mean, I probably would have been lost without it. When I took the professional development workshop and was introduced to the ebook at the beginning, I really was lost." She mentions feeling that professional development instructors were initially "talking above my head." However, she says that the ebook offered her scaffolds to better understand the face-to-face professional learning: "I mean, I know that sounds awful, but it was just like overwhelming. Then as I went on throughout the summer and I took some other courses and as I was exposed to ebook, I could understand things."

Teacher A wanted more opportunities to write code from scratch. "I still think it would have been more helpful if in sections they would have prompted me to write my own code and me have to figure it out, or if I get stuck, be able to contact someone and say, 'I can't get this code to work.' That kind of thing instead of just always answering the multiple-choice questions or doing the drop and drag (Parsons problems)."

All three teachers mentioned that they plan to return to the eBook in the future.

3.6.5 Feedback from CSP Pilot Teachers

For more detailed feedback, we paid a CSP pilot teacher in Georgia to review the teacher ebook, which she did in the spring of 2015. She found errors in the ebook, told us where she thought we needed more exercises or better descriptions, and also suggested adding answers for some of the more difficult practice problems to reduce frustration for teachers who were new to programming. These changes were done to version 2 in June before our in-person teacher professional development at Georgia Tech.

Another pilot CSP teacher in Georgia used version 2 of the teacher ebook with her students and gave us feedback on which chapters needed additional information. She said, "I loved the data unit at the end." She made specific recommendations on additional material that should be added to particular chapters. For example, she asked that the chapter on strings include a note to highlight the fact that printing a variable prints the value of the variable and printing a string prints the exact characters in the string. She also recommended more content for some of the introductory chapters based on how she was using the ebook with her students in class.

3.6.6 Log File Analysis

We conducted an analysis of the log file from before logging was accidently turned off in late June of 2015 to gather more evidence about how the teachers actually used the interactive features.

Figure 3 below shows how many of the teachers, who completed a particular section of chapter three (on the use of variables with numeric values), did each of the interactive activities in the section. The largest number of teachers (66) used the first code lens (black) and a large number also ran the first code (blue) using the active code feature. However, use of these features mostly decreased from the beginning to the end of this section. A large percentage (77%) of the teachers watched the videos (purple), attempted Parsons problems (73%) (green), and answered multiple-choice questions (74%) (gold). The number of teachers who used these last three features remained fairly steady over the course of this section. However, only 7 (11%) to 11 (16%) of the teachers listened to the audio tours (red), even though this chapter explicitly directed the reader to listen to one of the audio tours.

Table 2: Color to Activity Legend for Figure 3

Black	Code lens
Blue	Active Code Run
Gray	Active Code Edit
Red	Audio Tour
Gold	Multiple Choice Question
Green	Parsons Problem
Purple	Video

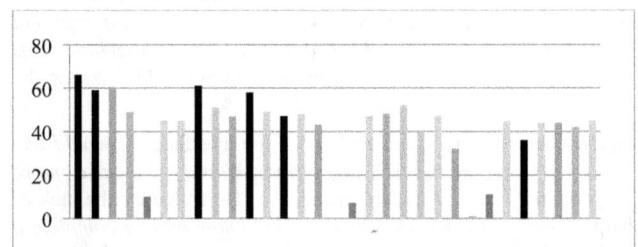

Figure 3. Num. who did Each Activity in Part of Chapter 3

The number of unique teachers who did each of the activities in chapter 10 (Repeating Steps with Turtles) appears in Figure 4. The analysis shows that most of teachers ran the active code (blue), solved Parsons problems (green), and answered multiple-choice questions (gold). As seen before, very few teachers edited the code, except for the fifth active code in the chapter, which would not run until the user edited the code. In this chapter only 1-2 (6% to 11%) of the teachers listened to the audio tours.

One of our questions was, "How much do teachers actually engage with code in the ebook?" Consistent with teacher self-report (Figure 2), log file data shows that most teachers ran the code. Surprisingly, few teachers actually *edited* the code, even when they were directed to by the ebook. One of the teachers that we interviewed said that she answered the questions and if she got those correct, she didn't feel the need to actually edit the code. Some teachers reported the code lens visualizer as being very valuable in their feedback. However, one of the interviewed teachers said she didn't bother using the code lens since she already understood the code.

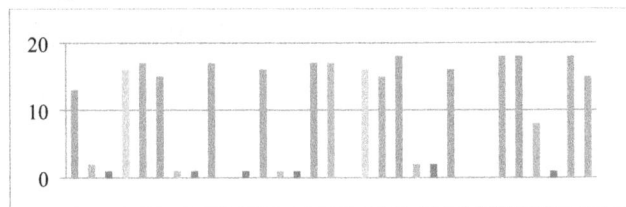

Figure 4. Unique Users who did Each Activity in Chapter 10

Some teachers listened to the audio tours as a supplement to reading the program code and did report finding them valuable in their feedback surveys. However, the log files show that the audio tours are not used as much as running the code and doing the practice activities. However, audio tours may particularly help new computer science teachers by modeling how to talk about code.

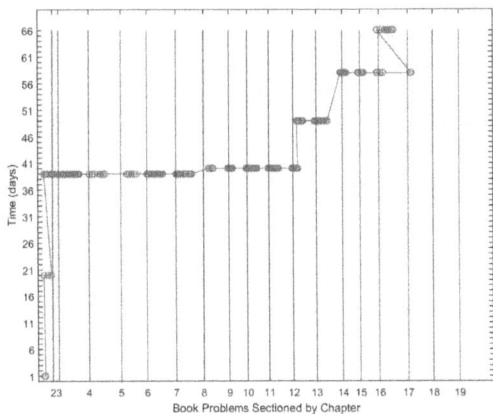

Figure 5. Teacher A's progression through the ebook

We reviewed how one of the teachers who we interviewed progressed through the ebook for additional insight into her behavior. Figure 5 shows numbered days of the study on the vertical axis, and the sequence of activities in the book (by chapter) horizontally, with a mark for each activity attempted. The teacher started with a few interactions in chapter 1, then about 20 days later did a few more actions in chapter 1 and then about another 20 days later she began to work through the ebook more consistently. She then had some long sessions working through many chapters in the same session. As she said in her interview, she was told to work through a certain number of chapters before

her in-person professional development, which may be why she suddenly seemed to focus on completing many chapters quickly.

3.7 Version 3: TeacherCSP Ebook
We ended the teacher study in September of 2016. Based on the feedback from the teachers we added the following.

- End of chapter summaries of the Python functions

- Additional material to the chapters of the ebook that teachers had pointed out as needing more examples and better explanations. For example we added a side-by-side comparison of a **while** and **for** loop, and additional examples using **while** loops.

- We added 10 end-of chapter exercises, even though that broke our *Examples+Practice* format. We added at least one exercise per chapter that required the teacher/student to write all of the code from scratch. Each of the exercises included the answer in a separate tab. An additional tab was added with a link to a discussion forum so that teachers could discuss the question.

Also in response to teacher requests, we released a companion student ebook in the fall of 2015 that has the same content, but removes the answers and pedagogical content knowledge notes. We are pleased to note that several of the teachers from the teacher study used the ebook with their high school students during the 2015-2016 academic year. They have also told us that they intend to use it again next year.

We haven't analyzed the data from version 3 of the teacher ebook yet. However, we are pleased that some of the teachers from the version 2 teacher study have continued working with the version 3 teacher ebook.

4. DESIGN PRINCIPLES
The design principles listed here are the ones that we have the most confidence in based on our multiple iterations, teacher observations, teacher feedback, teacher interviews, log file data analyses, and laboratory experiments. Evidence from the ebook iterations and experiments supports our belief that building upon educational psychology design principles is the right first step in developing our ebooks. However, we still don't completely understand what makes learning in computer science challenging. We cannot assume that the educational psychology principles will work as predicted. We have to test, and sometimes modify our approach, because of the unique challenges of learning computing.

4.1 Use Worked Examples + Practice
The teacher feedback provides evidence that the teachers appreciated the interactive nature of the ebook with worked examples in the form of active code or code lens paired with multiple-choice, fill in the blank or Parsons problems. The log file analysis shows that the majority of the teachers ran the examples and did the practice problems.

4.1.1 Use Subgoal Labels
As we started this project, a collaboration with Psychology professor Richard Catrambone and Ph.D. student Lauren Margulieux led to studies supporting the belief that subgoal labeling of worked examples facilitated student learning, retention, and transfer [24]. A follow-up experiment showed that the effect was twice as strong for teachers as for participants drawn from the undergraduate psychology pool [23]. Morrison

continued the experiments and showed that the subgoal labeling effects extended to C-like textual languages [27].

It can be challenging to invent good subgoal labels, as has been noted in the literature on worked examples [2]. We do not use subgoal labeling on all examples. We do not use the *same* subgoal labels on all program examples. When we do use them, we use them consistently across a chapter.

Morrison and Margulieux investigated different ways of using subgoal labels (e.g., giving students the labels compared with asking students to fill in the blank to construct subgoal labels) on program examples. Their results were contrary to the results predicted by previous literature [40]. They hypothesize that the implicit cognitive load of program understanding was so high that it swamped different uses of subgoal labeling (which might also explain the modality results). When they used a more sensitive learning measure in their subgoal labeling experiment (based on Parsons problems), they got results that matched the educational psychology predictions [34].

4.1.2 Use Low-Cognitive Load Practice Problems
Evidence from the teachers' feedback and the log file analyses show that teachers are using the low-cognitive load practice problems. Parsons problems, in particular, were mentioned as being valuable 10 times in the feedback, compared to five times for multiple choice or fill in the blank questions. Log file analysis also shows that Parsons problems were used as much as the multiple-choice questions and running code and far more than editing code. The most recent set of experiments also support the belief that Parsons problems have lower cognitive load than the same practice problem as a code-writing activity, and that subgoal labels also improve performance on Parsons problems [26].

4.1.3 Maybe Provide Audio Tours
Morrison attempted to measure the benefits of audio tours in an experiment where she compared textual, auditory, and combined text plus narration explanations of program code. However, she found no difference between the three conditions. Another experiment in the research literature also failed to find a difference between modality conditions on explanations of program code [34]. However, feedback from the teachers provides evidence that at least some teachers found the audio tours valuable. Yet, the log file analysis showed that only a small percentage of teachers actually listened to the audio tours. Audio tours are probably most beneficial for the teachers who have not taught programming before.

4.2 Provide lots of content
The teacher feedback included many requests for more content. They want more examples, more exercises, and more coverage of the CS principles course. They want answers to all the practice problems and exercises. In addition, teachers also asked for external resources such as lesson plans, quizzes, pacing guides, and project ideas.

4.3 Provide what teachers expect
Part of the answer to what teachers need is not about cognition, but about teacher expectations.

- Teachers wanted end-of-chapter exercises, even if our theoretical framework recommends pairing Examples+Practice. We recommend providing end of chapter summaries of both the computing concepts and Python procedures and functions covered in the chapter. Teachers explicitly asked for this and several teachers mentioned the concept summaries as being useful.

- Part of what we are testing with our ebook is how much programming teachers can learn and how much we can improve their confidence in their ability to teach programming *without* requiring them to do significant amounts of programming. However, teachers studying computer science expect to program, and some expect to code from scratch.

We ignore these requests at the risk of losing participation.

4.4 Support teachers understanding code
Reading and understanding programs is a challenging task, especially for novices. It's also an important task since it's one of the most common activities of expert CS teachers [30]. The teacher feedback shows that teachers found the code lens and audio tours useful for improving their understanding of code. Evidence from controlled experiments also shows that subgoal labels improve learners understanding of code.

4.5 Save teachers time
Teachers don't have a great deal of time for professional development. They often work in relatively small chunks of time. Add features to save teachers time.

- Provide a way to mark a section as completed and a way to return a teacher to where he or she was last.

- Break the material into chapters and sections. Make each section short enough to allow a teacher to complete it in 15-20 minutes, which makes it easier to fit into the day and to schedule.

- Provide answers for all the practice problems to help reduce teacher frustration and to scaffold teachers with no prior programming experience.

5. LIMITATIONS
Since logging was accidently turned off from late June till fall 2015, we don't have all the data from the teachers' use of version 2 of the ebook. In particular we don't have the end of chapter tests for many of the teachers who worked through the ebook, so we can't comment on how much the teachers learned from using the ebook. In addition, we are basing some of our recommendations on teacher feedback, however we only received feedback from thirty-eight teachers.

6. CONCLUSIONS
The teacher feedback and interviews serve as an existence proof that an Examples+Practice ebook approach (versus a MOOC-based, or in-class coding-centric approach) can achieve our goal of greater teacher self-confidence. We do not yet know how to design so that *all or most* teachers come away with increased self-confidence.

The contribution of this paper is a set of design principles that others can use when developing interactive ebooks for computer science teachers. We have presented evidence to support using a worked examples plus practice approach. The ebook provided worked examples using the active code and code lens features, and practice problems using multiple-choice, Parsons problems, and fill-in-the-blank questions.

7. ACKNOWLEDGMENTS
This material is based on work supported by the National Science Foundation under Grant No. 1432300. Any opinions, findings, and conclusions or recommendations expressed in this material are those of the authors and do not necessarily reflect the views of the National Science Foundation.

8. REFERENCES

[1] Astrachan, O., Briggs, A., Diaz, L., and Osborne, R.B., 2013. CS principles: development and evolution of a course and a community. In *Proceedings of the Proceeding of the 44th ACM technical symposium on Computer science education* (Denver, Colorado, USA2013), ACM, 2445382, 635-636.

[2] Atkinson, R.K., Derry, S.J., Renkl, A., and Wortham, D., 2000. Learning from Examples: Instructional Principles from the Worked Examples Research. *Review of Educational Research 70*, 2, 181–214.

[3] Barab, S. and Squire, K., 2004. Design-Based Research: Putting a Stake in the Ground. *The JOURNAL OF THE LEARNING SCIENCES 13*, 1, 1-14.

[4] Bell, T., Andreae, P., and Lambert, L., 2010. Computer Science in New Zealand high schools. In *Proceedings of the Proceedings of the Twelfth Australasian Conference on Computing Education - Volume 103* (Brisbane, Australia2010), Australian Computer Society, Inc., 1862223, 15-22.

[5] Bell, T., Andreae, P., and Robins, A., 2014. A Case Study of the Introduction of Computer Science in NZ Schools. *Trans. Comput. Educ. 14*, 2, 1-31.

[6] Benda, K., Bruckman, A., and Guzdial, M., 2012. When Life and Learning Do Not Fit: Challenges of Workload and Communication in Introductory Computer Science Online. *Trans. Comput. Educ. 12*, 4, 1-38.

[7] Brown, A.L., 1992. Design experiments: Theoretical and methodological challenges in creating complex interventions in classroom settings. *Journal of the Learning Sciences 2*, 2, 141-178.

[8] Brown, N.C.C., Kolling, M., Crick, T., Jones, S.P., Humphreys, S., and Sentance, S., 2013. Bringing computer science back into schools: lessons from the UK. In *Proceedings of the Proceeding of the 44th ACM technical symposium on Computer science education* (Denver, Colorado, USA2013), ACM, 2445277, 269-274.

[9] Brown, N.C.C., Sentance, S., Crick, T., and Humphreys, S., 2014. Restart: The Resurgence of Computer Science in UK Schools. *Trans. Comput. Educ. 14*, 2, 1-22.

[10] Caspersen, M.E. and Nowack, P., 2013. Computational thinking and practice: a generic approach to computing in Danish high schools. In *Proceedings of the Proceedings of the Fifteenth Australasian Computing Education Conference - Volume 136* (Adelaide, Australia2013), Australian Computer Society, Inc., 2667214, 137-143.

[11] Darling-Hammond, L., Wei, R.C., Andree, A., Richardson, N., and Orphanos, S., 2009. Professional learning in the learning profession. *Washington, DC: National Staff Development Council*.

[12] Denny, P., Luxton-Reilly, A., and Simon, B., 2008. Evaluating a New Exam Question: Parsons Problems. In *Proceedings of the International Computing Education Research Conference* (Sydney, Australia2008), ACM.

[13] Ericson, B. and Guzdial, M., 2014. Measuring demographics and performance in computer science education at a nationwide scale using AP CS data. In *Proceedings of the Proceedings of the 45th ACM technical symposium on Computer science education* (Atlanta, Georgia, USA2014), ACM, 2538918, 217-222.

[14] Ericson, B., Moore, S., Morrison, B., and Guzdial, M., 2015. Usability and Usage of Interactive Features in an Online Ebook for CS Teachers. In *Proceedings of the Proceedings of the Workshop in Primary and Secondary Computing Education* (London, United Kingdom2015), ACM, 2818335, 111-120. DOI= http://dx.doi.org/10.1145/2818314.2818335.

[15] Ericson, B.J., Guzdial, M., and Mcklin, T., 2014. Preparing secondary computer science teachers through an iterative development process. In *Proceedings of the Proceedings of the 9th Workshop in Primary and Secondary Computing Education* (Berlin, Germany2014), ACM, 2670781, 116-119. DOI= http://dx.doi.org/10.1145/2670757.2670781.

[16] Ericson, B.J., Guzdial, M.J., and Morrison, B.B., 2015. Analysis of Interactive Features Designed to Enhance Learning in an Ebook. In *Proceedings of the ICER* (Omaha, NE, USA, August 09-3, 2015 2015), ACM. DOI= http://dx.doi.org/http://dx.doi.org/10.1145/2787622.2787731.

[17] Freeman, S., Eddy, S.L., Mcdonough, M., Smith, M.K., Okoroafor, N., Jordt, H., and Wenderoth, M.P., 2014. Active learning increases student performance in science, engineering, and mathematics. *Proceedings of the National Academies of Science 111*, 23, 8410-8415

[18] Guo, P.J., 2013. Online python tutor: embeddable web-based program visualization for cs education. In *Proceeding of the 44th ACM technical symposium on Computer science education* ACM, 579-584.

[19] Guzdial, M., 2015. Learner-Centered Design of Computing Education: Research on Computing for Everyone. *Synthesis Lectures on Human-Centered Informatics 8*, 6, 1-165.

[20] Helminen, J., Ihantola, P., Karavirta, V., and Malmi, L., 2012. How Do Students Solve Parsons Programming Problems? - An Analysis of Ineraction Traces. In *Proceedings of the International Computing Education Research Conference* (Aukland, New Zealand2012), ACM, 119-126.

[21] Hubwieser, P., Magenheim, J., M, A., #252, Hling, and Ruf, A., 2013. Towards a conceptualization of pedagogical content knowledge for computer science. In *Proceedings of the Proceedings of the ninth annual international ACM conference on International computing education research* (San Diego, San California, USA2013), ACM, 2493395, 1-8.

[22] Jadud, M.C., 2006. *An exploration of novice compilation behaviour in BlueJ*. University of Kent.

[23] Margulieux, L.E., Catrambone, R., and Guzdial, M., 2013. Subgoal labeled worked examples improve K-12 teacher performance in computer programming training. In *Proceedings of the 35th Annual Conference of the Cognitive Science Society*, 978-983.

[24] Margulieux, L.E., Guzdial, M., and Catrambone, R., 2012. Subgoal-labeled instructional material improves performance and transfer in learning to develop mobile applications. In *Proceedings of the ninth annual international conference on International computing education research* ACM, 71-78.

[25] Mayer, R.E. and Moreno, R., 1998. A split-attention effect in multimedia learning: Evidence for dual processing systems in working memory. *Journal of Educational Psychology 90*, 2, 312.

[26] Morrison, B.B., Margulieux, L.E., Ericson, B., and Guzdial, M., 2016. Subgoals Help Students Solve Parsons Problems. In *Proceedings of the Proceedings of the 43rd ACM technical symposium on Computer Science Education* (Memphis, Tennessee2016).

[27] Morrison, B.B., Margulieux, L.E., and Guzdial, M., 2015. Subgoals, context, and worked examples in learning computing problem solving. In *Proceedings of the eleventh annual International Conference on International Computing Education Research* ACM, 21-29.

[28] Morrison, B.B., Ni, L., and Guzdial, M., 2012. Adapting the disciplinary commons model for high school teachers: improving recruitment, creating community. In *Proceedings of the ninth annual international conference on International computing education research* (Auckland, New Zealand2012), ACM, 2361287, 47-54. DOI= http://dx.doi.org/10.1145/2361276.2361287.

[29] Mousavi, S.Y., Low, R., and Sweller, J., 1995. Reducing cognitive load by mixing auditory and visual presentation modes. *Journal of Educational Psychology 87*, 2, 319.

[30] Ni, L., 2011. Building professional identity as computer science teachers: supporting secondary computer science teachers through reflection and community building. In *Proceedings of the seventh international workshop on Computing education research %@ 978-1-4503-0829-8* ACM, Providence, Rhode Island, USA, 143-144. DOI= http://dx.doi.org/10.1145/2016911.2016942.

[31] Parsons, D. and Haden, P., 2006. Parson's programming puzzles: a fun and effective learning tool for first programming courses. In *Proceedings of the 8th Australasian Conference on Computing Education* (Hobart, Australia2006), Australian Computer Society, Inc., 1151890, 157-163.

[32] Sadler, P.M., Sonnert, G., Coyle, H.P., Cook-Smith, N., and Miller, J.L., 2013. The influence of teachers'   knowledge on student learning in middle school physical science classrooms. *American Educational Research Journal 50*, 5, 1020-1049.

[33] Smith, M., Computer Science for All. , https://www.whitehouse.gov/blog/2016/01/30/computer-science-all, Accessed 2016, July 13

[34] Solomon, H.M., 2005. *The effect of audio narration in computer-mediated instruction on procedural fluency by students of varying reading levels*. Florida State University.

[35] Sorva, J., 2012. *Visual program simulation in introductory programming education*. Aalto University.

[36] Spradling, C., Linville, D., Rogers, M.P., and Clark, J., 2015. Are MOOCs an appropriate pedagogy for training K-12 teachers computer science concepts? *J. Comput. Sci. Coll. %@ 1937-4771 30*, 5, 115-125.

[37] Sweller, J., 1988. Cognitive load during problem solving: Effects on learning. *Cognitive Science 12*, 2, 257-285.

[38] Sweller, J. and Cooper, G., 1985. The Use of Worked Examples as a Substitute for Problem Solving in Learning Algebra. *Cognition and Instruction 2*, 1, 59-89.

[39] Taylor, K. and Miller, C.C., De Blasio to Announce 10-Year Deadline to Offer Computer Science to All Students, http://www.nytimes.com/2015/09/16/nyregion/de-blasio-to-announce-10-year-deadline-to-offer-computer-science-to-all-students.html, Accessed 2016, July 13

[40] Trafton, J.G. and Reiser, B.J., 1993. The contributions of studying examples and solving problems to skill acquisition. In *Proceedings of the Proceedings of the 15th Annual Conference of the Cognitive Science Society* (Hillsdale, NJ1993), Lawrence Erlbaum Associates, Inc., 1017–1022.

With a Little Help From My Friends: An Empirical Study of the Interplay of Students' Social Activities, Programming Activities, and Course Success

Adam S. Carter and Christopher D. Hundhausen
Human-centered Environments for Learning and Programming (HELP) Lab
School of Electrical Engineering and Computer Science
Washington State University
Pullman, WA 99164 USA
+1 509-335-6602
cartera@wsu.edu, hundhaus@wsu.edu

ABSTRACT

Computing education researchers have become increasingly interested in leveraging log data automatically collected within computer programming environments in order to understand students' learning processes and tailor instruction to student needs. While data on students' *programming activities* has been positively correlated with their learning outcomes, those data tell only part of the story. Another part of the story lies in students' *social* activities, which, according to social learning theory, can also be predictive of students' learning outcomes. In order to gain further insight into how computing students' learning processes influence their learning outcomes, we present an empirical study that explores the interplay of students' social activities, programming activities, and course outcomes in an early computing course. By analyzing log data collected through a programming environment augmented with a social networking-style activity stream, we found that answers to questions posed through the activity stream were positively correlated with students' ability to make programming progress, and their eventual success in the course. Based on our findings, we present recommendations for the design of pedagogical environments to support a more social programming process.

Keywords

Learning analytics, Predictive models of student performance and achievement, Educational data mining, Activity streams, Social networking.

1. INTRODUCTION

In recent years, the ease with which learning process data can be collected, coupled with the availability of low-cost, high-power machines to store and process such data, has led to an explosion in the field of learning analytics [29]. Computing education researchers, for instance, have collected data on students' programming processes, and have used those data to identify programming difficulties and how they are resolved [2]. Similarly,

researchers have created predictive models that relate students' programming behaviors to course outcomes [1, 7, 27]. While these models have achieved only modest predictive power, they do pave the way toward a future in which computing educators, with minimal effort and involvement, can leverage continuous updates on individual student learning processes and achievement.

Even though programming activities figure prominently in learning success, any approach that attempts to predict student success based solely on programming activities may overlook other factors critical to students' success or failure. For example, according to social learning theory, it makes sense to consider students' *social activities*: how they interact with their peers during the programming process. Indeed, past research provides evidence that a student's social behavior is a significant predictor of learning outcomes in computing courses [12]. This suggests that a broader picture of student achievement might be obtained by examining the *interplay* of a student's social behavior and programming activities.

In an effort to observe students' social and programming behaviors as they work on course programming assignments, we have developed a *social programming environment* (SPE), which augments a traditional IDE with features commonly found in social networking software [8]—most prominently, an activity stream in which students can asynchronously communicate about their ongoing programming activities. Our SPE provides an empirical foundation for studying the interplay of social behavior, programming behavior, and student achievement in computing courses. As a starting point for such an investigation, we propose three basic research questions:

RQ1: What kinds of programming questions do students pose within an SPE?

RQ2: How does programming behavior influence social behavior and vice versa?

RQ3: What is the relationship between students' social participation and course grades?

In this paper, we present an empirical study that uses log data collected within our SPE to address these questions. We found that students who pose questions, receive a suggestion, and make a follow-up post were significantly more likely to have made positive progress towards correct programming solutions. Furthermore, the scores received for programming solutions produced by these students were significantly more likely to exceed the class average.

ICER '16, September 08-12, 2016, Melbourne, VIC, Australia
© 2016 ACM. ISBN 978-1-4503-4449-4/16/09…$15.00
DOI: http://dx.doi.org/10.1145/2960310.2960322

Our study makes two key contributions to the computing education literature. First, while others have studied the relationship between students' programming activities and course outcomes, this paper presents the first-ever empirical study that uses automatically collected log data to explore the interplay between students' programming activities, social activities, and course outcomes. As such, it presents a more rounded attempt to characterize the relationship between computing students' learning processes and learning outcomes. Second, our study contributes evidence-based recommendations for the design of future pedagogical environments to support a more social computer programming process in early computing courses.

2. BACKGROUND AND RELATED WORK

This research draws on two lines of related research work that (a) has used students' programming data to predict their learning outcomes, and (b) has explored the influence of students' social activities on their learning outcomes. Guided by social learning theory, this research also builds on our prior effort to build a social programming environment to study the interplay of programming and social activities. Below, we review these lines of related and foundational work.

2.1 Using Programming Data to Predict Learning Outcomes

A large body of educational research has explored the extent to which various learner variables are able to predict learning outcomes or future learning behaviors. These variables include the learner's background [e.g. 6, 16], prior knowledge [e.g. 6, 19], cognitive abilities [e.g. 23], time-on-task [e.g. 24] and learning attitudes [e.g. 5]. While this line of research shares our interest in drawing associations between students and course outcomes, it differs from our work in that it is based on written surveys administered periodically, rather than on continuous learning process data automatically collected through a learning environment.

A more recent line of research has focused on leveraging a continuous stream of data in order to identify patterns of learning associated with positive learning outcomes. As such, it falls within the emerging areas of educational data mining and learning analytics [3, 25], which, in many STEM fields, have been used to gain insights into the processes that underlie student learning, and ultimately to better tailor instruction. A foundational idea is to build learner models that infer learners' background knowledge, learning strategies, and motivations from learning process data [19]. In turn, such models are used to adapt instruction to learner needs.

Duval and Verbert [26] categorize two approaches for the application of learning analytics: one that focuses on identifying patterns of behavior, and another that focuses on deriving interventions aimed at improving the learning process. In computing education, the former approach has been used to describe compilation behavior [e.g. 2, 15] and to identify behaviors associated with eventual success or failure in a course [e.g. 1, 7, 14, 28]. In computing education, the latter approach (developing learning interventions) has been less explored, although there are some notable exceptions [e.g. 10, 20]. In both cases, researchers have yet to seriously capitalize on data generated from students' online social interactions.

2.2 The Influence of Social Activities on Learning Outcomes

Students' online social interactions have been widely studied. For example, researchers have examined the impact of social

participation on course performance [12] or on particular skills [e.g. metacognition see 21]. Alternatively, researchers have created online social environments to facilitate pedagogically beneficial activities such as peer code reviews [11] or to generate and critique test questions [9]. In these cases, researchers correlate usage of the system with a proxy for course performance—often an exam or final grade [e.g. 11, 18]. In contrast to prior work, the research presented in this paper directly studies the influence of students' unstructured question-asking behavior on their future coding behaviors.

2.3 Social learning Theory

This work is predicated on the theoretical frameworks of social learning. Situated Learning Theory [17] holds that participation in a community of practice, which involves both the observation of others and actual participation in community activities, facilitates learning. Furthermore, Bandura's self-efficacy theory [4] posits that students develop a positive sense of their own programming abilities (so-called self-efficacy) by being able to observe the activities of their peers, by being able to evaluate themselves relative to their peers, and by engaging in their own performances. Resonant with this theory, Rosson et al. [22] identified strong positive correlations between a number of attitudinal variables, including self-efficacy, and a learner's orientation towards the computing discipline. Both of these social theories of learning suggest that learners may have difficulties making progress if they are forced to program in isolation from a broader community, as has traditionally been the case in computing education. This is especially true with the type of individual programming assignments that are common in early computing courses.

2.4 Social Programming Environments

Guided by these theories, our research lab has been investigating the impact of social programming environments (SPEs; see Figure 1, next page) on learning processes and outcomes in early computing courses. In previous work, we found that SPEs can have a positive impact on students' sense of community [8], and that regular participation in such an online social environment is positively correlated with course outcomes [12]. Furthermore, we found that data collected within our SPE can be used to construct predictive models of student success [7]. While our SPE has allowed us to collect the data necessary to explore the interplay between programming behavior, social behavior, and student performance within the context of early computing courses, we do not claim that an SPE is a necessary component for facilitating online social discourse within a classroom. Indeed, in past research, we have studied computing students' social discourse within a variety of online environments, including Facebook and more traditional learning management systems [12, 13].

3. STUDY METHODOLOGY

3.1 Participants

Participants in this study were enrolled in the spring 2014 offering of CS2 at Washington State University. Focusing on the C and C++ programming languages, this 15 week course had three 50-minute lectures and one 170-minute lab period per week, three exams (two midterms and a final), and seven individual programming assignments. The course enrolled 140 students, 129 of whom finished the course and received a grade. 108 of these students (100 men, 8 women) consented to releasing their learning process data (automatically collected within the SPE) and course grades data for this study.

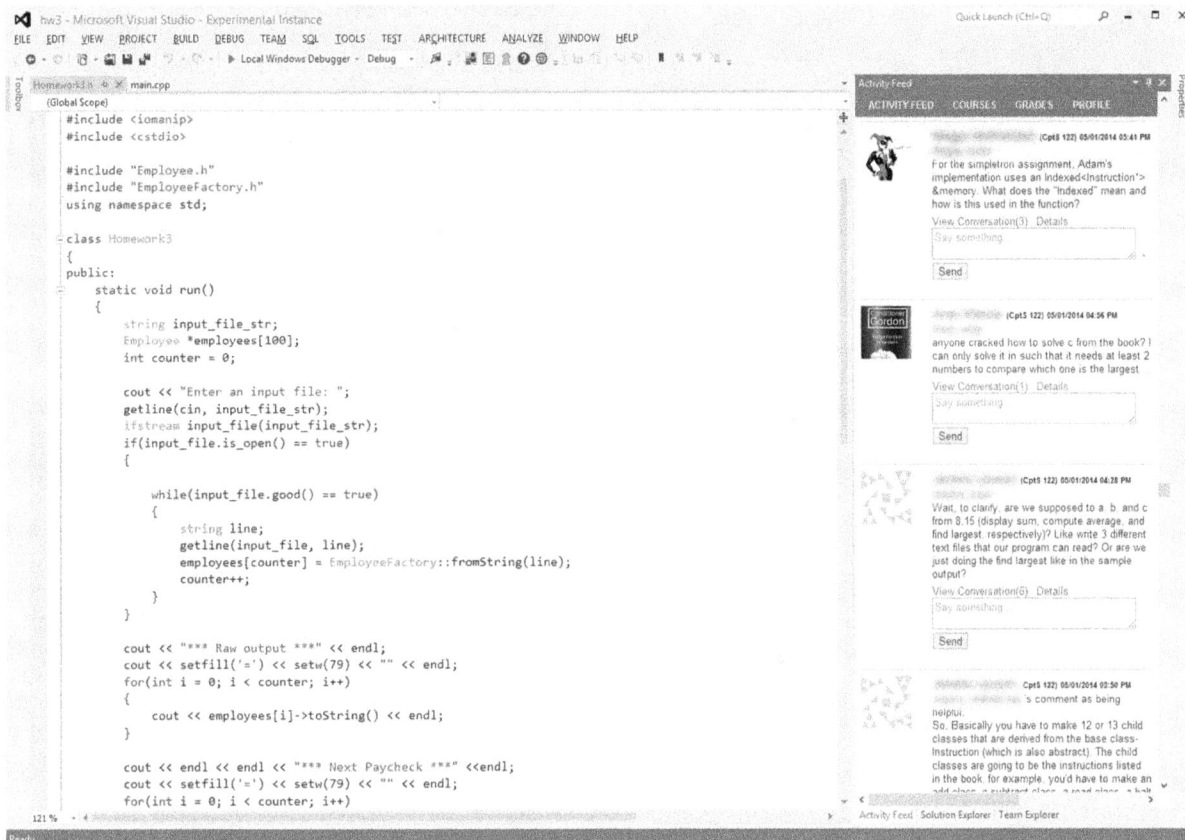

Figure 1: The OSBLE+ social programming environment

3.2 Data Collection, Sampling, and Analysis Method

Our SPE (see [8]) was used to collect students' online social activity and programming behaviors. The SPE collected 21,952,494 points of interaction and 10,720 discussion posts. In an attempt to make the data manageable, we employed a principled approach to sampling the content. To this end, we randomly sampled 10 students who received each of the five possible course grades (A, B, C, D, and F). While we were able to sample 10 students from each of the A, B, and C levels, only four students were available who received D's in the course, and only two students were available who received F's. Therefore, our sample could include only 36 students, instead of the 50 that we targeted.

Having chosen our sample, we next identified the 2,352 instances in which students in our sample were involved in some kind of social activity—either a post or reply on the SPE's activity stream. Since our research questions related to the interplay of social and programming behaviors, we opted to focus only on social activities (posts and replies) that had to do with *programming* activities. This refinement yielded 461 posts. Finally, in order to focus our study even more intently on our research questions, we further pruned the sample to include only posts and replies that were part of a thread that was initiated by a *programming* question. This resulted in a final sample of 93 threads.

For each of the 93 threads of social activity in our sample, we carried out the analyses described in Table 1 in order to provide a foundation for addressing our research questions.

In order to categorize question content (#1 in Table 1), we extended a previously used content coding scheme (see [13]), which we

Table 1. Analyses of Programming Questions

#	Description of Analysis	Relevant RQs
1	Categorize question content	RQ 1
2	Determine whether question related to question author's current build state	RQ 2, RQ3
3	Determine whether responses to question were posted	RQ 2, RQ3
4	Determine whether programming suggestions to address question were posted	RQ 2, RQ3
5	Determine whether question author explicitly acknowledged suggestions (with, e.g., "thank you")	RQ 2
6	Determine whether question author resolved the question in a future build	RQ 2

present in Table 2. To verify the validity of this coding scheme for the present analysis, the two authors independently coded a 20% sample of the corpus (n = 19 posts), attaining an overall agreement of 88% (0.83 kappa). Having established a sufficiently high level of inter-rater reliability for this coding scheme, the first author coded the remaining posts.

In order to determine whether a question was related to the student's current build state (#2 in Table 1), we examined the build that came immediately before or immediately after the question was posed. We considered these builds to be related to the question only if we could find clear evidence connecting the question to the state of the code in the build. For example, if a student's question asked about substrings, the student's previous or subsequent build would need to contain code that uses substrings, attempts to use substrings, or calls a function that uses substrings. In cases in which both builds occurred more than a day before or after a question was posed, we coded the question as *not* related to the current build state.

Table 2. Programming Question Content Categories

Category	Description	Example
COMPILE	Question relates to an issue encountered during program compilation.	"After I debug my code, I got this error, can anyone explain it to me? thank you Error 1 error LNK2019: unresolved external symbol [...]"
IDE	Question relates to the operation of Visual Studio	"Okay, does anybody else consistently get the problem where cin and cout are underlined with red and VS gives you the error "cout is ambiguous"?"
IMPLEMENTATION	Question asks for tips on how to best implement an algorithm or function. This is often, but not always, related to the requirements of a given lab or assignment.	"If both the player and the computer draw the same type of hand(say two pairs), who wins?"
RESOURCES	Question asks about the C/C++ language, or about a programming issue related to the misunderstanding of syntax.	"Does anyone know if the strtok() keeps the old string or does it fully erase it?"
RESOURCES	Question requests external programming resources or tips.	What did you guys use to create your UML diagrams?
RUNTIME	Question relates to an issue encountered during the runtime execution of a student's code	Does anyone know what "vector subscript out of range" means and to fix it?

Whether a given question had responses (#3 in Table 1) could be gleaned directly from a transcript of the activity stream. If at least one of the responses to a question suggested concrete action that the question author might take to address the question, we concluded that a suggestion was present (#4 in Table 1). Evidence of a question author's acknowledgment of a suggestion (#5 in Table 1) came in the form of any follow-up post by the author indicating that the author had read the post (e.g., "Thank you" or "What about...").

Finally, in order to determine whether the question author altered his or her code in a future build so as to resolve the original question posed (#6 in Table 1), we looked for clear evidence that the student's code had moved towards a resolution of the issue. For example, if the student asked a question about how to resolve a syntax error with using substring in her program, the error mentioned in the question would need to be resolved in a subsequent build.

In order to increase the likelihood that any progress made by question authors was influenced by their interaction in the corresponding activity stream thread, we considered subsequent builds that occurred within a reasonable time—two days—of the question author's last post to the thread. However, given that some students compiled their code infrequently, we required that a minimum of five compilations be considered. In some cases, examining a minimum of five compilations led us to consider compilations beyond the two-day window.

Two caveats come with the analysis approach just described. First, because it requires evidence that (a) programming questions be related to programming context, and (b) programming progress fall within a reasonable time after related programming questions are answered, our analysis approach may be seen as overly conservative. For example, it would have been possible for students to have asked a related coding question *before* they started coding their solution. Likewise, it would have been possible for students to have made positive strides towards a correct solution outside of our two-day, five-build window. Thus, it is possible that our analysis approach failed to identify some relationships between programming and social behavior.

Second, just because we are able to find evidence of positive programming progress that closely follows related social activity, this does *not* mean that such progress was made *because of* the social activity; indeed, such an assumption would fall prey to the *post hoc, ergo proctor hoc* fallacy. Clearly, our study is correlational, not causal. These two caveats should be borne in mind in interpreting the results that follow.

4. RESULTS

Using the categories of Table 2, Figure 2 presents a high-level breakdown of the content of the 93 questions in our sample. In this figure, the bars represent the *percentage* of questions that fall into each content category; all bars add up to 100%. The shading of each bar indicates the proportion of questions in each content category that were related to the question author's immediate coding context. As this figure suggests, a strong majority of the questions (74%) focused on IMPLEMENTATION (46%) or LANGUAGE (28%). The least common questions focused on COMPILE (4%) and IDE (4%) issues. Moreover, we see that questions having to do with RUNTIME, COMPILE, and LANGUAGE issues were most commonly associated with a student's active coding solution. In contrast, we see that none of the questions in the RESOURCES category was related to an active coding solution. This makes sense given that, by definition, RESOURCE questions ask for external programming resources or tips.

4.1 Relationship between Suggestions Received and Programming progress

82 of the 93 questions (88%) received a response; Slighter fewer (75, or 81%) received a response containing a programming suggestion to address the question. Did question authors' participation in the activity stream relate to their subsequent ability to make programming progress? To explore this question, Figure 3 considers the extent to which we found evidence that question authors made positive progress when they (a) did not receive a suggestion, (b) received a suggestion but did not acknowledge the response, or (c) received a suggestion and acknowledged the response. This figure illustrates a clear increase in success rates: only 38% of question authors made progress without a suggestion, versus a success rate of 85% when authors received and acknowledged a suggestion from another student.

According to chi-squared test, there was a significant association between the type of feedback received (no suggestion, suggestion + no acknowledgement, suggestion + acknowledgement) and whether or not a future build demonstrated progress towards a correct solution ($\chi^2(2) = 7.80$, $p = 0.02$). A post-hoc z-test revealed a significant difference ($p < 0.05$) between question authors who did not receive a suggestion and those who received and acknowledged a suggestion.

The middle condition—question authors who received a response but did not acknowledge the response—did not differ significantly from the other two categories.

4.2 Relationship between Social Activity and Course Outcomes

We next consider the relationship between discussions anchored in code and course outcomes, in order to further explore whether talking about code was a general indicator of success within the course. We begin by examining the relationship between the number of programming questions posed by a student and both the student's final grade, and the average programming assignment grade. We failed to find a significant relationship between the number of questions posed and the student's final grade ($F(1,18) = 0.2, p = 0.66$) or assignment average ($F(1,18) = 0.2, p = 0.66$). Next, we compared students who posted coding questions to those who did not. Again, we did not find a significant relationship between these groups and final grade ($F(1,105) = 0.03, p = 0.87$) or assignment average ($F(1,86) < 0.01, p = 0.96$).

The data indicate that simply posting a question about code bears no relationship to a student's overall class performance. However, it is possible that receiving programming suggestions on a given assignment might have positively impacted the grade received for that assignment. To investigate this possibility, we examined the 23 instances in which a student asked a question, received a suggestion, and acknowledged the suggestion with a response. For each instance, we compared the grade the student received on that assignment to the average grade of students that did not receive help on the assignment. Figure 4 depicts this relationship. Out of these 23 observations, only three observations were below the class average. When taken as a whole, we see that the average score received by this group was 10% higher (88% vs 78%) than the class average. A two-sample t-test with equal variance not assumed found this difference to be statistically significant ($t(23) = 2.65, p < 0.01$).

5. VIGNETTES

The prior section discovered statistically-significant positive relationships between participation in online discussions about code, coding progress, and course outcomes. In this section, we consider a series of vignettes, transcribed directly from the activity stream data collected in our study, that illustrate the interplay between student's coding behavior and social interactions. In exploring these vignettes, we see how rich discussions centered around coding can positively impact a student's coding progress. Likewise, these vignettes give us insights of what might happen when these kinds of discussions fail to materialize.

5.1 Vignette 1: Multiple Inheritance

The concept of inheritance in object oriented programming has recently been introduced in class and James[1] would like to use inheritance in his game of Battleship. James would like to build a subclass that inherits from multiple parents. He can get his program to compile when inheriting from a single parent, but cannot figure out the syntax for multiple inheritance. He asks for help with the issue on the OSBLE+ activity stream:

James: How do I make a class that is composed of two other classes? This is giving me an error: class Player : public Board : public Stats

Seeing James' question, Sharon provides a suggestion on how to accomplish multiple inheritance:

---

[1]All names used in these vignettes are pseudonyms.

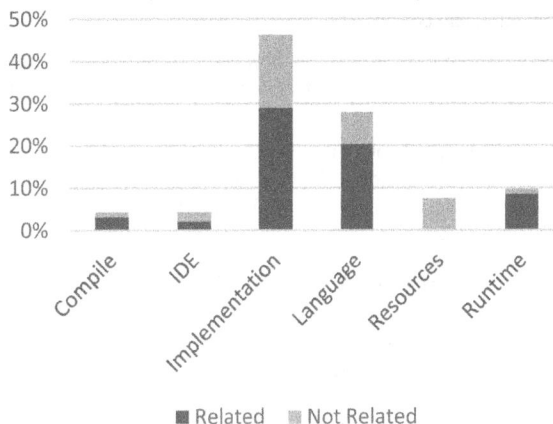

Figure 2: Percentage of questions in each content category, broken down according to whether or not they were related to immediate coding context

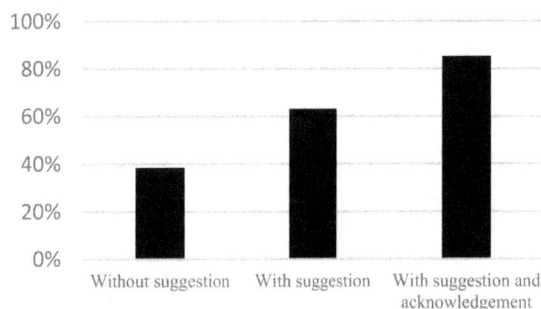

Figure 3: Percentage of future builds that demonstrate progress based on social feedback received

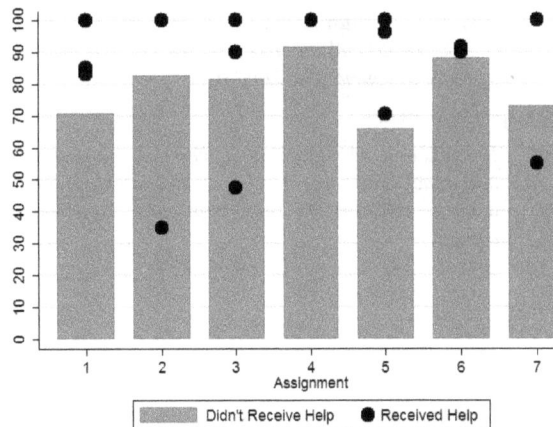

Figure 4: Grades of students who received help on assignment compared with those that did not for a given assignment

Sharon: Never done it myself, but this might help [url]... Try class Player : public Board, public Stats

James sees Sharon's question, modifies his class definition as suggested. His project compiles and he reports back his progress:

James: That's it. Crisis averted!

Timothy, who is also toying with multiple inheritance, sees James' conversation and confirms Sharon's suggestion:

Timothy: *This works. I have for instance, 5 different boat classes, all of which are inherited from a mothership parent class...*

Once again, James thanks Timothy for his confirmation. In the final post of the conversation, Steven, an upperclassman, offers a cautionary message regarding multiple inheritance:

Steven: *While you are all correct and multiple inheritance does work in c++. It can lead to a lot of errors, and stuff like the diamond problem...*

Less than three hours after posing the question, James was back on track.

5.2 Vignette 2: Understanding Requirements

Jessica has started work on her homework assignment, but her unfamiliarity with the game of poker is preventing her from making progress on how to properly implement a required function. Unable to make headway, she uses OSBLE+ to ask the class how about how the function should operate:

Jessica: *In highCard(), it returns one card which has the highest rank and the highest suit, right? I just want to make sure since I am unfamiliar with [poker]*

Stacie responds first:

Stacie: *Your function wants to return the highest rank over the highest suit. However, if you had, say 2 jacks in your hand, it would return the Jack of Spades, before the Jack of hearts. But say you had an Ace no matter what the suit is it would return the ace over the jacks. Hope this makes sense.*

Fred, who is also working on his poker assignment, asks a clarifying question:

Fred: *Isn't high card just for a no hand combination? Meaning 2 jacks would make a pair, high card only returns in the instance of you have no hand right?*

Barry responds to Fred:

Barry: *It would only be relevant if you had a jack and the dealer had a jack. Suits are only there to be compared if there is a tie if both have the same high card ...and flushes of course.*

Fred replies to Barry:

Fred: *I took the said suit function out, but I'm putting it back in [...]*

To close out the conversation, Jessica thanks the discussion participants:

Jessica: *Thanks guys*

Jessica continues to work diligently, and a day later, she has a working implementation of her function. However, not only did Jessica help herself, she also helped Fred, who might otherwise have been too shy to ask a question.

5.3 Vignette 3: Learning a New Concept

In the latest homework assignment, Beau is required to implement a basic factory pattern for creating different employee types. As this concept was recently introduced, Beau has no experience writing

factories and is thoroughly confused. He uses OSBLE+ to reach out for help:

Beau: *Any ideas to write studentFromString, staffFromString, facultyFromString? How do those function help the fromString funtion?*

Justin responds with an explanation of how the factory pattern works:

Justin: *The fromString function determines whether the employee is student, staff, or faculty then calls studentFromString, staffFromString, facultyFromString respectively. In those functions it sets all the information it gets from the string then returns it back to the fromString function. The fromString function then returns that.*

Apparently, other students are, like Beau, also struggling to understand how to implement a factory. Jessica writes:

Jessica: *So a majority of the code should be in the Factory and not in main? [...] What I'm having trouble with is bringing it back into main [partial code snippet]*

Steven responds that in his case, the majority of his code is indeed inside the factory. James follows this with a code snippet of how he "brought it back into main":

Stephen: *I just use: Employee *employ; and then in the while loop, just write: employee = factory.fromString(temp); cout<<employee->toString()<<endl; Hopefully, it can help you.*

Sandwiched between the discussion between Justin, Jessica, and Steven, Beau thanks the students for their suggestions. At the time Beau originally posed his question, he had not written any factory-related code. Less than a day later, Beau had implemented a fully-operational factory.

5.4 Vignette 4: Unacknowledged Question #1

Like Beau from Vignette 3, Rachel is having trouble implementing a factory for her homework assignment. Also like Beau, Rachel decides to seek help on OSBLE+. Unfortunately, she accesses OSBLE+ a day after Beau's discussion. Therefore, the help she seeks has fallen from the first page of the activity feed. Unaware of the previous discussion, Rachel makes her own post asking for implementation strategies:

Rachel: *I'm not sure what I should do in employeeFactory class, anyone can give me some ideas? Thank you.*

Unfortunately, Rachel's post does not receive the same attention as Beau's post; she receives no responses. Without help, Rachel has to go it alone. Over the course of the next two days (the maximum window of observation), Rachel makes progress towards correctly implementing a factory. However, at the end, she has still not implemented a fully working solution.

5.5 Vignette 5: Unacknowledged Question #2

Sean encounters an issue related to IFNDEF/ DEFINE preprocessor directives in his code. For some reason, large chunks of his code are being categorized as an "inactive preprocessor block." Confused, he poses his question on OSBLE+:

Sean: *So, in one of my header files I accidentally hit some key that made everything within that ifndef an "Inactive Preprocessor Block" (when I minimize it says that)... so, what key did I hit and how do I reactivate it?*

Unfortunately, nobody responds to his post. In an effort to solve his problem, Sean alters his preprocessor directives in a way that fixes his immediate error, but also introduces a potential bug that may cause issues in the future.

5.6 Vignette 6: Unacknowledged Response

Jon would like to create an array of pointers to use in his homework implementation, but he cannot figure out how to properly initialize the data structure. Looking for guidance, Jon poses his question on OSBLE+:

Jon: *I'm trying to use an Employee ** employee1 in my main function to hold all the employees in my .csv file. However there is no way of initializing that. So how would I hold an array of employees in main so I can access them whenever I want (i.e. for the paycheck)?*

Tyler responds with a code snippet demonstrating how he had initialized his array of pointers:

Tyler: *I did employee1 = new Employee*[100] to initialize my array of employees*

Jon never responds. Inspecting Jon's code, one finds that he appears to have implemented a different solution strategy. Future builds of Jon's solution do not include code related to 2D array initialization.

6. DISCUSSION

We organize our discussion of the results around our original research questions.

6.1 What Kinds of Programming Questions Do Students Pose Within an SPE?

Based on the content coding scheme presented in Table 2, nearly three-quarters (74%) of the programming questions posed within the OSBLE+ activity stream related to either language or implementation. The remaining questions had to do with runtime (10%), resources (8%), IDE (4%) and compilation (4%) issues. Given that this study focused on a CS2 course, it is perhaps unsurprising that so few questions had to do with IDE and compilation issues, which students at the CS2 level likely had already grappled with in previous computing courses. However, we found it somewhat surprising that such a small percentage of questions related to runtime issues (e.g., unexpected runtime behavior or runtime exceptions), which are notoriously difficult. We speculate that social interaction in an activity stream could provide a strong basis for addressing such issues.

6.2 How Does Programming Behavior Influence Social Behavior, and Vice Versa?

As illustrated in Figure 2, we found that at least half of all programming questions relate to the author's most recent program solution at the time the question was posed. Questions related to language, compile, and runtime issues were most commonly associated with the question author's current programming solution. This makes sense, as each of these question types is likely to arise as these issues are encountered by students. In contrast, not a single question about coding resources was related to the student's active programming solution. Again, this makes sense: students who are looking for programming resources are probably still formulating the problem and have not yet transitioned to writing actual code.

The vignettes presented in the previous section illustrate some ways in which social activity can influence coding behavior. In cases in which questions generated a healthy back-and-forth between their authors and other students, authors were likely to ultimately fix their issues. Furthermore, the vignettes illustrate the way in which discussions can attract students with similar issues. In this respect, we can see social activity as a mechanism for disseminating knowledge and creating bonds. The results of a previous study (see [8]), in which students using our SPE exhibited a significant increase in sense of community, provide additional empirical support for this observation.

6.3 What Is the Impact of Social Participation on Students' Ability to Successfully Complete Their Assignments?

Our quantitative results indicate that social behavior can have a significant influence on future coding behavior. When we examined conversations that contained a suggestion and an acknowledgement by the post's author, we saw the likelihood of the author making progress towards a correct solution increase significantly. Without a suggestion, only 38% of question authors' future compilations demonstrated evidence of progress. With an unacknowledged suggestion, this figure increased to 63%. And this number increased to 85% when the author received and acknowledged a suggestion. This result suggests that students who notice a helpful suggestion are likely to incorporate the suggestion into their own code, and that by doing so, they increase their chances of developing a correct solution.

In addition to helping students make positive solution progress, asking questions and receiving help also led to statistically-significant improvement in homework grades—at least for students who asked a question, received a suggestion, and acknowledged the suggestion. This finding suggests that asking for and receiving help on an assignment not only leads students towards a correct solution in the immediate sense; it also increases the likelihood of ultimately receiving a high grade on an assignment.

7. DESIGN IMPLICATIONS

Having addressed our original research questions, we next consider the implications these results might have for future pedagogical environments that aim to support individual programming assignments in early computing courses. Given the positive association between social interaction and programming behavior we identified, we believe that providing a space for students to discuss programming problems should be a key feature of any such pedagogical environment. Moreover, the results presented here provide guidance on how such pedagogical environments should be designed to support social discussions. We consider three specific design implications below.

First, as illustrated by our quantitative analysis, code-centric social interaction becomes more effective when a student receives a suggestion. The impact becomes significant when the question author acknowledges the suggestion. This finding implies that a pedagogical environment should specifically highlight unanswered questions. For example, a revised version of our SPE might have a section of the activity feed dedicated to unanswered questions.

Second, to ensure that those who ask for help actually read answers to their questions, an effective pedagogical environment needs to somehow bring potential solutions to the attention of question authors. To this end, the environment might contain a notifications area that is updated whenever a new solution has been submitted to a question. Along these lines, it might be helpful to incorporate a mechanism for both marking a potential solution and for marking the "best" solution, similar to what is currently provided by StackOverflow (2012).

Third, as highlighted by Vignettes 3 and 4, students may pose similar questions. Due to the ephemeral nature of an activity feed, students could easily be unaware that their current question has already been asked and answered. This implies the need for students to be made aware of prior questions. Such awareness could be provided through, for example, an ability to search past questions, perhaps using hashtags common on social media sites. Alternatively, the environment could recommend other posts based on the content of the question (e.g. "The following posts may be related to your current question"). Yet another approach could leverage the continuous nature of data logging to relate conversations. For example, for a question related to a compiler error, the pedagogical environment might be able to automatically suggest a discussion that was created by another student under similar coding circumstances.

8. LIMITATIONS
It is important to underscore three limitations of the research presented in this paper. First, while we were able to identify *when* students incorporated suggestions into their homework, our data does not indicate *how* students actually used online discussions to solve their programming issues. Understanding the process by which students incorporate feedback into their solutions would require us to augment our log data with retrospective interview or survey or survey data—an important direction for future research.

Second, it is possible that our study suffers from a sampling bias. It is possible that the sample of students selected for this study are not representative of the entire dataset. Alternatively, the inclusion of more A, B, and C students in our sample may have resulted in artificial significance findings. We can address the first threat by increasing the number of students in our sample; however, addressing the second threat would require us to gather more data.

Lastly, while we established inter-rater reliability for the content coding scheme (see Table 2), inter-rater reliability was not established for the other judgments required to perform the data analyses described in Table 1, item 6. We will need to address this shortcoming in future research.

9. CONCLUSION
In this paper, we have empirically investigated the relationship between programming activities and programming-focused activity stream discussions within the context of individual programming assignments in an early computing course. We began with a quantitative analysis that showed that questions posed by students are likely to be related to a current coding issue. We also discovered that students who received and acknowledged a suggestion to their questions were significantly more likely to fix their issues. Furthermore, these students were likely to turn in assignments whose scores were significantly higher than the class average. These findings were elucidated through a series of vignettes that illustrated how programming discussions can influence eventual success, how programming discussions can positively impact other students, and what happens when such discussions do not occur.

The work presented in this paper provides a compelling foundation for future work. First, we would like to broaden our analysis by expanding our selection criteria to include programming questions that occur as a sub-thread of another post. Second, we would like to explore how programming discussions impact students other than the question author. This includes both students who participate in the discussion and students who merely "lurk." Third, we would like to explore factors that contribute to question asking and answering. For example, do students with high social capital receive more responses? Alternatively, are successful students more likely to ask for and receive help? Does this create a divide between students who are capable of clearly formulating programming questions and those who are not? Finally, we would like to explore

the impact of the design modifications suggested by the results of this study, in order to further harness the potential for online social interaction to positively influence learning outcomes in early computing courses.

10. ACKNOWLEDGMENTS
This project is funded by the National Science Foundation under grant no. IIS-1321045. Carla DeLira assisted with the coding of the activity stream logs. We are grateful to the participants in the Social Analytics Workshop at ICER 2015 for their suggestions on how to pursue the analyses presented in this paper.

11. REFERENCES
[1] Ahadi, A. et al. 2015. Exploring Machine Learning Methods to Automatically Identify Students in Need of Assistance. *Proceedings of the Eleventh Annual International Conference on International Computing Education Research* (Omaha, NE, USA, 2015).

[2] Altadmri, A. and Brown, N.C.C. 2015. 37 Million Compilations: Investigating Novice Programming Mistakes in Large-Scale Student Data. *Proceedings of the 46th ACM Technical Symposium on Computer Science Education* (Kansas City, MO, USA, 2015), 522–527.

[3] Baker, R.S.J. and Siemens, G. 2014. Educational data mining and learning analytics. *The Cambridge Handbook of the Learning Sciences.* Cambridge University Press. 253–274.

[4] Bandura, A. 1997. *Self-efficacy: the exercise of control.* Worth Publishers.

[5] Bergin, S. et al. 2005. Examining the role of self-regulated learning on introductory programming performance. *Proc. 2005 ACM International Computing Education Research Workshop.* ACM Press. 81–86.

[6] Bransford, J. et al. eds. 1999. *How people learn: Brain, mind, experience, and school.* National Academy Press.

[7] Carter, A.S. et al. 2015. The Normalized Programming State Model: Predicting Student Performance in Computing Courses Based on Programming Behavior. *Proceedings of the Eleventh Annual Conference on International Computing Education Research* (2015).

[8] Carter, A.S. and Hundhausen, C.D. 2015. The Design of a Programming Environment to Support Greater Social Awareness and Participation in Early Computing Courses. *J. Comput. Sci. Coll.* 31, 1 (Oct. 2015), 143–153.

[9] Denny, P. et al. 2011. PeerWise: Exploring Conflicting Efficacy Studies. *Proceedings of the Seventh International Workshop on Computing Education Research* (Providence, Rhode Island, USA, 2011).

[10] Hartmann, B. et al. 2010. What would other programmers do: suggesting solutions to error messages. *Proc. 28th Conference on Human Factors in Computing Systems.* ACM. 1019–1028.

[11] Hundhausen, C.D. et al. 2011. Online vs. face-to-face pedagogical code reviews: An empirical comparison. *Proceedings 2011 SIGCSE Symposium on Computer Science Education.* ACM Press. 117–122.

[12] Hundhausen, C.D. et al. 2015. Supporting programming assignments with activity streams: an empirical study.

Proceedings of the 46th ACM Technical Symposium on Computer Science Education (New York, 2015), 320–325.

[13] Hundhausen, C.D. and Carter, A.S. 2014. Facebook me about your code: An empirical study of the use of activity streams in early computing courses. *Journal of Computing Sciences in Colleges.* 30, 1 (2014), 151–160.

[14] Jadud, M.C. 2006. Methods and tools for exploring novice compilation behaviour. *Proce. Second International Workshop on Computing Education Research.* ACM. 73–84.

[15] Jadud, M.C. and Dorn, B. 2015. Aggregate Compilation Behavior: Findings and Implications from 27,698 Users. *Proceedings of the Eleventh Annual International Conference on International Computing Education Research* (Omaha, NE, USA, 2015).

[16] Jeske, D. et al. 2014. Learner characteristics predict performance and confidence in e-Learning: An analysis of user behavior and self-evaluation. *Journal of Interactive Learning Research.* 25, 4 (2014), 509–529.

[17] Lave, J. and Wenger, E. 1991. *Situated Learning: Legitimate Peripheral Participation.* Cambridge University Press.

[18] Luxton-Reilly, A. et al. 2012. The Impact of Question Generation Activities on Performance. *Proceedings of the 43rd ACM Technical Symposium on Computer Science Education* (Raleigh, NC, USA, 2012).

[19] Ma, W. et al. 2014. Intelligent tutoring systems and learning outcomes: A meta-analytic survey. *Journal of Educational Psychology.* 106, 2007 (2014), 901–918.

[20] Mujumdar, D. et al. 2011. Crowdsourcing suggestions to programming problems for dynamic web development languages. *CHI '11 Extended Abstracts on Human Factors in Computing Systems* (Vancouver, BC, Canada, 2011), 1525–1530.

[21] Pifarre, M. and Cobos, R. 2010. Promoting metacognitive skills through peer scaffolding in a CSCL environment. *Computer-Supported Collaborative Learning.* 5, (2010).

[22] Rosson, M.B. et al. 2011. Orientation of Undergraduates Toward Careers in the Computer and Information Sciences: Gender, Self-Efficacy and Social Support. *ACM Transactions on Computing Education.* 11, 3 (Oct. 2011), 1–23.

[23] Schunk, D.H. 2012. *Learning theories: An educational perspective.* Merrill Prentice Hall.

[24] Slavin, R.E. 2011. *Educational psychology: Theory and practice.* Pearson Education.

[25] U.S. Department of Education, Office of Educational Technology 2012. *Enhancing Teaching and Learning through Educational Data Mining and Learning Analytics: An Issue Brief.*

[26] Verbert, K. and Duval, E. 2012. Learning Analytics. *Learning and Education.* 1, 8 (2012).

[27] Watson, C. et al. 2014. No tests required: comparing traditional and dynmaic predictors of programming success. *Proceedings of the 45th ACM Technical Symposium on Computer Science Education* (2014), 469–474.

[28] Watson, C. et al. 2013. Predicting Performance in an Introductory Programming Course by Logging and Analyzing Student Programming Behavior. *Proceedings of the 2013 IEEE 13th International Conference on Advanced Learning Technologies* (2013), 319–323.

[29] Wise, A.F. 2014. Designing Pedagogical Interventions to Support Student Use of Learning Analytics. *Proceedings of the Fourth International Conference on Learning Analytics And Knowledge* (New York, NY, USA, 2014), 203–211.

Learning to Program: Gender Differences and Interactive Effects of Students' Motivation, Goals, and Self-Efficacy on Performance

Alex Lishinski
Michigan State University
College of Education
East Lansing, MI
lishinsk@msu.edu

Aman Yadav
Michigan State University
College of Education
East Lansing, MI
ayadav@msu.edu

Jon Good
Michigan State University
College of Education
East Lansing, MI
goodjona@msu.edu

Richard Enbody
Michigan State University
Department of Computer
Science and Engineering
East Lansing, MI
enbody@cse.msu.edu

ABSTRACT

Previous research in computer science education has demonstrated the importance of motivation for success in introductory programming. Theoretical constructs from self-regulated learning theory (SRL), which integrates several different types of metacognitive processes, as well as motivational constructs, have proved to be important predictors of success in most academic disciplines. These individual components of self-regulated learning (e.g., self-efficacy, metacognitive strategies) interact in complex ways to influence students' affective states and behaviors, which in turn influence learning outcomes. These elements have been previously examined individually in novice programmers, but we do not have a comprehensive understanding of how SRL constructs interact to influence learning to program. This paper reports on a study that examined the interaction of self-efficacy, intrinsic and extrinsic goal orientations, and metacognitive strategies and their impact on student performance in a CS1 course. We also report on significant gender differences in the relationships between SRL constructs and learning outcomes. We found that student performance had the expected motivational and SRL precursors, but the interactions between these constructs revealed some unexpected relationships. Furthermore, we found that females' self-efficacy had a different connection to programming performance than that of their male peers. Further research on success in introductory programming should take account of the unique and complex relationship between SRL and student success, as well as gender differences in these relationships that are specific to CS.

Permission to make digital or hard copies of all or part of this work for personal or classroom use is granted without fee provided that copies are not made or distributed for profit or commercial advantage and that copies bear this notice and the full citation on the first page. Copyrights for components of this work owned by others than the author(s) must be honored. Abstracting with credit is permitted. To copy otherwise, or republish, to post on servers or to redistribute to lists, requires prior specific permission and/or a fee. Request permissions from permissions@acm.org.

ICER '16, September 08 - 12, 2016, Melbourne, VIC, Australia

© 2016 Copyright held by the owner/author(s). Publication rights licensed to ACM.
ISBN 978-1-4503-4449-4/16/09...$15.00

DOI: http://dx.doi.org/10.1145/2960310.2960329

Keywords

self-efficacy, goal orientation, metacognitive strategies, CS1, predictors

1. INTRODUCTION

Self-Regulated learning (SRL) constructs have been found to be important factors that can help predict students' academic outcomes [42]. SRL refers to a number of different student characteristics and behaviors (e.g. motivational characteristics, goal-setting behavior, metacognitive self-regulation, and cognitive strategies) that reciprocally interact with one another over time.

Previous research in computer science (CS) education has examined motivation and subcomponents of SRL as possible predictors of success, particularly in the context of introductory programming courses [9, 46]. Results from this research have shown that SRL and motivational constructs are useful for predicting programming success. However, these previous studies have mainly focused on examining the relationships between individual SRL constructs and course outcomes, rather than investigating how multiple components of SRL interact in introductory programming students over time as they learn to program. A detailed examination of the relationships and between motivation, SRL, and student CS outcomes requires a more complex structural model than what has previously been used. This model should also include repeated measures of the important constructs to capture reciprocal effects as students move through the process of learning to program. Therefore, the goal of this study was to provide such an analysis, detailing the relationships between SRL constructs in an introductory programming course. Furthermore, previous research has suggested that there are gender differences with respect to self-efficacy which may be important in learning to program [11, 53]. Therefore, this study also investigated gender differences in the relationship between self-efficacy and performance to see if any conclusions could be drawn about gender differences in the way that students approach an introductory programming course.

211

1.1 Research Questions

- RQ1: What are the relationships between self-efficacy, goal orientation, metacognitive strategies, and course outcomes in introductory programming students?

- RQ2: How does self-efficacy relate to programming performance, and how does this relationship change over time in CS1?

- RQ3: Are there gender differences in the ways that self-efficacy affects performance in CS1?

2. LITERATURE REVIEW

2.1 Self Regulated Learning: Motivation, Goals, and Metacognitive Strategies

Self-regulated learning theory (SRL) is a broad theoretical framework consisting of a number of behavioral (e.g., goal setting, strategy use) and affective (e.g., motivational states, self-efficacy) characteristics of students. SRL also includes students' views of the learning process; a self-regulated student is someone who is behaviorally, metacognitively, and motivationally an active participant in his/her own learning ([63], as cited in [64]). Within the SRL framework, motivation and learning strategies are an essential part of students' academic performance [64]. Use of metacognitive strategies is key as well. Self-regulated learners are characterized by their use of metacognitive strategies to achieve academic goals, and their awareness of the connection between these strategies and learning outcomes [64]. Most of all, self-regulated learners are responsive to feedback from the learning process, modifying their strategies and self-beliefs through self-monitoring of their learning outcomes. In summary, SRL is a theory of effective learning that includes motivation, goal-setting behaviors, and metacognitive strategies, in an iterative process that uses self-monitoring and feedback to modify the application of these learning behaviors. Hence, explaining student learning involves exploring the relationships between these cognitive, affective, and behavioral dimensions.

2.1.1 Motivation: Self-Efficacy

Self-efficacy is an important motivational construct that has its origins in Bandura's social-cognitive theory [4, 5]. Bandura originally presented self-efficacy as the belief that one can successfully execute behaviors needed to produce a desired outcome [4]. Self-efficacy beliefs determine the amount of effort people are willing to expend and how well they cope and persist in the face of challenges [4]. Within Bandura's social-cognitive theory, self-beliefs play a self regulatory role, mediating between goals or values and the behavior that individuals engage in to pursue those goals or values [5]. The strength of this framework is that weak linkages between prior ability and achievement are often explained by these sorts of self-beliefs [5].

Since Bandura's original discussion of self-efficacy [4], it has become one of the most important motivational variables that helps explain the relationship between past performance and future results in education research ([43], see also [39, 38, 14, 2]). Self-efficacy is related to a number of other self-beliefs (e.g., self-concept, attributions of success and failure) that are also important in motivation the-

ory, but it differs in that self-efficacy beliefs are more context and task specific than other self-beliefs, which are more global characteristics of individuals [35]. The specificity of self-efficacy beliefs is relevant for their use as a predictor of performance, as more general expectancy self-beliefs tend to be more weakly related to student outcomes [5].

The importance of self-efficacy in predicting academic success and choices has been well documented in a number of subject areas, such as mathematics [38], science [14], and language arts [39]. For example, students' sense of self-efficacy in mathematics has been shown to be more significantly related to their continuing to pursue mathematics than their previous math achievement [38]. Choice of mathematics and science careers has also been found to be strongly predicted by self-efficacy beliefs [31]. Valentine et al. conducted a meta-analysis on the effects of self-efficacy on achievement outcomes and found a consistently significant, albeit small, effect across disciplines, controlling for prior achievement [55]. However, the authors note that in practice, so-called self-efficacy measures often include a mixture of more task specific and more global measures of self-concept, which would cause a shrinkage from the true self-efficacy effect.

Research has also examined the accuracy of self-efficacy beliefs, showing that overconfident self-efficacy beliefs can have detrimental effects on later performance [37]. Prior work has suggested that self-efficacy influences performance by initiating more adaptive behaviors and causing students to pursue more opportunities for practice and feedback [42]. Along these lines, self-efficacy has been shown to be related to more resiliency in response to complex and difficult tasks. Self-efficacy has strong effects on transfer performance as well. A study by Ford et al. found effects of self-efficacy on transfer performance that went beyond the effects of knowledge and skills obtained on the original task [21].

2.1.2 Goal Setting: Goal Orientations

Another important component of self-regulated learning theory is goal orientation, which refers to the types of outcomes students desire for academic achievement situations. Goal orientation connects students' desired outcomes to the behaviors they engage in and the standards that they use to judge their performance, which in turn affect later performance [33]. Goal orientation theory originally described students' goal orientations with two main categories - mastery and performance. Students with mastery goal orientations value learning and personal growth, whereas students with performance goal orientation value social demonstration of success and relative achievement. Pintrich and Schunk called these two goal orientations intrinsic and extrinsic, and these terms are used in the current study [44]. Prior research has consistently linked intrinsic motivation to academic achievement and extrinsic motivation to academic difficulties [62]. These results imply that an intrinsic goal orientation focused on mastery and learning is more conducive to academic success and needs be fostered in academic settings.

The initial goal orientation categories have been revised and refined as the theory has developed. Intrinsic goals remained the same, whereas extrinsic goals were divided into two subtypes, performance approach and performance avoidance goals [23, 19]. Performance approach goals are based on the desire for the appearance of success to others, or success measured relative to others, whereas performance avoidance goals are based on the desire to avoid failure, particularly in view of others [34]. Empirical studies have shown a functional distinction between the two types of performance goals. Performance-approach goals predict adaptive behaviors in academic contexts, whereas performance-avoidance goals predict maladaptive behaviors [34].

2.1.3 Strategies for learning: Metacognitive strategies

Another important concept in self-regulated learning theory is metacognitive strategies. Metacognitive strategies are the self-monitoring and control processes used by students to select and implement appropriate behaviors to address an academic challenge [17]. Such strategies include, for example, asking oneself questions to check comprehension, or setting specific goals when studying. These strategies are a necessary component in the larger process by which self-regulated learning leads to increased academic outcomes [17]. Metacognitive strategies are important because they mediate between cognitive strategies and academic performance [61]. Whereas cognitive strategies are the strategies employed to complete a specific task that are connected to the substantive content of that particular task, metacognitive strategies are more general strategies that involve awareness and executive control of the cognitive strategies. Previous research has found that students might use the appropriate cognitive strategies, yet still fail to successfully perform the task because they fail to appropriately use metacognitive strategies [17, 21].

2.1.4 Relationships between Constructs

Previous research has also shed light on the relationships between these different self-regulated learning constructs. For example, self-efficacy has been found to be positively associated with the use of more metacognitive strategies [42]. Similarly, intrinsic goal orientations have been shown to be positively associated with self-efficacy, whereas extrinsic goal orientations are negatively associated with self-efficacy [62]. Metacognitive strategy use has also been found to be significantly related to later self-efficacy, possibly mediated by the effects of performance on self-efficacy [1]. When considering all three constructs, a meta-analysis by Crede and Phillips found that self-efficacy consistently has the strongest relationship with academic outcomes, followed by metacognitive strategies and then goal orientation [18]. These previous results provided the basis for the model of the relationships between these constructs used in the present study.

Self-efficacy is unique among the SRL concepts being examined in this study because of its malleability and reciprocal relationships with learning outcomes [22, 36]. Initial self-efficacy beliefs affect performance, which in turn affects later self-efficacy beliefs. Bandura argued that self-efficacy should be assessed at significant points in a learning process in order to explain how this self-efficacy feedback loop functions in a given academic setting [4]. Previous research shows that the reciprocal effects of self-efficacy and performance lead to a correction of self-efficacy beliefs over time. As students have more opportunities for self-evaluation, the correspondence between self-efficacy beliefs and performance becomes greater [50]. In other words, students' beliefs about what they can do become more accurate through feedback.

2.1.5 In CS Education

Previous research in computer science education has examined the individual relationships between the SRL constructs examined in this study (self-efficacy, achievement goals, and metacognitive strategies) and student learning outcomes in CS courses. Self-efficacy has been studied the most, with previous studies mostly confirming that self-efficacy predicts performance in CS contexts as it does in other academic settings. Ramalingam et al. found that students' self-efficacy was positively associated with course grades and previous experience, and that it increased over time [46]. Wiedenbeck found that self-efficacy was positively associated with overall course grade and outcomes on a debugging task [58]. Wilson and Shrock unexpectedly found that self-efficacy was not significantly related to course midterm grades [60]. Watson and Godwin found that self-efficacy was by far the strongest predictor of performance in CS1, above many other predictors of success [56]. A qualitative study by Kinnunen and Simon found that self-efficacy judgments are continually evolving during the process of working on programming assignments in CS1, that positive and negative self-efficacy judgments are possible in response to both positive and negative results in programming, and that task difficulty and achievement goal orientation are possible moderators of these changes [28]. A precursor to this study found that programming assignments tend to catch students off guard with difficulties when they think that they understand what they are doing. These "struck by lightning" experiences produce particularly intense emotional reactions in students which have accordingly larger effects on students' revisions to their self-efficacy beliefs [27]. These observations fit with the concept of the self-efficacy feedback loop, and suggest that this reciprocal process is worth further investigation in the context of students learning to program.

Goal orientations have been studied in CS classes multiple times as well, with the existing studies focusing on positive correlations between intrinsic goal orientations and grades. For example, Bergin and Reilly found that intrinsic goal orientations were associated with higher exam scores in a CS1 course [8], as did Zingaro and Porter [65]. Metacognitive strategies have been studied in CS as well, with observed results matching theory-based expectations. Bergin, Reilly, and Traynor found that the use of metacognitive strategies was associated both with intrinsic goal orientations and higher course grades in CS1 [9]. A qualitative study of students in an object oriented programming course showed that failures of metacognitive control accounted for problem solving failures [25]. Another qualitative study detailed the CS-specific and general types of metacognitive strategies used by introductory programming students [20]. These results confirm the importance of self-regulated learning constructs in explaining performance in introductory programming, with most of the findings aligning with previous research on precursors for success in other content areas [24]. Overall, studies of SRL constructs in CS have largely confirmed theoretically expected associations between these variables in the CS context, which supports the use of this theory to explain student outcomes in CS classes.

2.1.6 SRL and Gender in CS

The gender participation gap in CS has been widely noted and researched (see for example [49, 29, 54]). Recent data has shown that men outnumber women in CS bachelor's degrees 4 to 1 [13]. Many factors relating to the gender gap have been researched, including the lack of female role models, differences in previous programming experience, hostile culture, and differential rates of attrition [59, 13]. These authors have argued that aspects of the culture, such as the often competitive character of assessment in CS classes, encouragement of obsessive, socially isolated focus when doing work, and the small number of female role models, cause female students to feel isolated, which can lead to differential attrition rates [59].

The role of self-regulated learning constructs in the gender gap is an important dimension that has been underexplored. General research on self-efficacy has shown that, despite equal aptitude and performance, girls exhibit systematically lower levels of self-efficacy than boys [40]. Previous studies in the CS context have also found gender differences in comfort level and self-efficacy in CS classes, finding that compared to their male peers, females have less self-efficacy and lower comfort levels with respect to complex computer tasks [15, 12]. Research has also found correlates of success in CS that are unique to women. Women's success in CS courses is uniquely related to comfort level [10], as well as their having positive stereotypes of CS students and positive perceptions of the gender equity in their classes [12]. Previous research has hypothesized that differences in attribution theory and self-efficacy differences between boys and girls may be involved in the gender gap. Empirical studies have shown that women are more likely than men in a CS context to attribute success to luck rather than ability, which studies in science show may be responsible for differential attrition rates [59, 16]. It has also been hypothesized that the relative lack of role models in CS for females may be related to their lower initial self-efficacy levels, which reduces their propensity to seek out experiences that would be opportunities to increase their self-efficacy [59]. These previous results suggest that self-beliefs and affective characteristics may be very important for explaining the gender gap in CS. Therefore, this study examined gender differences in the self-efficacy feedback loop have not been previously examined.

2.2 Need for study

The previous research in CS education on the motivational precursors for success has confirmed the importance of motivational and SRL constructs in introductory programming courses [25, 56, 65]. However, we still know little about the relationships between these factors and their influence on student outcomes. To date, no studies have looked at the relationships between self-efficacy, goal orientation, and metacognitive strategies in introductory programming courses. Previous studies from other disciplines have suggested relationships between these constructs, but it is unknown whether these relationships hold in the context of introductory programming.

In particular, the self-efficacy feedback loop has been little studied in CS. Kinnunen and Simon's qualitative study suggested that something like a reciprocal self-efficacy feedback process occurs in introductory programming students, and the authors offered suggestions for keeping the feedback loop from becoming negative and driving students to failure [28]. The present study builds upon that study by further exploring the nature of the self-efficacy feedback loop in introductory programming by presenting the results of a larger quantitative study that also relates data on the self-efficacy feedback loop to other SRL constructs.

Another shortcoming of the previous work on motivation and CS is that programming performance has typically been measured by single course grade or exam grade, with little discussion or attention given to the implications of the choice of outcome measure. As has been argued elsewhere, different sorts of programming assignments appear to assess qualitatively different aspects of students' learning in introductory programming courses [32]. For this reason, this study takes a multiple outcome measures approach to examining motivation-performance relationships, by using multiple indicators of programming performance. Furthermore, previous studies on motivational variables have only measured them at one time point rather than examining student trajectories over time. This study used repeated measures of self-efficacy to enable a finer-grained examination of the reciprocal self-efficacy-performance relationship.

While previous research has suggested the importance of affective processes in explaining gender differences, the reciprocal interaction between self-efficacy and learning outcomes in CS, as mediated by gender, has not been previously examined. The gender gap in CS is a significant issue, and a full understanding of it needs to include an examination of the gender-specific ways that the self-efficacy feedback loop operates and influences student learning. Hence, this study presents results on the gender differences in the nature of the self-efficacy feedback loop in introductory programming courses.

3. METHODS

3.1 Participants and Setting

This study investigated the relationships between SRL constructs and student performance on a sample of 346 students in a CS1 course at a large midwestern university. Of these students, 248 (73.1%) were male, 93 (26.9%) were female and 5 were unidentified. The class was taught by the fourth author of this paper, but he was not involved in the data collection and analysis process. The course was taught in a mostly flipped format; students watched video lectures and attended lab sessions with a TA in which they completed lab exercises.

3.2 Self-Regulated Learning Measures

The motivational and self-regulated learning constructs were measured using subscales from the Motivated Strategies for Learning Questionnaire (MSLQ). The MSLQ is a widely used self-report instrument designed to measure student motivation and learning strategies [41]. The MSLQ comprises 81 likert-scale items across 15 subscales, six of which are designed to measure dimensions of motivation, and nine of which are designed to measure learning strategies. The MSLQ has also been used previously in CS education research to examine the relationships between individual subscales and student outcomes (see for example: [6, 56, 9, 51]). Beyond CS education, the MSLQ has been used in hundreds of studies, and its validity and reliability have been well substantiated.

For this study, 4 of the 15 subscales were chosen to measure the theoretical constructs of interest discussed previously. The scales used were self-efficacy, metacognitive self-regulation, intrinsic goal orientation and extrinsic goal orientation. Of note is the extrinsic goal orientation subscale. When the MSLQ was developed, the theory on goal orientations had not yet divided extrinsic goal orientations into performance-approach and performance-avoidance. The items that comprise the extrinsic goal orientation subscale on the MSLQ are all oriented towards assessing the performance-approach dimension. For that reason, the extrinsic goal orientation scale will be interpreted as measuring performance-approach goal orientation. The scales chosen for this study have been found to predict student outcomes consistent with self-regulated learning theory [18].

3.3 Programming Performance Measures

The programming performance dimension was assessed using student grades on different types of assessment. Previous CS education studies have generally used the overall course grade or final exam grade as outcomes. Other previous research, however, has suggested that different sorts of course assessments can measure qualitatively different aspects of student ability [3, 30], and so choice of outcome measure can have significant effects on the validity and interpretation of study results. For this reason, this study used 2 different measures of student performance, programming projects and multiple choice exams. The programming projects involved students writing complete programs, whereas multiple choice exams involved students answering questions about syntax, and tracing small bits of code. By using both measures, we can get a more fine grained picture of how motivation and learning strategies affect student performance.

4. DATA COLLECTION AND ANALYSIS

For this study, students were given an online survey containing the self-efficacy (Self-Eff init.), metacognitive self-regulation (Metacog Str.), intrinsic goal orientation (Intrin G.O.), and extrinsic goal orientation (Extrin G.O.) subscales in the second week of the course. Programming projects were due weekly starting the second week of the course, with the exception of weeks with midterm exams, which were given weeks 6 & 11. Course grade data consists of 7 programming projects and 2 multiple choice exams. Additionally, the self-efficacy subscale of the MSLQ was given to students on two subsequent occasions, 1 week before each exam, in week 5 (Self-Eff. R1) and week 10 (Self-Eff. R2). The data collection timeline is shown in figure 1.

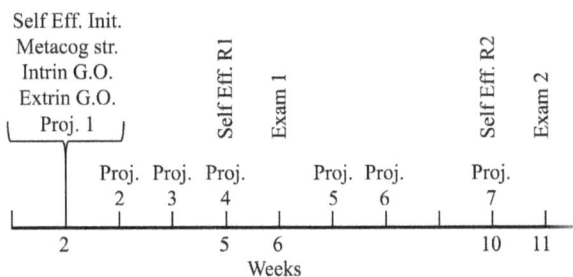

Figure 1: Data Collection Timeline

The data for this study was primarily analyzed with a path analysis model. Path analysis is a structural equation modeling technique that allows one to model the explana-

tory relationships, including mediating relationships, for a set of variables with complex interactions [47]. A path analysis model was fit to explain the observed direct and indirect relationships between the observed variables, based on theoretical expectations for these relationships. This type of analysis is appropriate because the relationships between the motivation and learning strategies constructs are theoretically and empirically well-grounded. The goal of this analysis is to build upon previous research, which has shown evidence for relationships between motivation, learning strategies and performance, and to provide a more fine grained model of these relationships in the particular context of CS1. Sample size was not large enough to enable separate path models to be fit by gender, so gender differences were analyzed by looking at individual correlation and correlation pattern differences between males and females, which were tested for significance. All analysis was done using R version 3.2.1 and the lavaan package [45, 48], and visualizations were produced using the ggplot2 and DiagrammeR packages [57, 52].

5. RESULTS

5.1 Descriptive Statistics

Descriptive statistics on the four MSLQ subscales, as well as the two self-efficacy repeated measurements and the course grades, are shown in table 1. Data was collected at multiple points and there was some attrition. The final data set was 218 students who provided complete data on all measures. The MSLQ items are on a 7 point likert scale, and sum scores were used as overall scores for these constructs. The intrinsic and extrinsic goal orientation scales have a maximum possible score of 28, the self-efficacy scale has a maximum possible score of 56, and the meta-cognitive strategies scale has a maximum possible score of 96. Exam 1 was worth 100 points, exam 2 was worth 150 points, and the 7 projects were worth a total of 235 points.

Table 1: Descriptive Statistics: MSLQ and Grade variables

	vars	n	mean	sd
Metacog. Strat.	1	346.00	56.77	10.16
Self Eff. Init.	2	346.00	43.02	9.91
Intrin G.O.	3	346.00	20.40	4.61
Extrin G.O.	4	346.00	22.32	4.78
Total pts	5	433.00	362.12	103.78
Exam1 pts	6	433.00	74.13	19.37
Exam2 pts	7	433.00	101.86	34.79
Proj pts	8	433.00	186.13	60.07
Self Eff. R1	9	269.00	42.47	10.70
Self Eff. R2	10	218.00	41.68	12.05

Gender differences on these variables were also calculated, and there were no significant differences by gender, with the exception of the initial self-efficacy measurement, on which females scored significantly lower than males (t = 2.92, p-value = 0.004).

5.2 Path Analysis

The path model used total exam scores and total project scores as outcomes, with the MSLQ variables as independent variables. In accordance with previous research, self-efficacy was hypothesized to have the greatest direct effect on performance, with metacognitive strategies and goal orientation having an indirect effect on performance through their effect on self-efficacy. Self-efficacy was measured 3 times, so the effects of earlier self-efficacy on later self-efficacy was modeled as well, as was the effect of earlier performance on later self-efficacy. In keeping with previous theory, goal orientation was hypothesized to influence both outcomes directly and indirectly through an effect on self-efficacy. Meta-cognitive strategies was hypothesized to have direct effects only on projects scores, because the monitoring and reflecting processes involved in meta-cognitive strategies do not show strong relationships with overall grades [18].

The model parameter estimates are shown in table 2. Model fit was good ($\chi^2 = 1.439$, df = 2, p = 0.487; CFI = 1.000; RMSEA = 0.00, 90% CI = (0.00, 0.122)) [26]. Previous theory suggested that that self-efficacy would produce the strongest direct effects, and that the other MSLQ scales would have largely indirect effects, and the model results are consistent with these expectations. For exam scores, the strongest direct effect was self-efficacy, in particular the second repeated measurement ($\beta = 1.215$, p < 0.001). Project scores were also significantly related but the magnitude of the effect was much smaller than that of self-efficacy ($\beta = 0.290$, p < 0.001). As expected, extrinsic goal orientation had a negative effect on exam performance, but this effect was not significant, nor was the effect of intrinsic goal orientation. Interestingly, the first repeated self-efficacy measure had a negative effect ($\beta = -0.594$, p = 0.010). These results suggest a self-efficacy correction, as performance feedback made later self-efficacy more accurate than earlier self-efficacy. The variance explained for exam scores was moderate ($R^2 = 0.351$).

For project scores the only significant direct effect was that of the first repeated measurement of self-efficacy ($\beta = 1.215$, p < 0.001). This effect was similar in magnitude to that of self-efficacy on exam scores. Both extrinsic and intrinsic goal orientations had negative effects, but these were not significant, nor was the positive effect of metacognitive strategies. The nonsignificant effect of initial self-efficacy once again suggests a self-efficacy correction effect. As students progressed and received feedback, their self-beliefs became more accurate with respect to their actual performance. The second repeated measure of self-efficacy was not included in the model because it was measured after all of the projects, but its correlation with total project scores was greater than that of the first measure, which further supports this interpretation because later self-efficacy was more closely related to performance after there were more opportunities for performance feedback. The variance explained for project scores was small ($R^2 = 0.094$)

The path coefficients for the two repeated measurements of self-efficacy reveal the indirect effects of the other MSLQ variables. The second repeated measurement of self-efficacy was understandably most strongly related to the first repeated measurement and the initial measurement of self-efficacy ($\beta = 0.502$, p < 0.001; $\beta = 0.252$, p < 0.001). The larger effect of the first repeated measurement supports the interpretation that while self-efficacy had some continuity between measures, a correction effect occurred over time. Metacognitive strategies had only an indirect effect on the second repeated measurement of self-efficacy, with a significant direct effect on the first measurement ($\beta = 0.173$, p =

0.005). The same is true for intrinsic motivation ($\beta = 0.405$, p = 0.005). Extrinsic motivation had the expected negative effect on the first repeated measurement of self-efficacy, but it was not significant. The path diagram with the insignificant paths removed is shown in figure 2.

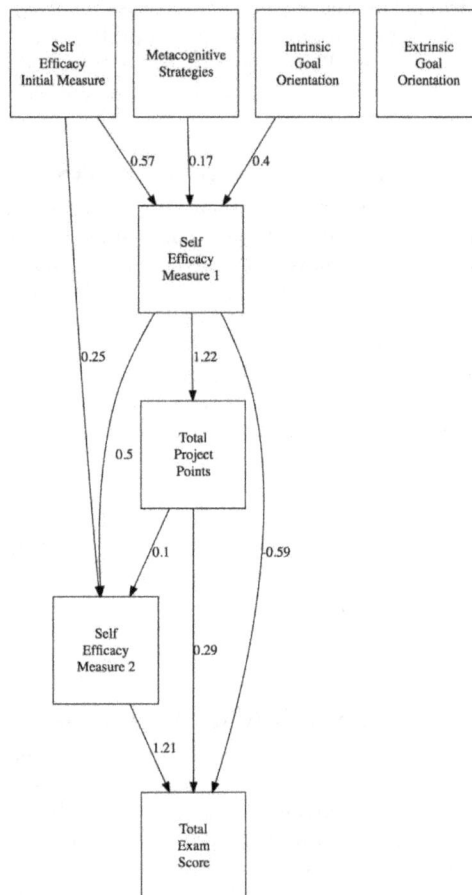

Figure 2: Path Model: Significant paths

Overall, the results of the path analysis were expected, because the best predictor of both performance indicators was a self-efficacy measurement. Another unsurprising, but interesting, aspect of the results of the path model is the difference in variance explained between the two outcome measures in terms of total variance explained. While 35.1% of the variance of the total exam score variance was explained by the MSLQ variables in the path model, only 9.4% of the variance of the project scores was explained by the MSLQ variables. Part of this difference is due to the fact that the second repeated measurement of self-efficacy was not used to predict project scores, because it was measured after all of the projects were completed. Adding this variable would increase the variance explained to 17.0%. Nevertheless, the difference is substantial. This difference may have to do with the standardized nature of the multiple choice tests versus the open-ended nature of programming projects, which makes the scores produced by the exam more reliable than project scores, and therefore easier to predict. Another possibility, however, is that projects and exams differ significantly in the self-regulatory processes that are involved in completing them. Metacognitive strategies, for instance, may play more of a role in completing a programming project than an exam, because projects require more planning and troubleshooting. The most likely possibility is that the factors involved in programming project performance are more multifaceted than those involved in exam performance. More complex interactions between the MSLQ variables and other cognitive and/or affective variables are likely involved, but the data collected in this study is insufficient to determine this.

Table 2: Path model: direct effects

Dep. Var	Ind. Var	est	se	z	p-value
Exams	SE R2	1.21	0.21	5.71	0.00
Exams	SE R1	-0.59	0.23	-2.56	0.01
Exams	Projects	0.29	0.05	5.49	0.00
Exams	Extrin G.O.	-0.72	0.39	-1.85	0.06
Exams	Intrin G.O.	-0.06	0.44	-0.14	0.89
Projects	SE Init.	-0.43	0.32	-1.35	0.18
Projects	SE R1	1.22	0.30	4.03	0.00
Projects	Intrin G.O.	-0.85	0.65	-1.30	0.19
Projects	Extrin G.O.	-0.96	0.56	-1.71	0.09
Projects	Metacog str.	0.26	0.28	0.92	0.36
SE R2	SE R1	0.50	0.07	7.13	0.00
SE R2	SE Init.	0.25	0.07	3.50	0.00
SE R2	Metacog str.	0.01	0.06	0.20	0.84
SE R2	Projects	0.10	0.02	6.45	0.00
SE R2	Intrin G.O.	0.06	0.15	0.41	0.68
SE R2	Extrin G.O.	-0.00	0.13	-0.03	0.98
SE R1	SE Init.	0.57	0.06	9.57	0.00
SE R1	Intrin G.O.	0.40	0.14	2.82	0.00
SE R1	Metacog str.	0.17	0.06	2.84	0.00
SE R1	Extrin G.O.	-0.13	0.13	-1.02	0.31

5.3 Gender differences

In addition to the results on the overall path analysis, there were significant differences in the self-efficacy feedback loop by gender. Unfortunately, the obtained sample sizes were not sufficient to fit separate path models by gender, so significant gender differences on correlation patterns are reported instead. Correlations between the self-efficacy and performance indicators show a consistently distinct pattern for males and females. The correlation matrix for the self-efficacy and performance measures (exam and project totals) for men and women are shown in table 3.

Table 3: Self-Efficacy/Performance Correlations; *Male values below diagonal, female values above*

	SE Init.	SE R1	SE R2	Proj.	Exam
SE Init.	1.00	0.71	0.67	0.23	0.14
SE R1	0.61	1.00	0.78	0.30	0.39
SE R2	0.47	0.63	1.00	0.31	0.42
Proj. pts	0.20	0.31	0.48	1.00	0.67
Exam pts	0.17	0.17	0.47	0.62	1.00

Correlations between the initial self-efficacy measurement and exam and project outcomes were not significantly different between male and female students, and these correlations increased across subsequent self-efficacy measurements, for both groups. However, for the remaining two

self-efficacy measurements a distinct pattern emerged. In the case of both the projects and exams, female self-efficacy - performance correlations increased between the initial self-efficacy measurement and the first repeated measurement. However, between the first and second repeated measurements of self-efficacy, the self-efficacy - performance correlation did not increase significantly. For males on the other hand, there were sharp, statistically significant increases in the self-efficacy/performance correlation between the first and second self-efficacy repeated measurements, for both projects and exams. These results are shown in figure 3.

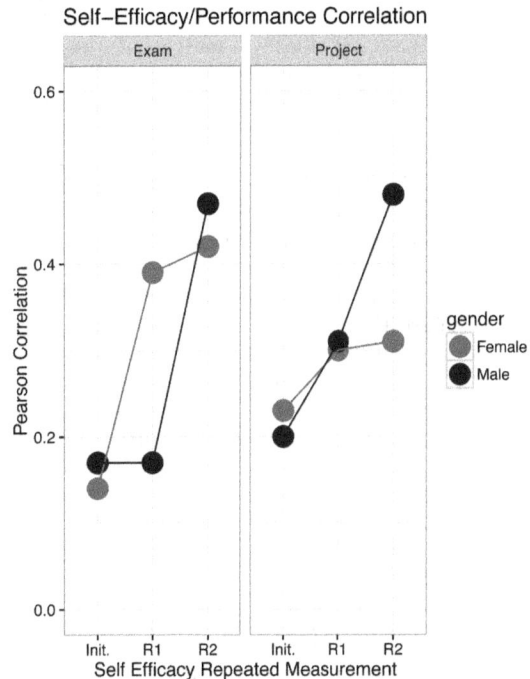

Figure 3: Gender differences in Self-Efficacy correction effect

Hypothesis tests showed that the correlation changes for males between the first and second repeated measurements of self-efficacy were significant, whereas the corresponding change was not significant for females. As shown in the chart, the effect is more pronounced for the exam scores, where the male self-efficacy - exam correlation does not increase at all between the initial self-efficacy measurement and the first repeated measurement, but it sharply increased by the second repeated measurement. This difference is consistent with the result from the path analysis, which showed that self-efficacy better predicted exam scores than project scores. However, the project/SE R2 correlation was statistically significantly higher for males than females, by contrast with the exam/SE R2 correlation, which was the same for both groups.

Change scores between the 3 self-efficacy measurements were also calculated and correlations with outcomes were computed. These tell the same story as the self-efficacy - performance correlations. For females, the change in self-efficacy from the initial measurement to the first repeated measurement had a greater association with scores on projects and exams than did the change from the first repeated measurement to the second repeated measurement. For males, the exact opposite was true for each outcome. The first change in self-efficacy had a weak correlation with performance, but the second change in self-efficacy had a significantly larger correlation. This difference in correlation patterns may be explained by the fact that between the initial self-efficacy measurement and the first repeated self-efficacy measurement, several projects were completed which would provide self-efficacy feedback whereas the first exam did not take place until after the first repeated self-efficacy measurement.

These results suggest that a self-efficacy correction occurs for both males and females as they progress through the course, but that the correction happens more quickly for females. The female self-efficacy - performance correlation reaches its plateau before students have even taken the first exam. Males on the other hand, are modifying their self-beliefs in response to performance feedback at least until the second exam. In the case of exam scores, the correlation with self-efficacy does not change at all for males until after the first exam, whereas it shows a modest (not statistically significant) increase before the first exam for the project - self-efficacy correlation. In each case, there is a clear pattern that suggests that females stop modifying their self-efficacy beliefs in response to performance feedback before exam 1 whereas males modify their self-efficacy beliefs significantly after exam 1. The change score correlations likewise corroborated this pattern. Overall, the correlation patterns suggest that for males the self-efficacy correction process takes longer and requires more performance feedback than for females. The flip side then is that males are more responsive to feedback, as there is a larger window of time during which performance feedback will significantly change their self-efficacy beliefs.

6. DISCUSSION AND CONCLUSIONS

The results of the path analysis reveal interesting patterns about the way that students' self-efficacy beliefs can influence their course outcomes and vice versa. The path analysis model showed that self-efficacy was the most important predictor of students' outcomes, but the model also shows the reciprocal effects of performance on self-efficacy. The important thing to take from these results is not that self-efficacy influences students' outcomes in CS1. This finding is not surprising given that prior research in both CS and non-CS classes has reported similar results. The important thing to take from these results is that metacognitive strategies and goal orientation impact self-efficacy, which impacts performance, and then performance impacts self-efficacy, which then impacts performance again. This self-efficacy feedback loop is the reason why self-efficacy is so important for performance and why managing it throughout the learning process has great potential to improve student learning outcomes in programming.

The results of the analysis also show a very interesting pattern in how male and female students modify their self-efficacy beliefs differently in response to performance feedback. Female students respond to performance feedback early in the course, revising their self-efficacy beliefs earlier. The implication of this result is important. It suggests that responses to early failures in CS could be causing female students to disengage from CS. As Kinnunen and Simon showed, programming assignments are characterized by their propensity to catch novice students completely off

guard with difficulties, and produce intense emotional reactions [27]. If female students are more prone to internalize these early failures by revising their self-efficacy beliefs, this may discourage them from continuing to engage with programming. The gender participation gap in CS is a very significant issue, and the results of this study may offer one piece of of the explanation of this gap. Female students did just as well as male students in this course by all indicators, but how that success is related to their self-beliefs is quite different. Understanding how the self-efficacy feedback loop operates differently could perhaps be used to modify pedagogical approaches to reduce the attrition rate of females in CS.

Another important result to notice is the disconnect between the programming project outcome and the exam outcome. Earlier work has shown that programming projects and multiple choice exams can assess fundamentally different things, so it is not particularly surprising that we see different results in the path analysis. The different results in the path analysis show that variables outside of the ones we looked at are more important for predicting project scores than exam scores. This could mean a few different things. Perhaps there is an distinct self-efficacy feedback loop for programming projects. There may be additional cognitive factors that affect the self-efficacy feedback loop, or perhaps more complex relationships between the cognitive and motivational processes that occur when students do programming projects. Future research should delve deeper into these connections and investigate more of these complex relationships.

Overall, these results reinforce the notion that self-efficacy beliefs are part of a reciprocal relationship with performance. The self-efficacy feedback loop is important to CS researchers and educators because self-efficacy, unlike metacognitive strategies and goal orientations, is very malleable. Self-efficacy interventions could offer a unique opportunity to improve student retention in CS, particularly for female students. Many cognitive and affective factors are known to be correlated with success in CS [7] but few are as malleable as self-efficacy. The potential for interventions to redirect the self-efficacy feedback loop is great, and targeted self-efficacy interventions could potentially help reduce the gender participation gap. Self-efficacy is very important for success, and a better understanding of how self-efficacy develops helps improve our understanding of how students learn CS. Self-efficacy is of course just one piece of the larger puzzle, but these results represent an important step in our understanding of that piece.

7. REFERENCES

[1] I. S. Al-Harthy and C. A. Was. Knowledge monitoring, goal orientations, self-efficacy, and academic performance: A path analysis. *Journal of College Teaching and Learning*, 10(4):263–279, 2013.

[2] S. Andrew. Self-efficacy as a predictor of academic performance in science. *Journal of Advanced Nursing*, 27(3):596–603, 1998.

[3] P. Azalov, S. Azaloff, and F. Zlatarova. Work in Progress - Comparing Assessment Tools in Computer Science Education: Empirical Analysis. *Proceedings of 34th ASEE/IEEE Frontiers in Education Conference, 20-23 October 2004*, 2:18–19, 2004.

[4] A. Bandura. Self-efficacy: toward a unifying theory of behavioral change. *Psychological review*, 84(2):191–215, 1977.

[5] A. Bandura. *Social Foundations of Thought and Action: A Social Cognitive Theory*. Prentice-Hall, Englewood Cliffs, NJ, 1986.

[6] S. Bergin, A. Mooney, J. Ghent, and K. Quille. Using Machine Learning Techniques to Predict Introductory Programming Performance. *International Journal of Computer Science and Software Engineering*, 4(12):323–328, 2015.

[7] S. Bergin and R. Reilly. Programming: Factors that Influence Success. *ACM SIGCSE Bulletin*, 37(1):411–415, 2005.

[8] S. Bergin and R. Reilly. The influence of motivation and comfort-level on learning to program. *Ppig 17*, (June):293–304, 2005.

[9] S. Bergin, R. Reilly, and D. Traynor. Examining the role of self-regulated learning on introductory programming performance. *First International Workshop on Computing Education Research*, pages 81–86, 2005.

[10] D. R. Bernstein. Comfort and Experience with Computing: Are They the Same for Women and Men? *SIGCSE Bull.*, 23(3):57–61.

[11] S. Beyer. Gender differences in the accuracy of self-evaluations of performance. *Journal of Personality and Social Psychology*, 59(5):960–970, 1990.

[12] S. Beyer. Predictors of Female and Male Computer Science Students' Grades. *Journal of Women and Minorities in Science and Engineering*, 14(4):377–409, 2008.

[13] S. Beyer. Why are women underrepresented in Computer Science? Gender differences in stereotypes, self-efficacy, values, and interests and predictors of future CS course-taking and grades. *Computer Science Education*, 24(2-3):153–192, 2014.

[14] S. L. Britner and F. Pajares. Sources of science self-efficacy beliefs of middle school students. *Journal of Research in Science Teaching*, 43(5):485–499, 2006.

[15] T. Busch. Gender Differences in Self-Efficacy and Attitudes Toward Computers. *Journal of Educational Computing Research*, 12(2):147–158, 1995.

[16] J. Cohoon. Must there be so few? Including women in CS. *25th International Conference on Software Engineering, 2003. Proceedings.*, pages 668–674, 2003.

[17] L. Corno. The metacognitive control components of self-regulated learning. *Contemporary Educational Psychology*, 11(4):333–346, 1986.

[18] M. Credé and L. A. Phillips. A meta-analytic review of the Motivated Strategies for Learning Questionnaire. *Learning and Individual Differences*, 21:337–346, 2011.

[19] A. J. Elliot. Approach and avoidance motivation and achievement goals. *Educational Psychologist*, 34:169–189, 1999.

[20] K. Falkner, R. Vivian, and N. Falkner. Identifying Computer Science Self-Regulated Learning Strategies. *Proceedings of the 2014 conference on Innovation & technology in computer science education, ITiCSE '14*, pages 291–296, 2014.

[21] J. K. Ford, E. M. Smith, A. Consulting, D. A. Weissbein, S. M. Gully, and E. Salas. Relationships of Goal Orientation, Metacognitive Activity, and Practice Strategies With Learning Outcomes and Transfer. *Journal of Applied Psyc*, 83(2):218–233, 1998.

[22] M. E. Gist. Self-Efficacy: A Theoretical Analysis of its Determinants and Malleability. *Academy of Management Review*, 17(2), 1992.

[23] J. M. Harackiewicz, K. E. Barron, P. R. Pintrich, A. J. Elliot, and T. M. Thrash. Revision of achievement goal theory: Necessary and illuminating. *Journal of Educational Psychology*, 94(3):638–645, 2002.

[24] H. M. Havenga. An investigation of students' knowledge, skills and strategies during problem solving in object-oriented programming. 2008.

[25] M. Havenga. The role of metacognitive skills in solving object-oriented programming problems: a case study. *The Journal for Transdisciplinary Research in Southern Africa*, 11(1):133–147, 2015.

[26] D. Iacobucci. Structural equations modeling: Fit Indices, sample size, and advanced topics. *Journal of Consumer Psychology*, 20(1):90–98, 2010.

[27] P. Kinnunen and B. Simon. Experiencing Programming Assignments in CS1 : The Emotional Toll. *Icer'10*, pages 77–85, 2010.

[28] P. Kinnunen and B. Simon. CS Majors' Self-Efficacy Perceptions in CS1: Results in Light of Social Cognitive Theory. *Proceedings of the seventh international workshop on Computing education research - ICER '11*, pages 19–26, 2011.

[29] S. Krieger, M. Allen, and C. Rawn. Are Females Disinclined to Tinker in Computer Science? In *Proceedings of the 46th ACM Technical Symposium on Computer Science Education (SIGCSE '15)*, pages 102–107, 2015.

[30] W. Kuechler and M. Simkin. How well do multiple choice tests evaluate student understanding in computer programming classes? *Journal of Information Systems Education*, 14(4):389–399, 2003.

[31] R. W. Lent and G. Hackett. Career self-efficacy: Empirical status and future directions. *Journal of Vocational Behavior*, 30(3):347–382, 1987.

[32] A. Lishinski. Cognitive, Affective, and Dispositional Components of Learning Programming. In *ICER Doctoral Consortium*, 2016.

[33] E. A. Locke and G. P. Latham. *New Developments in Goal Setting and Task Performance*. Routledge, 2012.

[34] C. Midgley, A. Kaplan, and M. Middleton. Performance-approach goals: Good for what, for whom, under what circumstances, and at what cost? *Journal of Educational Psychology*, 93(1):77–86, 2001.

[35] F. Pajares. Self-Efficacy Beliefs and Mathematical Problem-Solving of Gifted Students. *Contemporary educational psychology*, 21(4):325–44, 1996.

[36] F. Pajares. Self-Efficacy Beliefs in Academic Settings. *Review of Educational Research*, 66(4):543–578, 1996.

[37] F. Pajares and L. Graham. Self-Efficacy, Motivation Constructs, and Mathematics Performance of Entering Middle School Students. *Contemporary educational psychology*, 24(2):124–139, 1999.

[38] F. Pajares and M. D. Miller. Role of self-efficacy and self-concept beliefs in mathematical problem solving: A path analysis. *Journal of educational psychology*, 86(2):193, 1994.

[39] F. Pajares and G. Valiante. Influence of Self-Efficacy on Elementary Students' Writing. *Journal of Educational Research*, 90(6):353–360, 1997.

[40] M. Pajares, F. & Johnson. Self-efficacy beliefs and the writing performance of entering high school students. *Psychology in the Schools*, 33(April):163–175, 1996.

[41] R. Paul, S. Smith, M. L. Genthon, G. G. Martens, C. L. Hauen, G. G. Martens, M. Genthon, and P. Wren. A Manual for the Use of the Motivated Strategies for Learning Questionnaire (MSLQ). *Technical Report No. 91-B-004*, (The Regents of The University of Michigan.), 1991.

[42] P. R. Pintrich and E. V. de Groot. Motivational and self-regulated learning components of classroom academic performance. *Journal of Educational Psychology*, 82(1):33–40, 1990.

[43] P. R. Pintrich and D. H. Schunk. *Motivation in education: Theory, research, and applications.* Prentice-Hall, Englewood Cliffs, NJ, 1995.

[44] P. R. Pintrich and D. H. Schunk. Motivation in education: Theory, research, and practice. *Chapter*, 5:153–197, 1996.

[45] R Core Team. *R: A Language and Environment for Statistical Computing.* R Foundation for Statistical Computing, Vienna, Austria, 2015.

[46] V. Ramalingam, D. LaBelle, and S. Wiedenbeck. Self-efficacy and mental models in learning to program. *Proceedings of the 9th annual SIGCSE conference on Innovation and technology in computer science education - ITiCSE '04*, page 171, 2004.

[47] T. Raykov and G. A. Marcoulides. *A First Course in Structural Equation Modeling.* Lawrence Erlbaum Associates, London, 2006.

[48] Y. Rosseel. {lavaan}: An {R} Package for Structural Equation Modeling. *Journal of Statistical Software*, 48(2):1–36, 2012.

[49] M. A. Rubio, R. Romero-Zaliz, C. Mañoso, and A. P. de Madrid. Closing the gender gap in an introductory programming course. *Computers & Education*, 82:409–420, 2015.

[50] D. H. Schunk. Self-Efficacy and Education and Instruction. In *Self-Efficacy, Adaptation, and Adjustment: Theory Research and Application*, pages 281–303. 1995.

[51] J. Sheard, S. Simon, M. Hamilton, and J. Lönnberg. Analysis of research into the teaching and learning of programming. *Proceedings of the fifth international workshop on Computing education research workshop - ICER '09*, page 93, 2009.

[52] K. Sveidqvist, M. Bostock, C. Pettitt, M. Daines, A. Kashcha, and R. Iannone. *DiagrammeR: Create Graph Diagrams and Flowcharts Using R*, 2016.

[53] A. Syzmanowicz and A. Furnham. Gender differences in self-estimates of general, mathematical, spatial and verbal intelligence: Four meta analyses. *Learning and Individual Differences*, 21(5):493–504, 2011.

[54] J. Tsan, K. E. Boyer, and C. F. Lynch. How Early Does the CS Gender Gap Emerge? A Study of Collaborative Problem Solving in 5th Grade Computer Science. *Proceedings of the 47th ACM Technical Symposium on Computer Science Education (SIGCSE '16)*, pages 388–393, 2016.

[55] J. C. Valentine, D. L. Dubois, and H. Cooper. The Relation Between Self-Beliefs and Academic Achievement: A Meta-Analytic Review. *Educational Psychologist*, 39:111–133, 2004.

[56] C. Watson, F. W. B. Li, and J. L. Godwin. No Tests Required: Comparing Traditional and Dynamic Predictors of Programming Success. *Proceedings of the 45th ACM Technical Symposium on Computer Science Education (SIGCSE '14)*, 2014.

[57] H. Wickham. *ggplot2: elegant graphics for data analysis.* Springer New York, 2009.

[58] S. Wiedenbeck. Factors affecting the success of non-majors in learning to program. *Proceedings of the 2005 international workshop on Computing education research - ICER '05*, pages 13–24, 2005.

[59] B. C. Wilson. A Study of Factors Promoting Success in Computer Science Including Gender Differences. *Computer Science Education*, 12(1-2):141–164, 2010.

[60] B. C. Wilson and S. Shrock. Contributing to success in an introductory computer science course: a study of twelve factors. *ACM SIGCSE Bulletin*, 33(1):184–188, 2001.

[61] P. H. Winne. A metacognitive view of individual differences in self-regulated learning. *Learning and Individual Differences*, 8(4):327–353, 1996.

[62] C. Wolters and S. Yu. The Relation Between Goal Orientation and Students' Motivational Beliefs and Self-Regulated Learning. *Learning & Individual Differences*, 8(3):211–238, 1996.

[63] B. J. Zimmerman. Becoming a self-regulated learner: Which are the key subprocesses? *Contemporary Educational Psychology*, 11(4):307–313, 1986.

[64] B. J. Zimmerman. Self-Regulated Learning and Academic Achievement: An Overview. *Educational psychologist*, 25(1):3–17, 2010.

[65] D. Zingaro and L. Porter. Impact of Student Achievement Goals on CS1 Outcomes. *Proceedings of the 47th ACM Technical Symposium on Computer Science Education (SIGCSE '16)*, pages 279–284, 2016.

Learning Loops: A Replication Study Illuminates Impact of HS Courses

Briana B. Morrison
College of Information Science & Technology
University of Nebraska at Omaha
6001 Dodge Street
Omaha, NE 68182
bbmorrison@unomaha.edu

Adrienne Decker
School of Interactive Games and Media
Rochester Institute of Technology
152 Lomb Memorial Drive
Rochester, NY, 14623
adrienne.decker@rit.edu

Lauren E. Margulieux
School of Psychology
Georgia Institute of Technology
654 Cherry Street
Atlanta, GA, 30332-0170
l.marg@gatech.edu

ABSTRACT

A recent study about the effectiveness of subgoal labeling in an introductory computer science programming course both supported previous research and produced some puzzling results. In this study, we replicate the experiment with a different student population to determine if the results are repeatable. We also gave the experimental task to students in a follow-on course to explore if they had indeed mastered the programming concept. We found that the previous puzzling results were repeated. In addition, for the novice programmers, we found a statistically significant difference in performance based on whether the student had previous programming courses in high school. However, this performance difference disappears in a follow-on course after all students have taken an introductory computer science programming course. The results of this study have implications for how quickly students are evaluated for mastery of knowledge and how we group students in introductory programming courses.

Keywords
Subgoal labels, Cognitive Load, Contextual Transfer.

1. INTRODUCTION

In the nascent field of computer science education, we have become particularly good at two things: publishing new studies and establishing that our students don't know what we think they should know. Looking at any recent conference proceedings in the discipline, you would be hard pressed to find any papers that are replication studies. And we have many examples, from Soloway [36] to McCracken [26], of our students performing below our expectation levels on supposedly relatively easy programming tasks. This paper tackles both of these issues directly: we present the results of a replication study done with a new population of students at a different institution and provide evidence that students really do learn programming constructs, but perhaps not as quickly as we, the educators, would hope.

A recent study presented results on the effectiveness of subgoal labeling with students in introductory programming courses learning to write `while` loops to solve programming problems [28]. Subgoal labeling is a technique used to promote subgoal learning that has been used to help learners recognize the

fundamental structure of the procedure being exemplified in worked examples [10–12]. Subgoal labels are function-based instructional explanations that describe the purpose of a subgoal, or functional piece of the problem solution, to the learner. Some of results presented in the original study agreed with previous subgoal label research: learning with subgoal labels produces higher learning gains and better problem solving performance than learning without subgoal labels. The study compared students who learned from unlabeled worked examples (i.e., conventional examples) to those who learned from worked examples labeled with subgoal labels created by the experimenters and worked examples that prompted students to generate their own subgoal labels.

Also tested in the original study was the effect of transfer between worked examples and practice problems. Problem sets of worked example-practice problems came in two varieties: either *isomorphic* or *contextual transfer*. In the isomorphic transfer group the problem to be solved in the worked example-practice problem (WE-PP) pair was identical to the worked example in both procedural steps and cover story (i.e., context). The only thing changed was the actual values of the numbers to be calculated. In the contextual transfer group, the problem to be solved in the WE-PP pair involved the same procedural steps but the cover story and numeric values changed.

Both the unlabeled groups and the generate subgoal labels groups performed as expected in the code writing task whether or not they were in the isomorphic or contextual transfer treatment groups. In both of these cases, the isomorphic group outperformed the contextual transfer group, which cognitive load theory [27, 37, 39] would predict. Cognitive load theory (CLT) suggests that having an additional piece to figure out – the contextual transfer – may overload the cognitive processing of novices resulting in poorer performance on the assessment task. However, perhaps the most puzzling result came from the group of students who were given subgoal labels. In this treatment, the students who received problems with contextual transfer performed statistically better than the group of students receiving the isomorphic problems. This outcome was unexpected, and we are still exploring why the group receiving subgoal labels made by the experimenters would behave differently than the other groups.

To explore whether the original study was an anomaly, we set out to replicate the study with a different population at a different institution. In the original study, the average score on the post-test, which comprised items from the AP CS test, was only 31%, indicating that the students had not learned very much from the intervention. Perhaps the assessment tasks were too difficult and once again we were asking more from our students than they were capable of (a la McCracken [26]). To test this hypothesis we also asked students in a follow-on programming course to participate in the study to compare their performance with those in the introductory course. We found that the original results were not an anomaly – they repeated. We also found that students in the follow-on course performed better on the assessments (than the introductory students) indicating that writing `while` loops can be mastered. In addition, we found that students in the introductory programming course who had taken computing courses in high school performed better than those who did not. However, this difference in performance due to high school experience was not present for students in the follow-on course.

2. BACKGROUND
This section reviews the details of the previous study and examines current literature for the effect of previous coursework on programming performance in novices.

2.1 Previous Study
The original study [28] tested hypotheses related to whether using subgoal labels to teach a programming construct would produce results similar to those achieved in other disciplines. The study proposed that using subgoal labels to help students learn would reduce the cognitive load imposed in learning.

2.1.1 Cognitive Load Theory
Cognitive load can be defined as "the load imposed on an individual's working memory by a particular (learning) task" [40]. The cognitive load required to comprehend materials directly affects how much students learn, and affects their performance scores on assessments related to that task. If students have to keep too many things in working memory in order to understand a concept, learning suffers. The central problem identified by Cognitive Load Theory (CLT) is that learning is impaired when the total amount of processing requirements exceeds the limited capacity of working memory [31]. Currently CLT [27, 37, 39] defines two different types of cognitive load on a student's working memory: intrinsic load and extraneous load.

Intrinsic load is a combination of the innate difficulty of the material being learned as well as the learner's previous knowledge [21]. Extraneous load is the load placed on working memory that does not contribute directly toward the learning of the material. For example, the extra resources consumed to understand poorly written text or diagrams without sufficient clarity contributes to extraneous cognitive load [21].

The intrinsic and extraneous loads can be controlled through instructional design and care should be given to eliminate any possible extraneous load while attempting to optimize the level of intrinsic load so that the learner is challenged but not overly so. It is believed that worked examples, when carefully designed, can accomplish both of these goals [24].

2.1.2 Worked Examples
Worked examples are one type of instruction used to teach procedural process to students for problem solving activities. Worked examples give learners concrete examples of the procedure being used to solve a problem.

Eiriksdottir and Catrambone argue that learning primarily from worked examples does not inherently promote deep processing of concepts [15]. While learning from worked examples may result in better initial performance, it is less likely result in the retention and transfer [15]. When studying examples, learners tend to focus on incidental features, like those necessary for the cover story of the problem, rather than the fundamental features, like the concepts required to solve the problem. This happens because incidental features are easy to grasp and novices do not have the necessary domain knowledge to recognize fundamental features of examples [13]. A focus on incidental features leads to ineffective organization and storage of information that, in turn, leads to ineffective recall and transfer [8].

2.1.3 Subgoal Labeling
To promote deeper processing of worked examples and, thus, improve retention and transfer, worked examples have been manipulated to promote subgoal learning. Subgoal learning refers to a strategy used predominantly in STEM fields that helps students deconstruct problem solving procedures into subgoals, functional parts of the overall procedure, to better recognize the fundamental components of the problem solving process [1].

Subgoal labeling is a technique used to promote subgoal learning. Studies [3, 4, 10–12, 24, 25] have consistently found that subgoal-oriented instructions improved problem solving performance across a variety of STEM domains, such as programming [24] and statistics [12]. Studies have also found that giving subgoal labels in worked examples improves performance while solving novel problems without increasing the amount of time learners spend studying instructions or working on problems [24]. This format highlights the structure of examples, helping students focus on structural features and more effectively organize information [2].

By helping learners organize information and focus on structural features of worked examples, subgoal labels are believed to reduce the extraneous cognitive load that can hinder learning but is inherent in worked examples [32]. Worked examples introduce extraneous cognitive load because they are necessarily specific to a context, and students must process the incidental information about the context even though it is not relevant to the underlying procedure [39]. Subgoal labels can reduce focus on these incidental features by highlighting the fundamental features of the procedure [32]. Subgoal labels further improve learning by reducing the intrinsic load by providing a mental organization (i.e., subgoals) for storing information.

2.1.4 Results
The original study tested its hypotheses by dividing the participants into three treatment groups, each with its own instructional materials: learning with no subgoal labels, learning with given pre-defined subgoal labels, and asking participants to generate their own subgoal labels after some initial training. Each treatment group was then subdivided into two sections: *isomorphic* or *contextual transfer*. In the isomorphic transfer condition, the procedure and context used to solve the WE-PP were exactly the same but the exact values in the problem changed. For example, if a worked example asked participants to find the average of quiz scores with values 70, 80, and 90, then the practice problem asked participants to find the average of quiz scores with values 75, 85, and 95. In the contextual transfer condition, the procedure used to solve the WE-PP were the same except the context of the problem changed. For example, if a worked example asked participants to find the average of quiz scores, then the practice problem asked participants to find the average of money amounts.

The original study found that, similar to previous research in other disciplines, students who learned with subgoal labels (either given or generated) performed better on the code writing assessments than those who learned without subgoal labels. The participants who generated their own subgoal labels did not perform better on the code writing tasks requiring transfer, unlike previous research.

The unexpected results occurred with the given subgoal label group. Cognitive Load Theory would predict that learning with given subgoal labels and no contextual transfer should impose lower cognitive processing than learning with given subgoal labels *and* contextual transfer. The contextual transfer would require additional working memory to process. However the results from the original study directly contradict this. The original study found, unlike the other two treatment groups, that the participants that learned with given subgoal labels *and* contextual transfer significantly outperformed the given subgoal labels with isomorphic problems. This is the main finding we wished to test in the replication to determine if the original findings were an anomaly or if something else was happening.

2.2 Previous Coursework

Recent previous work has identified problems with student understanding and learning in introductory courses. McCracken et al. [26] showed that students were unsuccessful at writing correct code to answer problems involving programming by the end of the introductory course. Lister et al. [22] took this investigation further by examining students' abilities to read and trace code. They concluded that weak students are often weak in their ability to read (and trace) code which is a precursor to writing code. In an attempt to better understand how reading and tracing are related to abilities to write code, Lopez et al. [23] created an instrument to determine a hierarchy of concepts (reading, tracing, solving Parsons problems, writing) with regard to code. Their work found that solving Parsons problems might actually be more difficult than tracing iterative code.

In an effort to prevent students from performing poorly, many have turned to trying to determine what best predicts computing proficiency, presumably as a way to determine how to better teach students and/or determine which student may be more likely to need extra support during their first course. The research on success predictors goes back decades, with numerous factors being identified such as comfort level [45], math and/or science background [5, 6, 20, 43, 45], spatial visualization skills [35], attributions of success and/or confidence [6, 34, 45], learning style [9, 35]. Watson [42] has argued that programming behavior was better predictor of success in the course than the traditional test-based prediction metrics and/or demographics.

Many believe that prior exposure to programming is a positive predictive factor in success in the first course. Hagan and Markam [17] showed that prior programming experience did in fact help students in the introductory course. They showed that the number of programming languages used was also important to students' initial success in the course. However, Evans and Simkin [16] showed that prior academic experience (including computing experience) did not factor strongly into a predictive model for success, but rather worked in concert with other behavior and cognitive factors to determine success. This was shown again by Wiedenbeck [44] in regards to non-majors taking a programming course and with Ventura [41] when looking at students taking an objects-first curriculum.

One thing from the predictors research that stands out is that there are likely a number of factors that contribute to a student's success in a course. Prior experience, whether it be in programming or other disciplines, is an important factor in some studies, but not as important in others. What we are interested in here is whether or not the prior experience impacts the understanding of a particular concept, not necessarily overall student success in the course.

3. METHOD OF STUDY
3.1 Purpose

Participants in introductory programming classes who had already been introduced to loops within their course were given additional instructional material designed to reinforce the practice of solving programming problems using `while` loops. Participants were recruited from 3 different first and second year programming courses at a technical university in the northeast United States and the study was conducted over a one month period.

Table 1 summarizes the differences between the three courses. The first two courses are first year, first semester courses serving primarily two different populations of students. The first course (101) serves as the first programming course (CS1 equivalent) for students intending to major in New Media Interactive Design (a College of Imaging Arts and Sciences major), or New Media Interactive Development (a College of Computing and Information Sciences major) and is taught using Processing [33]. The "New Media" majors are focused on the interaction of art and technology through media. The difference between the students is the focus of the major, the "design" major attracts primarily students who may consider themselves artists, while the "development" major attracts those who are more "technologists". The second course (105) serves as the first programming course (CS1 equivalent) for students intending to major in Game Design and Development (a College of Computing and Information Sciences major) and is taught in C# [33]. The game design and development degree is a technically focused degree in game design and development and the coursework has many similarities to a computer science degree. The department does not give credit for either 101 or 105 for Advanced Placement (AP) credit. Students earning high scores on the AP exam earn credit for another course from another department, but still need to take 101 or 105 to complete the requirements for their respective majors.

Table 1. Classes Participating in Study

Course	Programming Language	Majors	Experiment Delivery Method
101	Processing	New Media Interactive Design, New Media Interactive Development	Closed lab in-class exercise
105	C#	Game Design & Development	Optional at-home assignment
202	C# (some Processing)	New Media Interactive Design, Game Design and Development	Closed lab in-class exercise

The second year course (202) is designed to bring together the groups from New Media Interactive Development and Game Design and Development and is taught primarily in C# (with some limited time devoted to Processing) and focuses on the use and integration of media and media artifacts into interactive experiences [33]. It should be noted that students who take the 101 course take 2 more courses (102 and 201) before taking the follow-on course while those who take the 105 course take only 1 more course (106) before taking 202. So students from the 101 course path have a 3 semester sequence while those in the 105 track have a 2 semester sequence.

The study was conducted either in a closed lab setting with up to 30 computers in a single room, or as an optional at-home assignment (see Table 1). The participating instructors decided how to structure the exercise in their particular course and what weighting it had on a student's grade, but participation in the study was strictly voluntary. That is, even in classes where there was a closed lab around the exercise, participation in the study described here was voluntary – consent to use the data for the study was given at the end of the exercises. All of these courses are taught in a computer lab of at most 30 students. Exercises where students are given a set of tasks to perform during the class period for their grade are a common part of these courses.

Students received an introduction to the study explaining that the material in the study was designed to help them learn how to write loops. Students were then given a URL to the first page of the study, which was housed in SurveyMonkey. Participants worked independently. The in-class sessions were an entire class period for the course (110 minutes). For the students who completed at home, the assignment was posted for them and they were given a due date by which they needed to complete the exercise. At the end of the window, the SurveyMonkey materials were closed.

3.2 Instructional Materials
The materials used were identical to those used in [28], other than placement of the consent. To learn the procedure for using `while` loops to solve programming problems, participants were given three worked examples and three practice problems. The worked examples and practice problems were interleaved so that after studying the first worked example, participants solved the first practice problem before moving on to the second worked example. The worked examples came in three formats, which varied between participants. The first format was not subgoal oriented, meaning that steps of the examples did not provide any information about the underlying subgoals of the procedure. The second format grouped steps of the example by subgoal and provided meaningful subgoal labels for each group as is typical in subgoal label research (e.g., [24]). The third format grouped steps of the example by subgoal and provided a spot for participants to write generated subgoal labels for each group. Each of the groups was numbered as "label 1," "label 2," etc., and groups that represented the same subgoal had the same number; therefore, groups that represented subgoal 1 were numbered as "label 1" regardless of where in the example they appeared (see Figure 1). Participants were told that each of the worked examples would have the same subgoals, and they were encouraged to update and improve upon their generated labels as they learned more.

No labels	Given Labels	Placeholder for Label

sum = 0
lcv = 1
 	
WHILE lcv <= 100 DO
 	
lcv = lcv + 1
ENDWHILE
	Initialize Variables
	sum = 0
	lcv = 1
	Determine Loop Condition
	WHILE lcv <= 100 DO
	
	Update Loop Var
	lcv = lcv + 1
	ENDWHILE
		Label 1: _____
		sum = 0
		lcv = 1
		Label 2: _____
		WHILE lcv <= 100 DO
		
		Label 3: _____
		lcv = lcv + 1
		ENDWHILE

Figure 1. Partial worked example formatted with no labels, given labels, or placeholders for generated labels.

Participant groups also received different practice problems to test how contextual transfer may affect learning – the *isomorphic* transfer condition and the *contextual* transfer condition, just as in the original study. The contextual transfer was intended to be harder for participants to map concepts from the worked example to the practice problem. More difficult mapping can improve learning by reducing illusions of understanding caused by shallow

processing thus inducing deeper processing of information [7, 15, 29]. However it can also increase cognitive load and potentially hinder learning [39].

After completing the instructions, participants completed novel programming assessments to measure their code writing performance. The assessments included two tasks. First, the code writing task asked participants to use the problem-solving structure that they had learned during the WE-PP pairs to solve four novel problems. Two of these problems required contextual transfer, meaning that they followed the same steps found in the instructions but in a different context. The other two problems required both contextual and structural transfer. In these problems the context was new to the participants and the solution to the problem required a different structure than the problems found in the instructional material (e.g., the practice problem is summing values, the assessment is counting matching values). These tasks were intended to measure participants' code writing and problem solving performance as a 'far' transfer.

After the code writing task, participants completed a Parsons problem. Parsons problems [30] involve correct code which is broken into code fragments that have to be put in the correct order. The Parsons problem used for assessment was a version of the "rainfall problem" [18]. The problem had 13 different code pieces with between 1 and 3 lines of code in each code piece. The participants were asked to put the code pieces in order with no consideration of indentation. In other words, they indicated the order of the code segments by numbering them.

3.3 Design
The experiment was a 3-by-2, between-subjects, factorial design: the format of worked examples (unlabeled, subgoal labels given, or subgoal labels generated) was crossed with the transfer distance between worked examples and practice problems (isomorphic or contextual transfer). The dependent variables were performance on the pre- and post-test, code writing tasks, and time on task.

3.4 Participants
Participants were 100 students from a technical university in the northeast United States (Table 2). To account for prior experience, participants were asked about their prior programming experience in high school (either regular or advanced placement courses) and college and whether they had experience using while loops. Other demographic information collected included gender, age, academic major, high school grade point average (GPA), college GPA, number of years in college, reported comfort with computer, expected difficulty of the programming task, and primary language. There were no statistical differences between the groups for demographic data, which is expected because participants were randomly assigned to treatment groups.

Age	Gender	GPA	Major
M = 19	72% male	M = 3.5/4	33% New Media 63% Game Design 3% CS, SWE, CEngr

Table 2. Participant Demographics

Participants who did not attempt all tasks were excluded from analysis. For the replication piece of the study, participants who answered more than two questions correctly out of the five on the pre-test were excluded from analysis because the instructions were designed for novices. However, for the second piece of analysis within the paper, we looked at the success rate of all students who completed all the tasks. Based on these exclusion criteria, we analyzed data from 27 participants for the replication study and 100 participants for overall performance.

3.5 Procedure
The procedure used in this study was identical to that used in [28], other than granting consent was moved from the beginning of the survey to the end. Students completed the demographic questions followed by a pre-test. The pre-test was comprised of multiple choice questions about `while` loops from previous Advanced Placement Computer Science A exams.

When participants finished the demographic questionnaire and pre-test, they began the instructional period which consisted of training followed by the worked example-practice problem (WE-PP) pairs. Participants who generated their own subgoal labels received training on how to create subgoal labels. Participants who did not generate their own subgoal labels received training to complete verbal analogies. Verbal analogies (e.g., water : thirst :: food : hunger) were considered a comparable task to subgoal label training because they both require analyzing text to determine an underlying structure. Participants who were not asked to generate their own labels were not given subgoal label training because it might have prompted them to process the instructions more similarly than would be expected of participants who were asked to generate their own labels, which might confound the results. The subgoal label training and the analogy training included expository instructions, worked examples, and activities.

Three WE-PP pairs were then presented to the participants. The worked example format differed between subjects among three levels: unlabeled, subgoal labels given, and subgoal labels generated. Furthermore, the transfer distance between worked example and practice problem differed between subjects between two levels: isomorphic or contextual transfer.

After the instructional period, participants moved to the assessment period. The assessment period included the problem solving tasks discussed earlier: 4 code writing problems and a Parsons problem.

At the end of the session, participants completed a post-test with the same questions as the pre-test to measure their learning. Throughout the procedure we recorded the time taken to complete each task. We also collected process data throughout the instructional period. We collected performance on the training activities and practice problems to ensure that participants were completing tasks.

We entered into the study with the following research questions:

R1. Do participants who learn with given subgoal labels and no contextual transfer perform better or worse on programming assessments than those who learn with given subgoal labels and contextual transfer?

R2. Do participants further along in their computing studies outperform novices on both the pre/post-test and programming assessments?

4. ANALYSIS AND RESULTS
4.1 Accuracy – Code Writing
We scored participants' solutions for accuracy to generate a code writing score. Participants earned one point for each correct line of code that they wrote. This scoring scheme allowed for more sensitivity than scoring solutions as wholly right or wrong. If participants wrote lines that were conceptually correct but contained typos or syntax errors (e.g., missing a parenthesis), they

received points. We scored logic errors (having < rather an <=) as incorrect. We considered scoring for conceptual and logical accuracy more valuable than scoring for absolute syntactical accuracy because participants were still early in the learning process. Participants could earn a maximum score of 44.

In the statistics reported below, we include two types of effect sizes. The first, est. ω^2, describes how much of the variation in scores can be attributed to the manipulation. For example, for the code writing assessment, an est. ω^2 of .10 means that 10% of the variation in performance can be attributed to the instructional manipulations. The second, f or d, describes the difference between groups using the standard deviation as the unit of measurement. For example, for the code writing assessment, a d of .5 would mean that the difference- between the means of two groups is half of the standard deviation for those groups.

The effect of the interventions on code writing performance depended on the interaction of the worked example manipulation and transfer distance manipulation. We found no main effect of worked example format, $F (2, 21) = 0.26$, $MSE = 105.6$, $p = .78$, est. $\omega^2 = .02$. In addition, we found no main effect of transfer distance, $F (1, 21) = 1.47$, $MSE = 105.6$, $p = .24$, est. $\omega^2 = .07$. There was, however, a statistically significant interaction between worked example format and transfer distance, $F (2, 21) = 5.19$, $MSE = 105.6$, $p = .015$, est. $\omega^2 = .33$, $f = .44$ (see Figure 2[1]).

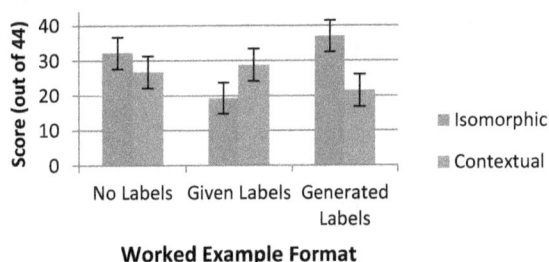

Figure 2. Code writing performance for novice programmers

In this interaction, the difference between the group that was given subgoal labels with isomorphic transfer ($M = 18.4$, $SD = 13.0$) and the group that was given subgoal labels with contextual transfer ($M = 31.2$, $SD = 13.8$) was not statistically significant, $t (8) = -1.50$, $p = .17$, but the difference between groups was large with an effect size of $d = 0.95$. Based on these results, the difference between groups is meaningful, even though it is not statistically significant, likely due to a small sample size. The sample size was small because this was a replication study thus we did not need as much statistical power to ensure the pattern of results was reliable. Because the effect size is large and matches previous results we conclude that this is a meaningful difference. Furthermore, the difference between the group that generated subgoal labels with isomorphic problems ($M = 18.0$, $SD = 4.6$) and the group that generated subgoal labels with contextual transfer ($M = 37$, $SD = 4.5$) was statistically significant, $t (4) = 7.18$, $p = .002$, with a large effect size, $d = 4.18$. This effect size is based on a sample of six, therefore, it is likely not reliable. The effect size is likely inflated due to the small sample; however, the effect of the intervention is still valid and in the correct direction. These results mean that participants who were given subgoal

---

[1] Error bars on all bar graphs represent the 95% confidence interval.

labels performed better when they had contextual transfer, and participants who generated subgoal labels performed better with isomorphic problems.

Performance on the post-test was similar to that on the pre-test. Average scores on the post-test were low, 36% (1.8 out of 5 points). We found no statistical differences for main effect of worked example format, $F(2, 21) = .07$, $MSE = 1.21$, $p = .93$, est. $\omega^2 = .01$, main effect of transfer distance, $F(1, 21) = .28$, $MSE = 1.21$, $p = .60$, est. $\omega^2 = .01$, or interaction, $F(2, 21) = .93$, $MSE = 1.21$, $p = .41$, est. $\omega^2 = .09$.

4.2 Accuracy – Parsons Problem

We scored participants' Parsons problem answers for correct order to create their score. Participants ranked the 13 code pieces from the Parsons problem; we gave them one point for each code piece that was in the correct order relative to the pieces around it. For example, if participants ranked the 4th, 5th, and 6th pieces of the problem as the 5th, 6th, and 7th pieces of their solution, they would receive two out of three possible points for those three pieces. The first piece would be counted as wrong because it is not following the 3rd piece, but the other two pieces would be counted as correct because they are following the correct piece. This scoring scheme better captures participants' understanding than scoring for absolute correct order as it does not penalize correct sequences of code that follow incorrect sequences.

Based on the analysis of Parsons problem responses, performance did not seem to depend on the worked example or transfer manipulations. We found no statistical differences for main effect of worked example format, $F(2, 21) = 1.20$, $MSE = 9.70$, $p = .32$, est. $\omega^2 = .10$, main effect of transfer distance, $F(1, 21) = .61$, $MSE = 9.70$, $p = .45$, est. $\omega^2 = .03$, or interaction, $F(2, 21) = .24$, $MSE = 9.70$, $p = .79$, est. $\omega^2 = .02$.

4.3 Time Efficiency

4.3.1 Time on Worked Example-Practice Pairs

For time spent studying worked examples and solving practice problems, we found a meaningful difference based on worked example format even though there was not a statistically significant ANOVA, $F(2, 21) = 3.37$, $MSE = 202.2$, $p = .06$, est. $\omega^2 = .27$, $f = .35$. We found no main effect of transfer distance, $F(1, 21) = 1.94$, $MSE = 202.2$, $p = .18$, est. $\omega^2 = .10$. In addition, we found no interaction, $F(2, 21) = 1.80$, $MSE = 202.2$, $p = .19$, est. $\omega^2 = .17$ (see Figure 3).

4.3.2 Time on Code Writing Assessments

Time spent on the code writing assessments was not affected by the subgoal or transfer manipulations. We found no statistical differences for a main effect of worked example format, $F(2, 21) = 2.22$, $MSE = 49.9$, $p = .13$, est. $\omega^2 = .17$, main effect of transfer distance, $F(1, 21) = .63$, $MSE = 49.9$, $p = .44$, est. $\omega^2 = .03$, or interaction, $F(2, 21) = .53$, $MSE = 49.9$, $p = .60$, est. $\omega^2 = .05$.

4.3.3 Time on Parsons Problems

Time spent on the Parsons problem was not affected by the subgoal or transfer manipulations. We found no statistical differences for main effect of worked example format, $F(2, 21) = 1.14$, $MSE = 8.75$, $p = .34$, est. $\omega^2 = .10$, main effect of transfer distance, $F(1, 21) = .21$, $MSE = 8.75$, $p = .65$, est. $\omega^2 = .01$, or interaction, $F(2, 21) = .26$, $MSE = 8.75$, $p = .77$, est. $\omega^2 = .02$.

5. PREVIOUS COURSEWORK EXPERIENCE

As mentioned earlier, we also asked students in a follow-on

programming course to participate in the study. This section reviews their performance and compares it with the novice performance. For this analysis we looked at all students who completed the tasks regardless of their pre-test score.

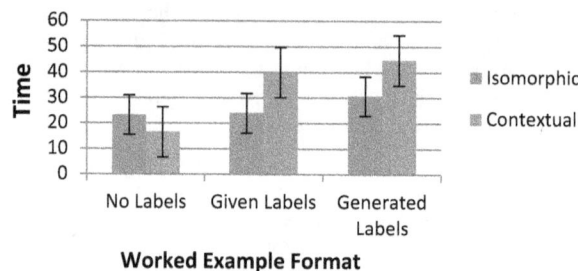

Figure 3. Time (in minutes) on instructional tasks

5.1 Results of All Introductory Students

Students considered for the results in Section 4, the replication study, had to match the qualifications of the original study. This meant that we excluded all introductory students that correctly answered 3 or more questions on the pre-test correctly. This eliminated 24 students, almost as many as we analyzed (27). It became clear that many of the students in the introductory courses had significant loop writing knowledge prior to our intervention. This led us to further investigate if this prior knowledge could be attributed to prior coursework.

Looking at all participants in the introductory courses ($n = 51$), the average score on the pre-test was 46% (2.3 out of 5). Participants scored about the same on the post-test with an average of 54% (2.7 out of 5).

Within this group, no manipulation by itself made a statistical difference in code writing performance. There was no main effect of worked example format, $F(2, 45) = .32$, $MSE = 106.1$, $p = .73$, est. $\omega^2 = .01$. There was also no main effect of transfer distance, $F(1, 45) = 1.88$, $MSE = 106.1$, $p = .18$, est. $\omega^2 = .04$. There was, however, an interaction, $F(2, 45) = 4.04$, $MSE = 106.1$, $p = .024$, est. $\omega^2 = .15$ (see Figure 4). This interaction resembles the pattern of results seen in the analyses reported earlier in this paper.

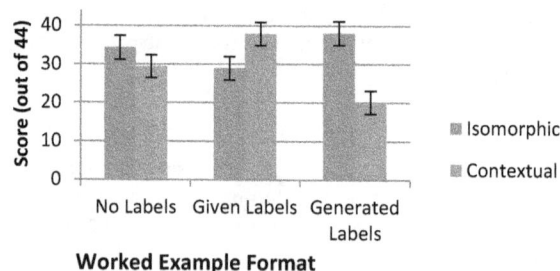

Figure 4. Code writing performance for participants in introductory courses

On the Parsons problem, there were no statistical differences among groups on performance. There was no main effect of worked example format, $F(2, 45) = 1.69$, $MSE = 12.6$, $p = .19$, est. $\omega^2 = .07$. There was no main effect of transfer distance, $F(1, 45) = .75$, $MSE = 12.6$, $p = .39$, est. $\omega^2 = .02$. There was no interaction, $F(2, 45) = .02$, $MSE = 12.6$, $p = .98$, est. $\omega^2 = .001$.

5.2 Results of Students in Follow-On Course

Participants in the follow-on course (i.e., the course after the

226

introductory college course) were excluded from previous analyses because they had at least a semester of programming instruction, and the instruction in the study was designed for novices. Participants in this course scored on average a 73% (3.6 out of 5) on the pre-test. After instruction on the post-test, participants scored about the same with an average of 70% (3.5 out of 5). Within this group, participants who were given subgoal labels performed better on the code writing assessments than those who were not given labels or those who generated labels, F (2, 43) = 7.33, MSE = 15.9, p = .002, est. ω^2 = .25, f = .37. There was no main effect of transfer distance, F (1, 43) = .25, MSE = 15.9, p = .62, est. ω^2 = .01, nor was there an interaction, F (2, 43) = 2.30, MSE = 15.9, p = .11, est. ω^2 = .10 (see Figure 5).

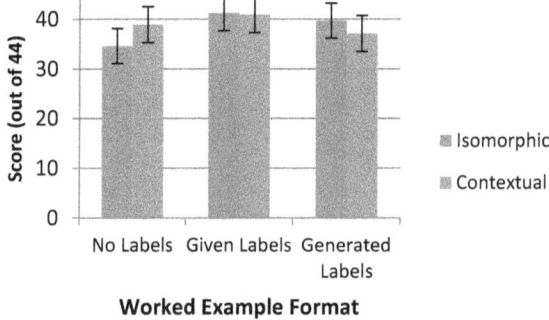

Figure 5. Code writing performance for 202 students

On the Parsons problem, participants who generated subgoal labels performed worse than those who were not given labels or those who received labels, F (2, 43) = 4.75, MSE = 10.9, p = .014, est. ω^2 = .18, f = .31. There was no main effect of transfer distance, F (1, 43) = 2.17, MSE = 10.9, p = .15, est. ω^2 = .05, nor was there an interaction, F (2, 43) = .62, MSE = 10.9, p = .54, est. ω^2 = .03 (see Figure 6).

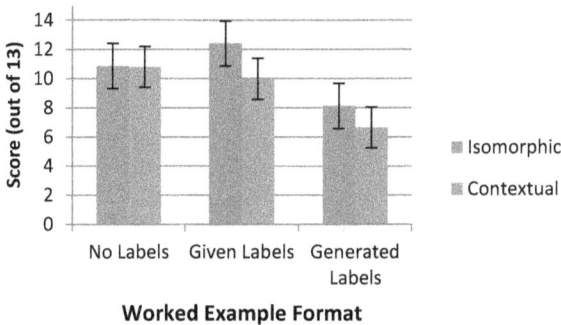

Figure 6. Parsons problem performance for 202 students

5.3 Effect of Previous Coursework

To explore the effect of computing courses in high school and the effect of prior computing courses in college on performance, we used these two variables as random independent variables in ANOVA to determine if they affected performance. Participants who took computing courses in high school performed better on the code writing assessment than those who did not, F (1, 96) = 12.0, MSE = 56.2, p = .001, est. ω^2 = .11, f = .35. Participants who had taken prior computing courses in college performed better, F (2, 96) = 14.3, MSE = 56.2, p < .001, est. ω^2 = .13, f = .38. There was an interaction, F (2, 96) = 11.1, MSE = 56.2, p = .001, est. ω^2

= .10, f = .33, such that participants who took computing courses in high school did not perform better that those who did not in later college computing courses (Figure 7). In other words, it does not matter if the previous course was taken in high school or college – the fact that the student had a previous course predicts better performance; but that advantage does not continue into the next course.

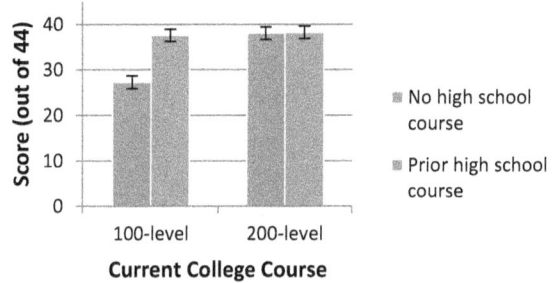

Figure 7. Code writing performance by course level

Similar to the code writing task, participants who took computing courses in high school performed better on the Parsons problem than those who did not, F (1, 96) = 9.85, MSE = 11.6, p = .002, est. ω^2 = .09, f = .31. Participants who had taken prior computing courses in college also performed better, F (2, 96) = 6.78, MSE = 11.6, p = .011, est. ω^2 = .07, f = .26. For this assessment, however, there was no interaction, F (2, 96) = 1.66, MSE = 11.6, p = .20, est. ω^2 = .02, suggesting that those who had computing courses in high school performed better than those who did not, even after their first computing course in college.

6. DISCUSSION

Here we summarize our findings related to our original research questions and discuss the implications for computing education.

6.1 Replication

Our replication of [28] yielded results that support the original findings. This study confirms that novice participants who learn by generating subgoal labels (using isomorphic WE-PP pairs) perform the best, and statistically better than if they had been WE-PP pairs with contextual transfer (Figure 2). We conclude that for the best learning results novice students should be taught to generate their own subgoal labels but be given WE-PPs that are very similar.

We hypothesize that teaching novice students to generate their own subgoal labels does require additional time, both for instruction and for the student during the WE-PP instruction time. Additionally it should be noted that within this experiment participants did not receive any feedback on the appropriateness of their generated labels. To obtain maximum benefit from generating subgoal labels, students should receive feedback on the correctness of their labels. Alternately, similar learning results may be obtained by using given subgoal labels.

However, if pre-defined given subgoal labels are used, the WE-PP pairs should utilize contextual transfer to ensure maximum learning. As mentioned earlier, this is contradictory to what would be predicted by CLT. This is certainly one phenomenon that needs further research. It may be that with given subgoal labels and isomorphic problems students do not adequately self-explain the process associated with each subgoal as the steps are identical within both the worked example and practice problem. Just as in the first study, we reviewed student code submissions to ensure that they were not copied from the worked example and they were not. Also the time spent in the instructional period indicates that participants spent similar amounts of time regardless if they received isomorphic or contextual transfer WE-PP pairs.

It may be that with given subgoal labels students require multiple examples for comparison to be able to determine the generalities of the labels and the process. It would be interesting to determine if more examples or additional practice problems would improve the learning performance of these groups. It may also be possible to present the worked example with no contextual story at all – just as a simple problem to be solved. If students are presented with a "vanilla" worked example with given subgoal labels followed by a practice problem embedded within a context, would the performance differ? Looking into these and other possibilities are planned as future research areas.

6.2 Previous Coursework

We were surprised at the number of students in the introductory courses that were excluded due to their pre-test scores. In looking at the demographics, we noticed many of the introductory students had a previous computing course in high school and their pre-test scores reflected this prior experience. In examining their performance along with the students in the follow-on course, we found that having that prior coursework experience made a significant difference in the performance on the assessment tasks.

Participants in the introductory courses with high school coursework experience performed statistically better on both the code writing and Parsons problem assessments than students in the same courses without high school computing coursework. These students performed similarly to those in the follow-on course (202). Students in the 202 course performed statistically better on the Parsons problem assessments than the students in the introductory courses, regardless of high school coursework. We have evidence that students with some coursework experience, whether in high school or a previous college class, have actually mastered this concept given the pre-test score above 70% and the performance on the code writing assessment (Figure 5 for 202 students only).

However, as can be seen in Figure 7, students in the follow-on course that did not have a high school computing course performed approximately the same as those who did have a high school computing course on the code writing assessment task. Thus, those without the previous coursework advantage had "caught up" to those who started with more knowledge. This has significant implications for those teaching introductory programming. If students with prior programming experience are in the same class as those with previous computing coursework, we cannot expect them to perform the same on assessment tasks, especially after a short exposure. The participants in the introductory courses had been exposed to loops in their current courses for approximately 2 weeks and were preparing for a graded test which would include loops. Even without knowing the scores for the exam, we predict that the students with previous computing courses in high school would significantly outperform those without that experience.

As instructors we need to be cognizant of the potential influence that prior coursework may have on student performance. We should not expect those being exposed to concepts for a minimal amount of time to be as proficient as those who have had a semester's worth (or more) of practice. Perhaps students with prior experience should be in a separate class from those without prior coursework, even for introductory courses. The evidence from this study suggests that by the next course, any advantage

those with prior coursework in high school once had, has been eliminated; at least for code writing tasks.

On the Parsons problem assessment, results from this study indicate that those who took a high school course continue to outperform those who did not. Further research is needed to determine if this result is repeatable and why this might be the case. It may be that continuous code writing practice improves performance on Parsons problems. We are unaware of research that compares novice to expert performance on Parsons problems but this study suggests that additional practice in programming continues to improve Parsons problem performance.

We found one additional interesting result in this study. Students in the follow-on course who generated subgoal labels performed statistically worse than those in the same course who were not given labels or those who received labels. This may be an example of the expertise reversal effect [19]. The expertise reversal effect occurs when the learner is presented with information that causes them to think below their automatized schema. The instructional design material, in this case the generation of subgoal labels, uses working memory that would not have been necessary if the learner were just solving the problem. In other words, the participant could have solved the problem without any instructional material at all because of their prior knowledge. The instructional material interfered with their problem solving process. Further research into when subgoal labels should no longer be used with those learning programming should be explored.

7. CONCLUSION

This study was originally conceived as a means to replicate an existing study to determine if the puzzling results would be confirmed. The data gathered in this study confirms that students who learn with given subgoal labels perform better with contextual transfer between the WE-PP pair than those who received isomorphic WE-PP pairs. While we still have no evidence as to why this occurs, contrary to cognitive load theory, we now know that the result is repeatable and deserves further research to investigate why this group in computing differs from those in other disciplines.

Because of the number of participants eliminated from the replication analysis we explored reasons for the difference in performance. Students who had previous computing coursework outperformed those without previous coursework in both code writing and Parsons problem assessment tasks. Students with previous computing coursework should be assessed at a different standard than those with minimal time exposure to the concept. However, in the follow-on course this performance difference disappears indicating that those without previous coursework do "catch up". This indicates that the students with differing experience backgrounds can be merged into a single class.

While some may think the results of this paper, students with previous experience perform better, are obvious, we demonstrate that our students actually do eventually learn and master a concept (writing loops) unlike so much previous research [22, 26, 36]. We also provide evidence that any advantage gained through previous coursework disappears, with regard to this introductory concept, in the follow-on course. We find these facts, that our students actually do learn and that students without previous experience can catch up, very encouraging.

8. ACKNOWLEDGMENTS

We would like to thank the students who participated in the study and their instructors who graciously gave us the time. We also thank the anonymous reviewers who supplied comments which improved this paper.

This work is funded in part by the National Science Foundation under grant 1138378. Any opinions, findings, and conclusions or recommendations expressed in this material are those of the authors and do not necessarily reflect the views of the NSF.

9. REFERENCES

[1] Atkinson, R.K. et al. 2003. Aiding Transfer in Statistics: Examining the Use of Conceptually Oriented Equations and Elaborations During Subgoal Learning. *Journal of Educational Psychology*. 95, 4 (2003), 762.

[2] Atkinson, R.K. et al. 2000. Learning from examples: Instructional principles from the worked examples research. *Review of educational research*. 70, 2 (2000), 181–214.

[3] Atkinson, R.K. 2002. Optimizing learning from examples using animated pedagogical agents. *Journal of Educational Psychology*. 94, 2 (2002), 416.

[4] Atkinson, R.K. and Derry, S.J. 2000. Computer-based examples designed to encourage optimal example processing: A study examining the impact of sequentially presented, subgoal-oriented worked examples. *Fourth International Conference of the Learning Sciences* (2000).

[5] Bennedsen, J. and Caspersen, M.E. 2005. An investigation of potential success factors for an introductory model-driven programming course. *Proceedings of the first international workshop on Computing education research* (2005), 155–163.

[6] Bergin, S. and Reilly, R. 2005. Programming: factors that influence success. *ACM SIGCSE Bulletin* (2005), 411–415.

[7] Bjork, R.A. 1994. Memory and metamemory considerations in the training of human beings. *Metacognition: Knowing about Knowing*. MIT Press.

[8] Bransford, J. 2000. *How people learn: Brain, mind, experience, and school*. National Academies Press.

[9] Campbell, V. and Johnstone, M. 2010. The significance of learning style with respect to achievement in first year programming students. *Software Engineering Conference (ASWEC), 2010 21st Australian* (2010), 165–170.

[10] Catrambone, R. 1996. Generalizing solution procedures learned from examples. *Journal of Experimental Psychology: Learning, Memory, and Cognition; Journal of Experimental Psychology: Learning, Memory, and Cognition*. 22, 4 (1996), 1020.

[11] Catrambone, R. 1994. Improving examples to improve transfer to novel problems. *Memory & Cognition*. 22, 5 (1994), 606–615.

[12] Catrambone, R. 1998. The subgoal learning model: Creating better examples so that students can solve novel problems. *Journal of Experimental Psychology: General*. 127, 4 (1998), 355.

[13] Chi, M. et al. 1989. Self-explanations: How students study and use examples in learning to solve problems. *Cognitive science*. 13, 2 (1989), 145–182.

[14] Denny, P. et al. 2008. Evaluating a new exam question: Parsons problems. *Proceeding of the Fourth international Workshop on Computing Education Research* (Sydney, Australia, 2008), 113–124.

[15] Eiriksdottir, E. and Catrambone, R. 2011. Procedural instructions, principles, and examples how to structure instructions for procedural tasks to enhance performance, learning, and transfer. *Human Factors: The Journal of the Human Factors and Ergonomics Society*. 53, 6 (2011), 749–770.

[16] Evans, G.E. and Simkin, M.G. 1989. What best predicts computer proficiency? *Communications of the ACM*. 32, 11 (1989), 1322–1327.

[17] Hagan, D. and Markham, S. 2000. Does it help to have some programming experience before beginning a computing degree program? *ACM SIGCSE Bulletin* (2000), 25–28.

[18] Johnson, W.L. and Soloway, E. 1985. PROUST: Knowledge-based program understanding. *Software Engineering, IEEE Transactions on*. 3 (1985), 267–275.

[19] Kalyuga, S. 2007. Expertise reversal effect and its implications for learner-tailored instruction. *Educational Psychology Review*. 19, 4 (2007), 509–539.

[20] Leeper, R.R. and Silver, J.L. 1982. Predicting success in a first programming course. *ACM SIGCSE Bulletin*. 14, 1 (1982), 147–150.

[21] Leppink, J. et al. 2013. Development of an instrument for measuring different types of cognitive load. *Behavior research methods*. 45, 4 (2013), 1058–1072.

[22] Lister, R. et al. 2004. A multi-national study of reading and tracing skills in novice programmers. *ACM SIGCSE Bulletin* (2004), 119–150.

[23] Lopez, M. et al. 2008. Relationships between reading, tracing and writing skills in introductory programming. *Proceedings of the fourth international workshop on computing education research* (2008), 101–112.

[24] Margulieux, L.E. et al. 2012. Subgoal-labeled instructional material improves performance and transfer in learning to develop mobile applications. *Proceedings of the ninth annual international conference on International computing education research* (2012), 71–78.

[25] Margulieux, L.E. and Catrambone, R. 2014. Improving problem solving performance in computer-based learning environments through subgoal labels. *Proceedings of the first ACM conference on Learning@ scale conference* (2014), 149–150.

[26] McCracken, M. et al. 2001. A multi-national, multi-institutional study of assessment of programming skills of first-year CS students. *Working group reports from ITiCSE on Innovation and technology in computer science education* (Canterbury, UK, 2001), 125–180.

[27] van Merriënboer, J.J. and Sweller, J. 2005. Cognitive load theory and complex learning: Recent developments and future directions. *Educational psychology review*. 17, 2 (2005), 147–177.

[28] Morrison, Briana B. et al. 2015. Subgoals, Context, and Worked Examples in Learning Computing Problem Solving. *ICER 2015* (Aug. 2015).

[29] Palmiter, S. and Elkerton, J. 1993. Animated demonstrations for learning procedural computer-based tasks. *Human-Computer Interaction*. 8, 3 (1993), 193–216.

[30] Parsons, D. and Haden, P. 2006. Parson's Programming Puzzles: A Fun and Effective Learning Tool for First Programming Courses. *Proceedings of the 8th Australasian Conference on Computing Education - Volume 52* (Darlinghurst, Australia, Australia, 2006), 157–163.

[31] Plass, J.L. et al. 2010. *Cognitive load theory*. Cambridge University Press.

[32] Renkl, A. and Atkinson, R.K. 2002. Learning from examples: Fostering self-explanations in computer-based

learning environments. *Interactive learning environments.* 10, 2 (2002), 105–119.

[33] Rochester Institute of Technology 2014. Undergraduate Course Descriptions.

[34] Rountree, N. et al. 2004. Interacting factors that predict success and failure in a CS1 course. *ACM SIGCSE Bulletin* (2004), 101–104.

[35] Simon et al. 2006. Predictors of success in a first programming course. *Proceedings of the 8th Australasian Conference on Computing Education-Volume 52* (2006), 189–196.

[36] Soloway, E. and Ehrlich, K. 1984. Empirical studies of programming knowledge. *Software Engineering, IEEE Transactions on.* 5 (1984), 595–609.

[37] Sweller, J. et al. 1998. Cognitive architecture and instructional design. *Educational psychology review.* 10, 3 (1998), 251–296.

[38] Sweller, J. et al. 2011. *Cognitive load theory.* Springer.

[39] Sweller, J. 2010. Element interactivity and intrinsic, extraneous, and germane cognitive load. *Educational psychology review.* 22, 2 (2010), 123–138.

[40] van Gog, Tamara and Paas, Fred 2012. Cognitive Load Measurement. *Encyclopedia of the Sciences of Learning.* Springer.

[41] Ventura Jr, P.R. 2005. Identifying predictors of success for an objects-first CS1. (2005).

[42] Watson, C. et al. 2014. No tests required: comparing traditional and dynamic predictors of programming success. *Proceedings of the 45th ACM technical symposium on Computer science education* (2014), 469–474.

[43] White, G. and Sivitanides, M. 2003. An empirical investigation of the relationship between success in mathematics and visual programming courses. *Journal of Information Systems Education.* 14, 4 (2003), 409.

[44] Wiedenbeck, S. 2005. Factors affecting the success of non-majors in learning to program. *Proceedings of the first international workshop on Computing education research* (2005), 13–24.

[45] Wilson, B.C. and Shrock, S. 2001. Contributing to success in an introductory computer science course: a study of twelve factors. *ACM SIGCSE Bulletin* (2001), 184–188.

Examining the Value of Analogies in Introductory Computing

Yingjun Cao
Computer Science and
Engineering Department
UC San Diego
La Jolla, CA, USA

Leo Porter
Computer Science and
Engineering Department
UC San Diego
La Jolla, CA, USA

Daniel Zingaro
Mathematical and
Computational Sciences
Univ. of Toronto Mississauga
Toronto, ON, Canada

ABSTRACT

Although computing students may enjoy when their instructors teach using analogies, it is unknown to what extent these analogies are useful for their learning. This study examines the value of analogies when used to introduce three introductory computing topics. The value of these analogies may be evident during the teaching process itself (short term), in subsequent exams (long term), or in students' ability to apply their understanding to related non-technical areas (transfer). Comparing results between an experimental group (analogy) and control group (no analogy), we find potential value for analogies in short term learning. However, no solid evidence was found to support analogies as valuable for students in the long term or for knowledge transfer. Specific demographic groups were examined and promising preliminary findings are presented.

Categories and Subject Descriptors

K.3.2 [**Computer Science Education**]: Computer and Information Science Education

Keywords

CS1; CS2 ; analogies; programming

1. INTRODUCTION

Analogies are considered a powerful instructional tool for improving student learning [11]. As such, it is unsurprising that, in a recent study, eight out of ten instructors report employing analogies when teaching CS1 [21]. In addition, there is evidence that computing students value the use of metaphors [13, 16].

Using analogies for teaching has its theoretical basis in constructivist theory [2] and Peirce's theory of signs [22] as analogies aim to connect student prior understanding of a familiar base topic to a new topic [10]. Given this basis, we would expect to find that student learning is improved when introducing material in the context of one or more appropriate analogies. Indeed, in education and cognitive

ICER '16, September 08-12, 2016, Melbourne, VIC, Australia
© 2016 ACM. ISBN 978-1-4503-4449-4/16/09... $15.00
DOI: http://dx.doi.org/10.1145/2960310.2960313

psychology, analogies have been shown to be valuable for learning [3, 4].

In computing, the results have been conflicting. [16] examines the value of analogies for college students learning Pascal, and finds evidence of small learning benefits for far transfer, but no difference in near transfer and other measures of learning (time to take an exam, etc.). By contrast, [5] finds more convincing evidence of analogies helping 15-17 year-old students learn programming.

Given that the majority of instructors use analogies to teach introductory computing, it becomes paramount to examine whether there is evidence to support this practice. As such, this work aims to answer our primary research question: Does introducing a topic with appropriate analogies improve student learning of that topic?

In our experiment, two sections of an introductory course alternate between control group (no analogies) and experimental group (analogies) for three CS1.5 topics: recursion, events, and multithreading. Student learning is measured by performance on technical clicker questions (short term), quizzes or exams weeks after the learning (long term), and exam questions that have students apply their understanding to new areas (transfer).

The results suggest a potential benefit from analogies in the short term, though the results are not conclusive. However, we find no strong evidence to suggest that there is a benefit from the analogies in later assessments, nor is there a benefit for transfer to new topics. Demographic factors are investigated, and we find that analogies may help students from certain demographic groups. After presenting the experimental methods and results, we explore the implications of these findings, potential limitations of the study, and suggestions for follow-on experiments.

2. BACKGROUND

Analogies and metaphors have been widely used in educational settings across disciplines including computer science [3, 4, 5, 16]. Computer science is a field that embodies many new concepts: concepts that are unique to the computational domain and not encountered in daily life. Analogies can bridge this gap between domains [7]. A large portion of analogy-related work in CS education focuses on proposing new analogies [1, 8, 9, 18], analyzing existing analogies and exploring how they should be used [21], and analogy-related instructional design [14, 15, 24].

Advances in cognitive and educational psychology have helped researchers to analyze analogies as rigorous mappings from the base domain to the target domain [10, 23]. Novices learning a new concept tend to focus on surface, contextual aspects of the problem domain rather than its core features [6]. Thus, Gentner et.al. proposed the use of analogical encoding to promote learning [11]. In analogical encoding, learners compare analogies from multiple domains, and the primary objective is for learners to capture the inherit relationships that exist in both the base and target domains. For example, Greer [12] investigated how three approaches for introducing recursion, namely theory-oriented, architecture-oriented and task-performance-oriented, affect student learning. In particular, the theory-oriented approach used an analogy between recursion and mathematical induction. No performance difference was observed in test scores, though the author discovered that students with strong mathematical background benefited more in the theory-oriented approach.

Relevant experimental work in CS education predominantly focuses on the effectiveness of analogies in student-centered analogical encoding. In [16], the authors examined the issues around the timing to introduce analogies when learning arrays, and observed that when an analogy was introduced before technical content, student performance significantly improved compared with the group where analogies were introduced after technical content. Chee [5] studied the effectiveness of analogies with respect to their relative goodness. The experimental subjects were high school students with no prior programming experience. The conclusion of that study is that learning outcomes are positively related to the quality of mapping between the material and the analogy. [13] designed a lecture format that incorporates student analogical encoding into the study of computer networks. Comparisons were conducted but the results did not reveal significant differences on student performance.

The aforementioned works provide evidence that student-centered analogical encoding has some learning benefits in terms of conceptual understanding of computing topics. Yet, these studies tend to scaffold the analogical reasoning rather than present the analogy directly, and results for introductory post-secondary CS courses are sparse.

In the present work, we study the effectiveness of analogies and examples in a typical post-secondary setting where an instructor briefly uses an analogy before the introduction of a new concept. We argue that this instructional setting is quite common in traditional lectures. This is the first study in computing, to our knowledge, that examines whether this standard use of analogies impacts student learning of technical content. The outcome measures of this study span short term effectiveness, long term effectiveness, and knowledge transfer. This study is also the first CS education experimental study that investigates the impact of analogies on particular demographic groups.

3. METHOD

The study was conducted in two CS1.5 sections (Java) at a large research-intensive North American university. One section, **Section A**, is at 10am and the other section, **Section B**, at 11am. One of the authors is the primary instructor of both sections. At our institution, students without a programming background can take a two-term CS1 sequence, with this CS1.5 course being the latter half of the sequence. More than 95% of students in this class completed the first-term introductory Java course. A few students with either extensive prior programming experience or no experience at all elected to start with the CS1.5 course.

The course was taught using Peer Instruction [19]. Each lecture consisted of mini-lectures, intermixed with clicker questions that followed the standard Peer Instruction protocol of an individual vote, group discussion, group vote, and class-wide discussion. The course instructor has taught introductory computing multiple times and used Peer Instruction multiple times.

Table 1: Student composition in the two sections. χ^2 test was used to test if there was a composition difference between the two sections.

Categories	Sub-categories	Sec. A	Sec. B
Gender ($p_{\chi^2} > .05$)	Male	120	116
	Female	64	60
Race ($p_{\chi^2} > .05$)	Caucasian	27	27
	Latino	13	15
	Asian	132	117
	Other	7	11
International ($p_{\chi^2} > .05$)	International	66	50
	Domestic	122	130
First generation ($p_{\chi^2} > .05$)	First-generation	47	35
	Not first-generation	142	146
Prior programming experience ($p_{\chi^2} > .05$)	Some experience I	78	69
	Some experience II	108	106
	Extensive experience	5	4
	No experience	6	4
Major ($p_{\chi^2} > .05$)	Computer Science	25	33
	Other	176	175
Class level ($p_{\chi^2} < .05$)	Freshman	63	58
	Sophomore	107	80
	Junior	22	50
	Senior	9	19

3.1 Section Composition

Student consent was obtained at the beginning of the term. Of the 559 enrolled students at that time, 498 students (89.25%) gave consent to use their data for research purposes. At the end of the term, 409 students in the consenting group remained in the class. Thus, the total number of students in this study is 409.

Table 1 provides student demographic data for the two sections. The "some experience I" group in the prior programming experience category includes students who had no programming experience before CS1 while the "some experience II" group includes those who had some programming experience before CS1. Students in the "no experience" group had no programming experience before taking this CS1.5 course. Demographic data was self-reported by students, using clickers, in the second lecture. These questions included a choice of "prefer not to answer" per approved Human Subjects guidelines. As such, totals may sum to less than 409. Other student demographics such as class level and major status were obtained from the campus database.

As shown in Table 1, the demographic composition of students between sections A and B are not statistically different (χ^2 test) concerning gender, race, nationality, first-generation status, prior programming experience, and major. The two sections differ on class levels.

3.2 Experimental Topics and Structure

An outline of the experiment can be found in Figure 1. Topics were selected to be introduced in the context of analogies (the experimental group) or without analogies (the control group). To help control for potential differences between sections, the experimental group and the control group alternated between section A and section B for different topics.

Four separate topics were initially selected: Polymorphism, Recursion, Events, and Multithreading.

These topics were selected both because of their perceived independence and because they were perceived to have strong

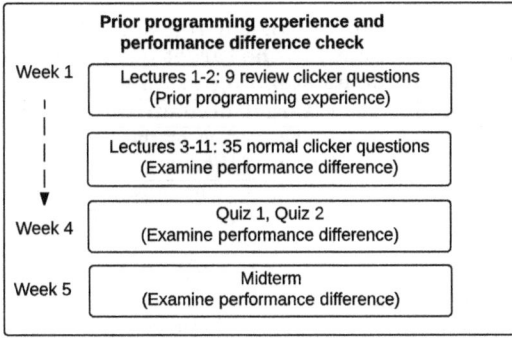

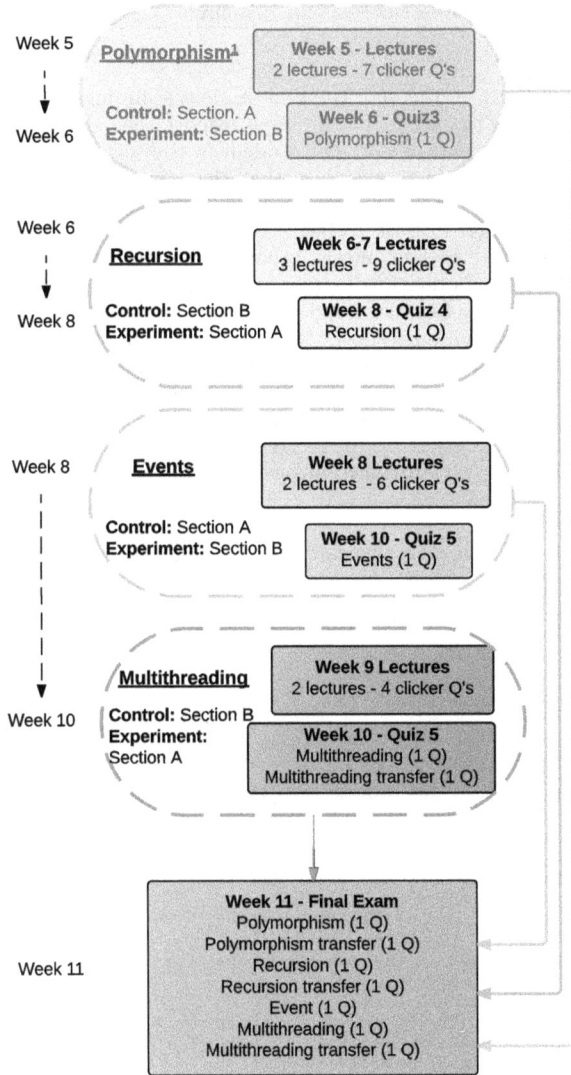

Figure 1: Experimental procedure[1]

analogies. The four CS topics were covered in the second half of the quarter, with between one and three lectures dedicated to each topic. Assessments of student learning were performed periodically throughout the term, including

---

[1]Although Polymorphism appears in the experimental setup, confounding effects caused the data to be unusable. Please see Section 3.3 for details.

Table 2: Results for prior programming experience and week 1-5 performance. The comparison of means between sections A and B all have $p>.05$.

Category	$\mu_A(\%)$	$\mu_B(\%)$
Nine review questions (prior programming experience)	61.9	60.7
Thirty-five clicker questions (in-class performance)	88.0	88.4
Quiz 1 (in-class performance)	75.9	77.5
Quiz 2 (in-class performance)	84.1	83.6
Midterm (in-class performance)	80.4	79.4

clicker questions, quizzes, and exams. Assessments from the first half of the term, before the experiment began, are used to examine whether the two sections had similar baseline performance. In addition, we measured student prior programming experience using nine "review" clicker questions on concepts related to the prior programming course. The means of these clicker questions were compared between the two sections. Table 2 shows the results of comparing prior programming experience and in-class performance.

After the experiment had begun, the following measurements were used to examine whether students benefit from being taught in the context of analogies:

- **Short Term - Clicker Questions:** After a mini-lecture introducing the analogy (usually less than 7 minutes), normal technical content was covered for the remainder of lecture (about 40 minutes). During the coverage of technical content, multiple clicker questions were given to formatively assess student understanding of the topic. Results of those clicker questions were analyzed for differences across sections.

- **Long Term - Quizzes and Exams:** Selected technical questions from quizzes and the final exam pertaining to the experimental topics were analyzed. These questions were given in a technical context, not a context related to the original analogies. Here we refer to "Long Term" as several weeks later than the experiment. Longer term effects (e.g. months after the course ended) were not examined in this work.

- **Transfer - Quizzes and Exams:** Selected questions asked students to transfer their knowledge of one experimental topic to another related non-technical area. Transfer questions were designed for three of our four topics: Polymorphism, Recursion, and multithreading. We unintentionally omitted a transfer question for Events.

3.3 Data Processing and Validation

We followed the guidelines below when processing clicker and exam/quiz data.

- *Clicker data*: Clicker data can be particularly noisy as students are only graded on participation, rather than correctness, and students often fail to answer all questions. We adopt a similar methodology for handling the clicker data as [20] in that the correctness of a student's clicker questions is calculated as the number of correct answers divided by the number of questions to which they responded. A student's clicker data is only included in the analysis if the student responds to more than half of the clicker questions being analyzed.

- *Exam/Quiz data*: For each topic being analyzed, the correctness for each student is calculated as the average correctness of all exam/quiz problems associated with that topic.

As the experimental manipulation (i.e. analogy or no analogy) occurred in the first lecture when the topic was introduced, we exclude from analysis the students who missed this first lecture. These students represented less than 10% of the students in the study. To verify that this exclusion did not impact the composition of the class, we reanalyzed the section compositions after performing the exclusions and found that excluding the aforementioned students did not statistically change demographics or pre-experiment performance between sections.

We reviewed all topics for potential confounding effects. We found a number of concerning issues with the polymorphism topic that ultimately resulted in this topic being removed from the evaluation. First, two questions that we designed to be comparable were shown by student comments to be quite different. Second, we failed to mention a core element of the way that Java handles polymorphism in the experimental section. Finally, we had a student give away the answer to one of our short term questions in the control group. The result of discarding the polymorphism topic is an unbalanced experimental setup where Section A is the experimental group twice, but both sections are still the experimental group for at least one topic.

4. ANALOGIES AND MEASUREMENTS

Each of the pre-selected topics was introduced in the context of one or more analogies or with only technical Java content. In the experimental group, the instructor started with analogies before technical content was introduced. In the control group, technical content was presented without any analogical examples. In this section, we outline the analogies used for each topic and provide a subset of the questions (common to both groups) asked about each topic. The analogies chosen in this study are from those commonly used by the authors. A detailed mapping of the base domain and the target domain for each analogy was constructed, and the analogies with the best mappings were then selected for the experimental group.

4.1 Recursion

We used three analogies for recursion in the experimental group: determining the total number of students standing in a line, a display of Sierpinski triangles, and a casual mention of the movie Inception[2].

The primary analogy is the calculation of the total number of students standing in a straight line. Suppose a group of students stands in a line and the student at the very end wants to know how many students there are in the line. The strategy she adopts is to tap the person in front of her and ask how many students are in front of that student. In turn, the student in the second-last position repeats this

---

[2]During the lecture in the experimental group, a student sitting in the back accidentally dropped his water bottle, and it bounced loudly towards the front of the classroom until someone caught it, and the water bottle was passed student by student back to the owner. The instructor also used this ad hoc analogical phenomenon to illustrate the idea of recursion.

Table 3: Mapping of analogical relations from the base domain (recursion) to the target domain (count the number of students standing in a line).

Base domain	Target domain
Has a base case	The student at the front of the line
Has recursive relationship	Each student taps the student in front of him/her
Has backtracking	A student tells the person behind him/ her the total number of students ahead
Guarantee the base case will be reached	Students standing in a line, not in a circle

action until, in the end, the first student standing in line is reached. That student can simply report that there are 0 students in front of her. The student in the second position will now be able to calculate that there is one student in front of her (1 student in front of her + 0 students returned by the person in front of her). This backtracking behavior repeats until the final answer is obtained by the last student. This analogy's relational mapping is shown in Table 3.

Nine clicker questions and two exam/quiz questions were included to measure short term and long term learning, respectively. There is one transfer question related to recursion in the final exam. We provide a sample question for each category (clicker, exam/quiz, and transfer).

Recursion sample questions

—Clicker

What happens when we call with argument 5 to the following method?

```
public static void foo(int x)
{
    if (x>1)
        foo(x-1);
    System.out.println(x);
}
```

—Exam/Quiz

What is the output produced by the following recursive program? (Hint: draw stack frames)

```
public class Mystery{
    public static void main( String[] args ){
        // print returned value
        System.out.println( mystery( 5 ) );
    }
    public static int mystery( int a ){
        int b = a + 1;
        if ( b < 10 ) {
            // print a and b separate by a space
            System.out.println( a + " " + b );
            b = a + mystery( b + 1 ); }
        else {
            // print Stop!
            System.out.println( "Stop!" );
            b = a - 2;
        }
        // print a and b separate by a space
        System.out.println( a + " " + b );
        return a + b;
    }
}
```

—Transfer

Suppose you moved into a new neighborhood but you don't know the street number of your house (hypothetically). You asked your neighbor to the right of your house for her house

234

number, but she doesn't know hers either. So she went ahead and asked her next door neighbor on the right. Suppose, in the end, someone will know their own house number, and this information will be used to figure out your own house number. What do you think about the validity of this approach?

A. It will always work.

B. It may fail if some of the houses in the neighborhood are arranged in a circle.

C. It may fail if the houses in the neighborhood are arranged in a straight line.

4.2 Events

The analogy used for events is how a police department processes different types of events. A police department carries out normal police activities most of the time. If there are special events such as terrorist attacks or participation in Christmas parades, then the police department allocates resources to handle those scenarios. This process is analogous to how Java Events work. The mapping of relations in the base and target domains is in Table 4.

Table 4: Mapping of analogical relations from the base domain (events) to the target domain (how a police department works)

Base domain	Target domain
Normal execution with event-driven responses	Normal police activity with special responses to events such as terrorist attacks
Must be able to register an event listener	911 phone calls
Resume normal execution after event handling	Resume normal activity after processing an emergency event
Each event is handled by a thread	Each policeman handles certain events
Allow different types of events	Handles terrorist attacks, parade, traffic, etc

We included six clicker questions and two exam/quiz questions, and provide one of each here.

Events sample questions

–Clicker
What will happen when the user clicks the "Deposit $20" button for the following code?

```
public class BankAccount extends Application {
  public static void main(String[] args) {
    launch(args);
  }

  @Override
  public void start(Stage primaryStage) {
    int balance = 100;
    primaryStage.setTitle("Bank Events!");

    //formatting details omitted
    HBox p = new HBox();
    TextField b = new TextField();
    b.setText("$ "+balance);
    Label text = new Label("Balance:\t");
    p.getChildren().addAll(text,b);

    HBox hbox = new HBox();
    Button btnDeposit = new Button("Deposit $20");
```

```
    Button btnWithdraw = new Button("Withdraw $20");
    hbox.getChildren().add(btnDeposit);
    hbox.getChildren().add(btnWithdraw);

    BorderPane bP = new BorderPane();
    bP.setCenter(p);
    bP.setBottom(hbox);

    Scene scene = new Scene(bP, 300, 150);
    primaryStage.setScene(scene);
    primaryStage.show();
  }
}
```

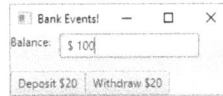

A Nothing

B An error

C Java will print a message

D The balance variable will increase to 120

E The text field with balance will increase to 120

–Exam/Quiz
(*The code used in this exam question is very similar to the code in the sample clicker question; Thus, it is omitted here*) For the code above, fill in the code for the deposit button handler. Make it so that the act of pressing the button adds $20 to the balance text field.

```
// assume DepositHandlerClass is declared
// inside BankAccount

class DepositHandlerClass
          implements __A.__ <__B.__> {

  @Override
  public void handle(ActionEvent e){
    // increase balance by 20
    __C.__

    // display balance on the textfield
    __D.__
}
```

4.3 Multithreading

In the experimental group, we used two analogies: morning routines where multiple actions can happen at the same time, and summing up 1000 receipt costs with help from friends in comparison with summing them up alone. The primary analogy is morning routines where a person may run various chores at the same time (such as listening to the news and brushing teeth). There are also naturally sequential activities, such as pouring and then eating cereal. Table 5 contains the mapping of base and target domains for the morning routine analogy.

Table 5: Mapping of analogical relations from the base domain (multithreading) to the target domain (morning routine)

Base domain	Target domain
A problem can be divided into subtasks	Morning routine contains multiple tasks
Threads have different stacks	Different routines happen at different places
Ordering of thread execution may matter	Ordering to execute routines may matter

Four clicker questions for multithreading were selected for analysis, and the focus of these questions is on the calculation of task completion time given a specified number of threads and subtasks. The two long term performance questions also focus on these types of calculations. The transfer question is based on the analogies discussed in [18]. We provide a sample question for each category (clicker, exam-/quiz, and transfer). The three sub-problems for knowledge transfer cover overhead, contention and communication, and diminished returns for multithreading.

Multithreading sample questions

—Clicker

Suppose I have a program that runs in 100 seconds. I find that it is doing something I could divide up into small chunks and allocate to different cores. It takes 10 seconds (of the 100) to setup the work to be done, and after that point, I can divide the work perfectly. Assume I have 4 cores. How long will my new program run (approximately)?

A 100 seconds   D 33 seconds
B 50 seconds   E 25 seconds
C 55 seconds

—Exam/Quiz

You have a program which runs in 100 seconds with a single core. You look into the code and find 20% of the work is serial, but 80% could be divided up perfectly (parallel). For this program:

A If you have 4 cores and use 4 threads for the parallel portion, how long will it take (roughly)?

B If you have 4 cores and use 8 threads for the parallel portion, how long will it take (roughly)?

C If you have 8 cores and use 4 threads for the parallel portion, how long will it take (roughly)?

—Transfer

Suppose that student A is working on a jigsaw puzzle, and that it takes A an hour to complete the puzzle. Now, suppose that another student, B, sits down at the table across from A, and works with A on the puzzle. For simplicity, let's assume that half the puzzle is grass and the other half is sky. Pick the best answers for the following questions.

- If A does the grass and B does the sky, how long will it take the two of them to complete the puzzle?

  A Exactly 30 minutes
  B Slightly longer than 30 minutes
  C Slightly shorter than 30 minutes

- Can A and B work completely independently, or will they need to work together at the horizon – that is, at the shared interface between their parts?

  A Yes, they can work completely independently.
  B No, they have to work together at some point.

- If we keep adding more people around the table to build the puzzle, do we keep speeding up?

  A Yes, it will speed up at the same pace.
  B Yes, but the benefit diminishes as more people begin to work on the puzzle. If too many people are added, there won't be any benefit anymore.
  C It won't speed up if more than 2 people work on the puzzle

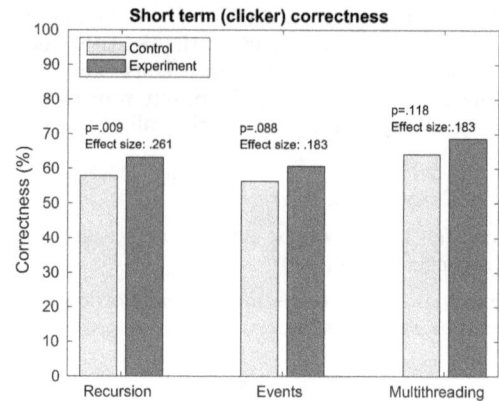

Figure 2: Clicker correctness for control and experimental groups for the three CS concepts. p-value and effect size are listed for each concept.

5. RESULTS

In this section, we present the results for short term learning (in-class clicker questions), long term learning (quiz and exam questions), and knowledge transfer.

5.1 Short Term Effectiveness

The overall clicker correctness mean was compared between the control group and the experimental group. Figure 2 shows the comparison of results.

Normality was tested before using the 2-sample t-test. The effect size based on Cohen's d is calculated for each concept. As seen in Figure 2, the experimental group noticeably outperformed the control group. Recursion showed significant differences between the control group and the experimental group ($p < .01$) with a moderate effect size. For events, the p-value is near significant and the effect size confirms the near significant difference between the control and experimental group. No significant difference is observed for multithreading.

We argue that the observed results suggest that commonly used instructor-led analogies have moderate impact on students' short term performance.

5.2 Long Term Effectiveness

Figure 3 provides the comparison of long term effectiveness. Differences between the two groups do not show any statistical significance. These results suggest that the moderate gain for the experimental group in the short term vanishes fairly quickly.

5.3 Transfer Effectiveness

Two transfer questions were given during the last quiz or final exam for recursion and multithreading. Figure 4 provides the comparison of results. The results show mixed conclusions for the two concepts. For recursion, the control group has higher correctness than the experimental group, though this difference is not statistically significant. For multithreading, the difference between the experimental group and control group is statistically significant with a moderate effect size. The effectiveness of knowledge transfer is therefore inconclusive.

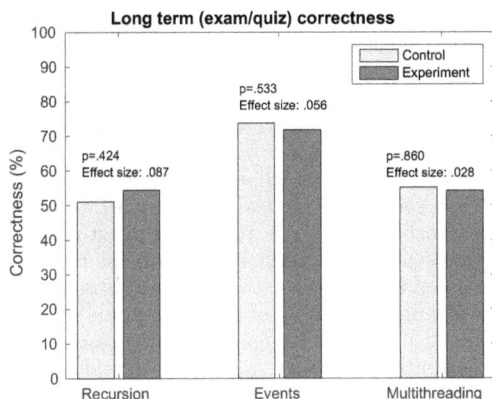

Figure 3: Exam/quiz correctness for control and experimental groups for the three CS concepts. p-value and effect size are listed for each concept.

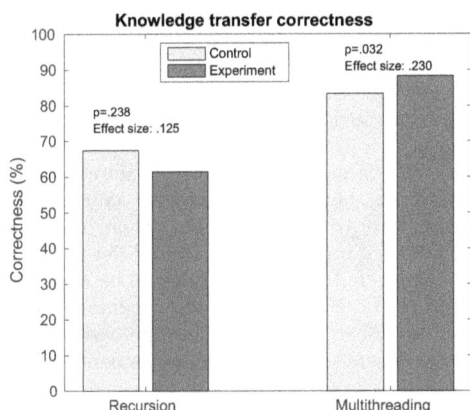

Figure 4: Transfer correctness for control and experimental groups for two CS concepts. p-value and effect size are listed for each concept.

5.4 Demographic Differences

The results to this point have all examined the classes as a whole. There is a potential that, by averaging across an entire class, subgroup effects are being masked. To determine whether a particular demographic subgroup was being differentially affected by analogies, we used multiple linear regression to test relationships and interactions between subgroups and outcomes.

The demographics we added to the linear regression model were major, gender, 1st-generation status, international student status, race, prior programming experience, and class level. There was no consistent trend among these groups of students not already explained by the experimental/control condition. No group was consistently helped (or hindered) beyond those findings already discussed.

Although not part of any general trend, there were some significant effects identified which may deserve further inquiry:

Short Term: For recursion, a significant interaction ($p=.0004$) was found in that students who were not majors were particularly aided by the analogy. On the short term clicker questions on recursion, non-CS majors answered 57% and 70% correctly in the control and experimental group, respectively. By contrast, short term clicker accuracy for majors was 74% and 62% in the control and experimental group, respectively. Non-majors were not significantly different from majors for the other concepts in terms of short term performance. Nevertheless, this potential benefit for non-majors is encouraging.

Long Term Performance: Multiple demographic categories show statistically significant differences on long term performance. For the first exam question on recursion, males scored higher in the experimental group than the control group but females scored lower in the experimental group than the control group ($p=.041$). This trend is also significant for the overall performance on recursion. The overall performance on recursion also shows that international students and first-generation students score higher in the experimental compared with the control group ($p=.01$ and $p=.04$, respectively). These results are promising as first-generation and international students are important demographic groups for recruitment and retention. For the second question on multithreading, there is an interaction between class level and experimental condition. Results show that the experimental condition helps lower-level students (freshmen and sophomores) while hindering juniors and seniors ($p=.03$).

Transfer: For the second question on transfer for multithreading, majors scored statistically significantly lower than non-majors ($p=.01$) in both the experimental and control group. On average, 86% of non-majors and only 73% of majors answered this question correctly. This could hint at a difficulty for majors to apply a non-technical analogy to technical topics.

6. DISCUSSION

Given the suggestively positive but sometimes conflicting results, we revisit our research question and explore the findings with respect to our theoretical expectations. We then address additional confounding factors that may limit the applicability of our results or threaten the validity of our findings.

6.1 Research Question Revisited

Our research question asks whether introducing technical introductory computing concepts in the context of analogies improves student learning. We measured and evaluated learning on three time scales.

6.1.1 Short Term

The theoretical basis for the benefits of analogies is in the connections between analogies and prior student understanding. The small time frame between introducing the material and presenting the clicker questions suggests that we would find evidence of learning in this data if such differences do indeed exist.

One potential influence on these results is that these topics spanned multiple lecture periods. Due to the timing of the lessons, it was not possible to cover the entire topic in one lecture period, so there were multiple days between the experimental condition (introduction with/without analogies) and some of the questions used in the analysis.

We found potential evidence that providing a meaningful analogy when introducing the topic can facilitate student learning in the short term, although only recursion did so statistically significantly. The effect sizes were also not large (between 0.18 and 0.26). There are two reasons that may help remedy the disparity between these effect sizes and our theoretical expectations. First, again the delay over multiple lectures may cause the treatment to be compounded with outside effects (studying outside class, programming assignments, etc.). Second, clicker data is known to be noisy [20] and this noise can increase variance, and hence standard deviation, which impacts effect size.

6.1.2 Long Term

We hypothesized that the experimental group may benefit from the analogy in the long term. If initial learning is more effective, then perhaps that learning benefit would endure. However, we were aware that any boost to learning, particularly a small boost, might be lost over time as students further engage with the material through assignments and studying. The nonsignificant results for long term benefit are likely due to these concerns. A small boost in the short term does not appear to persist in the long term.

This result dovetails with the ineffectiveness of animations in promoting long term student learning [17]. However, this finding conflicts with Peer Instruction results suggesting that performance on clicker questions impacts final exam outcomes [25]. In that study, the clicker scores across an entire term were used to show that in-class learning corresponds to exam outcomes. In the present study, the selected clicker questions covered a subset (about 30%) of all clicker questions over the term, so it is possible that the relationship between clicker scores and exam scores is reduced. Further inquiry is required to confirm this hypothesis.

6.1.3 Transfer

Students in the experimental group were offered a connection between the technical concept and another non-technical area. If students are given such a connection, does it make them better at making other connections? We can provide only tentative conclusions as we found a statistically significant effect for one of the two topics but not the other. Although this effect was in favor of the experimental group, the size of the effect, combined with the non-result for the other topic, limits potential conclusions. Again, it may be possible that such an effect exists in the short term but disappears when measured on later assessments.

6.1.4 Demographic Differences

Students in different demographic groups may have different programming and social backgrounds. It is therefore expected that responses to analogies from demographic groups would vary. We hypothesize that students who tend to be negatively affected by abstract or technical content will benefit more from the use of analogies. The results presented in Section 5.4, such as the effect on non-majors and international students, revealed partial support for this hypothesis. However, further study is needed to investigate why inconsistent trends were observed.

6.2 Additional Threats to Validity

A number of additional confounding factors may impact the validity of this study beyond those that led us to drop the data on polymorphism. Here we outline these issues and their potential impact.

1. The lectures from the experimental and control group are both podcast and students can watch either section. Based on informal discussions with students, we believe the majority of students watch the podcast for their corresponding section. However, students watching the podcast for the other section could impact the results.

2. We chose topics believed to be fairly independent of one another. That said, if better learning of one topic impacts learning of another, then it is possible that students who benefited from the experiment (or control) for prior topics may have carried this benefit with them into subsequent topics (e.g., better understanding of recursion made students in the experimental group stronger for multithreading). The swapping of control/experimental group should help mitigate this effect, but it remains a concern.

3. Both sections were taught using Peer Instruction. It is possible that this pedagogical practice impacted student learning of these topics. Results may differ in a standard lecture class and is hence motivation for study replication in a lecture course (albeit with a different mechanism for measuring short term learning).

4. The analogies used in this study, though carefully analyzed in advance, may not represent the best possible analogies for the selected CS1.5 concepts. A careful study of widely-used analogies from the CS education community might reveal more insights on the quality of analogies for a certain concept.

5. Although we examined a number of factors to identify potential differences between sections and only found a difference in class level, it is possible that there were student differences that were not measured. Any difference between the sections could confound the results. The experimental setup of altering the control and experimental group may mitigate such an effect, but it remains the case that this is not a true experiment with random assignment of students to class sections.

7. CONCLUSION

The majority of instructors use analogies to teach introductory computing. Are such analogies effective? This study begins to explore this question by using analogies to introduce introductory computing topics. In an experiment that switched lecture sections between control and experimental group, we find potential evidence that may support the value of analogies for short term learning. No significant difference was found for long term learning and ability to transfer. Our results also highlight difficulties involved in such inquiry. Analogies are not available in the literature for all relevant topics, so sometimes analogies must be constructed from scratch or personal experience. Short term learning data cannot be captured in a traditional lecture course offering without concomitant changes to course structure. Validated tests of understanding are not available, necessitating the creation of locally-produced test questions. Our study suggests that overcoming these hurdles will be important as we seek to learn more about the use and misuse of analogies to help our students learn.

8. ACKNOWLEDGMENTS

The authors would like to thank the anonymous reviewers for their helpful suggestions, and Hans Yuan and Soohyun Nam for providing programs for analyzing clicker data.

9. REFERENCES

[1] J. Bergin. Teaching Polymorphism with Elementary Design Patterns. In *Companion of the 18th Annual ACM SIGPLAN Conference on Object-oriented Programming, Systems, Languages, and Applications,* pages 167–169, 2003.

[2] J. D. Bransford, A. L. Brown, and R. R. Cocking. *How people learn: Brain, mind, experience, and school.* National Academy Press, 1999.

[3] J. D. Bransford, J. J. Franks, N. J. Vye, and R. D. Sherwood. New approaches to instruction: because wisdom can't be told. In *Similarity and analogical reasoning,* pages 470–497. Cambridge University Press, 1989.

[4] J. A. Bulgren, B. K. Lenz, J. B. Schumaker, D. D. Deshler, and J. G. Marquis. The use and effectiveness of a comparison routine in diverse secondary content classrooms. *Journal of Educational Psychology,* 94(2):356–371, 2000.

[5] Y. S. Chee. Applying Gentner's theory of analogy to the teaching of computer programming. *International Journal of Man-Machine Studies,* 38(3):347–368, 1993.

[6] M. T. Chi, P. J. Feltovich, and R. Glaser. Categorization and representation of physics problems by experts and novices. *Cognitive Science,* 5:121–152, 1981.

[7] T. R. Colburn and G. M. Shute. Metaphor in computer science. *Journal of Applied Logic,* 6(4):526–533, 2008.

[8] J. Edgington. Teaching and Viewing Recursion As Delegation. *Journal of Computing Sciences in Colleges,* 23(1):241–246, 2007.

[9] M. Forišek and M. Steinová. Metaphors and Analogies for Teaching Algorithms. In *Proceedings of the 43rd ACM Technical Symposium on Computer Science Education,* pages 15–20, 2012.

[10] D. Gentner. Structure-mapping: A theoretical framework for analogy. *Cognitive Science,* 7(2):155–170, 1983.

[11] D. Gentner, J. Loewenstein, and L. Thompson. Learning and transfer: A general role for analogical encoding. *Journal of Educational Psychology,* 95(2):393–405, 2003.

[12] J. E. Greer. A Comparison of Instructional Treatments for Introducing Recursion. *Computer Science Education,* 1(2):111–128, 1989.

[13] S. Iyer and S. Murthy. Demystifying networking: Teaching non-majors via analogical problem-solving.

Proceedings of the 44th ACM Technical Symposium on Computer Science Education, pages 77–82, 2013.

[14] S. Kurkovsky. Teaching Software Engineering with LEGO Serious Play. In *Proceedings of the 2015 ACM Conference on Innovation and Technology in Computer Science Education,* pages 213–218, 2015.

[15] T. Lapidot and O. Hazzan. Song Debugging: Merging Content and Pedagogy in Computer Science Education. *SIGCSE Bulletin,* 37(4):79–83, 2005.

[16] K. N. Macfarlane and B. T. Mynatt. A Study of an Advance Organizer As a Technique for Teaching Computer Programming Concepts. In *Proceedings of the 19th ACM Technical Symposium on Computer Science Education,* pages 240–243, 1988.

[17] J. B. Morrison and B. Tversky. The (in)effectiveness of animation in instruction. *Human factors in computing systems (CHI '01),* page 377, 2001.

[18] H. Neeman, L. Lee, J. Mullen, and G. Newman. Analogies for teaching parallel computing to inexperienced programmers. *ACM SIGCSE Bulletin,* 38(4):64, 2006.

[19] L. Porter and B. Simon. Retaining nearly one-third more majors with a trio of instructional best practices in CS1. In *Proceedings of the 44th ACM Technical Symposium on Computer Science Education,* pages 165–170, 2013.

[20] L. Porter, D. Zingaro, and R. Lister. Predicting student success using fine grain clicker data. *Proceedings of the tenth annual conference on International computing education research,* pages 51–58, 2014.

[21] J. P. Sanford, A. Tietz, S. Farooq, S. Guyer, and R. B. Shapiro. Metaphors we teach by. *Proceedings of the 45th ACM technical symposium on Computer science education,* pages 585–590, 2014.

[22] T. L. Short. *Peirce's theory of signs.* Cambridge University Press, 2007.

[23] R. J. Sternberg and J. L. Ketron. Selection and implementation of strategies in reasoning by analogy. *Journal of Educational Psychology,* 74(3):399–413, 1982.

[24] V. J. Traver. Can User-centered Interface Design Be Applied to Education? *SIGCSE Bulletin,* 39(2):57–61, Jun. 2007.

[25] D. Zingaro and L. Porter. Peer instruction: A link to the exam. In *Proceedings of the 2014 Conference on Innovation Technology in Computer Science Education,* pages 255–260, 2014.

Distractors in Parsons Problems Decrease Learning Efficiency for Young Novice Programmers

Kyle J. Harms, Jason Chen, Caitlin Kelleher
Department of Computer Science & Engineering
Washington University in St. Louis
One Brookings Drive
St. Louis, MO 63130, United States
{kyle.harms, chenjy, ckelleher}@wustl.edu

ABSTRACT

Parsons problems are an increasingly popular method for helping inexperienced programmers improve their programming skills. In Parsons problems, learners are given a set of programming statements that they must assemble into the correct order. Parsons problems commonly use distractors, extra statements that are not part of the solution. Yet, little is known about the effect distractors have on a learner's ability to acquire new programming skills. We present a study comparing the effectiveness of learning programming from Parsons problems with and without distractors. The results suggest that distractors decrease learning efficiency. We found that distractor participants showed no difference in transfer task performance compared to those without distractors. However, the distractors increased learners cognitive load, decreased their success at completing Parsons problems by 26%, and increased learners' time on task by 14%.

General Terms

Human Factors

Keywords

Independent Learning, Parsons Problems, Distractors, Completion Problems, Cognitive Load

1. INTRODUCTION

Parsons problems are a popular way to help individuals learn computer programming. In a Parsons problem, a learner is given a program where the statements have been placed out of order. Learners solve the Parsons problem by assembling the statements into the correct order [47]. Frequently, Parsons problems also include extra statements that are not part of the solution, known as distractors [22, 47]. Parsons problems are typically used for drill and practice exercises that complement traditional classroom and online learning [10, 47], or for assessing learners' programming skills [8, 41]. More recently, they have also been used to help children learn programming independently [17].

Distractors are a common feature of many Parsons problem implementations [8, 10, 22, 47]. Yet, little is known about how distractors affect learning. Broadly, distractors in Parsons problems

are often described as unnecessary code [10], extra fragments [18], or erroneous code [21]. Fortunately, some researchers provide a more precise explanation: distractors should be used to "illustrate a particular point" or to "highlight programming principles the student may ignore" [47]. Distractors based on these principles often attempt to illustrate common programming misconceptions and syntax errors [25, 47]. While this seems like a reasonable approach for using distractors, we are unaware of any empirical evidence on the effectiveness of distractors in Parsons problems.

In this paper, we present a study investigating middle school children's ability to learn programming concepts independently from Parsons problems with distractors. We conducted a formative evaluation exploring the potential use of distractors to encourage and foster a beneficial learning experience. We then report the results of a summative evaluation comparing the effectiveness of using *partial suboptimal path* distractors when learning programming concepts on transfer task performance. Our results show that distractors increased cognitive load for independent learners, reduced learners' ability to successfully complete Parsons problems, and significantly increased time on task. Distractor participants also showed no difference in transfer task performance compared to participants who trained without distractors.

2. RELATED WORK

At its core, a distractor is an *error*. Some suggest that the errors generated from distractors in Parsons problems may aid learning [25, 47]. Further, the reasons cited for using distractors in Parsons problems are similar to the reasons for using distractors in multiple choice tests [27, 33, 47]. In this section, we review research on the impacts of 1) generating errors on learning and 2) the use of distractors in testing.

2.1 Learning with Errors

Learners may encounter errors when learning from traditional educational materials or learning based games. We first discuss how errors affect learners in traditional education situations, followed by game based learning.

Humans naturally make errors as part of our learning process. Generating errors during learning can have both positive and negative consequences that educators must be careful to either leverage or mitigate. One approach to reducing errors made during learning is to teach common misconceptions to students when introducing new material [42]. This is especially important for low performing students, who benefited from learning about common misconceptions [42]. Errors can also affect high and low performing learners differently. Only high performing students benefited when learning via worked examples that contained errors [13]. Fortunately, providing students with corrective feedback on the errors mitigated the harmful effects for low performing students

[61]. Another common approach to learning with errors is using *trial and error*. Researchers demonstrated that generating errors when learning via trial and error helped younger learners, but impaired older adult learners [7]. Specifically in the context of programming, errors did not benefit learners. Students who learned programming using a method that deliberately encouraged them to make errors had their rote learning efficiency reduced and they tended to make the same errors later [9]. The inconsistency among the literature suggests that educators must take into consideration learners' abilities and age, feedback and even the educational domain when considering the effects of errors during learning.

There is also a growing body of evidence on the effectiveness of game based learning for several disciplines [58]. Some of these games leverage correcting errors as a central game mechanic [19, 30], while others use distractors to lure players into generating errors [55]. Correcting errors as part of a debugging game has been shown to be an effective strategy for helping children learn programming [30]. While Parsons problems are not a game, they have puzzle-like qualities and have been shown, without distractors, to be effective for learning [17]. We are unaware of any empirical evidence of the benefit or harm that generating errors from distractors in Parsons problems may cause.

2.2 Distractors and Errors in Testing

Multiple choice questions typically have several incorrect answers designed to distract lower level learners away from the correct answer [27]. Test takers also acquire new information from the act of taking a test [51]. Depending on the circumstances, the errors generated from distractors during testing may benefit or harm learners [5]. We discuss how testing affects learning and how the errors generated by distractors impact learners.

While testing may be viewed as assessing learned material, it also plays an important role in learning [51, 52]. When testing, individuals must retrieve information from their memory. Information is not stored statically in memory, but rather it is reconstructed upon retrieval; retrieval can change the information itself [26]. The act of retrieving information from memory can be an effective way to promote learning and even retention of information [52]. This is known as the *testing effect* [51]. The key to the testing effect is the retrieval process itself. The act of trying to retrieve information during testing, even if unsuccessful, was found to enhance future learning [29, 49]. Further, if an individual fails to retrieve the information, guessing the answer did not hurt future performance [23]. The testing effect persists across testing formats, including multiple choice tests with distractors [34, 53].

If a test taker constructs an incorrect answer during retrieval, there is the possibility that the error is committed to memory which can impair future performance [1]. Test authors should be especially careful when authoring multiple choice tests with distractors because individuals may acquire false information from any errors [5, 36–38, 53]. Additionally, low performing students are more likely to acquire false information from multiple choice testing [5, 37], while higher performing students actually benefit from the errors [5]. Learning false information in testing appears to be due to faulty reasoning when selecting answers [38]. If faulty reasoning is at play, this can be mitigated by providing corrective feedback after testing [4, 6]. Feedback was found to improve learning when test takers generated errors during multiple choice testing [4, 6, 20, 48]. Given the potential for learning false information from multiple choice testing, test administrators should take measures, like feedback, to limit the potential for false learning.

Guidelines based on empirical evidence may also help test authors write better multiple choice tests with distractors [15, 16]. Even then, writing good distractors is often difficult for test authors [57]. Part of the difficulty in writing quality distractors is providing responses that separate low and high performers [50], but that also provide insights about students' misunderstandings [27, 33]. One approach to authoring multiple choice distractors is to utilize common misconceptions [15, 39]. In our context, misconceptions can be common programming mistakes, for example, failing to properly nest statements in a control flow construct [2].

Overall, generating errors during learning may help learners under the right conditions. However, there is the potential that generating errors may also decrease the effectiveness of learning. Little empirical evidence exists to suggest how generating errors in Parsons problems will affect learners. Beneficial use of distractors in Parsons problems may only be effective under certain circumstances, similar to the learning with errors research. In this paper, we explore the potential for using distractors in Parsons problems to help novices learn programming independently.

3. LOOKING GLASS

For our study, we chose to use the blocks-based novice programming environment, Looking Glass [35]. In Looking Glass, users author programs that are 3D animations. Looking Glass also has support for Parsons problems as shown in Figure 1-A/B.

The Parsons problems in Looking Glass (known as programming completion problems) were influenced by prior work that demonstrated that high school students who completed partially written programs (i.e. completion problems) later constructed better quality programs than students who authored programs from scratch [59, 60]. To further aid independent learners, these code puzzles in Looking Glass include additional scaffolding within the interface to reduce the cognitive load that impairs learning (i.e. extraneous cognitive load) and increase the cognitive load that fosters learning (i.e. germane cognitive load) [17]. This includes a rich feedback mechanism designed to help learners correct errors without providing the answer [17]. In an evaluation, novices who learned programming constructs using programming completion problems demonstrated more evidence of learning compared to novices who learned using tutorials [17]. In the remainder of this paper, we refer to these Parsons problems simply as *puzzles*.

4. FORMATIVE EVALUATION

We conducted a formative evaluation to explore how to author distractors in puzzles to exploit the benefits of learning with errors while reducing the potential harm they may cause. Even though the most cited use of a distractor in Parsons problem is the programming syntax distractor [8, 10, 18, 22, 25, 47], we did not explore this distractor in our study. Blocks-based programming languages forgo syntax in an effort to reduce the barriers for learning programming. From our evaluation, we share three guidelines for distractors in code puzzles: 1) distractors that create *extra noise* are easy to ignore, 2) distractors should encourage learners to follow a *familiar, but suboptimal path*, and 3) allow only *one possible solution* to a puzzle.

For our formative study, we recruited 16 participants between the ages of 10 and 15 (10 female, 6 male; age: $M = 11.94$, $SD = 1.57$) from the Academy of Science of St. Louis mailing list. The Academy of Science is a not-for-profit organization dedicated to science outreach in the St. Louis metropolitan area. We compensated participants with a $10 gift certificate.

4.1 Extra Noise is Easy to Ignore

Prior work described distractors as extra code or unnecessary code in Parsons problems [10, 18]. We initially came up with three unnecessary code distractors: 1) create additional *unrelated* random noise, 2) create additional *tangentially related* noise, and 3) insert *unrelated control flow constructs*.

For the *unrelated noise* distractors we added random method invocations to the puzzles, for example: *ufo.resize(2.0)*. Users very quickly realized that the random statements are easy to eliminate from their possible solution space, as one participant stated, "the extra actions (statements) contradict, so you can ignore them." We also tested *tangentially related* distractors by inserting additional method invocations that could plausibly be part of an animation. For example, in an animation about a dolphin rescuing a sinking boat, we inserted a method call to a background ship object, *ship.sail_towards(boat)*. However, participants gave similar explanations that they knew they could just ignore it because the ship never sailed the boat.

Given that participants were quick to dismiss the *extra noise*, we tried another distractor designed to encourage participants to make decisions about which control flow blocks they might need for the solution. We inserted several types of *unrelated control flow blocks* as distractors. We knew that this approach better engaged some participants when they asked, "Do I have to use all of them?" Further, the extra control blocks appeared to encourage thinking for some participants, as one participant stated: "It's sorta tricky, but it also makes you think harder, like what does the computer want me to do?" However, we note that adding unrelated control blocks were also easy to dismiss as unnecessary.

4.2 Use a Familiar, but Suboptimal Path

Instead of adding extra noise to the puzzles, we tried to engage participants by creating distractors that encouraged them to follow a *familiar, but suboptimal path*, when solving the puzzle. The idea is similar to the *misconception* distractors mentioned in Parsons problems [47]. The distractors allow a user to create a suboptimal solution for a puzzle that follows a familiar strategy that they have likely used before. For example, using identical duplicate statements instead of using a loop as shown in Figure 1-E. We used three strategies for suboptimal path distractors: 1) insert distractor statements into the solution for the puzzle's *initial state* (Figure 1-C), 2) *initially nest* constructs incorrectly (Figure 1-C), and 3) add *alternative statements* that can lead to a suboptimal solution (e.g. duplicate statements instead of a loop) (Figure 1-E).

Compared to the previous *noisy* distractors, participants engaged with the suboptimal path distractors frequently. For the *initial state* distractor one participant stated, "This one you have to think that you can move the pieces on the board already off." In *initial nesting* distractors, participants would recognize that they needed the combined effects of both constructs for the solution. Yet, participants had difficulty realizing that they needed to switch the nesting order, "I'm a little bit irritated. I've checked over and over the difference between my video and the correct one."

When participants followed the suboptimal path, it often led to them failing to recover and failing to discover the optimal solution. This was especially true for the *alternative statement* distractors. Participants had difficulty understanding why their solution's output looked correct even though the feedback indicated it was incorrect, as one participant stated, "It makes me feel a little frustrated. Well I looked at the video many times. I figured out what I was missing. I corrected my animation. But looking at it… and it tells me that it's wrong [and that] makes me feel frustrated." Even if many participants failed to recover, the suboptimal path distractors are a promising approach given that participants were frequently actively engaged with the distractors.

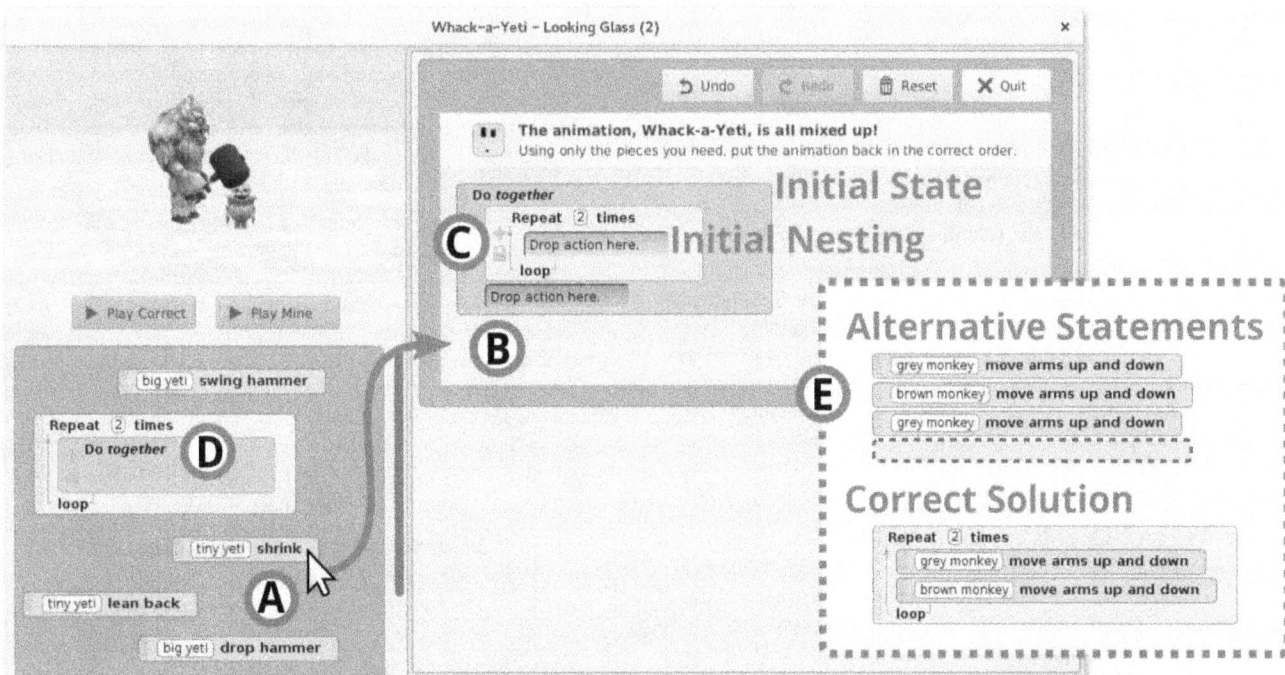

Figure 1. A puzzle (training task 5) in its initial state demonstrating *partial suboptimal path* distractors. Users solve a puzzle by assembling unused statements (A) into the correct order (B). In the *initial state* distractor (C), an incorrect *Do together* block is initially placed into the puzzle's solution. The *repeat* block is initially nested incorrectly into the *Do together* block for the *initial nesting* distractor; the correct solution is nested block (D). For the *alternative statements* distractor (E) (training task 2), users are given almost enough extra statements to create a suboptimal solution; the last statement is missing for the suboptimal solution.

4.3 Allow Only One Solution

The *familiar, but suboptimal path* distractors succeeded in leading participants down a suboptimal path, but they frequently failed to bring participants towards the optimal solution. The biggest problem with the suboptimal path distractors is that they create several suboptimal solutions in addition to the optimal solution. For example, the *alternative statement* distractors for a loop produce a complete suboptimal solution with the duplicate statements instead of the optimal loop solution. To gently nudge participants towards the optimal solution, we modified the distractors by removing the possibility of suboptimal solutions while still keeping the ability to make some progress down a partial suboptimal path.

One frequent source of suboptimal solutions is empty control flow blocks inserted by participants into the solution. Extra control flow statements can lead to no operation behavior (NOP) in Parsons problems [22]. For example, a *Repeat* block with no nested statements does nothing when executed. The NOP makes the program output match the correct output, even though the solution is incorrect because of the unused block. This can be particularly confusing for novices when their output looks correct but the puzzle feedback indicates that their solution is incorrect. The *initial nesting* distractors have a high tendency to produce NOP behavior. For example, a participant may unnest an incorrectly nested control block and then forget to remove the block from the solution. Yet, novices see nothing wrong with this behavior, as one participant stated, "I get that it's extra, but I don't agree…"

To help participants realize the existence of the optimal solution, we eliminated the existence of suboptimal solutions. For the *alternative statement* distractors we provided enough statements to lead a user down the suboptimal path, but not enough statements to actually finish the suboptimal solution. For example, in Figure 1-E the last duplicate statement is missing from the puzzle, so a user can start the suboptimal path, but must seek out the optimal solution to solve the puzzle. We also removed the NOP suboptimal solutions typically produced by the *initial nesting* distractors by locking nested control flow blocks together as shown in Figure 1-C/D. Because the blocks are locked together, the user can explore the suboptimal path (Figure 1-C), but because they cannot unnest the blocks, they cannot produce a puzzle with NOP behavior. Instead a user must swap out the incorrectly nested blocks with the correctly nested one (Figure 1-D). We also carefully authored and tested our puzzles to ensure that only one solution existed for each puzzle.

Not allowing participants to complete the suboptimal path had the desired effect of encouraging participants to seek out the optimal solution: "Are there any other pieces? Looks like I'm missing one." The *partial suboptimal path* distractors also appeared to lead to greater success. Several participants commented on how they enjoyed the distractors, as one participant stated, "I actually like that. I think it's pretty cool that you throw in some random ones because that's kinda how puzzles work." For the remainder of our study, we used the *partial suboptimal path* distractors.

5. SUMMATIVE EVALUATION

Using what we learned in the formative evaluation, we conducted a between subjects study to assess the impacts that distractors have on learning new programming knowledge. Our study contained two phases: training and transfer. In the training phase participants learned new programming skills using code puzzles that we then evaluated in the transfer phase. We developed a series of six puzzles using the *partial suboptimal path* distractors. Our puzzles introduced participants to three programming nested constructs: *Repeat* nested in a *Repeat*, *Do Together* nested in a *Repeat*, and *Repeat* nested in a *Do Together*. From this evaluation, we intended to answer the following questions: 1) What effect do distractors have on task completion time, task success, and mental effort? and 2) Do distractor participants show more evidence of learning than those who learned programming concepts without them?

5.1 Participants

We recruited 102 participants between the ages of 10 and 15 from the Academy of Science of St. Louis mailing list. We screened participants for participation in any of our previous studies. We removed nine participants from our data set for prior participation. We also removed one participant from our data set for not completing most of the study materials. In total we analyzed the data for 92 participants (32 female, 60 male; age: $M = 12.01$, $SD = 1.67$). We compensated participants with a \$10 gift certificate.

5.2 Materials

We developed, tested, and refined our study materials through a pilot study. For the pilot study we recruited 14 participants (9 female, 5 male; age: $M = 12.93$, $SD = 2.23$).

5.2.1 Familiarization Tasks

For each phase of the study, we developed familiarization tasks to help introduce participants to the format of the tasks and the mechanics of the programming environment.

5.2.2 Training Tasks

We developed six puzzles for the training tasks. The six tasks were designed to be completed sequentially. We developed two sets of training tasks: one set without distractors, the other with distractors. See Table 1 for the programming concepts and distractor types for each training task. The training familiarization task is identical in format to the actual training tasks. However, the training familiarization task did not contain any distractors.

5.2.3 Transfer Tasks

In the transfer phase, we wanted to acquire evidence that the participants learned the programming concepts from the training phase. Specifically, we wanted to know if participants could identify the correct programming concepts and the proper nested structure when given a novel problem. We developed three transfer tasks to evaluate participants' mastery of nesting a *Repeat* block within a *Repeat*, nesting a *Do Together* within a *Repeat*, and nesting a *Repeat* within a *Do Together*.

Each transfer task is a complete program with existing and correctly ordered statements as shown in Figure 2. The existing statements are only method invocations; there are no control flow constructs. To complete each task, participants need only identify and insert the correct control flow constructs from the programming environment as shown in Figure 2-A. Once a construct is inserted into the program, participants drag the appropriate existing statements, maintaining their order, into the newly inserted control block. Each transfer task also included a video of the correct animation, written instructions for completing the task, and inline

Table 1. Training Task Summary

Task	Programing Concept	Partial Suboptimal Path Distractors
1	Do Together	Alternative Statements
2	Repeat	Alternative Statements × 2
3	Repeat { Repeat }	Initial State; Alternative Stat.
4	Repeat { Repeat }	Initial State; Alternative Stat.
5	Repeat { Do Together }	Initial State; Initial Nesting
6	Do Together { Repeat }	Initial Nesting; Alternative Statements

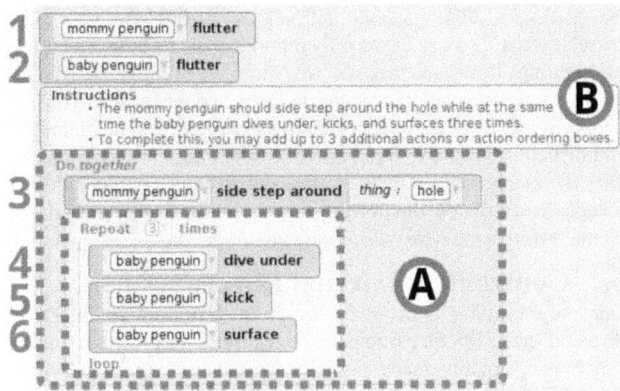

Figure 2. Example Transfer Task.
Statements 1-6 are already inserted and correctly ordered.
Participants need to insert additional control blocks (A) to
make the animation match the instructions (B).

comments describing the correct program output (Figure 2-B). The instructions noted that the existing statements are in the correct order and that participants are limited to only inserting three additional blocks into the program. We designed the transfer tasks to focus participants' time on demonstrating their programming knowledge, not authoring programs from scratch.

The transfer phase had two separate familiarization tasks. The first familiarization task introduced participants to the mechanics of authoring a sequential program in the programming environment. The second task is identical in format to the actual transfer tasks.

5.2.4 Surveys

We included three surveys in our evaluation: a self-developed programming experience survey, cognitive load task survey, and the Computer Science Cognitive Load Component Survey (CS CLCS) [40]. The programming experience survey gathered information about participants' age, gender, schooling, prior study participation, and prior programming education and experience.

The cognitive load task survey included two validated and reliable scales [45] for measuring cognitive load: mental effort [44] and difficulty [24]. Both scales are Likert item surveys with nine items from 1 (very, very low mental effort / extremely easy) to 9 (very, very high mental effort / extremely difficult). Historically when measuring cognitive load, researchers used either mental effort [44] or difficulty [24] scales to measure cognitive load. However, research now suggests that while mental effort and difficulty are correlated, they are not the same thing [12]. Because prior work on code puzzles used the difficulty scale [17], we included both scales for comparison. Please note that when we discuss cognitive load, we only refer to the mental effort scale.

We used a validated survey to measure the different types of cognitive load. The CS CLCS is an adaptation of an existing validated survey, the Cognitive Load Component Survey [31, 32], for the domain of computer science. The CS CLCS is a ten item Likert survey with three separate cognitive load scales: intrinsic, extraneous, and germane [40]. Each question is rated on an eleven-point scale from 0 (not at all the case) to 10 (completely the case).

5.3 Methods

We conducted our evaluation over several different multi-user sessions. Each participant attended a single two hour session. We seated participants to minimize viewing other participants' screens and to minimize interaction between participants.

We conducted a between subjects study with two conditions: control (no distractors) and distractors. We randomly assigned

participants to either the control or the distractors condition (control: 47, distractors: 45). The study contained two parts: the training phase and the transfer phase as shown in Figure 3. In the training phase, participants completed puzzles with or without distractors as assigned in their condition. In the transfer phase, participants completed three transfer tasks. After completion of the transfer phase, we allowed participants to create their own animation or work on additional puzzles.

Before the study, we asked participants to complete the programming experience survey. Once completed, a member of the research team followed up on the survey responses by interviewing each participant about their responses. This follow up interview allowed us to correct any misreported data about participants' prior programming experience.

5.3.1 Training Phase

In the training phase, we asked participants to complete a familiarization task, six training tasks, and the CS CLCS. The familiarization task used the same format as the training tasks.

At the start of the training phase, we gave participants an instruction sheet with directions on how to complete a training task. We gave participants twelve minutes to complete each training task; there was no time limit for the familiarization task. We permitted participants to ask for help during the familiarization task. However, after completion of the familiarization task, we required participants to complete the remaining six training tasks without assistance. Each participant completed the training tasks in the same order. After completing each task, we asked participants to complete the cognitive load task survey where they rated their mental effort and difficulty for that task.

Upon completion of all training tasks, we gave participants a reminder sheet with a picture and the title for each of the training task animations (i.e. not the familiarization task). We then asked participants to complete the same cognitive load task survey ranking their mental effort and difficulty across all six tasks. We then asked them to complete the CS CLCS. We encouraged participants to reference the reminder sheet when completing these surveys to help them recall their experience.

5.3.2 Transfer Phase

After completing the training phase, participants began the transfer phase of the study. Similar to the training phase, participants first completed two familiarization tasks, three transfer tasks, and then the CS CLCS.

With each familiarization task, we provided an instruction sheet. The first familiarization task's instruction sheet demonstrated the basics of the Looking Glass programming environment. In the second familiarization task, the instruction sheet provided directions on how to complete the transfer tasks in the study. We allowed participants to keep both instruction sheets for the remainder of the transfer phase as a reference. During the familiarization tasks, participants could ask for help. However, we provided no assistance during the actual transfer tasks. We assigned the three transfer tasks using a balanced "Williams" Latin squares

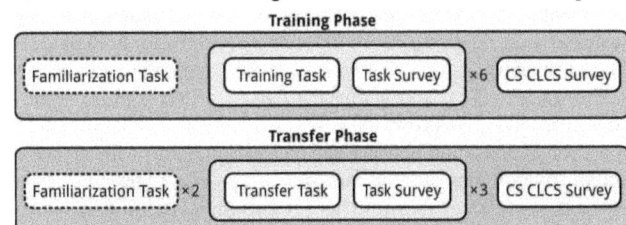

Figure 3. Summative Evaluation Procedure

design to control for learning effects [62]. Participants were given six minutes to complete each transfer task. Following the second familiarization task and each transfer task, we asked participants to complete the cognitive load task survey. Finally, upon completion of all transfer tasks, we gave participants a reminder sheet with each of the three transfer tasks' titles and pictures of each animation. We then asked them to complete a cognitive load task survey ranking their overall mental effort and difficulty for all transfer tasks and the CS CLCS using the reminder sheet.

6. ANALYSIS
We analyzed the data gathered in the training and transfer phases in the study. We also discuss how we control for external factors, like prior programming experience, in our analysis.

6.1 Training & Transfer Tasks
For the training and transfer tasks, we analyzed task time and performance, as well as the cognitive load scales. We collected cognitive load using several scales: mental effort across all tasks, difficulty across all tasks, overall intrinsic, extraneous, and germane cognitive loads. For each scale, we computed Cronbach's alpha for reliability ($\alpha > .70$).

Recall that we asked participants to rate their cognitive load for each task as well as rate their overall cognitive load after completing all tasks. Prior research has found that ratings completed at the end of a phase, as opposed to after each task, are often slightly higher than the mean of the ratings from all tasks [11]. The cognitive load task survey required minimal time (pilot testing revealed that this is typically less than 30 seconds) for participants to complete after each task. However, due to timing constraints and concerns over participant fatigue, we decided to only ask participants to complete the CS CLCS once, at the end of each phase. Because the CS CLCS was completed at the end of the phase the results may be slightly higher compared to the per task cognitive load ratings. To account for this potential difference in the CS CLCS results, we use both the immediate cognitive load task survey ratings and the overall ratings in our analysis.

6.1.1 Training Tasks
For the training tasks, we analyzed time on task, task completion, the cognitive load surveys, and distractor usage. Because task completion may have been affected by other factors, we analyzed whether participants ran out of time or gave up on the task. We also analyzed distractor usage within the distractors condition to evaluate the effectiveness of the distractors. We analyzed the percent of participants who used the distractors in each task and the percent of time participants used distractors in each task.

6.1.2 Transfer Tasks
Similar to the training tasks, we analyzed the time each participant took to complete each transfer task and their performance for each transfer task. For the transfer tasks, we measured performance by whether the participant's solution matches the correct solution exactly; we did not score with partial credit.

6.1.3 Cognitive Load
The mental effort scales ($\alpha_{training} = .90$; $\alpha_{transfer} = .89$) and difficulty scales ($\alpha_{training} = .89$; $\alpha_{transfer} = .79$) are both reliable for both phases. The intrinsic ($\alpha_{training} = .89$; $\alpha_{transfer} = .92$), extraneous ($\alpha_{training} = .78$; $\alpha_{transfer} = .71$), and germane ($\alpha_{training} = .87$; $\alpha_{transfer} = .92$) cognitive load scales from the CS CLCS were also reliable. There is a strong correlation between the mean mental effort for all tasks and the overall mental effort $r_{training} = .82$, $p_{training} < .001$; $r_{transfer} = .80$, $p_{transfer} < .001$. Likewise, there is a strong correlation between the mean difficulty for all tasks and the overall difficulty $r_{training} =$ .85, $p_{training} < .001$; $r_{transfer} = .80$, $p_{transfer} < .001$. Because these correlations are so strong, we only report the results of mental effort using ratings from each task (i.e. we ignore the overall ratings). Due to this strong correlation, we have not adjusted the results of the CS CLCS. We also see a strong correlation between mean mental effort and difficulty $r_{training} = .92$, $p_{training} < .001$; $r_{transfer} = .88$, $p_{transfer} < .001$. This suggests that mental effort and difficulty are very closely related. Because of this strong correlation, we only report the mental effort scale when discussing cognitive load.

6.2 Controlling External Effects
Our programming experience survey with follow-on interview revealed that 71% of participants had limited prior programming experience, notably many participants had used Scratch [54] or participated in an Hour of Code activity [19]. Because prior programming experience may influence the outcome of our results, we controlled for prior programming experience, as well as age, formal programming education, and gender, using covariates in our analysis. For all statistical results, where appropriate, we used ANCOVA or MANCOVA with Pillai's trace to compare the dependent variables from all six training tasks or all three transfer tasks against the control and distractor conditions.

Our analysis revealed that the age and prior experience covariates are significant for most results. In general, older participants and participants with prior experience performed better, while needing less time. The formal education and gender covariates are not significant for any results. This suggests that at the middle school level formal education may not differ much from informal learning. Researchers have also advocated for gender inclusiveness in software, including programming environments, in part because problem solving strategies tend to cluster by gender [3]. Reassuringly, we found no evidence of any gender differences.

When reporting our results, we also include effect size alongside p values. P values are heavily influenced by sample size; the larger the sample size, the more likely a statistical test will return significance ($p < .05$) [56]. Effect size removes the influence of sample size by measuring the magnitude a variable differs between conditions [56]. When reporting effect size for ANCOVA results we report omega squared (ω^2) and eta squared (η^2) for MANCOVA. We report the magnitude (small, medium, and large) based on the following values: .01, .06, and .14 [28].

7. RESULTS
We share the results of our summative evaluation in terms of how they address our research questions. However, before we report on our research questions we first verify that the distractors in our study performed as expected.

7.1 Distractor Usage
We expected participants to interact with the distractors or use the distractors when solving the training tasks. We used two measures to identify whether participants made use of the distractors: whether participants interacted with the distractors and the percent of time spent using those distractors.

Table 2. Training Task Distractors Usage

Task	% of Participants	Time Spent
1	69%	$M = 21\%$, $SD = 23\%$
2	69%	$M = 22\%$, $SD = 25\%$
3	100%	$M = 68\%$, $SD = 20\%$
4	64%	$M = 19\%$, $SD = 22\%$
5	98%	$M = 74\%$, $SD = 26\%$
6	53%	$M = 13\%$, $SD = 20\%$

All distractor participants used distractors in at least two of the training tasks ($Mdn = 5$). In fact, the majority of distractor participants (84%) used distractors in four or more of the six training tasks. When authoring multiple choice tests, researchers recommend removing infrequently chosen distractors; distractors should have a response frequency greater than 5% [14, 16]. Across each training task, a majority of participants used distractors in each task ($M = 76\%$, $SD = 19\%$). See Table 2 for the percentage of participants who used distractors for each task. We also note that participants spent on average 36% of their time interacting with the distractors ($SD = 27\%$). Table 2 also shows the average percent of time that participants used the distractors for each training task.

In general, we believe that this evidence suggests that participants used the distractors an appropriate amount. All participants in the distractors condition used distractors and spent an average of 36% of their time during the training phase using the distractors. While the specific numbers vary across tasks and participants, we believe that spending roughly 30% of task time generating errors, is a reasonable amount of time. We are confident that the distractors worked as intended and so we spend the remainder of the results section investigating our research questions.

7.2 How do distractors affect task completion time, task success, and cognitive load?

In this section, we report how the distractors affected the training task experience for participants. Overall, we found that distractors caused participants to spend 14% more time on the training tasks, while completing 26% less tasks and increasing participants' cognitive load. See Table 3 for a summary of the training results.

7.2.1 Training Task Time
Distractor participants spent more time completing the training tasks ($M = 6.15$, $SD = 1.00$ minutes) compared to the control condition ($M = 5.42$, $SD = 1.11$ minutes). There was a significant and large effect of distractors on training task completion time $V = .17$, $F(6, 81) = 2.86$, $p < .05$, $\eta^2 = .17$.

7.2.2 Training Task Performance
Distractor participants ($M = 65\%$, $SD = 23\%$) correctly completed fewer training tasks than the control participants ($M = 88\%$, $SD = 11\%$). This effect was significant and large, $V = .30$, $F(6, 81) = 5.65$, $p < .001$, $\eta^2 = .30$. Roughly, this translates to control participants correctly completing about five tasks ($Mdn = 6$) while the distractor participants only completed close to four tasks ($Mdn = 4$).

Recall that participants were given twelve minutes to complete each training task along with the option to quit working on a task at any point. Quitting a task early is analogous to giving up on the task. Distractors participants were significantly more likely to give up on a task compared to control participants, $V = .20$, $F(6, 81) = 3.33$, $p < .01$, $\eta^2 = .20$. In fact, distractor participants quit an average of 1.8 tasks ($SD = 2.16$, $Mdn = 1$) compared to an average of 0.45 tasks ($SD = 1.00$, $Mdn = 0$) for control participants.

Table 3. Mean Training Task Results

Task	Time (min.)*		% Complete***		% Quit Early**	
	Con.	Dis.	Con.	Dis.	Con.	Dis.
1	5.17	6.43	98%	78%	2%	13%
2	4.47	5.59	96%	80%	2%	18%
3	7.30	7.90	72%	29%	11%	40%
4	5.87	6.25	83%	58%	11%	33%
5	4.22	5.79	94%	60%	2%	36%
6	5.47	4.93	77%	53%	17%	40%

*** $p < .001$, ** $p < .01$, * $p < .05$

Table 4. Mean Transfer Task Results

Transfer Task	Time (min.)		% Complete	
	Con.	Dis.	Con.	Dis.
Do Together { Repeat }	3.49	3.07	55%	49%
Repeat { Do Together }	3.58	3.08	66%	42%
Repeat { Repeat }	4.56	3.95	43%	38%

There is not a significant effect of distractors on participants running out of time while working on a task, $V = .06$, $F(6, 81) = .92$, $p = .49$, $\eta^2 = .06$. This suggests that participants in both conditions had sufficient time to complete to the training tasks. Overall, we see that distractors appear to have a negative impact on participants' ability to complete the training tasks.

7.2.3 Training Task Cognitive Load
Across all training tasks, distractor participants reported higher cognitive load than control participants. On average control participants reported their mental effort as $5.18 \approx$ *neither low nor high* ($SD = 1.67$), whereas distractor participants reported their mental effort as $5.73 \approx$ *rather high* ($SD = 1.57$). The effect of distractors on cognitive load is significant and large, $V = .21$, $F(6, 81) = 3.55$, $p < .01$, $\eta^2 = .21$. These results suggest that distractors increase cognitive load for learners.

The CS CLCS reveals that the distractors increased extraneous cognitive load, but not intrinsic or germane load. Intrinsic and germane cognitive load are beneficial to learning. Extraneous cognitive load is imposed by the presentation of an instructional task and it is considered harmful to learning. Distractors did not have a significant effect on intrinsic and germane cognitive load; intrinsic: $F(1, 86) = .01$, $p = .94$, $\omega^2 = .01$; germane: $F(1, 86) = .35$, $p = .56$, $\omega^2 = .01$. The effect of distractors on extraneous cognitive load is significant, but small, $F(1, 86) = 6.03$, $p < .05$, $\omega^2 = .05$.

7.3 Do distractors participants show more evidence of learning?

Lastly, we wanted to know how distractors affected participants' ability to learn programming knowledge. Overall, we found no differences in control and distractor participants' transfer task time, transfer task performance, and cognitive load. See Table 4 for a summary of the transfer task results.

7.3.1 Transfer Task Time
Control participants ($M = 3.88$, $SD = .60$ minutes) spent roughly the same amount of time working on the transfer tasks as distractor participants ($M = 3.37$, $SD = .51$ minutes). There is not a significant effect of distractors on transfer task completion time, $V = .06$, $F(3, 84) = 1.73$, $p = .17$, $\eta^2 = .06$.

7.3.2 Transfer Task Performance
Control participants ($M = 55\%$, $SD = 12\%$) completed roughly the same number of transfer tasks correctly as distractor participants ($M = 43\%$, $SD = 6\%$). There is not a significant effect of distractors on correctly completing transfer tasks, $V = .06$, $F(3, 84) = 1.78$, $p = .16$, $\eta^2 = .06$.

7.3.3 Transfer Task Cognitive Load
Across all transfer tasks control and distractor participants reported roughly the same cognitive load. On average control participants ($M = 4.36$, $SD = 1.77$) and distractor participants ($M = 4.44$, $SD = 1.73$) reported *rather low* mental effort. The effect of distractors on cognitive load is not significant, $V = .001$, $F(3, 84) = .03$, $p = .99$, $\eta^2 = .001$. Further, there is no significant difference between conditions for intrinsic, $F(1, 86) = .52$, $p = .47$, $\omega^2 = .005$, extraneous, $F(1, 86) = .63$, $p = .43$, $\omega^2 = .004$, and germane, $F(1, 86) = .02$, $p = .89$, $\omega^2 = .01$, cognitive load.

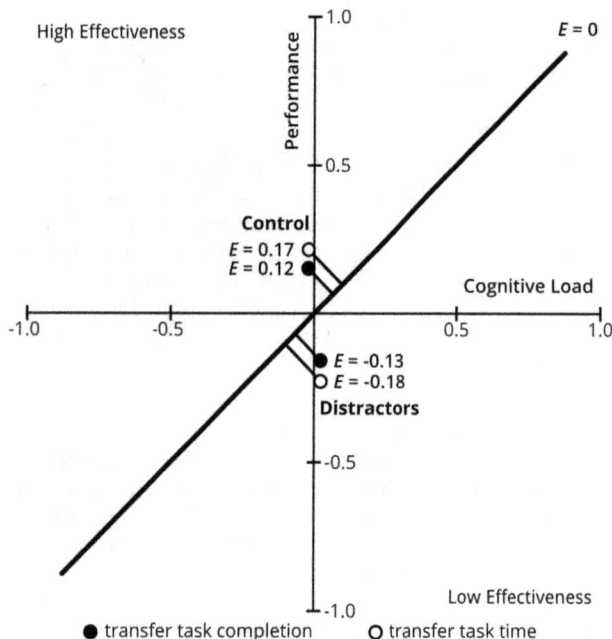

Figure 4. Instructional Efficiency (E)

7.4 Instructional Efficiency

To get an idea of how participants' cognitive load related to their performance in the transfer tasks, we computed instructional efficiency. Instructional efficiency is a measure that combines the transfer phase's cognitive load and performance in order to compare the effectiveness of instructional conditions [43, 46]. We decided to use two performance measures for computing the instructional efficiency: transfer task completion and transfer task time. Both can be considered valid measures since time on task is often related to performance [12, 46]. Figure 4 shows the instructional efficiency for our evaluation. Above the line $E = 0$ is the high effectiveness area of the graph (top-left corner); below the line $E = 0$ is the low effectiveness area (bottom-right corner). From Figure 4, we see that for both measures of performance, the control condition is more effective than the distractors condition.

8. DISCUSSION & FUTURE WORK

The results of this study suggest that distractors in code puzzles provide little benefit for novices learning programming. In this section, we highlight several questions requiring additional investigation.

8.1 Transfer Performance

Distractor participants experienced reduced learning efficiency during the training phase, while experiencing no difference in performance in the transfer phase. Based on our related work, we expected distractors to increase or decrease transfer task performance: the Parsons problem literature often hypothesizes that distractors are beneficial, [25, 47], suggesting increased transfer task performance; alternatively, based on the learning with errors and testing literature we would have expected distractors to decrease transfer task performance. However, the lack of difference in transfer performance is inconsistent with either expectation. This is an unexpected result that requires further study.

8.2 Programming Experience

Most participants had little prior exposure to the programming concepts tested in the transfer phase and on average performed poorly on all transfer tasks (control: 55%, distractors: 43%). The overall low performance suggests that participants were struggling

to simply understand the basic concepts. Learners with an existing basic understanding of a programming concept may find that distractors help them transition their understanding of that concept towards mastery.

8.3 Educational Context

In this study, we specifically targeted independent learning as a context for using distractors. Yet, Parsons problems are frequently used as practice alongside traditional classroom instruction [10, 47]. While these contexts may differ, many new programmers often struggle to learn programming, even with access to classroom resources. Given the low transfer performance, it is likely that distractors may reduce learning gains for these struggling students. Future work is needed to understand how distractors affect students' learning in different educational contexts.

8.4 Motivation

The higher failure rate for completing the puzzles in the distractor condition is worrisome (mean completion: control 88%, distractors 65%). Lower success may leave users feeling deflated and less motivated to continue learning programming. Future research is necessary to understand how distractors may affect learners' motivation to continuing learning programming from code puzzles.

9. THREATS TO VALIDITY

This study looked at one type of code puzzle distractor, the *partial suboptimal path* distractor, in a very specific context: middle school children learning programming independently. There are other types of distractors and contexts that this study did not explore. For example, Parsons problems frequently contain *syntax error* distractors [25, 47]. Considering that syntax is often a significant hurdle for new programmers, future research is necessary to understand how other types of distractors affect learners.

We also note that our recruiting mailing list often includes parents who consistently seek additional learning opportunities for their children, possibly enabling selection bias towards higher performing students. Thus our results may not fully represent the wide range of abilities of middle school children.

10. CONCLUSION

The results of our study suggest that distractors in code puzzles provide no clear benefit while reducing learning efficiency. This result can better help computer science educators to understand the potential implications that using distractors in code puzzles may have on their students. Educators should use caution if they choose to use distractors in code puzzles because the result may not match their expectations. We also encourage researchers to explore and evaluate circumstances where distractors in code puzzles have a clear benefit. Understanding how distractors impact learners is just one step towards improving the effectiveness of code puzzles to better meet the needs of future programmers.

11. ACKNOWLEDGMENTS

This material is based upon work supported by the National Science Foundation under Grant No. 1054587.

12. REFERENCES

[1] Bridger, E.K. and Mecklinger, A. 2014. Errorful and errorless learning: The impact of cue–target constraint in learning from errors. *Memory & Cognition.* 42, 6 (Mar. 2014), 898–911.

[2] Buffum, P.S. et al. 2015. A Practical Guide to Developing and Validating Computer Science Knowledge Assessments with Application to Middle School. *Proceedings of the 46th*

ACM Technical Symposium on Computer Science Education
(New York, NY, USA, 2015), 622–627.

[3] Burnett, M. et al. 2010. Gender Differences and Programming Environments: Across Programming Populations. *Proceedings of the 2010 ACM-IEEE International Symposium on Empirical Software Engineering and Measurement* (New York, NY, USA, 2010), 28:1–28:10.

[4] Butler, A.C. et al. 2007. The effect of type and timing of feedback on learning from multiple-choice tests. *Journal of Experimental Psychology: Applied.* 13, 4 (2007), 273–281.

[5] Butler, A.C. et al. 2006. When additional multiple-choice lures aid versus hinder later memory. *Applied Cognitive Psychology.* 20, 7 (Nov. 2006), 941–956.

[6] Butler, A.C. and Roediger, H.L. 2008. Feedback enhances the positive effects and reduces the negative effects of multiple-choice testing. *Memory & Cognition.* 36, 3 (Apr. 2008), 604–616.

[7] Cyr, A.-A. and Anderson, N.D. 2015. Mistakes as stepping stones: Effects of errors on episodic memory among younger and older adults. *Journal of Experimental Psychology: Learning, Memory, and Cognition.* 41, 3 (2015), 841–850.

[8] Denny, P. et al. 2008. Evaluating a New Exam Question: Parsons Problems. *Proceedings of the Fourth International Workshop on Computing Education Research* (New York, NY, USA, 2008), 113–124.

[9] Elley, W.B. 1966. The Role of Errors in Learning with Feedback. *British Journal of Educational Psychology.* 36, 3 (Nov. 1966), 296–300.

[10] Ericson, B.J. et al. 2015. Analysis of Interactive Features Designed to Enhance Learning in an Ebook. *Proceedings of the Eleventh Annual International Conference on International Computing Education Research* (New York, NY, USA, 2015), 169–178.

[11] van Gog, T. et al. 2012. Timing and Frequency of Mental Effort Measurement: Evidence in Favour of Repeated Measures. *Applied Cognitive Psychology.* 26, 6 (Nov. 2012), 833–839.

[12] Gog, T. van and Paas, F. 2008. Instructional Efficiency: Revisiting the Original Construct in Educational Research. *Educational Psychologist.* 43, 1 (Jan. 2008), 16–26.

[13] Große, C.S. and Renkl, A. 2007. Finding and fixing errors in worked examples: Can this foster learning outcomes? *Learning and Instruction.* 17, 6 (Dec. 2007), 612–634.

[14] Haladyna, T.M. and Downing, S.M. 1988. Functional Distractors: Implications for Test-Item Writing and Test Design. (Apr. 1988).

[15] Haladyna, T.M. and Downing, S.M. 1993. How Many Options is Enough for a Multiple-Choice Test Item? *Educational and Psychological Measurement.* 53, 4 (Dec. 1993), 999–1010.

[16] Haladyna, T.M. and Downing, S.M. 1989. Validity of a Taxonomy of Multiple-Choice Item-Writing Rules. *Applied Measurement in Education.* 2, 1 (Jan. 1989), 51–78.

[17] Harms, K.J. et al. 2015. Enabling independent learning of programming concepts through programming completion puzzles. *2015 IEEE Symposium on Visual Languages and Human-Centric Computing (VL/HCC)* (Oct. 2015), 271–279.

[18] Helminen, J. et al. 2013. How Do Students Solve Parsons Programming Problems? – Execution-Based vs. Line-Based Feedback. *Learning and Teaching in Computing and Engineering (LaTiCE), 2013* (Mar. 2013), 55–61.

[19] Hour of Code: *http://csedweek.org/*.

[20] Huelser, B.J. and Metcalfe, J. 2011. Making related errors facilitates learning, but learners do not know it. *Memory & Cognition.* 40, 4 (Dec. 2011), 514–527.

[21] Ihantola, P. et al. 2013. How to Study Programming on Mobile Touch Devices: Interactive Python Code Exercises. *Proceedings of the 13th Koli Calling International Conference on Computing Education Research* (New York, NY, USA, 2013), 51–58.

[22] Ihantola, P. and Karavirta, V. 2011. Two-dimensional parson's puzzles: The concept, tools, and first observations. *Journal of Information Technology Education.* 10, (2011).

[23] K, H. et al. 2011. Does incorrect guessing impair fact learning? *Journal of Educational Psychology.* 103, 1 (2011), 48–59.

[24] Kalyuga, S. et al. 1999. Managing split-attention and redundancy in multimedia instruction. *Applied cognitive psychology.* 13, 4 (1999), 351–371.

[25] Karavirta, V. et al. 2012. A Mobile Learning Application for Parsons Problems with Automatic Feedback. *Proceedings of the 12th Koli Calling International Conference on Computing Education Research* (New York, NY, USA, 2012), 11–18.

[26] Karpicke, J.D. 2012. Retrieval-Based Learning Active Retrieval Promotes Meaningful Learning. *Current Directions in Psychological Science.* 21, 3 (Jun. 2012), 157–163.

[27] King, K.V. et al. 2004. The distractor rationale taxonomy: Enhancing multiple-choice items in reading and mathematics. *Assessment Report. Pearson.* (2004).

[28] Kirk, R.E. 1996. Practical Significance: A Concept Whose Time Has Come. *Educational and Psychological Measurement.* 56, 5 (Oct. 1996), 746–759.

[29] Kornell, N. et al. 2009. Unsuccessful retrieval attempts enhance subsequent learning. *Journal of Experimental Psychology: Learning, Memory, and Cognition.* 35, 4 (2009), 989–998.

[30] Lee, M.J. and Ko, A.J. 2015. Comparing the Effectiveness of Online Learning Approaches on CS1 Learning Outcomes. *Proceedings of the Eleventh Annual International Conference on International Computing Education Research* (New York, NY, USA, 2015), 237–246.

[31] Leppink, J. et al. 2013. Development of an instrument for measuring different types of cognitive load. *Behavior Research Methods.* 45, 4 (Apr. 2013), 1058–1072.

[32] Leppink, J. et al. 2014. Effects of pairs of problems and examples on task performance and different types of cognitive load. *Learning and Instruction.* 30, (Apr. 2014), 32–42.

[33] Lin, J. et al. 2010. Distractor rationale taxonomy: Diagnostic assessment of reading with ordered multiple-choice items. *American Educational Research Association, Denver, CO.* (2010).

[34] Little, J.L. and Bjork, E.L. 2012. The persisting benefits of using multiple-choice tests as learning events. *Proceedings of the 34th Annual Conference of the Cognitive Science Society* (2012), 683–688.

[35] Looking Glass: *http://lookingglass.wustl.edu/*.

[36] Marsh, E. and Cantor, A. 2014. Learning from the Test: Dos and Don'ts for Using Multiple-Choice Tests. *Integrating Cognitive Science with Innovative Teaching in STEM Disciplines.* (Sep. 2014).

[37] Marsh, E.J. et al. 2009. Memorial consequences of answering SAT II questions. *Journal of Experimental Psychology: Applied.* 15, 1 (2009), 1–11.

[38] Marsh, E.J. et al. 2007. The memorial consequences of multiple-choice testing. *Psychonomic Bulletin & Review*. 14, 2 (Apr. 2007), 194–199.

[39] Mkrtchyan, A. 2011. Distractor Quality Analyze In Multiple Choice Questions Based On Information Retrieval Model. *EDULEARN11 Proceedings*. (2011), 1624–1631.

[40] Morrison, B.B. et al. 2014. Measuring Cognitive Load in Introductory CS: Adaptation of an Instrument. *Proceedings of the Tenth Annual Conference on International Computing Education Research* (New York, NY, USA, 2014), 131–138.

[41] Morrison, B.B. et al. 2016. Subgoals Help Students Solve Parsons Problems. *Proceedings of the 47th ACM Technical Symposium on Computing Science Education* (New York, NY, USA, 2016), 42–47.

[42] Muller, D. a. et al. 2008. Saying the wrong thing: improving learning with multimedia by including misconceptions. *Journal of Computer Assisted Learning*. 24, 2 (Apr. 2008), 144–155.

[43] Paas, F. and Van Merrienboer, J. 1994. Variability of worked examples and transfer of geometrical problem-solving skills: A cognitive-load approach. *Journal of Educational Psychology*. 86, 1 (1994), 122–133.

[44] Paas, F.G. 1992. Training strategies for attaining transfer of problem-solving skill in statistics: A cognitive-load approach. *Journal of Educational Psychology*. 84, 4 (1992), 429–434.

[45] Paas, F.G.W.C. et al. 1994. Measurement of cognitive load in instructional research. *Perceptual and Motor Skills*. 79, 1 (Aug. 1994), 419–430.

[46] Paas, F.G.W.C. and Merriënboer, J.J.G.V. 1993. The Efficiency of Instructional Conditions: An Approach to Combine Mental Effort and Performance Measures. *Human Factors: The Journal of the Human Factors and Ergonomics Society*. 35, 4 (Dec. 1993), 737–743.

[47] Parsons, D. and Haden, P. 2006. Parson's Programming Puzzles: A Fun and Effective Learning Tool for First Programming Courses. *Proceedings of the 8th Australasian Conference on Computing Education - Volume 52* (Darlinghurst, Australia, Australia, 2006), 157–163.

[48] Potts, R. and Shanks, D.R. 2014. The benefit of generating errors during learning. *Journal of Experimental Psychology: General*. 143, 2 (2014), 644–667.

[49] Richland, L.E. et al. 2009. The pretesting effect: Do unsuccessful retrieval attempts enhance learning? *Journal of Experimental Psychology: Applied*. 15, 3 (2009), 243–257.

[50] Rodriguez, M.C. et al. 2014. Distractor Functioning in Modified Items for Test Accessibility. *SAGE Open*. 4, 4 (Oct. 2014), 2158244014553586.

[51] Roediger, H.L. and Karpicke, J.D. 2006. Test-Enhanced Learning Taking Memory Tests Improves Long-Term Retention. *Psychological Science*. 17, 3 (Mar. 2006), 249–255.

[52] Roediger III, H.L. and Butler, A.C. 2011. The critical role of retrieval practice in long-term retention. *Trends in Cognitive Sciences*. 15, 1 (Jan. 2011), 20–27.

[53] Roediger III, H.L. and Marsh, E.J. 2005. The Positive and Negative Consequences of Multiple-Choice Testing. *Journal of Experimental Psychology: Learning, Memory, and Cognition*. 31, 5 (2005), 1155–1159.

[54] Scratch: *https://scratch.mit.edu/*.

[55] Smith, A.M. et al. 2012. A Case Study of Expressively Constrainable Level Design Automation Tools for a Puzzle Game. *Proceedings of the International Conference on the Foundations of Digital Games* (New York, NY, USA, 2012), 156–163.

[56] Sullivan, G.M. and Feinn, R. 2012. Using Effect Size—or Why the P Value Is Not Enough. *Journal of Graduate Medical Education*. 4, 3 (Sep. 2012), 279–282.

[57] Tarrant, M. et al. 2009. An assessment of functioning and non-functioning distractors in multiple-choice questions: a descriptive analysis. *BMC Medical Education*. 9, (2009), 40.

[58] Tobias, S. et al. 2014. Game-Based Learning. *Handbook of Research on Educational Communications and Technology*. J.M. Spector et al., eds. Springer New York. 485–503.

[59] Van Merriënboer, J.J.G. 1990. Strategies for Programming Instruction in High School: Program Completion vs. Program Generation. *Journal of Educational Computing Research*. 6, 3 (Jan. 1990), 265–285.

[60] Van Merrienboer, J.J.G. and De Croock, M.B.M. 1992. Strategies for Computer-Based Programming Instruction: Program Completion Vs. Program Generation. *Journal of Educational Computing Research*. 8, 3 (Jan. 1992), 365–394.

[61] Wang, M. et al. 2015. Using Feedback to Improve Learning: Differentiating between Correct and Erroneous Examples. *2015 International Symposium on Educational Technology (ISET)* (Jul. 2015), 99–103.

[62] Williams, E. 1949. Experimental Designs Balanced for the Estimation of Residual Effects of Treatments. *Australian Journal of Chemistry*. 2, 2 (Jan. 1949), 149–168.

A Study of Code Design Skills in Novice Programmers using the SOLO taxonomy

Cruz Izu   Amali Weerasinghe   Cheryl Pope

School of Computer Science, The University of Adelaide
Adelaide, South Australia
{cruz.izu, amali.weerasinghe, cheryl.pope}@adelaide.edu.au

ABSTRACT

There is a wealth of literature dealing with the difficulties of novice programmers with basic programming constructs such as variables, assignment and conditionals. In this paper we extend the study to two other core CS1 topics: loops and vectors (represented as single dimensional arrays). By the end of their first semester of instruction, students are expected to have acquired both the ability to reproduce given syntactic structure and basic design skills that allow them to write small pieces of code that extend, modify or combine in new ways the basic programming constructs.

This work presents an evaluation framework that uses the SOLO taxonomy to assess programming questions' complexity. Our framework extends SOLO by using the term "building block" as an adaptable parameter that explicitly defines the student's ability to increasingly write more complex pieces of code. The granularity of a "building block" is determined by the amount of programming practice students have carried out up to that point.

The analysis of final exam answers using this framework allows us to quantify the progress made by one cohort of novice programmers in the mastery of basic design skills and to study correlations between mastery of these skills and overall course performance. Furthermore, we identify common errors that illustrate the challenges students face when trying to combine programming constructs in non-trivial ways.

CCS Concepts

•Social and professional topics → Computer science education;

Keywords

Novice programmers, SOLO, code design

ICER '16, September 08-12, 2016, Melbourne, VIC, Australia

© 2016 ACM. ISBN 978-1-4503-4449-4/16/09. . . $15.00

DOI: http://dx.doi.org/10.1145/2960310.2960324

1. INTRODUCTION

Despite over 30 years of research into the teaching and learning of novice programmers, the challenge of designing effective pedagogy for programming remains. One approach to understanding how novice programmers learn to code is to analyse student performance in exams [8, 14, 15] moving from anecdotal evidence to more quantifiable data on what our students know. To cite Soloway [18]:

> A reasonable pedagogical philosophy is *The more we know about what students know, the better we can teach them.*

Most introductory courses cover a range of programming concepts starting with variables, assignment and basic I/O commands . They then introduce selection, iteration and arrays and finally present user-defined functions. Novice programmers' difficulties in understanding programming concepts have been well documented [18, 3], with particular emphasis on problems understanding variables and assignments [6, 9] as well as tracing small pieces of code [8].

We are specifically interested in the ability of novice programmer to not just learn but to integrate two key concepts: iteration and vector structures. This is not an uncommon expectation for a CS1 course, that students could write small pieces of code that manipulate a vector in various ways, such as finding the highest or lowest value, or the location of a given element.

To evaluate this expectation, we carried out a detailed analysis of students' performance (after 12-weeks of instruction) for two exam questions that involved single dimensional arrays as a common representation of vectors using an extended SOLO [1] taxonomy. The SOLO taxonomy is a popular choice to classify student answers to code writing questions[16, 20, 13]. Our analysis uses an extension of the SOLO taxonomy proposed in [5] for algorithm design.

This study aimed to explore the following questions:

- Are novice students, after 12 weeks of instruction, able to design and write correct code to manipulate vectors above the unistructural level?

- Do students exhibit the same SOLO level on different problems?

- Does the SOLO level in these questions correlate with their overall exam performance?

The rest of the paper is organised as follows: first we present a review of the literature on this topic, then we describe the student cohort and exam questions under analysis.

Next, we analyse the results of the coding of student responses with particular interest in students that *nearly* succeed and on common misunderstandings. Finally, we outline some recommendations for educators and some conclusions.

2. BACKGROUND

Many computer programs iterate over large data sets with hundreds, thousands or even millions of items. Therefore, programmers need to master both iteration and vector manipulation skills. These are core skills in an introductory course as listed in the *Fundamental Programming Concepts* of the CS 2013 curricula [7]. As such, they also constitute a significant part of the course assessment as shown in [17].

It is not only important to master each programming construct individually, but also to be able to edit, extend or combine basic iteration patterns practiced during formative assessment to solve related problems. This ability to develop code is tested using integrative questions, which are common in summative assessment [12], while the mastery of each individual pattern can be tested in shorter questions, which Zingaro calls concept questions [21].

This background section will present a literature review of the use of SOLO taxonomy for exam coding questions, and on the ability of novice programmers to master iteration and array manipulation.

2.1 SOLO Taxonomy to assess novice programmers

SOLO, which stands for the Structure of Observed Learning Outcomes [1], is a means of classifying learning outcomes in terms of their complexity, enabling us to assess students' work in terms of its quality, instead of how many lines or bits of code that are correct. At first students pick up only one or few aspects of the task (unistructural), then several aspects but they are unrelated (multistructural), then students learn how to integrate them into a whole (relational), and finally, they will be able to generalise that whole to as yet untaught applications (extended abstract).

In the area of CS education, the SOLO taxonomy was initially used to assess students' performance in code comprehension [14, 16], and later was extended to code writing [20] and algorithmic design [5]. Whalley et al. explicitly refer to the notion of *direct translation* of the specifications and the notion of redundancy. In other words, when they assess code writing in a novice programmer, they are testing their ability to translate a detailed specification into correct code in a programming language. Ginat's description of SOLO levels is the closest to our study, as it expects students to do the design, using and combining the patterns taught in a CS2 course and is included here in Table 1 as a reference.

2.1.1 Revised SOLO Taxonomy for code design & write

One of the goals of this study is to measure whether by the end of 12 weeks of instruction, novice programmers have developed basic design skills which allow them to solve small problems. To achieve this we focused on questions that did not sketch a step-by-step algorithm to be translated. Instead students must develop a solution by decomposing the problem into a combination of iteration, conditionals and assignment commands, reusing and extending the programming constructs and templates they have learned and practiced. To achieve this, we revised the descriptions given in Table 1

Table 1: SOLO Classification for algorithm design

SOLO Level	Algorithmic design
Prestructural (P)	Substantial lack of knowledge of selection and implementation of generic design patterns.
Unistructural (U)	Direct translation of the specifications into a straightforward implementation of a generic design pattern
Multistructural (M)	A translation of the specifications into flexible manipulation of a generic design pattern; or a simple, elementary composition of more than one generic pattern.
Relational (R)	A valid well-structured solution that involves the composition of two or more design patterns, integrated in a non-simple, interleaved manner, to form a logical whole.
Extended Abstract (A)	Insightful capitalization on hidden task characteristics; and/or a generalized structure that encapsulates abstraction beyond the required solution.

so they apply to the simpler construct patterns taught in a CS1 course, and generated a revised version shown in Table 2. Note we have omitted the extended abstract category for two reasons: firstly, it is not possible to determine from the exam answers if they can extend their current knowledge to other topics or areas; secondly, as most CS1 courses are heavy on content, there is hardly any space in summative assessments for questions at that level.

We should note the SOLO taxonomy can be applied to both exam questions and exam answers. It is common in exams to have a mix of short questions that test the basic knowledge of a single programming construct, similar to the concept questions presented in [21], as well as longer, integrative questions that combine two or more constructs. If a question is written at the given level, it can only be answered at that level or below. Although most times a lower level answer will be incomplete or incorrect, this is not always the case as we will see later in this analysis.

Table 2: Generic SOLO Classification for code design

SOLO Level	Algorithmic design
Prestructural (P)	Substantial lack of knowledge of basic building blocks and their use to solve the given task.
Unistructural (U)	Use of one building block or template to partially or completely solve the given task.
Multistructural (M)	Modify/extend a building block, or combine sequentially two or more blocks to partially or completely solve the given task.
Relational (R)	Combine and integrate in a non-simple manner two or more building blocks to solve the given task.

Petersen's work [12] considered both Bloom and SOLO taxonomies to evaluate exam questions from multiple institutions. The study found with both taxonomies the level will depend on the particular examples and exercises covered during course delivery. For example, if the code pattern of the sample answer has been presented or discussed in class, the level in Bloom's taxonomy will be *knowledge*,

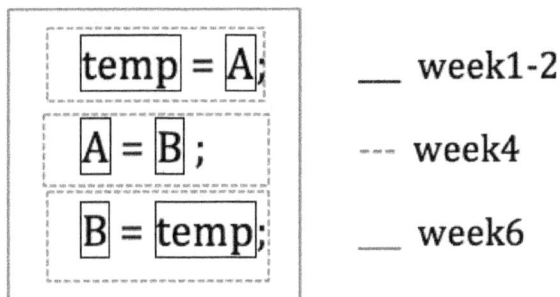

Figure 1: Swap template's building block evolution as novice programmers become more experienced with use of assignments and sequential flow control.

and the level in the SOLO taxonomy will be unistructural. But if this is not the case, the student must generate the solution either from scratch or by extending another simpler pattern he is already familiar with, then the question level will increase to *synthesize* in Bloom's taxonomy or to multistructural or relational in SOLO. We agree with Petersen's insight that any SOLO classification of questions is highly dependent on course content and depth of coverage.

Furthermore, if we compare SOLO mappings from the literature [14, 20, 6] we can see they all differ in their choice of the basic constructs that are considered to be at the unistructural level. This selection is determined by the amount of instruction the students have received so far.

We try to overcome this problem by using the term *building blocks* as an abstract entity that should be mapped to the current course content and assumed knowledge. A building block can be thought of as a pattern or template that students have mastered such that they see the code involved as a whole rather than as individual parts. Figure 1 illustrates how the list of unistructural blocks will evolve during the first weeks of instruction with the example of the Swap template. During the first two weeks, novice programmers are introduced to variables and assignments. At that point, the concept of a variable is still complex and writing a single assignment is viewed as a multistructural task in which both the variable on the left side and the expression on the right side are both basic blocks. After some practice we will expect students to easily write assignment commands, so by week 4 we consider each assignment to be a basic block (as indicated by their red frames). The Swap operation is still a multi structural task that requires students to consider the correct sequence of assignments. Assuming they have some practice swapping elements in week 4 or 5, we will expect by the end of week 6 that students are able to implement a swap operation as a single unistructural task (as indicated by the green frame), with any pair of values. Of course, there will be students that move faster from the relational to the unistructural level, and could do a swap earlier than that, but we aim to capture the progress expected from the class as a whole.

Table 3 lists the basic building blocks that we considered our novice students should be using at the unistructural level after 12 weeks of instruction. Note the course has also covered nested loops, 2-dimensional arrays and user functions but we don't expect student to have internalised these blocks yet, and hence they are not included in the current list.

Table 3: List of building blocks used for the analysis

Type	No	Description
Assignment	1	Simple assignment, i.e. x = 1
	2	Assignment of value from expression $x = 4*(a+3)$
	3	Sequence of assignments x = 10; y = x+1
Swap Template	4	swap two variables a and b as below temp = a; a = b; b = temp
Conditional statements	5	If statements with simple condition
	6	if-else statement
	7	switch or case statement
Complex Conditions	8	Two or more conditions combined by logical operators (and, or)
Basic input	9	accept number from user input
Basic output	10	display text or variable values i.e. fprintf('result is %d \n', res)
For loop	11	loop upwards by 1 for i= 1:n
	12	loop with increment (for i = 1:3:30)
	13	loop downwards (for i:n:-1:1)
Conditional loop	14	while(true) with break statement
	15	while with simple condition (ie. n > 0) where the variable tested has been initialised, and it will be updated in the body
Vector access	16	Access by location A[3] = 4
Vector concatenate	17	Add element to vector V = [V 10]
Vector templates	18	read/print all vector elements
	19	find min/max/sum of a vector
	20	simple update of all elements

2.2 Iteration and vector manipulation studies

This section summarises the literature that covers **novice** programmers' challenges with iteration and vector manipulation skills (note that most vector manipulation by default will include the use of iteration). Table 4 lists the papers in the last decade, organised by topic and level. The term *novice programmer* usually refers to a student in their first programming course at tertiary level, which matches our definition of this term, although Ginat [4] studied students in a CS2 course and also referred to them as novices.

In a standard CS1 course, iteration is usually introduced with a *while* or *for* loop over scalar data (i.e. print a sequence of integers), followed by iteration over a given vector (i.e. calculate the sum of the elements). After that, students will learn to create or modify the content of a vector. Finally, students will learn how to use nested loops to navigate over the elements of a multidimensional array and consider code efficiency As shown in Table 4, iteration has been explored in the literature mainly focusing on reading and tracing skills. Students are asked to describe the output or explain in their own words the outcome of an operation such as calculating the sum[8] or the average[14, 11] of an array, or printing a multiplication table [2]. Shihudan et al.[16] tested code comprehension using 20 multiple-choice questions which included a range of simple and nested loop examples.

Regarding writing iterative code, there is only one study

Table 4: Summary of studies focused on programming skills in novice programmers

Task	Basic	Intermediate	Advanced
Iteration	Single Loop	Nested Loops	Efficiency
	Read [2, 8, 11, 14, 16] Write [20]	Read [2, 8, 11, 16] Write [20]	Write [4]
Vector	Access	Create/Modify	Multi-dimensional
Manipulation	Write [16, 20]	Write [20, 5, 19]	none

[20] that analysed students' performance in coding two iterative tasks: one basic (loop to calculate average) and one medium (nested loop to print a box of asterisks). Ginat [4] studied CS2 students' difficulties in selecting the loop ranges for nested iteration, specifically investigating the strategies they used to encode enumeration problems. His focus was on generating *efficient* solutions, whilst many novices at the end of their first semester are still struggling to generate *correct* solutions to any non-trivial iteration task.

Regarding vector manipulation, [16] analysed a code writing task to find the minimum and the maximum of a data series using SOLO; this was a small part of a larger study of multiple choice tracing questions. There are other studies that analysed students' vector manipulation skills at the intermediate level, as shown in Table 4. However, each work had a different goal: Whalley et al.'s focus was on refining the framework to use SOLO for writing tasks [20], Ginat et al. focused on algorithmic efficiency [4] and Teague et al. [19] focused on the ability to reverse the effects of a given piece of code.

This study contributes to that body of work by analysing two intermediate writing tasks that combine iteration and vector manipulation, and by looking in more detail at common errors and misconceptions.

3. ANALYSIS OF EXAM ANSWERS USING SOLO

Our student cohort was a first year class of electrical engineering students taking their first programming course, although for most of them this was their second semester of university study. The course is organised to teach basic programming concepts in Matlab for the first 7 weeks, followed by 5 weeks of C programming. As we mentioned in the previous section, we restrict our definition of novices in this analysis to students taking their first programming course at tertiary level.

3.1 Data Collection

Students give their best effort in the final exam, in order to pass the course. Furthermore, such effort is devoid of any collaboration or external consultation so the exam answers are the best source of individual skills and programming difficulties. The final exam consisted of 8 questions, of which we selected 2 subquestions related to iteration over one or more arrays. The exam was completed by 100 students; therefore, the number of students in each category matches its percentage. The exam answers were anonymised and copied prior to the coding phase.

We focused on questions which solution goes beyond the simple iteration examples covered in the course (such as adding the elements of an array or printing their values).

```
Write a function interleave which takes two vectors of the same length and
returns a vector which is the result of interleaving the elements of the two
input vectors as shown in the examples below.
interleave([1 2 3], [10 11 12]) = [1 10  2 11 3 12]
interleave([1], [-5]) = [1 -5]
interleave([1 2 3 4], [-1 -2 -3 -4]) = [1 -1  2 -2  3  -3 4 -4]
```

Figure 2: Loop2vectors description

```
The following C code shifts all characters in a string one place to the right,
and moves the last character to the front:
void shift(char str[])
{
    int len = strlen(str);          // Assume string is not empty
    char last = str[len - 1];
    int i;

    for (i = len - 1; i > 0; i--) {
        str[i] = str[i - 1];
    }
    str[0] = last;
}
```
Modify the code so that it shifts all characters one place to the left, and moves the first character to the end of the string. You can assume the string contains at least one character.

```
Solution:
void shiftL(char str[])
{
    int len = strlen(str);
    char first = str[0];

    for (i = 0; i < len - 1; i++) {
        str[i] = str[i + 1];
    }
    str[len - 1] = first;
}
```

Figure 3: LoopReversal description and sample solution

Therefore, they cannot rely on simple recall of that pattern, and students must work above the unistructural level.

The first subquestion (Q4.(a) in the exam), which we will refer to as **Loop2vectors**, is shown in Figure 2. This question required students to create a vector C by interleaving the elements of two vectors A and B of the same length. Although it can be done with a single iteration, they cannot use the same index for all three arrays. Thus, they need to choose a strategy that either (1) iterates over A and B with the correct ranges and copy their elements into the right location of C or (ii) iterates over C inserting one element in each iteration from either A or B in sequential order. As we will see in the analysis, this question helps to identify which students understand the semantics of loops beyond the basic iteration with a single index and a single vector.

The second subquestion (Q5.(c) in the exam), which we will refer to as **LoopReversal**, is shown in Figure 3. It provides the code for a shift right and asks the students to reverse that operation with a shift left. Note they don't need to write a solution from scratch but can edit the code provided to reverse the action. This question was presented in another study [19] focusing on the cognitive development of the concept of reversibility in novice programmers in neo-piagetian terms. However, in our work we are interested in finding out how many students are able to do a **LoopRe-**

versal and to understand what the others failed.

In order to apply our revised SOLO taxonomy we need to clearly identify the building blocks that students will use in their design. Similarly to [20], we did an iterative coding process for Loop2Vectors to identify the salient elements of each task. Firstly, we listed all the design strategies that students used which are shown in Table 5.

Table 5: Observed Loop2Vectors design strategies(note L is the length of the input vectors and C is the final interleaved vector)

CORRECT INTERLEAVING STRATEGIES	
Single loop (L)	built C using concatenate
Single loop (L)	updates C with loop index i
Single loop (L)	updates C with extra index j
Single loop (2L)	updates C with extra index j
Single loop (2L)	updates C with extra indexes j,k
Two loops (L)	updates C from A (or B in the 2nd loop) with extra index j

INCORRECT INTERLEAVING STRATEGIES	
Single loop (2L)	index i out of bounds
2 nested loops*	over L
2 nested loops*	one over 2L and one over L
2 nested loops*	with i == j (redundant)
3 nested loops*	one loop per vector
No iteration	attempt to enumerate updates

* Note the nested loops are used with the wrong assumption that they run in parallel instead of being nested.

Table 6: Program constructs required for each task

Loop2vectors	
1	Iteration over one vector
2a	Concatenate: build C by adding elements from A and B
or	
2b	Vector element update - set C[i] with alternating values from A and B

LoopReversal	
1	Assignment - edit loop body to implement right shift
2	Iteration - (a) change decrement to increment and (b) reverse start and end values
3	Swap - correct update of the first and last values

Then, from this classification we were able to identified the building blocks (from Table 3) that are required to implement any valid strategy: the code must iterate over a vector (either the final interleaved vector, C, or the two input vectors) and in each iteration update (or concatenate) one value in C. Table 6 lists the building blocks they have

to use and integrate in order to produce a correct answer. The task decomposition for loopReversal was simpler as all students were editing the same coding block provided and shared the same design which has three well-defined components.

The Loop2Vectors task can be solved correctly at two levels of the taxonomy. Figure 4 shows two correct answers to this question; the first student answer combines block (1) and (2a) in a simple manner so it maps into the multistructural (M) level of our taxonomy. The second answer combines blocks (1) and (2b) but requires a non trivial addition of index j, so it maps into the relational (R) level.

The LoopReversal task is considered to be relational as we need to combine 3 patterns in a non-trivial way. The code provided by the question provides clues to which constructs are required for the task, but to achieve the desired reverse effect requires a good understanding of how these basic blocks interact together. We consider the loop reversal as a multistructural subtask, in which reversing direction is easy but identifying the start and end values requires a non-trivial edit of the loop template. Finally, to complete the shift operation, the code needs to preserve the original value of the first element to update the last location after the iteration completes. In other words, we are extending the swap pattern by swapping the last (or first) element with the original value but with code interspersed within the standard linear Swap building block.

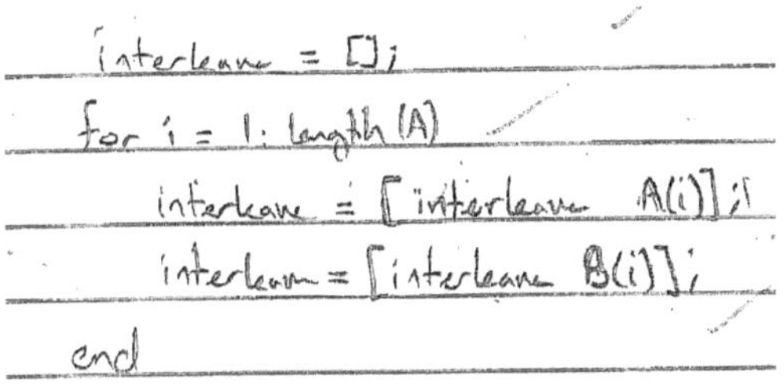

(a) Multistructural answer

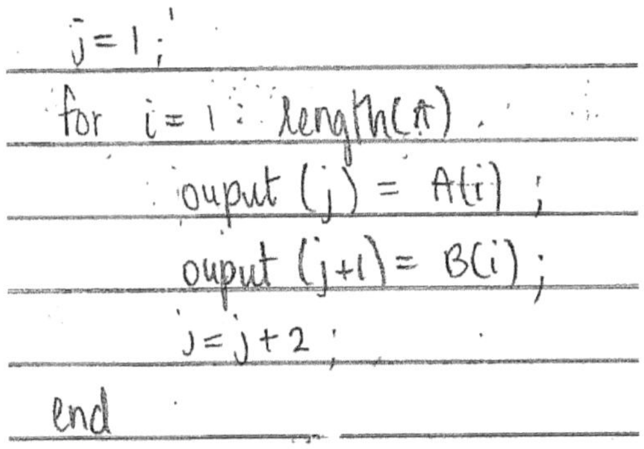

(b) Relational answer

Figure 4: Correct answers for Loop2Vectors at two levels of the SOLO taxonomy

Based on this table the SOLO level of each student answer was classified by two of the authors. Differences in classification were minimal (less than 5% percent) and always were for adjacent levels. The differences were due to answers which had student crossing out some code (as shown in line 2 of figure 5) that was correct or extra code that could be subjectively interpreted by the coders. Figure 5 shows an example of a case which was classified as unistructural (the Assignment construct as given in Table 6 is correct) by one coder. The second coder noted that the answer also had some aspects of the Swap construct and was also close to correctly implementing the Iteration construct (off by one), so it might be considered multistructural due to these partial implementations. However, returning to the notion of building blocks, it is clear that the student does not have a complete knowledge of these building blocks and the ability to integrate even two of these is not shown. Therefore the original classification of unistructural was agreed to be the correct one. In summary, these few cases were resolved by consensus to ensure consistency in our interpretation.

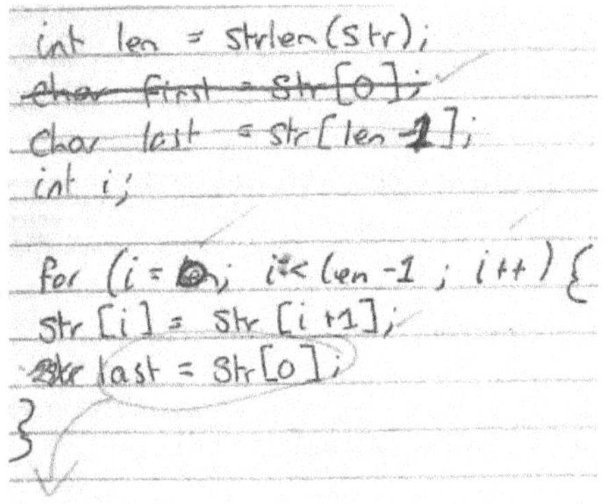

Figure 5: Coding consensus example of a LoopReversal answer

3.2 Overview of SOLO responses

Table 7 shows the distribution of students reposes as per SOLO classification. We created a sub-category *Mc*, which represents the students that provided a correct multistructural answer for Loop2Vectors. Note that these students working at this "lower" level, are not behind but may be ahead of the students classified as R, because they were able to identify a simpler way to combine the basic blocks. This again points to the need to carefully select questions in the context of student exposure and experience in the course; besides, some students may be ahead if they have done some additional programming practice outside the course. Taking account of this, we considered both sets of students (Mc and R) to be at the top of the SOLO responses for this question and in the quantitative analysis.

We can observe that the class is quite evenly spread over the 3 top SOLO levels. For the *loop2vectors* task, 35% of students worked at the relational level, 26% at the multistructural level and 30% at the uni-structural level. For the *loopReversal* task, 25% of students worked at the relational level, 21% at the multi-structural level and 37% at the uni-structural level.

If we allocate a number to each solo level, from 1 (pre structural) to 4(relational) and 0 for a blank response, we obtain an average of 2.81, and a median value of 3 for *loop2vectors* and an average of 2.45 and a median of 2 for the *loopReversal*. The fact that the SOLO mean score and the median is lower for *loopReversal* compared to *loop2vectors* may indicate that students find it harder to modify code compared to writing their own code from scratch or that

Table 7: Summary of SOLO responses

SOLO Level	Loop2vectors	LoopReversal
R (Mc)	24 (11)	25
M	26	21
U	30	37
P	7	11
Blank	2	6

Table 8: SOLO score Distribution Matrix

	SOLO	Loop2vectors				
	Level	0	1	2	3	4
LoopReversal	(B) 0	**0**	0	2	1	2
	(P) 1	1	**2**	5	2	1
	(U) 2	1	4	**13**	11	9
	(M) 3	0	1	6	**7**	7
	(R) 4	0	0	4	5	**16**

the reversing task itself is more difficult.

3.2.1 How many students have reached the top level?

Table 8 shows the distribution of SOLO levels for both questions. Looking at the data we can conclude that 44% of students (the sum of values from row 4 and column 4) are working at the relational level for at least one of the two questions, and only 3% of students have not reached the unistructural level for either of the questions, which we consider reasonable progress for 12 weeks of programming instruction.

This progress (i.e. SOLO mean of 2.63 across the two questions) is similar to that reported in other SOLO studies of first year undergraduates, i.e. Sheard [14] reported a mean score of 2.15 for a reading skill task that required students to explain the effect of code that contains a loop over an array (the code checks if the array is in order). Shuhidan's evaluation [16] of a simple vector iteration resulted in a mean score of 2.51.

The *loopReversal* task was also used in [19] but no SOLO analysis was applied. Instead, the percentage of correct answers were given. As we have 19 correct answers (excluding the 6 relational answers that have a minor syntax error), the performance of this class is 19% which is within the performance range of 8%-32% reported in the cited study for similar cohorts of novice students with 12 weeks of programming instruction.

3.2.2 Does a student work at the same SOLO level for both questions?

Most students show consistency amongst the two questions: 38% (the sum of the long diagonal in Table 8) of students are working at the same solo level and an additional 39% provide answers at adjacent levels. On the other hand, 13% answered one question at the relational level and the other at the uni-structural level and 3% answered one question at the multi structural level and the other at the pre-structural level.

3.2.3 Was there a relationship between exam results and SOLO responses?

Figure 6 shows the relationship between SOLO response levels and students final exam results. To facilitate visu-

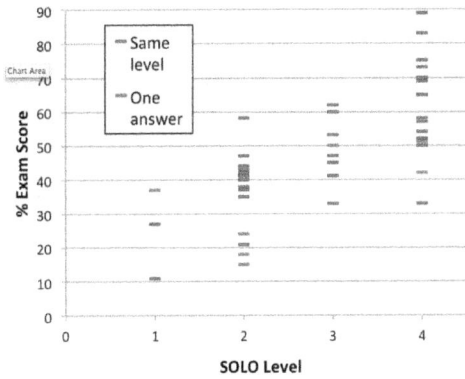
(a) One SOLO score.

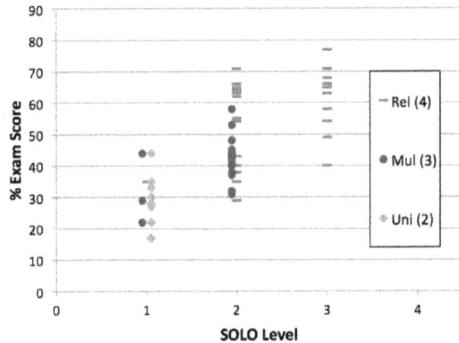
(b) Two SOLO scores (legend label shows 2nd)

Figure 6: SOLO response levels versus Exam result.

alisation of both scores, we split the class into two groups: students with one SOLO response level (both questions have the same level, or one question was blank), and students with two SOLO scores, and display the exam scores for each group in separate plots.

As expected, average exam mark decreases as the level of SOLO response decreases, from relational to prestructural. Spearmans' R correlations conducted on the SOLO responses and exam mark were significant for *loop2Vectors* (R = 0.65) and *loopReversal* (R=0.61) , as well as for the combined SOLO score (R=0.74).

4. COMMON ERRORS

The previous section provided a quantitative analysis of the writing/modifying skills of this cohort. In this section we identify the most common mistakes that students made at each level of the SOLO taxonomy for each task. We are particularly interested in major mistakes that show student challenges and misconceptions at lower levels of the SOLO taxonomy. Such errors highlight the need to provide scaffolding activities to improve student understanding of both loop semantics and vector manipulation.

4.1 Loop2vectors: common errors

At the relational level there are no significant errors to report. Six students had minor syntax errors that would be easily detected on the first compilation (i.e. $2n$ instead of $2 * n$). Four students provided working solutions that exhibited some code redundancy, i.e. using multiple indexes,

one for A and one for B, that advanced at the same rate. After only 12 weeks of instruction we focus on the ability to write correct code and leave efficiency for advance students.

Common mistakes at the **multistructural level** include: initialisation of an index within the loop that increments it (as shown in Figure 7(a)), confusion over which index to use with each vector, and using the wrong calculation for the position of the vector element to be updated. In other words, they choose the right design strategy but failed to implement it correctly. In most cases, their mistakes could be easily detected if they did a paper trace of their code for two or more iterations.

Most of the students at the **unistructural level** chose the wrong strategy to achieve interleaving, and we identified two clear misconceptions:

- Out-of-bounds logical error: six students iterated over the longer vector C, but used the same loop index to read from A and B (see code in Figure 7(b)). Although this is a common mistake for novice programmers, we should note this is not an off-by-one error as it is clear from the problem description that vector C should have twice the number of elements as the starting vectors.

- Wrong semantics of nested loops: using a nested loop with the intention of iterating over two separate vectors (see sample answer in Figure 7(c)). This approach reflects a lack of understanding of the semantics of nested loops: they assumed that each vector carries its own loop range and the two indexes advance independently.

Although we were initially surprised by the second misconception, Cetin[2] reported a similar case for *student3* of his study, who explicitly stepped over two loops simultaneously; the error was attributed to the increased cognitive load of nested loops. This mistake has also being described as a parallelism bug by Pea[11]. In other words, they assume that each index iteration applies *only* to the vector that uses that index. Note this is the most common misconception, exhibited by 13 students (43% of students at this level).

A small group at the unistructural level attempted the question by enumerating the assignments for the first 4 or 6 elements of C. Thus, although they showed a good understanding of vector updates, they have not grasped yet how to extend the the loop construct to iterate over two vectors.

Students working at the **pre-structural** level failed to use an iterative command. Their attempts reflected a lack of knowledge of the syntax and/or semantics of loops. Thus, we could not identify any relevant errors at that level.

4.2 LoopReversal: common errors

This question requires students to deal with the 3 building blocks listed in Table 6. Most students (83%) changed the assignment statement correctly but they failed to update the loop command to go upwards within the correct range. The remaining students either gave a blank answer (6%), edited the loop but did not change the assignment (3%) or edited the indexes but the assignment still shifted the elements to the left (8%).

Most students who performed below the relational level had problems dealing with the iteration block. To understand the problems we further revised the loop range lines

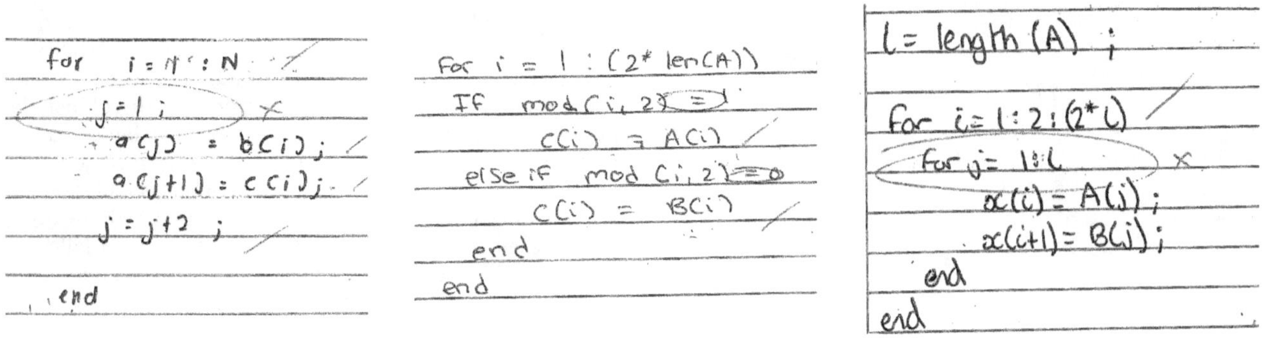

(a) Multi - wrong initialization   (b) Uni- Out of bounds read A, B   (c) Unistructural - nested loops

Figure 7: Examples of SOLO level mapping for Loop2vectors answers

Table 9: Sample of Loop command errors

	Command line	Count
Off-by-one (M)	$i = 0; i < len; i + +$	14
	$i = 0; i < len - 2; i + +$	2
Off-by-two (M)	$i = 0; i < len + 1; i + +$	2
	$i = 2; i < len; i + +$	2
infinite loop (Uni)	$i = len + 1; i > 0; i + +$	7
	$i = len - 1; i > 0; i + +$	6
	$i = 1; i > 0 ; i + +$	3
empty loop (Uni)	$i = len + 1; i < len; i + +$	2
	$i = 0; i > 0 ; i + +$	2
unedited loop (U/P)	$i = len - 1; i > 0; i - -$	10

they wrote. Table 9 provides a summary of the most common loop command errors and their frequency. As expected, the most frequent mistakes at the **multistructural** level were variations of the off-by-one error (OBOE). Fourteen students used the most common loop template to iterate upwards; this approach will cause the program to attempt to read one element beyond the end of the array (i.e. try to read str[len]). Other students missed the update to the next to last element by exiting the loop one iteration too early (a sign they were trying to avoid the out-of-bound access), while others wrote code to read not one but two elements past the end of the array.

At the unistructural level, most students attempted a *naive* reversal of the loop by *independently* reversing one or more components of the *for command*. For example, the 5th command line in Table 9 is the result of replacing each minus symbol of the original loop with a plus (the 8th command line also reverses the condition). These changes resulted in either an empty loop or an infinite loop, indicating this group haven't yet grasped the loop semantics beyond the basic template. Finally, 10 students at the unistructural level or below did not edit the given loop at all, resulting in code that copies the last element to all other positions.

4.3 Implications for educators

The analysis presented in this study has helped us to identify the issues that prevent novice programmers from us-

ing and combining building blocks to write correct pieces of code. For example, some students have a superficial understanding of loop semantics that led them to write infinite or empty loops. We hypothesise that most of their iterative practice has used a limited set of loop ranges, with the simple upward loop (counting up to n) dominating their use. To make students reflect on loop semantics we will add a multiple-choice review quiz that will ask them to trace or analyse a range of loop commands, including the cases of empty ranges and infinite ranges. The quiz's feedback should not just show the correct answer but provide an explanation for each incorrect answer. We are interested to measure whether this approach will increase students' ability to combine loops and vector manipulation commands in non-trivial ways, or whether they still show only the ability to use patterns through recall.

The description of SOLO levels in combination with the list of building blocks for a course as shown in this study makes it a good point of reference for instructors to set both summative and formative assessment that tests students at the right level of difficulty. As not all students progress at the same rate, the list should reflect the minimum level required to keep up with the course. In other words, students that perform at pre-structural level are considered to be behind and will need remedial support.

Although most instructors use their experience to align their assessment with the coding practice, we think this framework will help to better describe the spiral process of code and design skills acquisition in a CS1 course. For example, our course introduces the *for loop* in week 3, tests its usage in a practice session in week 4 and regularly uses the loop pattern in both examples and exercises afterwards. We can explain our minimum progress expectations to students by defining a lists of building blocks that should be unistructural at each stage of the course. For example, we could provide 3 checkpoints, at the end of weeks 4, 8 and 12. Writing a loop would be a relational task in the week 4 list, should become a multistructural task in week 8 and may be unistructural by week 12. We believe that the exercise of writing the list of unistructural tasks at certain stages of the course will help experienced instructors to consider question complexity relative to the list of building blocks mastered so far, reducing the expert blind spot effect [10].

Finally, instructors could use the SOLO scores measured early in the semester to tailor, when possible, the weekly coding practice to the current ability of each student.

5. CONCLUSIONS

Iteration and vector manipulation skills are core to introductory programming courses and constitute a significant part of their assessment. However, we often don't have a clear picture of the progress made by students after 12 weeks of instruction, or the challenges they face when learning to integrate iteration and vector structures. This work helps cover that gap by measuring the design and coding skills of a class of novice students answering two final exam questions that require vector manipulation. Students exhibited a wide performance range, but overall this novice cohort made significant progress over one semester of study: 44% of them reached the relational level for at least one of the two questions, and only 3% were still working below the unistructural level. The overall class performance is in a similar range as that of other published studies of CS1 courses.

As expected, novice programmers produced a range of syntax and logical errors. At the unistructural level, students showed a poor grasp of loop semantics, both for simple and nested loops. At the multistructural level, students failed to carefully consider the integration of loop ranges and vector access to avoid off-by-one errors.

This work in combination with the previous literature supports the use of the SOLO taxonomy to assess student ability to program and see higher level relationships. Future work will explore using the proposed SOLO framework (SOLO definitions combined with the list of basic building blocks at the unistructural level) as a tool to define the instructor's expectations of coding progress for a CS1 course. The same framework will also be used to obtain feedback from students on the accuracy of these expectations.

6. REFERENCES

[1] J. B. Biggs and K. F. Collis. *Evaluating the quality of learning: The SOLO taxonomy (Structure of the Observed Learning Outcome)*. Academic Press, New York, NY, USA, 1982.

[2] I. Cetin. Students' Understanding of Loops and Nested Loops in Computer Programming: An APOS Theory Perspective. *Canadian Journal of Science, Mathematics and Technology Education*, 15(2):155–170, Feb. 2015.

[3] B. Du Boulay. Some difficulties of learning to program. *Journal of Educational Computing Research*, 2(1):57–73, 1986.

[4] D. Ginat. On Novice Loop Boundaries and Range Conceptions. *Computer Science Education*, 14(3):165–181, Sept. 2004.

[5] D. Ginat and E. Menashe. SOLO Taxonomy for Assessing Novices ' Algorithmic Design. In *SIGCSE '15 Proc. 46th ACM Tech. Symposium on Computer Science Education*, pages 452–457, 2015.

[6] A. Jimoyiannis. Using SOLO taxonomy to explore students' mental models of the programming variable and the assignment statement. *Themes Sci. Technol. Educ.*, 4(2):53–74, 2011.

[7] Joint Task Force on Computing Curricula, Association for Computing Machinery (ACM) and IEEE Computer Society. *Computer Science Curricula 2013: Curriculum Guidelines for Undergraduate Degree Programs in Computer Science*. ACM, New York, NY, USA, 2013.

[8] M. Lopez, J. Whalley, P. Robbins, and R. Lister. Relationships between reading, tracing and writing skills in introductory programming. *Proc. 4th Int. Workshop on Computing education research - ICER '08*, pages 101–112, 2008.

[9] L. Ma, J. Ferguson, M. Roper, and M. Wood. Investigating and improving the models of programming concepts held by novice programmers. *Computer Science Education*, 21(1):57–80, 2011.

[10] M. J. Nathan and A. Petrosino. Expert blind spot among pre-service mathematics and science teachers. *Am Educational Research Journal*, 40(4):905–928, 2003.

[11] R. D. Pea. Language-independent conceptual" bugs" in novice programming. *Journal of Educational Computing Research*, 2(1):25–36, 1986.

[12] A. Petersen, M. Craig, and D. Zingaro. Reviewing CS1 exam question content. *42nd ACM Tech. Symp. Comput. Sci. Educ.*, pages 631–636, 2011.

[13] L. Seiter. Using SOLO to Classify the Programming Responses of Primary Grade Students. In *Proc. 46th ACM Tech. Symp. Comput. Sci. Educ. - SIGCSE '15*, pages 540–545, 2015.

[14] J. Sheard, A. Carbone, R. Lister, B. Simon, and E. Thompsom. Going SOLO to assess novice programmers. In *ITICSE'08*, number 3, pages 209–213, 2008.

[15] J. Sheard, Simon, A. Carbone, D. Chinn, M.-J. Laakso, T. Clear, M. de Raadt, D. D'Souza, J. Harland, R. Lister, A. Philpott, and G. Warburton. Exploring Programming Assessment Instruments : A Classification Scheme for Examination Questions. *7th Int. Workshop on Computing Education Research*, pages 33–38, 2011.

[16] S. Shuhidan, M. Hamilton, and D. D'Souza. A taxonomic study of novice programming summative assessment. In *Proc. 11th Australasian Conf. on Computing Education - Volume 95*, ACE '09, pages 147–156. Australian Computer Society, Inc., 2009.

[17] Simon, J. Sheard, A. Carbone, D. Chinn, M.-J. Laakso, T. Clear, M. de Raadt, D. D'Souza, R. Lister, A. Philpott, J. Skene, and G. Warburton. Introductory programming : examining the exams. *14th Australasian Computing Education Conference*, pages 61–70, 2012.

[18] J. C. Spohrer and E. Soloway. Novice mistakes: are the folk wisdoms correct? *Communications of the ACM*, 29(7):624–632, July 1986.

[19] D. Teague and R. Lister. Programming: Reading, writing and reversing. In *Proc. 2014 Conference on Innovation & Technology in Computer Science Education*, ITiCSE '14, pages 285–290, 2014.

[20] J. Whalley, T. Clear, P. Robbins, and E. Thompson. Salient elements in novice solutions to code writing problems. *Conferences in Research and Practice in Information Technology Series*, 114:37–45, 2011.

[21] D. Zingaro, A. Petersen, and M. Craig. Stepping up to integrative questions on CS1 exams. *Proc. 43rd ACM Tech. Symp. Comput. Sci. Educ. - SIGCSE '12*, page 253, 2012.

Cognitive, Affective, and Dispositional Components of Learning Programming

Alex Lishinski
Michigan State University
620 Farm Ln
East Lansing, MI, 48824, USA
lishinsk@msu.edu

ABSTRACT

Programming is a complex cognitive skill that develops over an extended period of time. The development of programming ability is the product of a number of different cognitive, affective, and dispositional factors. Furthermore, programming ability itself is a complex learning outcome that cannot be measured simply. Prior research on the individual factors that are associated with success in programming is extensive, but detailed pictures of the interactions over time of the many factors involved are rare to non-existent. My dissertation research focuses on building such a detailed picture of the factors that contribute to students developing programming ability. If these processes were better understood by CS education researchers, then interventions to improve student learning in introductory programming contexts could be more theoretically informed and effectively applied.

Keywords

Theory, Student Success Factors

1. PROGRAM CONTEXT

I have completed 3 years of my Ph.D program in Educational Psychology and Educational Technology at Michigan State University. I have completed all coursework requirements, as well as my research practicum and comprehensive/qualifying exam requirements. I am currently writing my dissertation proposal, which I plan to defend in early Fall 2016. I then plan to complete and defend my dissertation no later than Summer 2017.

2. CONTEXT AND MOTIVATION

Programming is an important skill that many students would benefit from. There are national movements to increase the prevalence of CS teachers and CS classes at every level [9]. The importance of programming sits at the center of this push. Programming is the core CS competency that makes the field relevant for students in many other fields outside CS, which is why most CS education research focuses on programming. Most computer science education researchers have the sense that something about programming makes it uniquely difficult to learn for beginners, and this is reflected in high attrition rates in early level CS courses [3]. A lot of research is conducted to determine what makes programming so hard to learn, what factors contribute to individual differences in outcomes, and how we can change pedagogical practices to address these factors. A lot of progress has been made, but major difficulties remain. We lack comprehensive, empirical accounts of the multifarious interacting factors that are involved in learning to program.

3. BACKGROUND & RELATED WORK

Programming is a complex skill with a difficult learning curve, which students often find difficult to overcome. Furthermore, programming can be an emotionally challenging skill to develop [6]. Much of the existing research on student factors that influence success in programming is rather piecemeal, with individual studies typically examining the impact of a small number of factors [4]. Broader models to explain the difficulty of learning programming have also been proposed. For example, the learning-edge momentum model explains the difficult learning curve of programming through the hierarchical interdependence of different programming competencies [10]. The hierarchy of programming skills [8] is another model of the cognitive complexity in programming, dividing component skills (i.e. syntax knowledge, code tracing, code explaining, and code writing) into a hierarchical ordering that students progress through as they increase in proficiency. This is a good high level model of the developmental trajectory of programming, but it focuses only on the characteristics of the tasks, not the students. Therefore, a model that explains the student factors involved in progressing through the hierarchy of programming skills would be desirable.

Programming is a complex cognitive skill and so there are important cognitive components. However, affective factors (e.g. self-efficacy) and dispositional factors (e.g. personality traits) may be just as important. Research on complex cognitive skill acquisition has shown how the interaction of component cognitive skills can explain student learning on complex tasks [1]. This type of model could be brought to programming, but incorporating non-cognitive factors as well as cognitive. Both global and context-specific affective and dispositional characteristics have been shown to interact with cognitive characteristics to influence complex skill

ICER '16 September 08-12, 2016, Melbourne, VIC, Australia

© 2016 Copyright held by the owner/author(s).

ACM ISBN 978-1-4503-4449-4/16/09.

DOI: http://dx.doi.org/10.1145/2960310.2960338

development [2]. Research on complex skill acquisition has shown these factors to be just as important as cognitive factors [5]. Therefore, any model of skill development for programming should incorporate cognitive as well as non-cognitive factors.

4. STATEMENT OF THESIS/PROBLEM

The goal of this research is to develop a detailed model of factors that affect introductory programming students' learning outcomes. This involves these research questions:

- How do cognitive, affective, dispositional, and background factors interact and influence learning outcomes for beginning programming students?

- All things considered, what are the most important factors affecting student programming outcomes?

- What are significant junctures where interventions could improve the learning process for students?

5. RESEARCH GOALS & METHODS

The main goal of this research project is to provide a detailed model of the significant cognitive, affective, and dispositional factors in students learning to program. To create this model, data will be collected from a large cohort of introductory programming students on important cognitive, affective, and dispositional characteristics at various time points. This data will then be used to create a model of student developmental processes in learning to program.

The constructs of interest include, among others, problem solving, self-efficacy, and big 5 personality traits. Problem solving ability will be assessed using problem solving items from the Programme for International Student Assessment (PISA). The Motivated Strategies for Learning (MSLQ) instrument will measure motivation and self-regulated learning constructs. Big 5 personality traits will be assessed with Goldberg's (1992) big 5 factor inventory.

The study will use structural equation modeling to map the interactions between the various student characteristics and student learning outcomes. Cross-lagged models will be used to chart the development of programming ability over time with respect to cognitive, affective, and dispositional covariates. Item response theory (IRT) models will also be used to analyze assignment and exam data at a more fine-grained level. This will allow for a detailed examination of what information is being collected by the exams and assignments in the programming course. IRT provides the best quality information from these multiple types of outcome measures.

6. DISSERTATION STATUS

I have been collecting data from introductory programming students for a year and a half, and I already have an empirical basis for the variables that are important to examine further (See Lishinski et al (2016) [7]). I will collect more data from new cohorts of students on these variables of interest. I have thus far completed a detailed outline of my dissertation proposal covering the questions that I am interested in, and what analyses I plan to do to answer them. I plan to complete my dissertation proposal over the summer, incorporate feedback from the ICER doctoral consortium, and defend my proposal to my dissertation committee shortly thereafter in the fall. I will continue to collect data

in the fall semester while writing my literature review and methodology sections. In the spring I will be analyzing data and writing up results, and I plan to defend my dissertation in the late spring or early summer.

7. EXPECTED CONTRIBUTIONS

The outcome of this analysis will be a model that describes how cognitive, affective, and dispositional factors interact in introductory programming students. This will support general conclusions about the processes involved in learning to program as well as conclusions about how different groups of students experience these processes differently. The end goal is to have a better sense of what is causing student attrition and differential performance by accounting for these factors and their interactions in one cohesive model. The goal is to have a theoretical overview of important student factors and experiences so that future interventions to help students learning to program can be better informed and targeted to the right factors, time points, and groups of students.

8. REFERENCES

[1] P. L. Ackerman. Determinants of Individual Differences During Skill Acquisition: Cognitive Abilities and Information Processing. *Journal of Experimental Psychology: General*, 117(3):288–318, 1988.

[2] M. Ainley, S. Hidi, and D. Berndorff. Interest, Learning, and the Psychological Processes That Mediate Their Relationship. *Journal of Educational Psychology*, 94(3):545–561, 2002.

[3] J. Bennedsen and M. E. Caspersen. Failure rates in Introductory Programming. *ACM SIGCSE Bulletin*, 39(2):32–36, 2007.

[4] S. Bergin and R. Reilly. Programming: Factors that Influence Success. *ACM SIGCSE Bulletin*, 37(1):411–415, 2005.

[5] R. Kanfer and P. L. Ackerman. Motivation and Cognitive Abilities: An Integrative/ Aptitude-Treatment Interaction Approach to Skill Acquisition. *Journal of Applied Psychology*, 74(4):657–690, 1989.

[6] P. Kinnunen and B. Simon. CS Majors' Self-Efficacy Perceptions in CS1: Results in Light of Social Cognitive Theory. *Proceedings of the seventh international workshop on Computing education research - ICER '11*, pages 19–26, 2011.

[7] A. Lishinski, A. Yadav, J. Good, and R. Enbody. Learning to Program: Gender Differences and Interactive Effects of Students' Motivation, Goals, and Self-Efficacy on Performance. *Proceedings of the 12th Annual International ACM Conference on International Computing Education Research (ICER '16)*, 2016.

[8] M. Lopez, J. Whalley, P. Robbins, and R. Lister. Relationships Between Reading, Tracing and Writing Skills in Introductory Programming. *Proceedings of the fourth international workshop on Computing education research - ICER '08*, pages 101–112, 2008.

[9] National Science Foundation. CS For All, 2016.

[10] A. Robins. Learning edge momentum: a new account of outcomes in CS1. *Computer Science Education*, 20(1):37–71, 2010.

Early Identification of Novice Programmers' Challenges in Coding Using Machine Learning Techniques

Alireza Ahadi

University of Technology, Sydney
Sydney, NSW, 2008, Australia
Alireza.Ahadi@uts.edu.au

ABSTRACT
It is well known that many first year undergraduate university students struggle with learning to program. Educational Data Mining (EDM) applies machine learning and statistics to information generated from educational settings. In this PhD project, EDM is used to study first semester novice programmers, using data collected from students as they work on computers to complete their normal weekly laboratory exercises. Analysis of the generated snapshots has shown the potential for early identification of students who later struggle in the course. The aim of this study is to propose a method for early identification of "at risk" students while providing suggestions on how they can improve their coding style. This PhD project is within its final year.

Keywords
Source Code Snapshot Analysis; Novice Programmers; Machine Learning

1. CONTEXT AND MOTIVATION
http://dx.doi.org/10.1145/2960310.2960339Every year, tens of thousands of students fail introductory programming courses world-wide. As a consequence, studies are retaken or postponed, careers are reconsidered, and substantial capital is invested into student counseling and support. World-wide, on average one third of students fail their introductory programming course. Even when looking at statistics describing pass rates after teaching interventions, as many as one quarter of the students still fail the courses. Thus, automated early identification of students' performance within the course is important. The output of this PhD study will not only contribute to shaping assessment/automated tutoring systems, but also help improve our understanding of the ways novices develop their coding patterns and suggest changes to the pedagogy of introductory programming courses.

2. BACKGROUND & RELATED WORK
In "Methods and Tools for Exploring Novice Compiling Behavior", Jadud presented a method to quantify a student's tendency to create and fix errors, which he called the *error quotient* [1]. In his study, the correlation between the error

quotient and the average score from programming assignments was mediocre but statistically significant ($r = 0.36$; $p = 0.012$), while the correlation between the error quotient and the grade from a course exam was high ($r = 0.52$; $p = 0.0002$). Rodrigo et al. used an alternative version of Jadud's error quotient, and found that in their context the correlation between the error quotient and the midterm score of an introductory programming course was strong and statistically significant ($r = -0.54$; $p < 0.001$) [2]. In essence, this suggests that the fewer programming errors students make, and the higher the midterm grade.

Watson et al. also conducted a study using Jadud's error quotient, and found a significant correlation between the error quotient and their programming course scores ($r = 0.44$) [3]. They proposed that the amount of time that students spend on programming assignments should be taken into account, and that one should consider the files that a student is editing as a part of the error quotient calculation. They proposed an improvement to the error quotient called *Watwin*, and found that with this improvement the correlation increased from ($r = 0.44$) to ($r = 0.51$). They also noted that a simple measure, the average amount of time that a student spends on a programming error, is strongly correlated with programming course scores ($r = -0.53$; $p < 0.01$).

3. STATEMENT OF THESIS/PROBLEM
The current formulation of this PhD study's research question is as follows:

What, if there is any, would be an environmental independent common attribute of the data collected from novices in different programming languages which could automatically classify students according to their ability of coding?

The research goals are as follows:

Data Collection: data used in this study is collected from source code snapshots generated by novices enrolled in an introductory programming courses at a) University of Helsinki, Finland. b) University of Technology, Sydney, and c) snapshots generated by novices enrolled in an database fundamental course at University of Technology, Sydney. The collected programming snapshots represent line-edit level [4] snapshots of the students' main source code while working on a programming task, while the database SQL SELECT statements represent different attempts of novices in writing SQL code.

Replication: analyzing the collected data in an unsupervised machine learning framework to assess the state of the art techniques described above. The collected source code snapshots will be used to identify possible clusters of novices according to different features extracted from their source codes.

Proposition and Comparison: analyzing the collected data in order to compare the performance of new methods proposed as a part of this PhD with the state of the art methods. Based on the output of different machine learning tools, a set of context-independent features extracted from the data as well as a systematic approach for analyzing them will be proposed.

4. PROGRAM CONTEXT

Accomplishing the final output of this research project involves fulfilling the objectives of three main phases. The first phase is dedicated to analysis of snapshot data in different contexts [5]–[9] to understand the data and find possible links to what previously has been reported [10]–[16]. The second phase is devoted to designing machine learning derived techniques for snapshot data analysis [6]. The third and last phase of the project is dedicated to performing the comparative analysis of the proposed techniques of analyzing snapshot data with the state of the are techniques in a large scale on different datasets.

5. DISSERTATION STATUS

This PhD project is within a year of completion. The data collection has been completed successfully and some preliminary results have been generated based on an original hypothesis. Replication and comparison stages are almost completed. Based on findings so far, there is a significant and strong negative correlation between the number of steps a novice takes to complete a coding task successfully and her overall performance in the programing subject.

6. REFERENCES

[1]   M. C. Jadud, "Methods and tools for exploring novice compilation behaviour," *Proc. 2006 Int. Work. Comput. Educ. Res. ICER 06*, vol. 09, no. Figure 1, pp. 73–84, 2006.

[2]   M. M. T. Rodrigo, E. Tabanao, M. B. E. Lahoz, and M. C. Jadud, "Analyzing online protocols to characterize novice java programmers," *Philipp. J. Sci.*, vol. 138, no. 2, pp. 177–190, 2009.

[3]   C. Watson, F. W. B. Li, and J. L. Godwin, "Predicting performance in an introductory programming course by logging and analyzing student programming behavior," in *Proceedings - 2013 IEEE 13th International Conference on Advanced Learning Technologies, ICALT 2013*, 2013, pp. 319–323.

[4]   A. Ahadi, "Applying Educational Data Mining to the Study of the Novice Programmer , within a Neo-Piagetian Theoretical Perspective" in *Psychology of Programming Interest Group*, 2014, pp. 197–202.

[5]   A. Ahadi, R. Lister, H. Haapala, and A. Vihavainen, "Exploring Machine Learning Methods to Automatically Identify Students in Need of Assistance," *Icer'15*, pp. 121–130, 2015.

[6]   A. Ahadi, A. Vihavainen, and R. Lister, "On the Number of Attempts Students Made on Some Online Programming Exercises During Semester and their Subsequent Performance on Final Exam Questions," in *ACM conference on Innovation and Technology in Computer Science Education*, 2016.

[7]   A. Ahadi, J. Prior, V. Behbood, and R. Lister, "Students ' Semantic Mistakes in Writing Seven Different Types of SQL Queries," in *ACM Conference on Innovation and Technology in Computer Science Education*, 2016.

[8]   A. Ahadi, V. Behbood, A. Vihavainen, J. Prior, and R. Lister, "Students ' Syntactic Mistakes in Writing Seven Different Types of SQL Queries and its Application to Predicting Students ' Success," in *SIGCSE '16: Proceedings of the 47th ACM Technical Symposium on Computer Science Education*, 2016.

[9]   A. Ahadi, J. Prior, V. Behbood, and R. Lister, "A Quantitative Study of the Relative Difficulty for Novices of Writing Seven Different Types of SQL Queries," in *Proceedings of the 2015 ACM Conference on Innovation and Technology in Computer Science Education*, 2015, pp. 201–206.

[10]   A. Ahadi and R. Lister, "Geek genes, prior knowledge, stumbling points and learning edge momentum: parts of the one elephant?," *Proc. Ninth Annu. Int. ACM Conf. Int. Comput. Educ. Res. (ICER 2013)*, pp. 123–128, 2013.

[11]   D. Teague, M. Corney, A. Ahadi, and R. Lister, "Swapping as the ' Hello World ' of Relational Reasoning□: Replications , Reflections and Extensions," pp. 87–94, 2012.

[12]   A. Ahadi, R. Lister, and D. Teague, "Falling Behind Early and Staying Behind When Learning to Program," in *25th Anniversary Psychology of Programming Annual Conference*, 2014.

[13]   D. Teague, M. Corney, C. Fidge, M. Roggenkamp, A. Ahadi, and R. Lister, "Using Neo-Piagetian Theory , Formative In-Class Tests and Think Alouds to Better Understand Student Thinking□: A Preliminary Report on Computer Programming Design□: Neo-Piagetian Theory of Cognitive Development," 2012.

[14]   D. Teague, R. Lister, and A. Ahadi, "Mired in the Web□: Vignettes from Charlotte and Other Novice Programmers," 2014.

[15]   M. Corney, D. Teague, A. Ahadi, and R. Lister, "Some Empirical Results for Neo-Piagetian Reasoning in Novice Programmers and the Relationship to Code Explanation Questions," *14th Australas. Comput. Educ. Conf.*, pp. 77–86, 2012.

[16]   D. Teague, M. Corney, A. Ahadi, and R. Lister, "A qualitative think aloud study of the early neo-piagetian stages of reasoning in novice programmers," in *Proceedings of the Fifteenth Australasian Computing Education Conference*, 2013, vol. 136, pp. 87–95.

The Role of Spatial Reasoning in Learning Computer Science

Amber Solomon
Georgia Institute of Technology
85 5th Street NW
Atlanta, GA, 30308
asolomon30@gatech.edu

ABSTRACT

Spatial reasoning concerns the locations of objects, their shapes, their relations to each other, and the paths they take as they move. People with high spatial reasoning scores are more likely to major in degrees in STEM disciplines and go into STEM careers than those with low scores. Spatial reasoning tends to be low amongst students of low socioeconomic status. We need to understand the the relationship between spatial reasoning, socioeconomic status, and success in learning computer science. If there are causal relationships among these variables, we will need appropriate interventions in order to broaden participation and improve success in computing education.

Keywords
Spatial Reasoning; Socioeconomic Status

1. PROGRAM CONTEXT

I have completed my first year of the Human-Centered Computing (HCC) Ph.D. program at Georgia Tech. I anticipate passing my qualifying exams in Spring 2017 and hope to finish all coursework and propose by Spring 2018. I expect to defend my dissertation by Spring 2020. I have worked on projects exploring novel pedagogies and spatial reasoning. One project attempts to understand the effects of using design studio pedagogy in a computer science classroom [9]. Another project is a study to measure the interaction between socioeconomic status (SES), access to computer science learning opportunities in high school, and spatial reasoning abilities as predictors for performance in computer science. Lastly, I have been working on a review of literature that connects spatial reasoning ability and success in computer science education with SES. I am currently determining potential research questions pertaining to SES and spatial reasoning in regards to performance in computer science education.

2. CONTEXT AND MOTIVATION

Scores of high-quality studies conducted over the past 50 years indicate that spatial reasoning is central to STEM success [10]. Significant visual ability is a strong predictor for an Engineering career, followed by a career in Computer Science or Mathematics [10].

Even more than being a potential predictor, spatial reasoning may be an important factor for learning computer science. A study found, "spatial ability was the best predictor of knowledge of basic commands; and a combination of spatial ability and field independence best predicted scores on generated graphics programs [3]." Jones and Burnett found participants with high spatial abilities completed programming exercises faster than those with lower spatial abilities [4]. A study with 30 students with experience in Java found "programmers use equivalently strategies for program comprehension and spatial cognition [5]." Thus similar cognitive skills are used for spatial cognition and program development.

Cooper *et al.* noticed an unintended consequence when they were attempting to understand the relationship between a student learning to program and his or her spatial ability. They found some evidence to suggest that, "the spatial skills training helped the low SES students, so that their CS knowledge gain was not distinguishable from the middle/high SES students. In other words, in the group given spatial skills training, the lower SES students improved just as much as the higher SES students did in CS [2]."

Spatial reasoning concerns the locations of objects, their shapes, their relations to each other, and the paths they take as they move [8]. We think spatially everyday when "we consider rearranging the furniture in a room, when we assemble a bookcase using a diagram, or when we relate a map to the road ahead of us [8]." Spatial abilities have been linked to higher-level thinking, reasoning, and the creative process. However, it is unclear exactly why and how spatial abilities lead to success in STEM. It is thought that spatial abilities may be linked to students' abilities to think at different levels of abstraction, an essential skill for engineers and computer scientists to develop [2].

Studies have shown that people from low SES backgrounds have lower spatial abilities and are underrepresented in computer science [1, 6, 8]. If students from low SES backgrounds were trained to have better spatial reasoning, would they be more successful in computer science, and would more of them pursue computer science?

However, very little research has been done to investigate the relationship between SES backgrounds and spatial reasoning scores. There has also been little to no targeted interventions aimed at increasing the spatial reasoning abilities of those from low SES backgrounds. There are some hypotheses that suggest students of lower SES do not score as well due to environmental reasons [1]. Minorities make up a significant portion of students from low SES groups, and "poorly developed spatial skills for these students could have serious implications for broadening participation in STEM [1]."

To broaden participation in computer science, we need to study the spatial reasoning of students with different SES backgrounds. By establishing potential causes, better interventions to increase spatial reasoning for students of low SES backgrounds can be made.

3. BACKGROUND & RELATED WORK

Most research conducted on spatial reasoning and computer science is focused on gender. Many studies note spatial reasoning differences between males and females, with females having lower spatial abilities [7, 8]. Potential causes of these differences are broad and varying, including stereotype threat, and biological or environmental factors [7]. Spatial training has been shown to help close the gender gap [7, 8].

There is some evidence suggesting students of middle and high SES backgrounds have better spatial skills than students of low SES backgrounds [1, 6]. Levine et al. found that spatial reasoning for students from low SES groups were significantly lower than the skills for students from middle or high SES groups [6]. Casey et al. discovered that, "spatial skills were related to measurement performance in the affluent but not in the low-income community [1]."

Cooper *et al.* were able to find some evidence, on a small scale, that spatial training can help close the gap between students of different SES backgrounds [2]. However, besides this research, very little has been done in computer science education research on spatial reasoning and SES; this area is generally not well understood. Thus, my research will contribute to this area by understanding the relationship between computer science performance, SES, and spatial reasoning. My research will also provide reasons why students' of low SES have lower spatial reasoning and how to best improve their spatial reasoning.

4. STATEMENT OF THESIS/PROBLEM

This research will explore potential relationships between SES, spatial reasoning, and computer science success. Potential research questions could be expansive and include the following:

- Is there a relationship between computer science performance, SES, and spatial reasoning?
- What are some potential reasons for the gap between spatial reasoning scores for students of differing socioeconomic status?
- How do we best provide spatial reasoning training for this population?

5. RESEARCH GOALS & METHODS

To discover if there is a relationship between computer science performance, SES, and spatial reasoning, I will run a study comparing students' SES with their scores on the Revised Purdue Spatial Visualization Test, and their scores on a computer science test, SCS1. Running statistical analyses on this data will help determine correlations.

If there are correlations, then a better understanding of potential reasons why students of low SES have lower spatial reasoning may be useful in determining what is necessary to create effective spatial reasoning training for this group. As environmental factors may be the best explanation of this occurrence, I will conduct a study collecting quantitative and qualitative data comparing what students from low SES had access to as children (toys, experiences like going to museums, video games, etc.) to students from high SES. While doing this study, a more exhaustive literature review will be conducted on other indicators or predictors of spatial reasoning.

If environmental factors are a reason for this gap, then creating a culturally relevant intervention may be necessary to increase students of low SES spatial abilities. After developing this intervention, a study will be conducted to determine whether it affected how well students of low SES perform in computer science. The computer science performance of two groups of students of low SES, one group receiving the intervention and the other not, will be compared to determine if the training was useful.

6. DISSERTATION STATUS

I expect to take my qualifying exams in Spring 2017. I hope to propose my dissertation by Spring 2018. My expectation from participating in this consortium is to have a better understanding of how to design the studies for this research and to learn about other work that could impact my own.

7. EXPECTED CONTRIBUTIONS

I hope to contribute a more nuanced understanding of low SES students' cultures that cause effects like low spatial reasoning. I also expect to develop computer based, culturally relevant spatial reasoning training. The broader implication of my research is to broaden participation within the computer science field by helping increase spatial reasoning amongst students of low SES.

8. REFERENCES

[1] Casey, B. M., Dearing, E., Vasilyeva, M., Ganley, C. M., & Tine, M. (2011). Spatial and numerical predictors of measurement performance: The moderating effects of community income and gender. *Journal of educational psychology*, *103*(2), 296.

[2] Cooper, S., Wang, K., Israni, M., & Sorby, S. (2015, July). Spatial Skills Training in Introductory Computing. In *Proceedings of the eleventh annual International Conference on International Computing Education Research* (pp. 13-20). ACM.

[3] Fincher, S., Baker, B., Box, I., Cutts, Q., de Raadt, M., Haden, P., & Petre, M. (2005). Programmed to succeed?: A multi-national, multi-institutional study of introductory programming courses.

[4] Jones, S., & Burnett, G. (2008). Spatial ability and learning to program. *Human Technology: An Interdisciplinary Journal on Humans in ICT Environments*, *4*(1), 47-61.

[5] Jones, S. J., & Burnett, G. E. (2007, June). Spatial skills and navigation of source code. In *ACM SIGCSE Bulletin* (Vol. 39, No. 3, pp. 231-235). ACM.

[6] Levine, S. C., Vasilyeva, M., Lourenco, S. F., Newcombe, N. S., & Huttenlocher, J. (2005). Socioeconomic status modifies the sex difference in spatial skill. *Psychological Science*, *16*(11), 841-845.

[7] Linn, M. C., & Petersen, A. C. (1985). Emergence and characterization of sex differences in spatial ability: A meta-analysis. *Child development*, 1479-1498.

[8] Newcombe, N. S. (2010). Picture This: Increasing Math and Science Learning by Improving Spatial Thinking. *American Educator*, *34*(2), 29.

[9] Solomon, A., Zhang, D., Jones, R., Disalvo, B., Macintyre, B., Guzdial, B. (2016). Using Projection AR to Add Design Studio Pedagogy to a CS Classroom. *IEEE VR KEVLAR*.

[10] Wai, J., Lubinski, D., & Benbow, C. P. (2009). Spatial ability for STEM domains: Aligning over 50 years of cumulative psychological knowledge solidifies its importance. *Journal of Educational Psychology*, *101*(4), 817.

Bringing the Innovations in Data Management to Secondary CS Education

Andreas Grillenberger
Computing Education Research Group
Friedrich-Alexander-Universität Erlangen-Nürnberg (FAU)
Martensstraße 3, 91058 Erlangen, Germany
andreas.grillenberger@fau.de

ABSTRACT

Data Management is a field of CS that has changed significantly with the innovations of recent years. With increasing amounts of data that is being collected, stored and processed today, this field evolved from the traditional field databases. While storing data in databases is a typical topic in (secondary) CS education, more modern aspects are hardly covered at all. However, as these innovations have a high impact on our daily lives and in society, not only can they help convey a realistic impression of CS, but they have also the potential to support students when handling (their own and others') data. In my research project, I investigate the field data management from an educational point-of-view in order to identify central aspects relevant and practical for CS classes in secondary schools. To ensure that the identified concepts and ideas are central to CS education, the field will be analyzed not only from a CS point-of-view, but also from the students', teachers' and the societal perspective.

Keywords

data management; databases; big data; secondary CS education; educational reconstruction

1. PROGRAM CONTEXT

I am a doctoral student at the computing education research group at the University of Erlangen-Nürnberg, Germany, since 10/2013. My advisor is Prof. Dr. Ralf Romeike. As it is common in Germany, I am not enrolled in a PhD program, instead I work as research assistant at the university. I intend to finish my work by late 2018. So far, I have set my focus on finding an appropriate research framework [7], analyzing the science content structure of data management as well as on characterizing the gap between data management in CS and in CS education [5]. The next step is to go through a first iteration of the research framework.

ICER '16 September 08-12, 2016, Melbourne, VIC, Australia

© 2016 Copyright held by the owner/author(s).

ACM ISBN 978-1-4503-4449-4/16/09.

DOI: http://dx.doi.org/10.1145/2960310.2960341

2. CONTEXT AND MOTIVATION

Besides algorithms and data structures, databases have been a central topic of CS education (CSE) for years. In CS, various innovations in this field led to a shift of focus from databases to data management in general. Not only have new topics evolved, but various of the topics in this field are also considered from a wider perspective today. These innovations strongly affect society and our daily lives—e.g. when talking about systems like online shops or social media. Yet, they are hardly covered in current CSE: aspects like handling meta-data are only considered marginally, new methods of data analysis are missing, and the increasing parallelization of data processing is not part of current teaching, even though these aspects are generally accepted as being central to CS. Additionally, next to providing a realistic perspective on CS, an important task of CS teaching is fostering competencies that are needed for daily life, like using and handling data in a self-determined and responsible way.

3. BACKGROUND & RELATED WORK

Data Management is frequently discussed from various perspectives. This field was characterized in detail by the Data Management Association in their Data Management Body of Knowledge [2]. Also, established database textbooks are central to data management. In CSE, many publications on big data / data management can be found, too. However, most of them are related to learning analytics, which is not covered by my research. Only few articles can be found on data management as topic in class: while databases were discussed intensively in the early 1990s (e.g. [8]), there have hardly been any publications for years. But in recent years, the attention on this topic has increased: e.g. Buffum et al. describe an approach for integrating big data principles into other subjects [1], and the topic is also mentioned in the draft for the revised K–12 CS Standards[1].

4. STATEMENT OF THESIS/PROBLEM

As shown in [5], there is a clear gap between the current state-of-the-art in data management and its representation in CS education. In parts this gap may be explained by the complexity of some topics or because they are only relevant in specific contexts. But as described in [6], students also need to acquire competencies on various aspects of data management in their own daily lives. Topics like synchronization and backup can serve as interesting contexts,

---

[1]http://www.csteachers.org/page/SubmitYourFeedback (checked on 19/05/2016)

e. g. for discovering the problems but also the advantages of redundant data storage, while today's teaching focuses only on avoiding redundancy (e. g. when normalizing data schemes). Finding such concepts and ideas of data management is a central aspect of my work. Hence, my key question is: *"Which are the influences of the current developments in data management on secondary CS education, and how can CS education handle the challenges and requirements that are accompanying these changes and innovations?"*.

5. RESEARCH GOALS & METHODS

As a research framework for my project, I will use the model of educational reconstruction for CSE [3]. A detailed research plan for my project was described in a work-in-progress paper [7], so I will not describe the application of the framework here. Instead, I will concentrate on the goals and methods. The framework considers four perspectives: science, society, students and teachers. While in the model all these perspectives are equally relevant, not all of them can be examined during one PhD project in equal depth. Hence, I set my focus is on the content-related aspects of the model in particular and on the science perspective, while other aspects are covered in a less detailed way. Consequentially, the most important questions are:

1. How is everyone affected by data management in their daily lives ?

2. Which are the fundamental and long-lasting aspects of data management that are central to CS education?

3. What knowledge, competencies and skills concerning data management does everyone need to have?

4. Which prior knowledge, attitudes and perceptions do learners currently have on this topic as well as on the opportunities and threats of data management?

For answering these questions, I will use several methods: As the focus of the project is on the content-oriented aspects, methods like the qualitative content analysis are central. For investigating questions 2 and 3, I plan to analyze documents like current curricula, educational standards, but also scientific material. For example, to determine the gap between the scientific point-of-view and CS teaching on this topic [5], I conducted an analysis of current CS curricula and standards in comparison to the the DAMA-DMBoK [2]. Also, to ensure the validity of the results, I plan some expert interviews. For dealing with question 4, I am investigating alternative methods to surveys, as directly questioning students is hardly possible in Bavaria because of regulations by the ministry of education. Yet the students' perspectives should not be neglected in this project. A possible option to include at least a general impression of the learners' attitudes and interests is a meta-analysis of studies like the German JIM Study [4] on youth, information and media.

6. DISSERTATION STATUS

In addition to choosing the model of educational reconstruction as a research framework and adapting this model for my project (cf. [7]), some aspects have already been investigated: from the societal perspective, central competencies that everyone needs for handling personal and others'

data in the daily life were analyzed and proposed at the KEYCIT conference (cf. [6]). The scientific perspective was considered by characterizing the gap between current CS education and data management in CS [5]. Also, for gaining a more comprehensive overview of data management, I started creating an overview map of of this field which should help to find central ideas as well as appropriate contexts and phenomena for linking these ideas with students' experiences. In addition I started to investigate students' perspectives by analyzing studies on the media use of teenagers, and I collected feedback from the teachers' perspectives in various teacher training workshops I conducted. At the moment, the thesis document itself only exists as an outline and partly in a rough draft version. However, several of the already published papers will be reused in the thesis.

7. EXPECTED CONTRIBUTIONS

Today, data management is hardly considered in CSE, even though it has a strong relevance in daily life as people use and produce data continuously. By analyzing data management from an educational point-of-view and by finding its central and long-lasting ideas, this project can strongly contribute to the further development of teaching in this field. This will, on the one hand, help modernizing current teaching, but, on the other hand, also prevent just following trends. In addition, by adapting the model of educational reconstruction for analyzing this complete field, it will be investigated if this model is suitable for bringing innovative topics to CSE.

8. REFERENCES

[1] P. Buffum et al. CS Principles Goes to Middle School: Learning How to Teach "Big Data". In *Proceedings of SIGCSE '14*, pages 151–155. ACM New York, USA, 2014.

[2] DAMA International. *The DAMA Guide to the Data Management Body of Knowledge - DAMA-DMBOK*. Technics Publications, LLC, USA, 2009.

[3] I. Diethelm, P. Hubwieser, and R. Klaus. Students, Teachers and Phenomena: Educational Reconstruction for Computer Science Education. In *Proceedings of Koli Calling 2012*, pages 164–173. ACM New York, USA, 2012.

[4] S. Feierabend, T. Plankenhorn, and T. Rathgeb. *JIM-Studie 2015*. Medienpädagogischer Forschungsverband Südwest, 2015.

[5] A. Grillenberger and R. Romeike. A Comparison of the Field Data Management and its Representation in Secondary CS Curricula. In *Proceedings of WiPSCE 2014*, pages 29–36. ACM New York, USA, 2014.

[6] A. Grillenberger and R. Romeike. Teaching Data Management: Key Competencies and Opportunities. In *Proceedings of KEYCIT 2014*, pages 133–150. University Press Potsdam, 2014.

[7] A. Grillenberger and R. Romeike. Bringing the Innovations in Data Management to CS Education: An Educational Reconstruction Approach. In *Proceedings of WiPSCE 2015*, pages 88–91. ACM New York, USA, 2015.

[8] H. Witten. Datenbanken - (k)ein Thema im Informatikunterricht? *LOG IN*, 2:14–19, 1994.

Dynamically Adaptive Parsons Problems

Barbara J. Ericson
Georgia Institute of Technology
801 Atlantic Drive
Atlanta, GA, 30332, USA
+1-404.385.2107
ericson@cc.gatech.edu

ABSTRACT

Parsons problems are code segments that must be placed in the correct order with the correct indention. Research on Parsons problems suggests that they might be a more effective and efficient learning approach than writing equivalent code, especially for time-strapped secondary teachers. I am exploring this hypothesis with empirical experiments, observations, and log file analyses. Our research team also plans to modify the open-source js-parsons software to allow Parsons problems to be dynamically adaptive, which means that the difficulty of the problem will change based on the user's past performance. I plan to compare dynamically adaptive Parsons problems to the current non-adaptive Parsons problems to determine which learners prefer and to see if solving dynamically adaptive Parsons problems leads to more efficient and effective learning than solving non-adaptive Parsons problems.

General Terms

Design, Experimentation, Measurement

Keywords

Parsons problems; Learning programming; Online learning; Ebook; Adaptive Learning

1. RESEARCH SITUATION

I have just completed the 4th year of my Human-Centered Computing (HCC) PhD program. I am working on my PhD part-time while working full-time. I passed my written and oral qualifying exams in the spring of 2014. I passed my proposal in December of 2015.

My research group is creating and testing features for e-books to help people learn programming. One of the features that I have focused on is Parsons problems [8]. Parsons problems are code segments that are mixed up and have to be placed into the correct order and may have to be indented correctly as well. Parsons problems can also have extra code segments, called distractors, which are not needed in a correct solution. The distractor code segments can be displayed in a random order along with the correct code segments or can be displayed paired with the correct code segments.

ICER '16, September 08-12, 2016, Melbourne, VIC, Australia
ACM 978-1-4503-4449-4/16/09.
http://dx.doi.org/10.1145/2960310.2960342

I created 11 Parsons problems for a chapter of the *How to Think Like a Computer Scientist – Interactive Edition* Python e-book. Teachers that I observed solving the Parsons problems said that they wanted the Parsons problems to be harder. However, log file analysis of student use of the ebook showed that while the majority of students got most of the Parsons problem right in one to two tries, there were four questions that took three to nine tries for 75% of the people to solve. Some students had as many as 109 tries before correctly solving one problem. We also found that for some of the easier problems 50% of the students, who gave up, did so after only 2 tries. For harder problems 50% of the students, who gave up, did so after six to nine tries.

I also created Parsons problems for an ebook for CS Principles teachers and another one to help students prepare for the Advanced Placement Computer Science A exam. Advanced Placement courses are high school (secondary) courses intended to be equivalent to introductory university courses.

2. CONTEXT AND MOTIVATION

National Science Foundation (NSF) wants to prepare 10,000 United States of America high school teachers to teach a new course, Advanced Placement (AP) Computer Science Principles (CS-P), by the beginning of the 2016-2017 school year. This effort is called the CS 10K effort. Many researchers in the computer science education community are focusing on this effort, including the members of the CS Learning 4U project at Georgia Tech.

The new AP CS-P course covers several big ideas in computing, including programming. It would be very expensive and difficult to provide face-to-face professional development for thousands of teachers. Much of the professional development will have to be done using distance learning.

One of the difficulties in preparing teachers to teach programming is that programming can be difficult to learn. Reported failure rates in introductory computer science courses at the university level are as high as 90% [2]. A large multi-institutional study found that many undergraduate students can't program as well as expected after either their first two computer science courses [5].

The pace of on-line learning can be problematic for teachers. A study of adult learners in two online introductory computer science university courses found that success in the course was dependent on having sufficient time to dedicate to the course work and that working adults often did not have sufficient time [1]. Students had difficulty in learning to program and the time it took to create working programs was unpredictable. Even simple syntax errors like having a comma out of place could take hours to fix [1].

Studies of expert programmers show that experts recognize and apply many "programming plans" [7]. Teachers who are new to programming will need to learn these "programming plans". Soloway and Guzdial recommend using scaffolding to support learners as they learn a new task [8]. Parsons problems are a type of scaffolding.

3. BACKGROUND & RELATED WORK

One way to make the learning of computer science more efficient and effective is to reduce the amount of time that beginners struggle with syntactic and semantic errors. One possible approach is to use Parsons problems [6] instead of requiring learners to write lots of code. There are several variants of Parsons problems, such as including extra code as distractors and pairing the distractor and correct code.

Work in this area [3] has found that Parsons problem scores highly correlate with code writing scores. This means that Parsons problems might be a more effective and efficient way to learn than the traditional approach, which requires beginners to spend an unpredictable number of hours writing code. Denny, Luxton-Reilly et al. suggested that students should be able to solve the Parsons problems more quickly than writing the equivalent code, but they did not test this hypothesis. They also tested several variants of Parsons problems and found that students had the most trouble with Parsons problems with one distractor per code block with all blocks in a random order and had the easiest time solving Parsons problems when they were given the structure of the solution (the number of lines in each code block and the indention). Students also had an easier time when the distractors were paired with the correct code.

In the e-books we are using an open-source tool called js-parons. Researchers using this tool have found that even though Parsons problems remove syntax errors, users can get stuck and repeat the same incorrect solution [4]. Some users also exhibit a "trial and error" approach [4]. They drag a single code block into the solution area and ask for feedback to see if it is in the correct place.

4. STATEMENT OF THESIS/PROBLEM

Do paired distractor dynamically adaptive Parsons problems help beginners learn programming more effectively and efficiently compared to writing code or fixing code? Our research group has modified js-parsons to allow for paired distractors. Our research group also plans to extend the js-parsons tool to allow for dynamically adaptive Parsons problems, which means that the difficulty of the problem will change based on the user's performance.

5. DISSERTATION STATUS

I created one set of Parsons problems and observed teachers solving those problems. The teachers wanted the Parsons problems to be harder. However, log file analysis of students solving the same problems revealed that some students had a great deal of difficulty solving the Parsons problems. By making the Parsons problems dynamically adaptive we should improve learning by keeping the learner in the Zone of Proximal Development.

I created experimental materials for comparing solving Parsons problems that have paired distractors with syntactic and semantic errors, against fixing code that contains the same syntactic and semantic errors, and also against writing the equivalent code. I plan to run that experiment this summer. Our research group is changing js-parsons to allow dynamically adaptive Parsons problems this summer. I plan to observe teachers solving current Parsons problems and dynamically adaptive ones in the fall of 2016. In the spring of 2016 I plan to compare the effectiveness and efficiency of learning from current Parsons problems versus dynamically adaptive ones. I hope to defend by the end of 2017.

6. EXPECTED CONTRIBUTIONS

Research on Parsons problems suggests that they might be a more effective and efficient learning approach than writing equivalent computer programs. However, more research is needed to solidify this claim and to test if dynamically changing the difficulty of the Parsons problems results in more effective and efficient learning. If this research helps teachers learn programming on-line in an efficient and effective manner, it could provide a scalable solution to allow the US to prepare 10,000 computing teachers by 2016-2017.

7. ACKNOWLEDGEMENT

This work is supported by the National Science Foundation grant CNS-1138378.

8. REFERENCES

[1] Benda, K. and A. Bruckman (2012). "When life and learning do not fit: Challenges of workload and communication in introductory computer science online." ACM Transactions on Computing Education.

[2] Bennedsen, J. and M. E. Caspersen (2007). "Failure rates in introductory programming." SIGCSE Bull. 39(2): 32-36.

[3] Denny, P., et al. (2008). Evaluating a New Exam Question: Parsons Problems. International Computing Education Research Conference. Sydney, Australia, ACM.

[4] Helminen, J., et al. (2012). How Do Students Solve Parsons Programming Problems? - An Analysis of Ineraction Traces. International Computing Education Research Conference. Aukland, New Zealand, ACM: 119-126.

[5] McCracken, M., et al. (2001). "A multi-national, multi-institutional study of assessment of programming skills of first-year CS students." SIGCSE Bull. 33(4): 125-180.

[6] Parsons, D. and P. Haden (2006). Parson's programming puzzles: a fun and effective learning tool for first programming courses. Proceedings of the 8th Australasian Conference on Computing Education - Volume 52. Hobart, Australia, Australian Computer Society, Inc.: 157-163.

[7] Soloway, E. and K. Ehrlich (1984). "Empirical Studies of Programming Knowledge." IEEE Transactions on Software Engineering SE-10(5): 595–609.

[8] Soloway, E., et al. (1994). "Learner-Centered Design: The Challenge For HCI In The 21st Century." Interactions 1(2) 36-48

Accounting for the Role of Policy in the Underrepresentation of Women in Computer Science

Elizabeth Patitsas
Department of Computer Science
University of Toronto
Toronto, Ontario, Canada
patitsas@cs.toronto.edu

ABSTRACT

Since the 1990s, a great deal of effort has been toward improving female participation in computing. Yet the numbers in North America haven't budged: women continue to make up 18% of CS majors. Current efforts and research focus on societal, cultural, and psychological reasons for this underrepresentation. I argue that the political dimension also needs to be considered both in terms of why women are underrepresented and how to change it. I have found that admissions policies have a profound effect on how many women study undergraduate CS. I've also observed that diversity is not being considered in mainstream CS department policy-making, and "women's issues" are expected to be solved by women's groups. And in the women's spaces, I've observed a focus on individual career advancement ("Lean In") rather than a push for political, collective action.

1. PROGRAM CONTEXT

I am a PhD candidate in the Department of Computer Science at the University of Toronto. My supervisors are Steve Easterbrook and Michelle Craig. I have finished my coursework, passed my qualifying exam, and presented a research proposal to my thesis committee.

I've written four papers related to my research, but I feel that a fifth study would be needed to properly tie everything together. I'm currently planning that final study and would like feedback from the DC on the study and how to fit everything together.

2. CONTEXT AND MOTIVATION

A great deal of effort has been put into trying to improve the percentage of women in CS in North America. Yet the numbers haven't budged: women continue to make up around 18% of CS majors [1]. I'm interested in understanding why the existing gender diversity initiatives in CS are not impacting this percentage, and what can be done to effectively improve female representation in CS.

3. BACKGROUND & RELATED WORK

There's a plethora of literature on women in computing [4], to which I cannot do justice in a short abstract. NCWIT's "Girls in IT: The Facts" provides an excellent representation of the existing literature and how the research area is typically conceived. The report describes the low numbers of girls in computing as a result of five factors [1]: educational environments; media and popular culture; families, communities and role models; peer influences; and girls' perceptions, interests, confidence and career decisions.

The latter is centred in the middle of this model, reflecting a focus on the individual and their psychology. The four other factors can be distilled as reflecting the culture of computer science and larger societal factors.

Existing initiatives tend to reflect this understanding of female underrepresentation. Women in Computing (WIC) initiatives often focus on providing mentors, role models, and a supportive community for women/girls, to give women/girls a "safe space" from the negative culture of computing. In 2005–06, Sturman conducted an institutional ethnography of the WIC clubs at three universities as well as the Grace Hopper Celebration [8]. She found that in WIC events, it was typical for hyperfeminine and highly successful white women to be used as role models [8]. Furthermore, she found these events focused on individual success rather than collective action—what today would be called "Lean In" culture.

4. STATEMENT OF THESIS/PROBLEM

My thesis statement is that appreciating gender politics is vital for understanding the underrepresentation of women in computer science—and, crucially, how to change it.

Put most simply, "politics" refers to the processes in which a limited number of resources are allocated amongst a set of people [5]. Politics need not be on a grand scale. "Micropolitics" refers to the politics that occur within organizations, such as in schools or universities [2]. These micropolitics have a significant impact over what is taught, who teaches, the goals of instruction, who is taught, and the overall learning environment of students [2].

5. RESEARCH GOALS & METHODS

I've been using soft systems methodology (SSM) as an overarching approach to study the underrepresentation of women in computing. SSM is a systems-thinking approach to tackling wicked problems in social systems [3].

In SSM, one first needs to express the "problem situation" and then articulate different framings of the situation. From there, one identifies and justifies a choice of framing. Then one conducts research to produce a conceptual framework of the system, then to compare this model with the real world, then to define possible changes, and to take action to improve the problem situation [3].

5.1 Problem framing

My problem situation is that the percentage of women studying undergraduate CS in North America has been largely unchanged despite three decades of ubiquitous gender diversity initiatives.

A few of the problem framings I first considered were that the diversity initiatives have unintended and counter-productive side-effects, that there are successful initiatives but they lack scale, and that the initiatives lack leverage [7].

In order to choose a problem frame, I conducted a historical analysis of the percentage of women in CS [6]. I found that CS department policies during enrollment booms have a large impact on the percentage of female students. When departments enact more stringent gate-keeping practices, there are fewer women in CS. Indeed, gate-keeping practices during the enrollment boom of the late 1980s appear to have contributed to the decline in the percentage of women in CS from around 40% to the approximate 25% of the 1990s. This study led me to see a new problem frame: that the existing understanding of female underrepresentation neglects the role of educational policies.

5.2 Enrollment Booms

Given that we are currently in an enrollment boom, I conducted a survey of CS faculty about how their departments are responding to the boom. I found that many CS departments are once again restricting access to their majors and classes. I also found that diversity is not generally considered in discussions of how to handle the enrollment boom. Efforts to improve diversity are seen as separate from "normal" CS department policy like admissions policy, despite the effect admissions policy can have on diversity.

5.3 Women's Issues at the Sidelines

In Sturman's 2005–6 ethnographic work of WIC organizations and events [8], she found that these efforts diverted people away from advocating for women in their departments. Rather than being places where women could come together to advocate as a group, the events were apolitical. I conducted an autoethnography of a recent WIC Celebration to follow up her work, and performed critical discourse analysis of relevant texts.

I found many of the same characteristics of WIC events which Sturman did ten years ago: a neoliberal approach which foregrounds individualism over collective action, ubiquitous use of gender essentialism, the use of hyperfeminine role models, and the perception held by young women that these events were merely networking opportunities.

5.4 Field Work

My studies have led me to see gender politics as vital for understanding the underrepresentation of women in CS; and that the existing view of underrepresentation being a result of cultural, societal, and psychological factors is incomplete. I've observed that department policy can affect diversity. I've also observed that the discussion of diversity is largely absent from undergraduate affairs discussions, and

that instead efforts to improve diversity are focused on targeted women-in-CS initiatives, rather than on policies which would enact systemic change. Having built a conceptual model of underrepresentation being a political issue, my next step in SSM would be to compare it the real world.

I plan to visit 6–8 CS departments, and examine how policymakers and stakeholders conceive of admissions policies, the enrolment boom, diversity, and whether they see links between them. I want to interview key informants about how their department is responding to the enrolment boom, what has influenced relevant policy decisions, and how they perceive gender diversity efforts. I plan to analyse the results with critical discourse analysis [5].

6. DISSERTATION STATUS

So far, I've completed four studies which will contribute to my thesis, and I see a fifth study as necessary to properly tie them all together. I've begun drafting my thesis document, which currently sits at a rough and unedited 113 pages. My programme requires both an internal defense and an external defense: I'm planning for the former to be in December 2016 and the latter to be in spring 2017.

7. EXPECTED CONTRIBUTIONS

I expect that my thesis will contribute to our community's understanding of the underrepresentation of women in CS and how to more effectively promote gender diversity. I plan to produce an accessible report for policymakers based on my findings.

8. REFERENCES

[1] C. Ashcraft, E. Eger, and M. Friend. *Girls in IT: The Facts*. National Center for Women & Information Technology, 2012.

[2] S. J. Ball. The micro-politics of the school. *London: Methuen*, 67:79, 1987.

[3] P. Checkland. Soft systems methodology: a thirty year retrospective. *Systems Research and Behavioral Science*, 17(S1):S11, 2000.

[4] J. M. Cohoon and W. Aspray. A critical review of the research on women's participation in postsecondary computing education. *Women & info. tech.: Research on under-representation*, pages 137–79, 2006.

[5] J. P. Gee. *An introduction to discourse analysis: Theory and method*. Routledge, 2014.

[6] E. Patitsas, M. Craig, and S. Easterbrook. A historical examination of the social factors affecting female participation in computing. In *Proceedings of the 2014 Conference on Innovation & Technology in Computer Science Education*, ITiCSE '14, pages 111–116, New York, NY, USA, 2014. ACM.

[7] E. Patitsas, M. Craig, and S. Easterbrook. Scaling up women in computing initiatives: What can we learn from a public policy perspective? In *Proceedings of the eleventh annual International Conference on International Computing Education Research*, pages 61–69. ACM, 2015.

[8] S. M. Sturman. *'Women in Computing' as Problematic: Gender, Ethics and Identity in University Computer Science Education*. PhD thesis, University of Toronto, 2009.

Pedagogy and Measurement of Program Planning Skills

Francisco Enrique Vicente G. Castro
Department of Computer Science
Worcester Polytechnic Institute
Worcester, Massachusetts 01609 USA
fgcastro@cs.wpi.edu

ABSTRACT

Students in first-year computing courses deal with programming problems that can be solved through various solutions that organize the problem's tasks in different ways. Selecting among these organizations of code or program *plans* and implementing them depends on various factors such as prior knowledge of solutions and features of programming languages used. Additionally, problem solving through effective program planning continues to be difficult for students; instruction in many first-year courses focuses on low-level constructs without discussing higher-level plans and students are left to figure out strategies for problem decomposition and code composition on their own. My research explores ways to teach planning strategies effectively so students will be able to learn to apply these strategies as well as transfer the use of these strategies across problems.

Categories and Subject Descriptors

K.3.2 [**Computers and Education**]: Computers and Information Science Education—*Computer Science Education*.

Keywords

Program design, programming pedagogy, plan composition

1. PROGRAM CONTEXT

I am a full-time doctoral student and research assistant beginning the third year of my PhD program in Computer Science at WPI. I have gained candidacy by completing my research qualifying requirement and PhD breadth requirement in Spring 2016. My program coursework includes learning science courses to inform my research.

My research qualifier was an exploratory study of planning behavior of CS1 students; results of this study were also presented in a conference. I am doing follow-up studies that explore the effect of planning-focused pedagogical interventions on how students structure their solutions to programming problems and exploring how to measure planning skill acquisition and the transfer of these skills to other problems. The findings will contribute to the development of a dissertation proposal in the coming academic year.

ICER '16 September 08-12, 2016, Melbourne, VIC, Australia

© 2016 Copyright held by the owner/author(s).

ACM ISBN 978-1-4503-4449-4/16/09.

DOI: http://dx.doi.org/10.1145/2960310.2960344

2. CONTEXT AND MOTIVATION

Students make various choices when developing solutions for programming problems. These choices range from lower-level concerns of selecting programming constructs to use (e.g. choosing between looping constructs) to higher-level concerns such as how to cluster the subtasks of a problem into functions or code blocks. The organization and clustering of subtasks is called a *plan* [7]. Consequently, programming is a process that involves both the implementation of plan components using lower-level constructs and the composition of these implementations into a solution that meets the goals of the programming problem.

Arguably, program planning is a useful skill, not only for students who study computing or intend to work in software development, but also for casual programmers who write code to, say, process data for lab experiments. These people encounter situations such as noisy data and changing process requirements that require planning and not just low-level construct choices. However, the landscape of first-year programming courses focuses instruction on the use of low-level programming constructs while expecting students to develop problem-solving and programming strategies on their own through extensive trial-and-error [2]. A recent study I have conducted showed that students struggle with programming even with the use of scaffolding code when there is no explicit instruction on program planning [1].

3. BACKGROUND & RELATED WORK

Developing and integrating programming plans has been identified as a difficult task among programming students [7]. While more recent studies have shown students succeed in program planning in specific contexts [4, 6], the pedagogic choices that help students with this task, as well as the prior knowledge that students bring with them remain poorly understood. Students who take their first computing courses in college vary in terms of programming background – some will carry some experience from high school while for others, this is their first exposure to programming.

Alongside the resurgence of planning studies [1, 6] is a growth in the body of research that addresses the improvement of planning skills through pedagogical frameworks and curricula that teach problem solving strategies in programming. Muller *et al.* used the concept of programming *patterns*, known solutions for recurring design or programming problems, in developing pattern-oriented instruction [5]. This approach teaches students to attach labels to algorithmic patterns and encourages them to look for common patterns across problems. De Raadt *et al.* used a 'strategy guide' that discusses *abutment*, *nesting*, and *merging* for integrating programming strategies and explicitly required their students to apply specific strategies in their solutions [3]. My research builds on these by focusing on *problem-level techniques* (e.g. cleaning data) rather than *code-level techniques* (e.g. merging code). Additionally, I am exploring students' discussions on design tradeoffs as a way of surveying what they understand about patterns and their motivations for choosing between them.

4. STATEMENT OF THESIS/PROBLEM

My work explores how to make students effective at planning programs with multiple subtasks. Specifically, I want to develop (a) techniques for measuring planning and related skills in students, and (b) techniques for teaching these skills in ways that improve students' planning performance.

Based on preliminary findings and lessons learned in my previous studies, I propose that students who have acquired sufficient planning skills should be able to do the following:

1. **Planning:** apply planning in producing programs by decomposing the problem into relevant tasks, implementing the tasks in code, and composing the implementations into an overall program.
2. **Assessment:** provide a technically accurate assessment of plans using a vocabulary of planning terminology.
3. **Transfer:** apply planning to other problems requiring similar plans but in different contexts.

5. RESEARCH GOALS & METHODS

I will focus on the following concrete goals and methods:

Develop a framework for teaching planning. An integral part of this is exposing students not only to problems with multiple subtasks, but also to multiple plans for each problem. At this stage, I am building a library of problems that can be used for teaching and assessment and determining what techniques and principles to teach students for designing plans.

Measure the acquisition of planning skill. Measuring learning gains requires assessing students' prior knowledge. I will collect data on students' programming backgrounds and ability to write programs for simple problems. This will provide a baseline of what plans students know before instruction on planning in a first-year computing course. To measure acquired planning knowledge, students' solutions to assessment problems will be analyzed to determine (a) what plans students use, (b) ability to develop correct plans for problems, and (c) whether they can develop multiple plans for a problem - this last measure gives insight into students' skills in approaching a problem in multiple ways.

Measure planning assessment skill. Programming problems can be solved through multiple approaches that each have design tradeoffs. Good planning education enables students to produce multiple plans for each problem and appreciate tradeoffs between plans. I will collect and analyze data on issues and principles students raise when discussing programming solutions before and after instruction. Doing so allows me to determine whether students gain richer and more accurate planning vocabulary and whether being made aware of multiple solutions changes their plans when solving problems. This also aids in gaining insight into their problem solving knowledge and processes.

Measure transfer of planning skill. This enables the assessment of the transfer of learning in planning across problems. Multiple problems with different contexts but sharing common plans will be used for assessment to determine whether students are able to recognize similarities in plan requirements and are able to utilize their planning knowledge to solve these problems.

6. DISSERTATION STATUS

I have published an exploratory study [1] that looked at student programming behavior when working on problems for which they have not seen techniques for solving. Findings show that even when scaffolding is provided (i.e. template code for traversing input data), students struggled to develop working solutions. This shows that we clearly need to figure out richer approaches to teach them about planning.

A follow-up study was done where students from different universities were given a lecture on planning between assignments. Students were given programming problems in the pre-test and then assigned a new set of problems in the post-test. Students were also asked to produce two solutions for the post-test that embody different plans and preference-rank their solutions to see what criteria they used to evaluate their plans. We observed some positive impact, but not as much as we wanted in one course, so studies are continuing.

At this stage, I am in the process of developing (a) follow-up studies, (b) material for planning instruction, and (c) methods for measuring student planning performance. I am also building the literature for my dissertation proposal. The findings from the studies to be conducted will be used to inform my proposal which I hope to present at the end of the coming academic year.

7. EXPECTED CONTRIBUTIONS

The contributions of this work to computing education include a pedagogical framework for integrating programming instruction with planning instruction and methods of measuring student performance in planning, planning assessment, and transfer of learning in planning. Findings from studies conducted provides insights into students' planning and programming methodologies and their understanding of their own knowledge.

8. REFERENCES

[1] F. E. V. Castro and K. Fisler. On the Interplay Between Bottom-Up and Datatype-Driven Program Design. In *Proceedings of SIGCSE*, SIGCSE '16, pages 205–210, New York, NY, USA, 2016. ACM.

[2] M. de Raadt, M. Toleman, and R. Watson. Training Strategic Problem Solvers. *SIGCSE Bull.*, 36(2):48–51, June 2004.

[3] M. de Raadt, R. Watson, and M. Toleman. Teaching and Assessing Programming Strategies Explicitly. ACE '09, Darlinghurst, Australia, Australia, 2009.

[4] K. Fisler. The Recurring Rainfall Problem. ICER '14, pages 35–42, New York, NY, USA, 2014. ACM.

[5] O. Muller, D. Ginat, and B. Haberman. Pattern-oriented Instruction and Its Influence on Problem Decomposition and Solution Construction. ITiCSE '07, pages 151–155, New York, NY, USA, 2007. ACM.

[6] O. Seppälä, P. Ihantola, E. Isohanni, J. Sorva, and A. Vihavainen. Do We Know How Difficult the Rainfall Problem is? Koli Calling '15, pages 87–96. ACM, 2015.

[7] E. Soloway. Learning to Program = Learning to Construct Mechanisms and Explanations. *Commun. ACM*, 29(9):850–858, Sept. 1986.

Geospatial Analysis of Computer Science Course Offerings in Wisconsin Public High Schools

Heather Bort
Marquette University
MSCS Department – Cudahy Hall
1313 W. Wisconsin Ave.
Milwaukee, WI 53233, USA
heather.bort@marquette.edu

ABSTRACT
Many fields within the social sciences utilize geospatial analysis to explore the importance of place in their research context. This dissertation will extend these methods to the area of high school computer science course offerings in the state of Wisconsin. My research will look at spatially clustered occurrences of course offerings over time in order to classify the strength of CS programs in individual schools, identify areas of need for intervention, and determine whether there is behavioral diffusion or common attributes driving the process.

Categories and Subject Descriptors
K.3.2 [**Computers and Education**]: Computer and Information Science Education – *computer science education.*

Keywords
Computer Science Education, Geospatial Analysis

1. PROGRAM CONTEXT
I am a fifth year Computational Science PhD student at Marquette University. At this point, all of my course work has been completed and I have passed my written comprehensive exam. I am working on the dissertation portion of my program while working full time. I have been working with my advisor, Dr. Dennis Brylow, to put together a proposal for my dissertation research and I expect to present the proposal to my committee before the Fall 2016 semester. I expect to defend my dissertation in the Summer of 2017.

2. CONTEXT AND MOTIVATION
The Preparing the Upper Midwest for Principles of Computer Science (PUMP-CS) project at Marquette University has the ambitious goal of preparing at least 100 high school teachers for computer science classrooms by the 2016-17 school year. This goal will be met in an effort to contribute to Wisconsin's share of the 10,000 teachers requested for the NSF's CS10K Project. While Wisconsin is one of the few states with clearly defined licensing standards for K-12 computer science teachers, we suffer from a lack of programs that provide the necessary courses for a teacher to qualify for the license required by the WI Department of Public Instruction to teach those course that have more than

ICER '16, September 08-12, 2016, Melbourne, VIC, Australia
ACM 978-1-4503-4449-4/16/09.
http://dw.doi.org/10.1145/2960310.2960345

25% computer programming content [1]. With almost 500 public high schools in the state, there were fewer than 40 of those schools with students enrolled in an AP CS face-to-face course for the 2014-15 school year.

As part of the effort to meet the PUMP-CS goal of preparing teachers for offering computer science courses, Marquette is hosting annual cohorts of high school teachers for Exploring Computer Science (ECS) professional development sessions. We have been leveraging the ECS program to develop the diverse teaching talent recruited for PUMP-CS, providing ECS training as part of an alternative pathway to secondary licensure for K-12 computer science.

While we continue to fill our cohorts each summer and have increased the number of schools offering computer science courses in our state by just over 10%, we are not reaching the level of successful adoption reported in places like Los Angeles [2], Ohio [3], or Chicago [4]. Even programs that are not based on ECS have reported success and provided insight to the factors affecting the high school computer science landscape [5]. We have found that many of the teachers that go through our program are at schools that already have some experience with offering computer science or they have been involved in some other program\activity to promote CS ED (i.e. CS4HS, SIGCSE, CSTA, etc.). We would like to find a way to increase the participation by schools outside of our current community of practice, to find a way to identify schools in our state that could benefit from a CS ED initiative and to determine what type of help we could offer. Can we identify CS ED "density-challenged" regions [1] and improve the likelihood of sustainable CS programs in the schools that make them up.

3. BACKGROUND & RELATED WORK
Identifying why phenomena occur in certain places and not others is a common theme throughout social science research. Indeed, there is a common interest in geography across social science fields where certain theories allude to assumptions that spatially proximate groups are likely to behave in a similar way and the groups that are more distant are less likely to exhibit those behaviors. The role of space and geography has been explored in many ways; the geographic patterns of suicide [6], democratization [7], spatial patterning of homicide rates [8], and of course Snow's work on the London cholera epidemic [9]. Geospatial analysis methods have been used within education research as well, for example, to study regional science attainment in St. Louis [10] and educational level changes in Finland [11]. While all of these research efforts have very different contexts, they are all focusing on principles of geospatial analysis. All of the researchers found that, within their context, place matters.

Geographical place is an inherent factor in scaling CS ED initiatives and there have not yet been publications exploring, in geospatial context, the patterns of adoption and geographic clustering of CS courses at the high school level.

4. STATEMENT OF THESIS/PROBLEM

My dissertation will focus on geospatial modeling of the state of high school computer science in Wisconsin. The main research question being: What can we learn from a geospatial model of Computer Science courses offered at the high school level in the state of Wisconsin?

The specific problems that need to be solved are:

- How can we define an appropriate, theoretically based, spatial weights matrix?

- What class of spatial model will best fit the data that we have available?

- What are the conclusions that we can draw from our model that can lead to actionable measures toward growing high school CS ED in Wisconsin?

5. RESEARCH GOALS & METHODS

This research is being conducted in three parts, each related to a specific problem. The first part will focus on defining areal units and specification for spatial weights, for the second part we will develop appropriate models from the data, and the third part will look at what statements we can make from the model results.

The first part of this research deals with reconciling disparate data, knitting together an appropriate shape file for partitioning the state into attendance polygons as areal units. Once we have defined areal units we will be able to specify a theoretically based spatial weights matrix. We must extend what have been found to be likely contributing factors in the adoption of computing programs by other research efforts [2,3,4,5], combined with interview data from teachers in our program, to develop a likely definition of neighbor for the purpose of our weights specification as it is a too common occurrence, with spatial modeling, to define an empirically convenient matrix.

To develop an appropriate model, we must begin by identifying the presence of spatial dependence in the data. Then we attempt to address Galton's problem to accurately determine which type of process is responsible for the spatial dependence. Galton's problem focuses on how there is an important and substantive distinction between spatial dependence produced by either diffusion or independent adoption [12]. We can then choose between two classes of models, spatial lag models and spatial error models, to begin the work of developing models that will give insight to the state of CS ED in our state.

The final part of this research will be to use the models to classify the strength of CS ED programs in schools throughout our state, identify areas of the state that are in the most need of help to gain access to CS ED resources, and determine where we can focus efforts to expand our current initiatives.

6. DISSERTATION STATUS

I have data for carrying out this research, including 5 years of course offering data with student enrollment counts and demographics for each publicly funded school in the state. An initial study to classify attributes in the data has identified spatial dependence at a global level. Design decisions still need to be made in this study and I will be using independent coders to help classify and reconcile disparate data. I am on track to finish with

the data generation process and begin working on the models in the fall 2016 semester.

7. EXPECTED CONTRIBUTIONS

This research will contribute to the CS ED research community by extending the use of the geospatial theoretical framework. This work will show that the perceived patterning of high school CS course adoption is more than apophenia and provide a useful guide for other researchers in CS ED to explore the importance of place in their own research contexts.

8. REFERENCES

[1] Brylow, D. PUMP-CS. NSF CS21 Grant Proposal. 2013.

[2] Margolis, Goode, Chapman (2015). An Equity Lens for Scaling: A Critical Juncture for Exploring Computer Science. *ACM Inroads*. Sept. 2015, Vol. 6, No. 3. Pp. 58-66. PDF.

[3] Hu, H., Heiner, C. and McCarthy, J. 2016. Deploying Exploring Computer Science Statewide. *In Proceedings of the 47th ACM Technical Symposium on Computing Science Education* (SIGCSE '16). ACM, New York, NY, USA, 72-77.

[4] Dettori, L., Greenberg, R.I., McGee, S., and Reed, D. 2016. The Impact of the Exploring Computer Science Instructional Model in Chicago Public Schools. *Computing in Science and Engg.* 18, 2 (March 2016), 10-17.

[5] Guzdial, M., Ericson, B., Mcklin, T. and Engelman, S. 2014 Georgia Computes! An Intervention in a US State, with Formal and Informal Education in a Policy Context. *Trans. Comput. Educ.* 14, 2, Article 13.

[6] Baller, R. and Richardson, K. 2002. Social Integration, Imitation, and the Geographic Patterning of Suicide. *American Sociological Review* 67(6):873-888.

[7] Gleditsch, K. and Ward, M. 2006. Diffusion and the International Context of Democratization. *International Organization* 60(4): 911-933.

[8] Messner, S., et al. 1999. The Spatial Patterning of County Homicide Rates: An Application of Exploratory Spatial Data Analysis. *Journal of Quantitative Criminology.* 15(4):423-450.

[9] John Snow. 1855. *On the Mode of Communication of Cholera.* London: John Churchill.

[10] Hogrebe, M., Kyei-Blankson, L. and Zou, L. 2008. Examining Regional Science Attainment and School-Teacher Resources Using GIS. *Education and Urban Society.* 40(5):570-589.

[11] Vilkama, K. and Tammilehto-Luode, M. 2015. Using geocoded urban and regional statistics to monitor change in the educational level in Finland. *Statistical Journal of the IAOS.* 31:91-96.

[12] Darmofal, D. 2015. Spatial Analysis for the Social Sciences. *Cambridge Press.*

Computational Thinking as a Computer Science Education Framework and the Related Effects on Gender Equity

Jon Good
College of Education
Michigan State University
620 Farm Lane
East Lansing, MI 48824, United States
goodjona@msu.edu

ABSTRACT
This submission describes my current status in implementing a dissertation study around the themes of gender equity, computational thinking, and teacher practice. The scholarly and social context for the study is presented, reviewing some of the work related to gender equity and computer science over the past decade. Computational thinking provides a framework for computer science education centered on the learning of mental skills and "big ideas" of the field. The effect this framing has on female students' performance and interest in computer science is unclear. Establishing any possible benefits would be instructive for researchers, as would isolating teacher practices that support any possible benefits for equitable interactions.

Keywords
Computational thinking, gender equity, secondary education

1. PROGRAM CONTEXT
I have recently completed my third year of study in the Educational Psychology and Educational Technology doctoral program at Michigan State University. I have successfully completed all of my coursework and comprehensive/qualifying exams. I will be proposing my dissertation study in the Fall semester of 2016 and expect to defend my dissertation in the Fall semester of 2017. My prior research has been focused on issues related to computational thinking, creativity, and computer science education. I am currently developing my literature review and honing my core research questions. I hope to subsequently develop my research methods and measures more fully, with plans to begin fieldwork in Fall of 2016.

2. CONTEXT AND MOTIVATION
My research examines how a computational thinking approach toward the teaching of computer science at the secondary level can influence female students' interest in computer science. Gender inequity has been known to be a critical problem within computer science, along with other STEM fields. It would be helpful to both secondary teachers and educational researchers to identify practices within the secondary classroom that may affect

ICER '16, September 08-12, 2016, Melbourne, VIC, Australia
ACM 978-1-4503-4449-4/16/09.
http://dx.doi.org/10.1145/2960310.2960346

female students' interest and success in pursuing computer science in their future studies and careers.

There is a continuing need for practical advice on how teachers' classroom practices and curricular choices can aid in retaining female students in computer science. Considering the efforts over the last decade to institute forms of computational thinking within various age levels and disciplines, it is worth investigating whether these efforts have a gender-based difference in their effectiveness. Empirical research regarding these effects could inform both classroom practice and further research regarding computational thinking and gender.

Research shows that students' motivations for engaging in computer science courses can differ by gender [9]. Considering the recent focus on expanding access to computer science education, such as seen in "CS for All" and the efforts of Code.org, the importance of equitable access to these resources becomes more urgent. The existing work of computer science educational researchers has already called for reframing existing practices to appeal to a more diverse audience and to reflect more closely the work of computer scientists in multiple contexts [6]. Computational thinking could possibly be another lens for reframing these practices. Rather than providing only a difference in context, the curriculum can be reframed along the "big ideas" of computer science, similar to the AP Computer Science Principles or Exploring Computer Science framework.

The main focus of this research is to provide actionable recommendations for teachers of computer science. The increase in funding and focus on computer science education will likely create an influx of students into computer science at the secondary level and below, with some educators working with the subject matter for the first time. This presents an opportunity to address teacher practices before they become entrenched and habitual for new instructors.

3. BACKGROUND & RELATED WORK
The literature regarding computational thinking has often focused on how the cognitive skills used within computer science can be developed and used within multiple subjects and grade levels [3, 5]. One could interpret the concept of computational thinking as an introduction to computer science concepts, without using programming as the central phenomenon around which computer science is taught.

Given the existing research regarding computer science and equity [1, 6, 8], computational thinking may be able to add another set of curricular recommendations for teachers. Male and female students can attain similar levels of computational thinking, although initial results suggest that females students may need more time to develop these skills [2]. Similar to the work of the Exploring Computer Science curriculum [4], focusing on the larger principles may increase female students' interest in computer science during secondary school.

Adding to this, Goode, Margolis, and Chapman [4] state that curriculum alone is not enough to have an impact on student learning. Teacher practice in the classroom has a direct effect on how any curriculum is portrayed to and interpreted by learners. In regards to equity, teacher practice can play a role in encourage equitable interactions that strengthen students' learning. Identifying these practices and establishing their effectiveness can provide useful guidance for teachers.

4. STATEMENT OF THESIS/PROBLEM

My main research question is:

- Does presenting a broad perspective of computer science curriculum around computational thinking ideas and practices have a positive effect on female students' level of interest in computer science?

- Which specific practices of computer science teachers, encourage equitable interactions between teacher-student and student-student groups?

At this time the dissertation is still under development in its early stages. I expect to generate further research questions to add to the project as it progresses. Attending the ICER doctoral consortium would allow me to further refine these questions and their related methods with the input of other consortium attendees and faculty present.

5. RESEARCH GOALS & METHODS

I expect to develop a week-long unit of study for students in a secondary computer science course. This lesson would focus on the computational thinking skills being developed alongside the programming statements. A classroom with the subject taught in the standard manner will serve as the control. Along with measuring students' pre-post levels of interest in the chosen CS topic and CS overall, the class sessions will be recorded for subsequent qualitative coding related to teacher practices and student interactions with both peers and the instructor. I will employ a coding strategy similar to that of Lewis and Shah [7] in their study of pair-programming interactions and its relation to equity. As for the measuring of skills, this will be measured via formative quizzes and programming assignments, with analysis done between genders.

The outcomes of these methods are twofold: First, we can establish whether using computational thinking as a curricular frame increases girls' interest in computer science and whether the methods have any effect on the learning of the programming skills. Second, we can discover through the qualitative coding how the interactions differ between the computational thinking and control classroom, and whether specific teacher practices can be tied to these interactions. Establishing the efficacy of these methods, along with actionable recommendations for teachers, are the end goals

6. DISSERTATION STATUS

As part of my practicum study, I have already completed a study of in-service teachers' conceptions of computational thinking as a framing for computer science curriculum. This dissertation builds upon that work by investigating whether the teachers' positive impressions of this approach translate into measurable benefits for the learners. The work on the proposal has begun, with the literature review and research questions being further developed and refined. Additionally, I have assisted in the revisions of a study regarding gender equity in computer science, particularly as it relates to gender-based perceptions of the practice of computer science. By the time of the ICER conference, I expect to have my proposal ready, using my time at the doctoral consortium to solicit feedback from consortium attendees and leaders.

7. EXPECTED CONTRIBUTIONS

To contribute to the research community for computer science education, I want to establish whether there are any gender-equity ramifications for the use of computational thinking as a computer science curriculum framework. If the effects are found to be positive, I hope to offer initial observations regarding how the interactions are affected by this framing and specific teacher practices that support equitable interactions.

8. REFERENCES

[1] Ashcraft, C., Eger, E. and Friend, M. 2012. *Girls in IT: The Facts.* National Center for Women & Information Technology. https://www.ncwit.org/resources/girls-it-facts

[2] Atmatzidou, S. and Demetriadis, S. 2016. Advancing students' computational thinking skills through educational robotics: A study on age and gender relevant differences. *Robotics and Autonomous Systems.* 75, (Jan. 2016), 661–670.

[3] Barr, V. and Stephenson, C. 2011. Bringing Computational Thinking to K-12: What is Involved and What is the Role of the Computer Science Education Community? *ACM Inroads.* 2, 1 (2011), 48–54.

[4] Goode, J., Margolis, J. and Chapman, G. 2014. Curriculum is not enough: the educational theory and research foundation of the exploring computer science professional development model. (2014), 493–498.

[5] Grover, S. and Pea, R. 2013. Computational Thinking in K–12: A Review of the State of the Field. *Educational Researcher.* 42, 1 (Jan. 2013), 38–43.

[6] Kafai, Y.B. and Burke, Q. 2014. Beyond Game Design for Broadening Participation: Building New Clubhouses of Computing for Girls. *Proceedings of Gender and IT Appropriation. Science and Practice on Dialogue - Forum for Interdisciplinary Exchange* (Siegen, Germany, 2014), 21.

[7] Lewis, C.M. and Shah, N. 2015. How Equity and Inequity Can Emerge in Pair Programming. *Proceedings of the Eleventh Annual International Conference on International Computing Education Research* (New York, NY, USA, 2015), 41–50.

[8] Margolis, J., Ryoo, J.J., Sandoval, C.D.M., Lee, C., Goode, J. and Chapman, G. 2012. Beyond Access: Broadening Participation in High School Computer Science. *ACM Inroads.* 3, 4 (Dec. 2012), 72–78.

[9] Sax, L.J. 2012. Examining the Underrepresentation of Women in STEM Fields: Early Findings from the Field of Computer Science. *CSW Update.* (Apr. 2012), 3–8.

Mixed Methods for the Assessment and Incorporation of Computational Thinking in K-12 and Higher Education

Joshua Levi Weese
Kansas State University
2184 Engineering Hall
Manhattan, KS, 66506, USA
weeser@ksu.edu

ABSTRACT

A movement to include computer science in K-12 curriculum standards has sparked a significant interest in computational thinking (CT). This paper describes current and future work in the development of visual programming curricula for teaching CT at the K-12 level and self-efficacy surveys for evaluating the effectiveness of the curricula at fostering CT. Current work on a comprehensive system for automated extraction of assessment data for descriptive analytics and visualization is also described. To complement attitude surveys, a translation of *Scratch* to *Blockly* is proposed. Data on student programming behaviors at the collegiate level will be collected and quantitatively analyzed to help assess CT in support of self-efficacy.

Keywords
Computational Thinking; assessment; self-efficacy; outreach

1. PROGRAM CONTEXT

I am currently at the end of my third year as a doctoral student in the Department of Computer Science at Kansas State University. I have passed all preliminary written examinations, as well as the research proficiency exam (RPE) and was admitted to candidacy at the end of my second year. The RPE is a semester-long project with an oral and written report to assure the student is ready to do research at the doctoral level. I also just passed my dissertation proposal defense. In my proposal, I discussed and presented my current results in studying self-efficacy in computational thinking (CT) in a summer STEM outreach program during the summer of 2015. I also presented my current work done developing a web portal which can automatically extract assessment data uploaded to provide descriptive analytics and recommendations. For work that is still in progress, I am proposing to continue studies with the summer STEM outreach program to improve my self-efficacy survey. I am also preparing to collect data from another STEM outreach program for 4th-6th grade. I have also proposed an initial design for implementing features of the *Scratch* programming language in Google's *Blockly* language in order to collect data on programming behaviors to study CT in a CS0 course.

ICER '16, September 8-11, 2016, Melbourne, VIC, Australia.
ACM 978-1-4503-4449-4/16/09.
http://dx.doi.org/10.1145/2960310.2960347

2. CONTEXT AND MOTIVATION

Since Jeanette Wing's ACM Viewpoint in 2006 [1], CT has gained traction as an essential 21st century learning skill. CT draws from computer science fundamentals; however, few definitions of CT give a succinct synopsis of what fundamentals CT includes. This is an important distinction to make as computer science standards are being formed for K-12 education in the United States. CT in K-12, as well as higher education, gives students a firm foundation for a higher level of thinking not only in computer science, but also a plethora of other STEM fields. As Barr and Stephenson state, an interpretation or definition of CT "must ultimately be coupled with examples that demonstrate how computational thinking can be incorporated in the classroom [2]."

In recent years, countries such as the United Kingdom and Australia have begun to incorporate computing in the K-12 education system. From these curricula and reports, succinct definitions of CT provide broader impacts in terms of education and career readiness. Currently, the US does not have nation-wide CS education standards; however, some organizations, such as the CSTA, have been dedicated in creating CS standards that incorporate CT, although their standards are not widely officially adopted. The variety of interpretations of CT, as well as the lack of methods for assessing CT, are motivations for my dissertation. Unifying various interpretations of CT and what it entails, as well as pedagogy and methods for assessing CT, will further help incorporate CT into education standards at all levels, not just K-12.

3. BACKGROUND & RELATED WORK

Visual programming languages have been a popular, low overhead method, for teaching computer science and CT to students and educators who do not have any formal training in computer science. Using visual programming languages in outreach programs has been proven to be a successful method for training educators and students alike in computer science and CT. For example, Repenning et al. developed an outreach program, *Scalable Game Design*, which used *AgentSheets* and *AgentCubes* for developing video games [3]. This program was designed to increase understanding of CT concepts, which in turn allowed students to transfer those concepts to developing scientific simulations. Assessing student understanding of CT concepts was done using an automatic tool which detected common design patterns, rather than strict static analysis of the student programs [3]. Another outreach program developed a *Scratch* curriculum centered on music and measured CT learning outcomes by using self-efficacy surveys [5]. Apart from K-12 outreach, Bean et al. developed a workshop for pre-service teachers [4]. This workshop focused on teaching CT concepts using *Scratch* and how CT can be incorporated into their future classrooms.

Outreach and visual programming languages have helped capture the essence of CT. A foundational study for this dissertation developed a CT framework based on *Scratch* [6]. Brennan and Resnick define CT in terms of concepts, practices, and perspectives. Seiter and Foreman take a similar approach by creating the progression of early computational thinking (PECT) model for evaluating *Scratch* programs [7]. The PECT model assessed CT by looking for evidence of programming constructs, design patterns, and CT concepts. While PECT is used for assessment of CT, it gives a practical definition and view of CT.

4. STATEMENT OF THESIS/PROBLEM

This dissertation aims to provide a clear and practical definition of computational thinking, as well as effective pedagogy and mixed methods for assessing CT. The research questions aligned with this statement are as follows:

1. Do the computer science principles chosen to be included computational thinking align with student learning outcomes?

2. Can the attitude surveys created reliably assess student ability in computational thinking?

3. Are the computer science principles taught through outreach curricula reflected in student confidence in CT?

4. Is there a link between qualitative and quantitative analysis of computational thinking? If so, does quantitative analysis support or refute self-efficacy as a method of measuring CT?

5. Can student personas be extracted from traditional physics assessments, and if so, can the method be generalized to apply to CT assessments?

5. RESEARCH GOALS & METHODS

There are three main goals for my dissertation research. The first goal is to develop a practical definition of computational thinking. This will mainly be accomplished through an extensive literature review, as well as my own experience in teaching CT in outreach programs. The second goal is to develop pedagogy for teaching CT in K-12 outreach programs. The current proposed pedagogy is centered on cognitive load theory, problem-based learning, and inquiry learning. This pedagogy will be tested during a summer STEM outreach program for 5th-9th grade students, as well as a STEM program for 4th-6th grade students during two academic years. This leads to my third goal: develop mixed methods for the assessment of CT. This goal will be done in two stages. The first will be done qualitatively by designing self-efficacy surveys for measuring CT learning outcomes of both STEM programs, as well as an introductory course on computer science in an undergraduate program. In support of the self-efficacy surveys, the second stage will include quantitative analysis of student programming data, including problem solving traces, collected by a custom implementation of *Blockly*.

6. DISSERTATION STATUS

Currently I have completed a study on a STEM program during the summer of 2015. This study included the development of two different themed curricula (on based on artificial intelligence and the other on game design). A pre and post self-efficacy survey measured 21st century learning skills and CT concepts for four

week-long classes encompassing 91 students. A follow-up study is planned for this coming summer with similar curricula, though game design is being changed to be microcontroller-themed to fit the needs of the program. The survey language has been adapted to measure CT in computer science and problem solving, to see whether students understand CT better when framed in different contexts. For the study involving the 4th-6th grade outreach program, an hour-long *Scratch* music exercise was developed; the results of which will be analyzed through pre- and post-survey data being collected through the next academic year. The quantitative study will also be carried out this coming academic year once the development of the custom *Blockly* implementation is complete. Also coming this next year will be a study on large-scale physics assessment data. While not directly related to CS or CT, this provides a vehicle for developing a generalized model to extract student personas from traditional assessments with potential application to the CT assessment data collected through outreach programs.

7. EXPECTED CONTRIBUTIONS

The novel contributions of this work will include new curricula and methods for teaching CT. I expect the proposed approach for assessing CT, along with the proposed pedagogy and definition of CT, will provide educators with a clear view of CT and reliable methods for incorporating it into their classrooms.

8. REFERENCES

[1] Wing, J. M. (2006). Computational Thinking. *Communications of the ACM, 49*(3), 33-35.

[2] Barr, V., & Stephenson, C. (2011). Bringing Computational Thinking to K-12: What is Involved and What is the Role of the Computer Science Education Community? *ACM Inroads, 2*(1), 48-54.

[3] Repenning, A., Webb, D. C., Kho, K., Nickerson, H., Miller, S. B., Brand, C., . . . Repenning, N. (2015). Scalable Game Design: A Strategy to Bring Systemic Computer Science Education to Schools though Game Design and Simulation Creation. *ACM Transactions on Computing Education, 15*(2), 1-31.

[4] Bean, N., Weese, J. L., Feldhausen, R., & Bell, R. (2015). Starting From Scratch: Developing a Pre-Service Teacher Program in Computational Thinking. *Frontiers in Education*, 1307-1314.

[5] Bell, R. S. (2014). Low Overhead Methods for Improving Capacity and Outcomes in Computer Science (Doctoral dissertation). Manhattan, KS: Kansas State University. Retrieved from http://krex.k-state.edu/dspace/handle/2097/18168

[6] Brennan, K., & Resnick, M. (2012). Using artifact-based interviews to study the development of computational thinking in interactive media design. *Annual meeting of the American Educational Research Association - AERA '12.* Vancouver, BC, Canada.

[7] Seiter, L., & Foreman, B. (2013). Modeling the learning progressions of computational thinking of primary grade students. *Proceedings of the ninth annual international ACM conference on International computing education research - ICER '13*, 59-66.

Teaching – Learning of Troubleshooting Skills for Computer Science Undergraduates

Kavya Alse
Inter-disciplinary Program in Educational Technology
Indian Institute of Technology - Bombay
Mumbai, Maharashtra, 400076, India
kavyaalse@iitb.ac.in

ABSTRACT

Every CS graduate working with different technologies will need troubleshooting in one or other way. This document provides an overview of the research work I am pursuing on teaching troubleshooting skills. The focus of my thesis is building a learning environment for teaching troubleshooting in Computer Networks. At the end of my thesis, I intend to come up with some design principles for building learning environments in related domain. Both of these will be contributions for the CS education Research community.

Keywords

Troubleshooting Skill; Computer Networks; Thinking Skill; Design Based Research

1. PROGRAM CONTEXT

I am a second year full time research scholar in Inter-disciplinary Program (IDP) in Educational Technology at the Indian Institute of Technology, Bombay. The university requires the doctoral students to complete a course work which takes 6 months to one year, which I have completed.

As a department, IDP- Educational Technology has a focus on teaching and learning of pan-domain thinking skills and teacher professional development. I am investigating teaching and learning of troubleshooting skills for computer science undergraduates. I have chosen computer networks as the domain to teach troubleshooting skill. I have done a literature review of existing teaching strategies for troubleshooting in general and network troubleshooting in specific. Based on that, I have designed an instructional strategy for troubleshooting in Computer Networks. I am building a technology enhanced learning environments (TELE) for teaching troubleshooting skill.

2. CONTEXT AND MOTIVATION

Computer Science undergraduates are expected to work with diverse technologies in diverse situations like integrating different systems, building a system from scratch, using code written by others and change or improve it etc. All these tasks will require them to do troubleshooting in one or other way. Moreover, the specific details of troubleshooting in each of these tasks might differ from each other. So it is desirable to teach troubleshooting as a problem-solving strategy for CS undergrads.

3. BACKGROUND & RELATED WORK

Troubleshooting in Computer Science usually manifests as debugging or network troubleshooting. Tools like gcc and packet tracer [3] are used for this purpose. The approach taken is to debug/troubleshoot a specific problem using that tool. It is desired that the focus be given to the process of troubleshooting as well since the technologies change. For this the tools should explicitly focus on the process of troubleshooting.

Troubleshooting has been taught with respect to mechanical and electrical systems as a type of problem solving. Many instructors or researchers have come up with a set of steps for troubleshooting [2, 4]. I have synthesized a list of sub-skills for troubleshooting from this as appropriate for Computer Networks. The sub-skills are: i) Problem Representation ii) Hypothesis generation and linking iii) Experimenting and Evaluation iv) Reflection.

Another area research related to troubleshooting is related to the behavior of experts and novices in troubleshooting. It has been reported that experts have 'compiled knowledge' related to the domain and have 'functional understanding' of the components of the system [5] whereas novices have difficulties such as information overload, unable to have the complete troubleshooting process in mind [5]. I have considered these to design features and scaffolds in the learning environment.

4. STATEMENT OF THESIS/PROBLEM

The broad problem that I am considering is "How to develop troubleshooting skills in Computer Science undergraduates in the domain of Computer Networks?". More specific research problems are:

1. What are the sub-skills of troubleshooting skill?
   a. How to develop each of these sub-skills?
2. How to evaluate/measure troubleshooting skill?

5. RESEARCH GOALS & METHODS

As of now, I have identified the following goals for my thesis:

1. Identify the sub-skills of troubleshooting skill as appropriate for Computer science undergraduates and thus derive learning objectives for Computer Networks.
2. Create a measure for evaluating troubleshooting skill according to the sub-skills identified.
3. Design of learning activities for the identified sub-skills and learning objectives that is appropriate for CS undergraduates studying Computer Networks.

ICER '16, September 08-12, 2016, Melbourne, VIC, Australia.
ACM 978-1-4503-4449-4/16/09.
http://dx.doi.org/10.1145/2960310.2960348

4. Analyze the difficulties faced by the novices during troubleshooting. This would help in designing the type of scaffolds required, the time at which it should be given etc.,

5. Analyze the troubleshooting process of experts in Computer Networks. Here, I am intending to identify the actions/strategies that enable the experts to troubleshoot efficiently.

6. Build a technology enhanced learning environment (TELE) with designed learning activities and scaffolds.

7. Evaluate students' learning of troubleshooting skill with the TELE according to the designed measure.

I am following the research method of Design Based Research (DBR) in which the intervention is designed and built in an iterative manner using inputs from all participants like students, teachers, researchers and practitioners. For this, the research studies will have to be both qualitative and quantitative in nature. Also, as parts of DBR, domain specific theories or design principles are expected be derived during the iterative design process.

At this moment I am in the first cycle of DBR. This cycle starts with the detailed description of context and sub-skills of troubleshooting. Then the broad level details about technology and intervention strategy are obtained by doing literature survey. The details of instructional strategy and scaffolds are designed with the help of expert and novice studies. The experts and novices observed while they are solving troubleshooting problems in Computer Networks followed by interviewing them. The first cycle of DBR ends with the detailed design of instructional strategy and scaffolds for TELE. The next cycles include the implementation of the TELE and its iterations.

6. DISSERTATION STATUS

As of now, I have done literature review and synthesized a set of sub-skills for troubleshooting skill. These sub-skills are: i) Problem Space Representation, ii) Hypotheses generation and linking iii) Experimenting and evaluation iv) Reflection. I have designed the learning activities and a paper prototype of the TELE. I am working on doing expert and novice studies. I have explored virtual worlds, HTML5 + JavaScript as options of technology to build TELE. I have a rudimentary rubric of evaluating the sub-skills of troubleshooting. I am planning to build the TELE, do iterations of improvement and evaluate students' learning in the TELE in next 3 years.

7. EXPECTED CONTRIBUTIONS

Troubleshooting, as other pan-domain thinking skills, requires knowledge of concepts related to the domain (Computer Networks here). My TELE will be aiming at troubleshooting in Computer Networks primarily. However, I expect that because of the focus on the process of troubleshooting in the TELE, the students who interact would be better equipped with what questions to ask, what kind of hypothesis to frame etc., given a troubleshooting problem in a new context or domain.

At the end of my thesis, I intend to contribute the following to Computer Science Research Community:

1. A TELE for teaching troubleshooting for Computer Science undergraduates.

2. A measure for evaluating troubleshooting skill according to the sub-skills identified.

3. An understanding of expert-novice troubleshooting process in Computer Networks.

4. Design principles for developing similar TEL environments.

8. REFERENCES

[1] Cobb, P., Confrey, J., Lehrer, R., & Schauble, L. Design experiments in educational research. Educational researcher 32,1, (2003), 9-13.

[2] Jonassen, D. H. Learning to solve problems: A handbook for designing problem-solving learning environments. Routledge. (2010), 77-105

[3] Janitor, J., Jakab, F., & Kniewald, K. Visual learning tools for teaching/learning computer networks: Cisco networking academy and packet tracer. Sixth IEEE International Conference on Networking and Services (ICNS), (2010), 351-355.

[4] Ross, C., & Orr, R. R. Teaching structured troubleshooting: integrating a standard methodology into an information technology program. Educational Technology Research and Development 57,2 (2009), 251–265.

[5] Schaafstal, A. S., Cognitive Task Analysis and Innovation of Training: The Case of Structured Troubleshooting. Human Factors: The Journal of the Human Factors and Ergonomics Society 42, 1 (2000), 75-86.

Learning and Collaboration in Physical Computing

Kayla DesPortes
Georgia Institute of Technology
85 5th Street NW
Atlanta, GA, 30308, USA
ksdesportes@gatech.edu

ABSTRACT

My research expands our understanding of CS education in the context of physical computing. Specifically I examine how the tools used when creating physical computing projects affect how students work and learn. Using distributed cognition (DCog) within a classroom environment, I will investigate the effect that information representation has on students' conceptions of CS and electronics. These explorations will be complemented by an application of cognitive load theory (CLT) to understand the difficulty of physical computing tasks and the effect tools have on the load students experience. Completion of this work will uncover mistakes and misconceptions students have in physical computing and highlight ways to effectively design tools for novice learners.

Keywords
Distributed Cognition, Cognitive Load Theory, Physical Computing.

1. PROGRAM CONTEXT
I have completed my first three years within Georgia Tech's Human Centered Computing PhD program. I have successfully passed my qualifying exam and am looking to propose my dissertation work by the end of the year.

2. CONTEXT AND MOTIVATION
http://dx.doi.org/10.1145/2960310.2960349Physical computing combines CS with electronics, expanding the possibilities for design and creation of computing artifacts. This has been shown to open up avenues for engaging a diversity of students (ex. [4,6]). However, many complexities arise when working in the intersection of computer science and circuitry [2]. Individually, research has shown that both computer science and electronics involve concepts that are difficult to teach and learn [3,7]. When combined in the physical computing domain, there is little research on the educational challenges that arise. While we can hypothesize what might transfer from the individual domains, we still have many unanswered questions about the processes of working and learning in this intersectional discipline. Furthermore, while many tools have been developed for this domain [1], we do not yet have a comprehensive understanding of

how they affect the learning environment. My work will begin to address this gap in the literature with two avenues of exploration. The first uses DCog to analyze the educational environment in which students work on physical computing projects *in the wild*. This will allow for an analysis of the roles the tools play in the learning and collaboration in a real-world environment. The second will apply cognitive load theory (CLT) to analyze the use of various tools for prototyping circuits during physical computing activities.

3. BACKGROUND & RELATED WORK
Vygotsky brought attention to the ability of *tools* to expand humans' capabilities of thinking, emphasizing their importance in education [11]. Within physical computing, complexities arise out of the vast array of tools used. The environment usually includes an IDE, a programming language, symbolic circuit representations, tools for building circuits, and electronic circuit components; however, little is known about how these tools affect learning. This work proposes to use DCog and CLT to understand how students use and appropriate the tools in this domain.

Distributed cognition was proposed as a way to understand socio-technical systems through applying a cognitive science approach, to the entire system rather than an individual agent. DCog highlights how information is processed and transferred between agents within this system [9]. Deitrick et al. were the first to apply DCog to the computing domain. They reported on a case-study in which two students and a facilitator worked on developing code for a musical instrument using the tools around them. DCog enabled the researchers to capture how knowledge about a song transformed into various representations [4]. We build upon this work in the first study, by applying DCog to analyze an educational environment with an explicit focus on analyzing how the tools for prototyping circuits affect the system.

This study will be complemented by laboratory based studies, which offer an alternative perspective on the tools and allow us to measure cognitive load in a controlled environment. Cognitive load theory integrates what we know about available working memory to the design of instructional materials. CLT distinguishes between the load on the working memory that is essential for learning material (intrinsic) and the load on working memory that is irrelevant (extraneous) [10]. We propose to understand differences in the load through laboratory studies that have identical objectives and learning goals, but integrate different tools for building circuits. Within these studies we will measure load using the NASA task load index (NASA-TLX), which can quickly gather data on difficulty of tasks performed while reducing the irrelevant between-subject variability that you get from other subjective measures [8].

4. STATEMENT OF THESIS/PROBLEM

The work presented falls into one overarching research question:

RQ. *How do tools affect learning and collaboration in physical computing activities?*

1. How do tools affect the distribution of cognition within a collaborative learning environment?
   a. How do the tools affect students' collaborative practices?
   b. How do the tools affect information flow through the cognitive system?
2. How do various designs within the circuit prototyping tools affect the difficulty of physical computing projects?
   a. What are students' common misconceptions and mistakes in programming/circuit construction?
   b. How does information representation within circuit building tools affect students' errors and understanding of code/circuits?
   c. How does information representation within circuit building tools affect the cognitive load of programming/circuit construction tasks?

5. RESEARCH GOALS & METHODS

The research questions above will be approached through laboratory and *in-situ* classroom studies. The DCog questions (1a. and 1b.) can only be answered through *in-situ* studies where the entire cognitive system is present. I will run a comparative study of two classrooms in which novice students work in pairs on physical computing projects with different tools for building circuits. The activity will last several class periods and have students complete various tasks with a set of associated learning goals within CS and electronics. Data collection will comprise of video and audio recording, pre-/post-study tests, formative assessments during the class periods, and post-study interviews with a subset of the students. A DCog analysis of the videos will be used to understand students' work processes and collaborative practices (1a and 1b). The videos will also be used to assess the difficulty of the tasks (2a 2b 2c) through: gathering time to complete activities, coding for student errors and misconceptions, and analyzing performance on the formative assessments. The pre-/post-study tests will supplement this data. The post-study interviews will provide a way to understand the students' experience through self-reflection.

The laboratory studies will involve individual novice students working on physical computing tasks as they perform a think-aloud protocol. Each of the tasks will have CS and electronics learning goals associated with them. Data collection will involve video and audio recording, pre-/post-study tests, and NASA-TLX assessments to measure load. The think-aloud protocol will give us a better understanding of what students are thinking when they make certain mistakes and give us a clearer understanding of their misconceptions (2a). It will also clarify what they do understand and how the tools affect this (2b). The NASA-TLX assessment on each of the tasks will enable us to compare tools and understand the difficulty of the tasks (2c).

6. DISSERTATION STATUS

I have completed one pilot study in a comparative classroom study investigating two tools for prototyping circuits during a physical computing activity. This study indicated the importance of organizational capabilities within the tools, which effected the number difficulties the students experienced. Furthermore, the diverse student appropriation of the tools led us to question how this might relate to their conceptual understanding [5]. Within the next two years I will complete the studies presented here that build on this work and investigate these findings further.

7. EXPECTED CONTRIBUTIONS

With a rise in the *maker movement* promoting DIY projects physical computing is becoming more intertwined with computing education. It is important for the CS Ed community to understand the complexities of the socio-technical system involved in these learning environments. My dissertation on physical computing will provide the research community with: (1) an understanding of the learning processes involved, (2) misconceptions and difficulties students' have, and (3) an understanding of how tools affect the learning environment. This will enable us to construct more effective and efficient educational experiences for students as they pursue computing in a 3D medium.

8. REFERENCES

1. Paulo Blikstein. 2013. Gears of our childhood: constructionist toolkits, robotics, and physical computing, past and future. *Proceedings of the 12th International Conference on Interaction Design and Children*, ACM, 173–182.
2. Tracey Booth, Simone Stumpf, Jon Bird, and Sara Jones. 2016. Crossed Wires: Investigating the Problems of End-User Developers in a Physical Computing Task. *ACM Press*, 3485–3497.
3. Michelene T. H. Chi. 2005. Commonsense Conceptions of Emergent Processes: Why Some Misconceptions Are Robust. *Journal of the Learning Sciences* 14, 2: 161–199.
4. Elise Deitrick, R. Benjamin Shapiro, Matthew P. Ahrens, Rebecca Fiebrink, Paul D. Lehrman, and Saad Farooq. 2015. Using Distributed Cognition Theory to Analyze Collaborative Computer Science Learning. *ACM Press*, 51–60.
5. Kayla DesPortes, Aditya Anupam, Neeti Pathak, and Betsy DiSalvo. 2016. BitBlox: A Redesign of the Breadboard. *Interaction Design and Children* In Press.
6. Kayla DesPortes, Monet Spells, and Betsy DiSalvo. 2016. The MoveLab: Developing Congruence Between Students' Self-Concepts and Computing. *ACM Press*, 267–272.
7. Mark Guzdial. 2010. Why is it so hard to learn to program. *Making Software: What Really Works, and Why We Believe It. O'Reilly Media*: 111–124.
8. Sandra G. Hart and Lowell E. Staveland. 2005. Development of NASA-TLX (Task Load Index). *Ergonomics: Skill, Displays, Controls, and Mental Workload* 2: 408.
9. Edwin Hutchins. 1995. How a cockpit remembers its speeds. *Cognitive science* 19, 3: 265–288.
10. John Sweller, Jeroen JG Van Merrienboer, and Fred GWC Paas. 1998. Cognitive architecture and instructional design. *Educational psychology review* 10, 3: 251–296.
11. Lev Semenovich Vygotsky. 1978. *Mind in society: The development of higher psychological processes*. Harvard university press.

Mobile Learning Application for Computer Science Students: A Transactional Distance Perspective

Pakapan Limtrairut, Stuart Marshall, Peter Andreae
School of Engineering and Computer Science, Victoria University of Wellington
PO BOX 600, Wellington 6140, New Zealand
lili.limtrairut, stuart.marshall, peter.andreae@ecs.vuw.ac.nz

ABSTRACT

The advance of mobile technology has transformed our society and altered many facets of our daily lives. Furthermore, its use within the context of education are becoming more critical as more educational institutions deliver their courses through the use of mobile technology and engage with their students via distance learning tools. However, mobile learning applications only have a few design guidelines that are grounded in learning principle to ensure their effectiveness. We applied principles from the Transactional Distance Theory (TDT) to formulate design guidelines specifically for designing effective mobile learning applications for computer science students. To evaluate the appropriateness and effectiveness of these guidelines in a mobile learning context, we developed application prototypes that teach computer related topics based on these guidelines, which will then be evaluated for their effectiveness on student engagement.

CCS Concepts

•**Human-centered computing** → *HCI design and evaluation methods; User models; Graphical user interfaces;* Laboratory experiments;

Keywords

Distance Education; Mobile Learning Application; Transactional Distance Theory; Application Design

1. PROGRAM CONTEXT

I have begun my PhD program in Software Engineering at the School of Engineering and Computer Science, Victoria University of Wellington in New Zealand since April 2013. My previous background and experience as a lecturer in my home country, Thailand, fueled my interest in applying well-designed and relevant computing technology to the teaching and learning processes, thus helping computer science students increase their levels of engagement and enjoyment in the course of their education. My research pri-

marily focuses on proposing a set of design guidelines for mobile learning applications that are grounded in learning principles and evaluate if the resulting design could engage the students during their learning process. My research is divided into three parts; draw the design guidelines based on TDT, design two mobile learning application prototypes and evaluate the prototypes to compare their effectiveness on student engagement. There will be three iterations to this research process. Each iteration will provide an opportunity to review and improve the mobile application design.

2. CONTEXT AND MOTIVATION

In recent years, learning experience in the traditional classroom has been supplemented with Internet-enabled modes of learning. The accelerated proliferation of mobile phones also increases the potential of mobile learning (m-learning), "enabling any time, any place" learning for a much larger target audience. However, the software and hardware limitations of the mobile devices may have significant impact on the types of learning content and interaction that can be meaningfully and appropriately delivered to learners. Currently there are many m-learning projects being launched. However, m-learning design lacks design guidelines that are grounded in learning principles to help drive effective design and evaluation. Our research will contribute to the resolution of this problem by establishing design guidelines that are based the principles from TDT.

Our research will measure the levels of students' engagement and their experience in using the application, in order to gage the success of the application design based on TDT. Theoretically, the findings could suggest if a long-standing theory in distance education (i.e., TDT) can effectively engage learners during their learning process when it is used to guide the design of a modern education platform such as m-learning application. Practically, the qualitative and quantitative findings from the m-learning application design development process, regardless of whether the outcomes are positive or negative, can inform the future development of guidelines or best practice towards the design of m-learning applications.

3. BACKGROUND & RELATED WORK

TDT [3] explored issues in the physical separation between instructors and learners in distance education during the 1970s. It suggested that learners felt disconnected with learning and named this feeling as transactional distance. Based on TDT, there are three key factors that control the transactional distance: dialogue - forms of communication;

ICER '16 September 08-12, 2016, Melbourne, VIC, Australia

© 2016 Copyright held by the owner/author(s).

ACM ISBN 978-1-4503-4449-4/16/09.

DOI: http://dx.doi.org/10.1145/2960310.2960350

structure - the actual design, course management and various media presenting the learning content; and learner autonomy - the individual ability of a learner to control his/her own learning process.

TDT had been actively applied to modern ICT-based education. For example, it was also used to categorize (but not guide the design of) current m-learning applications [4]. The TDT factors also exist in several current m-learning projects. For example, dialogue and structure factors were also present in a mobile learning project using MobileWeb 2.0 tools [2]. This project aimed to facilitate collaborative learning and engage students in tertiary education.

Despite these past efforts, mobile learning design only has a few design guidelines that will consider and respond to all three important TDT factors, in order to support individuals' learning and create opportunities for learners to express their individual preferences and resolve their own specific learning problems.

4. STATEMENT OF THESIS/PROBLEM

Mobile learning applications lack design guidelines that are grounded in learning principle to ensure their effectiveness. TDT is a long-standing theory primarily applied in the field of distance education. It has never been used to guide the design of m-learning application.

There are three keys questions in the research:

- Can guidelines based on TDT be used to inform the design of a modern education platform such as a m-learning application in a practical situation i.e., the design of m-learning applications for first year computer science and students?

- How the designs of a m-learning application based on TDT affect students' learning quality with respect to student engagement?

- Is there any correlation between engagement and learner autonomy?

5. RESEARCH GOALS & METHODS

There are three goals in this research:

- The first goal is to examine TDT, which was originally proposed in a distance-learning context, and determine how its factors can be applied in an m-learning context.

- The second goal is to create application prototypes that teach the subjects on curriculum guidelines for undergraduate degree programs in computer science (i.e., ethics and Agile management) [1] based on the design knowledge and guidelines we harnessed in our first goal.

- The third goal is to evaluate the TDT-based design guidelines using the prototypes and draw conclusions indicating whether TDT can effectively engage learners during their learning process.

The evaluation will be conducted in a laboratory setting. We will provide a smart phone with the designed application installed to every participant. We plan to use various evaluation techniques. For example: a video recording (only on the smart phone screen and the face of participants will not be shown in the video) to evaluate the interface design qualitatively, a set of questionnaire for participants to perform self-evaluation of engagement, Google Mobile Analytics to provide information about the usage quantitatively We plan to repeat these evaluation processes for three times. In between each evaluation time, we will improve the applications design based on our findings during the evaluation. This will assist us in creating a final user interface design that is appropriate and effective for our target learners.

6. DISSERTATION STATUS

The research has reached approximately 60 percent of its progress. We are currently in our last testing phase for the first iteration of the research (There will be three iterations in total). The first version of design guidelines has been drawn, and prototype I and II have both been developed. The two prototypes are ready to be tested for the first time with our target learners. We have also completed a primary user study which observed the participants experience towards the provided features. This primary finding has been documented, published and presented at the International Conference on Computer Supported Education (CSEDU2016). It will form a chapter in my final thesis, although it is yet to be presented in a thesis format.

Approximately 20 percent of the actual thesis document has been completed. Some chapters, specifically those focusing on the development of the design guidelines and the prototypes have been drafted. These chapters will require further literature review to ensure they are up-to-date.

As the first-round testing of the prototypes has yet to begun, the findings and evaluation of the design guidelines and the prototypes have yet to be written. Once all three evaluation rounds are completed, a full chapter will be used to present the entire design and development process.

7. EXPECTED CONTRIBUTIONS

Drawing on the Transactional Distance Theory, the research will contribute new design knowledge that emphasizes the notions of dialogue, structure, and learner autonomy to the development and design process of mobile learning applications. Theoretically, we will present a critique of TDT's ability in guiding the design of modern education platform such as m-learning application design. From a practical perspective, research findings may be used by institutions or application developers to develop effective strategies in designing and evaluating mobile learning application.

8. REFERENCES

[1] ACM/IEEE-CS Joint Task Force on Computing Curricula. Computer science curricula 2013. Technical report, ACM Press and IEEE Computer Society Press, December 2013.

[2] T. Cochrane and R. Bateman. Smartphones give you wings: Pedagogical affordances of mobile web 2.0. *Australasian Journal of Educational Technology*, 26(1):1–14, 2010.

[3] M. G. Moore. Toward a theory of independent learning and teaching. *Journal of Higher Education*, 44(9):661–680, 1973.

[4] Y. Park. A pedagogical framework for mobile learning: Categorizing educational applications of mobile technologies into four types. *The International Review of Research in Open and Distance Learning*, 12(2):78–102, 2011.

Situating Physical Computing in Secondary CS Education

Mareen Przybylla
Didactics of Computer Science
University of Potsdam
August-Bebel-Str. 89, 14482 Potsdam, Germany
przybyll@uni-potsdam.de

ABSTRACT

Physical Computing is the design and creation of interactive objects, which are programmed tangible media that integrate sensors and actuators. It uses methods and ideas, for example, of embedded systems, cyber physical systems and IoT devices. In Physical Computing, learners dive into the role of inventors and learn in creative and constructionist settings. The work described here aims at examining what opportunities are offered by Physical Computing and how these can be used most effectively in computer science education at secondary school level.

Keywords

Physical Computing; embedded systems; secondary CS education; educational reconstruction, constructionism

1. PROGRAM CONTEXT

I am research assistant and PhD candidate at the professorship for Didactics of Computer Science at the University of Potsdam, Germany, with Prof. Dr. Andreas Schwill as my adviser. As common in Germany, I am not enrolled in a PhD program, but do an individual doctorate. I started in 2013 and have scheduled myself a time line that aims at finishing 2017. Until now, I have worked on the theoretical framework of my research, implementation of lesson series, data collection and partly analysis. Data collection will be finished by the end of summer so that I plan to start writing the thesis document by the end of this year.

2. CONTEXT AND MOTIVATION

This research project aims at contributing to the scientific study of Physical Computing trends from a computer science (CS) education perspective. Physical Computing covers the design and realisation of interactive objects and installations and allows learners to develop concrete, tangible products of the real world that arise from their imagination. In contrast to other hardware-centred approaches such as robotics activ-

ICER '16 September 08-12, 2016, Melbourne, VIC, Australia

© 2016 Copyright held by the owner/author(s).

ACM ISBN 978-1-4503-4449-4/16/09.

DOI: http://dx.doi.org/10.1145/2960310.2960351

ities, Physical Computing involves arts and design processes. It encourages learners to become creative inventors and enthuses teachers and students alike [6, 8]. Despite its potentials to offer modern state-of-the-art CS education, Physical Computing is often used as 'just another teaching method' to introduce students to topics and contents already existing in the curricula. But Physical Computing has a lot more to offer: sensing and actuating technology, hardware in general and embedded systems (feedback and control, concurrency, trade-offs, etc.) are no longer discussed on a theoretical level, but actually "done" in class. In my research, I use the model of educational reconstruction for CS education (MER-CSE, [2]) to identify and examine relevant contents, contexts and phenomena for teaching in this topic area.

3. BACKGROUND & RELATED WORK

Physical Computing has a comparatively long tradition. Blikstein's historical overview of Physical Computing devices in educational settings dates back to the 1980s when the LEGO/Logo platform was developed [1]. With the large availability of suitable hard- and software tools for all purposes and experience levels in the last couple of years, this trend has regained popularity (e. g. [8, 4]). Within the Physical Computing community tinkering is very popular. This includes two basic activities: exploring existing systems and expressing ideas in creating new systems. This way, constructionist learning [5] takes place: guided by their own interest and for a personally relevant purpose, learners actively construct knowledge. From a scientific point of view, many perspectives were considered, e. g. from interaction design, embedded systems design or the maker movement. The findings of analysing those perspectives show that Physical Computing integrates many methods and underlying ideas of embedded systems, cyber physical systems, interactive systems and smart objects and combines these topics with arts, crafting and engineering (e. g. [3, 4]).

4. STATEMENT OF THESIS/PROBLEM

Despite its potentials for constructionist learning environments, Physical Computing has not been suitable for classroom use for many teachers. My work is guided by the hypothesis that Physical Computing bears many new contents that are relevant for CS education and that need to be didactically prepared. The aim of this research is to situate Physical Computing within the field of CS education. Questions that need answering in this context are:

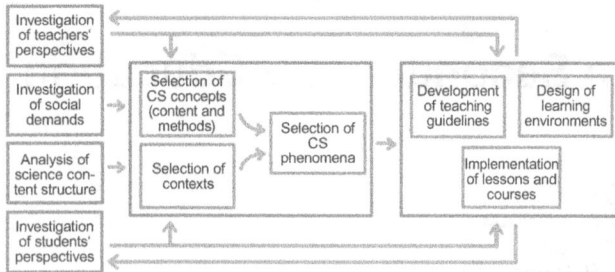

Figure 1: Application of the MER-CSE (Grillenberger & Przybylla)

1. Which aspects of Physical Computing are relevant and appropriate for CS education at secondary school level?

2. What are the potential benefits and drawbacks of Physical Computing in school student learning?

3. How can Physical Computing be implemented most effective in the CS classroom?

5. RESEARCH GOALS & METHODS

This research project examines what opportunities are offered by Physical Computing and how these can be used most effectively in CS education. When analysing Physical Computing from a CS education point-of-view, not only the scientific content, but also students' and teachers' perspectives and social demands are considered in order to answer the above-mentioned questions. It is the goal of this research to take into account all those different perspectives using the MER-CSE in a slightly adapted version (Fig. 1) and this way to provide the community with teaching guidelines and evaluated settings, activities and examples for classroom use. Different methods and instruments are used for data collection, e. g. surveys (interviews with teachers and student questionnaires including scales on intrinsic motivation, perception of CS lessons, creativity, constructionist learning, interest and self-efficacy, both prior to and after teaching lessons series on physical computing), observations during interventions, learner reports and concept maps. These outcomes are evaluated together with teachers and students, so that through the reflection of their experience the resulting learning environments can be adjusted to the particular demands of a given setting. This is similar to design-based research in that it involves iterations to create and constantly refine design principles and best practice examples for lessons and courses.

6. DISSERTATION STATUS

In my research, I started with an existing lesson series called My Interactive Garden (MyIG, cf. [6]), which I developed with the aim of offering a constructionist, creative and motivating learning environment that empowers students to learn principles of computing by constructing meaningful interactive objects. This concept has been developed over three years with several iterations in different classes. More than twenty teachers were accompanied in different Physical Computing projects of which about ten collaborate closely. They and their students were surveyed, so that now there is quantitative and qualitative data from more than 200 students and almost 100 teachers that only partially were analysed so far. Thus, currently, I'm in the process of evaluating all these data with regard to the research questions. Intermediate results are manifold and affect all the earlier perspectives, e. g. in a concept maps analysis we found that students have only a very vague understanding how hardware can be used in combination with software in order to perceive changes in the environment and interact with it [7]. In teacher surveys we learnt they are concerned about the balance between crafting and tinkering and the actual study of CS but they also see a lot of value in it because they assume that it boosts their students' motivation and creativity. Most sections of the intended thesis document are in a rough draft version, the data analysis and results chapters are missing at the moment.

7. EXPECTED CONTRIBUTIONS

When I started with my research, Physical Computing had not been suitable for classroom use for many teachers. The continuous development of MyIG and other Physical Computing projects is supposed to help changing the situation. Despite the already mentioned guidelines, activities and learning environments, one major outcome of this thesis will be a systematically created curriculum with concepts, contexts and phenomena.

8. REFERENCES

[1] P. Blikstein. Gears of Our Childhood: Constructionist Toolkits, Robotics, and Physical Computing, Past and Future. In J. P. Hourcade, E. A. Miller, and A. Egeland, editors, *Proceedings of the 12th International Conference on Interaction Design and Children*, pages 173–182, New York, 2013. ACM.

[2] I. Diethelm, P. Hubwieser, and R. Klaus. Students, teachers and phenomena: Educational reconstruction for computer science education. In *Proceedings Koli Calling 2012*, pages 164–173, New York, 2012. ACM.

[3] D. D. Gajski and F. Vahid. Specification and design of embedded hardware-software systems. *IEEE Design and Test of Computers*, 12(1):53–67, 1995.

[4] D. O'Sullivan and T. Igoe. *Physical Computing: Sensing and Controlling the Physical World with Computers*. Thomson Course Technology PTR, Boston, 2004.

[5] S. Papert. A Word for Learning. In Y. Kafai and M. Resnick, editors, *Constructionism in Practice: Designing, Thinking, and Learning in a Digital World*, pages 9–24. Routledge, 1996.

[6] M. Przybylla and R. Romeike. My Interactive Garden – A Constructionist Approach to Creative Learning with Interactive Installations in Computing Education. In C. Kynigos, J. E. Clayson, and N. Yiannoutsou, editors, *Constructionism: Theory, Practice and Impact. Proceedings of Constructionism 2012*, pages 395–404, 2012.

[7] M. Przybylla and R. Romeike. Concept-Maps als Mittel zur Visualisierung des Lernzuwachses in einem Physical-Computing-Projekt. In J. Gallenbacher, editor, *Informatik allgemeinbildend begreifen - INFOS2015*, pages 247–256. Gesellschaft für Informatik (GI), 2015.

[8] N. Rusk, M. Resnick, R. Berg, and M. Pezalla-Granlund. New Pathways into Robotics: Strategies for Broadening Participation. *Journal of Science Education and Technology*, 17(1):59–69, 2008.

Improving Scientific Inquiry through Physical Computing

Sandra Schulz
Humboldt-Universität zu Berlin
Department of Computer Science
Unter den Linden 6, 10099 Berlin, Germany
saschulz@informatik.hu-berlin.de

ABSTRACT

Physical Computing is used to improve computer science competences in school. For this purpose numerous devices and tools for earning knowledge exist, but only with few didactic concepts. Theoretically, there are a lot of overlaps between physical computing and scientific inquiry. The aim of my research is to learn from other sciences to improve physical computing in computer science education. It appears that computer science skills and especially scientific inquiry skills can be improved in this context. Thus we learn more about student's problems in computer science and can find supporting mechanisms.

CCS Concepts

•**Social and professional topics** → **K-12 education;**
•**Computer systems organization** → **Embedded and cyber-physical systems;** *Robotics;*

Keywords

Physical Computing, Scientific Inquiry, Computer Science Education, STEM Education

1. PROGRAM CONTEXT

I am a doctoral candidate advised by Prof. Dr. Niels Pinkwart. Since spring 2015 I conduct research and participate in a structured doctoral program at Humboldt-Universität zu Berlin. This program is called "ProMINTion", which is aimed at STEM education (MINT is the German equivalent for the English STEM). Integrating computer science in STEM teaching subjects is innovative for empirical learning and teaching research in Germany.

Until now I did literature research and pilot studies related to my research questions. I will conduct a further pilot study in summer 2016 to start the main studies in spring 2017 and finish my dissertation in the same year. A more detailed summary of my research is included in section 6.

ICER '16 September 08-12, 2016, Melbourne, VIC, Australia

© 2016 Copyright held by the owner/author(s).

ACM ISBN 978-1-4503-4449-4/16/09.

DOI: http://dx.doi.org/10.1145/2960310.2960352

2. CONTEXT AND MOTIVATION

Scientific inquiry (SI) is a subset of the general problem solving theory. An often used description to explain what computer scientists are actually doing is problem solving. It is obvious that SI skills and ways to gain them are necessary in computer science education, but only little research has been done in this field. To use physical computing (PhC) in schools concrete didactic concepts need to be researched. PhC is increasingly used to improve computer science skills in different topics like programming or algorithmic thinking. It appears also to be suitable for STEM education. The positive influence of PhC on motivation and skills sets the goal for a wider use with a theoretical grounded concept.

3. BACKGROUND & RELATED WORK

SI is well-researched and developing inquiry skills is demanded by numerous organizations and researchers as a key competence [4] independent of domains. The process is divided in the phases: (observation,) hypothesis, inference, test, and feedback. Several passes of this cycle and potentially even in a different order are common [1]. Results also exist which concern student's problems [6] (e.g. drawing conclusions based on experimental data). Some guidelines for supporting these deficits are provided as well. Physical computing is defined by O'Sullivan and Igoe as "[it] is about creating a conversation between the physical world and the virtual world of the computer" [3][p. xix]. It is realized using sensors, actuators, and processing with microcontroller. Concrete devices are robots, Arduinos etc. The use of PhC is increasing in schools and other learning environments. The most popular goal is to improve computer science competences. Okita observed the process of evaluating outcomes in robotic activities and did find difficulties too [2] – in this case for PhC. She linked to problem solving and states that robotics provide a special (recursive) feedback. Problems during hands-on activities in computer science need to be observed in detail, and the development of supporting techniques to compare real-world outcomes and the virtual program is desirable. The educational view on PhC is quite new in computer science education and could improve PhC and the connection to STEM. It appears to be an overlap between the structure and the process of SI and PhC, but it is not investigated.

4. STATEMENT OF THESIS/PROBLEM

PhC has the potential to improve competences in computer science and natural sciences as well. SI holds a strong theoretical base and practical experience, which could be adapted for computer science education to provide a theoretical based concept. It is a core hypothesis of my research, that computer science students can improve their inquiry skills using PhC.

To investigate this problem, several problems need to be addressed. These include measurement instruments, a theoretical PhC model to develop an educational PhC model, and to find similarities to scientific inquiry literature. It is necessary to figure out specific hurdles computer science students have during PhC activities. If these are also similar to scientific inquiry, supporting mechanisms can be adapted for computer science education.

5. RESEARCH GOALS & METHODS

The first research question includes a theoretical comparison of scientific inquiry with the PhC process. Therefore a model for the PhC process is necessary. This theoretical base is then used to find critical parts of the process, which need to be supported, and to anticipate further problems for computer science and STEM education. The second research question focuses on different levels of problems provided by PhC. It encompasses a devision of the predefined levels: hardware, software, and environment. If we know more about concrete problems and errors, we can support the transition between performance and – that is where the greatest challenge lies – evaluation. Identifying is just as important as handling them. We need concrete ways to overcome these problems. My research questions are:

Q 1 What are the challenges and what is the benefit of using physical computing as a scientific inquiry working technique? Do the similarities of the processes even support the theory that PhC is a working technique in scientific inquiry?

Q 2 Which problem sources and errors can occur in the PhC process? What is appropriate for debugging or troubleshooting?

Q 3 What type of support do students need to improve inquiry skills and in more specific which methodological supports for typical problems in the evaluation phase, e.g. matching input and outcomes?

Methodologically I expand my literature review in order to find evidence for Q 1. After finishing that, I will continue recording videos of students during computer science tasks in PhC without inquiry instructions, to observe the "natural" PhC process. Therefore and to tackle Q 2 the students are requested to work in pairs of two to discuss their problems and to find a solution together. Analyzing their discussions I will get deeper insights of the cognitive processes and problem solving strategies of the students. In a qualitative analysis I code concrete problems and group these by their characteristics and by their occurrence. For Q 3 a support shall be created and integrated into this experimental setting. Because of previous results a methodological aid for the evaluation phase appears to be most required. This could either be a simple structuring of the working process to an inquiry process or a worksheet. This worksheet should be an instrument, which supports the evaluation of the observed outcomes and handling problems. To compare the influence of scientific inquiry components on inquiry skills, a closing interview will be conducted in addition to the qualitative analysis of the videos.

6. DISSERTATION STATUS

Within the last year I conducted two pilot-studies regarding to different research questions. The first of which was exploratory in nature: to figure out the effort for science learning during physical computing (PhC) activities [5]. We did find initial evidence PhC devices can improve STEM competences. I analyzed the PhC process described in the literature to conduct a theoretical comparison of SI and PhC process. In pilot-studies in spring 2016 I investigated if PhC is suitable for inquiry learning. Therefore I included scientific inquiry (SI) components to improve inquiry skills (paper status: submitted). Students at the age of 14 to 17 got the task to solve a specific problem in PhC activities. During summer 2016 I plan to conduct further pilot-studies related to Q 3. For this I will design an instrument which supports students inquiry during PhC activities. The instrument will be tested in a qualitative study. My dissertation contains the theoretical base and first results for Q 1 and first indications for Q 2, which need to be confirmed in further studies. In spring 2017 I will conduct main studies and complete the dissertation until the end of the year. In the doctoral consortium I would like to discus preliminary results, get a feedback to my methodology and the supporting instrument.

7. EXPECTED CONTRIBUTIONS

Exploring these problems provides a strong base for PhC and gaining competences in computer science. I will establish a SI method, which is suitable for computer science education, and test the effectiveness in research studies. A side product will be the design of SI material for computer science lessons. This is directly connected to inquiry learning in PhC and improves SI skills. I will build a base for an interdisciplinary STEM education with PhC.

8. REFERENCES

[1] R. W. Bybee. Scientific inquiry, student learning, and the science curriculum. *Learning science and the science of learning*, pages 25–35, 2002.

[2] S. Y. Okita. The relative merits of transparency: Investigating situations that support the use of robotics in developing student learning adaptability across virtual and physical computing platforms. *British Journal of Educational Technology*, 45(5):844–862, 2014.

[3] D. O'Sullivan and T. Igoe. *Physical computing: sensing and controlling the physical world with computers*. Course Technology Press, 2004.

[4] J. W. Pellegrino, M. R. Wilson, J. A. Koenig, A. S. Beatty, et al. *Developing assessments for the next generation science standards*. National Academies Press, 2014.

[5] S. Schulz and N. Pinkwart. Physical computing in stem education. In *Proceedings of the Workshop in Primary and Secondary Computing Education*, WiPSCE '15, pages 134–135, New York, NY, USA, 2015. ACM.

[6] C. Zimmerman. The development of scientific thinking skills in elementary and middle school. *Developmental Review*, 27(2):172–223, 2007.

Examining Graduateness through Narratives

Sebastian Dziallas
School of Computing
University of Kent
Canterbury, CT2 7NF, England
sd485@kent.ac.uk

ABSTRACT
Graduateness as a concept describes attributes that all graduates should have developed by the time they leave university. In my work, I take a different view and explore graduateness as constructed through graduates' individual narratives.

Keywords
Qualitative Research, Narrative Methodology, Graduateness

1. PROGRAM CONTEXT
I am currently in my second year of the computer science PhD program at the University of Kent and will enter my third year in September. At this point, I have conducted hour-long interviews with 35 graduates from the School of Computing and begun analysis of interviews with a subset of participants who completed a "year in industry". Going forward and into the fall, I plan to explore the entire set of interviews for themes and trajectories.

2. CONTEXT AND MOTIVATION
The effects of higher education are often described in terms of students' individual development and specific socio-economic outcomes. Part of the discussion surrounding graduate outcomes is the term *graduateness* which is used predominantly in the UK to describe a set of generic skills that all graduates should (or will) have attained by the time they graduate. [4] But graduates from different institutions and in different disciplines do not necessarily develop the same kind of attributes. For instance, in computer science, graduates have to be able to adopt to changing disciplinary knowledge and work environments post-graduation.

Definitions of graduateness have in the past focussed on specific knowledge and skills, such as problem-solving and communication skills. In this work, I intend to expand the definition of graduateness to include other aspects of practice, such as graduates' own interpretation of what it means to engage in disciplinary activities.

3. BACKGROUND & RELATED WORK
My previous submission to the Doctoral Consortium focussed on the narrative methodology I employ in my research. [2] Here, I want to instead consider relevant work within the wider ICER community.

Permission to make digital or hard copies of part or all of this work for personal or classroom use is granted without fee provided that copies are not made or distributed for profit or commercial advantage and that copies bear this notice and the full citation on the first page. Copyrights for third-party components of this work must be honored. For all other uses, contact the Owner/Author.
Copyright is held by the owner/author(s).
ICER '16, September 08-12, 2016, Melbourne, VIC, Australia
ACM 978-1-4503-4449-4/16/09.
http://dx.doi.org/10.1145/2960310.2960353

Begel and Simon, for instance, explore the experiences of recent graduates who are in their first positions as software developers. [1] Through direct observations of participants at work and reflections (which participants recorded as video diary entries), they identify issues recent graduates face in working as part of larger teams and on legacy codebases. They also suggest instructional techniques educators at university may use to alleviate these issues.

In contrast, McCartney and Sanders focus on students' development at university. They conducted yearly interviews with 12 undergraduate students in computing as part of a longitudinal study to explore their professional identities. In their work, they describe the cases of two participants in detail and examine the way *critical incidents* that occurred during their time at university affected their experience. [8] These incidents fall into two distinct categories: events relating to coursework and to work and employment beyond university.

The work of McCartney and Sanders, as well as that of other researchers working to explore student development in (and as a result of) university, centers on identity. Sfard and Prusak provide a perspective that explicitly connects learning to a person's identity. They propose a framework consisting of *actual* and *designated* identities and argue that learning "closes the gap" between the two. [11] For them, identities can be equated with the collective stories about a person. For Mary Juzwik, who draws on and proposes a revision to their work, it is instead the *life story* – on which I rely in my work – that forms a person's identity and reflects their own, continually evolving view of who they think they really are. [6]

4. PROBLEMS, GOALS, AND METHODS
The overall goals of my study have not changed significantly over the past year. [2] I am still looking to explore how graduates from the School of Computing at the University of Kent make sense of their computing education within their wider learning trajectories (and what this reveals about their graduateness). And methodologically, I still rely on life story approaches developed by McAdams and others. [7] Elliot Mishler writes that "[u]nderstanding identity formation through analysis of life stories requires a critical vantage point that contextualizes the individual life course – culturally, socially, and historically." [9] I have already worked to explore the historical context (within the computing discipline) of my participants' life course through my work on the development of the ACM curriculum reports. [3] Culturally and socially, I follow Phil Hammack, who uses the term *master narrative* to describe cultural scripts against which we position stories of our individual experiences. [5]

One aspect of my research that has evolved over the past year and that I want to focus on here is the approach I plan to take in presenting and analyzing my work. My approach is inspired by Elliot Mishler's work on the identity of craft workers. In his book

Storylines, he use a case-centered method to focus on specific aspects of his participants' narratives (such as how they originally became involved in craft work). He explores "similarities and differences among intra-individual or intra-case patterns of change," rather than across groups of individuals. [9] In my work, I plan to adopt a similar approach that allows me to highlight nuances in individual cases beyond surface similarities.

This approach stands in contrast to predominantly quantitative approaches. I am not concerned with how *much* graduateness a graduate has "achieved" on a quantifiable scale by the time they leave university. Indeed, such a metric would not be able to describe the idiosyncrasies of my participants' lived experiences.

My approach is also different from traditional qualitative methods of analysis, such as grounded theory, where researchers aim to establish common themes through multiple readings of data, develop coding schemes in the process, and, in some cases, ultimately quantify these themes. Such work generally relies on individual text segments which are coded and presented. However, in the context of my work, this approach is problematic for two reasons. First, by sharing their life story a person is making a series of identity claims. These identity claims are open to interpretation by the audience. Removing them from the context of the interview then affects our interpretation as researchers. As Mishler writes, it removes limits on interpretation and "allows us to do too much with too little." [9] Second, traditional qualitative methods do not always preserve the wider trajectories in the participant's narrative. But one of the goals of my work is to explore students' conception of their learning experiences within their wider learning trajectories: I am not concerned with a generic construction of graduateness which all graduates develop regardless of their individual experience and instead view graduateness as a construct that emerges longitudinally and in reflection. Thus, these trajectories are of particular interest to me. As Scutt and Hobson observe: "Allowing individual narratives space further allows us to recognize that if something is happening among a group of people, the same thing is not happening to each person. This is a vital insight for educational research." [10]

In terms of analytical frameworks, I currently plan to engage with the work by Shove et al. [12] They divide *practice* into three components: materials, competence, and meanings. For them, materials are "things" (including tangible artefacts, but also technologies); competence refers to skills and knowledge; and meaning broadly describes the "social and symbolic significance of participation," which includes the sense we make of our experiences. Practices are constituted when all three aspects are linked. Within this framing, I am interested in how the different elements evolve in graduates' narratives and in the role of meaning in relation to the other elements.

5. DISSERTATION STATUS
In addition to the work I completed during my first year (reviewing work on narrative methodologies and exploring the changing context of a computing education over time) I have now collected data. And in a publication currently under review I have, together with my supervisor, analyzed aspects of graduateness through the lens of the year in industry experience. Preliminary findings suggest that narratives provide a fruitful means of examining graduates' own construction of their graduateness.

I expect that the methodology, the historical context of computing curricula, and the examination of the year in industry will each become a chapter in my dissertation. As I continue over the summer with the analysis of the interviews I conducted, I expect that further aspects of graduateness will emerge.

6. EXPECTED CONTRIBUTIONS
The contributions of this work are twofold. First, it provides insight into graduates' conception of graduateness and the wider effects of a specific computer science department on their lives beyond short-term outcomes. It may also indicate specific (and otherwise unapparent) aspects of practice that can be distilled into guidelines and recommendations for other departments. Second, the narrative methodology I use here may prove useful not only in this work, but also in other computing education research efforts.

7. REFERENCES
[1] Begel, A. and Simon, B. 2008. Novice Software Developers, All over Again. *Proceedings of the Fourth International Workshop on Computing Education Research* (New York, NY, USA, 2008), 3–14.

[2] Dziallas, S. 2015. Characterizing Graduateness in Computing Education. *Proceedings of the Eleventh Annual International Conference on International Computing Education Research* (New York, NY, USA, 2015), 257–258.

[3] Dziallas, S. and Fincher, S. 2015. ACM Curriculum Reports: A Pedagogic Perspective. *Proceedings of the Eleventh Annual International Conference on International Computing Education Research* (New York, NY, USA, 2015), 81–89.

[4] Glover, D. et al. 2002. Graduateness and Employability: student perceptions of the personal outcomes of university education. *Research in Post-Compulsory Education*. 7, 3 (Oct. 2002), 293–306.

[5] Hammack, P.L. 2008. Narrative and the Cultural Psychology of Identity. *Personality and Social Psychology Review*. 12, 3 (Aug. 2008), 222–247.

[6] Juzwik, M.M. 2006. Situating Narrative-Minded Research: A Commentary on Anna Sfard and Anna Prusak's "Telling Identities." *Educational Researcher*. 35, 9 (2006), 13–21.

[7] McAdams, D.P. 1997. *The stories we live by: personal myths and the making of the self*. Guilford Press.

[8] McCartney, R. and Sanders, K. 2015. School/Work: Development of Computing Students' Professional Identity at University. *Proceedings of the Eleventh Annual International Conference on International Computing Education Research* (New York, NY, USA, 2015), 151–159.

[9] Mishler, E.G. 2004. *Storylines: Craftartists' Narratives of Identity*. Harvard University Press.

[10] Scutt, C. and Hobson, J. 2013. The stories we need: anthropology, philosophy, narrative and higher education research. *Higher Education Research & Development*. 32, 1 (Feb. 2013), 17–29.

[11] Sfard, A. and Prusak, A. 2005. Telling Identities: In Search of an Analytic Tool for Investigating Learning as a Culturally Shaped Activity. *Educational Researcher*. 34, 4 (May 2005), 14–22.

[12] Shove, E. et al. 2012. *The Dynamics of Social Practice: Everyday Life and how it Changes*. SAGE Publications.

Improving Students' Knowledge Integration in Data Structures

Shitanshu Mishra
Inter-disciplinary Program in Educational Technology
Indian Institute of Technology Bombay
Mumbai, Maharashtra - 400076, India
E-mail: shitanshu@iitb.ac.in

ABSTRACT

In order to create deep conceptual understanding, students need to integrate knowledge pieces into coherent knowledge structures. When students first engage with new knowledge, it is fragmented and weakly connected with their existing knowledge and they need to do the integration process. However, current teaching - learning methods do not explicitly train students in order to do so. The Ph.D. work discussed in this paper aims at designing and evaluating a technology enhanced learning environment to train students in knowledge integration. The theoretical foundation of the technology enhanced learning environment is exploratory question posing, i.e., asking new questions related to a given concept. By the end of doctoral research I expect the following contributions: 1) an empirically evaluated online intervention for knowledge integration 2) cognitive scaffolds for knowledge integration (specific to data structures domain) based on exploratory questioning strategies and 3) a validated assessment framework to evaluate knowledge integration performance. I am carrying out this research in the domain of data structures and the target population is first year CS engineering undergraduates.

1. RESEARCH SITUATION

I am currently a fulltime Ph.D. candidate in the Interdisciplinary Program in Educational Technology at Indian Institute of Technology, Bombay. I had successfully completed the academic credit requirements and enrolled as a fulltime research scholar in teaching assistant category in July 2013, and anticipate that I will graduate in the next 1 year.

As far as my state of research is concerned, I have completed one cycle of my design based research (DBR), where in I have explored how does the exploratory questions, in a semi-structured question-posing (QP) situation [8] supports the cognitive activity of knowledge integration. I found seven exploratory question-posing (EQP) strategies using which students integrate their prior knowledge with the given knowledge (in the form of classroom or video lecture). Based on these seven EQP strategies I have designed and tested a learning intervention that aims at scaffolding and improving students' Knowledge Integration (KI) performance. In the ongoing DBR cycle I am refining the intervention based on the results obtained from series of pilot implementations of the initial intervention. Later in my research I aim at devising a concept mapping based evaluation rubric to assess students' KI performance.

ICER'16, September 08-12, 2016, Melbourne, VIC, Australia
ACM 978-1-4503-4449-4/16/09.
http://dx.doi.org/10.1145/2960310.2960354

2. CONTEXT AND MOTIVATION

In order to make sense of new knowledge and attain deep conceptual understanding, it is desired that students integrate different knowledge pieces into a coherent whole [3]. To ensure that students can successfully do knowledge integration, they must be scaffolded during their exploration of new knowledge [7]. My thesis focuses on devising cognitive scaffolds for exploration in data structures domain to improve students' KI performance. Results from the first cycle of DBR show that exploratory question posing is an indicator of exploration and integration. The integration of knowledge is caused by (if anything) the exploration process, which comes before and after the questioning.

My thesis identifies different exploration mechanisms employed by the students in the form of EQP strategies. My thesis aims at designing and developing a technology enhanced learning environment which would train students on how to better explore with an aim to do a good KI. I hypothesize that training students on exploratory questioning strategies would enable students to improve their knowledge integration performance.

3. BACKGROUND & RELATED WORK

Slotta & Linn presented KI as a theoretical framework of learning and defined it as "a dynamic process where students build connections between their existing knowledge and the curriculum content." [7]. KI has been described as "the process of adding, distinguishing, evaluating, and sorting out accounts of phenomena, situations, and abstractions in science" [3]. Davis [1] has presented a framework for KI environment and provided guidelines of how to scaffold students' knowledge integration process in science education. Alison King [2] suggested that questioning could promote connections between the concepts, which would in turn lead to improved knowledge integration.

To the best of our knowledge there is a dearth of research that focus on exploiting questioning as a way to provide cognitive scaffold to knowledge integration. Moreover, the student question posing research community resides mostly in the mathematics education domain and QP has not been explored much in CS education research [4].

As far as the assessment of KI is concerned, previous research [3] has presented an evaluation rubric for analyzing text responses from the students and assessing their KI performance. In my thesis I am adapting this rubric for assessing KI from student generated concept maps.

4. STATEMENT OF THESIS/PROBLEM

With a broad goal of devising a technology enhanced learning environment that could improve students' KI performance, the broad research question (RQ) is "*How to Improve Students' KI performance?"* More specific research questions that I would be answering in this research are:

1. What EQP strategies do students organically use to integrate their prior knowledge with given knowledge to generate questions in data structures?
2. Can engaging students at different cognitive levels with different EQP strategies improve students' KI performance?
3. How to assess the KI performance using concept maps?

5. RESEARCH GOALS & METHODS

Following research goals (and research methods) have been identified till now:

(1) Identifying a range of EQP strategies that students employ to integrate their prior knowledge with given knowledge to generate questions.

To achieve this goal, I performed series of field implementations of QP activity in data structures class, where students were asked to generate questions in a semi-structured QP situation [8] to either propose a new idea, or to unfold new knowledge, or to clarify any muddy points. All generated questions were collected and analyzed using an inductive qualitative data analysis method that provided insights into the mechanisms of knowledge integration associated with EQP.

(2) Devising a learning strategy to improve students KI.

I have developed a learning intervention, which engages students with different types of EQP strategies. These engagements are at different cognitive levels: (1) Firstly students use the listed EQP strategies to *analyze* their own questions (the activity of **categorization**); (2) then they evaluate and comment on the categorizations done by one of their peers (the activity of **criticizing**); (3) then, in pairs they confront and resolve their categorizations (the activity of **discussion**). I am further refining the learning strategy in the ongoing DBR cycle.

(3) Measuring the effectiveness of the learning strategy devised in the goal 2.

The previously discussed learning strategy has been operationalized as an online learning environment. 1st year computer science undergraduates would be hired to participate in the experimental studies. We are using concept-mapping tasks to assess the KI performance of any student. The concept map analysis rubric has been adapted from the KI evaluation rubric presented by [3].

6. DISSERTATION STATUS

To address the first research goal, field implementations of QP activity were conducted and questions generated by students were collected and qualitatively analyzed. The aim of the study was to understand how students integrate their prior knowledge and the given knowledge while posing exploratory questions. The key finding of this study was that students employed one or more of the seven EQP strategies to pose any exploratory question. Each EQP strategy involved certain kind of integrations of prior knowledge with given knowledge. These 7 EQP strategies are: Apply, Organize, Probe, Compare, Connect, Vary, and Implement. (The details of this study can be found in [5]). As discussed in the goal 2, we have proposed an intervention:

Categorize-Criticize-Discuss (CCD), which aims at training students on how to better explore for quality EQP by cognitively engaging students with EQP strategies.

Key publications that came out of this exploratory research include, one paper [5] that discusses the qualitative study that led to identification of seven EQP strategies in data structures; another paper that has proposed a QP based instructional strategy: Student Query Directed (SQDL) learning that enables student directed learning through questioning posing [6].

From the ICER community I want to discuss if same EQP strategies are possible in other CS topic and how to generalize for other topics and domains? I hope to gain ideas and appropriate research methodology that should be employed to decide 'goodness' measures of KI performance (goal 3). Also, I would like to get feedback about how to ensure authentic engagement of students with our technology enhanced learning environment.

7. EXPECTED CONTRIBUTIONS

One of the key contributions of my research (till date) is the identification of QP strategies to generate exploratory questions in CS applications domain. By the completion of my dissertation, I anticipate that we would have validated concept map based KI assessment instrument/ guidelines, an efficient learning strategy to improve students' QP skills in CS applications domain.

8. REFERENCES

[1] Davis, E. A. (2000). Scaffolding students' knowledge integration: Prompts for reflection in KIE. International Journal of Science Education, 22(8), 819-837.

[2] King, A., & Rosenshine, B. (1993). Effects of guided cooperative questioning on children's knowledge construction. The Journal of Experimental Education, 61(2), 127-148.

[3] Liu, O. L., Lee, H. S., Hofstetter, C., & Linn, M. C. (2008). Assessing knowledge integration in science: Construct, measures, and evidence. Educational Assessment, 13(1), 33-55.

[4] Mishra, S. & Iyer, S. (2013), Problem Posing Exercises (QPE): An Instructional Strategy for Learning of Complex Material in Introductory Programming Courses. Technology for Education (T4E).151-158.

[5] Mishra, S. & Iyer, S. (2015). Question-Posing strategies used by students for exploring Data Structures. In international conference on Innovation technology in computer science education. ITiCSE 2015.

[6] Mishra, S. & Iyer, S. (2015). An Exploration of Problem Posing Based Activities as an Assessment Tool, and as an Instructional Strategy. Research and Practice in Technology Enhanced Learning (RPTEL), June 2015.

[7] Slotta, J. D., & Linn, M. C. (2000). The knowledge integration environment: Helping students use the Internet effectively. Innovations in science and mathematics education: Advanced designs for technologies of learning, 193-226.

[8] Stoyanova, E., & Ellerton, N. F. (1996). A framework for research into students' problem posing in school mathematics. Tech. in mathematics education. Melbourne: Mathematics Education Research Group of Australia.

Identify and Help At-Risk Students Before It Is Late

Soohyun Nam Liao
University of California at San Diego
9500 Gilman Drive, Mail Code 0404
La Jolla, CA, 92093-0404, USA
snam@ucsd.edu

ABSTRACT

Identifying at-risk students early in the term is valuable. It is because an instructor can have more time to provide extra support, and students can also estimate how much extra effort they should put on to succeed in class. Prior work showed it is possible to predict at-risk students, but they either did not provide a specific prediction method or are too onerous to implement. Thus, my dissertation will develop and evaluate more robust, universal, and simple prediction methodology to classify at-risk students and propose how to automatically generate customized practice materials for early intervention. Once the methodology becomes robust, I will implement publicly accessible educational software application so that other CS instructors can easily adopt this method.

Keywords

At-risk students; Early-intervention; Clicker data; Final exam scores

1. DEGREE PROGRAM CONTEXT

I am in the third year of my PhD program in computer science and engineering. I have been working on computer science education research for six months and plan to do my thesis proposal for advancement to candidacy at the end of this year. According to the department policy of my school, I am not allowed to change my PhD dissertation topic after the thesis proposal examination. Therefore, it is crucial for me to ensure my dissertation topic to be worthwhile.

To date I have investigated how to recognize at-risk students at the beginning of a term, based on in-class clicker question responses of the students. Next steps will be applying this methodology to different courses taught by different instructors and developing proper customized early-intervention material based on the each at-risk student's misconceptions. An educational software framework implementing these ideas will be my last step to finish my PhD dissertation.

ICER '16 September 08-12, 2016, Melbourne, VIC, Australia
© 2016 Copyright held by the owner/author(s).
ACM ISBN 978-1-4503-4449-4/16/09.
DOI: http://dx.doi.org/10.1145/2960310.2960355

2. CONTEXT AND MOTIVATION

Identifying at-risk students as early as possible is valuable for both instructors and students. First of all, instructors can diagnose who needs additional help. This information is helpful considering the increasing demand of CS1 classes yet resources such as teaching assistants, office hours, and discussion sessions are limited. Moreover, students can estimate how much more effort they should put or how to utilize the given resources better to succeed in class. Previous studies modeled student's final performance [1, 4] based on in-class clicker responses or several programming assignments, but their methodologies are heavy to implement or do not include intervention process. In addition, there is no available educational software framework for this purpose, so the entire data collection and analysis process needs to be done by an instructor on his/her own.

Therefore, three things need to be addressed: 1) a simple identification method of struggling students with satisfying accuracy rate; 2) efficient early-intervention strategies such as customized practice materials, extra discussion sessions, and so on; and 3) development of a publicly accessible software framework for an instructor to acquire prediction results and intervening materials, using any kind of formative assessment result.

3. BACKGROUND & RELATED WORK

Porter, Zingaro, and Lister [4] demonstrated the possibility of predicting a student's final exam scores with his/her in-class clicker questions responses. The authors previously adopted Peer Instruction methodology [2, 3], so clicker responses were collected naturally in each lecture. This work observed that final exam scores are highly correlated with clicker question correctness during the first three weeks of a term. Although it mentioned an instructor may be able to identify at-risk students early enough to offer intervention, it did not suggest any prediction process or early-intervention strategy for at-risk students.

Ahadi, Lister, Haapala, and Vihavainen [1] proposed the specific methodology of predicting student's final grade based on 24 different programming assignments given during week 1 of the academic term. Although the prediction accuracy is satisfying, it is dependent on the prior programming experience of students and demanding to implement. My dissertation will build on these two prior works to generate more robust and easier-to-implement prediction methodology. Then, extra data analysis on each at-risk student will give information on the misconceptions of each individual and enable building an effective early-intervention strategy.

4. STATEMENT OF THESIS/PROBLEM

The first milestone of my dissertation is to propose a more robust, universal, and lightweight methodology in classifying at-risk students. I plan to make the methodology to be applicable to essential computer science classes. My dissertation goal also includes whether any formative assessment data such as online quizzes can be used for modeling, so instructors do not have to adopt Peer Instruction. The next step is to identify individual misconceptions of the classified at-risk students. Misconceptions will be categorized by the learning goals of each course. That way, I can create personalized extra materials such as additional readings or practice questions for each at-risk student. To do so, each misconception category on every course should have a set of available practice materials in the database so that the personalized extra material can be created purely automatically. Lastly, these ideas will be implemented as an educational software application so that other CS instructors can use with the formative assessment data including clicker data to generate customized intervening materials.

List of the problems needs to be addressed is below:

- Classify at-risk students at the early stage of a term in a more robust, universal way

- Identify the misconceptions of each at-risk students

- Create and embed intervening materials such as practice questions, additional readings for CS1 courses

- Automatically generate customized intervening materials for the classified at-risk students

- Build a publicly available software framework which any CS1 instructor can use

5. RESEARCH GOALS & METHODS

I am currently evaluating whether my latest prediction methodology works for different CS courses. The data I have are collected from four different courses in two North American research universities. Each course was taught by a same instructor and each course has at least two consecutive class data. For each course subjects, the earlier term data is defined as train set and the later term data as test set. Train set is subdivided into pure train set and validation set, so my training algorithm can optimize some training parameters including intervention threshold (i.e. below what score you would like to intervene). Linear regression is used for prediction modeling and principal component analysis is used to avoid over-fitting. For now, the model predicts student's final exam score using 3-week-worth clicker data. The initial evaluation is done for one CS1 course and the result showed up to 76% of the final prediction accuracy rate.

Once my prediction method works nicely on all four different CS courses, the next goal is listing up the learning goals of all four courses. Learning goals describe what concepts a student should learn in class, so it can be an excellent set of categories of possible misconceptions as well.

Next milestone is collecting a good amount of intervening materials to input to the database. For some subjects which already have many available Concept Inventory questions, I can simply import those questions and add some reading materials such as interactive textbook chapters. For the other subjects, I will need to generate practice questions and this process must be done very carefully.

Lastly, when all the three previous steps are done, I will implement a web-based software framework so that any CS instructor who teaches available course subjects can feed the formative assessment input from his/her class and the framework returns at-risk students information with personalized extra intervening materials for each of them.

6. DISSERTATION STATUS

Thus far, I devised a more lightweight prediction modeling methodology with in-class clicker question responses. The course subject is introductory Python programming and was taught by a same instructor with almost identical lecture materials. This method is considered to be lightweight, because the input data for modeling can be from other formative assessments such as online quiz results instead of clicker responses.

What is left to do is improving this prediction methodology to have better accuracy rate and applying the same methodology to the different course data. Then, once more detailed analysis to identify the misconceptions of each at-risk students is done and intervening-materials are ready, I can implement an actual educational software application. My dissertation is documented only the overall outline at this point, but I plan to propose thesis topic at the end of this year so will start documenting more details soon.

7. EXPECTED CONTRIBUTIONS

Recognizing at-risk students at the early stage of a term is important, because an instructor can have more time to provide intervention. Thus, I plan to devise more robust, universal, and lightweight classification methodology of at-risk students by using any available formative assessment data and automatically generate customized intervening materials for them. This way, both an instructor and students can be more efficient in teaching and studying respectively.

8. REFERENCES

[1] A. Ahadi, R. Lister, H. Haapala, and A. Vihavainen. Exploring machine learning methods to automatically identify students in need of assistance. In *Proceedings of the Eleventh international Conference on Computing Education Research*, pages 121–130, 2015.

[2] C. Lee, S. Garcia, and L. Porter. Can peer instruction be effective in upper-division computer science courses? In *Transactions on Computing Education*, pages 12–22, 2013.

[3] L. Porter, D. Bouvier, Q. Cutts, S. Grissom, C. Lee, R. McCartney, D. Zingaro, and B. Simon. A multi-institutional study of peer instruction in introductory computing. In *Proceedings of the 47th ACM Technical Symposium on Computing Science Education*, pages 358–363, 2016.

[4] L. Porter, D. Zingaro, and R. Lister. Predicting student success using fine grain clicker data. In *Proceedings of the tenth annual conference on International computing education research*, pages 51–58. ACM, 2014.

Author Index